Cases on Public Information Management and E–Government Adoption

Christopher G. Reddick
The University of Texas at San Antonio, USA

Information Science
REFERENCE

Managing Director:	Lindsay Johnston
Senior Editorial Director:	Heather A. Probst
Book Production Manager:	Sean Woznicki
Development Manager:	Joel Gamon
Acquisitions Editor:	Erika Gallagher
Typesetter:	Adrienne Freeland
Cover Design:	Nick Newcomer, Lisandro Gonzalez

Published in the United States of America by
Information Science Reference (an imprint of IGI Global)
701 E. Chocolate Avenue
Hershey PA 17033
Tel: 717-533-8845
Fax: 717-533-8661
E-mail: cust@igi-global.com
Web site: http://www.igi-global.com

Library of Congress Cataloging-in-Publication Data

Cases on public information management and e-government adoption / Christopher G. Reddick,
editor.
    p. cm.
  Includes bibliographical references and index.
  Summary: "This book provides real world examples of the successes and pitfalls faced by public
sector organizations, including coverage of the process of adopting technology from the perspective of complicated social, practical, administrative, cultural, and legal pitfalls and opportunities"--
Provided by publisher.
  ISBN 978-1-4666-0981-5 (hardcover) -- ISBN 978-1-4666-0982-2 (ebook) -- ISBN 978-1-4666-
0983-9 (print & perpetual access) 1. Public administration-- Technological innovations--Case
studies. 2. Public administration-- Information technology--Case studies. 3. Electronic government
information-- Case studies. 4. Internet in public administration--Case studies. I. Reddick,
Christopher G.
  JF1525.A8C367 2012
  352.3'802854678--dc23
                                        2011051298
British Cataloguing in Publication Data
A Cataloguing in Publication record for this book is available from the British Library.

Table of Contents

Chapter 18

Tanja Arh, Jožef Stefan Institute, Slovenia
Vlado Dimovski, University of Ljubljana, Slovenia
Borka Jerman Blažič, Jožef Stefan Institute, Slovenia

Chapter 19

Shafi Al-Shafi, Brunel University, UK

Detailed Table of Contents

Section 1
Politics and Policy

Chapter 1

Adenekan (Nick) Dedeke, Northeastern University, USA

In 2003, Eric Kriss, of the Executive Office of the Governor of Massachusetts, advised all employees that the Executive Branch would begin a transition of its information technology resources into open standards. The intent of the plan was the standardization of the IT infrastructure and the improvement of interoperability across agencies. The Executive Office later extended the open standards policy to electronic documents. In the quest to make documents accessible across agencies, Open Document Format (ODF) was declared to be the preferred format for storing data. This decision provoked a serious conflict between Microsoft and the Executive Branch after it became clear that proprietary open document formats, such as the one that was being offered by Microsoft, were declared to be unacceptable. This case explores the decisions that the champions made, the role that politics played in the process and the impact of these decisions on the ODF implementation.

Chapter 2

Kevin Y. Wang, University of Minnesota-Twin Cities, USA

This chapter examines the extent to which the Internet can represent a place for negotiation, consensus building, and civic participation using Singapore's online consultation portal and the debate over the decision to build the nation's first casino resort as a case study. The structural design of the consultation portal and the entire content of a discussion thread with 508 posts were analyzed with a conceptual framework drawn from previous studies of democratic deliberation. Findings suggest that while the forum reflects some criteria for deliberation, the lack of transparency and government participation raises the question over the quality of the discourse and overall effectiveness of this online medium. Current challenges, recommendations, and directions for future research and development are discussed.

E-governance systems in India have witnessed prolific advancement over the years. India has strategically adopted e-governance as a part of its policy. In recent times each state has its own e-governance plan to deliver services as planned. National policy also aims to provide formalized services across the nation while recognizing the importance of state specific services. This approach includes various mission mode projects under national e-governance plan (NeGP). Manifestation of such approach has resulted in 100,000 common service centers (CSC) in rural areas. It is expected that rural citizens would find them useful and it may contribute for effective governance. In this chapter it is argued that such an initiative would be successful if rural citizens find these CSCs useful for their livelihood security. Various dimensions of this phenomenon are also examined through some cases in this chapter to understand their contributions to successful CSCs in India.

A significant shift has occurred in the nature of policing over the past 30 to 40 years across jurisdictions and contexts. The paradigm of policing as a purely government function is under challenge. Policing is becoming more "pluralised" with a range of actors, both public and private. This shift has significant social implications for the general public, together with the public and private organisations that provide policing services. These implications are discussed and highlighted through the use of information technology by private police in two areas—CCTV surveillance and intelligence gathering. This case discusses this shift between public and private sectors in policing. The situation is more complex than a simple public/private divide and plays host to a range of interactions that bring many actors into contact, competition, and alliance in networks and assemblages. Most research and regulation remains focused on public policing even though, numerically, private policing is now a major provider of policing services in an increasingly fragmented, pluralized, and commodified market. This case considers the regulation of private policing as it exists in the Australian context and how it applies to the use of information technology, together with issues for human rights, especially privacy.

Chapter 5

Sherif Kamel, The American University in Cairo, Egypt

Over the last 20 years, the international postal sector has changed drastically due to several forces, including globalization, changing technology, greater demands for efficient services, and market liberalization. For Egypt, keeping up with the changing atmosphere in the global market meant investing in information and communication technology. The Ministry of Communication and Information Technology (ICT), as part of its efforts to transforming government performance using ICT, chose the Egyptian National Post Organization (ENPO) as a model for ICT integrated government portal. The selection was due to ENPO's extensive network, and the public's confidence and trust in the organization. The case of ENPO, capitalizing on public-private partnership models, proved successful when reflecting ICT deployment for organizational transformation within the context of an emerging economy. In addition to its importance in providing eGovernment services to citizens, ENPO is evolving as a critical medium for effectively developing Egypt's eCommerce. This case study takes an in-depth look at how ICT has improved the quality and range of services offered by ENPO, while asserting the magnitude of its impact on the country's emergence as a competitor in today's global postal market.

Chapter 6

Francesco Molinari, ALTEC S.A. Thessaloniki, Greece
Christopher Wills, Kingston University, UK
Adamantios Koumpis, ALTEC S.A. Thessaloniki, Greece
Vasiliki Moumtzi, ALTEC S.A. Thessaloniki, Greece

This chapter describes experiences acquired during the research work conducted as part of the European Project Tell Me (www.tellmeproject.eu). The project envisaged to support the pan-European creation of Living Labs as new forms of cooperation between government, enterprises, citizens, and academia for a successful transfer of e-Government, e-Democracy, and e-Services state-of-the art applications, solutions, know-how, and best practices. In this chapter authors explore the potential of providing an existing system (DEMOS) allowing moderated and goal-oriented discourses between the citizens and the policy makers to become parts of open-ended ventures to allow the creation of collaborative networks for Electronic Democracy. This work also recommends that this form of support network elevates e-Democracy of a country and thus improves e-governance systems at the grassroots.

Section 2
Public Management Issues

The evolution of e-Government services moves quickly. There is a limited time for adaptation to the new environment in terms of legislation, society, and economy. Maintaining reliable services and a secure IT environment is even more difficult with perpetual changes like mergers and acquisitions, supply chain activity, staff turnover, and regulatory variation. The nature of the changes has become discontinuous; however, the existing approaches and IT solutions are inadequate for highly dynamic and volatile processes. The management of these challenges requires harmonized change management and knowledge management strategy. In this chapter, the selected change management strategy, the corresponding knowledge management strategy, and their IT support are analyzed from the public administration point of view. SAKE project (FP6 IST-2005-027128 funded by the European Commission) approach and IT solution are detailed to demonstrate the strategic view and to solve the knowledge management and change management related problems and challenges in public administration. The current situation of economic downturn and political change forces public administration to follow the reconfiguration of existing resources strategy, which is appropriate on the short run; moreover, the combined application of personalization and codification strategy can result in long-term success.

This chapter presents a case study concerning the development of a Statistical Information System (SIS) out of data coming from administrative archives of the PAs. Such archives are a rich source of up to date information, but an attempt to use them as sources for statistical analysis reveals errors and incompatibilities among each other that do not permit their usage as a statistical and decision support basis. These errors and incompatibilities are usually undetected during administrative use, since they do not affect their day-by-day use in the PAs; however they need to be fixed before performing any further aggregate analysis. The reader is engaged with the basic aspects involved in building a SIS out of administrative data, such as design of an integration model for different and heterogeneous data sources, improvement of the overall data quality, removal of errors that might impact on the correctness of statistical analysis, design of a data warehouse for statistical analysis, and design of a multidimensional database to develop indicators for decision support. Finally, some examples are presented concerning the information that can be obtained by making use of a SIS constructed out of Registry and Income Office archives.

For first generation (1G) wireless communications technology standards, the Japanese government's early decision provided an opportunity for its national manufacturers to be first movers in the global market, while the late development of wireless communications in Korea made the Korean market dependent on foreign manufacturers by adopting the U.S. standard (AMPS). Moving toward the 2G wireless technology market, both countries decided to develop standards instead of adopting a technology from outside their regions. Japan developed its own standard, PDC, while Korea developed CDMA systems with Qualcomm, the U.S. technology provider. Although these governments' decisions on technologies looked only slightly different, the socio-economic consequences were greatly distinctive. The Korean success brought not only the rapid development of its domestic market but also opportunities for its manufacturers to become global leaders, while the PDC standard only provided the fast growth of the Japanese domestic market without any opportunities for the Japanese manufacturers to grow further internationally in the 1990s. By the end of 1990s, two nations again had to decide a 3G technology standard with vast challenges and pressures.

Fiscal transparency today is considered as an essential element of both good governance and e-governance. Therefore, in the new public management and budgeting reforms made by governments, it is clearly observed that fiscal transparency is one of the key elements. E-government technologies, and especially the internet, are supportive to the efforts on the part of governments offering unprecedented opportunities to public administrations enabling the dissemination of fiscal information and improving the e-governance system. In Turkey, where there is the tradition of Continental Europe, the reforms made through new laws in early 2000 contain various legal and institutional regulations to improve fiscal transparency and encourage the public administrators to use websites in an attempt to enhance fiscal transparency. This chapter, within the context of evaluating the endeavors in question, examines the websites of municipalities in Turkey in terms of fiscal transparency and eventually presents some suggestions for the improvement of the e-governance system.

Chapter 11

Reima Suomi, Turku School of Economics, Finland
Irene Krebs, Brandenburgische Technische Universität, Germany

The visually-impaired are in a distinctive disadvantage when using computer screens based on visual presentation of data. Their situation becomes increasingly critical, as most society services, including issues such as e-Commerce, e-Business, e-Health, and e-Government go on-line. Yet modern technologies can too offer solutions to their problems, both at hardware and software level, and often with reasonable cost. Effective ICT can open up new communication channels and functionalities for say totally blind people, which would not have been available for them otherwise. General sensitivity for this issue, and especially, sensitivity among designers of governmental e-services must be developed. E-Government is an especially demanding activity area as it comes to all sorts of imparities (not just vision impairment), as governmental services are often in a monopoly service delivery situation: citizen have to use them, and there is often no other alternative. The issue binds it to the wider discussion on digital divide, where vision impairment is one cause for digital divide, and often very devastating, especially if still combined with other sources of digital divide.

Chapter 12

Rachel Lawry, Deakin University, Australia
Dianne Waddell, Deakin University, Australia
Mohini Singh, RMIT University, Australia

This chapter presents a model that depicts the critical factors and assists in understanding the demands and effectiveness of Chief Information Officers (CIO) in public sector organisations. The chapter explores the literature on public sector CIO addressing personal and professional characteristics. It also reviews the literature pertaining to the responsibilities, career advancement, and future directions in government departments. The authors adopt a qualitative methodology, by which semi-structured interviews are conducted with CIO representatives from a State Government in Australia. From collation of the interview results, utilising a mind mapping strategy, the chapter identifies a model that adequately reflects the critical factors required for a public sector CIO. The chapter concludes that there are certain unique characteristics and responsibilities that a public sector CIO must possess yet a private sector CIO does not require. The chapter also acknowledges the importance of outlining a future direction of the role, something that is neglected by the literature.

The emergence of faster delivery service required a faster mechanism of transaction between government and its people. But such a transaction is not without issues that have to be addressed by the governments of the public sectors. The primary issues addresses by this chapter include the relationships between the perceived: security tightening, facilitating conditions, usefulness, eases of using e-filing system, and users' retention. The second issue addressed by the chapter is differences in gender of the users with respect to factors that influence their state of retention. The findings of the study show a strong relationship between the predicting factors and user's intention to continuing using the system. The findings also show that the retention of users is highly affected by the differences in the gender of the users. This research would like to recommend that a faster transaction mechanism between the government and the people enhances the e-governance system and in this context, this chapter focuses on some potential implications of e-filing system of Malaysia.

Section 3
Issues and Constraints

"Stop Stopping, Get Going." The commonwealth of Virginia's Web site slogan tells much of the E-ZPass story. E-ZPass uses computer technology to automate vehicle toll collection and payments across most of the northeastern and eastern sections of the United States. E-ZPass participants have radio frequency identification (RFID) tags installed in their cars to signal their trip through a tollbooth. Each entry and exit is recorded in a database and charged against an account on file. Bills for tolls may be paid automatically through a credit card charge or from deposits in a cash account. Electronic toll collection reduces delays at tolls, eliminates fumbling for change, trims air pollution from idling vehicles, and accelerates travel. By most accounts, E-ZPass has been a resounding success. Within the northeastern and midwestern United States, over 9 million account holders subscribe to the program, recording over 2 billion transactions each year for road, bridge, and tunnel use in 2006. Customer satisfaction is high, and program enrollments continue to grow. E-ZPass represents a state-of-the-art practice in electronic toll collection as well as a significant success in the use of RFID technology for consumers.

There is a growing belief that IT can improve public management in general. The Dutch policy and services with regard to the elderly are no exception. Obviously, IT opportunities in the healthcare domain play a central role in this, since the main objective of policies is to sustain the independent functioning of the elderly in everyday social life. In this research four IT opportunities for elderly policy in The Netherlands are explored through discussion meetings with elderly, and consultation of experts in the field of elderly policy and services. The IT opportunities are designed to align the different levels of motivation and skills of elderly to use IT. Four IT pilot projects are defined, which take into account the costs and benefits of these opportunities to improve the elderly policy chain in The Netherlands.

This case presents the possibility that commercial mobile tracking and monitoring solutions will become widely adopted for the practice of non-traditional covert surveillance within a community setting, resulting in community members engaging in the covert observation of family, friends, or acquaintances. This case investigates five stakeholder relationships using scenarios to demonstrate the potential socio-ethical implications that tracking and monitoring will have on society. The five stakeholder types explored in this case include: (i) husband-wife (partner-partner), (ii) parent-child, (iii) employer-employee, (iv) friend-friend, and (v) stranger-stranger. Mobile technologies like mobile camera phones, global positioning system data loggers, spatial street databases, radio-frequency identification, and other pervasive computing can be used to gather real-time, detailed evidence for or against a given position in a given context. Limited laws and ethical guidelines exist for members of the community to follow when it comes to what is permitted when using unobtrusive technologies to capture multimedia and other data (e.g., longitude and latitude waypoints) that can be electronically chronicled. In this case, the evident risks associated with such practices are presented and explored.

Information Communication Technology (ICT) has played an important role in today's global economy. Many countries have gained successful growth due to the implementation of ICT. In Malaysia, increased utilization of ICT has contributed significantly to the total factor productivity. One of the main contributing factors is the e-commerce and Internet based services. Therefore, this case study aims to examine the contribution of the newly introduced E-government application, namely E-filing system. E-filing system is a newly developed online tax submission services offered by the government to the tax payers in the country where they are able to easily, quickly, and safely file their tax returns. The primary discussion in this case study concerns Malaysia's ICT revolution, followed by the introduction of E-Filing system, the challenges and barriers faced by the government, and the chapter concludes with future trends in the implementation of this system.

Chapter 18

Tanja Arh, Jožef Stefan Institute, Slovenia
Vlado Dimovski, University of Ljubljana, Slovenia
Borka Jerman Blažič, Jožef Stefan Institute, Slovenia

This chapter aims at presenting the results of an empirical study, linking the fields of technology-enhanced learning (TEL), Web 2.0 technologies and organizational learning, and their impact on the financial and non-financial business performance. The chapter focuses on the presentation of the conceptualization of a structural model that was developed to test the impact of technology-enhanced learning and Web 2.0 technologies on the organizational learning and business performance of companies with more than 50 employees. The authors provide detailed definitions of technology-enhanced learning, Web 2.0 technologies, and technical terms related to it, its scope and the process of organisational learning, as well as a method for business performance assessment. Special attention is given to the findings related to the observed correlations between the aforementioned constructs. The results of the study indicate a strong impact of ICT and technology-enhanced learning on organizational learning and the non-financial business performance.

Chapter 19

Shafi Al-Shafi, Brunel University, UK

This chapter examines the adoption of free wireless Internet parks (iPark) by Qatari citizens as a means of accessing electronic services from public parks. The Qatar government has launched the iPark concept with a view of providing free internet access for all citizens while enjoying the outdoors. This concept is enabled by an ICT infrastructure and broadband facilities, which is considered as regional good practice. By offering free wireless Internet access, the Qatari government encourages its citizens to actively participate in the global information society with a view of bridging the digital divide. Using a survey based study this research set out to examine the Qatari citizens' perceptions of the iPark initiative. Results of the survey showed that there is a positive level of relation between the independent variables, usefulness, ease of use, Internet safety, and Internet speed/response time and one dependent variable, intention to use the iPark in Qatar. The chapter provides a discussion on the key findings, research implications, limitations, and future directions for the iPark initiative in Qatar.

Preface

This book examines the important issue of public management and electronic government (or e-government) adoption through case studies. Electronic government is the use of Information Technology (IT), such as the Internet, to interact with citizens in public sector organizations. Research has questioned if e-government will implement real transformational change in government or just incremental change (Kraemer & King, 2006; Bekkers, & Homburg, 2007).

This book takes a public management perspective. Public management is the examination of how to make public sector organizations more efficient, effective, and accountable. Public management is derived from the New Public Management (NPM) literature. This literature is a rejection of the Old Public Administration (OPA) model in which organizations are viewed as being reactive to situations, bureaucratic, and red tape bound, which inhibit IT reform (Bannister, 2001; Fountain, 2001; Welch, & Pandey, 2006; Denhardt & Denhardt, 2000).

E-government is said to change the way that bureaucracy interacts with its citizens (Bovens, & Zouridis, 2002). NPM argues that organizations need to be dynamic and take into account many of the principles of business administration and apply them to public settings. The focus on NPM is on results and outcomes, rather than just producing outputs in OPA (Denhardt & Denhardt, 2000). Essentially, public management is the counterpart of business administration, but with the focus on public sector organizations. However, existing IT and public administration research challenges the presupposition that you can apply private sector principles to public administration (Bretschneider, 1990). The issues that public organizations face are viewed, according to the literature, as being vastly different than business administration. The case studies discussed in this book show the differences between public and private sector organizations.

This book provides case studies of public management and e-government adoption in both developing countries and developed nations. Developing countries have unique challenges with the adoption of e-government since they lack the requisite resources needed for successful adoption, and access to technology is more of an issue for these nations (Heeks, 2002). For developed countries, the adoption of e-government is inhibited many times by being too expensive to adopt and uncertainty about the willingness of citizens to use this technology. Essentially, there is a lack of willingness politically to change existing systems because of the lack of incentives and uncertain returns on investment from e-government projects.

Case studies are a way of examining important issues in public administration (Stillman, 2010). The case study is a method to determine whether a certain theory or concept is applicable to a situation-specific context. For public managers, the case study becomes a tool for them to apply what they have learned in their business settings or in the classroom. Case studies should be dynamic, in that they offer more than just descriptions of events that have taken place; essentially they are more than just retelling a story. They have impacts beyond the immediate case study, and help in understanding important issues in public administration and management. With case studies public managers can learn more about the effectiveness of e-government programs (West, 2005; Reddick, 2008). The case studies provided in this book are able to discuss broader issues that impact e-government and IT adoption in the public sector.

This book has case studies that follow the socio-technical perspective (Pasmore, 1988). In this theory, case studies can be understood as a mixture of social dynamics within a technical setting. IT cannot be divorced from the social setting, and adoption of this technology must take into account the social dynamics of the organization. This means addressing not only change within the organization, but its broader impacts on citizenship. In the e-government and public administration literatures, citizens are viewed as playing a key role in the successful adoption of IT (Welch, Hinnant, & Moon, 2004). As many of these case studies in this book show, having citizens involved in the implementation of e-government projects has a great impact on the success of the project.

The importance of citizens in public administration can be shown through the New Public Service (NPS) literature (Denhardt, & Denhardt, 2000). This literature is a rejection of the NPM, in that it argues that public sector organization should focus on more than just using private sector principles and applying them to public settings. With the movement to NPM in the 1980s, citizens have taken a back seat to their important role in public service delivery (Chadwick, & May, 2003). The adoption of e-government in the late 1990s showed the extent to which citizens were viewed as being important. As many of the case studies examined in this book show that citizens' are the key for successful implementation of e-government.

Denhardt and Denhardt (2000) have examined the differences between OPA, NPM, and NPS and the editor has examined these theories with application to IT and public administration research. The core differences between the three theories of OPA, NPM, and NPS are shown in Table 1. These three theories are explored in this preface by an examination of each of the case studies in this book. There has been much theory building in e-government research, with most of it examining (or criticizing) the linear stages of growth model (Grant, & Chau, 2005). This research is different with its application of the Denhardt and Denhardt (2000) model to public administration and IT research.

In Table 1 the roles of technology, citizens, politics, policy, and public management influence on the three theories of public administration is examined. This table can be used to view the role that technology plays in the organization along with the other dimensions of organizational change and reform. Technology in OPA is viewed as a way to automate production of public service delivery. An example of an emblematic technology for OPA is the use of transaction processing systems for payroll. The focus on OPA is on providing more outputs for a given input; there is no concern in this theory for achieving results. While for NPM the role of technology for government is to be more responsive to its customers. Citizens as "customers" are viewed critical for e-government development and customer relationship management technology is an emblematic technology in NPM (King, 2007). Governments can use e-government technology to provide more services to citizens and satisfy their service delivery needs. Notice in Table 1 that for NPM there is no role for citizens and democratic governance. The role of citizens comes out fully in NPS, where citizens are viewed as the drivers of policy change. Governments do not merely respond to customers by providing more services. Social media sites are

Table 1. Old public administration, new public management, and new public service in public information management and e-government adoption

Roles	Old Public Administration	New Public Management	New Public Service
Technology and Example	**Passive to automate organizations (e.g., transaction processing systems for payroll)**	**To be more responsive to citizens (e.g., customer relationship management technology)**	**E-government used for greater access for citizens to enhance democracy (e.g., social media technology)**
Citizens	Citizens viewed as being inferior to the organization	Citizens viewed as being customers	Citizens are viewed as the most important for enhancing democracy
Public Managers	Increase productivity of workers	Provide incentives through market-based principles	To facilitate and collaborate with citizens
Policy Making	To administer change from the top-down	Considers input from its customers, but government makes the final decision	Citizens initiate policy changes from the bottom-up
Politics	Separation of politics from administration	Intermingling of politics and administration to focus on more efficient and effective service delivery.	Politicians are responsive to the needs of citizens; they collaborate and facilitate change through governance
Processes	Output-oriented	Results-oriented	Outcome-oriented

examples of empowering citizens to use technology for transformation change of government. E-government provides citizens with the ability to collaborate with government in the policy making process. Scholars argue that e-governance will replace NPM as the new reform agenda (Dunleavy, Margetts, Bastow, & Tinkler, 2005).

This book is composed of three distinct parts. The first part of the book examines the policy and politics of public information management and e-government adoption. In order to successfully adopt e-government within public organizations public managers need to take into account the politics of the organization (Danziger, Dutton, Kling, & Kraemer, 1982). If there is no support politically for e-government, the chances of it being successfully implemented will be slim. In addition, there must be an examination of the policy making process of e-government. What role does the policy-making process have on the adoption of e-government? The case studies in this book show the importance of policy and politics on the adoption of IT in public sector organizations.

Besides the importance of politics and policy, the management of IT in public sector organizations is also viewed as critically important for a book on this subject. E-government projects are ultimately implemented by public managers and understanding the issues that they face is fundamental to know (Brown, & Brudney, 1998). In addition, the underlying technical issue of e-government adoption is shown in these case studies, which public managers must understand the technical as well as the social dynamics for successful implementation.

The third part of this book examines the issues and constraints that these public sector organization's face in the adoption of e-government. Any case study book would not be complete without a discussion of some of the topical issues in the area such as mobile government (m-government), wireless Internet access to government, and Global Positioning Systems (GPS), among others, and their impact on government. These technologies are the future of e-government and will impact its adoption.

In this book there are 19 case studies that fall in three parts that cover *Politics and Policy* in Section 1, *Public Management Issues* in Section 2, and *Issues and Constraints* in Section 3. Each of the case studies will be discussed along with their key contribution to the literature on OPA, NPM, and NPS theories. This book shows one cannot understand e-government adoption without knowing the three core areas.

POLITICS AND POLICY

The first section of this books deals with the politics and policy of public information management and e-government adoption. Chapter 1, by Dedeke, examines the important issue of open standards in public sector organizations through an examination of IT developments and policy in the state of Massachusetts in the United States. This case study discusses some of the issues that public sector organizations face in the movement to open standards in IT architecture. This case study addresses the importance of the consideration of politics in the process of selecting a vendor for open source software, where there are various vested interests that prevent an easy option path. This case study shows the importance of IT in public organizations, since funding for these projects rest with the legislative branch, which involves politics. As the case study illustrates, it was in the late 1990s that government agencies throughout the world became more concerned about the issue of un-integrated IT infrastructures. The issue is that when you there are not open standards, it is difficult to have scalable systems that grow with the organization. As the authors mention, their case study shows the extent in which e-government has a major impact on public sector reforms. NPM had an influence on governments that wanted to adopt more open standards for their IT infrastructure. This case study shows the importance of understanding the political situation for e-government reform, where there was much turnover in state government CIOs as a result of a new administration coming to office and having a different agenda than the previous.

Chapter 2, the case study by Wang, discusses the importance of democratic deliberation in the formulation of a new policy on casinos in Singapore. Singapore used an online consultation form to engage their citizens on the debate over whether they should build the nation's first casino. This case shows the importance of the Internet for civic engagement through social media sites and other web-based forums. Singapore is an interesting case study of e-government because it shows an increase in the use of the Internet, but there are also issues of the government using censorship and control of the Internet. This government used an online consultation portal to get feedback on this policy idea. The findings from this study indicated that the online consultation forum might have the potential to become a place for civic engagement and consensus building. Participates were able to make comments on casino gambling, but making their comments they rarely referenced sources other than their own experiences and values. The author suggests that perhaps a moderator of the discussion would have been helpful to provide more focus on the conversation. The key contribution of this study is seen through the examination of NPS, in which citizen involvement is the key for successful e-government adoption.

In Chapter 3, Misra points out one of the greatest challenges for developing countries is to address issues of the digital divide and generally low usage of the Internet for e-governance. Studying the digital divide is a very important and growing area of e-government research (Norris, 2001; Helbig, Gil-Garcia, & Ferro, 2009). Another challenge that has not been addressed as much in the literature is that of the rural versus urban digital divide. Efforts in e-governance are county specific, depending upon the national level policies, the socio-economic situation, and governmental system. India is a country, according to many reports, that needs dramatic improvements to bridge the digital divide. One of the most important issues that this chapter addresses is the idea of e-inclusion. These are the efforts governments are taking to address the challenges of lack of infrastructure, integration, and transformation of government through e-governance. Most of the reform so far, in many developing countries, have been supply driven by government's themselves. The author points out that the livelihood of rural citizens is dependent on providing more access to e-governance in these communities. Therefore, this case study falls under the framework of NPS since it shows the importance of citizens in the adoption of e-government.

Chapter 4, by Aspland, discusses the important topic of the use of IT to support surveillance and intelligence gathering by private policing. For example, the use of Closed Circuit Television (CCTV) by private police organizations can help to fight crime, but there are also privacy issues as well that should be acknowledged. CCTV is used to monitor public and private spaces, which has been a critical component of law enforcement for years. However, more recently, CCTV has enabled the private policing of large numbers of areas to practice proactive policing. A major concern is the anonymity of the individual and their right to privacy has been diminished. Therefore, the greatest concern with CCTV is the misuse of this information and invasion of privacy for those unaware that they are being observed. For example, in the United Kingdom there are 4.2 million CCTV cameras, or 1 for every 14 Britons. This case study shows the importance of NPM on the adoption of this technology for society, in that its use reflects a serious concern of using private entities to assume the role of public law enforcement.

Kamel, in Chapter 5, provides a case study that examines the evolution and issues with the National Post Organization in Egypt. Postal organizations throughout the world have had to change the way that they do business as a result of the Internet. Egypt is trying to implement an aggressive strategy to modernize the National Post Organization for the purpose of economic development, with IT being used for these efforts. Three important initiatives adopted by the Egyptian government are citizen-centric service delivery, community participation, and efficient allocation of government resources that are reflected in postal reforms. Through IT, the post offices can provide innovative and secure services, with products and services that citizens and businesses want. Many of the IT reforms involve providing electronic means of processing mail and other methods to improve the efficiency and effectiveness of business operations. These principles applied to the National Post Organization in Egypt are consistent with NPM theory.

Chapter 6, by Molinari et al., discusses the use of citizen-centric software in Europe to enhance electronic democracy or e-democracy. Their chapter examines the feasibility of having a Trans-European service integrated to produce greater e-democracy. Their methodology can be used so that citizens can co-design and co-produce e-government services. The power of the Internet is that it enables users to get involved in the production of public service delivery. These authors stress that politicians are beginning to realize that connecting directly with citizens to shape policy is becoming possible and important as a result of e-government. There is a movement from government merely providing information online, to consultation, and ultimately active participation of citizens in public policy. The key contribution is that the authors show how this is feasible with e-government; this is consistent with NPS and the importance of citizens for enhancing democracy.

PUBLIC MANAGEMENT ISSUES

The second section of this book examines chapters that deal with important public management issues. Chapter 7 by Kő, Kovács, and Gábor, discusses the importance of knowledge management in public administration. Knowledge management is critically important for governments, because public sector agencies need this resource to manage their programs. In order to manage the proliferation of knowledge, special knowledge management software must be used in these organizations. As the authors discuss, knowledge management is a strategic resource for public sector organizations. They discuss a case study of a project in the European Union to show the importance of knowledge management for the utilization of more efficient and effective public administration, which is consistent with the principles of NPM.

Fugini, Cesarini, and Mezzanzanica, in Chapter 8, discuss that one of the most important things to consider for the public sector organization is effective database management. There are administrative databases that are good for administrative purposes, but these databases may be faulty for statistical analysis. This is a result of the presence of errors in the data, duplications, inconsistencies, and instability in the database. These databases can look up information on citizens for public service delivery, but provide inaccurate information for the analysis of the statistics of the populations that they serve. Sometimes these errors go undetected by the administrative agencies, as the authors in this chapter explain. The solution to this problem is to provide data cleansing in order to correct for errors and duplication in the data. This case study recalls that data can have two purposes, one being the day-to-day operations and the other knowledge management and examining trends in agency operations and performance. The first use can sometimes be perceived as more important because it is immediate, but the statistical analysis is equally important for policy making and management, impacting the long-term viability of the public sector organization. This case study shows the importance of NPM principles of providing for more efficiency and effectiveness in database management for public sector organizations.

Seo, in the case study in Chapter 9, discusses the importance of wireless communication industry and the government's role in creating standards in two Asian countries. In the chapter, the importance of the government's role in South Korea and Japan is examined with their choice of national technology standards for wireless communication. Other countries like the U.S. have led industry through competition to determine the standards, while South Korea and Japan are examined as two countries that have used regulation of the communications industry to create standards. The case illustrates the importance of government's role in the regulation of industry, which can have an impact on the development of e-government, an area that deals with NPM and the role of privatization of government oversight.

In Chapter 10, Demirbaş discusses the importance of fiscal transparency in a case study of Turkish Websites. The Internet offers governments an unprecedented ability to increase the level of transparency in their operations. The Internet has enabled governments to make fiscal information more easily accessible, in a cost effective way, and to a large audience of citizens and business users. Fiscal transparency is part of the NPM reforms efforts, with governments offering more of these types of accountability reforms since the 1990s. The authors mention some important obstacles to fiscal transparency in their case study of Turkey, which include: lack of leadership and coordination, funding issues, the digital divide, and the lack of public interest in fiscal information.

Chapter 11, by Suomi and Krebs, discusses the issue of vision impairment and access to e-government. These authors argue that since e-government in intended for the masses, it leaves out a small minority of the population, the visually impaired. This case shows the importance of e-government research addressing the digital divide, or the inequality in access to online public services. This chapter discusses some of the activities that governments are using to assist vision-impaired individuals in e-government in Finland and Germany. The authors conclude by saying that the technology currently exists to aid those that are vision impaired to access e-government; however, the technology has not been used to the full extent that it should. This case study shows the importance of NPS in e-government adoption, in that citizens can be left out of e-government adoption, if governments just follow what the majority of what citizens want through NPM.

In Chapter 12, Lawry, Waddell, and Singh examine the critical factors that are important for public sector Chief Information Officers (CIO) in Australia. The CIO's role is becoming increasingly important in public sector organizations because of e-government. The authors compare some of the differences between public and private sector organizations as being important to know to understand the constraints that public sector CIOs face. Some of these include the increased level of bureaucracy, more red tape, and lower managerial autonomy than their private sector counterparts. Through a series of interviews with CIOs, the authors concluded that there are unique difference between the sectors and that public sector CIOs need to appreciate their distinctive roles. Therefore, a focus on understanding the unique differences between public and private sectors, as this case study discusses, is an important area of research in NPM.

In Chapter 13, there is a discussion by Ambali of e-government and the e-filing system in Malaysia. The case study shows that the overall usage of the e-filing system in this country is very low, despite media efforts to increase e-filing. There are concerns by the public of the security and privacy of this e-government. Since e-government involves trust, there is a less trusting relationship with government in Malaysia, which impedes use of the e-filing system. In addition, the digital divide is a factor that prevents usage of the e-filing system. Governments throughout the world would like to use e-government to improve public service delivery, and the e-filing system is a good example of a program with that purpose. This case falls right into the NPM framework, with the adoption of e-government technology to improve public service delivery.

ISSUES AND CONSTRAINTS

The final section of this book deals with some of the most important issues and constraints that public administrators need to know when dealing with e-government adoption. Rich, in Chapter 14, examines the use of IT to integrate toll collection in the State of Ohio in the United States. This is an interesting case study in the use of IT to improve the performance of public service delivery for motorists. The E-ZPass system is the introduction of technology whereby drivers have the convenience of automated toll collection, allowing them to move through the toll areas quickly. This system use Radio Frequency Identification (RFID) tags as an inexpensive way to collect tolls from the motorist. However, the cost of the technology *is* expensive, and this is especially so with the need to maintain existing toll operators for those motorists that do not have access to the technology. This shows the application of NPM for improving the performance of toll collection.

Chapter 15 discusses the importance of elderly population and e-government adoption. This is a challenge that governments must address throughout the world, making sure the elderly have access to e-government. The elderly have traditionally been a group that strongly relies on government support. Governments tend to use e-government in ways that neglects the elderly population. Batenburg, Versendaal, and Breedveld, in Chapter 15, provide evidence of this in the case of the Dutch elderly population. Their main contribution of their study is that governments should design e-government systems that take into account the elderly population. This case study shows the impact of NPM reforms through e-government that can marginalize a population from access to this technology.

In Chapter 16, Abbas et al. discuss the impact of Global Positioning Systems (GPS) that can track the movements of individuals. These devices can be used to display location specific information along with other characteristics of individuals can be gathered. These authors argue that these technologies have in the past only been used by law enforcement, but now they are readily available to the community at large. The issue is that the use of this technology by private citizens and organizations does not have the checks that have been placed on law enforcement. This type of technology subverts democracy and prevents citizens' access to privacy, which runs counter to NPS theory.

In Chapter 17, Thominathan and Thurasamy discuss some of the challenges of e-filing of income taxes in Malaysia. Some of the most important issues are the low use of personal computers and broadband use in this country that may impede adoption. There also is the impact of the digital divide on the use of the e-filing system. There are some advantages of the e-filing system such as the immediate knowledge that their taxes have been filed. In addition, there is 24/7 availability of this service for citizens, something that is critically important if focusing on customer satisfaction with NPM. There are potential costs savings for both government and citizens from filing online which can be realized from the e-filing system.

In Chapter 18, Arh, Dimovski, and Blažič, examines mobile government with a case study of Saudi Arabia. As in many Middle East countries, there is a high rate of mobile technology adoption by its citizens. The numbers of mobile phones have skyrocketed in Saudi Arabia compared to Internet subscribers for this country. There have been rapid advances in mobile technology, which have opened up the opportunities for mobile government (m-government). Mobile technology is a more cost effective and convenient way to deliver government services, especially in developing countries that lack Internet infrastructure. Mobile government may replace e-government and has some unique characteristics that should be noted. There is more personalization of information, it is always on, and the mobility of the individual is consistent with empowering citizens and accessing their government in NPS. There are some issues with mobile devices for m-government such as limited memory of processors, small display areas, short battery life, and lack of security.

Chapter 19, the final chapter in this book, examines the role of free wireless Internet connection in Qatar. Al-Shafi in this chapter examines the use of wireless Internet parks in Qatar, as providing citizens with a free way of accessing the Internet in a public space. The government has adopted a policy of "Broadband for All" as a way of fostering a more knowledge-based economy for Qatar. The way Qatar is doing this is by creating "hot spots" in public parks. The authors of this case recall that because of the digital divide, the benefits of the Internet are not available to all, and free wireless Internet access is one way to bridge the digital divide. This shows the importance of understanding citizens and e-government adoption, which is important for the theory of NPS.

As mentioned, this book can be read using the framework provided in Table 1 showing the unique roles of OPA, NPS, and NPM. This framework provides a way of understanding the development of e-government and public information management adoption through an analysis of case studies.

Christopher G. Reddick
The University of Texas at San Antonio

REFERENCES

Bannister, F. (2001). Dismantling the silos: Extracting new value from IT investments in public administration. *Information Systems Journal, 11*(1), 65–84.

Bekkers, V., & Homburg, V. (2007). The myths of e-government: Looking beyond the assumptions of a new and better government. *The Information Society, 23,* 373–382.

Bovens, M., & Zouridis, S. (2002). From street-level to system-level bureaucracies: How information and communication technology is transforming administrative discretion and constitutional control. *Public Administration Review, 62*(2), 174–184.

Bretschneider, S. (1990). Management information systems in public and private organizations: An empirical test. *Public Administration Review, 50*(5), 536–545.

Brown, M. M., & Brudney, J. L. (1998). Public sector information technology initiatives: Implications for programs of public administration. *Administration & Society, 30*(4), 421–442.

Chadwick, A., & May, C. (2003). Interaction between states and citizens in the age of the internet: "E-government" in the United States, Britain, and the European Union. *Governance: An International Journal of Policy, Administration and Institutions, 16*(2), 271–300.

Danziger, J. N., Dutton, W. H., Kling, R., & Kraemer, K. L. (1982). *Computers and politics: High technology in American local governments.* New York, NY: Columbia University Press.

Denhardt, R. B., & Denhardt, J. V. (2000). The new public service: Serving rather than steering. *Public Administration Review, 60*(6), 549–559.

Dunleavy, P., Margetts, H., Bastow, S., & Tinkler, J. (2005). New public management is dead-Long live digital-era governance. *Journal of Public Administration: Research and Theory, 16*(3), 467–494.

Fountain, J. E. (2001). *Building the virtual state: Information technology and institutional change*. Washington, DC: Brookings Institution Press.

Grant, G., & Chau, D. (2005). Developing a generic framework for e-government. *Journal of Global Information Management, 13*(1), 1–30.

Heeks, R. (2002b). E-government in Africa: Promise and practice. *Information Polity, 7*, 97–114.

Helbig, N., Gil-Garcia, J. R., & Ferro, E. (2009). Understanding the complexity of electronic government: Implications from the digital divide literature. *Government Information Quarterly, 26*, 89–97.

King, S. F. (2007). Citizens as customers: Exploring the future of CRM in UK local government. *Government Information Quarterly, 24*(1), 47–63.

Kraemer, K., & King, J. L. (2006). Information technology and administrative reform: Will e-government be different? *International Journal of Electronic Government Research, 2*(1), 1–20.

Norris, P. (2001). *Digital divide: Civic engagement, information poverty, and the internet worldwide*. Cambridge, UK: Cambridge University Press.

Pasmore, W. A. (1988). *Designing effective organizations: The sociotechnical systems perspective*. New York, NY: John Wiley & Sons.

Reddick, C. G. (2008). Perceived effectiveness of e-government and its usage in city governments: Survey evidence from information technology directors. *International Journal of Electronic Government Research, 4*(4), 89–104.

Stillman, R. J. (2010). *Public administration: Concepts and cases* (9th ed.). Cengage Learning.

Welch, E. W., Hinnant, C. C., & Moon, M. J. (2004). Linking government satisfaction with e-government and trust in government. *Journal of Public Administration: Research and Theory, 15*(3), 371–391.

Welch, E. W., & Pandey, S. K. (2006). E-government and bureaucracy: Toward a better understanding of intranet implementation and its effect on red tape. *Journal of Public Administration: Research and Theory, 17*, 379–404.

West, D. M. (2005). *Digital government: Technology and public sector performance*. Princeton, NJ: Princeton University Press.

Section 1
Politics and Policy

Chapter 1
Politics Hinders Open Standards in the Public Sector:
The Massachusetts Open Document Format Decision

Adenekan (Nick) Dedeke
Northeastern University, USA

EXECUTIVE SUMMARY

In 2003, Eric Kriss, of the Executive Office of the Governor of Massachusetts, advised all employees that the Executive Branch would begin a transition of its information technology resources into open standards. The intent of the plan was the standardization of the IT infrastructure and the improvement of interoperability across agencies. The Executive Office later extended the open standards policy to electronic documents. In the quest to make documents accessible across agencies, Open Document Format (ODF) was declared to be the preferred format for storing data. This decision provoked a serious conflict between Microsoft and the Executive Branch after it became clear that proprietary open document formats, such as the one that was being offered by Microsoft, were declared to be unacceptable. This case explores the decisions that the champions made, the role that politics played in the process and the impact of these decisions on the ODF implementation.

DOI: 10.4018/978-1-4666-0981-5.ch001

ORGANIZATIONAL BACKGROUND

Government and IT Organization Structure

The Massachusetts State Government consisted of three branches, the Legislature, the Judicial and the Executive Branches. The Executive Branch consisted of the Office of the Governor and fifteen executive departments. The Executive Office for Administration and Finance (EOAF) had fifteen divisions and Bureaus, one of which was the Information Technology Division (Exhibit 1). The Information Technology Division (ITD), which is the primary focus of this article, was a unit that reported to the head of the Executive Office for Administration and Finance.

The ITD was charged with the responsibility of providing information technology (IT) services for the 170 plus agencies in the Executive Department. These services included Internet access, enterprise applications, wide area networks, Web portal services, a central e-mail system, and Web and application hosting services. The ITD also set the IT standards for all other Executive Department agencies. By an action of the Legislature, the Office of the Chief Information Officer (CIO) was created to head the ITD in 1996 (ITD, 2006a). The CIO reported to the Secretary of the EOAF. The ITD had ten operational groups.

In the fiscal year 2005, the ITD employed over 250 technologists and IT financial, legal and policy experts. All the executive's offices reporting to the Office of the Governor had about 1700 technologists. Some 95 percent of IT employees were union employees. Microsoft supplied over 80 percent of the installed desktop software within the Executive Branch. Most of the agencies reporting to the Office of the Governor had their own Chief Information Officers and Chief Security Officers. The agency Chief Information Officer (CIO) was the expert in the agency, department or other branch of government who had the delegated authority for all information technology resources in use within the entity. The responsibilities included, in some cases, the day-to-day planning, budgeting, deploying, maintaining and controlling of the information technology resources of the entity. The agency Chief Security Officer (CSO) was the individual, within an agency, department or bureau, who had the delegated authority for ensuring that the information and the IT systems of an entity had adequate security controls in place. The CIO and the CSO may or may not be the same person. The agency CIOs and CSOs were independent in the sense that they did not report directly to the Office of the CIO within the EOAF. The agency CIOs that reported to the Office of the Governor were required to submit their projects for review and the approval of the Office of the CIO only if a planned information technology development project or purchase by the agency had a total projected cost, including the cost of any related hardware, software and consulting fees, that exceeded $200,000. All agency CIOs were also regular civil servants rather than political appointees of the Governor. Because the Office of the CIO and the Chief Technology Officer positions were created during the Administration of Governor Mitt Romney, a Republican governor, political appointees filled the two positions. It was the norm in Massachusetts for political appointees to leave their jobs every four years, owing to the change in governorship. However, Democrat politicians dominated both houses of the Legislature.

GOVERNMENT STAFF STRUCTURE AND POLITICAL CONTEXT

The Commonwealth, as well as its Information Technology Divisions, also had a tiered structure. First, there were the career civil servants who worked permanently for the Government. Second, there were politicians and third there were politically elected personnel. This case focuses on the decisions of the political appointees of the Information Technology Division of the Executive Branch of the Government of Massachusetts. In the context of this case, the Legislature consisted primarily of elected politicians, who were Democrats, while the leadership of the Executive Branch, the host of political appointees to cabinet and senior level positions and advisory boards, were mostly Republican or Conservatives.

SETTING THE STAGE

The IT Decision-Making Process

Generally, decisions in regard to the acquisition of IT resources involved the appropriation of funds. Hence, the process was tightly linked to the State's budgeting process. The process begins with each agency CIO creating and submitting the request for funds for the next fiscal year to the EOAF. The head of the EOAF works with each agency to cut costs and prepares the budget that the Governor submits to the Legislature. All IT decisions that required funding went through the Legislature's budgetary process. The Legislature created the Office of the CIO and CTO and also funded all the ITD projects. The Senate Oversight Committees had the subpoena power over the officials of the ITD. Though the Legislature could not prohibit the ITD from initiating or pursuing technology projects, it could withhold funds from specific or all ITD projects.

Electronic Records Storage in the Executive Branch

In 2000, the citizens of Massachusetts increasingly interacted with the agencies of the State electronically. Hence, the IT divisions had to store, manage, support, and provide access to increasing volumes of electronic records. Furthermore, the diversity of the electronic channels that were used increased. State employees were equipped with heterogeneous IT assets including desktop PCs, laptops, notebooks, software systems, cell phones, handheld devices, Palm Pilots, and Blackberry devices. Owing to the rapid proliferation of the IT channels, the capability of the IT agencies to exchange and guarantee access to these information assets became more complex. Because of the administrative and legal requirements, a sizeable amount of electronic records had to be retained by the agencies over decades. According to the Secretary of the Commonwealth's Records in Common Schedule, agencies had to retain certain electronic records, even though the agency had no operative need for them. Though the Records in the Common Schedule set forth records retention rules for all of the records generated by the Executive Branch, it did not specify where or for how long documents must be held. Owing to the lack of a digital archive, agencies retained records in their own custody, though the Records in Common Schedule mandated the records be in the custody of the Secretary of the Executive branch. The Schedule did not prescribe the use of digital archives for public records.

The Commonwealth's State Archive primarily captured information only on paper. Hence, the Archive faced the challenge of migrating its paper documents into an electronic format. Furthermore, the ITD had to seek a solution that would allow it to capture and store electronic data that were in disparate data formats in its Archive. Some of the paper records were transformed into nondigitized electronic forma. Hence, the Executive Branch increasingly faced the challenge of managing digital and nondigital electronic formats over the decades. Furthermore, the Executive Branch suffered from systems integration challenges. The State agencies maintained a diverse array of hardware and network assets. Massive legacy systems and silo applications created data interoperability problems and delivered suboptimal customer service. Moreover, most agencies bought the IT systems that addressed their internal needs rather than those that enhanced interoperability among the agencies. Furthermore, much of the State's data were stored in proprietary formats, primarily Microsoft-based files that, potentially, limited the means by which the public could access the data. Nevertheless, Microsoft's proprietary Office products were the standard across the agencies.

CASE DESCRIPTION

Emergence of IT Strategies and
E-Government in the Public Sector

In the late 1990's, government agencies around the world were becoming increasingly concerned about the challenges of unintegrated IT infrastructures. The concept of e-government and that of an enterprise strategy began to evolve. E-government could be defined as the effective conceptualization, redesign, reorganization and use of information technologies in a manner that delivered better, faster, reliable, secure and more responsive services to citizens at the lowest cost to the public sector. The Government of Ontario developed and deployed what was called an enterprise model of information technology (Cisco Systems, 1998). The Government strategy called for the integration of 21 separate IT departments into 7 organizational units serving multiple public agencies. The Ontario experience underscores what was called IT consolidation. This strategy focused on ways of reorganizing the existing IT services to make service delivery, faster, efficient and cost effective. It was a strategy that worked effectively within the environments in which different products were being used for a standard service, such as e-mail services and Web services. The consolidation of the IT resources within the government context was normally mandated by executive order or by statute. The second IT strategy that emerged was not focused on the delivery in the most efficient manner of a particular service that was present in the different software products. For example, three unique software products that were used by different agencies might all offer the same service of payment of fees in their unique ways. The IT strategy that was called the shared services development sought to centralize specific IT functions across the agencies. This strategy was implemented whenever agencies voluntary agreed to participate. They did this by signing service level agreements (Gartner, February, 2006; NASCIO, March 2006).

Generally, the centralization of IT in the public sector was driven by the desire to reduce overall IT costs. Whenever such a transformation was undertaken, studies found that the strategies were resisted by the autonomous agencies that stood to lose a profound level of IT autonomy and control (Harris & Kost, 2008). The Massachusetts State Government was also involved in this wave of transformation of IT in the government. In 2002, a Government statute called for the creation of an IT commission, whose task was to make recommendations on how the public service could enable technology to deliver services faster and cheaper. Assisted by IBM consulting services, the body met six times from November 2002 to February 2003 to assess the best practices and to formulate guiding principles, establish the weaknesses and the strengths of the State's IT organization and to formulate

5

recommendations. The commission also made a host of findings. In the realm of IT architecture and standards, it found that the architectures across the agencies were not aligned nor were they clearly understood. Hence, the State was not enjoying the maximum benefit that a coherent architecture could offer. The commission also recommended that the Office of the CIO for the State be elevated in rank and that formal reporting relationships be created between the Office of the CIO and the agency CIOs. In the sphere of IT strategy, the commission recommended that the State develop a comprehensive IT infrastructure plan and update its existing architecture. It also recommended that the position of a Chief Technology Officer be created.

The idea of shared services evolved into the services oriented architecture (SOA) strategy. This transformation strategy sought to create an IT architecture in which business processes were separated from technology, such that any software product that was used by one agency could offer some of its functions for use on request from software products that were used by other agencies. In a sense, the IT of such a government enterprise becomes spontaneous and flexible to change. An agency of the Federal Government took a notable step in this direction in 2003. The General Services Administration, under the guidance of Unisys, implemented an SOA-based architecture that was based on open standards (Mayo, 2004). The deployment of a services-oriented architecture was embraced by the organization representing the Chief Information Officers of States as the philosophy that would enable State Governments across the U.S. to become agile enterprises (NASCIO, May 2006).

Though, the strategies of the services-oriented architecture was already being deployed in the U.S. private sector in 2003, the framework for the deployment of the approach in the public sector had just been completed by the NASCIO. The State of Massachusetts was one of the first attempting to adopt a services-oriented architecture in the public sector. This case is also unique because Massachusetts had the first CIO that connected the services-oriented approach with the data formats. This connection may have been coincidental to the State's archives production of challenges. Extant literature shows that e-government does play a major role in public sector reform. Foreign governments, such as the Dutch (Korteland & Bekkers, 2007), the Canadian (Cullen, 2007), the Spanish (Navaro, Gabriel, Dewhurst, Penalver & Juan, 2007) and the Singaporean (Sharma, 2007) public sectors have all deployed e-government initiatives. Our case contributes to this body of knowledge.

Who Should the State Employ to Help Solve its Electronic Archives Problem?

The Romney Administration was newly elected on a reform-based platform. The new Governor brought in people with business and IT competencies. The Administration was open to new approaches and ideas and transformative solutions. In

January 2002, the then-Governor Romney appointed Eric Kriss to be Secretary of the EOAF. He left his position as Partner at Bain and Company to become the Assistant Secretary of the EOAF in the early 1990's under the administration of Governor Weld. Thereafter, Eric Kriss led other firms, including MediQual Systems, Cardinal Health, and Workmode. Bethann Pepoli, Chief Operating Officer within the ITD, described Eric as being technically minded, passionate, and driven to implement as many technology solutions as possible. She stated that he was a high-energy person who was not unnecessarily concerned about political processes. Eric hired Peter Quinn to be the CIO and to head the ITD in September 2002. Peter resigned his position as the CIO of Boston Financial Data Services to become the State's CIO. He took the job, despite his lack of experience in the public sector, because he wanted to achieve a meaningful institutional IT reform in the Government. Peter Quinn enlisted the support of Bob Stack after he had assumed his CIO position. Bob had over 20 years experience in the Information Technology field. He resigned as the CIO of a communications firm to become the State's Chief Technology Officer (CTO). He, too took the CTO job because he believed that it offered him the opportunity to help deploy change in the Government.

What Should the State do to Help Resolve its Electronic Archives Problem?

Eric Kriss had the full support of Governor Romney to move forward with his transformational efforts. Eric hired two experts who helped implement the changes. Although Eric publicly championed the open standards initiative by being the executive defender of the policy, Peter and Bob were accountable and responsible for the details of the implementation. Trust was an essential ingredient in the relationship of the three champions. Eric, Peter, and Bob had less than four years as their time-horizon for the change, because of the four-year electoral cycle. If Mitt Romney, the Republican governor, failed to compete for re-election or if he campaigned for the post but lost the election, all those who were political appointees of the administration had to vacate their positions. This "time crunch" created a sense of urgency for the team. After consultation with his team, Eric announced the first initiative of the ITD. The vision proposed that the Executive Branch of the Government move towards the adoption of an open source software wherever possible. To enforce the new policy, Eric issued a memo to all agency CIOs to inform them of the strategy.

In that September memo, Eric stated that effective immediately, the Executive Branch of the Commonwealth of Massachusetts would adopt, under the Chief Information Officer's (CIO) guidance, a comprehensive open standards, open source policy for future IT investments and operating expenditures. His memo provided three reasons for the shift to open standards. First, software developed in compliance with open standards requirements made systems integration and data sharing simpler and more efficient. Second, agencies could share software modules rather than each having to develop individual programs. Third, products licensed under open standards specifications, also known as open-source software, were cheaper to acquire, develop and maintain. Eric was surprised at the response that the memo provoked. The October 27, 2003, the column of *Washington Technology* ran the headline, "Open source riles of software makers – Massachusetts ignites furor with new strategy." The article revealed that Eric's memo had been leaked to the media. The article stated that the memo advocated a greater use of open standards and open source code in the State. The pushback from proprietary firms was immediate. Steve Balmer, CEO of Microsoft Corporation, argued that the Government should choose the software that offered the best value (Welsh, 2003).

The State's Senate Post Audit and Oversight Committee also held a hearing on the issue of open standards. During the hearing, Senator Marc Pacheco mentioned his concerns that the new policy might force the State Government to use open-source software even when these were inferior to the traditional software (Bray, 2003):

Prior to the memo, open-source software products were already in use in the Massachusetts public sector, though the State had not approved of their use. However, certain issues limited the adoption of open-source software on a wide scale. Wick Keating, Chief Technology Officer, summarized these concerns. He stated that one needed to know if the open source software components were secure, robust and scalable, and not riddled with defects (Peterson, 2004). Eric responded to the detractors of his plan by clarifying his intention. He argued that the State wanted to put more focus on where open-source products could fill some of the needs in the public sector, not kick-out proprietary products (Welsh, 2003).

The leaked memo and the resulting ruckus were certainly not how Eric had planned to introduce the transition process. Though Eric Kriss, Peter Quinn, and Bob Stack faced opposition from the proprietary firms, they stuck to their open standards plan rather than abandoning it. They had to clarify the way forward by defining what open standards meant and specify how the IT managers in the executive branch would integrate it into purchasing decisions. To achieve these goals, the three leaders led the Information Technology Division (ITD) to develop a policy on open data formats and a reference framework for open standards. The specification of an open data formats policy put the ITD and Microsoft on a collision course. As push came to shove, Peter had to decide whether the executive branch should accept, reject or delay for two years the acceptance of Microsoft's open data format into the State's framework for open standards.

Understanding Systems Integration and Open Standards Approaches

The ITD could have chosen either of two paths to achieve integration and interoperable architectures, systems integration or the open standards approaches. These strategies were not unique to the public sector. The systems integration approach focused on the creation of software bridges (middleware) and programming that enabled different (heterogeneous) proprietary hardware operating systems and software to understand each other. However, the risk of the failure of these projects was considerable because each software system to be integrated had to be 'taught' the language of all the other systems with which it had to communicate by using middleware software. Some software products were impossible to modify in this manner. This systems integration approach was also vendor-dependent.

The open standards approach differed from the systems integration approach in several ways. First, the purpose of the open standards approach was to create unified standards that would ensure that future technology purchases and implementations understood each other. In a sense, the approach does not change the existing IT infrastructure: rather, it targets new IT investments.

Under this regime, the firms that adopt the standards achieve the interoperability of information systems and applications because their departments use open standards specifications for their systems and infrastructure development and purchasing decision-making. Open standards advocates believed that it was better to make the technologies that were built to work together rather than to try to *force* them to do so *after* the development was completed.

However, the open standards approach had a major limitation. The rate of adoption of open standards by vendors and software developers determined its impact on an industry. Practically speaking, software developers could ignore a publicly published open-standards specification without any repercussions. Costs of adoption was an important reason for considering open-source and open standards-based software, such as Linux operating systems, the Open Office suite and the MySQL database. Though ITD did not initiate a business case or a comparison of proprietary to open source applications, in the fall 2003, the Defense Research & Development Canada produced a special report, which determined the role of free and open source software in its information system architectures and in the whole government of Canada. Exhibit 3 presents the cost comparison of proprietary to open-source products that was part of the report. The data shows that costs per desktop computer was about half that of proprietary software. Similarly, while the hardware costs were comparable, people and software costs for proprietary costs were higher than those of open source products. However, the open standards approach had not yielded enterprise-level software. Open-source software and standards are royalty free. The specifications remain in the public domain and experts continuously modified them.

PATH TO OPEN STANDARDS: DEVELOPING THE ENTERPRISE TECHNICAL REFERENCE MODEL

After consultation with Peter and Bob, Eric wrote his memo to all Agency-level CIOs to inform them about the plan to move the Executive Branch in the direction of open-source software and open standards. In September 2003, Eric clarified how the plan would affect existing technology assets as follows (Welsh, 2003):

This does not mean we are kicking out proprietary products. Massachusetts wants to gradually use products whose standards are not proprietary to a company and are open to peer-review. These particular standards, which are widely used by government and industry, could provide a platform that moves us closer to interoperability and exchangeable data.

Exhibit 2 provides a detailed description of the desired degree of interoperability and objectives that should be accomplished by the open standards initiative. To initiate the move towards the open standards approach, Bob formed the Enterprises Architecture Council (EAC), which involved up to 15 agency CIOs and their representatives. In November 2003, the EAC developed the first version of the open standards framework, named the Enterprises Technical Reference Model (ETRM), in eight months.

The Council did not create the framework from scratch. Instead, it adapted and modified existing frameworks such as the National Association of State Chief Information Officers' (NASCIO) Enterprise Architecture Tool Kit and the U.S. Federal Government's Enterprise Architecture Program model. Bob noted that the ETRM project was a natural consequence of Eric's vision. He described the objective as follows:

ETRM was a construct that Eric, Peter, and I discussed a lot. It was a basic framework designed to help us discuss technology issues such as integration, openness and so on. These were called domains in the ETRM framework. As we created the ETRM, we proceeded from the general level to the more detailed level of technology specification. The members of the Council evaluated and discussed past IT decisions and debated to reach a consensus with regard to future decisions. The members evaluated each technology according to its appropriateness for the Service Oriented Architecture (SOA) objective of the Commonwealth.

The relevant drafts of the ETRM were posted online for public comments and distributed to the Executive Branch agency's CIOs. In response to these postings, the ITD received hundreds of comments from State agencies, citizens of Massachusetts, other states, other countries, and from technologists around the world. The ITD has made changes to the ETRM draft based on the comments received. The EAC created several drafts of the ETRM document.

The ITD adopted the versions 1.0 and 2.0 of the ETRM on April 21, 2004 and May 5, 2005, respectively. The ETRM consisted of two interdependent parts, the reference model and the reference architecture (shown in Exhibit 4). Although the ETRM model outlined the domains, disciplines and technology areas, the ETRM architecture compiled the technical specifications for the technical areas. The adoption of the ETRM was mandatory only for agencies within the Executive Branch of the Government. The ETRM incorporated the standards, specifications and technologies that were necessary for the State to achieve the Service Oriented Architecture (SOA). In an SOA-based environment (Exhibit 3), all IT systems made their resources available to other IT systems in the network as independent services. The interactions between the IT systems occurred in a standardized manner. This provided a more flexible coupling of resources than was possible using the systems integration approach. The systems integration approach created a rigid coupling of the IT systems; thus, access to the resources on such systems was not standardized.

From Open Standards to Open Formats

In 2004, the State's main archive was primarily a paper-only facility. Because the State lacked a digital archive, only a few agencies transferred their electronic records to a central location. Over decades of IT use, the Executive Branch had generated billions of electronic records. Consequently, the ITD was interested in improving the electronic archiving practices of the State. Maintaining the *status quo* of archiving records did not guarantee security, easy access or the easy exchange of information within agencies and between agencies and citizens. Moreover, agencies stored their electronic records in different proprietary formats. This posed the risk that State records would be inaccessible in the future because they were locked into proprietary formats.

On January 15, 2005, about a year after the adoption of the ETRM, Eric confirmed that the Executive Branch of the Commonwealth was poised to extend the open standards approach to the data format area (Kriss, 2005):

We are now ready to extend the concept of open standards to the next stage. We will extend the definition of open standards to include what we will be calling Open Formats. Open formats are specifications for data file formats based on an underlying open standards, developed by an open community, and affirmed by a standards body; or de facto format standards controlled by other entities that are fully documented and available for public use under perpetual, royalty-free, and nondiscriminatory terms. An example is text (TXT) and Portable Document Format (PDF) document files.

Eric proceeded to explain the reasons for the extension:

Why should we care about formats? Simply put, the question is whether, when we look back a hundred years from now, we will be able to read records of what we did today. It is an overriding imperative of the American democratic system that we cannot have our public documents locked up in some kind of proprietary format, perhaps unreadable in future, or subject to proprietary system license that restricts access.

Challenge: Choosing an Open Data Format for the ETRM

Once the open data format was defined as the new goal, the ITD faced the challenge of selecting an open data format for the ETRM version 3.0. In 2003, the Extensible Markup Language (XML) was emerging as an industry standard. XML was a set of reference definitions or schemas that allowed the user to create documents to be opened and processed by similar XML-compatible applications, regardless of vendor.

When the ITD adopted the ETRM, there were various kinds of XML reference schemas on the market. They were mostly incompatible with each other. Hence, the ITD seriously considered only two XML formats.

The first format was the OASIS Open Document Format (ODF) standard, which was developed through an open process and adopted by a standards-setting body. Its patents were held by Sun Microsystems, which had licenses that imposed minimal legal restrictions on the users. The second was Microsoft's 2003 Office XML Reference Schema, also called Office XML, which was copyrighted and patented by Microsoft. Neither Office XML nor the ODF standard required the State to abandon its existing investments in the legacy IT systems. The change would only affect office documents. While only Microsoft Office products supported the Office XML format, multiple vendors of office products had already implemented, or planned to implement, the ODF. The open-source productivity software, Open Office, already supported ODF. In 2003, the ITD staff piloted the use of open source-based Open Office applications side-by-side with Microsoft Office (see comparison charts in Exhibits 3 and 6).

Based on the satisfactory results, the ITD included both formats in its approved list of open data formats in the ETRM version 3.0. In summer 2004, the ITD began negotiations with Microsoft with the goal of making Office XML more open. The advantage of Office XML was that it worked well with all Microsoft applications. However, the license had legal restrictions that the ODF did not have. Furthermore, the code of Office XML had some proprietary XML codes. Despite these concerns, the ITD included Office XML under the list of Open Data Formats in ETRM version 3.0.

After the online posting of the draft, the ITD deleted Office XML from the draft to diffuse the negative feedback from the external stakeholders. In an effort to alleviate the fears expressed about Office XML, the ITD's Architectural Council hosted several public forums on the issue. Representatives from companies such as IBM, Sun, Adobe, Microsoft and OASIS participated in the forums. There was a consensus among participants that the "openness" criterion for data formats was a continuum; nevertheless, they concluded that the licensing terms and nature of Office XML reference schema did not meet the emerging criteria of openness. Before the June 16 2005 Open Data Format forum, the ITD upgraded its criteria for defining openness. Eric stated that the test for openness would thenceforth include three elements:

- It must be published and subject to peer review
- It must be subject to joint stewardship
- It must have no or absolutely minimal legal restrictions attached to it.

Stuart McKee, who represented Microsoft at the meeting, made the following comment:

We do have some concerns that we are now not on the list and, in fact, I think you stood before this body and talked about us being on the list. So, I guess the question is how does this policy evolve over time, what could we expect when we are on the list, off the list, can we get back on the list?

In response to the inquiry, Eric said the following:

If you dropped the patent entirely, if you were to publish the standard and then make provisions for future changes to that standard to be part of a joint stewardship that is no longer solely controlled by Microsoft Corporation, then we would be delighted to begin a true technical comparison of your standard with the open document standard and go from there.

Who has the Right to Make Architectural Decisions for IT?

In July 2005, Eric wondered what he should do. Based on the Open Data Forum discussions, it was clear to him that the participants did not believe that Office XML was 'sufficiently open'. The issue was to decide if Office XML should be included, delayed for two years or kept off the ETRM version 3.5 list. On July 28 2005, representatives of the Executive Office of Administration and Finance (EOAF) and ITD had a courtesy meeting with Microsoft. The CIO, Peter Quinn, formally informed Microsoft that Office XML would not be included in the ETRM version 3.5 because of its lack of openness. From August 29 to September 9, 2005, the ITD posted the draft of the new ETRM 3.5 online for public comments. The ITD announced that a final ratification of the open document format decision would be made after an 11-day public comment period. A total of 157 email and mail comments were submitted. Ninety-seven were endorsements of the included amendments to the ETRM, 46 submissions were critical of the ETRM's omissions and 13 contributors offered both praise and criticism. Seven of the negative comments were from Massachusetts's public officials. A significant number of the critical comments were from advocates of persons with disabilities. The advocates registered serious concerns that the ODF decision had ignored the needs of people with disabilities and the fact that their software products were not yet ODF-capable.

All submissions from the major corporations were positive except the comment from an individual from Microsoft. On September 21, 2005, the ITD adopted the final ETRM 3.5 version that excluded Office XML. After the adoption of the final ETRM version, Bob Stack resigned and moved back into the private sector.

In October 2005, The Senate Post Audit and Oversight Committee (SPAOC) hosted a public hearing on the ODF issue. Members of the committee challenged the authority of the ITD to adopt the ETRM. Some also raised the issue that the ITD was in a possible violation of the State or Federal Disabilities Law. The CIO, Peter Quinn and the Legal Counsel of ITD had to defend the decision before the committee. After the hearing was over, the committee requested that the implementation of the ODF be delayed until more facts were established. However, because of Massachusetts's law, the Commonwealth's Uniform Electronic Transaction Act, chapter 110G sections 17, authorized the ITD to define and adopt IT standards and policy. The unit decided to retain its ODF plan and its schedule to initiate the implementation of the plan in January 2007.

Shortly, after the SPAOC hearings, someone leaked a story to the Boston Globe in November 2005. The published article alleged that Peter Quinn was under investigation because of six unauthorized trips that he made. The allegations later proved to be false. Furthermore, in December 2005, news got to Peter Quinn that some legislators had taken steps to block the funds that were needed to finance the ITD projects. Some members of the House also prepared a legislation that was intended to eliminate the Office of the CIO altogether. Peter Quinn believed that certain members of the Legislature and of the Secretary of State's Office were prime instigators of the legislation. That was the last straw for Mr. Quinn. He resigned his position and left the State Government in December 2005.

What Would Happen to ODF?

ITD hired a new CIO in February 2006. Mitt Romney, who had but one year left as Governor, named Louis Gutierrez to replace Mr. Peter Quinn. Thomas Trimarco was named Secretary of the Executive Office for Administration and Finance. Gutierrez left his position as Chief Technology strategist at the University of Massachusetts Medical School. He had served in the State Government as the State's first CIO from 1996 to 1998. He returned in 2003 as CIO of the Executive Office of the Health and Human Services (HHS), where he worked through to June 2004. After he had assumed the CIO position, he remained committed to the ETRM framework and ODF as the open standard for the Massachusetts' Executive Branch. However, he showed a willingness to postpone the January 2007 ODF implementation schedule if the preconditions of the adoption were not met. Gutierrez believed that the ETRM and the ODF did not inherently advantage or disadvantage any particular office suite. Hence, under the leadership of Gutierrez, the ITD forged ahead with their plans to make the ODF the default standard for the Executive Branch.

In 2006, the ITD evaluated the software tools called ODF converters (plug-ins) that enabled regular Microsoft Office applications to create and read files in the ODF format. In May 2006, the CIO announced that third-party ODF-converters had enabled Microsoft Office users to open and save files in the ODF format. Microsoft Office products were then deemed to have satisfied the ETRM's requirement for open document formats. Furthermore, the ITD conducted pilot tests using ODF-enabled software. One of the purposes of the pilot tests was to examine the impact of the concurrent use of divers ODF-compatible products. For example, the ITD investigated if the ODF files that were created by one vendors product could be easily opened and undated by other products. The ITD successfully exchanged ODF files between Star Office and Open Office, and between Open Office and Microsoft Office. These results verified the assumption that the ODF files could be read across the software of different vendors.

Moreover, Gutierrez signed a Memorandum of Understanding in August 2006, which assured the Massachusetts Office on Disability and the Department of Health and Human Services that the ITD would design, procure, certify and develop training for software that was accessible to people with disabilities and implement an accessibility laboratory. He appointed a new accessibility group within the ITD and promised that future plans and the implementation of the ODF would consider the needs of people with disabilities. He also introduced a process whereby the ETRM would be reviewed and updated every six months to keep it current.

However, the activities targeting the ITD persisted in the Legislature. An amendment to the bill was proposed that was intended to largely strip the ITD of its decision-making authority. The amendment was to be attached to an economic stimulus bill. Senator Michael Morrissey sponsored the amendment. The backers of the amendment desired that the authority and decision rights for IT standards be assigned to a Government task force and the Secretary of State's Office for approval. Louis Brian Burke, a lobbyist for Microsoft Corp, was backing the amendment. Furthermore, the Legislature refused to set a date for the debate on the IT bond bill that was the tool for funding the ITD projects. With these political pressures, Gutierrez resigned his CIO position in October 4, 2006. His reason for resigning was that the Legislature had refused to fund the ITD's IT projects. A senior civil servant within the ITD, Bethann Pepoli, was named the acting state CIO.

CURRENT CHALLENGES/PROBLEMS FACING THE ORGANIZATION

A new administration under the leadership of Governor, Deval Patrick, took office in 2007. The new Governor, a Democrat, was elected partly due to his promise to bring a new unity between the branches of Government. Bethann Pepoli remained the acting State CIO. She had to decide how to move the ODF process forward. In a period in which the gulf between the ODF and the Office XML camps seemed to be entrenched by new developments. While the International Standards Organization (ISO) declared ODF to be a global standard, the European Computer Manufacturers Association (ECMA) standards body declared Microsoft's Office XML to be an open data format. Microsoft's data format was renamed Ecma-376 Office Open XML. Bethann had to revisit the ETRM decision again—Should Ecma-376 Office Open XML format be added to the list of open data formats in the ETRM version 4.0 or not?

At a higher level, ITD faced major organizational challenges. The agency CIO's were still autonomous of the office of CIO. So it was unclear if the office of the CIO had enough power to enforce its policies. It was also unclear if a new CIO and the ITD would really be able to exert their autonomy in IT matters without being frustrated by the legislature's power of funding. As listed in exhibit 5, CIO had no authority to require agency CIOs to implement his/her mandates. It was also unresolved if the CIO's position should be a civil servant position rather than a political appointee. Finally, the ITD IT governance structures needed to be fully enacted and integrated in the laws of the state.

REFERENCES

Bray, H. (2003, December 22). Open-source battle is heating up. *Boston Globe*. Retrieved August 4, 2008, from http://www.boston.com/business/technology/articles/

Canadian State Government. (2005). *Free and open source software—Cost comparison model*. Retrieved August 4, 2008, from http://www.tbs-sct.gc.ca/fap-paf/oss-ll/foss-llo/model-eng.asp

Cisco Systems. (1998). *Ontario Government pioneers next generation of e-government*. San Jose, CA: Cisco Systems, Inc.

Cullen, R. (2007). E-government in Canada: Transformation for the digital age. *Information and Polity, 12*(3), 187–191.

Gartner. (2006, February). *How to manage the consolidation of government IT infrastructure*. (Gartner Report # G00137407). Stamford, CT: Gartner.

Harris, R., & Kost, J. (2008, January). Dealing with roadblocks to centralized government IT. *Gartner Industrial Research*, G00151858. Retrieved August 4, 2008, from http://www.Cio.state.nm.us/content/cioCouncil/governmentITConsolidation-DealingWithRoadblocks.pdf

Information Technology Division. (2006a). *Facts about information technology division*. Retrieved November 18, 2006 from http://www.mass.gov/portal/site/massgovportal/

Information Technology Division. (2006b). *Information domain – Enterprise technical reference model v.3.5*. Retrieved August 4, 2008, from http://www.mass.gov/portal/site/massgovportal/

Korteland, E., & Bekkers, V. (2007). Diffusion of e-government innovations in the Dutch public sector: The case of digital community policing. *Information Polity, 12*(3), 139–150.

Kriss, E. (2005). *Informal comments on open document*. Retrieved August 4, 2008, from http://www.mass.gov/eoaf/open_formats_comments.html

Mayo, S. (2004). *E-Government case study analysis: Unisys lays a services-oriented architecture foundation for the GSA. IDC Report, October (No. 32079)*. Framingham, MA: IDC.

NASCIO. (2006, March). *IT consolidation and shared services: States seeking economies of scale, issue brief.* Retrieved August 4, 2008, from http://www.nascio. org/publications/documents/nascio-con_and_ss_issue_brief_0306.pdf

NASCIO. (2006, May). *Service oriented architecture: An enabler of the agile enterprise in state government, research brief.* Retrieved August 4, 2008, from http://www.enterprise-architecture.info/Images/Documents/NASCIO_SOA_Research_Brief_2006.pdf

Navaro, C., Gabriel, J., Dewhurst, F., Penalver, B., & Juan, A. (2007). Factors affecting the use of e-government in the telecommunications industry of Spain. *Technovation, 27*(10), 595–604. doi:10.1016/j.technovation.2007.03.003

Peterson, S. (2004). The open road. *Government technology.* Retrieved August 4, 2008, from http://www.govtech.net/magazine/story.php?id=87471

Sharma, S. (2007). Exploring best practices in public-private partnership (PPP) in e-government through select Asian case studies. *International Library Review, 39*(3/4), 203–210.

Welsh, W. (2003, October 27). Open source riles software makers – Massachusetts ignites furor with new strategy. *Washington Technology, 18*(15). Retrieved August 4, 2008, from http://www.washingtontechnology.com/print/18_15/22000-1.html

APPENDIX

Exhibit 1

Figure 1. Exhibit 1.

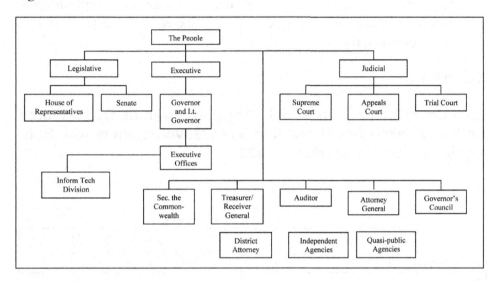

Exhibit 2

Target State (ITD, 2006b)

The Commonwealth is transitioning from a silo, application-centric and agency-centric information technology investments to an enterprise approach where applications are designed to be flexible, to take advantage of shared and reusable components, to facilitate the sharing and reuse of data where appropriate and to make the best use of the technology infrastructure that is available. Implementation of the ETRM will result in a Service Oriented Architecture (SOA) for the Commonwealth that uses open standards solutions where appropriate to construct and deliver online government services. Agencies are expected to migrate towards compliance with the ETRM as they consider new information technology investments or make major enhancements/replacement to existing systems. Projected benefits and goals:

- Ease of integration of applications to enable inter-agency collaboration and sharing
- Increase level of application interoperability within the Commonwealth

- Efficient sharing, and re-use, of current information technology assets
- Expand the consideration of possible alternatives as part of a best value evaluation of potential information technology solutions
- Reduce the level of resources and costs required to develop, support, and maintain government applications
- Enable the consolidation of the state's information technology infrastructure to reduce costs, improve service levels, and increase operational flexibility across the enterprise.

Exhibit 3

2003 Cost Comparison Model: Proprietary versus Open Source Software (taken from Canadian State Government report. Published in 2004 and updated in 2005)

		Costs per Desktop Computer			
Proprietary software installation		Initial	Annual Maintenance/ License	Annual Internal Support	Total Annual Expenditure
Desktop Type	3				
Setup Time (hrs)	4	48			
Hardware		850	125	60	185
Operating System		100	10	24	34
Office Productivity Tools		250	30	144	174
Client Access Licenses		0	0	0	0
Anti – Virus/Spam		20	6	901	907
TOTALS		1,268			1,301

		Costs per Desktop Computer			
Open source software installation		Initial	Annual Maintenance/ License	Annual Internal Support	Total Annual Expenditure
Desktop Type	1				
Setup Time (hrs)	0.5	8			
Hardware		675	75	84	159
Operating System		0	0	34	34
Office Productivity tools		0	0	202	202
Client Access Licenses		0	0	0	0
Anti – Virus/Spam		0	0	17	17
TOTALS		683			412

	YEAR	1	2	3	4	5
	Hardware	1,333,754	1,333,754	2,365,754	618,129	1,449,379
	Software	1,224,400	1,224,400	3,258,100	1,244,231	1,244,231
Cost of proprietary	**People**	4,113,582	4,113,582	4,159,255	4,069,712	4,111,779
	Total	6,671,735	6,671,735	9,783,108	5,932,071	6,805,388
	Hardware	1,153,407	1,153,407	1,153,407	1,153,407	1,153,407
Cost of free open-source software	**Software**	0	0	0	0	0
	People	1,798,185	1,798,185	1,798,185	1,798,185	1,798,185
	Total	2,951,592	2,951,592	2,951,592	2,951,592	2,951,592
	Hardware	109,250	14,250	14,250	14,250	14,250
	Software	2,480,000	0	0	0	0
Cost of migration	**People**	1,605,000	20,000	20,000	20,000	20,000
	Total	4,194,250	34,250	34,250	34,250	34,250

Exhibit 4

ETRM Reference Architecture

SUMMARY of TECHNOLOGY SPECIFICATIONS	
Technology Areas	**Technology Specifications**
ACCESS AND DELIVERY	
Web Browser	• **Must support 128 bit encryption and X.509 v.3 digital certificates**
Enterprise Portal	
Executive Office Sub Portals & Agency Web sites	• Java Specification Request (JSR) 168 for J2EE based applications • C# Portals for .Net based applications • **Web Services for Remote Portal (WSRP) v. 1.0 for Web services**
Formats	• Hypertext Markup Language (HTML) v. 4.01 • **Extensible Markup Language (XML) v. 1.0 (Third Edition) or v 1.1 when necessary**
Protocols	• Hypertext Transfer Protocol (HTTP)/1.1 • Secure Hypertext Transfer Protocol (HTTPS) – SSL, minimum 128 bit key length • **Simple Object Access Protocol (SOAP) v. 1.2**
INFORMATION	
XML Specifications	• Extensible Markup Language (XML) v. 1.0 • XML Schema Part 1: Structures and XML Schema Part 2: Data types • Extensible Stylesheet Language (XSL) v. 1.0 • **XML Query Language (XQUERY) 1.0**
Community of Interest XML	• **Global Justice XML Data Model (Global JXDM) v. 3.0.2**
Metadata	• **Web Service Description Language (WSDL) v. 1.1**

SUMMARY of TECHNOLOGY SPECIFICATIONS	
Open Formats	• **OASIS OpenDocument Format For Office Applications (OpenDocument) v. 1.0**
	• **Plain Text Format**
	• **Hypertext Document Format v. 4.01**
Other Acceptable Formats	• Portable Document Format v. 1.5 •
APPLICATION	
Development Model	• **Interoperability Basic Profile (WS-I Basic Profile) v. 1.0**
Development Methodology	• **Unified Process (UP)**
INTEGRATION	
Web Service Registry	• **Universal Description, Discovery and Integration (UDDI) v. 2.0**
Messaging Services	• Java Messaging Service (JMS) v. 1.1 • **Simple Object Access Protocol (SOAP) v 1.1**
SECURITY	
Identity Repository	• **Lightweight Directory Access Protocol (LDAP) v. 3.0**
Identity Assertion	• **Security Assertion Markup Language (SAML) v. 1.1**
Web Service Authentication	• **XML Signature**
Encryption	• **XML Encryption**
Web Service Message Header	• **WS-Security v. 1.0**

Exhibit 5

Challenges Facing the Massachusetts Public Sector

Challenges	Issues underlying the challenges
Definition of the scope of the decision authority of the CIO of the executive branch in matters of setting standards policy was unresolved.	- Most divisions of the state had agency CIOs, who had autonomous decision-making authority vis-à-vis the CIO of the Executive branch.
It remained unresolved if the CIO's position should remain a political appointment or if it should be made a civil servant position.	- At best, most political appointments lasted about three years. The appointments were made after the Governor was in inaugurated and the appointees left before the four years cycle expired.
The IT governance structure was still incompletely defined.	- The laws of the state did not define appropriate nor expected processes for making ITD policies. - The laws did not include mechanisms that would integrate inputs of the legislature in the processes of ITD.
It remained unclear how ITD could exert its legislatively granted autonomy to make policy in technical matters.	- Legislature had shown that it would reject and block ITD's projects, through its power over the annual funding cycle, if it disagreed with a technical policy of the division.

This work was previously published in the Journal of Cases on Information Technology, Volume 11, Issue 1, edited by Mehdi Khosrow-Pour, pp. 65-82, copyright 2009 by IGI Publishing (an imprint of IGI Global).

Chapter 2
Democratic Deliberation in Online Consultation Forums:
A Case Study of the Casino Debate in Singapore

Kevin Y. Wang
University of Minnesota-Twin Cities, USA

EXECUTIVE SUMMARY

This chapter examines the extent to which the Internet can represent a place for negotiation, consensus building, and civic participation using Singapore's online consultation portal and the debate over the decision to build the nation's first casino resort as a case study. The structural design of the consultation portal and the entire content of a discussion thread with 508 posts were analyzed with a conceptual framework drawn from previous studies of democratic deliberation. Findings suggest that while the forum reflects some criteria for deliberation, the lack of transparency and government participation raises the question over the quality of the discourse and overall effectiveness of this online medium. Current challenges, recommendations, and directions for future research and development are discussed.

DOI: 10.4018/978-1-4666-0981-5.ch002

BACKGROUND

The rapid diffusion of information communication technologies (ICTs) over the last two decades has brought changes to the political landscape throughout the world. It has been noted that the Internet's unique technological properties, such as interactivity, immediacy, connectivity, point-to-point and non-hierarchical modes of communication, low cost to users, and accessibility across national boundaries (Barber, Mattson, & Peterson, 1997), will reduce the distance and barriers between voters and politicians, and consequently facilitate a more direct citizen involvement in the political process (Agre, 2002). One of the many ways that such civic engagement can be seen is through the discussion of political issues *online* – in chatrooms, message boards, blogs, social media sites, and other types of web-based forums.

Although many previous studies of online political talk have noted that the Web provides a meeting place for people from different social, cultural and political backgrounds to form communities, build social relationships, share opinions, and discuss issues with one another (Baym, 1995; Rheingold, 1993; Wellman, 1999), others have observed that, rather than facilitating diversity, people tend to interact with users who share similar interests and values (Van Alstyne & Brynjolfsson, 1996) and hear the echoes of their own voices (Sunstein, 2001). Whether the Internet can truly represent a public sphere for negotiation, consensus building, and democratic deliberation remains to be seen, but the conditions in which online discussion may or may not flourish, and the criteria used to evaluate its outcomes are key to answering this question.

This chapter addresses these issues through the lens of a case study that explores the structure and the content of an online discussion thread in Singapore's online consultation forum. As the high-tech hub of Southeast Asia, Singapore is known for its adoption and development of information communication technologies in the private and public sectors. Recent studies indicate that Internet penetration rate in Singapore has reached 67.4%, with more than three million users (Internet World Stats, 2009). Singapore's electronic government scheme and the overall e-readiness have also consistently received high praises from benchmark reports (e.g., Economist Intelligence Unit, 2008; West, 2007). While these achievements are remarkable, Singapore is also known for its censorship and control over the Internet, a practice that has long attracted criticism domestically and abroad (e.g., Amnesty International, 2004; Gomez, 2000). The juxtaposition between the freedom afforded by technological advancement and the restrictions imposed by government regulation therefore makes Singapore a unique case.

In 2005, the Singapore government proposed plans to develop two casino-based entertainment resorts in an effort to stimulate its tourism industry. The decision to build the nation's first casino generated a vibrant debate among Singaporeans over whether the government should abandon its long held position against legalized gambling. In the months leading up to the final announcement, the government solicited views and feedback on the subject matter from the public through various communication channels, including several online discussion threads in its online consultation portal. By examining the effectiveness, or lack thereof, of this online medium to encourage public discussion and facilitate deliberation, this case study hopes to contribute to our understandings of online discussions in a political context and also to the broader conversation about the promise of the Internet as a public sphere.

SETTING THE STAGE

Online Consultation and Relevant Research

Online consultation, a term that refers to the government's use of web-based technologies to seek policy suggestion and feedback from the public, is an emerging trend in electronic government research and practice. The Organisation for Economic Co-operation and Development (OECD) defined online consultation as, "A two-way relation in which citizens provide feedback to government. It is based on the prior definition by government of the issue on which citizens' views are being sought and requires the provision of information" (OECD, 2001, p. 5). In other words, the government identifies the issues for consultation, sets the questions and manages the process, while citizens are invited to contribute their views and opinions through web-enabled applications.

From the government's perspective, online consultation represents one of the many communication *channels* that, in addition to other traditional means, are used to reach out to the public. From the citizen's perspective, it may be seen as an online meeting *place* where people interact with one another to express their opinions or discuss public policy issues. However, online consultation differs significantly from other online fora, such as blogs, bulletin boards, or social networking sites, in the sense that it is considered to be an official mechanism of the state and not merely a platform for social interaction. As such, the practice of online consultation is often guided by legislations that establish the implementation process or require the outcome of the consultation to be analyzed, archived, and relayed back to the policy circuit. Many countries around the world (e.g., Canada, Sweden, The Netherlands, United Kingdom, and the United States) have developed different forms of online consultation, but most vary along the lines of online public hearings, online town hall meetings, online guest or panel Q& A, live multimedia events, public comment forums, and online focus groups (Clift, 2004).

As a relatively new phenomenon, previous studies of online consultations have initially emerged from the government circle with a focus on the development of procedural guidelines and policies for implementation (Macintosh & Whyte, 2003; Poland, 2001). With online consultation and other similar e-government practices gaining popularity in recent years, a steady stream of scholarly research on citizen participation in policy making has also emerged. For example, Coleman and Gøtze (2001) argued that various forms of online public engagement platforms would strengthen the quality of representative democracy by creating opportunities for mutual learning between citizens and their representatives. Macintosh, Robson, Smith, and Whyte (2003) noted that increased level of civic participation may be particularly true among young people, who are often more comfortable with new communication technologies. Although the democratic and participatory potential of online consultation and related practices are widely recognized (e.g., Chadwick, 2003; Coglianese, 2005; Fountain, 2001; Shulman, Schlosberg, Zavestoski, & Courard-Hauri, 2003), there is also a general consensus on several areas of concerns.

For instance, Stephens, McCusker, O'Donnell, Newman, and Fagan (2006) found a culture of cynicism exists among citizens with respect to state/administration initiated consultation processes. This lack of trust in the authenticity of the process raises the question of whether the online consultation process can truly be effective. As Coleman (2004) suggested, "For online consultations to be seen as more than a gesture, there must be tangible evidence that [government officials] are interacting with the public and taking views online contributors into account in their deliberations" (p. 20). In addition, Noveck (2005) observed that in order to increase the level of participation, the design of the online platforms must facilitate and convey a sense of community to the participants. Finally, Whyte and Macintosh (2001) pointed out that the design of public consultation systems should promote shared awareness of activity and identity among users, while creating a sense of transparency in the consultation as well as the decision-making processes.

All of these issues indicate that, while online consultation represents a promising public practice and a rich subject for scholarly inquiry, more interdisciplinary dialogue and research is needed to develop guidelines for conducting consultation, identify criteria for evaluation and assessment, and design appropriate technological platforms that would facilitate citizen interaction and participation.

Theoretical Issue: Criteria for Democratic Deliberation

The idea that policy decisions should emerge from a dialogue involving citizens and their elected officials is the fundamental premise behind online consultation practices, and is also one of the central tenants of representative democracy. Many scholars (e.g., Cohen, 1989; Habermas, 1984; Rawls, 1971) have argued that a healthy democratic system requires not just conversation about political issues, but a unique process of "deliberation" that is significantly different from daily conversation. In the words of John Elster (1998), this is a process of collective decision that requires "the participation of all who will be affected by the decision of their representatives, and includes the decision making by means of arguments offer by and to participants who are committed to the values of rationality and impartiality" (p. 8).

Dahlberg (2001), drawing heavily from Habermas' earlier work on communicative action, constructed a model that specifies the criteria for democratic deliberation as: (a) being autonomous from economic and political manipulation; (b) demonstrating rational reasoning, rather than dogmatic assertions; (c) examining the issue with reflexivity to the larger social context; (d) demonstrating a commitment to mutual dialogue with respect; (e) displaying sincerity, with each participant making an effort to understand all relevant information; and (f) showing inclusion and equality toward all participants. Habermas was not alone in advocating specific criteria for this deliberative process. Barber (1984), in presenting his case for a "strong" democracy, also argued that a "strong political talk" should involve: (a) an articulation of interests; (b) persuasion; (c) agenda setting; (d) affiliation and affection; (e) mutuality; (f) self-expression; (g) re-formulation and re-conceptualization; and 8) community-building. Similarly, Dahl (1991) noted that effective participation, equality, enlightened understanding and control of agenda are the requirements for deliberation.

Although the specific terminology used by these scholars may differ, the central tenets overlap with one another to describe the ideal condition in which an informed citizenry can actively participate in the formation of public policy decisions through a process of democratic deliberation. The key criteria for democratic deliberation as described in previous literature can be summarized in Table 1.

Research Questions

If one were to accept that the goal of online consultation is to gather citizen feedback on public policy issues through dialogues and conversations, and that such interaction among citizens and their elected officials is at the heart of democratic governance, then the abovementioned criteria for democratic deliberation provide a framework for evaluating online consultation practices. Therefore, the broader question for the case study was: to what extent does Singapore's online consultation forum reflect the ideals of democratic deliberation?

More specifically, this larger issue could be further divided into two research questions that explore both *structural* and *content* perspectives. Here, "structure" referred to the design of the online platform, the guidelines for discussion, and the other characteristics of the online consultation practice that may create an en-

Table 1. Criteria for democratic deliberation

Criteria	Definition
Autonomy	The deliberation and the participants must be free from manipulation of political/economic power.
Transparency	The process should be visible from outside, and contributions should be fed to the policy making circuit by formal mechanisms.
Equality of access	Every person affected by the validity claims under consideration is equally entitled to participate.
Privacy and trust	Privacy and anonymity of the participants must be protected to encourage candid discussion and the level of trust.
Enlightened understanding	Participants must have a good understanding of issues being discussed in order to make sound judgment.
Reflexivity	Participants must critically examine their cultural values, assumptions, and interests, as well as the larger social context.
Mutuality	Participants must attempt to understand the argument from the other's perspective. This requires a commitment to an ongoing dialogue with difference in which participants respectfully listen to each other.

vironment to facilitate or impede democratic deliberation. For example, whether there were barriers to participate in consultation process might be an indicator the degree of equal access. Likewise, the extent to which background information of the policy issue being discussed was provided in the discussion forum might also signal whether an enlightened understanding of the subject matter could possibly be achieved.[1] Table 2 shows research question one and the criteria for democratic deliberation measured from the structural standpoint:

On the other hand, the "content" perspective referred to the actual posts and opinions expressed by participants in the discussion. For example, the type of arguments and the sources that users relied on to make their claims might reflect the level of reflexivity demonstrated by the users. Further, whether the interaction led to a sustained debate among participants, as seen in the frequency and diversity of participation, might indicate the level of mutuality in the discussion forum. Table 3 shows research question two and the criteria for democratic deliberation measured from the content point of view:

CASE DESCRIPTION

Online Consultation in Singapore

In Singapore, the practice of online consultation is administered by the Feedback Unit, an office set up in 1985 to solicit citizen feedback on public policy issues in

Table 2. Research question one and criteria for democratic deliberation

Research Question #1: To what extent does the *structure* of Singapore's online consultation reflect the ideals of democratic deliberation?	
Sub-Questions:	**Criteria for Democratic Deliberation Measured:**
What is the degree of administrative control on the online consultation forums?	Autonomy
What is the level of transparency in the management of the online consultation forum?	Transparency
What are the criteria for participating in the online consultation forum?	Equality of access
How are the issues of privacy and anonymity handled on the online consultation forum?	Privacy and trust
What kind of background information of the issues discussed in the online consultation forum does the government provide?	Enlightened understanding

order to help the government shape and fine-tune its policy decisions. Key operations of the Feedback Unit range from hosting dialogue sessions, tea sessions, or public forums, to publishing two publications, *Policy Digest* and *Feedback News*, that aim to help Singaporeans to understand the rationale behind these policies (Feedback Unit, 2005). The online consultation portal (http://www.feedback.gov.sg) was launched in March 1997 to reach out to Internet-savvy and younger Singaporeans. As seen in Figure 1, the portal includes several feedback mechanisms such as: online consultation papers on different policy topics, online polls, an online discussion forum, policy digests that provide relevant background information, a general feedback/reply area, a specific comment section for cutting red tape and government waste, and a separate section on integrated casino resort. In addition, the portal features a calendar of events, a newsroom for media relations, and an area where selected official responses to citizen feedbacks are posted.

Table 3. Research question two and criteria for democratic deliberation

Research Question #2: To what extent does the *content* of Singapore's online consultation reflect the ideals of democratic deliberation?	
Sub-Questions:	**Criteria for Democratic Deliberation Measured:**
What kinds of opinions are expressed? What is the level of flaming?	Reflexivity
What is the frequency of participation? What is the level of diversity among participants?	Mutuality

Figure 1. Singapore's online consultation portal. This screenshot was taken in June 2005. (© 2005, Government of Singapore. Used with permission.).

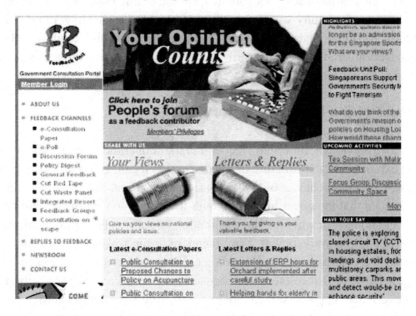

The Debate over Legalized Gambling

In Singapore, a debate involving government officials, political parties, religious groups, industry lobbyists, and concerned citizens took place after the government announced in April 2005[2] its plan to build two casino-based Integrated Resorts (IRs) – and thereby effectively legalized gambling in the country. While the Singapore government had for many years opposed the establishment of casinos for fear of creating social ills in the country, the decision to change the long-standing policy against casinos was primarily based on the economic benefits that integrated resorts might bring. It was projected that the two Integrated Resorts would boost Singapore's tourism industry, while creating about 35,000 jobs directly or indirectly (Ministry of Trade and Industry, 2005). On the other hand, opponents of legalized gambling cited the potential negative impacts on individuals or the society at large. Concerns about social order, public corruption, gambling addiction, and moral values were noted by several social and religious groups as reasons for opposition to the government plan (Au, 2004; Chia, 2004; Teo, 2004).

To address these potential social issues associated with legalized gambling, the Singapore government proposed a set of social safeguards that included: "a minimum age requirement, a membership system for Singapore residents, self-exclusion programs, guidelines on credit extension, voluntary loss limits, advertising guidelines and patron education" (Ministry of Trade and Industry, 2004, para. 3). At the same time, citizen feedback was solicited via the online consultation portal. The data for the present study was drawn from one such discussion entitled, "Social Safeguards for Integrated Resort with Casino Gaming," with a total of 508 posts between December 30, 2004 and April 24, 2005. The discussion thread was content analyzed in its entirety.

Structure of the Discussion Forum

As described previously, the criteria for democratic deliberation were used as a framework to explore both the structure of the discussion forum and online consultation portal, as well as the content of the discussion itself. First, the degree of administrative control that the government had over the discussion forum symbolizes the level of autonomy – or whether the consultation forum was free from manipulation of political and economic power. The Singapore forum was free from commercial influences as it clearly prohibited any direct selling, advertisement, or promotional messages. However, since the online consultation portal represents a subset of a larger government apparatus, it cannot be totally free from administrative control. Although prior approval was not a requirement for posting, government administrators had the right to remove posts that were deemed irrelevant to or inappropriate for the topic of discussion, and had taken such action against several participants' posts. The removal of these posts raised questions over the impartiality of the discussion, and such concern was expressed by many. For instance, one participant wrote:

Dear Webmaster, I am re-submitting my post after a little tweaking? Hope you can allow it this time since I have taken out a few things I thought which might have incurred your honorable wrath? I had also emailed you privately but got no reply. Please let me know where I am wrong so I can improve? (User comment, 2005)

Second, the level of transparency is another important criterion of democratic deliberation, as determined by whether the management of the consultation forum was visible from outside, and whether the contributions were fed to the policy making circuit. In this respect, the consultation portal clearly fell short of providing adequate information that allowed users and the public to understand the operations of the online platform, as well as the online consultation process in general. For example, while the website had clearly stated "Terms of Use" that described different guidelines ranging from the protection of intellectual property rights to many other important issues regarding proper usage, the government could change the general practices of the consultation portal in its sole discretion without notice (Feedback Unit, 2005). In addition, the consultation portal did not present adequate information that explained the consultation process (e.g., how are the posts handled/followed up), or the similarity of and differences between feedback channels available on the consultation portal. For the discussion forum, the government offered a brief netiquette guideline that prohibited defamatory statement, name-calling, obscene, vulgar, sexually-oriented, hateful, or threatening messages. The website, however, did not provide a clear definition of what content would be considered "irrelevant" or "inappropriate" that might warrant a post's removal.

Another area where the level of transparency can be evaluated is whether government officials respond to or participate in the consultation process. While official responses were posted in a general area, government officials did not participate in specific discussion fora, which invariably provoked questions from the users. For instance:

Hi people at Feedback Unit, Really... if you would be so kind as to post a note to say "Hi", I think we would feel less strongly that you're not capturing our opinions...In fact, I feel that if *consultation* is to be done effectively, someone from the government should be here probing us with questions and counter-arguments. Feedback can be one way, but to really call it consultation, there should be two way exchanges...That will really help in breaking the perception of an un-listening government. (User comment, 2005)

While participation from government officials was lacking, general contact information for the Feedback Unit, including its mailing address, phone or fax number, and email address, was listed on the website. A detailed staff listing or directory was not available.

Third, equal participation is another aspect of democratic deliberation. For the online consultation portal in Singapore, participation appeared to be open and without restrictions based upon citizenship, age, or gender. The website only made minimal technical recommendations with regards to web browsers, and mentioned nothing about Internet connection speed or other hardware requirements. The consultation portal also stated that the content of the website is accessible for the hearing and vision impaired. An evaluation of the portal using "WAVE 3.0 Accessibility Tool," proprietary software that assesses the level of web-accessibility using industry and government guidelines, confirmed that the website was compatible to various accessibility standards.[3]

In addition, the issues of privacy and anonymity are important factors in online discussion, as they would influence the degree of trust and dictate the level of participation. In this regard, the consultation forum offered an environment that protected privacy and anonymity. A privacy policy was found on the consultation portal, which stated that the government does not capture personally identifiable data if users were only browsing the website. However, when users were participating in the activities offered by the site, such as sending feedback or posting messages in the discussion forum, the government claimed that it could collect personal data and share them with relevant government entities. Although users had the option of creating an account – thereby transmitting personal information – to the Feedback Unit, there was no required registration process before participating in the forum. Therefore, it is unclear what and how personal data were gathered when users did not voluntarily provide them. Further, posts were displayed in the discussion thread without identifiable information, such as e-mail addresses or IP addresses, which could be used to track a user's geographical location. Only a screen-name chosen by the user and the date and time of the post were shown alongside the actual message. In other words, citizens could decide to remain totally anonymous when participating in the discussion fora.

Finally, for democratic deliberation to be successful, participants of the discussion must also have an enlightened understanding of the issues being discussed in order to make a meaningful judgment. Since it was not possible to assess individual participants' level of knowledge by simply examining the content of the posts, enlightened understanding could only be explored structurally, by looking at whether the background information of the issues being discussed was provided on the portal. Since the Singapore government defines the topic of discussion in the online consultation practice, it should follow that the government would present any relevant information, such as statistics, official statements, or white papers, for participants to peruse. However, Singapore's online consultation portal failed to provide adequate information in this regard. For the particular discussion thread analyzed by this case study, the government offered only a short introduction to the topic of discussion, and an external link to the Ministry of Trade and Industry website that outlined the social safeguards for casino gaming. No other information or additional links to relevant government offices were found.

Content of the Discussion

In terms of the content of the discussion itself, the frequency of posts and interactions among users are key indicators of the mutuality and diversity of the discourse. This discussion thread had a total of 508 posts contributed by 165 uniquely identifiable users and 30 anonymous users. The average word count for each post was 220, suggesting that participants did put in some efforts to their posts, while the longest post was 1579 words. Posts were skewed toward the latter end of the four-month period specified by the government, perhaps reflecting the gradual buildup of public opinion and increased media coverage throughout the consultation period.

It is worth noting that, although there were 165 uniquely identifiable users, the discourse was dominated by a small number of active participants. For instance, five users contributed 32% of the total posts, and four other users each contributed 10 or more posts. In contrast, there were 112 users with only a single post. In other words, the level of participation in this particular discussion forum may not be characterized as broad and diverse. Further, among the 508 posts, 347 were identified "new posts" while only 141 were considered to be in "response" to other participants, indicating that there was not a sustained engagement among the participants. Overall, these statistics indicate that a sense of mutuality was somewhat lacking in the consultation forum. Finally, there was very little evidence of flaming, defined here as exchanges that involve personal attacks, insults, or hostile provocations, perhaps due to the fact that government administrators were removing potentially objectionable messages from the forum.

In terms of content, a small portion of the discussion (53 posts) was identified as irrelevant to the topic of discussion. Although a great majority (465 posts) did touch upon the general issue of integrated casino resorts, only 90 posts commented specifically on question of social safeguards, which was the main subject for consultation. Here is an example of a post that focused on the issue at hand:

I understand and support cabinet's decision of proceeding with the IR with casino. I agree that safeguards are quite necessary to address any negative social impacts. I would like to add a couple of points on the present safeguards: (a) introduce a new subject named "To be a wise gambler - Gambling education" into our education system at secondary level or incorporate it into social studies; and (b) increase the taxation on the profit from gambling. Whereas we always talk about losing money from gambling, I believe some of gamblers could be luck enough to make profits in a short term. So the government should impose a higher tax on this part of income. (User comment, 2005)

To explore signs of reflexivity – that is, the participants' ability to critically examine the issue at hand beyond their personal experiences or circumstances – each post was qualitatively analyzed to identify any source of reference, as well as the viewpoint that upon which the argument was based. The analysis revealed that, when expressing their opinions, the great majority of the post (417 out of 508) referenced personal anecdotes and beliefs as the basis of the claims. Of the 91 posts that did draw from other sources, 32 referenced other participants' comments, 30 referenced the media, 27 used a combination of both media and user, and only two posts referred to government material provided on the consultation portal. The large number of posts that relied on personal sources indicates that participants rarely go out of their ways to retrieve other information to support their arguments.

However, as for the viewpoints and perspectives expressed in the discourse, 360 out of 508 posts were identified as going beyond personal interests and belief and connecting issue to the society at large. Among them, 52% argued from a moral and social standpoint, 23% referred to the commercial and economic issues behind the casino plan, while 25% used a combination of both. As discussed previously, opponents of the casino resort argued that gambling, like many other controversial issues such as prostitution or drug use, are matters of morality that would create more social problems when legalized. This argument was highly contested by many participants. For example:

Prostitution is wrong, is a sin. Who are we to judge? Why is it a sin? Always? If it is a matter of life and death, if it is part of a culture (as we know that some places do condone it), can we say that? Are you going to banish all 'prostitutes' to hell-fire? Gambling is a sin? Can it be a game? Can it be fun? It is the addiction that comes from compulsion that and how we try to feed that compulsion that brings on the woes of addiction. And that can come about with any activity. Gambling is so addictive because of the money factor, and the adrenalin that come about with the thought of making money the easy way. (User comment, 2005)

Other participants went a step further to criticize whether the Singapore government's reversal on its longstanding position against legalized gambling is consistent with other government policies, and to question whether the economic growth promised by the casino resorts may truly be realized:

Upfront, it looks like the introduction of Casino will create some 10,000 job vacancy, however, has it been assessed how many percent of these jobs could be filled by fellow Singaporeans and attribute to the reduction in local unemployment rate? Will it require even more foreign workers to fill the vacancy and introduce further social or management problems? Current government plans to develop Singapore into educational hub, cultural center, health care center, sports center are all in the line of ethical and healthy society. However, will the introduction of casino contradict with the above initiatives? (User comment, 2005)

These posts, along with other similar ones in the forum, reflect the complexity behind the casino plan, and demonstrate that many participants were able to consider the issue from multiple perspectives.

Finally, the tone of the post was analyzed to identify whether the message expresses a pro or anti-government stance. Given Singapore's record of media censorship, it was particularly relevant to see if strict government regulation over media content and information had any negative effect on people's willingness to articulate their true opinions toward public policy. Interestingly, 13% (68 posts) of the total messages expressed a clear "pro-government" position that either supported the creation of casino resorts in Singapore or approved the government's scheme for social safeguard. In contrast, 20% (100 posts) had an "anti-government" stance and opposed the government proposal for casino gambling. Although the vast majority of the posts in the discussion thread could not be clearly identified as falling into either category, a sense of cynicism over the authenticity of the consultation process and the government's seriousness in gathering citizen feedback was widespread. For instance, one participant remarked:

All along I already expected it. No matter what we common citizens say, if the Government say they are going to do it, they will do it. You can talk about the pros and cons until pigs fly. THEY DO NOT CARE, NEITHER DO THEY LISTEN. No wonder youths today could not care less about politics. They are very smart, they know there is no point talking so much because their views will never be taken into consideration. They might as well spend their time doing things which are so much more fun while they are still in the prime of youth. (User comment, 2005)

CURRENT CHALLENGES IN SINGAPORE'S ONLINE CONSULTATION FORUM

The results of the content analysis, as described above, illustrate the extent to which Singapore's online consultation forum reflected the various elements of a demo-cratic deliberation. Structurally, the forum created an environment where equal participation, privacy, and anonymity were protected. The participants of the forum also showed some signs of reflexivity by examining the casino plan from multiple perspectives beyond personal interests. Based on the findings, it is reasonable to conclude that the online consultation forum in Singapore may have the potential to become a place for civic engagement and consensus building. However, such an ideal cannot be realized without addressing a number of issues that prevent an open and productive dialogue from occurring.

The first issue facing Singapore's online consultation forum is that the discourse in the discussion forum appeared to be fragmented from both structural and sub-stantive standpoints. Structurally, it was difficult for viewers or other participants in the discussion thread to follow a specific line of reasoning or debate because the website only displayed 25 posts per page in reverse chronological order. For example, when users replied to one another, the original post to which he or she was responding to did not appear side-by-side, or could even be located on the same page because it was posted at an earlier time. This technical limitation created confusion and misunderstanding that eventually resulted in a lack of *sustained* discussion on the subject matter. In addition, the high number (121) of single post authors also indicates that ongoing discussion among participants was rare. The effort by government administrators to remove inappropriate or irrelevant content further increased the severity of this problem, as several authors responded to posts that had been deleted, making it difficult for others to follow the conversation.

Content-wise, with less than 20% of the posts (90 out of 508) specifically commenting on the topic set out by the government for discussion, it can be argued that the discussion failed to achieve its original purpose. In addition, while many participants did go beyond their personal interests and concerns to consider the issue in light of the larger society, the majority relied solely on personal anecdotes and beliefs as the basis of their opinions. Although drawing from one's own values or experiences is natural in interpersonal conversation, for the results of online consultation to be taken more seriously by elected officials or policy makers, the participants of these online discussions can also utilize other sources, such as media reports, government statements, or relevant websites, to build their arguments with more objective and credible evidence. This ability to approach an issue critically from multiple angles with diverse viewpoints is central to the idea of reflexivity in democratic deliberation, but it was not fully seen in the case of Singapore's online consultation forum.

The second issue that stems from the findings of this case study is that many participants had strong reservations about the government's intention to listen to and consult with the public on this particular issue. As noted previously, the sentiment of distrust and resignation were vividly expressed in many posts. Here is another example:

I think it has already been decided long ago that the casino WILL be built regardless of what we say. I suspect they purposely started a so-called "debate" just to hype it up, to get people interested, to get people to talk about it...if that was what they intended, they have succeeded...thanks to us! (User comment, 2005)

Although this study is limited by its methodological approach and cannot measure the true attitudes or beliefs behind these posts, the existence of such cynicism is not a particular surprise, given Singapore's history of one-party rule. However, it does suggest that many Singapore citizens may still remain unconvinced of the actual usefulness of the online consultation practice. It also serves as a reminder that the content of interpersonal discussion, whether online or offline, is shaped and influenced by the larger social and cultural context.

In addition, the level of government participation may be another factor that contributed the issue of distrust. As described previously, there was neither elected official nor moderator presence in the discussion forum, which led many users to believe that civic consultation is just another "formality" that the government had to go through in order to "legitimize" their policy decision, which was believed to have already been finalized. The lack of transparency on how citizen feedback is gathered and reported also cast doubt on the entire consultation process. In other words, if the purpose of the consultation portal is to engage in a deliberative policy-making process with citizens, then the government must also demonstrate its ability to follow the criteria of democratic deliberation as part of this exchange. In the case of Singapore, it is clear that the government failed to create an environment in which a sense of transparency, authenticity, and trust was established and conveyed to users of the online consultation portal.

It is important to point out that the descriptions of the issues associated with the online consultation forum only reflect what the portal looked like at the time of data collection in 2005. The particular website examined by this case study is no longer available today. Instead, a new online consultation portal (http://www.reach.gov.sg) has been launched to include features that address, to a certain extent, some of the issues discussed in this chapter. In the current online discussion forum, for example, users can quote or incorporate others' comments in their entirety in their responses, thereby making the conversation easier to follow. The issues or topics for discussion are still being defined by the government; however, a separate section now allows users to start their own discussion thread on matters of their concern. Government participation in these online forums remains extremely limited, although there are instances of administrator response to user inquiries. Finally, the website suggests that feedback posted on the discussion forum is compiled into summary reports that are then transmitted to the Cabinet and other government agencies every month. Figure 2 is a screenshot of the current online consultation portal.

SOLUTIONS AND RECOMMENDATIONS

To summarize, this chapter describes a case study that explores the extent to which Singapore's online consultation forum reflected the ideals of democratic deliberation by examining the *structure* or the portal as well as the *content* of a discussion thread using a framework of democratic deliberation. Data collected suggest that while the consultation portal provided an environment that ensured privacy, anonymity, and equal participation, the forum suffered from ambiguous administrative intervention characterized by the removal of posts, as well as a lack of information both in terms of guidelines to the consultation process and the background information of the topics being discussed. Further, analysis of the posts suggests that while the participation was not extremely broad and diverse, participants were able to make constructive

Figure 2. Singapore's current online consultation portal. This screenshot was taken in June 2009. (© 2009, Government of Singapore. Used with permission.).

comments on the issues of casino gaming and social safeguarding from a variety of social, moral, and economic perspectives. However, in making their arguments, participants rarely referenced sources other than their own experiences and values.

As discussed earlier, the online discussion forum faced two important challenges: (1) inadequate technical design contributed to the structural and substantive fragmentation of the discourse; and (2) the lack of government participation and transparency in the consultation process resulted in a culture of cynicism and distrust among participants toward the authenticity and usefulness of the discussion. These issues must be addressed in order for the online discussion forum and the practice of online consultation in general to fully live up to its democratic potential. To that end, several recommendations can be made to improve the effectiveness of online discussion.

First, as Singapore case illustrates, the technical interface of the online platform influences the way people interact with one another as well as the discourse itself. This observation has also been noted by many empirical investigations (e.g., Linna Jensen, 2003; Morison & Newman, 2001; Wilhelm, 2000; Wright, 2005; Wright & Street, 2007). With the advent of new technologies and the growing popularity of social media, the importance of designing a web environment that facilitates social interaction has also led to emergence of several research areas in recent years. For example, works on discourse architecture, defined as the design and implementation of technology base and features that structure computer-mediated communication (Jones & Rafaeli, 2000) may help create online platforms that support collaboration and community building. Similarly, research on the analysis of Very Large-Scale Conversation, which refers to large scale, network-based, and public dialogue like the one in the Singapore case, represents effort to develop techniques for identifying conversational structure and the forces that shape it (Sack, 2005). The advance in these research areas is likely to be important for online consultation and other related e-democratic practices. In addition, with the massive amount of information being generated through citizen interaction and feedback, the development of knowledge and information management systems are also essential.

Second, the fragmented content and the sense of distrust seen in the Singapore case also suggest that moderator presence and government participation is likely to increase the effectiveness of online discussion. As Kearns, Bend, and Stern (2002) noted, moderators can keep citizen engagement focused and ensure the process adds value to all parties involved. In the same vein, Wilhelm (2000) also argued that moderators could contribute to the success of political discussion forums because "a skilled and trusted facilitator is often necessary to manage the forum and to create order out of potential chaos" (p. 140). In addition, since goal of online consultation is to promote and strengthen the interaction between citizens and policy makers, government participation in the process is therefore crucial. Finally, Coleman (2004) observed, "For online consultations to be seen as more than a gesture, there must be tangible evidence that [elected officials] are interacting with the public and taking views of online contributors into account in their deliberations" (p. 20). Integrating various forms of moderation, as well as increasing the level of government participation, is likely to address many of the issues seen in the Singapore case.

As for the future scholarly research on the practice of online consultation, a more systematic investigation into the different stakeholders involved in the process may shed light on when, how, and why online consultation may be most effectively implemented. For instance, user demographic information can be gathered to construct a more representative picture of public opinion, and participants can be surveyed for their experiences and attitudes toward the practice. Experimental methods can be employed to test different technical deigns and their impact on usability, online collaboration, and interactivity. Content analysis of the discourse being generated through different online media may be used to evaluate the value and quality of these policy discussions. Interviews with elected officials and legislators could be valuable for understanding how the consultation practice may contribute to the decision-making process, and comparative studies can be conducted to analyze the lessons and experiences learned from different parts of the world. All of these potential research areas suggest that a mixed and multi-method approach is perhaps most appropriate for examining a complex and interdisciplinary subject such as online consultation. Finally, applying the abovementioned methods to study different stages of the process (e.g., pre-consultation, consultation, and post-consultation) may also generate useful insights.

REFERENCES

Agre, P. (2002). Real-time politics: The Internet and the political process. *The Information Society, 18*(5), 311–331. doi:10.1080/01972240290075174

Amnesty International. (2004). *Country summary: Singapore*. Retrieved May 20, 2005, from http://www.amnestyusa.org/countries/singapore/document.do?id=ar&yr=2005

Associated Press. (2005). *Singapore delays launching casino tender*. Retrieved June 20, 2005, from http://www.forbes.com/associatedpress/feeds/ap/2005/06/16/ap2095993.html

Au, A. (2004, November 11). Casino decision: A bigger question looms. *The Strait Times*. Retrieved August 4, 2009, from http://www.wildsingapore.com/sos/media/041111-2.htm

Barber, B. R. (1984). *Strong democracy: Participatory politics for a new age*. Berkeley, CA: University of California Press.

Barber, B. R., Mattson, K., & Peterson, J. (1997). *The state of 'electronically enhanced democracy': A survey of the Internet*. New Brunswick, NJ: Walt Whitman Center.

Baym, N. K. (1995). The emergence of community in computer-mediated communication. In Jones, S. (Ed.), *Cybersociety* (pp. 138–163). Newbury Park, CA: Sage.

Chadwick, A. (2003). Bringing e-democracy back in: Why it matters for future research on e-governance. *Social Science Computer Review, 21*(4), 443–455. doi:10.1177/0894439303256372

Cheney, S. (2007, May 22). Marina Bay Sands project on track for completion by 2009. *Channel News Asia*. Retrieved November 11, 2007, from http://www.channelnewsasia.com/stories/singaporelocalnews/view/277767/1/.html

Chia, S. (2004, November 26). Sizing up the casino critic. *The Strait Times*. Retrieved August 4, 2009, from http://www.wildsingapore.com/sos/media/041126-3.htm

Clift, S. (2004). *Online consultations and events - Top ten tips for government and civic hosts*. Retrieved November 20, 2004, from http://www.publicus.net

Coglianese, C. (2005). The internet and citizen participation in rulemaking. *I/S: A Journal of Law and Policy for the Information Society, 1*(1). Retrieved May 2, 2009, from http://www.is-journal.org/V01I01/I-S,%20V01-I01-P033,%20Coglianese.pdf

Cohen, J. (1989). Deliberative democracy and democratic legitimacy. In Hamlin, A., & Pettit, P. (Eds.), *The good polity* (pp. 17–34). Oxford, UK: Blackwell.

Coleman, S. (2004). Connecting parliament to the public via the Internet: Two case studies of online consultations. *Information Communication and Society, 7*(1), 1–22. doi:10.1080/1369118042000208870

Coleman, S., & Gøtze, J. (2001). *Bowling together: Online public engagement in policy deliberation.* London, UK: Hansard Society.

Dahl, R. A. (1991). *Democracy and its critics.* New Haven, CT: Yale University Press.

Dahlberg, L. (2001). Computer-mediated communication and the public sphere: A critical analysis. *Journal of Computer Mediated Communication, 7*(1). Retrieved December 20, 2005, from http://jcmc.indiana.edu/vol7/issue1/dahlberg.html

Economist Intelligence Unit. (2008). *E-readiness rankings 2008: Maintaining momentum.* Retrieved August 10, 2009, from http://graphics.eiu.com/upload/ibm_ereadiness_2008.pdf

Elster, J. (1998). *Deliberative democracy.* Cambridge, UK: Cambridge University Press.

Feedback Unit. (2005). *Government consultation portal.* Retrieved January 10, 2005, from http://www.feedback.gov.sg

Fountain, J. (2001). *Building the virtual state: Information technology and institutional change.* Washington, DC: Brookings Institution Press.

Gomez, J. (2000). *Self-censorship: Singapore's shame.* Singapore: Think Centre.

Grossman, L. (1996). *The electronic republic: Reshaping democracy in the information age.* New York, NY: Viking.

Habermas, J. (1984). *The theory of communicative action, volume one. Reason and the rationalization of society.* Boston, MA: Beacon Press.

Internet World Stats. (2009). *Asia Internet usage stats and population statistics.* Retrieved August 14, 2009, from http://www.internetworldstats.com/stats3.htm

Jones, Q., & Rafaeli, S. (2000). Time to split, virtually: Discourse architecture and community building as means to creating vibrant virtual publics. *Electronic Markets: The International Journal of Electronic Commerce and Business Media, 10*(4), 214–223.

Kearns, I., Bend, J., & Stern, B. (2002). *E-participation in local government.* London, UK: Institute for Public Policy Research.

Linaa Jensen, J. (2003). Public spheres on the Internet: Anarchic or government sponsored – A comparison. *Scandinavian Political Studies, 26*(4), 349–374. doi:10.1111/j.1467-9477.2003.00093.x

Macintosh, A., Robson, E., Smith, E., & Whyte, A. (2003). Electronic democracy and young people. *Social Science Computer Review, 21*(1), 43–54. doi:10.1177/0894439302238970

Macintosh, A., & Whyte, A. (2002). *An evaluation framework for e-consultations?* Paper presented at the International Association for Official Statistics conference, London, UK.

Ministry of Trade and Industry. (2004). *Social safeguards for integrated resort with casino gaming.* Singapore: Ministry of Trade and Industry. Retrieved June 20, 2005, from http://app.mcys.gov.sg/web/corp_press_story.asp?szMod=corp&s zSubMod=press&qid=674

Ministry of Trade and Industry. (2005). *Proposal to develop integrated resorts.* Singapore: Ministry of Trade and Industry. Retrieved August 20, 2009, from http://app.mti.gov.sg/data/pages/606/doc/Ministerial%20Statement%20-%20PM%20 18apr05.pdf

Morison, J., & Newman, D. R. (2001). On-line citizenship: Consultation and participation in New Labour's Britain and beyond. *International Review of Law Computers & Technology, 15*(2), 171–194. doi:10.1080/13600860120070501

Noveck, B. S. (2005). The future of citizen participation in the electronic state. *I/S: A Journal of Law and Policy for the Information Society, 1*(1). Retrieved April 28, 2009, from http://www.is-journal.org/V01I01/I-S,%20V01-I01-P001,%20Noveck.pdf

Organisation for Economic Co-operation and Development. (2001). *Engaging citizens in policy making: Information, consultation, and public participation.* Paris, France: OECD.

Poland, P. (2001). *Online consultation in GOL-IN countries: Initiatives to foster e-democracy*. Amsterdam, The Netherlands: Ministry of the Interior and Kingdom Relations.

Rash, W. (1997). *Politics on the Net: Wiring the political process*. New York, NY: W.H. Freeman.

Rawls, J. (1971). *A theory of justice*. Cambridge, MA: Harvard University Press.

Rheingold, H. (1993). *The virtual community: Homesteading on the electronic frontier*. Reading, MA: Addison Wesley.

Sack, W. (2005). Discourse architecture and very large-scale conversation. In Latham, R., & Sassen, S. (Eds.), *Digital formations: IT and new architectures in the global realm* (pp. 242–282). Princeton, NJ: Princeton University Press.

Shulman, S., Schlosberg, D., Zavestoski, S., & Courard-Hauri, D. Electronic rule-making: New frontiers in public participation. *Social Science Computer Review*, *21*(2), 162–178. doi:10.1177/0894439303021002003

Stephens, S., McCusker, P., O'Donnell, D., Newman, D., & Fagan, G. (2006). On the road from consultation cynicism to energizing e-consultation. *The Electronic. Journal of E-Government*, *4*(2), 87–94.

Sunstein, C. (2001). *Republic.com*. Princeton, NJ: Princeton University Press.

Teo, J. (2004, November 26). Anti-casino groups keep up the fight. *The Strait Times*. Retrieved August 4, 2009, from http://www.wildsingapore.com/sos/media/041117-1.htm

Thatcher, J., Waddell, C., Henry, S., Swierenga, S., Urban, M., & Burks, M. (2003). *Constructing accessible web sites*. San Francisco, CA: Apress.

Van Alstyne, M., & Brynjolfsson, E. (1996). *Electronic communities: Global village or cyberbalkans?* Paper presented at the 17th International Conference on Information Systems, Cleveland, OH.

Wellman, B. (1999). *Networks in the global village: Life in contemporary communities*. Boulder, CO: Westview Press.

West, D. (2007). *Global e-government 2007*. Providence, RI: Center for Public Policy, Brown University. Retrieved August 20, 2009, from http://www.insidepolitics.org/egovt07int.pdf

Whyte, A., & Macintosh, A. (2001). Transparency and teledemocracy: Issues from an e-consultation. *Journal of Information Science*, *27*(4), 187–198.

Wilhelm, A. (2000). *Democracy in the digital age: Challenges to political life in cyberspace*. New York, NY: Routledge.

Wright, S. (2005). Design matters: The political efficacy of government-run discussion forums. In Oates, S., Owen, D., & Gibson, R. (Eds.), *The Internet and politics: Citizens, voters, and activists* (pp. 80–99). London, UK: Routledge.

Wright, S., & Street, J. (2007). Democracy, deliberation and design: The case of online discussion forums. *New Media & Society, 9*(5), 849–869. doi:10.1177/1461444807081230

ADDITIONAL READING

Barber, B. R. (1984). *Strong democracy: Participatory politics for a new age*. Berkeley, CA: University of California Press.

Carlitz, R. D., & Gunn, R. W. (2002). Online rulemaking: A step toward e-governance. *Government Information Quarterly, 19*, 389–405. doi:10.1016/S0740-624X(02)00118-1

Chadwick, A. (2003). Bringing e-democracy back in: Why it matters for future research on e-governance. *Social Science Computer Review, 21*(4), 443–455. doi:10.1177/0894439303256372

Coleman, S. (2004). Connecting parliament to the public via the Internet: Two case studies of online consultations. *Information Communication and Society, 7*(1), 1–22. doi:10.1080/1369118042000208870

Coleman, S., & Gøtze, J. (2003). *Bowling together: Online public engagement in policy deliberation*. Retrieved from http://bowlingtogether.net

Dahlberg, L. (2007). Rethinking the fragmentation of the cyberpublic: From consensus to contestation. *New Media & Society, 9*(5), 827–847. doi:10.1177/1461444807081228

Dryzek, J. S. (2002). *Deliberative democracy and beyond*. Oxford, UK: Oxford University Press. doi:10.1093/019925043X.001.0001

Janssen, D., & Kies, R. (2005). Online forums and deliberative democracy. *Acta Politica, 40*, 317–335. doi:10.1057/palgrave.ap.5500115

Kearns, I., Bend, J., & Stern, B. (2002). *E-participation in local government*. London, UK: Institute for Public Policy Research.

Lazer, D., & Mayer-Schönberger, V. (2007). *Governance and information technology: From electronic government to information government.* Cambridge, MA: MIT Press.

Macintosh, A., Robson, E., Smith, E., & Whyte, A. (2003). Electronic democracy and young people. *Social Science Computer Review, 21*(1), 43–54. doi:10.1177/0894439302238970

McCusker, P., O'Donnell, D., Stephens, S., & Logue, A. M. (2005). Consultation cynicism: Whither e-consultation. In *Proceedings of European Conference on E-Government, Antwerp, Belgium.*

Morison, J., & Newman, D. R. (2001). On-line citizenship: Consultation and participation in New Labour's Britain and beyond. *International Review of Law Computers & Technology, 15*(2), 171–194. doi:10.1080/13600860120070501

Noveck, B. S. (2005). The future of citizen participation in the electronic state. *I/S: A Journal of Law and Policy for the Information Society, 1*(1). Retrieved from http://www.is-journal.org/V01I01/I-S,%20V01-I01-P001,%20Noveck.pdf

OECD. (2001). *Citizens as partners: Information, consultation and public participation, in policy-making.* Paris, France: OECD.

OECD. (2003). *Promise and problems of e-democracy: Challenges of online citizen engagement.* Paris, France: OECD.

Sack, W. (2005). Discourse architecture and very large-scale conversation. In Lathamand, R., & Sassen, S. (Eds.), *Digital formations: IT and new architectures in the global realm* (pp. 242–282). Princeton, NJ: Princeton University Press.

Schlosberg, D., Zavestoski, S., & Shulman, S. W. (2007). Democracy and e-rulemaking: Web-based technologies, participation, and the potential for deliberation. *Journal of Information Technology & Politics, 4*(1). Retrieved from http://www.jitp.net/files/v004001/JITP4-1_Democracy_and_E-Rulemaking_Schlosberg_%20Zavestoski_Shulman.pdf

Stephens, S., McCusker, P., O'Donnell, D., Newman, D., & Fagan, G. (2006). On the road from consultation cynicism to energizing e-consultation. *Electronic Journal of E-Government, 4*(2), 87–94. Retrieved from http://www.ejeg.com/volume-4/vol4-iss2/v4-i2-art6.htm

Stromer-Galley, J. (2003). Diversity of political conversation on the Internet: Users' perspectives. *Journal of Computer-Mediated Communication, 8*(3). Retrieved from http://jcmc.indiana.edu/vol8/issue3/stromergalley.html

Wilhelm, A. (2000). *Democracy in the digital age: Challenges to political life in cyberspace*. London, UK: Routledge.

Wright, S., & Street, J. (2007). Democracy, deliberation and design: The case of online discussion forums. *New Media & Society*, *9*(5), 849–869. doi:10.1177/1461444807081230

KEY TERMS AND DEFINITIONS

Autonomy: The participants and the online consultation process itself must be free from the manipulation or influence of external political or economic powers in order to maintain a sense of objectivity.

Democratic Deliberation: A process of collective decision that requires the participation of all who will be affected by the decision of their representatives, and includes the decision making by means of arguments offer by and to participants who are committed to the values of rationality and impartiality.

Enlightened Understanding: Participants of online consultation should have a good understanding of the issues in order to make sound judgment and meaningful contribution to the dialogue. To facilitate such understanding, the government must provide sufficient background information of the issues on which citizens' views are being sought.

Equality of Access: Every person affected by the issues being discussed in the online consultation process should be equally entitled to participate and provide their views.

Mutuality: Participants of online consultation should attempt to understand the issue or the argument from multiple perspectives. This requires a commitment to an ongoing dialogue and to listen and engage with each other.

Online Consultation: Use of web-based technologies by government agencies to seek policy suggestion and feedback from the public. It is based on the prior definition by government of the issue on which citizens' views are being sought and requires the provision of information.

Privacy and Trust: The online consultation process must protect the privacy and anonymity of the participants in order to facilitate a sense of trust and encourage candid discussions.

Reflexivity: Participants of online consultation should critically examine the issues in relation to their cultural values, assumptions, and interests, as well as the larger social context.

Transparency: The management of the online consultation process should be visible from outside, with clearly defined guidelines and information about how the feedbacks are gathered and relayed back to the policy makers.

ENDNOTES

[1]   The methodological limitation of content analysis prevented the study from measuring enlightened understanding at the individual level. Instead, the study focused on whether or not an environment that could facilitate enlightened understanding was created.

[2]   Singapore announced that it would defer issuing formal requests for proposals for its two casino resorts until the third quarter of 2005 (Associated Press, 2005). Bids were solicited and announced in 2006 and the resorts are to be completed in 2009 (Cheney, 2007).

[3]   Including Web Content Accessibility Guidelines (WCAG) and Section 508 standards of the US Rehabilitation Act. For more on website accessibility, see: Thatcher, J., Waddell, C., Henry, S., Swierenga, S., Urban, M., Burks, M., Regan, M., & Bohman, P. (2003). *Constructing accessible web sites*. San Francisco, CA: Apress.

This work was previously published in Cases on Online Discussion and Interaction: Experiences and Outcomes, edited by Leonard Shedletsky and Joan E. Aitken, pp. 263-281, copyright 2010 by Information Science Reference (an imprint of IGI Global).

Chapter 3
Citizen–Centric Service Dimensions of Indian Rural E–Governance Systems:
An Evaluation

Harekrishna Misra
Institute of Rural Management Anand, India

EXECUTIVE SUMMARY

E-governance systems in India have witnessed prolific advancement over the years. India has strategically adopted e-governance as a part of its policy. In recent times each state has its own e-governance plan to deliver services as planned. National policy also aims to provide formalized services across the nation while recognizing the importance of state specific services. This approach includes various mission mode projects under national e-governance plan (NeGP). Manifestation of such approach has resulted in 100,000 common service centers (CSC) in rural areas. It is expected that rural citizens would find them useful and it may contribute for effective governance. In this chapter it is argued that such an initiative would be successful if rural citizens find these CSCs useful for their livelihood security. Various dimensions of this phenomenon are also examined through some cases in this chapter to understand their contributions to successful CSCs in India.

DOI: 10.4018/978-1-4666-0981-5.ch003

BACKGROUND

E-governance initiatives, despite acceptance to an extent in the form of e-government systems, have so far remained hype in many parts of the world. Failure stories abundantly reflect that such initiatives with development perspectives have not yielded encouraging results. Estimates indicate that 35 per cent are total failures, 50 per cent are partial failures, and 15 per cent are successes in developing and transitional countries. It is argued that e-governance initiatives are often on project mode and each project forms island for deliveries creating an overwhelming gap between project design and on-the-ground reality (known as design-reality gaps). This gap contributes to failures (Heeks 2003). Despite such discouraging outcomes, e-government initiatives in developing countries have evolved to a level of acceptance among government agencies and backend service provisioning organisations. Most countries are now in the phase of assessing the "impact" on issues related to "efficiency," "effectiveness," and "equity" since they have gone beyond the initial phases of addressing primary challenges of "digital divide," "setting up infrastructure," and "spreading awareness" for ICT use and delivering citizen-centric e-governance services. Most of the countries are now able to showcase their e-governance services and declare the "availability" of these services uninterrupted crossing the spatial challenges (Figure 1). E-governance systems in many countries have evolved to the level of maturity. However, usage of such services has been a challenge. E-governance systems have so far remained supply-driven in most countries and their actual use largely depends on the type of services rendered. E-government services are "mandatory" in nature and citizens are expected to use them. However, usage of many services which have development perspectives like income generation, health and education depends largely on the success of these services related to citizen needs. Though it is argued that readiness, availability, and uptake phases of e-governance systems are not contemporary anymore for evaluation of success in managing such projects, most of the developing countries still grapple with this phenomenon. There is still use divide, low latent demand, and sub-optimal usage of e-governance services (Misra & Hiremath 2009; Misra 2009).

Discussion on global e-governance systems suggests a clear direction to policy makers and implementers which calls for provisioning of converged and value added services to citizens with least cost, time, and effort. It is also evident that e-governance systems need to evolve to connected governance through establishment of robust infrastructure, backend integration with all stakeholders, and transforming the government itself through innovation and value addition (UN, 2008). Information indicates that connected governance is possible through phases (Heeks, 2006; Heeks & Molla, 2009; Archmann,2008). It needs a concerted effort to graduate any e-government effort to connected governance.

Figure 1. Changing e-government issues over time

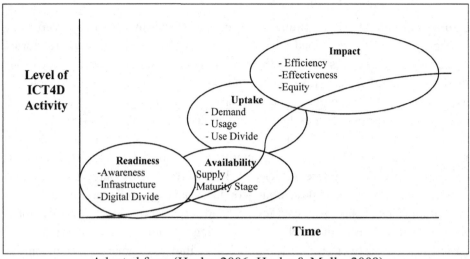

Adopted from (Heeks, 2006; Heeks & Molla, 2009).

As shown in Figure 1 and Box 1, it is mandatory for any country to ensure its readiness in each stage before going to the next higher stage. In the context of Indian e-governance efforts, the situation is not different when compared to global e-governance scenarios, experiences, and trends. In India, foundation of e-governance was laid during 1954 when the Planning Commission introduced computers followed by setting up of the Department of Electronics (DOE) in 1970 and establishment of the National Informatics Centre in 1970 as a national agency to make available necessary infrastructure across all states to provide required connectivity with the central government (Mishra 2007; Prabhu 2004; Planning Commission,2001). The government's policies to encourage digital empowerment are presented in Table 1.

Box 1. Three critical considerations for establishment of connected governance (UN, 2008)

In order to establish ICT enabled connected governance, UN recognizes following three areas:

a. **Infrastructure:** Creating an information infrastructure both within the public sector and across society at large, one based upon reliable and affordable Internet connectivity for citizens, businesses and all stakeholders in a given jurisdiction;

b. **Integration:** Leveraging this new infrastructure within the public sector in order to better share information (internally and externally) and bundle, integrate, and deliver services through more efficient and citizen-centric governance models encompassing multiple delivery channels; and

c. **Transformation:** Pursuing service innovation and e-government across a broader prism of community and democratic development through more networked governance patterns within government, across various government levels and amongst all sectors in a particular jurisdiction.

Table 1. Indian e-governance genesis

Year	Mile-stones for E-Governance Efforts	Goal
1984	New Computer Policy	Spread of Computer Use
1986	Policy on Software Export, Development and Training	To promote Sectoral growth in ITeS, Business Process Outsourcing
1987	Setting up of NICNET, DISNIC	Setting up of IT infrastructure in Government Sector
1994	Policy on National Telecommunication (NTP 94)	To ensure better Tele-density, focus on Rural Telephony
1995	Launching of Internet; Spectrum Allocation and Release	Web Access and bandwidth allocation for use
1997	Establishment of Telecom. Regulatory Authority (TRAI)	To unbundle telecommunication services (last mile)
1998	National Task Force on IT	To formulate an IT policy document
1999	Creation of Ministry of IT	To oversee implementation of IT policy
1999	Policy on National Telecommunication (NTP 99)	To accelerate tele-density
2000	Formulation of IT Act	To provide legal status to use of IT in business, government, and governance systems
2000	Formulation of Communication Convergence Bill	Convergence of content, convergence of carriage, and convergence of Terminal
2000	Telecom Disputes Settlement and	Fair and transparent telecom. services
	Appellate Tribunal (TDSAT)	
2000	Corporatization of DoT (formation of BSNL)	Unbundling of the telecommunication sector, private sector investments and managing USO
2004	Formulation of Broadband Policy	To implement broadband services in the last mile
2006	National E-Governance Plan (NeGP)	To formulate, plan, design, and deploy e-government solutions and establish citizen interfaces
2007	Mission 2007	To consider each village a knowledge centre

Adopted from (Misra & Hiremath, 2009).

E-governance efforts globally have been challenged by plethora of socio-technical, cultural and economic issues (Riga Declaration, 2006). In India, theses challenges are enormous because of the diverse nature of the issues concerning not only the socio-technical, cultural and economic dimensions but the rural citizens who constitute an integral part to contribute to the success of the e-governance efforts. Despite e-governance policies formulated and directed towards rural citizens, voluntary participation of rural citizens is yet to gain momentum. However, sporadic efforts are visible through pilot projects directed towards collaboration of rural citizens. Therefore, there is a considerable need to examine the influencing factors for ensuring participation of rural citizens in the national level effort for development. In this chapter, various dimensions influencing rural citizen participation are discussed aimed at fruitful delivery of e-governance services. In this chapter it is posited that demand driven information infrastructure needs to be developed for successful implementation of e-governance systems and especially demands of rural citizens need to be reflected adequately in the e-governance systems. In order to provide demand driven rural information infrastructure in India, it is argued that livelihood security based assessment of such information infrastructure would be beneficial. This chapter verifies the dimensions of such demands and assesses the status of e-governance efforts undertaken in one of the districts in Gujarat state, India.

The organization of the chapter is as follows. The chapter provides a global perspective of e-governance initiatives, their rationale to adopt such strategies, challenges and opportunities faced during implementations of e-governance projects. It includes underpinnings of current global e-governance initiatives. It then presents the e-governance scenario and initiatives taken up in India and discusses the challenges faced for its effective implementation. Subsequently, focus on rural e-governance scenario, role ICT for development in the context of rural India are examined through a model. The model is aimed at interfacing demand and supply characteristics of information infrastructure and relating them to e-governance models deployed nationally. The chapter also examines the of a village information system (VIS) with livelihood perspectives which needs to be established before any ICT infrastructure is deployed. It is argued that VIS should aim to provide information and "services" on demand through "stakeholder-ownership oriented development" initiatives. In order to appreciate the applicability of the proposed framework, results obtained through a survey undertaken in a sample district in Gujarat are discussed. Finally, the chapter discusses observations and elaborates on the direction for further research.

E-GOVERNANCE ASSESSMENT IN INDIA: THE NEED

As discussed in Figure 1 (Heeks 2006) and as recognized by UN (UN 2008), infrastructure is a critical contributor to the success of "connected governance." E-governance efforts in a country strongly reflect the role and contributions of infrastructure in their policies, projects and implementation strategies. Infrastructural readiness is one of the concurrent evaluation criteria which have been set for the countries globally. There are various agencies involved in assessment exercises globally. In Table 2 below a list of such agencies are presented. E-governance assessment frameworks have evolved with the intention to benchmark the e-government strategies, policies and provide an environment of learning from these ever dynamic processes. It is largely recognized that e-governance efforts are country specific,

Table 2. Profile of e-readiness assessment agencies (global)

Study	Focus
APEC (Asia Pacific Economic Cooperation)	E-Commerce Readiness
CIDIF (Centre International pour le Development de l'Inforoute en Francais)	Internet Service Market
EIU (Economist Intelligence Unit) with IBM	E-Business Readiness
IDC	Infrastructure
World Bank (KAM)	K-Economy
McConnell International (MI)	Infrastructure, Digital Economy, Education, and Government
MN (Metric Net)	E-Economy
MQ (Mosaic Group)	Internet
NRI (CID, Harvard)	Infrastructure, E-Society, Policies, Digital Economy, Education, and Government
CID (Centre for International Development)	Society
CIDCM (University of Maryland)	Qualitative Assessment based on past performance and current internet pervasiveness
World Telecommunication/ ICT Development Report; International Telecommunication Union (ITU)	Telecommunication; Measuring ICT for Social and Economic Development; Measuring ICT availability in Villages and Rural Areas (ITU, 2006a; ITU,2007b)
SIDA (Swedish International Development Cooperation Agency)	Mainly Strength, Weakness, Opportunity and Threat (SWOT) analysis of a Nation
USAID (US Agency for International Development)	Access, Government,
World Economic Forum; Global IT Report	E-Readiness
United Nations Development Programme	E-Governance
World Economic Forum	Global Competitiveness Report
Measurement of Information Society, ITU	ICT Opportunity Index
Economic and Social Commission for Asia and The Pacific (ESCAP), UN	Regulations, Polices, Legal Framework Related to ICT; UN's Global E-Government Survey
United Nations Development Programme (UNDP)	ICT Indicators for Human Development; Democratic Governance Indicators

Compiled from (Budhiraja & Sachdeva,2009; Misra & Hiremath, 2009)

related to national level policies, socio-cultural systems and government systems. Though it is not easy to map all the success factors of e-governance efforts made in other countries to the Indian scenario, overall learning from them would help the country to improve upon.

While the number of agencies involved in the assessment process is not important, their approaches lead to the conclusion that the e-readiness exercises have their importance in any phase of deployment of e-governance. E-governance efforts are continuous and these efforts require concurrent evaluation to add value progressively. In the Indian context, the global e-readiness exercises provide an insight to various challenges that the country faces to set up and use infrastructure. India, being a developing country, experiences harsh realities of e-readiness attributes explained in Figure 1. However, in recent times last mile dimensions of digital divide is increasingly being addressed through various policies like tele-density increase, broadband penetration, establishment of common service centers, and state and centre sponsored content management through state- wide area network backbones (SWAN) under NeGP. A close look at the global IT report indicates that India needs to improve upon many other dimensions of e-governance including digital divide (Misra & Hiremath, 2009).

E-readiness assessment exercise is an implicit phenomenon for all nations and there is a mechanism to display the status of e-readiness of each country in order to examine the progress and identify the areas of improvement. There are various components of e-readiness exercise and important among them are "infrastructure readiness," "individual readiness," "government readiness," and "political and regulatory readiness." In Figure 2 the e-readiness components in India vis-à-vis other countries are shown in a time line. It may be observed that infrastructure readiness needs considerable attention in India to achieve better e-governance service utilization. Other readiness indicators have shown appreciable improvements in global standards, despite diverse socio-economic ambience. Individual readiness, government readiness, and political and regulatory readiness indicators support the fact that awareness among stakeholders to accept ICT enabled services has increased. But as a nation, India has to traverse a long path to achieve all inclusive readiness in order to bring in overall development and appreciable use of e-governance services.

Availability of Integrated E-Governance Infrastructure and Services

Availability of integrated infrastructure in a nation is reflection of its sound policy and implementation strategy. In India ICT initiatives and their convergence are integral parts of its policies. Various policies and Five Year Plans have elaborated the role of connectivity and possible road maps for converged approaches. The tenth and eleventh five year plan documents (Planning Commission 2001) provide a comprehensive approach towards achieving convergence in ICT infrastructure and content management with special emphasis on rural development. Some among them are convergence bill, broadband policy, NeGP with MMPs, and universal service obligation (USO).

Figure 2. E-readiness indices of India Note: Percentile displays the rank among participating countries; higher percentile indicates better status; Adopted from (Misra, 2009)

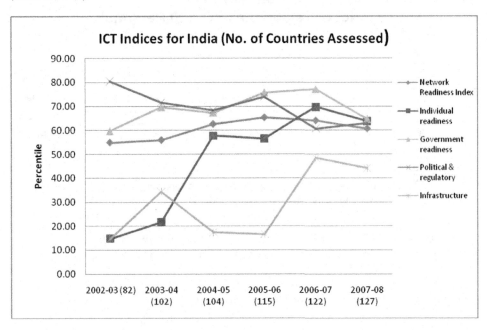

As a strategic move, spread of basic telephony to all citizens has been part of India's sound infrastructure policy. Telephony has been a powerful mode of establishing the required connectivity among citizens. It has catalyzed the convergence of other stakeholders in the governance system which is involved in provisioning of user services. Telephony has also been instrumental in spread of Internet services and the Internet is the backbone of e-governance infrastructure today. Tele-density has been a globally accepted metric for understanding the spread of telephony because of such critical contribution. A comparative assessment of urban-rural tele-density in India is provided in Figure 3. However, the picture is far from satisfactory and there is a huge disparity in urban-rural tele-density despite policy level support.

Internet and telephone users in India are way below world figures. From Figure 4, it is evident that there is tremendous scope to improve upon the infrastructure as India's rank ranges between 87 and 107 among 127 countries assessed. As regards Internet users in India, it is estimated that 12 per cent of urban population are using the Internet whereas only 1.2 per cent of rural population is using the Internet (JuxtConsultIndia Online 2008).

Availability of services is another important dimension of e-governance systems. Conceptualization, design, development, and deployment of electronic services

Figure 3. Tele density in India

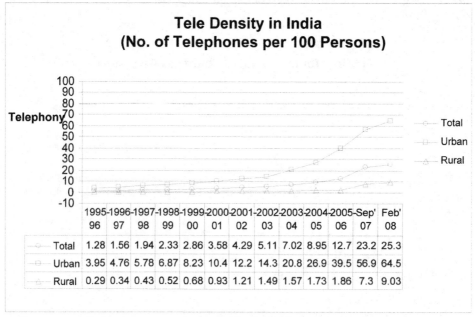

Source: www.Indiastat.com, accessed on 2 March, 2009

Figure 4. Status of internet and telephony in India

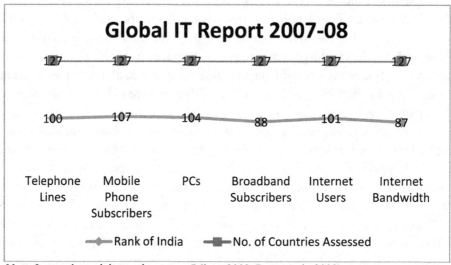

Note: Lower the rank better the status; (Misra, 2009, Dutta et al., 2008)

online are major responsibilities of content management. The Convergence Bill of India calls for convergence of content and convergence of carriage as national initiatives (Planning Commission 2001). Convergence of carriage calls for major changes in structures of the computer industry and more comprehensively the tele-communication and networking industry that are responsible for data communication and broadcasting of multi-media applications.

The National Task Force on IT and Software Development recommended in 1998 in addressing the last-mile connectivity problem. Convergence of content calls for efforts in e-government and e-governance, and provision of a single window service to the citizen. Another issue is to address the convergence of terminal in order to provide multilingual services on multimedia applications anywhere and anytime in India. Today there are various attempts made to provide the content in local languages including the operating system initiative of C-DAC named as the Bharat Operating System Solutions (BOSS). As regards service oriented contents, NeGP recognizes the scope for large-scale implementation of application under mission mode projects (MMPs) with emphasis on integrated services. Under NeGP, national level MMPs and state level MMPs are identified for implementation on scale-up mode as presented in Figure 5 (Ministry of Information Technology [MoIT] 2009a).

Every interested state government is now under a state wide area network (SWAN). Each state is now in the process of having state data centres under the NeGP policy. This endeavour is part of state readiness exercise which is adapted

Figure 5. MMPs under NeGP

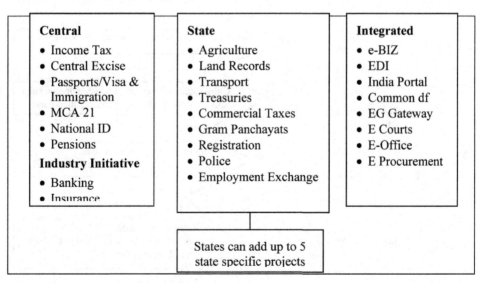

Central
- Income Tax
- Central Excise
- Passports/Visa & Immigration
- MCA 21
- National ID
- Pensions

Industry Initiative
- Banking
- Insurance

State
- Agriculture
- Land Records
- Transport
- Treasuries
- Commercial Taxes
- Gram Panchayats
- Registration
- Police
- Employment Exchange

Integrated
- e-BIZ
- EDI
- India Portal
- Common df
- EG Gateway
- E Courts
- E-Office
- E Procurement

States can add up to 5 state specific projects

Source: Adopted from (MoIT, 2009).

mostly from the global information technology report framework published annually by the World Economic Forum. This assessment commencing in 2003 has provided insight to the performance of states which are placed in six categories: Least Achievers (L1), Below Average Achievers (L2), Average Achievers (L3), Expectants (L4), Aspiring Leaders (L5), and Leaders (L6). The latest rankings of the participating states are given in Figure 6.

E-readiness for districts has been on the agenda of the e-governance policy in India. This readiness is essential to implement e-district services which are parts of the state level mission mode projects under NeGP. It envisages provisioning of services through CSCs planned to be made available in every sixth village across the country and these services include district administration and citizen- centric government services (MoIT 2009).

Figure 6. State e-readiness pyramid of the states

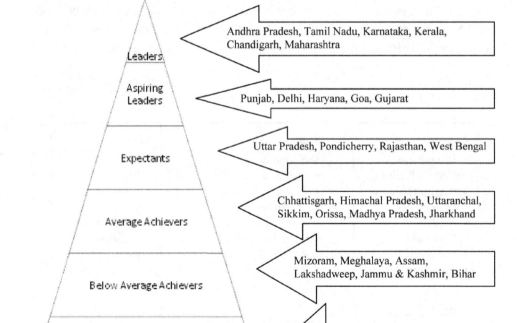

Source: www.mit.gov.in, accessed on 5 March, 2009

Uptake of E-Governance Services in India

It is quite evident that Indian efforts are in line with global e-governance scenarios and the Indian government is making all possible efforts to establish the e-governance infrastructure and provide converged services for the citizens. This supply mode of services has long lasting effect on the readiness of government systems and integration of backend services. As regards mission mode projects at the state and national levels, most of them are related to government systems and citizens would have no option but to accept them as made available to them. The real challenge, however, lies in assessing the net uptake of the services which largely depends on demand; usage and usage divide as shown in Figure 1. In the Indian context, these three dimensions of demand are quite relevant because of the digital divide. It is largely felt that the digital divide has now been converted to digital opportunities because of various policies/acts such as the Broadband Policy, NeGP, and RTI Act. There are many well documented challenges in India to maximize the uptake of services because of the diversity and disparities in the needs of rural-urban citizens. Despite many efforts, e-government services are yet to render the desired pro-citizen services and are mostly targeted towards internal efficiency (Bhatnagar 2006). Pro-poor services may be available through state and national MMPs in due course since the projects are in the phases of transition.

Impact of E-Governance Services in India

The current scenario e-governance efforts has provided the right platform to render effective services at the national and state levels through organized backbones, data centers, and MMPs. NeGP caters to the 100,000 CSCs and provides the platform for convergence of various services through the private-public-partnership (PPP) mode. There is a significant change in the way government systems are working now because of the impact of the information technology Act, and the RTI Act. MMPs alike NCA-21, Income Tax, and Railways have added the right impetus to citizen-acceptance of IT enabled services. Penetration of telephony (wire and wireless) has been phenomenal, triggering the right ambience for m-government (mobile government) applications. But the real challenges to improve upon the impacts are many. It is argued that mere provisioning personal computers, connectivity, and content do not correlate with actual use of services (Heeks et al. 2009). This situation is prevalent especially in rural areas.

NATIONAL E-GOVERNANCE PLAN IN INDIA: THE CASE

In the previous sections, e-governance efforts supporting the development process in developing countries are discussed. E-inclusion has been a critical consideration for global apex bodies such as UN, EU, UNDP, and ITU in provisioning of e-governance services to citizens (EU,2007). MDG efforts include ICT enabled services as one of the most critical indicators for understanding the success of goals set. It is also recognised that global e-governance efforts face challenges of infrastructure, integration, and transformation. There are many failures in implementing e-governance projects and some of the attributes leading to unsuccessful results are design-reality gaps, digital divides, supply-driven services and scanty usage of services.

In India, e-governance services have gone beyond the phases of incubation, prototyping and showcasing of standard software engineering processes. Despite sincere efforts, the services have remained supply driven and need to be transformed to a level of high use through creation of latent demand at village level. Along these lines, National e-Governance Plan (NeGP), has laid emphasis on deploying MMPs at state and central government levels and has provided the desired attention to integrate them so as to generate citizen-centric services on demand and to increase the latent demand. In Figure 7, the approach to integrate various services is presented.

In this integrated approach NeGP intends to provide a service grid through adequate connectivity, increased influx of capital with focused deliveries, increase in the capacity and capabilities of service provisioning agencies in the government, providing adequate content in local languages, establishing required policies and legal frameworks to encourage convergence of services and service providers, establish security standards, and channel the grid based services to citizens through an established channel of interface.

The citizen interface is the most critical element in the grid which largely influences the success of e-governance services. In this chapter, it is hypothesized that services supplied would meet their desired level of success through sustained use by end users. The study discusses the interface of NeGP services being planned, designed, and deployed with that of the latent demand and its influencing factors. The objective is to understand user-divides prevalent in rural areas in India since the success of e-governance efforts largely depends on their contributions to rural development indicators nationally and as per MDG imperatives. This study is largely a continuation of our work in the sample district in Gujarat in India (Misra & Hiremath, 2006). The study also posits that user-divides in rural India is intensely influenced by livelihood security metrics of the households. In this chapter, an attempt is made to explore the effects of livelihood metrics on the latent demand of the information and services network being deployed.

Figure 7. NeGP approach for integration

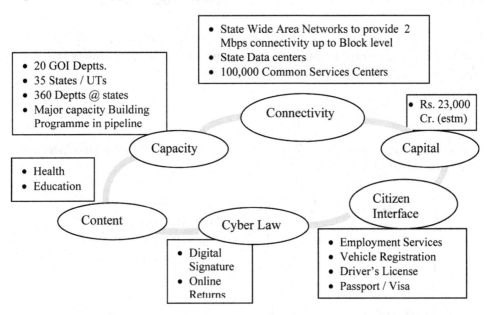

Source: www.mit.gov.in , accessed on 5 March, 2009, MoIT (2009).

NeGP, in its phase of implementation and scale up recognizes the fact that CSCs should work on sustainable basis with public-private-partnerships (PPP). This approach calls for a sustainable demand from the rural citizens and this demand largely depends on usability, usefulness and usability of services. User interfaces and user orientation of services have still remained a challenge for ICT planners, developers and implementers (Heeks et al., 2009; Misra, 2009). The situation is more complex in the Indian context where information infrastructure for ICT enabled governance systems grapple with development challenges. The challenges are not limited to "technology," but the "people" and the "processes." Specifically rural ICT enabled governance initiative face daunting task, not because it involves the rural infrastructure, but the complex process of involving the rural masses. These masses (the rural citizens), who lack access to basic livelihood opportunities, are oblivious of ICT initiatives. They continue to remain so because of poor reflections of their interests in such projects. Such apathy has contributed immensely to "poor user interfaces" which is termed as "citizen interfaces."

FRAMEWORK FOR ANALYSIS OF THE CASE

Considering the challenges in implementing e-governance services in Indian context, a framework is presented to reflect the contributors to the success of such endeavor (see Figure 8).

Figure 8. The framework to reflect demand influencers (Adopted from Misra & Hiremath, 2009; Misra, 2009)

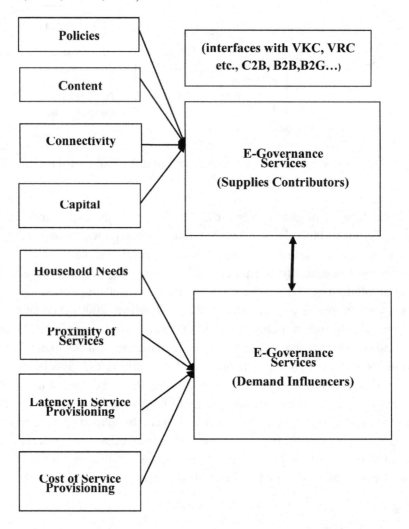

The framework suggests that success of e-governance services is dependent on the "demand" created locally in rural ambience in India (Misra, 2009). As discussed earlier, various agencies are engaged in extending services to rural citizens in villages/ Panchayats through entrepreneurship models. Thus there is a strong need for assessment of demand in the village/ Panchayat so that entrepreneurs engaged in providing the services earn their livelihood, make the service provisioning centre as an income generating avenue and establish the right linkage between service providing agencies and rural citizens.

The Influencers of Supply-Demand

The framework recognizes the need for a strong collaborative interface between "e-governance service- information supplies" and "e-governance service- Information demands." It is considered that e-governance centered information supplies are mostly contributed by policies, infrastructure for establishing connectivity, content developed for the purpose and capital invested in the process. These are mostly incubated, piloted and implemented within the framework of policies. The framework includes influencers discussed in the first method and uses them in the second method to understand the "supply-contributors" as shown in Figure 7. Readiness, availability, uptake and impacts are essentially influenced by policies, content, connectivity and capital which remain supply-driven. The framework suggests that parameters like e-readiness, availability of content, connectivity and capital would critically influence the uptakes and impact of e-governance services. However, the framework also considers the citizens' demand to be local, household specific. It also considers that "supply-demand interface" can be successful only when service is made available on demand, with better proximity at optimized cost and low latency. Suitable interface with information demands generated at the points of services is also necessary to build a sustainable and trustworthy relationship with the citizens. The citizens in general and rural citizens in India in particular, are influenced by the quality of services that are provided for better and sustained use. These influencers are household needs, proximity of services, latency in service provisioning and cost of services. The information supply mechanisms need to consider all these influencers well in advance and incorporate them in the supplies contributors discussed in the framework. In other words, policies, infrastructure for establishing connectivity, content developed for the purpose and capital invested in the process should recognize household needs, proximity of services, latency in service provisioning and cost of services. Besides, the services to be rendered need to recognize the intentions of citizen who look for support of agencies to have better infrastructure, income generation opportunities, and increased awareness etc.

The Framework for Impact Study

The village information system assumes a critical role in contributing to the national information services plan. Diversity in social, cultural, demographic, economic and infrastructural assets in a village influences the household livelihood security options and thus generates a unique scenario. Information economics principles has a far-reaching effect on VIS which argues that information is increasingly recognised as a capital and can add to the livelihood pentagon framework which has five faces of capital to assess the livelihood of a household: financial, human, natural, physical, and social. This information capital can be used for the advantages of citizens in developing countries to support livelihood options (Heeks et al. 2009; World Bank 1986). Box 2 explains these advantages.

Availability of information capital at the household level in developing countries can immensely influence local livelihood opportunities through information management at right time, at appropriate locations, and with right language interfaces. Therefore, it is important that information availability is measured through its proximity to the source and recipient, latency in extending information and its related services, decrease in the uncertainty in provisioning of information through integration, and ability of citizens to gain access to the information at affordable cost. The proposed framework aims to establish a synergy between the information provisioning agencies and citizens in the villages and map the services through these metrics. It is posited that VIS would assume this role in establishing the required synergy.

Methodologies

There are two aspects that the framework intends to address. First, the e-governance services-supplies are assessed. This is done through examination of two cases of e-governance efforts "NeGP" and "E-Gram" which are considered for scale up at national level and state level respectively. This assessment is based on the parameters explained in figure 7 under "e-governance services, supplies contributors." The

Box 2. Advantages of information capital for rural citizens in a developing country

• **Information absence:** key information that development actors need is not available.
• **Information quality:** key information that development actors need is available but of poor quality.
• **Information uncertainty:** key information that development actors need is available but its quality is uncertain.
• **Information asymmetry:** some development actors have access to key information that others lack.
• **Information cost:** key information can only be obtained at high cost (often a physical journey).

Source: (Heeks & Molla, 2009).

objective is to understand the rigor of the deliveries based on information supplies of the suggested framework. Second, these two cases are examined with viewpoints of interfaces with information demand influencers.

Primary surveys are conducted in seven sample villages to understand the efficacy of these influencers. These sample villages are drawn from a particular district in the state where both E-Gram and NeGP projects are co-existing. These samples are mostly homogeneous, small and therefore, there is a limitation in generalization of the findings. Research method included a sampling plan to elicit responses of rural citizens with respect to their aspirations and the limitations these endeavours attempt to meet them. There are 284 respondents who participated in the interview and participatory rural appraisal (PRA) exercises in the village. In the interview method, random sampling was adopted to avoid bias. However, seven villages provided a cluster scenario for the researcher. As regards PRA exercise, each village had one and interested villagers were encouraged to participate (Misra & Hiremath, 2009).

Readiness would relate critically to local infrastructure and local sources for information retrieval and integration among these sources in order to encourage citizens to avail such services. Availability largely depends on the readiness of infrastructure and integrated services. Besides, it is also largely influenced by the cost factor. Increase in uptake would depend on availability of integrated services and low latency with focus on livelihood-centric services because it might build trust in the system. Impact assessment is also an important stage in the evolution since it measures the net effect of e-governance services. Latency and integrated services in a sustainable manner are expected to provide a larger impact. While all stages of evolution in e-governance services are expected to be largely influenced by the integrated information infrastructure, latency in availing and providing services are the next most important metric for successful evolution. Proximity and cost of information and services are considered important metrics; they are largely critical for the readiness, availability, and uptake stages of the evolution process.

Village Information System: The Critical Interface

Village Information System (VIS) is the core issue in this study. The research propositions are as follows:

1. VIS is expected to provide the desired interface with the citizens and supplied services for supporting their livelihood prospects in local conditions.
2. VIS is treated as "atomic" in order to establish the uniqueness of the demand that the concerned village would place on the service providing agencies to meet livelihood security based challenges at the household level. It is argued

that each village has uniqueness in raising demand on e-governance services. Each village is therefore, a unit of study. Each village provides an aggregated ambience based on household level demand to understand prioritised information requirements.

3.   Proximity to information and service resources, latency, integrated information, and cost of services influence readiness, availability, uptake, and impact in provisioning e-governance services.

The research propositions demand a primary survey at the household level because of the premise that each household has uniqueness in placing its demand on the "orchestrated" information network available through the e-governance policy framework.

In this chapter, severity metrics are formed to support the measurements. Severity is presented as a term associated with difficulty/ importance attached to citizens' critical needs to support livelihood security. Severity metric depends on quantifiable parameters of the livelihood security profile of a household aggregated at the village level. This metric indicates the difficulty level of a household/village to get support from agencies for receiving information. In Table 3, this severity is explained for the purpose of benchmarking results that the proposed framework examines. These metrics are indicative of the perspectives of sample respondents who participated in the exercise. An assessment of these metrics indicates that rural citizens are not averse to payment for availing services provided desired services are rendered on demand and at a convenient place. Besides, the rural citizens are unanimous to argue that services need to be rendered as per their convenience and they also agree that service supplying agencies need to provided improved services keeping in view the rural citizen's livelihood centric requirements. It means a continuous innovation approach should be adopted for sustainability of services. Sample citizens also viewed that trust in the system would accrue if such an approach is taken in a concerted manner.

In the proposed framework, VIS metrics are posited to be the interfaces with the livelihood security oriented delivery systems for rural citizens. This delivery system needs to understand the ICT imperatives to provide livelihood-centric information. These metrics will be used to examine critically the processes and services available to citizens. In table 4, VIS metrics are mapped to the four stages of evolution in e-governance services, readiness, availability, uptake, and impact. As per the sample respondents, influencers discussed in the framework have a varied impact in the interfaces of services that VIS could manage.

Table 3. Information severity metrics and benchmarks

Livelihood Security Profiling	Severity Metrics			
	Description	Range	Metric	Demand on VIS
Food Security	Sufficiency of Food	0-4months	+++ (Most Severe)	Very High
		5-8 months	++ (Severe)	High
		9-12 months	+ (Less Severe)	Important
	Income Generation Opportunities (Information Asymmetry)	Proper Sale Value Realization in the Village		
		> 80 per cent said Yes	+ (Less Severe)	Important
		<80 per cent>40 per cent	++ (Severe)	High
		<40 per cent	+++ (Most Severe)	Very High
		Distance Travelled for Sale		
		< 5 Km	+ (Less Severe)	Important
		> 5 < 10 Km	++ (Severe)	High
		> 10 Km	+++ (Most Severe)	Very High
		Availability of Work Opportunity in Village		
		> 80 per cent said Yes	+ (Less Severe)	Important
		<80 per cent>40 per cent	++ (Severe)	High
		<40 per cent	+++ (Most Severe)	Very High
		Household Asset Sold for Purchase of Food		
		> 80 per cent said Yes	+++ (Most Severe)	Very High
		<80 per cent>40 per cent said Yes	++ (Less Severe)	High
		< 40 per cent said Yes	+ (Severe)	Important
Health Security	Human	Accessible to Health Infrastructure		
		< 5 Km	+ (Less Severe)	Important
		> 5 < 10 Km	++ (Severe)	High
		> 10 Km	+++ (Most Severe)	Very High
		Availability of Health Services in the Village		
		> 80 per cent said Yes	+ (Less Severe)	Important
		<80 per cent>40 per cent	++ (Severe)	High
		<40 per cent	+++ (Most Severe)	Very High
		Availability of Immunization /Health Training Services in the Village		
		> 80 per cent said Yes	+ (Less Severe)	Important
		<80 per cent>40 per cent	++ (Severe)	High
		<40 per cent	+++ (Most Severe)	Very High
	Livestock	Availability of Livestock Support Services in the Village		

continued on following page

Table 3. Continued

Livelihood Security Profiling	Severity Metrics			Demand on VIS
	Description	Range	Metric	
		> 80 per cent said Yes	+ (Less Severe)	Important
		<80 per cent>40 per cent	++ (Severe)	High
		<40 per cent	+++ (Most Severe)	Very High
Education Security	Formal Education Facility (Primary)			
		> 80 per cent said Yes	+ (Less Severe)	Important	Important
		<80 per cent>40 per cent	++ (Severe)	High	High
		<40 per cent	+++ (Most Severe)	Very High	Very High
	Access to Formal Education Facility (Primary)			
		< 5 Km	+ (Less Severe)	Important	Important
		> 5 < 10 Km	++ (Severe)	High	High
		> 10 Km	+++ (Most Severe)	Very High	Very High
	Formal Education Facility (Secondary)			
		> 80 per cent said Yes	+ (Less Severe)	Important	Important
		<80 per cent>40 per cent	++ (Severe)	High	High
		<40 per cent	+++ (Most Severe)	Very High	Very High
	Access to Formal Education Facility (Secondary)			
		< 5 Km	+ (Less Severe)	Important	Important
		> 5 < 10 Km	++ (Severe)	High	High
		> 10 Km	+++ (Most Severe)	Very High	Very High
	Formal Education Facility (Higher)			
		> 80 per cent said Yes	+ (Less Severe)	Important	Important
		<80 per cent>40 per cent	++ (Severe)	High	High
		<40 per cent	+++ (Most Severe)	Very High	Very High
	Access to Formal Education Facility (Higher)			
		< 5 Km	+ (Less Severe)	Important	Important
		> 5 < 10 Km	++ (Severe)	High	High
		> 10 Km	+++ (Most Severe)	Very High	Very High
Financial Security	Ability to meet Household Expenses			
		> 80 per cent said Yes	+ (Less Severe)	Important	Important
		<80 per cent>40 per cent	++ (Severe)	High	High
		<40 per cent	+++ (Most Severe)	Very High	Very High
	Availability of Credit/ Insurance Services			
		> 80 per cent said Yes	+ (Less Severe)	Important	Important
		<80 per cent>40 per cent	++ (Severe)	High	High

continued on following page

Table 3. Continued

Livelihood Security Profiling	Severity Metrics			
	Description	**Range**	**Metric**	**Demand on VIS**
	<40 per cent	+++ (Most Severe)	Very High	Very High
	Access to Credit/ Insurance Services			
	< 5 Km	+ (Less Severe)	Important	Important
	> 5 < 10 Km	++ (Severe)	High	High
	> 10 Km	+++ (Most Severe)	Very High	Very High
	Savings Activities			
	> 80 per cent said Yes	+ (Less Severe)	Important	Important
	<80 per cent>40 per cent	++ (Severe)	High	High
	<40 per cent	+++ (Most Severe)	Very High	Very High
Social Security	Activities in Groups (Social)			
	> 80 per cent said Yes	+ (Less Severe)	Important	Important
	<80 per cent>40 per cent	++ (Severe)	High	High
	<40 per cent	+++ (Most Severe)	Very High	Very High
	Activities in Groups (Religious)			
	> 80 per cent said Yes	+ (Less Severe)	Important	Important
	<80 per cent>40 per cent	++ (Severe)	High	High
	<40 per cent	+++ (Most Severe)	Very High	Very High
	Activities in Groups (Community Organisations)			
	> 80 per cent said Yes	+ (Less Severe)	Important	Important
	<80 per cent>40 per cent	++ (Severe)	High	High
	<40 per cent	+++ (Most Severe)	Very High	Very High

Table 4. Relationship of VIS metrics with e-governance evolution

Stages of E-Governance Evolution	VIS Metrics			
	Proximity of Source of Information/ Services	**Latency in Availing Information/ Services**	**Requirement of Integrated Information**	**Cost of Services**
Readiness	+++	+	+++	+
Availability	+	+++	+++	+++
Uptake	+++	+++	+++	+
Impact	+	+++	+++	+

Highly Critical: +++ Important: +

SOLUTIONS AND RECOMMENDATIONS

The framework is applied to understand two dimensions of e-governance services in India. The first one is to understand the supply contributors whereas the second addresses the demand influencers for the cases related to NeGP, and E-Gram services.

Result of the First Method

In this method e-readiness, availability, uptake and impact are examined to appreciate the efforts planned during development of information supplies and actual deliveries. In Table 5 below the status is presented. It is noted that both the e-governance initiatives are backed by state and national level polices. These two initiatives are in growth stages and their infrastructure is readily available in the Panchayat/ for a group of villages. As regards uptakes, e-gram has better uptake because of local contents, state managed and controlled by Panchayats. NeGP services, on the other hand, are driven by national policies and are based on entrepreneurship model. Business models are integrated with e-governance objectives. Maturity of the services is yet to be assessed which could have been examined during pilots. There were no pilots for both these services. Digital divide issues are not visibly addressed since the uptake is minimal. Impacts are also not visible since most the citizens resort to conventional governance procedures.

In Table 6 below the results obtained through primary survey are presented. These seven sample villages provide varying results in each of the assessment factors. Under e-readiness, it indicates that awareness and digital divide issues need immediate attention whereas infrastructure is adequately available in each sample village.

Table 5. Assessment of supplies contributors

Parameters	NeGP	E-Gram
E-Readiness	CSCs are established; Connectivity is in place; Services are through entrepreneurs; MMPs are being introduced; State level integrations are being implemented.	E-Gram centers are established and connected to state Head Quarters; Services are through Panchayats; State controlled applications are in place.
Availability	Available for every six villages	E-Gram centers are in Panchayats (a group of villages)
Uptake	Growth stage and Uptake is minimal	Growth stage and uptake is minimal
Impact	Non-availability of integrated services lead to low impact	Non-availability of integrated services lead to low impact

Table 6. Assessment of e-governance efforts in villages

Assessment Factors	Factors	Sample Villages						
		1	2	3	4	5	6	7
E-Readiness	Awareness	++	+++	+++	+++	+++	+++	+++
	Infrastructure	+	+	+	+	+	+	+
	Digital Divide	+++	+++	+++	+++	+++	+++	+++
Availability	Supply	+++	+++	+++	+++	+++	+++	+++
	Maturity	+++	+++	+++	+++	+++	+++	+++
Uptake	Demand	+++	+++	+++	+++	+++	+++	+++
	Usage	+++	+++	+++	+++	+++	+++	+++
	Use Divide	+++	+++	+++	+++	+++	+++	+++
Impact	Efficiency	+++	+++	+++	+++	+++	+++	+++
	Effectiveness	+++	+++	+++	+++	+++	+++	+++
	Equity	++	++	++	++	++	++	++

+ -> quite adequate, ++ -> moderately adequate and +++ -> poor

As regards availability, both supply and maturity issues are critically poised and they need to be addressed with due attention. Because of poor availability and moderate e-readiness, the uptake has been affected severely in terms of demand, usage and usage divides. Similarly, low impact has remained visibly dismal in terms of efficiency and effectiveness whereas equity has moderately improved. This is because of some increased inquisitiveness and acceptability among women, poor and children in the households.

Result of the Second Method

The second stage of the evaluation is to understand and capture influencers of information demands of the citizens. In Table 7 these influencers are discussed. The respondents were encouraged to contribute to the assessment based on their household needs, proximity of source or point of service, requirement of integrated services (single window service) and their cost.

Citizens' demands in Indian context are influenced by various factors. Some of them have been considered here for evaluation. It is considered important here that information on citizens' basic requirements need to be made available on demand, with least latency and at the village or nearby locations so that their opportunities to receive the desired services are adequately available at an affordable cost. Such a scenario needs appropriate integration of services, networking of service providing agency with ICT backbone.

Table 7. Understanding demand influencers

	Demand Influencers			
Household Needs	Proximity of Source of Information / Services	Latency in Availing Information / Services	Requirement of Integrated Information	Cost of Services
Income Generating Opportunities	In the Village	In Hours	Full Integration	Free Information
Providing Information on Doctors, Interaction with Doctors, Receiving advice from Doctors	Doctor/ Agency in the vicinity of the Village	No Latency	Full Integration	May be Priced for Access to Information
Information on the Institutions and Courses	In the Village	No such Criticality	Full Integration	May be Priced for Access to Information
Information on demand on Appropriate skills	In the Village	No such Criticality	Full Integration	May be Priced for Access to Information

In Table 8, results of the survey conducted on the influencers n the influencers considered for evaluation in seven sample villages are presented. In this evaluation process, information needs described in Table 3 are taken as the influencers in Table 8. This evaluation exercise indicates that in five out of seven sample villages, information needs for income generation opportunities is regarded as very critical and these services are poor. Health service related information is also poor in four

Table 8. Understanding demand influencers

Information Demand Influencers	Sample Villages						
	1	2	3	4	5	6	7
Income Generating Opportunities	++	+++	+++	+	+++	+++	+++
Providing Information on Doctors, Interaction with Doctors, Receiving advice from Doctors	+	++	+++	+	+++	+++	+++
Information on the Institutions and Courses	++	++	++	++	++	++	++
Information on demand on Appropriate skills and vocational courses	++	+++	+++	+	+++	+++	+++

+ -> quite adequate, ++ -> moderately adequate and +++ -> poor out of seven sample villages which need adequate attention. As regards formal education related information, the services are adequately available in all sample villages whereas skill development related information is not adequately available.

Recommendations

The chapter intended to set an agenda to appreciate rural citizens' aspirations for sustaining their livelihoods and incorporate them in the e-governance services being rendered at the local level. It argued that a VIS needs to be developed to assess demand influencers and supply contributors at the village level so that right information and services are rendered locally. The case analysis through the framework substantiated the argument and suggested that e-gram and NeGP should provide the desired synergy by including the demand influencers.

The framework provided a tool to assess the village level demand for establishing the desired interfaces with NeGP services being supplied. Application of this framework for ample villages indicated that VIS metrics are different and are dependent on the livelihood centric demands. Such diversity in demand makes VIS more critical and dynamic. It is thus important that e-governance projects should capture desired demand and provide citizen centered services so as to ensure desired impact. This is more prevalent in Indian context. In this chapter, it was argued uptake and impact are influenced by several citizen needs and especially these factors critically influence the success of e-governance services in Indian context. In India, e-governance services to be successful, rural citizens' needs are to be captured adequately and interfaced with e-governance service network being designed. Rural citizens' livelihood perspectives are important contributors to organize a sustainable interface between "e-governance service- information supplies" and "e-governance service- information demands."

This chapter focused on citizen interface in general and rural citizens in particular in Indian scenario and argued in favour of an interface with backend e-governance plan through an agile VIS. This VIS arguably concluded that rural citizens' would continuously access the services rendered by e-governance services if certain dimensions like proximity, latency, quality of services are taken care of and are related to their livelihood options. It concluded that mere supply of services through e-governance network would not sustain itself in the long run. Strategic planners need to take cognizance of the demands of rural citizens if overall development is to be assured in the context of rural India.

REFERENCES

Archmann, S., & Kudlacek, I. (2008). Interoperability and the exchange of good practice cases. *European Journal of ePractice, 2.*

Bhatnagar, S. (2006). *Paving the road towards pro poor e-governance*, (pp. 26-27). UNDP, APDIP, UNCRD Workshop Report, Bangkok.

Budhiraja, R., & Sameer, S. (2009). *E-readiness assessment (India).* Retrieved from unpan1.un.org/intradoc/groups/public/ documents APCITY/ UNPAN014673.pdf

Dutta, S., Lopez-Claros, A., & Mia, I. (2008). *The global information technology report. INSEAD.* New York, NY: Oxford University Press.

EU. (2007). *Inclusive e-government: Survey of status and baseline activities.* European Commission, DG Information Society and Media, e-Government unit, December.

Heeks, R. (2006a). *Most E-government projects-for-development fail: How can risk be reduced?* Working Paper 14, IDPM, University of Manchester, UK.

Heeks, R., & Molla, A. (2009b). *Impact assessment of ICT-for-development projects: A compendium of approaches.* Working Paper 36, IDPM, University of Manchester, UK.

ITU. (2006a). *World telecommunication/ict development report 2006.*

ITU. (2007b). *World information society report, beyond WSIS.*

Ministry of Information Technology. (2009). Retrieved from http://www.mit.gov.in/default.aspx?id=832

Mishra, D. C. (2007). *Sixty years of development of e-governance in India (1947-2007). Are there lessons for developing countries?* ICEGOV2007, December 10-13, Macao, ACM. 978-1-59593-822-0/07/12

Misra, H. K. (2009). Managing rural citizen interfaces in e-governance systems: A study in Indian context. *Proceedings of ACM ICEGOV2009*, November 10-13, 2009, Bogota, Colombia, (pp. 155-162).

Misra, H. K. (2009). *Governance of rural information and communication technology: Opportunities and challenges.* New Delhi, India: Academic Foundation.

Misra, H. K., & Hiremath, B. N. (2006). Citizen-led participatory e-governance initiatives: An architectural perspective. IIM Lucknow. *Metamorphosis, 5*(2), 133–148.

Misra, H. K., & Hiremath, B. N. (2009). *Livelihood perspective of rural information infrastructure and e-governance readiness in India: A case based study.* IRMA Working Paper Series 215, IRMA, Anand, India.

Planning Commission. (2001). *Government of India, report of the working group on convergence and e-governance for tenth five year plan (2002-2007),* (pp. 6-25). New Delhi, November.

Riga Declaration. (2006). *Internet for all: EU ministers commit to an inclusive and barrier-free information society.* Press release of June, IP/06/769.

UN. (2008). *UN e-government survey, from e-government to connected e-governance.* New York, NY: UN.

ADDITIONAL READING

E-Readiness Assessment Report. (2003a), Department of Information Technology. *Ministry of Communication and Information Technology.* Government of India, New Delhi.

E-Readiness Assessment Report. (2004b). Department of Information Technology. *Ministry of Communication and Information Technology.* Government of India, New Delhi.

E-Readiness Assessment Report. (2006c). Department of Information Technology, *Ministry of Communication and Information Technology.* Government of India, New Delhi.

EU. (2007). *Inclusive e-Government: Survey of status and baseline activities.* European Commission. DG Information Society and Media, e-Government Unit, December.

European Commission. (2005). *i2010 – A European information society for growth and employment.* SEC (2005)717, 01.06.2005 COM(2005) 229 final, Brussels (BE)

Kochhar, S., & Dhanjal, G. (2005). *Skoch e-governance report card 2005: From governance to e-governance.* Skoch Consultancy Services Pvt. Ltd., October, New Delhi.

Korten, D. C. (1980). Community organisation and rural development: A learning process approach. *Public Administration Review*, (September-October): 480–510. doi:10.2307/3110204

Levina, N., & Vaast, E. (2005). The emergence of boundary spanning competence in practice: Implications for implementation and use of information systems. *Management Information Systems Quarterly, 29*(2), 335–363.

Luftman, J. (2000). Assessing business – IT alignment maturity. *Communications of the AIS, 4,* December.

Rao, T. P., Rao, V., Bhatnagar, S., & Satyanarayana, J. (2004). *E-governance assessment framework.* EAF Ver-2.0, Department of Information Technology, Ministry of Communication and Information Technology, Governmnet of India, New Delhi, May.

Riley, T. B. (2003). *E-governance vs. e-government.* I4D, November 1-4, New Delhi.

Satyanarayana, J. (2004). *E-government, the science of the possible* (pp. 8–22). New Delhi, India: Prentice-Hall of India.

Shah, T. (1997). *Design issues in catalyzing peoples institutions for sustainable development.* (IRMA, Unpublished).

Signore, O., Chesi, F., & Pallotti, M. (2005). *E-government: Challenges and opportunities.* XIX Annual Conference, CMG-Italy, 7-9 June, Florence, Italy.

Subramanian, K., & Sachdeva, S. (2003). *Quantifying and assessing e-governance.* I4D, November 1-4, New Delhi

UN. (2008). *UN e-government survey, from e-government to connected e-governance.* New York.

UNDP. (2004). *ICT and human development: Towards building a composite index for Asia, realising the millennium development goals.* Elsevier.

Venkatesh, V., Morris, M. G., Davis, G. B., & Davis, F. D. (2003). User acceptance of information technology: Toward a unified view. *Management Information Systems Quarterly, 27*(3), 425–478.

Ward, J., & Peppard, J. (2002). *Strategic planning for information systems* (pp. 25–59). London, UK: John Wiley and Sons.

Weill, P., & Broadbent, M. (1998). *Leveraging the infrastructure: How market leaders capitalise on information technology.* Boston, MA: Harvard Business School Press.

World Bank. (1986). *Poverty and hunger: Issues and options for food security in developing countries.* Washington, DC: A World Bank Policy Study.

KEY TERMS AND DEFINITIONS

E-Governance: Electronic form of citizen interfaces and citizen service delivery

E-Government: Electronic form of back end and formalized services for citizens that bureaucracy provides

Governance: Participation of citizens in availing services of government

Government: Formalized bureaucracy for provisioning of citizen services

Information: Processed data for the benefit of users or intended recipients

Latency: Minimum delay in a system to render services

Livelihood: Sustaining opportunity provided for having better living conditions

Metrics: Measurement criteria for interpreting the result

Proximity: the distance for the citizen to travel for availing the services

This work was previously published in Cases on Adoption, Diffusion and Evaluation of Global E-Governance Systems: Impact at the Grass Roots, edited by H. Rahman 35-56, copyright 2011 by Information Science Reference (an imprint of IGI Global).

Chapter 4

The Other Side of "Big Brother":
CCTV Surveillance and Intelligence Gathering by Private Police

David Aspland
Charles Sturt University, Australia

EXECUTIVE SUMMARY

A significant shift has occurred in the nature of policing over the past 30 to 40 years across jurisdictions and contexts. The paradigm of policing as a purely government function is under challenge. Policing is becoming more "pluralised" with a range of actors, both public and private. This shift has significant social implications for the general public, together with the public and private organisations that provide policing services. These implications are discussed and highlighted through the use of information technology by private police in two areas—CCTV surveillance and intelligence gathering. This case discusses this shift between public and private sectors in policing. The situation is more complex than a simple public/private divide and plays host to a range of interactions that bring many actors into contact, competition, and alliance in networks and assemblages. Most research and regulation remains focused on public policing even though, numerically, private policing is now a major provider of policing services in an increasingly fragmented, pluralized, and commodified market. This case considers the regulation of private policing as it exists in the Australian context and how it applies to the use of information technology, together with issues for human rights, especially privacy.

DOI: 10.4018/978-1-4666-0981-5.ch004

1. INTRODUCTION

It is not just a case of "sleepwalking into" or "waking up to" a "surveillance society," as the UK's Information Commissioner famously warned, it feels more like turning a blind eye to the start of a new kind of arms race, one in which all the weapons are pointing inwards. – B. Hayes

What Hayes (2009, p. 5) highlights is the increasing use of information technology in support of surveillance and intelligence gathering in a range of policing methodologies that impact on the daily lives of an increasingly large part of the modern population. Most policing is intrusive and can infringe on individual rights and freedoms. The policing methodologies of surveillance and intelligence gathering are perhaps more intrusive than other models. Whether it be the right to privacy, freedom of speech or the right to come and go as the individual pleases, the actions of police have the potential to curtail these freedoms. One of the freedoms that is most often infringed is the right to privacy. This is done through many forms of surveillance ranging from search warrants, telephone taps, email sweeps, observation, CCTV, video recording to intelligence gathering (Bronitt, 1997). These technologies allow for large amounts of data to be gathered and stored on individuals and organisations often without their knowledge or permission (Fox, 2001).

The common paradigm of policing is that it is carried out by properly accountable government agencies with due authority of the law for good of the community. In a major shift to this paradigm, most of this infringement of personal freedoms in our society is no longer carried out by government organizations, but rather is carried out by private organisations in a context where security can be purchased as a commodity (Newburn, 2001). The nature of private policing makes it ideally suited to methodologies involving information technology, such as surveillance and intelligence gathering. Indeed this is often its main strength in situational crime control.

The social implications of these activities that infringe on the rights and privacy of the individual are significant. They raise questions of the accountability of the organisations that undertake them and may even shape community attitudes to a range of issues.

Most research into accountability and regulatory frameworks focuses on the public police with relatively little carried out into private policing or its interaction with public policing (Button, 2002, p. 1; Hummer & Nalla, 2003, p. 88; Zedner, 2006a, p. 273; Stenning, 2009). Shearing argues that the focus on public policing has caused a failure of comprehension of the full implications of private policing (1992, p. 424). What needs to be considered is the accountability of private policing in its use of information technology for surveillance and intelligence gathering, as much of it falls outside state oriented regulatory and human rights frameworks (Marx, 1987; Stenning, 2009; Leman-Langlois & Shearing, 2009).

This case aims to discuss the reasons for change and the social implications of the increasing use of surveillance and intelligence gathering. The starting point in this analysis is how and why the policing streetscape has changed in the latter 20th and early 21st centuries. A good understanding of this helps to create a greater understanding of modern private policing methodologies of which surveillance and intelligence gathering form a critical part.

The case then discusses some of the key points through the use of scenarios that illustrate the critical issues that underpin CCTV surveillance and intelligence gathering by private police. The reason for this is that much learning concentrates on the acquisition of facts and principles, often in isolation. The use of scenarios in this instance is aimed at developing critical thinking about the issues and problems created by the use of CCTV and intelligence gathering by private police organisations and engaging in an experiential problem solving methodology utilizing the facts and principles discussed in the case (Hmelo-Silver, 2004; Naidu, Menon, Gunawardena, Lekamge, & Karunanayaka, 2007). The use of scenarios also allows for the effective consideration of complexity in a rapidly changing social environment which more closely reflects a real life application in context (Richards, O'Shea, & Connolly, 2004).

2. SETTING THE STAGE: THE PARADIGM SHIFT FROM PUBLIC TO PRIVATE POLICING

The term "private policing" is perhaps more controversial than "private security" but when examined as part of the overall social function of "policing," this concept is now greater than just the conventional understanding of "the police" as an organized body in the public domain. Shearing defines the function of policing as "the preservation of peace" where people are free from unwarranted interference to go about their business safely (1992, p. 400). Given this breadth of definition it is logical to expand the concept of "policing" to engage many actors, both public and private.

Public and private policing have always existed side by side in a continuum. The issue of security, or rather insecurity, over the past 30 years has seen the rejuvenation of the private policing sector to a point where it now outweighs public policing in terms of numbers in many areas by a factor of 2 or 3 to 1 (De Waard, 1999).

A common misconception is that there remains a strict public/private divide, even if one ever existed. In modern policing there are a range of "assemblages" and "networks" that provide a complex mix of policing interactions and exchanges on many levels (Wood, 2006). This has seen services previously provided by government agencies, including policing and security, outsourced to the private sector or engaged in joint investigations. There are also private individuals contracting private organizations or organizations where public/private boundaries are blurred and organizations where staff circulate between the two (Marx, 1987; Hoogenboom, 2010, p. 87).

There have been several descriptions of this phenomenon and one of the most logical is that of the "pluralized" policing environment. Public policing remains, legislatively and socially, the dominant arm of policing and would be expected to remain so whilst the nation-state remains the primary political structure. But private policing, in all its forms, is now the largest policing *bloc* in the increasingly fragmented policing streetscape. Any consideration of crime prevention strategies in the 21st century, without considering the role of private policing, ignores a significant factor (Hummer & Nalla, 2003).

There has been an increased demand for policing services driven by many factors including increased fear of crime, insecurity and social unrest; increased levels of recorded crime; greater demands for protection caused by increased property ownership created by rising incomes of both individuals and corporations; shifts in public/private space and increases in mass private space. Also there has been a decline in the social "guardians" such as tram, rail and bus conductors and ticket inspectors; roundsmen/women such as milkmen and postal workers; together with other traditional social controls such as churches, schools, neighbourhoods and families that provided much "secondary" social control (Swanton, 1993; Nina & Russell, 1997, p. 7; De Waard, 1999; Johnston, 1999, p. 179; Jones & Newburn, 2002, p. 141; Neyroud & Beckley, 2001, p. 24; Schneider, 2006, p. 292; Fleming & Grabosky, 2009, p. 282; Caldwell, 2009, p. 114).

Since the 9/11 attacks in New York and the beginning of the "War on Terror" there has been an even greater focus on security at all levels (Perry, 2001). Also, the Global Financial Crisis (GFC) of 2008 has caused a significant reduction in public funding for public police (Gill, Owen, & Lawson, 2010, p. 6). Even before the GFC, increasing demand for policing services was pushing public police organizations to the limit of their capacity (Newburn, 2001, p. 841; Zedner, 2003, p. 153). Grabosky points out that the notion of policing as a "public good" has diminished and that it is unlikely that the state will be able to return to the dominant position of service provision thus ensuring an ongoing role and growth for private policing in a pluralised policing environment (2004, pp. 79-80). Sarre (2008) has noted that the private security sector in Australia grew from around 25000 in 1991 to around 50000 in 2006, whereas the numbers of public police increased from 36000 to 42000 in the same period. He highlights the fact that the increasing demand for policing services has continued unabated into the 21st century.

Another shift in policing style that has given application to the increased use of information technology has been to move away from the paradigm of "post crime" or reactive intervention by the public criminal justice system to the notion of "pre crime" or risk management based prevention strategies being more effective (Swanton, 1993; Zedner, 2006b). This style of crime prevention is in tune with the "risk society" philosophy of the post-modern world where issues are assessed on the basis of risk management and prevention, rather than reacting to the crime after the event, which may be virtually impossible in the globalised world of business and travel in the 21st century (O'Malley, 2010, p. 3).

Also, with the move to a globalised world where crime is also becoming globalised and macroeconomic, it is fair to expect that business will move to seek a globalised crime or loss prevention mechanism that is free of the geopolitical strictures of the nation state. This is an extension of the "vacuum theory" where private policing continues to exist and flourish in areas where the state cannot guarantee to safeguard the peace and well-being of its citizens. In the post-modern, globalised world this may become more the rule than the exception (Shearing, 1992, p. 406).

It is now a truism that the average member of the public is more likely to come into contact with private policing than public policing in their daily lives (Sklansky, 2006, p. 89). These encounters take place in a wide variety of locations and on a regular basis often without the individual really noticing as they have become second nature. There is the overt presence, whether it is the security guard patrolling the shopping mall, at the airport searching passengers as they board their flights or providing security at government or private buildings where people work. The use of private security guards has extended into other areas, previously the preserve of public police, e.g., private security personnel have been used to control crowds at public demonstrations and protests (Button & John, 2002).

Then there is the not so obvious presence of the CCTV operator, the insurance fraud investigator and the private intelligence organizations that gather data on other businesses and individuals. Much investigation by government agencies in such areas as welfare and taxation fraud is now outsourced to the private sector.

Much of what is referred to as "hidden crime" that impacts on our lives is now investigated by private security organizations (Prenzler, 2001). As these are not public order issues requiring some form of uniformed presence, these areas that are ideally suited to the subtle, persuasive and embedded styles of private policing (Shearing, 1992).

3. POLICING BY TELEVISION: CCTV SURVEILLANCE OF MASS PRIVATE SPACE

Closed Circuit Television (CCTV) and its use to monitor public and private space has led to significant changes in both public and private policing. The use of CCTV has become a critical tool in "situational crime prevention" (Von Hirsch, 2000, p. 59; Wakefield, 2000, p. 128; ASIAL, 2010b). The use of large numbers of CCTV cameras has allowed for surveillance of large areas of public and private space without the need to deploy large numbers of public or private police in an overt manner with the CCTV seen as a preemptive tool for proactive policing (McCahill, 2008). Wakefield makes the point that the "unremitting watch" of private police using CCTV is often a critical aid to public police in identifying serious offenders (2000, p. 142).

Modern cameras allow the CCTV operator to home in on individuals in a crowd and identify troublemakers. It is a tremendous aid to the main power that underpins private policing, exclusion from private property and public/private space (Von Hirsch & Shearing, 2000). The main ethical question that underscores the use of CCTV is that it records all persons present in an area, both persons of interest to the CCTV operator as well as passers-by. The anonymity of the individual in the public environment has been diminished, if not removed altogether (Johnston & Shearing, 2003, p. 69).

In the public environment the individual has a right to privacy and Article 17 of the International Covenant on Civil and Political Rights provides that no one shall be subject to arbitrary interference with their privacy. It would seem at face value that the random sweep of the CCTV is just such an arbitrary interference. But what of "mass private space" such as shopping malls, which are now becoming the hub of much community life?

The laws relating to private property when applied in mass private space preclude private citizens from claiming their civil and human rights to a large degree. When entering mass private space, i.e., shopping malls, mass public transport, residential communities, hotel complexes, factories, manufacturing centres, hospitals, office blocks and other areas that could be deemed to be "private property" (Lippert & O'Connor, 2006, p. 57), the citizen loses the right to privacy having bags or belongings inspected or being under surveillance from CCTV often as a condition of entry. Gone also is the right to come and go as the citizen pleases as the greatest power used by private policing is the arbitrarily applied power of exclusion from private property, with dissension regarding the powers of the property owners (or their agents in the form of private security) being resolved by the surrendering of rights being an implied or explicit condition of entry (Sarre, 1994, p. 264):

Scenario 1: Duncan Fanning worked as a senior retail loss prevention officer for a large chain of retail stores. During his career he had developed a skilled ability to observe and monitor groups and individuals via CCTV in the various retail centres where he had worked. Most people were in the retail centres to enjoy the ordered atmosphere and shopping that was available. Also however, Duncan had observed a wide range of shop stealing methodologies used by a significant number of individuals and groups. Duncan had made sure that he recorded these methodologies and as many individuals as he could identify. He compiled a database which he shared with other loss prevention professionals, both in the retail store where he worked and other retail outlets belonging to the same chain, and with the public police. In that database he compiled lists of identification, recent photographs available from CCTV, the types of goods favoured, seasonal factors and common modus operandi. This information provided a sound basis for Duncan and other loss prevention professionals to exclude "high risk" individuals and groups from the retail centres where they worked.

This scenario discusses several of the key issues concerning the use of CCTV in mass private space; firstly the invasion of privacy and the fact that some people may not wish to be recorded or observed, whilst doing nothing illegal. The CCTV is a "catch-all" technology which is being increasingly widely used and the civil and human rights which underpin our democratic legal system are greatly reduced while the individual is on private property (Fox, 2001). Von Hirsch points out that this covert surveillance by an "unobservable observer" takes people unawares when they think they are free of scrutiny and that the person can feel constrained by the "chilling effect" of covert surveillance even if this is not the case (2000, p. 68). Fox describes this chilling effect as

routine surveillance creates an abiding sense of communal unease in which awareness of such scrutiny tends to chill the exercise of accepted civic rights, such as freedom of movement, association, assembly and speech. Surveillance of citizens inhibits full participation in democratic society (2001, p. 261).

Research shows that the majority of Australians (92%) are aware of the use of CCTV in public space and 79% of those surveyed are not concerned with this. Those surveyed suggested a range of public places as being appropriate for surveillance including places where people congregate, public transport and stations, shopping malls and private institutions. Of those that were concerned about the use of CCTV in public places the greatest concerns were that the information may be misused or that it was an invasion of privacy. In spite of this the majority of those surveyed nominated "the police" as an appropriate organisation to have access to CCTV footage, with only a few nominating businesses, councils or even the organisation that installed the CCTV as being appropriate (The Wallis Group, 2007, pp. 74-79; Hummerston, 2007).

This raises what Leman-Langlois and Shearing describe as "function creep" (2009, p. 7). Surveillance of this nature was originally aimed at curbing harmful criminal acts, behaviours that degraded life or abuse of state systems. Now the concern is that as society's tolerance of surveillance grows, surveillance can be used at lower levels with less justification, e.g., surveillance methodologies and technologies originally designed for use by government against terrorism end up being used by private organisations to monitor minor anti-social behaviour.

Next there is the issue of the power of exclusion. This is the main power that private policing holds over the individual in order to ensure compliance although in the private context it can be arbitrarily applied (Wakefield, 2000, p. 133). The power of exclusion is used to remove or restrict undesirable elements from mass private space in order to ensure that the retail trade continues without undue interference. According to Nina and Russell:

instead of being concerned about individual civil rights or Human Rights, private security of the "new" public space is more concerned about how to create conditions which can assist in promoting the logic of capital accumulation and the avoidance of any interference in this process (1997, p. 3).

The social implications of this exclusion of certain individuals or groups from mass private space are that anti-social behaviour is increasingly concentrated in lower socio economic areas. These become subject to increasingly disorder-intolerant public policing styles such as zero-tolerance (Kempa, Stenning, & Wood, 2004, p. 577). Also, is there an increase in public anxiety when viewing quantities of CCTV images of minor crime and anti-social behaviour through media outlets?

The interaction between the CCTV operator and other agencies in the pluralistic policing environment raises the issue of what confidentiality requirements are placed upon him/her when communicating observations or releasing video or audio material to other agencies and the risks of unregulated exchanges of information (Von Hirsch, 2000, p. 70). McCahill makes the point that interaction in this environment has assisted the mixing of policing techniques with private police adding "crime fighting " and "law enforcement" to their existing concerns of "private justice" and "loss prevention."

The use of CCTV by security companies is regarded as cost effective and the trend is for continuing growth in this area (Prenzler, Sarre, & Earle, 2009). Walters (2007) states that, based on figures from the Australian Security Industry Association, there are some 40,000 to 60,000 cameras in the Sydney CBD alone and there have also been moves by the NSW State Government, along with many other governments, to compile biometric facial recognition databases for use by police, using photographs collected for drivers licence applications (Jones, 2010). The compiling of these databases without public debate raises the issue of what safeguards are in place to protect the use and sharing of these records both now and in the future (Fox, 2001).

The British experience is even greater with an estimated 4.2 million CCTV cameras deployed in the United Kingdom or about 1 for every 14 citizens (Welsh & Farrington, 2009, p. 19). In addition to the video and audio scanning capacity the British systems also feature sophisticated number plate recognition software that permits large numbers of vehicles to be tracked simultaneously as they travel around major metropolitan areas (McCahill, 2008, p. 215).

The Australian Security Industry Association Limited (ASIAL) provides a specific CCTV Code of Ethics which states, among other things, a CCTV is not to be used solely for monitoring and surveillance but must serve a crime prevention function. This is supported by the Office of the Privacy Commissioner, Australia, who suggests that the use of CCTV surveillance should have a clear objective and are a proportional response to the defined threat (Hummerston, 2007). The possible breaching of privacy by the use of CCTVs is now the subject of reports by the NSW and Australian Law Reform Commissions who recognise that modern technology, whilst a great aid in the workplace, is also a great hazard to confidentiality and privacy (Davitt, 2010, p. 16).

Technology, such as CCTV allows for the covert gathering of a large amount of information on private citizens. This leads to the discussion of another use of information technology by private organisations, the gathering of intelligence.

4. INTELLIGENCE GATHERING: INTRUSION INTO PRIVATE LIVES

Intelligence, the analysed information on which organizations base decisions, is a critical factor in the effectiveness of both public and private of policing. In the digital age it is an area where privacy and policing are often seen to be at odds (Curtis, 2007).

The gathering of intelligence on domestic citizens by public policing agencies has been seen as necessary, in the context of criminal investigations, to track both individual criminals and patterns of crime. It is also seen as a threat to democratic freedom as in the stories of Australian Police Special Branches being used to monitor political activists, especially Communists in the 1950 and 1960s, and in more recent times, others who were considered unreliable or a potential threat to the established order, until these organizations were disbanded in the 1990s (Campbell

& Campbell, 2007, p. 92). Domestic intelligence gathering by government is now subject to rigorous parliamentary oversight and is highly accountable.

The thought of private companies gathering intelligence on domestic citizens is the stuff of nightmares. It conjures up images of an unseen "Big Corporate Brother" watching in a futuristic scenario where all individual privacy has been stripped away by electronic corporate databases and information holdings on individuals in a "dataveillance" system that does not forget transgressions (Fox, 2001). This is seen as a threat to democracy itself (Kairys & Shapiro, 1980).

Intelligence gathering on individuals and organisations has increased dramatically since the 1970s as data gathering technology has improved and is carried out every day by many organisations, some as a part of their normal activities while for others it is their sole specialist function (Fox, 2001). The use of private intelligence services by corporations stems from issues of cost, need for specialized information to protect business interests (Hoogenboom, 2006, p. 380; Lippert & O'Connor, 2006). If not directly titled *Intelligence* this can go under the names of risk analyses, protective security services or consultancies (Hoogenboom, 2006, p. 375).

The databases gather an extraordinarily broad range of data and have the ability to retain it indefinitely with significant consequences for individual privacy, especially if there is an error in the data (Leman-Langlois & Shearing, 2009). This gathered intelligence is often shared within "Security Intelligence Networks" taking in public and private organisations (Lippert & O'Connor, 2006, p. 51).

At its most common and seemingly innocuous, the loyalty cards and credit card transactions offered by a wide range of businesses track the spending patterns of clients in order to target them for advertising material and E-tags track vehicle movements. At another extreme insurance companies hold intelligence information on clients claim histories and assessments on a clients insurance risk as a fraud prevention tool. Button cites examples of private security firms involved in retail loss prevention gathering intelligence on shoplifters and sharing that information with other retail organizations and police in intelligence gathering networks (2002, p. 104).

Private corporations hold a wide range of intelligence on individuals, ranging from credit ratings, loan default histories through to background employment checks. If one of the primary roles of private policing is to prevent loss for clients, then intelligence on potential risks is critical to the success of this role. Lippert and O'Connor (2006) make the observation that whilst private security organisations have developed a significant intelligence gathering capacity, they tend to share that intelligence with clients and public police mainly, with only a limited interaction with other corporations, as these are seen as competitors.

Wakefield states that private police, to aid situational crime control in mass private space, can and do develop risk profiles of individuals and groups based on such factors as anti-social behaviour, if they seem "out of place" or they are known offenders. She points out that much of the activity of private policing in this environment is directed toward gathering and sharing information through such activities as CCTV monitoring, data gathering, participating in security networks, engaging in informal liaison with public police and providing information to public police investigations (2000, p. 139). Some aspects of the issues raised are examined in the following scenario:

Scenario 2: In a continuation of Scenario 1, along with the lists, Duncan Fanning would provide a range of information from his own experience on the best way to identify and defeat shopstealing groups and individuals, to the other loss prevention officers within his company. At times he would also share this information with the local police, although not to any extent that would cause loss or embarrassment to his employer and only if it was a situation that he could not resolve without the intervention of public police. The information he gathering and analysed allowed him, and his company, to develop proactive strategies in loss prevention based on the methodologies and key times used by the main offenders. This analysis also permitted the extra resources and visible presence of the local police to be harnessed at times of peak risk. However Duncan was reluctant to share this information, on anything but a limited and informal basis, with loss prevention officers from other retail chains as they were competitors in the same field. Also he was aware of issues of privacy that could impact on any formal arrangement.

When gathering information and intelligence in the area of private security many companies operate without the need for legislative authorisation in many areas, although any organisation dealing in personal information is governed by the Privacy Act 1988 (Hayne & Vinecombe, 2008). The issue of the confidentiality of corporate databases and access to client information is one that will bedevil modern society with respect to the privacy of individuals and to what extent does the private security sector have the right to access confidential information, especially if the information has been supplied by the customer to the company, or another company, for alternative purposes than those for which they are being accessed. Williamson highlights the point, in the Australian context, by stating "most organisations do not have adequate governance over the collection, protection and destruction of personally sensitive data" (2010, p. 12).

In a Review of the Private Sector Provisions of the Privacy Act (Office of the Privacy Commission, 2005, p. 224), the Australian Institute of Private Detectives (AIPD) made a submission asking for private detectives to be considered as a law enforcement body on par with public police. The basis of this submission was that private detectives had limited access to information and that this could prejudice their clients. The submission was refused mainly on the grounds that, unlike public police, private detectives are not accountable to the government or the community (2005, p. 229).

Prenzler (2001) identified the area of information privacy as a key concern with a number of inquiries taking place in New South Wales and Queensland into the unauthorised trading of information between police, private investigators and their clients (often through "old boy" networks). Prenzler makes the point though that the unauthorised trade could be as much the result of lack of knowledge about the legalities, given the complexity of the regulations governing the sector, as much as any misconduct or wrongdoing (2001, p. 10). Shearing states that this can arise where former public police join private organizations as a career change and vice versa, as quite commonly happens (1992, p. 414). This is topical given that much data handling is now outsourced to organisations that may not even be within the same national borders. This was recently highlighted when a data processing company in India, which processes data from many countries worldwide, including Australia, decided to use inmates from a gaol as data entry staff (Farooq, 2010).

Examples exist of the sharing of information and intelligence between the public and private sectors in law enforcement. These are the Greater Manchester Community Safety Partnership Team in the UK, the Eyes on the Street Program in WA and Operation Piccadilly to reduce Ram Raids on ATMs in NSW, Australia (Lewis, 2008, p. 158; Crime and Research Centre, 2008; Prenzler, 2009). These may well serve as models for the future and have significant social implications as large quantities of data are gathered on citizens and shared across a range of public and private organisations.

However, at present the sharing of intelligence has been identified as one of the main stumbling blocks to partnership policing as indicated by a number of senior police officers (Gill et al., 2010, p. 45). In the Australian context there are significant legislative and policy barriers to the sharing of intelligence between public and private policing organizations. Yet the trading and exchange of information within a trusted network is one of the pillars for effectiveness in pluralistic policing (Wardlaw & Boughton, 2006, p. 141). But, whilst many public policing organizations are prepared to accept information and intelligence, they are unable or unwilling to reciprocate in return and this raises barriers of trust (Harfield & Kleiven, 2008).

5. THE CURRENT CHALLENGES: HOW IS PRIVATE POLICING REGULATED?

The regulation of surveillance and intelligence gathering by private police is becoming more important and has significant social implications as the increasingly fragmented and pluralized policing streetscape is becoming more difficult to regulate. This is partly due to the diversified nature of the private security sector and the complexities of pluralised policing networks. This makes developing partnerships or applying universal standards difficult (Gill et al., 2010, p. 29). The fragmented nature of the industry makes it difficult to regulate as there is no one entity that is "private policing." Included are a diverse range of manned security contractors, "in house" security, risk consultants, security advisors, technical staff and sales people working for any number of organizations ranging from one person, local operations to multi-national corporations. Also, given the state-based nature of regulation, staff working for the same company in different states of Australia can fall under different regulatory regimes.

Prenzler makes the point that it is difficult to prevent misconduct in public policing organizations which are heavily regulated. He raises the same question with regards to private policing and makes the point that there is a "very high opportunity factor for misconduct" based on "privileged knowledge about clients assets and vulnerabilities, and from the potential 'Dirty Harry' style conflict between noble ends and legal constraints" (2001, p. 7).

As previously stated most scrutiny, research and regulation in policing is focused on the public police, yet some of the larger private policing organizations have significant surveillance and intelligence gathering capacities, making them a substantial force in the marketplace. Well run and responsible organizations can be seen as an aid to government in promoting social and international order, yet they could also become a parallel force operating in a quasi-government fashion. The growth of private policing organisations in South Africa provides a useful case study in this area (Nina & Russell, 1997; De Waard, 1999; Defence Sector Program, 2007).

The American criminologist Elizabeth Joh (2006) offers a lesson from U.S. history, warning against the current enthusiasm for private policing organizations as an alternative to fill the void left by public funding shortfalls. She highlights the great risks if the corporate vested interests that control private policing are not properly regulated. As Marx (1987) points out, the regulatory frameworks in most democracies are aimed at limiting the power of the state over the private citizen, but not towards what private citizens do to each other unless that private citizen is in some way acting on behalf, and with the authority, of the state. Shearing advances the idea these experiences in the 19th and 20th century United States have coloured the attitudes of much present day analysis of private policing (1992, p. 405).

The regulation of private policing in Australia relies on state based legislation overseen by the Commissioner of Police for that state and industry codes of practice from bodies such as the Australian Security Industry Association Limited (ASIAL). There is also oversight in some states (notably New South Wales and Victoria) from Security Industry Advisory Councils which are made up of key industry stakeholders.

Sarre observes that while the role of private policing has increased unabated there is still much confusion over the role and powers of these organizations. He states that the "legal authority, rights and powers of private security providers is determined more by a piecemeal array of privileges and assumptions than by clear law" (2008, p. 303). There has been little by way of legislation to recognize any special role of the private security industry, with their powers and role still being largely defined as that of the ordinary citizen. Fox (2001) states that the legislative frameworks that protect citizens from overt and covert monitoring remain weak.

Much of the regulation of the industry in Australia is concerned with administrative issues and licencing rather than any ethical concerns of the interaction between the industry and the public (Button, 2007, p. 118). Queensland is unique in having legislated Codes of Practice at this time. However ASIAL provides a number of codes of practice that are specific in dealing with ethical issues in such areas a public interest, integrity, conflict of interest, unethical conduct, surveillance and privacy (2010a, 2010b).

Another significant basis of the regulation and control of private policing is the contract between the employer and the private policing organization. The employment contract, whether it be for contracted security or "in house" security defines the role, activities and functions of the security organization or employee and gives them the scope of their authority (Sarre, 1994, p. 263). Paradoxically, it is this contract based control that can lead to a number of ethical issues as the consumer of these commodified policing services generally purchases these services reluctantly and with a careful eye to the price, rather than quality (Zedner, 2006a, p. 271). This creates a downward pressure on costs which leads to low wages and high staff turnover in the private security sector which can create an increasing dependency on information technology. It also militates against the additional costs of training and accreditation which could lead to a decrease in the professional standards of the industry.

Regulation by customer complaint is not to be underestimated. Given that the role of much of private policing is to aid the profitability of the contractor, the industry can be very sensitive to the needs of customers. This includes both those who hold the contracts and those who interact with private police in retail situations in mass private space, although security guards do tend to act in accordance with private interests rather than in the public interest (Wakefield, 2000).

6. CONCLUSION

The rejuvenation and expansion of the private policing sector in the late 20th century leading into the 21st century has seen private police take up many of the roles previously thought to be the prerogative of the public police. This has now included areas such as surveillance and intelligence gathering and has developed to the point where the private citizen is more likely to encounter private policing organizations and forms of policing in their daily lives, than public ones even if they do not realize it, but the regulation of this area remains fragmented.

While it is believed that public policing will remain the dominant policing form, by virtue of its legislative and social position, private policing will continue to grow and further develop to fill roles and functions required in an increasingly commodified and fragmented policing market. These roles will include an expanding use of information technology such as CCTV and intelligence databases. Given the pressure being placed on public policing agencies by ongoing funding and staffing cuts caused by the recent Global Financial Crisis it is likely that this will be the policing model of the future.

The social implications of this for the community as a whole will be significant with accountability of the use of surveillance and intelligence gathering technology being reliant on the governance of a pluralised network. This is likely to become more crucial as the use of this technology increases as people and organisations seek to reduce their risk of being victims of crime.

REFERENCES

Australian Security Industry Association Limited (ASIAL). (2010a). *Code of professional conduct.* Retrieved November 26, 2010, from http://www.asial.com.au/CodeofConduct

Australian Security Industry Association Limited (ASIAL). (2010b). *CCTV code of ethics.* Retrieved November 26, 2010, from http://www.asial.com.au/CCTV-CodeofEthics

Bronitt, S. (1997). Electronic surveillance, human rights and criminal justice. *Australian Journal of Human Rights, 3*(2). Retrieved January 1, 2011, from http://www.austlii.edu.au/au/journals/AUJ1HRights/1997/10.html

Button, M. (2002). *Private policing.* Cullompton, UK: Willan Publishing.

Button, M. (2007). Assessing the regulation of private security across Europe. *European Journal of Criminology, 4*(1), 109–128. doi:10.1177/1477370807071733

Button, M., & John, T. (2002). Plural policing in action: A review of the policing of environmental protests in England and Wales. *Policing and Society, 12*(2), 111–121. doi:10.1080/10439460290002659

Caldwell, C. (2009). *Reflections on the revolution in Europe. Can Europe be the same with different people in it?* London, UK: Allen Lane, Penguin Books.

Campbell, D., & Campbell, S. (2007). *The liberating of Lady Chatterley and other true stories. A history of the NSW Council of Civil Liberties.* Glebe, NSW, Australia: NSW Council of Civil Liberties.

Curtis, K. (2007, November 20). *The social agenda: Law enforcement and privacy.* Paper presented at the International Policing: Towards 2020 Conference, Canberra, ACT, Australia.

Davitt, E. (2010). New laws needed to prosecute invasion of privacy cases. *Australian Security Magazine.* Retrieved from http://www.securitymanagement.com.au/articles/new-laws-needed-to-prosecute-invasion-of-privacy-cases-130.html

De Waard, J. (1999). The private security industry in international perspective. *European Journal on Criminal Policy and Research, 7,* 143–174. doi:10.1023/A:1008701310152

Defence Sector Program. (2007). *Conference report on the regulation of the private security sector in Africa.* Pretoria, South Africa: Institute for Security Studies.

Evans, K. (2011). *Crime prevention. A critical introduction.* Thousand Oaks, CA: Sage.

Farooq, O. (2010). *Company outsources work to Indian prison, plans to employ about 250 inmates.* Retrieved January 21, 2010, from http://www.news.com.au/business/breaking-news/company-outsources-work-to-indian-prison-plans-to-employ-about-250-inmates/story-e6frfkur-1225865832163

Fleming, J., & Grabosky, P. (2009). Managing the demand for police services, or how to control an insatiable appetite. *Policing. Journal of Policy Practice, 3*(3), 281–291.

Fox, R. (2001). Someone to watch over us: Back to the panopticon? *Criminal Justice, 1*(3), 251–276.

Gill, M., Owen, K., & Lawson, C. (2010). *Private security, the corporate sector and the police: Opportunities and barriers to partnership working.* Leicester, UK: Perpetuity Research and Consultancy International.

Grabosky, P. (2004). Toward a theory of public/private interaction in policing. In McCord, J. (Ed.), *Beyond empiricism: Institutions and intentions in the study of crime* (*Vol. 13,* pp. 69–82).

Harfield, C., & Kleiven, M. (2008). Intelligence, knowledge and the reconfiguration of policing. In Harfield, C., MacVean, A., Grieve, J., & Phillips, D. (Eds.), *The handbook of intelligent policing. Consilience, crime control and community safety* (pp. 239–254). Oxford, UK: Oxford University Press.

Hayes, B. (2009). *NeoConOpticon. The EU security-industrial complex.* Retrieved January 20, 2011, from http://www.statewatch.org/analyses/neoconopticon-report.pdf

Hayne, A., & Vinecombe, C. (2008, February). *IT security and privacy – The balancing act.* Paper presented at the Securitypoint 2008 Seminar.

Hmelo-Silver, C. (2004). Problem based learning: what and how do students learn. *Educational Psychology Review, 16*(3), 235–266. doi:10.1023/B:EDPR.0000034022.16470.f3

Hoogenboom, B. (2006). Grey intelligence. *Crime, Law, and Social Change, 45*, 373–381. doi:10.1007/s10611-006-9051-3

Hoogenboom, B. (2010). *The governance of policing and security. Ironies, myths and paradoxes.* Houndmills, UK: Palgrave Macmillan. doi:10.1057/9780230281233

Hummer, D., & Nalla, M. (2003). Modelling future relations between the private and public sectors of law enforcement. *Criminal Justice Studies, 16*(2), 87–96. doi:10.1080/0888431032000115628

Hummerston, M. (2007, October 2). *Emerging issues in privacy.* Paper presented at the SOCAP- Swinburne Consumer Affairs Course.

Joh, E. (2006). The forgotten threat: Private policing and the state. *Indiana Journal of Global Legal Studies, 13*(2), 357–398. doi:10.2979/GLS.2006.13.2.357

Johnston, L. (1999). Private policing in context. *European Journal on Criminal Policy and Research, 7*, 175–196. doi:10.1023/A:1008753326991

Johnston, L., & Shearing, C. (2003). *Governing security.* London, UK: Routledge.

Jones, G. (2010, June 3). NSW government recording features for facial recognition. *Daily Telegraph.*

Jones, T., & Newburn, T. (2002). The transformation of policing? Understanding current trends in policing systems. *The British Journal of Criminology, 42*, 129–146. doi:10.1093/bjc/42.1.129

Kairys, D., & Shapiro, J. (1980). Remedies for private intelligence abuses: legal and ideological barriers. *Review of Law and Social Change. New York University, 10*, 233–248.

Kempa, M., Stenning, R., & Wood, J. (2004). Policing communal spaces. A reconfiguration of the "mass property" hypothesis. *The British Journal of Criminology*, *44*(4), 562–581. doi:10.1093/bjc/azh027

Leman-Langlois, S., & Shearing, C. (2009). *Human rights implications of new developments in policing*. Retrieved January 20, 2011, from http://www.crime-reg.com

Lewis, S. (2008). Intelligent partnership. In Harfield, C., MacVean, A., Grieve, J., & Phillips, D. (Eds.), *The handbook of intelligent policing. Consilience, crime control and community safety* (pp. 151–160). Oxford, UK: Oxford University Press.

Lippert, R., & O'Connor, D. (2006). Security intelligence networks and the transformation of contract security. *Policing and Society*, *16*(1), 50–66. doi:10.1080/10439460500399445

Marx, G. (1987). The interweaving of public and private police undercover work. In Shearing, C., & Stenning, P. (Eds.), *Private policing* (pp. 172–193). Thousand Oaks, CA: Sage.

McCahill, M. (2008). Plural policing and CCTV surveillance. *Sociology of Crime. Law and Deviance*, *10*, 199–219. doi:10.1016/S1521-6136(07)00209-6

McGinley, I. (2007). Regulating "rent-a-cops" post 9/11: Why the Private Security Officer Employment Authorisation Act fails to address homeland security concerns. *Cardozo Public Law. Policy and Ethics Journal*, *6*(129), 129–161.

Naidu, S., Menon, M., Gunawardena, C., Lekamge, D., & Karunanayaka, S. (2007). How scenario based learning can engender reflective practice in distance education. In Spector, J. (Ed.), *Finding your voice online. Stories told by experienced online educators* (pp. 53–72). Mahwah, NJ: Lawrence Erlbaum & Associates.

Newburn, T. (2001). The commodification of policing: security networks in the late modern city. *Urban Studies (Edinburgh, Scotland)*, *38*(5-6), 829–848. doi:10.1080/00420980123025

Neyroud, P., & Beckley, A. (2001). *Policing, ethics and human rights*. Cullompton, UK: Willan Publishing.

Nina, D., & Russell, S. (1997). Policing "by any means necessary": Reflections on privatisation, human rights and police issues – Considerations for Australia and South Africa. *Australian Journal of Human Rights*, *3*(2). Retrieved January 25, 2010, from http://www.austlii.edu.au/au/journals/AJHR/1997/9.html

O'Malley, P. (2010). *Crime and risk*. Thousand Oaks, CA: Sage.

Office of the Privacy Commissioner. (2005). *Getting in on the act: The review of the private sector provisions of the Privacy Act 1988*. Melbourne, Australia: Author.

Perry, W. (2001). The new security mantra. Prevention, deterrence, defense. In Hoge, J., & Rose, G. (Eds.), *How did this happen? Terrorism and the new war* (pp. 225–240). New York, NY: Public Affairs.

Prenzler, T. (2001). *Private investigators in Australia: Work, law, ethics and regulation*. Retrieved from http://www.criminologyresearchcouncil.gov.au/reports/prenzler.pdf

Prenzler, T. (2009). Strike Force Piccadilly: A public-private partnership to stop ATM ram raids. *Policing: An International Journal of Police Strategies and Management, 32*(2), 209–225. doi:10.1108/13639510910958145

Prenzler, T., Sarre, R., & Earle, K. (2009). The trend to private security in Australia. *Australasian Policing. Journal of Professional Practice, 1*(1), 17–18.

Richards, L., O'Shea, J., & Connolly, M. (2004). Managing the concept of strategic change within a higher education institution: the role of strategic and scenario planning techniques. *Strategic Change, 13*, 345–359. doi:10.1002/jsc.690

Sarre, R. (1994). The legal powers of private police and security providers. In Moyle, P. (Ed.), *Private prisons and police. Recent Australian trends* (pp. 259–280). Leichardt, NSW, Australia: Pluto Press.

Sarre, R. (2008). The legal powers of private security personnel: Some policy considerations and legislative options. *QUT Law and Justice Journal, 8*(2), 301–313.

Schneider, S. (2006). Privatising economic crime enforcement: Exploring the role of private sector investigative agencies in combating money laundering. *Policing and Society, 16*(3), 285–316. doi:10.1080/10439460600812065

Shearing, C. (1992). The relation between public and private policing. In Tonry, M., & Norval, N. (Eds.), *Modern policing* (pp. 399–434). Chicago, IL: University of Chicago Press. doi:10.1086/449198

Sklansky, D. (2006). Private police and democracy. *The American Criminal Law Review, 43*(1), 89–105.

Stenning, P. (2009). Governance and accountability in a plural policing environment – The story so far. *Policing, 3*(1), 22–33. doi:10.1093/police/pan080

Swanton, B. (1993). *Police & private security: possible directions*. Trends & Issues in Crime and Criminal Justice.

The Wallis Group. (2007). *Community attitudes to privacy*. Melbourne, VIC, Australia: Office of the Privacy Commissioner.

United Nations. (1966). *International covenant on civil and political rights*. New York, NY: Author.

Von Hirsch, A. (2000). The ethics of public television surveillance. In Von Hirsch, A., Garland, D., & Wakefield, A. (Eds.), *Ethical and social perspectives on situational crime control* (pp. 59–76). Oxford, UK: Hart Publishing.

Von Hirsch, A., & Shearing, C. (2000). Exclusion from public space. In Von Hirsch, A., Garland, D., & Wakefield, A. (Eds.), *Ethical and social perspectives on situational crime control* (pp. 77–96). Oxford, UK: Hart Publishing.

Wakefield, A. (2000). Situational crime prevention in mass private property. In Von Hirsch, A., Garland, D., & Wakefield, A. (Eds.), *Ethical and social perspectives on situational crime control* (pp. 125–146). Oxford, UK: Hart Publishing.

Walters, C. (2007, September 22). There is nowhere to hide in Sydney. *Sydney Morning Herald*. Retrieved January 20, 2011, from http://www.smh.com.au/news/national/there-is-nowhere-to-hide-in-sydney/2007/09/21/1189881777231

Wardlaw, G., & Boughton, J. (2006). Intelligence led policing – The AFP approach. In Fleming, J., & Wood, J. (Eds.), *Fighting crime together. The challenges of policing and security networks* (pp. 133–149). Sydney, Australia: UNSW Press.

Welsh, B., & Farrington, D. (2009). *Making public places safer. Surveillance and crime prevention*. Oxford, UK: Oxford University Press.

Williamson, G. (2010). The problem with privacy. *Australian Security Magazine*, 10-12.

Wood, J. (2006). Dark networks, bright networks and the place of police. In Fleming, J., & Wood, J. (Eds.), *Fighting crime together. The challenges of policing and security networks* (pp. 246–269). Sydney, Australia: UNSW Press.

Zedner, L. (2003). The concept of security: an agenda for comparative analysis. *Legal Studies, 23*(1), 153–176. doi:10.1111/j.1748-121X.2003.tb00209.x

Zedner, L. (2006a). Liquid security: Managing the market for crime control. *Criminology & Criminal Justice, 6*(3), 267–288. doi:10.1177/1748895806065530

Zedner, L. (2006b). Policing before and after the police. *The British Journal of Criminology, 46*, 78–96. doi:10.1093/bjc/azi043

This work was previously published in the Journal of Cases on Information Technology, Volume 13, Issue 2, edited by Mehdi Khosrow-Pour, pp. 34-48, copyright 2011 by IGI Publishing (an imprint of IGI Global).

Chapter 5

The Egyptian National Post Organization Past, Present, and Future:
The Transformational Process Using ICT

Sherif Kamel
The American University in Cairo, Egypt

EXECUTIVE SUMMARY

Over the last 20 years, the international postal sector has changed drastically due to several forces, including globalization, changing technology, greater demands for efficient services, and market liberalization. For Egypt, keeping up with the changing atmosphere in the global market meant investing in information and communication technology. The Ministry of Communication and Information Technology (ICT), as part of its efforts to transforming government performance using ICT, chose the Egyptian National Post Organization (ENPO) as a model for ICT integrated government portal. The selection was due to ENPO's extensive network, and the public's confidence and trust in the organization. The case of ENPO, capitalizing on public-private partnership models, proved successful when reflecting ICT deployment for organizational transformation within the context of an emerging economy. In addition to its importance in providing eGovernment services to citizens, ENPO is evolving as a critical medium for effectively developing Egypt's eCommerce. This case study takes an in-depth look at how ICT has improved the quality and range of services offered by ENPO, while asserting the magnitude of its impact on the country's emergence as a competitor in today's global postal market.

DOI: 10.4018/978-1-4666-0981-5.ch005

INTRODUCTION

As Amr Badr Eldin, ENPO vice chairman for Information Technology (IT), and responsible for IT strategy, infrastructure deployment and utilization, approached his office at the headquarters of ENPO, which is ironically Egypt's oldest museum, located in Ataba square, one of the busiest squares in down town Cairo; the first object that immediately grabbed his attention was the 1865 automatic stamp vending machine. In a country like Egypt, where automatic vending machines were scarcely found and were still considered innovative, one immediately realized the great role that this place once had in the establishment of modern Egypt. The postal sector, on an international level, had changed drastically in the last 20 years. Several key forces had driven this evolution in the postal market including but not limited to changes in the volume of supply and demand of postal services, globalization effects, market liberalization, changing technology, dynamic communications shift, and regulatory progress, amongst other factors.

One other primary reason was the ever-growing competition from the private sector threatening the comfortable monopoly enjoyed by public operators for centuries. The level of services offered by the private sector had grown dramatically forcing public operators to change to meet the demand of the globally and growingly integrated mail market. Postal organizations across the world had started to transform their business and use Information and Communication Technology (ICT) in order to compete with the change in market trends. There were various successful models of services offered by various postal organizations. This included the United States Postal Service (USPS) offering email and eCommerce services; the South African Post Office offering hybrid mail services; and, Korea Post offering a synchronized information network (mobile, radio communication and RFID) whereby consumers have access to mail services and track the whereabouts of mail or packages anytime, anywhere. ENPO was determined to join that league in offering new services beyond the traditional mail services it used to over for decades.

Since 1999, Egypt had been implementing an aggressive ICT strategy as part of its national development plan; and ENPO was perceived as an integral part of such strategy. ENPO has been leveraging its capability to serve millions of consumers and trust to regain lost ground and compete, offering a plethora of services similar to those of other national postal organizations and pursuing further developments; thus turning it into a highly competitive organization. With images of newspaper titles racing in Badr Eldin's mind, celebrating ENPO's latest achievement in succeeding to become the only governmental institution to be part of Egypt's third mobile operator, he started to wonder where this organization once was, where it currently is and, most importantly, where it is going. The question immediately presented itself; was Egypt's National Post Organization rediscovering itself once again? The development of ENPO using ICT comes as an integral factor in the overall ICT development in Egypt. Table 1 demonstrates the evolution of ICT in Egypt.

BACKGROUND

ENPO volume and diversity of service had reached more than 18 million local customers and led to a long lasting trust between the national post and the local population from different segments and backgrounds. Such trust led to increasing the number of customers who took part in the financial services of ENPO to 2 million last year. A trust that has resulted in having *"Daftar Tawfeer"* (Arabic translation for a savings account) becoming the generic name for a saving account used by literally all segments of the society from all ages and from different social and economic segments and groups. ENPO was the main pillar for connecting Egypt with the outside world. This unmatched penetration within the Egyptian culture was made possible by the organization's large and extensive distribution network of more than 3,700 post offices located in every province and across the nation's 4,000 villages making ENPOs' distribution network the largest in Egypt coming in second to the network of national schools. One of the major characteristics of such a huge organization was the exceptionally large number of employees working in it; whereas, ENPO employed over 45,000 people of which 50% are located in remote offices in order to secure the quality and rate of the services provided to clients and enabling the same service on a nationwide scale.

Table 1. Development of the information society in Egypt

Programs	Year
Open Door Policy	1974
Economic Reform Program	1985
Information Project Cabinet of Ministers (IPCOM)	1985
Information and Decision Support Program (IDSC)	1986
National Information and Administrative Reform Initiative	1989
Egypt Information Highway	1994
Ministry of Communications and Information Technology (MCIT)	1999
National Information and Communications Technology Master Plan	2000
Egypt Information Society Initiative (EISI)	2003
Egypt ICT Strategy 2007-2010	2007

SETTING THE STAGE

Organizational History

ENPO was established on January 2, 1865. Located in the heart of Cairo, it is thought to be one of the oldest and most prestigious governmental organizations in Egypt. Since its inception, Egypt post was united with the ministry of occupation, under the British rule, which lasted from 1882 to 1954. Later on, its association was transferred to a number of ministries until 1965, when Egypt post was under the umbrella of the ministry of finance, which issued a regulation specifying that the transfer of letters and issuance of stamps is exclusive to the government of Egypt. In March 1876, all employees working for the post were required to wear a uniform. In 1899, services that were offered since the posts' inception were cancelled including salt and soda stamps, steamboat tickets and telegram and telephone services.

In 1919, the ministry of transportation was established and was given control of the post authority. Later on that year, law number 9 was issued to set all postage fees; and the post authority headquarters was moved from Alexandria to Cairo in Ataba Square. In 1934, the 10th conference of the International Post was held in Cairo, coinciding with the 70th anniversary of the established Egypt post. After the 1952 revolution, Egypt post was transformed into a cost center using revenue surplus to improve its services to the community. In 1957, Egypt post was replaced by the Egyptian Post Authority (EPA), and in 1966, EPA was replaced by the General Post Authority (GPA). In order to regulate Egypt, post law number 16 was passed in 1970. In 1982, the name was changed again to the National Post Authority (NPA) under law number 19. Finally, in 1999, the Ministry of Communications and Information Technology (MCIT) was established and became in charge of supervising the National Post Authority (NPA), Telecom Egypt (TE) and the National Telecommunication Institute (NTI). In 2008, Egypt Prime Minister, Ahmed Nazif, inaugurated the new headquarters of ENPO in the Smart Village. Table 2 demonstrates the development timeline of ENPO. This was perceived as a new phase in Egypt post evolution where its role was being repositioned as a tool to avail eGovernment and as a platform for services provision that can reach all segments of the community.

ENPO TRADITIONAL SERVICES

Since its redesigned services and repositioning under MCIT in 1999, ENPO has been focusing its services on three main areas: postal services, financial services and social services. Exhibit 1 demonstrates details of the services offered.

Table 2. ENPO timeline

Time Line	Evolution Phase
1865	Egypt Post Established (associated with ministry of occupation under British rule)
1919	Egypt Post was associated with ministry of transportation
1952	Egypt Post was transformed into a cost center
1954-1964	Egypt Post was associated with a number of ministries
1957	Egypt Post was replaced by the Egyptian Post Authority (EPA)
1965	EPA associated with ministry of finance
1966	EPA was replaced by the General Post Authority (GPA)
1982	GPA name was changed to National Post Authority (NPA)
1999	NPA was transformed to ENPA and became associated with MCIT

Postal Services

The postal services are considered one of the oldest and cheapest methods of communication between individuals provided by ENPO and they include:

- **Regular post**, which has enjoyed price stability over the years that is not available by any other service offered.
- **Fast/express mail**, which is the fastest means of sending parcels and documents, within 24 hours in Egypt, and 48-75 hours outside Egypt to over 215 countries. The service is totally insured with door-to-door delivery and confirmation provided to ensure efficiency.
- **Postal parcels**, which is a service that allows the transfer of parcels, luggage, and gifts that weigh more than 2 kilograms with fees fixed by the authority according to the weight, distance, kind and value of contents.
- **Public postal services**, which includes private post boxes, postal cards and stamps

Financial Services

Despite some minor unreliability in its postal services, ENPO's financial services have always enjoyed a good reputation as a reliable financial institution, owing to the fact that it has never defaulted in payment of interest to the depositors. This has allowed it to earn the trust of all segments of the society for more than 100 years. ENPO started its financial services in 1905 by issuing saving booklets (Postal Saving PassBook), which is one of the oldest financial services offered in Egypt. In addition to the benefits of privacy, flexibility of depositing and monthly awards, the saving booklet's main advantage lies in the fact that the government guarantees its balances as well as the interests. Additionally, ENPO offers individuals, companies and organizations safe money transfer from one post office to another. With the number of depositors reaching 14.4 million and an enormous amount of deposits reaching 6.3 billion US dollars, it was becoming obvious that ENPO was a hidden treasure waiting to be discovered, or more accurately, waiting to be correctly invested. Other services include GiroNil, which has been introduced as result of cooperation between ENPO, Misr bank and Commercial International Bank, a private bank operating in Egypt. The GiroNil Company specializes in utility payments, allowing customers to pay their bills to large corporations and multinationals via ENPO offices. Customers also have the option of simply signing a document that allows ENPO to pay utility bills on their behalf, thus avoiding the risk of forgetting bills or queuing long hours to pay.

Social Services

ENPO's social service initiatives began in 1963 based on its conviction with its role in Egypt's socioeconomic development. For instance, the organization started paying pensions to around 3 million citizens with a total pension of 1.6 billion US dollars per year (www.egyptpost.org). The service has allowed pensioners to receive their pensions from 3,600 national post offices distributed all over the country, thus facilitating the process. This is part of the new services offered by ENPO to the government and a disbursing agent. It is important to note that this service has also removed the pensioner's burden of commuting from different areas in Egypt and queuing for long hours. Moreover, for customer convenience, some pensions are delivered directly to the customer's homes free-of-charge. More than 300 thousand pensioners (many over the age of 70, ill, and people with special needs) benefit from this service. ENPO also manages to deliver parcels to customer's homes through post offices nationwide. Another social service is the housing project where customers through the post office can benefit by buying application forms and making housing reservations provided by the state to young graduates. Finally, there is the fourth social service known as "lost property", which involves ENPO's cooperation with police forces to return lost property to the original owners.

ENPO on the National ICT Agenda

"The main drive of the eGovernment initiative is to modernize the citizen's experience of public services and to improve the functionality of the government." Tarek Kamel, Minister of Communications and Information Technology.

ICT Sector Reform

In 1999, MCIT announced the formulation of the first national ICT plan. The plan was focused on upgrading the existing infrastructure in terms of information and technology and availing an ecosystem that can help diffuse ICT in Egypt in terms of laws and regulations. The success of this plan was intended to create more business opportunities through ICT-empowered products and services that can benefit all stakeholders. The convergence between information, media and telecommunications was one of the most important developments. Based on a number of amendments in 2000, 2004, and 2007, a new ICT strategy was developed focusing on three main pillars: (a) ICT sector restructuring, (b) ICT for development; and, (c) Innovation and ICT industry development. The strategy was formulated by MCIT in collaboration with leading expertise in the ICT sector. The aim is to continue the development of the ICT infrastructure to maximize its benefits, leverage public-private partnerships, create more community involvement and link Egypt globally.

ICT Sector Restructuring

MCIT stated that the ICT sector restructuring would be realized through the development of state-of-the-art telecommunications infrastructure and export of services, reform of the postal sector, and enhancing the framework governing the use of ICT networks and services.

ICT for Development

The use of ICT for economic development could be achieved through ensuring easy, affordable access to ICT for all citizens, diffusing education and lifelong learning through the Egyptian Education Initiative (EEI), integrating ICT in health services, supporting the production, use and distribution of Arabic digital content (eContent) and providing the necessary ICT support for the government. It is important to note that ICT for development is a collective effort by different government entities in collaboration with the private sector in an attempt to create industry-related opportunities using ICT.

Innovation and ICT Industry Development

Innovation and creativity using ICT is integral in the development process and MCIT formulated a plan to realize this objective through developing export-oriented IT-enabled services, developing the ICT capacity of Egypt, formulating strategic plans for research and innovation and promoting local and foreign direct investments in the ICT sector.

CASE DESCRIPTION

The Beginning

Since the inception of the eGovernment program, the government of Egypt was determined to deliver high quality government services to the public where they are and in the format that suits them. The vision was guided by three main principles:

- **Citizen centric service delivery** where the program slogan is *"government now delivers"* reflecting government intention to develop a one stop shop eServices approach focused at citizen's needs.
- **Community participation** where eGovernment is a project with nationwide impact, thus community participation is necessary. Citizens' demands are constantly being analyzed and reflected, and private/public sector companies are active participants in project's implementation and management.
- **Efficient allocation of government resources** where the emphasis was focusing on techniques to improve the level of efficiency, increase productivity, work on cost reduction, as well as the efficient allocation of resources.

When Egypt first launched its eGovernment initiative in 2001 in partnership with Microsoft Corporation to design and implement a web portal that would serve as a gateway to government services, the project was faced with much criticism for its low usage levels. According to the literature, the eGovernment initiative faced several challenges, illiteracy being the biggest challenge along with an Internet penetration rate of 20%, which endorsed the idea that eGovernment services are just for the rich educated segment of the society instead of being a nationwide targeting tool to improve the way governmental services are offered. There was a need for providing enabling technologies, products and services to underpin the development of Egypt as a knowledge economy in the global market. The initiative, which also aimed at crossing the boundaries between ministries by offering joint services, has been accused of being an unrealistic step towards improving governmental services, the reason being the low acceptance of the newly introduced eServices. Low acceptance is a problem, which, according to the minister of state for administrative development, Ahmed Darwish, lies in the word trust or more accurately, lack of it. According to Darwish, *"the process of gaining people's trust will take time, but we are working on building that trust by providing tangible results*". This is where the role of ENPO emerges.

Moreover, the emphasis of the role of ENPO was clearly highlighted in a speech by Tarek Kamel concerning Egypt's national ICT agenda, which included three objectives. First, developing and modernizing ENPO infrastructure; second, transforming ENPO as a delivery arm for financial and eGovernment services; and third, building on the trust with the citizens in maximizing the utilization of their postal savings. The positioning of ENPO was invaluable due to its constant interaction with different clusters of the community irrespective of the social or economic segment.

Reform of the Postal Sector

MCIT's investigation of ENPO showed that it was performing below potential. The services offered to both individuals and businesses were inefficient. The reform program was aimed at resolving these issues, achieving national development objectives and increasing national competitiveness. The following objectives were identified: (a) to develop a worldclass postal service in terms of quality, innovation and accessibility; (b) to increase overall levels of private sector investment in the postal market through open and fair competition and progressive regulation; and, (c) to create a new export-oriented postal industry in Egypt. It is important to note that all these objectives were formulated with a platform that reflects the notion that ICT is an enabler for service improvement, government efficiency and economic development.

Development of a State-of-the-Art Postal Network

A fundamental component of the MCIT strategy for developing the postal sector is modernizing Egypt Post by availing state-of-the-art ICT. MCIT is working tediously with ENPO to facilitate the development of services and systems that support eGovernment and eCommerce. Moreover, MCIT encourages ENPO to form partnerships with businesses and the private sector through outsourcing business models, bringing innovative products and services to customers by making use of the ICT industry. By restructuring ENPO through ICT, citizens have greater accessibility to information and government services. This is especially true for citizens who reside in rural areas and underprivileged communities in Egypt allowing them to easily register with the government, apply for licenses and obtain tax documents by simply visiting their nearest postal retail office. MCIT works with ENPO to develop new and innovative products that combine digital and physical communications systems, such as "*hybrid mail*". This will eventually result in the development of systems for sorting, tracing, addressing and customer care. An additional area of interest for MCIT is eCommerce, which can benefit by utilizing postal networks and ICT to manage global supply chains and enhance delivery. It is important to note that since the inception of MCIT and the leadership at the helm of ENPO selected was long-time ICT professionals and experts with extensive experience in diffusing ICT, which clearly indicates the intention of transforming ENPO to be ICT-enabled in terms of services offered.

Regulating the Postal Market

Creating an open and competitive postal market has been met with some success, but has also been accompanied with complications. Given the fact that ENPO is the entity that is granted the sole authority for issuing licenses to postal operators, it could easily utilize its power to monopolize the postal market. However, this has not been the case. On the contrary, ENPO has a high level of competition with 12 operators providing various forms of postal services. ENPO actually promotes private sector participation in the market by forming partnerships with a number of private sector individuals and businesses to expand services and products in the market. This has been very promising and indicated vast potentials in a fast growing and competitive marketplace.

It is important to note that increasing private sector investments has been a more difficult process for a number of regulatory reasons. This is problematic because, as the Egyptian economy grows and mail-heavy industries such as financial services and utilities expand, there will always be an increasing need for an efficient postal network to handle advertising, bill delivery and payment, and goods and cash transfers. In order to meet this anticipated increase in demand, the level of partnerships and private sector investment must increase and keep pace with the developments taking place. However, in order to increase private sector participation in the market, reform of the postal sector and effective policies was necessary. MCIT is brainstorming incentives to encourage private sector participation in projects that could stimulate further market progress. The biggest barrier hindering private sector investment in the postal market has been the lack of an effective regulatory oversight. A study carried out by the Universal Postal Union (UPU) concluded that the "postal market in Egypt is performing below capacity and that there is room for expansion and additional private sector investment". This has been the ENPO focus over the last few years while assessing what emerging ICT tools and techniques can bring in to the postal services.

However, lack of transparency concerning ENPO's dual role as a regulator and an operator in the market, as well as legitimate regulations of the sector, have affected the willingness of the private sector to invest. Respectively, a number of measures were taken by MCIT, postal operators and other stakeholders between 2007 and 2008 to develop effective postal regulatory policies, laws and regulations; in addition to establishing a neutral regulatory mechanism responsible for monitoring ongoing growth and innovation in the Egyptian postal market and benchmarking the sector's progress against international standards. It is hoped that, with proper regulation and market definition, private sector participation will significantly increase in the postal market.

Creating an Export-Oriented Industry

Faced with opportunities for global expansion, ENPO has been adapting itself to new international postal regulations. International regulatory advances, such as WTO's General Agreement for Trade in Services, are rapidly reducing or eliminating trade barriers, creating new opportunities for Egypt Post's penetration into the global market. Egypt Post envisions itself as a "*hub*" in the region, managing supply chains on a regional level. Egypt's geographic position, in conjunction with its growing ICT infrastructure, puts the country in a favorable position for regional expansion. When postal networks work with customs counterparts, import and export channels are strengthened, supporting the growth of Small and Medium Enterprises (SMEs) and other businesses.

MCIT continues to build on its successful experience with multinational telecom and IT companies to generate international appeal for its candidacy as a regional "*hub*". Working on a national level to create the first postal free zone in the Middle East, MCIT is mediating with governmental agencies responsible for transport and trade including aviation, transport, finance and investment, the Customs Authority, Egypt Post, private operators and other stakeholders. The establishment of the postal free zone will require that the current regulatory frameworks being developed will parallel those in prominent regional and international free zones. New infrastructure and supply systems are being created to connect the zone to global and regional markets, while appropriate regulatory processes and inspection mechanisms being developed to facilitate transactions and promote business. To promote Egypt's free trade zone as a regional hub and logistics center on an international level, MCIT is cooperating with the General Authority for Investment and Free Zones (GAFI), as well as other international postal and supply-chain operators. However, despite the developments in its ICT infrastructure, MCIT recognizes the postal sector's need to develop the regulatory laws necessary for liberalize services and complying with international trade regimes. Regulatory reforms will need to be introduced to prepare the postal sector for future changes in international postal regulatory systems, allowing it to succeed as a global market player.

Modernizing ENPO

Starting his position as ENPO Chairman, Alaa Fahmy knew that his job was going to be anything but easy. As Chairman, he is mainly responsible for providing strategic directions, explore business opportunities and promote ENPO in different market, business and industry circles. ENPO's history of being the oldest, most widely used and trusted governmental organization in Egypt simply represented the missing link between the government and the people. Fahmy knew that ENPO was desperately in need of a restructuring process, whether organizational or ICT-related. Moreover, he knew the burden of being the executing arm of Egypt's new eGovernment initiative that was being placed as part of ENPO's agenda. During Aly Moselhy tenure, the former ENPO chair, and current member of government, he realized that there was a potential for ENPO to do more for its customers and most importantly, for Egypt. He had a vision that with a comprehensive ICT infrastructure coupled with availing easy-to-use services by the community, ENPO could be the gateway for an eService-oriented society in Egypt.

During this time, the seeds of a new business model began to be planted. The former team started the first phase of creating an image that would turn this ever regarded, highly trusted governmental institution into an institution with a corporate image, objective and most importantly organizational infrastructure that enables service provision in a smooth and easy way. ENPO's new business model had to capitalize on the new, healthy investment atmosphere in Egypt and the ICT infrastructure made available by MCIT, and integrating the new offerings with the former products in order to create a better value proposition for ENPO customers. Based on this plan, and under the current chair, Fahmy, the image of ENPO started to manifest itself into a reality. In the early phase, some 920 post offices were modernized beginning with the main traffic offices located in Ramses, Alexandria, Tanta and Cairo international exchange centers at the Cairo airport.

The modernization process was done in three phases based to the location of the office. Many of the offices located in small alleys or villages, ironically, did not need to look too polished or else the regular customer would have started to have doubts and would have reconsidered dealing with ENPO, directly shattering the concept of trust, which is the edge that ENPO enjoys and intended to capitalize upon. However, in order to implement this business model and introduce a profit making culture to a governmental organization of more than 45,000 employees a lot had to be changed, and with an organization as old as ENPO, this was definitely a challenge.

ICT and Postal Services

"A strong postal network reaches all residents, many of whom have no other means of communicating with the outside world. By providing this universal level of communication, posts can also provide the increased access to information that is essential to poverty reduction in the information age. But postal services do much more: they connect people and raise their level of social development and cohesion."

- Nemat Shakif, Vice-President, Private Sector Development and Infrastructure, The World Bank Group

Although the core of the postal business would remain paper-based for years to come, ICT had created a new realization to the world's postal services. By applying ICT-based infrastructure, postal services could improve the quality of their *"traditional"* services and introduce new, reliable, affordable products and rapid services to meet the growing needs of the community. New ICT offers enormous potential to post offices that are reinventing themselves to remain the primary means of communication and continue playing a significant role in the world's economy and information society. Merging ICT and the post was a big challenge waiting to be transformed into an opportunity that would effectively lead to a powerful entity, which provides accessibility, trustworthiness, security and privacy.

Accessibility

Combining around 700,000 worldwide postal outlets with ICT facilitate Internet access to people in remote areas. Posts are often seen as attractive partners in the provision of eGovernment services.

Trust and Security

The post office has always been trusted with people's mail. As people start to send messages through new communication networks they expect to deal with a trusted party who can securely and confidentially deliver information. Through ICT, post offices can provide innovative and secure services and products to continue honoring their role.

Privacy

Direct or advertising mail delivered physically to consumers could be converted electronically to customers who specifically request to receive such information.

ICT Back Then, ICT Now

"The coming era will witness an expansion in the use of ICTs in developing Egypt's postal organization and providing the citizens with better services in a more efficient way".

Badr Eldin, ENPO Vice Chairman for IT, sat in his office reviewing his IT infrastructure development plan as he realized the long way they had come, and the longer way they were yet to go. The deadlines were strict and tangible benefits were awaited. Prior to the new developments, the concept of using IT as a tool to improve the quality and efficiency of the services offered by ENPO was simply non-existent. All services, such as opening accounts, invoices and payments were offered using paper. This was unfavorable to customers due to the time wasted. The lack of communication between offices made the process inefficient and costly in terms of paper and time wasted. Moreover, there were no networks, PC's or application software present in any of the offices.

During the period 2001-2005, the mission was to connect all offices through the postal network. However, this was easier said than done. Starting from scratch, the former ENPO team managed to connect 640 offices because of the threat ICT posed to the employees especially in poor and underprivileged communities where these offices were located, and the lack of the infrastructure needed to support it. Sometimes offices had to be connected through satellite, which involved high costs. The 640 offices being connected on a network marked the introduction of a new culture to the staff and to operations of ENPO in general.

In February 2006, Fahmy urgently continued to build on what was previously accomplished. Respectively, the total number of branches reached 3,688 at the end of the second quarter in 2009. With more advanced ICT came an even greater responsibly. Now the ICT team has to make sure that the four pillars of ICT in ENPO were present and functioning in a reliable way. The pillars could be demonstrates as follows:

- With respect to networks, reliability needs to reach 5-nine (99.999%) availability as a target. Currently, availability stands at 75% with backups for emergencies.
- With respect to application rings, there need to avail databases and applications working in parallel and reliably.
- With respect to PC penetration and PC support, the target is to reach 24 hours a day, 7 days a week reliability.
- With respect to servers and database center, the objective is that if any of the servers fail, backups should be ready for replacement. However, the cur-

rent problem is that some companies offer services using the NPO network, which sometimes causes confusion when a company's server fails and people think it is ENPO's server.

Establishing the ICT Platform

In his plan, Badr Eldin decided that his department's main mission was to provide quality IT products and services to help ENPO reach its goals. Consequently, the organizational structure and strategic goals of the IT department should pave the way towards achieving the objectives of ENPO as a whole "*by transforming itself into a quality focused, highly productive, responsive organization supporting a market driven system*". Realizing the importance of having a complete and up-to-date ICT infrastructure, major changes to the IT department's organizational structure had to be taken. Exhibit 2 demonstrates the former organization structure of the IT department. Depicted in the chart is a strategic business unit structure in which each department has IT as a complimentary tool integrated within the function itself. The functions, which are divided into finance, communication, human resources, security and IT sourcing all reported to the chief information officer (CIO) after passing through the steering committee. The vice chair for IT realized that several disadvantages were associated with such a structure, which would directly hinder the role of IT in the progress of ENPO. These disadvantages could be summarized as follows.

ICT Core Business

The structure is not placing IT as a core business behind the whole organization, which is the case in real life. Combining functions like communications, human resources and finance, which are not directly linked to ICT presents ICT as a tool rather than the main driver for the whole organization.

ICT Operational Methodology

Badr Eldin specifically objected to the idea of dividing the structure into small business units. In his own defense, he asserted that in a newly transforming giant organization like ENPO, a business unit structure (as demonstrated in Exhibit 2) is not suitable. It is only suitable for large multinationals where business units are set up like separate companies, with full profit and loss responsibility invested in the top management of the unit and the units are at a level to compete with each other. Such condition was neither present, nor currently requested within ENPO's ICT organization structure. Other disadvantages included the minimal strategy coordination that occurs across business units and the performance recognition, which is often very blurred. Making his point, the vice chair for IT suggested that the new organization structure would consolidate the role of ICT as the core business of ENPO. The structure mainly focused on creating six functions that are directly related to ICT including information centers, technical support, operations, services, infrastructure, and design and planning. Exhibit 3 demonstrates the new ICT structure. Each function has a vice president responsible for the subordinate sub-functions and eventually all departments report to the CIO, passing by the executive committee and reporting secondly to the financial services and human resources departments. The functions are further grouped into three phases, which represent the IT life cycle, beginning with design then implementation and lastly, technical support.

According to Robert Dailey, Organizational Behavior Professor at Drake University, there are numerous advantages to this structure. Firstly, the structure is based on specialization, which allows employees within each function to speak a common language. It also minimizes the extent of duplication and facilitates tight control. Badr Eldin was extremely convinced with the need to introduce a double reporting system in the ICT structure to ensure that the system will always function effectively. The department's manager will not only be reporting to financial services and human resources, but he/she will also be reporting to the main office, which ensures that each department is functioning as expected and that work is evaluated objectively. The new structure takes into consideration the maximum number of people that can report to the CIO which, in this case, are seven people reporting on behalf of their functions. Although the suggested changes were approved by senior management, there were a number of challenges that still faced the IT department including:

- ENPO is the largest organization (number of employees).
- Increased business dependency on ICT.
- Growth in business applications and storage requirements.
- National and international coordination.
- Increasingly remote workforce.
- Technology obsolescence cycles, which related to the employees' changing attitudes toward ICT requiring regular attempts to channel them from the inherited manual systems to the newly digital ones.

In an effort to instill this new concept in the minds of staff, and also to aid its transformation process, Fahmy had decided to take advantage of Egypt's new high-tech business district, the Smart Village, by relocating the Ataba office to relocate into a consolidated premises at the Smart Village. Often referred to as Egypt's Silicon Valley, the Smart Village hosts 54 buildings, providing 336 square meters of office space over 300 acres of land. The Village hosts 55,000 jobs, and is built using state-of-the art ICT infrastructure and high speed connectivity for integrated services, (whether data, audio or video) making it an ideal location for most of Egypt's ICT based companies both national and international. In conjunction with the move, ENPO planned to eliminate paper entirely within the organization in order to transform it into a digital workplace. Knowing the difficultly in implementing such a decision, the management decided to undertake dual operations during the phased implementation of the relocation. The management needed to develop an electronic file management system, including support and an operational system in order to process ENPO applications electronically allowing automated enterprise operations. In addition to this, a reliable IT infrastructure was needed to connect the main office in Ataba square with the Smart Village premises requiring the design, development, installation and testing of fiber connections, cable plants, data switches and telecommunications. The telecommunication services covered meeting room capabilities, electronic building directories, a facility help desk and a full-fledged security control system.

Human Capital: Investing in What Matters Most

With over 45,000 employees working at ENPO, the human factor was an essential part in the transformation process, if not the most important one. With such a huge number of employees, having a well-constructed organization structure was a necessity in order to manage and administer effectively, while also adding value to their development process. Unfortunately, that was not the case until the new transformations were introduced. In the former organizational structure, all functions reported to a single vice president who in turn reported directly to the CEO. According to El-Labban, director of international relations, *"how can anything be done effectively when you have 45,000 employees reporting to one person? It can never work"*. Based on this, the organizational structure itself was transformed in order to achieve decentralization; with six vice presidents, each concerned with a certain function/area.

Moreover, the new management team has tried to introduce the idea of having a human resources department, which was not common in most governmental organizations and the customary approach was to deploy a personnel department that mainly handled employee files as a storage room. However, the new human resource department could manage the appraisals and elevate the HR function as a whole by managing employee performance and most importantly concerning itself with the training necessary in the coming transformational period. In an attempt to introduce a market oriented and customer-focused culture, the marketing campaign began functioning instantly, with new marketing material announcing ENPO's services, as well as its new image and entrance into the market. Marketing material included pens, mouse pads, newspaper announcements and advertisements highlighting the new services offered by ENPO in Egypt's most wide spread daily newspapers like Al-Ahram and Al-Akhbar.

Public and Private Partnerships

"The post is based on the concept of connecting two parties together which is the same concept on which communication is based, so if any organization should be part of the new operator it should be ENPO, the oldest supplier of the service"

- Amr Badr El Din, Vice Chairman, IT

Etisalat

Outside the ICT Minister's office at the Smart Village, Fahmy and Badr Eldin were anxiously waiting to know the results for the long bidding process. The Minister came out and congratulated them, *"You took it"* he said, *"ENPO won the bid"*. They were thrilled. According to Badr Eldin, *"The feeling was indescribable, everyone was congratulating us and that is the moment when I felt that my post was most fulfilling"*. The next day the news was all over Egypt that ENPO would become the first governmental organization to be part of a huge corporation like Etisalat, UAE's number one operator and currently Egypt's third. The consortium included Etisalat, Egypt Post, National Bank of Egypt and Commercial International Bank; they won the bid for over 3 billion US dollars and a 6% of the annual revenues to be paid to the National Telecommunications Regulatory Authority (NTRA). Exhibit 4 demonstrates the public-private partnership model and the shareholders in this consortium. This step was one of Fahmy's major strategies to transform ENPO into a profit-making organization by diversifying their offerings and introducing some major public private partnerships that could capitalize on ENPO's competitive advantage, manifested in its distribution network and credibility within the society. According to Badr Eldin, *"Public Private Partnerships are arrangements between the government and private sector entities for the purpose of improving public infrastructure and community facilities. Although these partnerships entail sharing investment, risk and responsibility, this long term partnership is very rewarding in many ways"*.

Referring to his partnership with Etisalat, Badr Eldin knew that ENPO's capabilities would be important for the company to penetrate successfully the local market. Some of the partnership benefits include: (a) using ENPO's network of offices that extends all over Egypt as a distributor of the company for selling their prepaid charging cards and accessories; and, (b) using ENPO office buildings to install the company's antenna instead of using resident buildings and paying hefty amounts of money in return. Another similar agreement was made with Vodafone, Egypt's second mobile operator, according to which ENPO would provide prepaid charging cards for Vodafone consumers in its offices.

Egypt Air

ENPO Chairman Fahmy and Egypt Air Chairman Galal signed a memorandum of understanding (MoU) to utilize the post office for booking airline tickets. According to the Minister of ICT, *"The MoU reflects the collaboration between different stakeholders and Egypt Post to facilitate the service delivered to the community"*. This MoU is part of ENPO's bigger strategy to turn their post offices into full-fledged service centers.

Jordan Post Company

After studying, the executive and legislative framework of Jordan Post Company in cooperation with EFG Hermes and Jordanian Riyada Ventures, Egypt decided to bid for a share in the Jordanian postal service. Egypt Post is competing with La Poste France, Aramex Jordan and British Consultative Post Services over acquiring a share in this company. This was another strategic move through alliances in order to develop the investment volume of Egypt Post and derive revenues with limited risks. These different steps indicated the intention of the government of Egypt to transform the role played by ENPO in providing a diversified portfolio of digital services while being one of the tools and platforms to diffuse eGovernment services.

International Agreements

ENPO extended their activities to regional levels. In February 2007, ENPO signed off 1.8 million US dollars *"Institutional Twining Program"* with the French National Post Organization, *"La Poste"*. It was aimed at developing the various departments at ENPO in order to match European and international standards applied. The program allows exchange of expertise, allowing ENPO to capitalize on La Poste expertise in marketing, service monitoring and quality assurance. Furthering boosting their bilateral economic and technical relations, they signed a cooperation agreement. The agreement that went into effect in 2008 would aid in developing postal and financial services and marketing tools for these services. This was another step in the integrated plan to utilize international expertise to upgrade the Egyptian post. Moreover, another agreement between ENPO and the Italian Post (Poste Italiane) was concluded in order to develop the sector in both countries. The minister indicated that the postal sector is a key economic and service driver to Egypt's modernization system. It is important to note that the agreement involved training human resources and raising the value of its assets.

Moreover, Fahmy signed an agreement with 7 Arab countries to exchange the financial remittances through the congress postal conference which was held in July 2008 in Geneva. The seven countries included Egypt, UAE, Syria, Yemen, Morocco, Tunisia, and Qatar. Just recently, Fahmy signed a pact to run electronic remittances between both Egyptian and Jordanian postal services, which started functioning in January 2009. This new agreement will enable Egyptian citizens working in Jordan, around 1 million, to transmit their money through the post offices at extremely competitive prices.

SERVICES OFFERED BY ENPO

A plethora of ICT-powered services was added to the "traditional" list of services after restructuring the ICT sector.

Government Services

With about 5 million Egyptians using the Internet, the adoption of eGovernment services is a far-fetched idea. However, as previously mentioned, being a delivery arm to the government concerning these services and having an integral role in servicing its community became one of Fahmy's priorities. Capitalizing on its intensive distribution network, ENPO currently offers 3 million citizens their pensions with a total sum that exceeds 1.6 billion US dollars through its 3600 offices, which are geographically dispersed across Egypt. Additionally, the service has also extended to reach citizens who are ill or having special circumstances and those aging 70 years and above, who ca not make it to any of the offices by offering them a delivery of their pension to their doorstep.

The *"Tamween"* card is another practical application of ICT that is utilized to help provide better services to the citizens. Previously, everything regarding food subsidies, which citizens were entitled to receive was documented on paper, which made the system more liable to fraud and human error. However, in this project and after installing the electronic platform, citizens are given smart cards; a person passes his card through the point of sale (POS) that is connected to the post network. This in turn, is connected to the network of the ministry of social solidarity, which holds the files of all citizens who are entitled to receive monthly nutrition subsidies. These records show the utilization of every item supplied based on the needs of citizens. This provides feedback that helps the ministry to decide, which items to increase depending on consumption. According to Badr Eldin, this was just a prototype that was tested in the Suez province, because of the limited geographical coverage making it more controlled and possible to monitor. Moreover, the limited population was a very important determining factor making Suez an ideal place to test the new electronic platform. If proven successful, the *"Tamween"* card will be implemented in all of Egypt's 28 provinces.

Financial Services

During 2007, as demonstrated in Exhibit 6 showing the postal financial services, there was witnessed the launch of a new postal savings account based on investment in the stock market. Minister Kamel stated that the new service aims to facilitate changeable high revenues through long-term investments. The new savings account requires a minimum of 18 US dollars with no ceiling while enabling citizens to invest in the Cairo-Alexandria Stock Exchange (CASE) and raises their investment awareness. The service has proven to be a success collecting 2 billion US dollars of small savings in less than a week. During the Cairo ICT 2009 Trade Fair and Forum several new financial services were launched which continue to meet the needs of the post's wide spectrum of customers. The services included a variety of offerings including current accounts in US dollars and Euros and earning daily variable revenues for companies and individuals; *Hadiyati* (Arabic translation for *"My Gift"*), a prepaid electronic gift card that can be charged with up to 181 US dollars. It also include *Mahfazti* (Arabic translation for *"My Wallet"*), a prepaid rechargeable card that can be used for purchasing goods and services and to withdraw cash from ATM machines.

To complement the above, Egypt Post will launch Universal Windows in 600 post offices in June 2009 in order to offer a diversified portfolio of financial services that meets the needs of the citizens including different types of money orders. More than 20,000 employees have been trained to aid in the dissemination of these financial services nationwide. In order to keep pace with the introduction of these financial services, ENPO signed a cooperation agreement with SAP who will provide business software applications to speed up the implementation of postal and financial services offered. In addition

Misr Mail

"Now that our ENPO is entering the new era of ICT, certain applications cannot be ignored. E-mail is the new version of what we have always offered. Delivering mail is now done electronically, and we are doing it as well as anyone else". Amr Badr El Din, Vice Chairman, IT

ENPO introduced *"Misr Mail"*, which offers a list of services that include 2GB capacity mail, a portal with exclusive news from Egypt and high security that ensures privacy. Moreover, Misr Mail offers career and training opportunities for all those registered on it. Misr Mail is complemented by another service called *"hybrid mail"*. The service makes use of the new electronic signature to track and confirm the delivery, acceptance and delivery date of emails sent, which is an essential step along the way to governing and encouraging eCommerce activities in Egypt. Furthermore, they extended to reach other services like EPEM service, which is crucial for eCommerce. The service allows electronic checking of all electronic documents involved in any electronic transaction by verifying and validating the signatures on the documents, as well as the date and time of signature and automatically stores this information for future reference. This helps eliminate fraud in business transactions taking place over the Internet, and thus encourages the citizen use of these services by establishing trust. With these security measures, eCommerce has a greater chance of flourishing in Egypt. Finally, Egypt Post has recently introduced the International Post Service (IPS) system allowing the sender to *"track and trace"* their message from the time it leaves their home until it is delivered to the addressee.

Table 3. ENPO critical success factors

Critical Success Factors	Definition
Completing ENPO ICT infrastructure build-up	− Design, develop and implement a nationwide infrastructure connecting all ENPO offices across Egypt's 28 provinces
Availing value-added services	− Availing connectivity and develop value-added information networks between ENPO and the community of organizations and users
Linking Egypt globally-digitally	− Link Egypt to the growing information and postal networks across continents capitalizing on the outreach of ICT
Investing in human capital	− Invest in human capacities across different ENPO departments and units to be able to transform the organization and promote eServices
Building an online society	− Build an online electronically ready community that can appreciate and use ENPO services

CURRENT CHALLENGES/PROBLEMS FACING THE ORGANIZATION

Egypt has been gradually building its information society since the mid 1980s, adapting its strategy and approaches to the evolution of the global ICT sector. The steps taken included supplying accurate and timely information, encouraging private investment, formulating effective economic reforms, improving productivity, providing programs for lifelong learning, making public services more efficient, improving health care, optimizing the use of natural resources and protecting competition. Despite the major progress in IT deployment, policy and regulatory frameworks and implementation levels, many milestones must still be achieved to reach the critical mass of ICT users and critical level of ICT utilization that can enable organizational such as ENPO that are transforming themselves to become ICT-enabled to be successful. There needs to be an overall strategy that promotes electronic readiness and help create a critical mass of ICT-literate users that can appreciate and use the type of services that ENPO is offering. Table 3 demonstrates the critical success factors for ENPO.

REFERENCES

Badr, E. A. (2007, April 1). *ENPO Vice President for IT interview*.

Cairo ICT. (2009). Retrieved March 20, 2009, from, www.cairoict.com

Egypt Post. (2009). Retrieved March 25, 2009, http://egyptianpost.net/en/index.asp

El-Labban, D. N. (2007, April 1). *ENPO Director for International Relations interview*.

Gillingham, A. (n.d.). *Bulk mail takes notes and goes hi-tech*.

Roger, W. (1999) *Postal service getting wired*. Retrieved May 31, 2009 from www.interactive-week.com

Si-young, H. (2007, June 11). Korea post utilizes cutting-edge IT. *The Korea Herald*.

Universal Postal Union. (2003). *The role of postal services*. Bern: WSIS Summit.

World Summit on Information Society. (2009). Retrieved February 10, 2009, from www.wsis-egypt.gov.eg.

Zekri, N. (2006, April 16). Transformation of the post organization. *Al-Ahram Newspaper*.

ADDITIONAL READING

Daily Star Egypt. (2006). *Egypt's third mobile license to benefit from the Egypt National Post Offices distribution network.* Retrieved July 7, 2009, from, www. dailystaregypt.com

Editorial. (2006, April 16). Marketing and electronic signature as latest services offered. *Etisalat Al Mostaqbal.*

Information and Decision Support Center. (2008). Retrieved from http://www. idsc.gov.eg

Kamel, S. (1999). Information technology transfer to Egypt. In *Proceedings of the Portland International Conference on Management of Engineering and Technology (PICMET). Technology and Innovation Management: Setting the Pace for the Third Millennium,* Portland, Oregon, United States, 25-29 July (pp. 567-571).

Kamel, S. (2008). The use of ICT for social development in underprivileged communities in Egypt. In *Proceedings of the International Conference on Information Resources Management (Conf-IRM) on Information Resources Management in the Digital Economy*, Niagara Falls, Ontario, Canada, May 18-20.

MCIT. (2007). *Egyptian-European postal institutional twinning program under way.* Retrieved May 3, 2009, from, www.mcit.gov.eg.

Ministry of Communications and Information Technology. (2005). *Egypt Information Society Initiative* (4th ed.).

Ministry of Communications and Information Technology. (2009). *Egypt post launches new financial services at Cairo ICT 2009.* Retrieved April 22, 2009, from, www.mcit.gov.eg.

Ministry of Communications and Information Technology. (2009). Retrieved May 5, 2009, from, www.mcit.gov.eg.

Ministry of State for Administrative Development. (2008). Retrieved September 3, 2009, from, http://www.ad.gov.eg.

APPENDIX

Exhibit 1. Detailed List of ENPO Services Offered

Postal Services			Financial Services		
		Registered Mail			ATM Cards
		Ordinary Mail	Electronic Payment		Visa
		Net Courier			Mastercard
		Banking letters	GiroNil		
Letters		Direct Mail	Postal Savings Passbook		
		Cassette Post	Daily interest account		Golden Account >10000
		Fax Post			Silver Account <10000
		E-document exchange	Postal Investment Book		
		Publications			Internal remittances
Express Mail (EMS)			Postal Remittances		Governmental Remittances
Parcel Services		Domestic			Electronic remittances
		International			Cashed external remittances
		Postal Cards	Postal Proxy		
Public Postal Services		Private Post Box			
		Clearance Tools			
Social Services					
		Delivery of Pensions			
Home Delivery		Delivery of Parcels			
		Delivery of Remittance			
Housing Projects		Youth Housing Project			
		Miscellaneous			
Lost Property					

Exhibit 2. Former ICT Structure

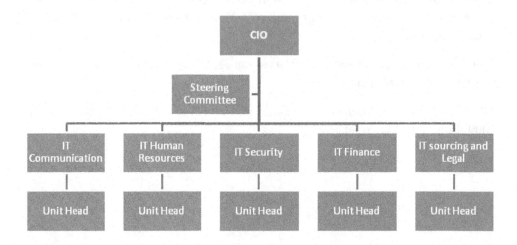

Exhibit 3. Current ICT Structure

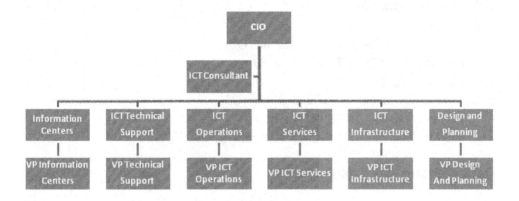

Exhibit 4. Public Private Partnerships

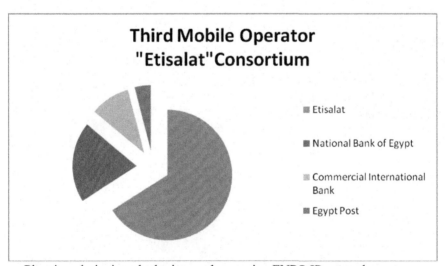

- Planning, designing, deploying, and managing ENPO IP network.
- Full responsibility of IP Network and voice services operation activities.
- Services will include network operations center, service desk, field operations, onsite support, customer care, third party support.

Exhibit 5. Action Timeline (2007)

Telecommunication

- Fiber cable, WiMax and Co-location (Q2)
- 640 Branch SDSL and ISDN (Running)
- Upgrade 512K (Q2)
- 450 Branch ADSL, VSAT and VPDN (Q3)
- Co-Location 40 TE POP (Q3 and Q4)
- 1000 Branch VPDN (Q4-2006/2007 and Q1-2007/2008)

Data Centers-Op & Mo

- Ramses (Q3 and Q4)
- Smart Village (Q3 and Q4)
- Alex (Q1-2007/2008 and Q2-2007/2008)
- Assiout (TBD)

Peripherals

- 3500 PCs + 450 LANs (Running)
- 1500 PCs + Printers (Q3)
- 3000 PCs (Q4)

Exhibit 6. Postal Financial Services

The total number of postal investment accounts invested in the Egyptian Stock exchange reached 33 thousand accounts since November 2007 with a total balance of 55.4 million US dollars until February 2008.

Figure 5.

Source: Ministry of communications & information technology, Egypt Post

This work was previously published in Cases on Technology Innovation: Entrepreneurial Successes and Pitfalls, edited by S. Ann Becker and Robert E. Niebuhr, pp. 246-266, copyright 2010 by Business Science Reference (an imprint of IGI Global).

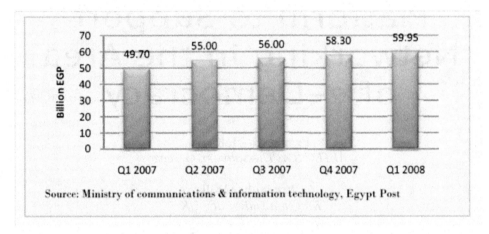

Chapter 6
A Citizen–Centric Platform to Support Networking in the Area of e–Democracy

Francesco Molinari
ALTEC S.A. Thessaloniki, Greece

Christopher Wills
Kingston University, UK

Adamantios Koumpis
ALTEC S.A. Thessaloniki, Greece

Vasiliki Moumtzi
ALTEC S.A. Thessaloniki, Greece

EXECUTIVE SUMMARY

This chapter describes experiences acquired during the research work conducted as part of the European Project Tell Me (www.tellmeproject.eu). The project envisaged to support the pan-European creation of Living Labs as new forms of cooperation between government, enterprises, citizens, and academia for a successful transfer of e-Government, e-Democracy, and e-Services state-of-the art applications, solutions, know-how, and best practices. In this chapter authors explore the potential of providing an existing system (DEMOS) allowing moderated and goal-oriented discourses between the citizens and the policy makers to become parts of open-ended ventures to allow the creation of collaborative networks for Electronic Democracy. This work also recommends that this form of support network elevates e-Democracy of a country and thus improves e-governance systems at the grassroots.

DOI: 10.4018/978-1-4666-0981-5.ch006

ORGANIZATION AND TECHNOLOGICAL BACKGROUND

After the "Helsinki Manifesto" (2006) put the "human-centric way" at the very centre of the measures needed "for turning the Lisbon Strategy (2000) into a living reality", the topic of competitiveness and innovation in Europe has been enriched of a further dimension, namely, co-creative collaboration with the forthcoming users of the developing products and services. This is especially useful in the field of (private and Government) e-Services, where the people can be considered as "twice" beneficiaries, namely of public services as such – impacting per se on their lives and businesses – and of ICT based or supported services, where the question becomes to which extent this novel user-centric approach can improve customization (if not "tailoring") to individual needs and requirements.

Some "champions" of this new dimension of innovation belong to the so-called ENoLL – European Network of Living Labs. In a purely business perspective, a Living Lab can be seen as a service providing organization in the topic of R&D and innovation, based on the "co-creation" concept, which focuses on people in their daily living environments as active, if not decisive, contributors to products and services design, development and testing.

In spite of a limited evidence on the known experiences – most of which could count on a significant external funding - it can be affirmed that the cost of building up and maintaining a Living Lab from scratch (i.e. deploying the communication and collaboration infrastructure, gathering and orchestrating the community of users, carrying out the requested evaluation services) can be substantial, thus preventing a long-term impact into the regional innovation systems.

Here is where the Tell Me project initiative starts up. Through the adaptation of a service already operational in Germany and other European Countries, originally thought for the animation of democratic discussions and participative public opinion formation at local and regional level, establishes a solution for the networking and interaction of Living Lab trials participants during the development and implementation of innovative projects. More specifically, Tell Me objectives were to investigate the administrative viability of the service on a European scale and to identify the conditions for future, pan-European deployment of the service under a juridical and a financial perspective.

The service is based on an existing infrastructure for moderated and goal-oriented discourses involving citizens and political institutions as well as project developers and investors, at national and European level.

The users who tested the service during the pilot phase of the Tell Me project falls into two categories:

1. Living Lab 'Owners' (as their staff validated the services from the technical and administrative point of view and assess their viability and usability);
2. Living Lab 'Members' (Public Administrations, Citizens, Enterprises, Non Profit Organisations, who are the ultimate beneficiaries of these services), mostly operating in the same territorial areas, but also coming from different cities/countries. After each trial/pilot, the results were analysed with a view to mapping the most relevant application areas and to replicating the service in one or more additional Living Labs in order to align the service to the national regulations (if any) and activate cross-fertilisation among the Living Labs through the exchange of **best practices** at European level.

In the light of the above, main purpose of this work is to provide a Trans-European service integrated with a proven methodology that can enable a co-creative user driven e-Democracy service development. The most important is the fact that the service can "link together" the different stakeholders in order to let them work more efficiently establishing an intimate communication channel between participants in a region. Besides, what is crucial is to increase the availability of easier-to-use eGovernment applications that have been validated in advance through online in-teraction with the potential users. This will potentially enlarge the scope for public sector innovation in Europe.

The aim is to establish what users (the local public) expect from e-Government, e-Democracy and e-Services applications and to explore the cross-fertilization ad-vantages of a "co-design/co-creation approach" using e-Democracy-like tools to plan, communicate and evaluate technologies, ideas, solutions and applications by moderated discourses. This implies the adaptation of a service already operational in Germany and other European Countries, originally thought for the animation of democratic discussions and participative public opinion formation at local and regional level.

In order to enhance the added value of the service deployment our target user fall into two categories, those who validate the services from the technical and adminis-trative point of view and those mostly operating in the same territorial areas, but also coming from different cities/countries. This relates to align the service according to the national regulations (if any) and exchange of best practices at European level.

Information and communication technologies and the Internet have great sig-nificance in a service-based economy. Just as service is not clearly defined in the literature, so too is the term e-service. Rust & Lemon (2001) consider that the term is used in general to denote transactions in which information is the primary value exchanged. Gronroos et al. (2000) claim that e-service is any product or service that is exchanged over the Internet. Others restrict their scope on services that are delivered electronically (Javalgi et al. 2004) or over electronic networks (Rust &

Kannan, 2003). In Tell Me, the focus is on any type of (web) service that can be found or exchanged via the Internet.

The Internet tends to shift bargaining power to end consumers in their transactions with businesses (Porter, 2001) because it allows the end consumer to get in contact directly with a great number of producers. On the other hand, the concepts of "mass customisation" (Gilmore & Pine 2000), "one-to-one marketing" (Peppers et al., 1999) and "long tail economics" (Anderson, 2006) are based on the premise that, with the support of information technologies, business firms are able to target each consumer separately, personalise their services and disseminate them efficiently.

This is taken into account in the Tell Me Framework. The Framework supports both 'one-to-one' and 'many-to-many' marketing and dialogues within a social network which enable the consumer to communicate with providers and other consumers able and willing to meet a need.

In order to design this network of consumers and providers ideas can be gleaned from current business networks and ecosystems. In the literature we can find different kinds of business networks, such as business constellations (Normann & Ramirez, 1993), extended enterprises (Prahalad & Ramaswamy, 2003), value nets (Bovet & Martha, 2000), virtual enterprises (Sawhney & Parikh, 2001; Walters & Lancaster, 1999), strategic networks (Jarillo, 1988) and business ecosystems (Moore, 1996; Iansity & Levien, 2004). The concept of business ecosystem is a metaphor that steps forward the movement towards symbiotic and co-evolutionary business networks.

Although Tell Me allows user-defined services as well, in the case of business services, the Tell Me Framework's network takes the form of a business and consumer ecosystem. Here, the role of the customer is of prime importance. Therefore, the network is crafted to respond to his/her special needs and where these needs cannot be met the social network would rise to fill this gap. This would also be of use in cases where the services sought are not related to business services, but rather of a voluntary nature.

The OASIS Group defines Service Oriented Architecture (SOA) as a powerful framework for matching needs and capabilities and for combining capabilities to address those needs (OASIS, 2006). Services in SOA are defined in a similar way to the definition of service in the business world that is as deeds performed by the service provider for the benefit of the service client. Consequently, from a conceptual point of view, SOA could be used to provide the technological foundations that are required for the empowerment of consumers in the selection, composition and consumption of products or services in electronic markets.

The services' world is discussing issues more closely related to providing Software as a Service (SaaS) components and how we can handle issues relating to security and transactions in web services. Security, the first of these issues, allows for secure usage of services regardless of the underlying platform and provides specifications (like WS-Security - Rosenberg & Remy (2004)) and languages (SAML – OASIS (2009)) for secure services. Additionally proposals for supporting transactions in web services have already been implemented, like the WS-AtomicTransaction - OASIS (2009)). Finally, the Software as a Service (SaaS) model promises to deliver "all" existing software that we use daily on our computers as services in the near future – this idea is now slowly emerging and it's being exploited in this project.

From an operational point of view, a SOA can be implemented with the use of Web Services. The basic Web Services model endorses three roles (service requestor, service provider and service registry) and three operations (publish, find and bind). Web Services follow the "find, bind and invoke" paradigm, where a service requestor performs dynamic service search by querying the service registry for a service; if the service exists, the registry provides the requestor with contact details for the service.

Such an operational model is clearly consumer-oriented and could support consumer-oriented value creation. The service requestor recognizes some need, searches for solutions, makes the selection, invokes the service and composes it with other services in his own context, in order to create value for him. Through a social network, other users can assist the service requestor in the composition and provide feedback.

Composition can be implemented with the use of mash-up technologies. Mash-ups are a new kind of data intensive and data integration applications which are based on the fusion of heterogeneous data sources that provide a public set of APIs. Depending on the API either a more traditional server based content generation process is followed or a client side scripting language or applet is used to mash-up the content. Most of the available mash-ups rely on the first solution and use the browser side technologies to produce an aesthetically pleasing result for the user. A technology or better an application model that characterizes mash-ups is AJAX (Asynchronous Javascript and XML) Lauriat (2007). AJAX has revolutionized the way web applications behave and provide a more robust and fulfilling user experience.

Other technologies involved in developing and supporting mash-ups include web services related protocols like SOAP (W3C, 2009) and REST Tyagi (2006). SOAP is the basic message exchange protocol used by services (including of course services used in the mash-ups) to communicate with each other. On the other hand REST provides a simple protocol for web services that supports only basic functions (like POST, PUT, DELETE, etc) but its simplicity makes it a prime candidate for mash-ups since it allows the easy fusion of different data sources.

An important issue in the mash-ups is the interoperability among the different data sources. This is addressed by the use of semantic web technologies like RDF/S based ontologies and RDFa (W3C, 2009) based annotations. That way data and their meaning can be seamlessly exchanged among the different sources and can carry their real meaning along. Mash-ups can be used as the main integration point for semantically described data bringing closer the concepts of Semantic Web and Web 2.0 by providing the best of both worlds.

Composition of services through mash-ups is also a consumer-oriented approach, as the consumer decides which services to mash-up and in which way in order to create value for him/herself and the community at large.

It must also be mentioned however that most existing research on Service-Oriented Architectures focuses on software services which are seen as software components providing access to "real" services (for example a software service for travel booking provides access to the actually service for travelling) (Pistore et al., 2009). In addition, software services are used, but not necessarily owned (in the sense of being able to customize them according to needs) by consumers (NESSI, 2006). This leads to the needs to define Service Level Agreements where appropriate (e.g. in chargeback mechanisms) as software services are not used exclusively by their producers.

In this project, authors recognize the importance of technical considerations (e.g. Service Level Agreements) for business services. However, we also aim to provide a more user-friendly approach to services, trying to contribute towards viewing the Internet as an enabler of "real" services aimed towards the end consumer, instead of pure "software" services created by the provider of these services.

As has been mentioned, there are two levels of users in the system, and for each of those different requirements (to be confirmed during the project) are foreseen to be essential:

- For the citizens (plain users), they may want to access services, and therefore issues such as Service Level Agreements, Quality of Service, chargeback according to different service models are still important. These considerations point to looking at the technical aspects of web services, therefore we are still looking at services from a "software" point of view.
- For institutional / public users, "real-world" considerations of services are of importance. It is for these reasons that some key assets relating to services must be defined with which the user (citizen) is able to construct / mash-up / configure services. Following the paradigm by Pistore et al. (2009), these assets (which can be enablers or constraints) are:
  1. Time, representing the temporal relation of the activities of the user, as well as conflicts and overlaps between these activities.
  2. Location, representing the (current and perspective) location of the user, the availability of (real-world) services in these locations, as well as the necessity of moving or travelling to use these services.

3. Social relations (representing other parties such as family, friends, colleagues) involved in the user activities.
4. Money and other values, representing costs and assets involved in the user activities.

NEEDS FOR E-DEMOCRACY AND CITIZEN PARTICIPATION

As indicated in the (OECD, 2001a) report: "A key challenge will be to make the transition from area wide (metropolitan) technical structures to area wide (metropolitan) political structures which empower citizens by addressing the 'democratic deficit' and thereby improve the effectiveness of policies at the local level. This implies central government building community policy frameworks, but leaving policy content largely in the hands of local actors".

"Achieving such a transition will involve a cultural change towards a people centre local democracy, not imposed from above, but achieved through strong community policy frameworks in which citizens are empowered to decide the changes they want to see.

This will require a more transparent and accountable decision-making process in which citizens are more fully informed and involved. Key elements of cultural change and improving the policy framework include: modernizing voting procedures, developing new leadership skills among the local political elites, encouraging new forms of participation, and ensuring that area-based approaches are linked to mainstream policy, are properly evaluated, and involve a long-term commitment by local government."

Identifying the "right" structures for local actors to participate may, however, present several difficulties. Municipalities are often both too big and too small to perform democratically. On the one hand, the gigantism of some contemporary metropolises tends to "alienate" the citizen who is far from decision-making centers. On the other hand, sub-national government may be too small to solve some problems that extend beyond its administrative boundaries, such as air pollution and traffic congestion.

Combined with the difficulty of encouraging a new sense of belonging and people's identification with topics of mutual concern is the additional problem of ensuring that the solutions allowing greater participation are not achieved at the cost of the socially and economically excluded. Making a transition to more effective forms of governance is, thus, not just a question of changing institutions, but crucially of moving to a political culture that is centered on the interests of people.

As indicated in another report (OECD, 2001b): "Engaging citizens is a sound investment in public policy-making. As these new relationships have evolved and matured, local governments have increasingly recognized their reliance upon the active contribution of citizens in making better decisions and achieving policy objectives. In this perspective, strengthening government relations with citizens may be seen as a sound investment in tapping new sources of policy-relevant ideas, information and resources for implementation".

Among the driving forces that have led governments to strengthen their relations with citizens, are the needs to:

- Improve the quality of policy, by allowing governments to tap wider sources of information, perspectives, and potential solutions in order to meet the challenges of policy-making under conditions of increasing complexity, policy interdependence and time pressures.
- Meet the challenges of the emerging information society, to prepare for greater and faster interactions with citizens and ensure better knowledge management.
- Integrate public input into the policy-making process, in order to meet citizens' expectations that their voices be heard, and their views be considered, in decision-making by government.
- Respond to calls for greater government transparency and accountability, as public and media scrutiny of government actions increases and standards in public life are codified and raised.
- Strengthen public trust in government and reverse the steady erosion of voter turnout in elections, falling membership in political parties and surveys showing declining confidence in key public institutions.

Three types of local Government-Citizen interaction might be present all along the *policy life cycle* – see Table 1 (adopted from OECD, 2001b).

The major contribution of the citizens' involvement into the public action is to make better decisions and achieve in a consensual way policy objectives. In this perspective a local government has to adjust public action by a continuous evaluation of objective and results along the policy life cycle. The Table 2 (adopted from QUALEG, 2004) includes the dynamically adjusted actions along the policy life cycle.

The "ideal" process of designing, implementing and evaluating public (e-)Services should come as a specific instance of the above scheme. However, what happens in reality – as noted, among others, by Følstad et al. (2007) – is that an insufficient care is given to users' involvement, in three respects:

Table 1. Types of local government-citizen interaction

Stage of policy making	Information	Consultation	Active participation
Formulation (Agenda Setting)	• White Papers, policy documents • Legislative programmes • Draft laws and regulations	• Large-scale opinion surveys • Use of discussion groups or citizens' panels • Invitation of comments on draft legislation	• Submission of alternative draft laws or policy proposals • Public dialogue on policy issues and options
Implementation	• New policy or regulations and their provisions	• Use of focus groups to develop secondary legislation	• Partnership with Civil Society Organisations to disseminate information on compliance with new laws
Evaluation	• Public notice of evaluation exercises and opportunities to participate	• Inclusion of stakeholders in reviews of government evaluation programmes and results	• Independent evaluation conducted by Civil Society Organisations

1. To introduce and gain experience with resource-effective methods from the multitude of user groups and stakeholders relevant in the development of e-Government systems and services;
2. To manage evolving goal structures for public e-Services, where the goals of different users are reflected;
   a. To give proper attention to the administrative and/or legislative reforms needed to align the new services to the underlying institutional and organizational framework.

Table 2. Dynamically adjusted actions along the policy life cycle

Stage of policy making	Continuous objectives evaluation	Continuous results evaluation	Continuous actions readjustment
Formulation (Agenda setting)	- Understand the citizen needs	- Proposal or action plan presentation to the citizens	- Change of objectives formulation and key indicators
Implementation	- Continuous actions adaptation to the citizen's solicited or unsolicited feed back	- Continuous measurement of quantitative or qualitative action's results	- Continuous change of the qualitative indicators in order to action evaluation
Evaluation	- Collect the qualitative and quantitative citizen feedback and reconfigure the objectives	- Collect the qualitative and quantitative results and reconfigure the means	- Reformulate a new action plan for the next cycle

DESCRIPTION OF THE SERVICE

Currently the DEMOS.2 platform facilitates large-scale e-participation and on-line deliberation projects. This flexible framework supports integration of nearly every discourse process model currently used by on-line moderators. The DEMOS.2 platform transcends the common approach of structuring user contributions (e.g. articles) in hierarchical and inflexible "threads". Instead, every contribution is deemed as equal; its position in e.g. listings of articles depends on meta information attributed to each article, for example the number of votes, hits, or comments. The moderators (as well as the users) may choose and combine these pieces of meta information to generate specific "views" (i.e. filtered and sorted lists of articles).

Together with innovative capabilities to structure discourses on a time-line and to integrate a huge variety of voting and rating mechanisms, the DEMOS.2 system fosters goal-oriented on-line deliberations. Most features of the system are easily switched on and off by the moderators in the administration backend, for example the option to comment on any contribution may be turned off for the whole system but turned on for one specific view.

However, the main strength of the system emerges from the user interaction; e.g. users are allowed to create links between articles or assign articles to a specific position on a map which results in visually stunning cluster effects. Furthermore, the content is effortlessly available, due to compliance with the relevant accessibility and syndication standards.

DEMOS.2 goes beyond the usual Internet chat or discussion forums to provide a powerful and integrated toolset with the following, configurable and customizable state-of-the-art features for supporting large-scale public participation in political discourses on the Web:

- Support for a wide range of types of discourses, from not moderated, ad hoc discussions and to complex moderated, structured and goal-directed deliberations differentiated user roles and access rights
- Modes for communication and feedback (direct/indirect, public/protected) supporting a variety of types of user interaction
- Support for analysing and visualizing the results of surveys, including sorting and aggregating quantitative data and qualitative semantic content (free answers, comments and statements)
- Participative "bottom up" specification of issues, construction of questionnaires, and selection of experts
- Conflict resolution strategies allowing differentiated outcomes (convergence, consensus, divergence, "rational dissent")

- Support for self-organization and subgroup formation, with different levels of aggregation and distribution

These features have presented various technical challenges to the software developers, including:

- Assuring scalability, to maintain process coherence and coordination in the face of a large numbers of participants
- Providing powerful and convenient administration features for moderators and mediators, especially for structuring and dynamically restructuring large scale participative discourses
- Using surveying, rating and voting to help discussions progress and to enhance conclusiveness of debates
- Supporting procedures, similar to "rules of order", for essential parts of the participation process.

Apart from Living Labs the DEMOS.2 system has been adapted and specialized either to the needs and demands of informal and formal processes especially public administrations are promoting themselves or even obliged to perform as well as several e- services.

Tell Me services have been identified and built upon the DEMOS.2 system and shifted to solution-oriented services in order to include a focused potential final users' analysis.

METHODOLOGY

Within this research, it builds and populates the targeted experiential service according to the following steps of a Living Lab configuration process:

Contextualization

Contextualization means a prior exploration of the technological and social challenges implied by the technology or service under investigation. Applicable methods are, consequently:

- A technological scan, giving an overview of current and future technologies but also to map the specific functionalities and characteristics related to them;
- A (state-of-the-art) study in order to determine the socio-economic implications of the research focus (framework as well as topic).

The contextualization phase is the starting point for the preparation of a Tell Me Living Lab process. Within this phase all important decisions on topic selection, process structure, user to be involved and evaluation issues have to be made.

Tell Me Living Labs can be adapted to the following application fields:

- Urban and regional planning (UP)
- E-services (E-S)
- Product innovation / product development (PI)
- Participative decisions on policies, projects or budget planning (BP)
- Idea development (ID)

These fields require using different tools and the adaptation of different evaluation criteria. For this reason it is important to draw a clear picture of the test application / service / technology and to focus on the crucial research question.

To achieve this, so-called technological scans can be performed to provide an overview of current and future technologies but also to map the specific functionalities and related characteristics. State-of-the-art studies can additionally determine the socio-economic implications of the topic under consideration.

The selection of topics to be discussed and processed in the context of the Tell Me Living Lab process have to be defined carefully and the particular context should be explored in detail. All following phases and activities and the configuration of the DEMOS 2 system are depending on this first decision about the issue to be debated.

It is left to the individual testbeds of the Tell Me project to clarify these aspects in more detail. Within the Contextualization Phase, five different tasks are specified:

1. Development of goals, quality standards and evaluation methods
2. Adaptation of DEMOS process and technology
3. Preparation of background information
4. User selection
5. Administration and moderation

Selection

Selection phase includes the identification of potential users or user groups, by means of non probabilistic or purposeful sampling. Useful criteria are, for instance:

- The maximum variation of underlying phenomenon (e.g. education or age);
- The search for a significant variation of observations (e.g. selective or criterion sampling)

- The theoretical variation of relevant concepts (according to some preexisting study).

The scope of participation has to be clarified in advance in order to avoid disappointments. The topic must be specified as well as the groups of people that have to be involved. It is recommended to write a list of daily activities to monitor the progress in this area.

The following issues have to be solved:

- Exploration of the user groups to be involved, e.g. experts, interest groups, members of authority etc.
- Investigation of already existing networks which can be directly addressed by the discussion
- Invitation of users to participate
- Preparation of a strategy and local activities in order to make people aware of the Tell Me Living Lab and motivate them to participate in advance and during the ongoing process.

The following Concretization Phase is based on the assumptions made here.

Concretization

Concretization phase means a thorough description of the current characteristics, everyday behavior and perceptions of the selected test users regarding the research focus. In this initial measurement authors looked at specific user characteristics (sociodemographic and economic) as well their relation towards the introduced technology or service. The methodology used depends on the size of the test panel: for instance, a quantitative survey can be integrated, depending on the sample scale, by qualitative interviews. The initial measurement of the sample is made before a technology or service is introduced or before the test panel becomes active in the Living Lab; it then enables to perform a second measurement and a full evaluation at the end of the project.

This phase is intended to mainly cope with the user registration. DEMOS 2 offers a registration mode that is adaptable to the needs of the trails. The registration process and the underlying threshold (low/high) have to be defined. It must be made clear which data are requested for the registration process, which information is mandatory or optional for registration. The Table 2 includes an example of registration checklist. Examples for optional data:

- Full name
- Gender
- Age
- Town
- District
- Education
- Occupation

Examples for different thresholds are:

- **Very low:** Within the registration process the user has to choose a login name and a password. No information else is mandatory or proved.
- **Medium:** Within the registration process, the user has to choose a login name and a valid email address. The mail is sent to the given address to validate the request.
- **High:** Just pre-invited users are able to register to the process.

User Rights are related to forum access, writing / reading and change documents, upload content etc. Typically three different types of users are to be distinguished:

- Moderators and administrators have all rights (read / write, access to all forums / wikis /documents etc., can change the content on the platform DEMOS 2)
- Normal users have restricted rights (access to public forums, right to read and write, access to wikis)
- Special or expert users have restricted rights (access to public and expert forums, right to read and write)

Table 3. Checklist registration

Tasks	Specification
Define set of registration information	• Necessary for all Tell Me Living Labs • More and specialised questions for target group related issues like UP, E-S
Distinguish between mandatory and optional information	• Necessary for all Tell Me Living Labs
Define registration threshold	• Necessary for all Tell Me Living Labs • Lower for ID

In the following, in order to gather information about current characteristics and every day life behavior of the users and their perceptions regarding the research focus, an initial online-survey has to be conducted. The participants who have registered to the platform should actively be motivated to take part in that survey.

Implementation

Implementation is actually the behavioral validation and operationally running test phase of the Living Lab. From a user-oriented and ethnographic viewpoint. Authors distinguish two major research methods:

- **Direct analysis**, using remote data collection techniques and strategies (like technological monitoring) and software logging tools (if applicable) on the device level (e.g. pda, mobile phone or digital television) as well as on the platform/network level;
- **Indirect analysis**, based on (thematically organized) focus groups, in-depth interviews and self-reporting techniques like diaries, all being applied to investigate the meaning and motivation for behavior.

The following description specifies the 3 different stages of the DEMOS 2 process with respect to their outcome and the moderator's intervention strategies. Due to the specification made within the Contextualization Phase, closed forums, polls, user diaries have to be put in place.

Stage 1

The purpose of the first phase is to initiate and facilitate the discussion, to generate different viewpoints and collect a widespread collection of opinions and statements and finally to identify the central and most important (sub) topics of the general subject matter. The phase concludes splitting up the main forum into different thematic sub forums dedicated to the most central issues in stage 2.

The moderators have to analyze and cluster the free text contributions in order to find out the issues most participants seem to be interested in. Additionally, the moderators will have to summarize the discussion during the course of the first stage following a specific procedure. These summaries consist of content and progress related parts and highlight and profile emerging lines of conflict. The first stage finally results in a set of proposed sub topics that can be more intensively discussed in separate discussion forums in the next phase. Since this procedure is relying on interpretations of the individual postings as well as of the entire discussion, the result may not exactly meet the preferences of the participants. At this point the survey method might come into play in order to evaluate whether or not the proposed sub forums meet the demands of the community and, if necessary, to generate ideas on how to revise the list of sub topics.

Stage 2

In the second stage a limited number (~3) of sub forums will be offered on the basis of the poll results. This phase is meant to intensively discuss the chosen topics among smaller discussion groups in thematic sub forums and to work out ascertained and feasible solution strategies.

In this stage specific aspects can intensively be discussed in smaller groups of interested participants, while the main forum still catches those participants who want to discuss the topic on a more general level. Again the moderators will summarise the developing debate on a regular basis and at the same time try to tease out and manage emerging conflicts. They clarify how and to what extent people are agreeing or disagreeing and at the same time try to reduce the distance between diverging positions by deliberation.

In order to generate concrete results or possible solution strategies the moderators invite the participants to fix their ideas in so called "wikis". Wikis are documents that can be developed collaboratively by different participants on the Internet. If the moderators foresee that a concrete idea is emerging, they will open a wiki that the participants can jointly work out or adapt to the discussion going on in the forum. At the end of this phase the sub forums and the wiki documents will be closed again. The participants can still read the content but not revise it any more. Finally, the moderators will close this phase with a summary of what was discussed so far and an outlook about what will happen in the last phase.

Stage 3

The third stage reintegrates the sub forums into the still existing main forum by transferring the summaries (wikis) and related survey results. Here the participants have the opportunity to see the particular sub topic as part of the general subject matter and a 'big picture' will emerge. Participants have the last chance to comment on the main topic and the assembled results of the sub forums. The community will be asked to rate the sub topics in terms of importance for the main topic that the DEMOS process was intentionally set up for. The final result will be a condensed document depicting both the results of a dynamic discussion and the importance accorded its different aspects in the view of its participants.

Stage 3 intends to open the single discussions again towards a wider perspective and the interrelations of the different aspects. The moderators have to keep track of the discussion and help the participants to finally scrutinize the results of the discussion and the wikis. By help of the rating system users can rank the different ideas (wikis) which were developed in the second phase with regard to their quality and feasibility for the underlying discussion topic.

In cooperation with the users the moderators will work out the final summary of the discourse and its detailed results.

Feedback

Feedback phase consists of two research steps:

1. An ex post measurement based on the same techniques of the initial measurement, to check if there is any evolution in the users perception and attitude towards the introduced technology or service, to assess changes over time in everyday life in relation to technology use and to detect transitions of usage over time.
2. A set of technological recommendations from the analysis of data, gathered during the previous implementation phase. This outcome of the feedback phase can be used as the starting point for a new research cycle within the Living Lab; in this way the iterative feature of our research cycle can be made operational.

At Tell Me project there are three different layers of feedback that have to be taken into account:

1. Ex-post measurement: conduct and analyse a final online survey. At the end of the Living Lab process a final survey has to be conducted, analysed and compared with the results of initial survey. The aim is to track a change of attitudes and opinions in the course of the Living Lab process.. The result of this comparison should be cross checked with the discussion.
2. Analysis of the contribution: if necessary, a thematic analysis within the feedback phase of a Tell Me Living Lab should provide an in-depth analysis of the content by
    a. Analysing the argumentation process in forums
    b. By analysing user diaries especially for PI
    c. In-depth comparison of the different proposals UP, BP, ID especially with regard to users agreement / disagreement
    d. Analysis of change between different version of the same wiki
3. Analysis of the quality of the outcome: to assess the quality of the outcome it is important to keep in mind the goal of the Tell Me Living Lab process.

EVIDENCE FROM A PRACTICAL CASE STUDY: TUSCANY REGION LIVING LAB

Case studies are generally regarded as particularly useful in depicting a *holistic portrayal of a experiences and results* regarding the application or implementation of a new concept or program as in the case of the Tell Me services. Though case studies are used to organize a wide range of information about a case and then analyze the contents by seeking patterns and themes in the data, and by further analysis through cross comparison with other cases. The case study's unique strength is its ability to deal with a full variety of evidence such as documents, interviews and observations. The multiple perspectives, methods and observations in the studies also provide a strategy of triangulation to add rigor, breadth and depth to the investigation.

The simple fact that what people say and what people do is not necessarily the same thing is also taken into consideration through observation and cross checking with the perspectives of others involved in various transactions in different settings. Evidence from the case studies highlighted many instances of the disparity between the language used to articulate the desire to collaborate and the organizational reality of how decision-making is exercised in implementing the practice. However, sufficient evidence has been collected that supports the efficacies of using the Tell Me service as a collaboration infrastructure for carrying out processes that are communications-intensive and exhibit a high degree of complexity as the result of the involvement of many actors and shareholders.

The Regional Government of Tuscany in the late 2007 published the Law n.69 on "Rules on the promotion of participation in the development of regional and local policies" also known as 'law on participation' (See Figure 1).

That law is an innovative tool for encourage and disseminate new ways and methods of participation, through the construction of new participatory institutions, new processes and shared rules to discuss any size issues within a community and to assess possible solutions through dialogue and confrontation, within a defined time.

The trial was dedicated to evaluate the citizenship knowledge of the law and their comments and expectation about the law.

Contextualization

In the Tuscany land there is a community network whose name is PAAS (Access Points to the Services see http://www.e.toscana.it/paas/). The 270 nodes are spread across the whole Tuscany region and at present have more than 25.000 subscribers. The network is an evaluable result of an e Inclusion initiative of Regional Government of Tuscany (RGT).

Figure 1. Home -Living-Lab.toscana.it (adopted from TELL ME project trial website http://www.living-lab.toscana.it/)

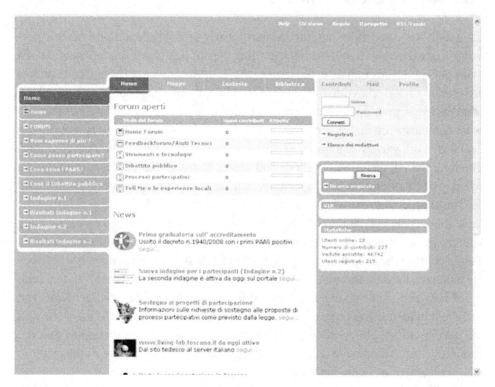

The PASS-LL has been built with the focus of e Participation, e Government and e Services, but, taking in account the importance of the law, the trial addressed only the e Participation theme.

The target group of the trial are the citizens of all 10 Provinces of Tuscany, with age between 18 and 80 and therefore all the PAAS subscribers are considered in that group.

By means of a call for proposal were selected 20 PAAS nodes using criteria like geographic coverage different (2 every Province) and knowledge and experience about participation and social network of every single node manager. This choice has been taken in order to have a simpler management of the trial and to include the more motivated node-owners.

In the following the four different areas of contextualisation phase are detailed, as stated in D4.1 Operational Methodology the contextualisation phase of TELL-ME.

Development of Goals, Quality Standards, and Evaluation Methods

During the initial phase of the trial discussion subject was about the Tuscany Regional Law n.69/2007 "participation give the chance of a new active citizenship". Trial main goal was a debate about the law's effectiveness and citizen's expectations.

Trial evaluation criteria were the definition of the number of participants registered on the platform, the number of contributions in the forum and the degree of satisfaction of the Regional Government of Tuscany Directorate. The last ones are responsible of the Participation Law publishing. Based on the above Table 4 includes the corresponding trial **Contextualization** phase checklist.

Adaptation of DEMOS.2 Process and Configuration of the DEMOS.2 Platform

The adaptation of DEMOS.2 has been carried out in two different phases.

The first phase has been used in order to learn the platform functions and complete the Italian translation of menus and windows. During the second phase the platform has been customised and settled for the trial (see Table 5).

Selection

The new regional law on participation affected all the citizenship of Tuscany and hence all the PAAS subscribers and visitors were interested by our survey. It has to be considered also that the goal of the trial was to highlight the powerfulness of the e Participation when used within a well-organised Community Network just like a Living-Lab.

Therefore, all the PAAS-LL node maintainers were instructed to invite all their own subscribers over 18 years old to participate to survey. The people selected were a good sample of Tuscany citizenship because of the presence in the Living-Lab of two PAAS node for every Province. In the following figures are shown the sample composition considering age, sex, and education (see Table 6).

Table 4. Checklist of contextualization phase

Tasks	Specification	Checked y/n
Definition of type of TELL ME Living Lab (UP, E-S, PI, BP, ID)	• Explain the purpose of the TELL ME Living Lab • Explain main research focus • Define evaluation standards	yes yes yes

Table 5. Checklist of DEMOS adaptation

Tasks	Specification	Checked y/n
Translation	• Translation of information material • Translation of advertising material • Translation of system and process description • Provide translation possibilities during the process	Yes
Layout specification	• Necessary for all types of TELL ME Living Labs • Logo integrated? • Typo correct? • Phrases and sentences integrated? • Wording correct? • Color scheme correct?	Yes Yes Yes Yes Yes

Concretization

In order to give to all the participants to the trial all the tools and information to understand the innovation of the web 2.0 and social network platforms during the month before the pilot itself it was started a common discussion and insight about the different ways to support debates within a network community. As a result all the subscribers and visitors could start the trial with a full awareness of what they were going for and hence endorse their trust on the survey goals.

Furthermore, in order to let every subscriber to take part to the initial online survey they were all registered to the DEMOS.2 platform as debate participants and therefore they get used to consider themselves as a member of the coming trial (see Table 7).

Table 6. Checklist of selection phase

Tasks	Specification	Checked y/n
Define user groups	• Necessary for all types of TELL ME Living Labs especially for E-S and UP	Yes
Define communication channels	• Necessary for all types of TELL ME Living Labs • Define communication channels and marketing strategies for each target group separately	Yes
Invitation to participate	• Necessary for all types of TELL ME Living Labs • Plan invitation waves for each target group during the whole process • Develop a schedule for invitations and reminders of participating	Yes Yes

Table 7. Checklist of concretization phase

Tasks	Specification	Checked y/n
Define user groups	• Necessary for all TELL ME Living Labs	Yes, not relevant
Define access rights for user groups	• Necessary for all TELL ME Living Labs	Yes
Define user profiles in Demos.2 for invited guests / experts	• Necessary for all TELL ME Living Labs	Yes
Conduct initial online survey	• Necessary for all TELL ME Living Labs	Yes

Implementation

The implementation phase duration was one month. The debates were divided in 5 different forums, two of them with the main topic of participation law and participative process, while the other topics were to support the discussion on web 2.0 tools, TELL-ME project, and user assistance. At the end of the 23 day of trial there were 215 registered subscribers that produced 227 contributions, having the amazing number of 11047 hits that means that the DEMOS.2 platform was visited by subscribers of all PAAS nodes, not by PAAS-LL only (see Table 8).

Feedback

In order to collect feedback from users two questionnaires were prepared. One questionnaire was sent to the entire registered user in order to get their feedback, while the other questionnaire was prepared for collecting qualitative feedback from the PAAS-LL maintainers and moderators. The summarized results are presented in the following sections (see Table 9).

BENEFITS AND CHALLENGES

Tell Me brings a subjective richness to bear on decision-making problems faced by Public Administrations. This research believes that Tell Me service, through more conscious attention and deliberate experimentation and adoption in the real world, it aims to offer the following benefits:

Improved functioning of Living Labs (public administrations)- With Tell Me, a basic infrastructure (integrated with a methodology) is provided to "link together" the different stakeholders in order to let them work more efficiently. Equally important

Table 8. Checklist of implementation phase

Tasks	Explanation	Checked y/n
Moderation	• Summarize topics • Report on rule violation • Comment on discussion process • Provide hand-over on shift change	Yes Yes Yes Yes
News announcement	• Produce daily news due current development • Report on events and summarize them • Produce news in advance • Report from the discussion	Yes Yes Yes Yes
Open wikis	• Name and implement subforums • Provide first structure for the wikis	Yes Yes
Edit final document	• Add user polls and rankings to this final document • Include results from starting / final questionnaire	Yes Yes

is that Tell Me establishes an intimate communication channel between participants in a Living Lab. This communication service is the first step towards the provision of user centred and customised services.

Co-creative e-Government- Another benefit of the Tell Me service is to develop trust between the people and stakeholders in a region, this is the first step to enable a co-creative user driven e-Government service development.

Improved quality of public services- It should not be forgotten that the main area of public interest for the project will be related to the online service provision to citizens by European public administrations. Tell Me will enable on one hand, improved staff efficiency and on the other hand, more citizens/customers oriented and "socially accepted" e-Services.

Easily available e-Government applications- Another benefit for the community will be the availability of easier-to-use eGovernment applications that have been

Table 9. Checklist of feedback phase

Tasks	Explanation	Checked y/n
Final survey	• Conduct a final survey and compare results with initial survey	Yes
Thematic analysis (main method: content analysis)	• Argumentation process in forums, necessary for all types of TELL ME Living Labs • Proposal comparison, especially for UP, BP, ID	Yes Yes
Evaluation of quality outcome (main method: content analysis, quantitative research)	• Quantitative Research to evaluate user profile (especially for UP, E-S, BP) • Content analysis to value the quality of the ideas, suggestions, arguments etc, necessary for all types of TELL ME Living Labs	Yes Yes

validated in advance through online interaction with the potential users. This will potentially enlarge the scope for public sector innovation in Europe.

Improved efficiency/effectiveness of the validation process- Outside and beyond the public sector, a number of additional benefits can be experienced by the repeated use of the Tell Me methodology in the private sector context.

SOLUTIONS AND RECOMMENDATIONS

The field of eDemocracy in Europe has been developed by different players on the European, national and local level over the course of the last years.

On the European level the different organisations (EuroParl, EC etc.) have tested and implemented a series of eDemocracy programmes and initiatives to support the development of the field: The European Commission funded ca. 20 Information Society Technology projects with more than 30 million euro and many of the sixth Framework Programme projects support the field of eDemocracy (Chrissafis, 2005). One major step forward to implementing "contribute to easing mobility of European citizens within the Internal Market, making European Citizenship a reality, supporting them as active citizens through innovative government services and through participation" (IST policy, 2004) on the European level is the Interactive Policy Making (IPM) project. The system has been put into place "to facilitate the stakeholders' consultation process by the use of easy-to-use and straightforward online questionnaires, making it easier both for respondents to participate and for policy makers to analyse the results" (Interactive Policy Making, 2007).

The Council of Europe supported the general development by the set up of the ad hoc Committee on E-Democracy of the Council of Europe (CAHDE, 2006). The goal of CAHDE is among others to "examine developments on e-democracy/e-participation at European and international level"; to "develop proposals for the Forum for the Future of Democracy as to how it could embrace issues of e-democracy". The recommendations on eDemocracy developed by CAHDE are finalized by the end of 2008 will certainly help to convince policy makers in the 47 member states to support the field of eDemocracy.

Another factor in the development of eDemocracy even thou it does not touch the four products to be marketed by the consortium is eVoting. Internet voting was assessed in the cybervote project with was "tested in 2003 during trial election that will be held in Germany, France and Sweden. These trials will involve more that 3000 voters and will allow full assessment of the system before any potential product launch". Electronic Voting machines however have been implemented in many European states on different organisational levels. eVoting in all of its forms is subject to critical discussion which is mainly focussed on security and transparency concerns. The technical and also procedural criticism related to eVoting resulted in a focus on deliberative and issue focused forms of implementing eDemocracy. In the following some projects will be described as examples to give an overlook on the wide diversity of eDemocracy projects in Europe established during the last years. The collection is manly based on the major comparative review of current practice by Prof. Ann Macintosh published in the OECD study "Promise and Problems of eDemocracy" (2003).

Summing up beyond the small list of examples given in this text there are many different eDemocracy projects beyond those given here. Various initiatives are already in place or planned on the European, national and local level and its count is still growing. This hints at a larger market potential lying ahead for electronic democracy in Europe or as Stephen Coleman puts it:

"Politicians are beginning to realise that connecting directly with the citizens they represent can lead to better policy-making and legislation, informed by public experience and expertise; a new kind of relationship between government and governed, based upon politicians' listening, learning and sharing ideas as well as steering and aggregating; and the reward of enhanced public confidence in democratic institutions and the renewed legitimacy of governance." Coleman (2003).

According to the "Helsinki Manifesto" issued on 20th November 2006, a further dimension, namely, co-creative collaboration with the forthcoming users of the developing products and services, has enhanced the issue of competitiveness and innovation in Europe. The most important impact to citizens is its usefulness in the he field of (private and Government) e-Services. As a result, the concept of e-Democracy networking can be an extremely beneficial toolset to bring together regions and industrial stakeholders with citizen academia and researchers.

Besides, it is obvious to us that citizens and community members develop a positive feeling for local authority budgets, both intuitively and through learning by playing; they also gain a better understanding of the scope and limits of budgetary planning.

Municipalities and regions acquire more information about the desires, preferences and needs of their citizens, enabling them to create opportunities for debating about future avenues for development or new projects.

Any sustainable solution would require to:

1. Communicate the scope and limits of local authority budget-setting in an intelligent and innovative way.
2. Use the tool to explain the meaning of individual budget items.
3. Let the public participate in making important decisions.
4. Identify citizens' desires and priorities at an early stage.
5. Generate acceptance for budget consolidation.

6.   Create more transparency – and thus more local democracy.
7.   Integrate the planner in the political process: create opportunities for discussion.

Users of the Tell Me platform learn what it means to implement political "dreams" against a background of limited resources and spending limits imposed by law. The complexity of the budget planner varies according to the degree to which the user goes deeply into the subject – from a smart game to a level verging on reality.

TELL ME is a European project, which focuses on the design of transnational public services built on ICT in e-Government related areas. We aimed at demonstrating the pilot implementation and exploring the market potential of what was originally presented as a (joint) methodology and toolset for the configuration and the pan-European deployment of Living Labs in the areas of e-Government, e-Democracy and e-Services. As a result, the existing and upcoming best practices in such domains have been considered as a first market segment for our service since the beginning of the project. This deliverable documents the steps ahead made by the TELL ME partners in the market validation of such a complex service during the 1st project year.

A Living Lab is a real-life environment, managed by a business/citizens/government partnership, which enables users to take an active part in the research, development and innovation process. Products and services are developed in a person-centric and co-creative way, based on continuous feedback from users to developers. As an open innovation platform, it creates an environment where users are confronted with ideas, concepts and prototypes or demonstrators of technology since the early stages of the research, development and innovation process, not only at its end, like in more classical field trials or product testing approaches.

The intuition behind the TELL ME project has been to replicate an existing service (DEMOS) - originally thought for the animation of democratic discussions and participative public opinion formation at local and regional level - and adapt it to the networking and repeated interaction of participants during the development and implementation of Living Lab trials. After a first phase where the TELL ME consortium focused into the preparation of five regional Living Lab trials in the domains of e-Government, e-Services and e-Participation, the second phase has been based on the most important findings derived from market analysis, project dissemination and the collection of the trials results, to build up a first draft of business plan for the consortium as a whole.

Ata higher level, our analysis has focused on the understanding of the TELL ME service "portfolio" composition i.e. what are the services making up the TELL ME suite?

In fact, a first piece of evidence has been that the DEMOS system – though very effective in allowing moderated and goal-oriented discourses between citizens and policy makers, as well as trial managers, developers and other stakeholders, at national and European level - simply adds up to a plethora of existing ICT solutions that are already operational at Living Lab level. It was then necessary to prepare an overview of the actual strengths and weaknesses of the service to lay the proper foundations for a good marketing action.

A second piece of evidence relates to the fact that, until now, very few Living Labs are actually operating in the areas of eGovernment, eParticipation and eDemocracy. This can be seen as a promising market scope, at the only condition that it should not hide the good or best practices that are already operating in these domains, though not (or not explicitly) under the Living Labs "umbrella". In that respect, what we thought was missing from our original approach is a deeper consideration of the original traits being born and brought up in the context of public administration and participatory policy making.

ACKNOWLEDGMENT

Our thanks to the European Commission for partially funding the Tell Me project and the architect of the Tell Me ideas and vision, Mr Rolf Luers. Tell Me is an eTEN Project, running as part of the European Union's Framework Programme 6 for Research in Information Society Technologies, aiming towards 'e-Government'. Official project Web site: http://www.tellmeproject.eu

REFERENCES

W3C. (2009). *RDF annotations (RDFa)*. Retrieved October 22, 2009, from http://www.w3.org/TR/xhtml-rdfa-primer/

W3C. (2009). *RDF schema (RDFS)*. Retrieved October 22, 2009, from http://www.w3.org/TR/rdf-schema/

W3C. (2009). *Resource description framework (RDF)*. Retrieved October 22, 2009, from http://www.w3.org/RDF/

W3C. (2009). *Simple object access protocol (SOAP)*. Retrieved October 22, 2009, from http://www.w3.org/TR/soap/

Ad Hoc Committee on E-Democracy of the Council of Europe (CAHDE). (2006). *Introduction to the Ad Hoc Committee on E-democracy (CAHDE)*. Retrieved from http://www.coe.int/t/e/integrated_projects/democracy/02_activities/002_e-democracy/00%20Intro%20CAHDE_en.asp

Anderson, C. (2006). *The long tail: Why the future of business is selling less of more*. New York, NY: Hyperion.

Ari-Veikko, A. (2003). Building strong e-democracy: the role of technology in developing democracy for the information age. *Communications of the ACM, 46*(9).

Bovet, D., & Martha, J. (2000). Value nets: Reinventing the rusty supply chain for competitive advantage. *Strategy and Leadership, 28*(4), 21–26. doi:10.1108/10878570010378654

boyd, d., & Ellison, N. B. (2007). *Social network sites: Definition, history, and scholarship*.

Cardoso, J., & Sheth, A. P. (Eds.). (2006). *Semantic Web services, processes and applications*. Springer. doi:10.1007/978-0-387-34685-4

Chrissafis, T. (2005). *E-democracy: Challenges and actions in the EU*. TED Conference on e-Government Electronic democracy: The challenge ahead, Bolzano, Italy.

Gilmore, J. H., & Pine, B. J. (2000). *Markets of one: Creating customer-unique value through mass customization*. Boston, MA: Harvard Business School Press.

Grönroos, C. (2000). Service management: A management focus for service competition. *International Journal of Service Industry Management, 1*(1), 6–14.

Iansiti, M., & Levien, R. (2004). *The keystone advantage: What the new dynamics of business ecosystems mean for strategy, innovation and sustainability*. Boston, MA: Harvard Business School Press.

Interactive Policy Making Online Consultations website. (2007). *Report on interactive policy making*. Retrieved from http://ec.europa.eu/yourvoice/ipm/index_en.htm

IST-507767 – QUALEG. (2004). *Deliverable 4.1 "marketing research."*

IST policy on the objective of ICT research for innovative Government website. (2004). Retrieved from http://cordis.europa.eu/ist/so/govt/home.html

Jarillo, J. C. (1988). On strategic networks. *Strategic Management Journal, 9*(1), 31–41. doi:10.1002/smj.4250090104

Lauriat, S. M. (2007). *Advanced AJAX: Architecture and best practices*. Upper Saddle River, NJ: Prentice Hall PTR.

Lisbon Strategy. (2000). *Lisbon European Council 23 and 24 March 2000 presidency conclusions*. Retrieved from http://www.europarl.europa.eu/summits/lis1_en.htm

Maglio, P., & Spohrer, J. (2008). Fundamentals of service science. *Journal of the Academy of Marketing Science, 36*, 18–20. doi:10.1007/s11747-007-0058-9

Moore, J. F. (1996). *The death of competition: Leadership and strategy in the age of business ecosystems.* Winchester, UK: J. Wiley & Sons.

NESSI. (2006). *Strategic research agenda, Vol. 1: Framing the future of the service.*

Normann, R., & Ramirez, R. (1993). From value chain to value constellation: Designing interactive strategy. *Harvard Business Review, 71*(4), 65–77.

O'Hear, S. (2006, June 20). Web's second phase puts users in control. *The Guardian, Education.* Retrieved from http://education.guardian.co.uk/elearning/story/0,1801086,00.html

OASIS. (2006). *Reference Model for Service Oriented Architecture 1.0.*Retrieved from http://www.oasis-open.org/committees/ tc_home.php?wg_abbrev=soa-rm, accessed August 2006.

OASIS. (2009). *Business process execution language v 2.0.* Retrieved from http://docs.oasis-open.org/wsbpel/2.0/OS/wsbpel-v2.0-OS.html, retrieved 22/10/2009

OASIS. (2009). *Security assertion markup language (SAML).* Retrieved from http://www.oasis-open.org/committees/tc_home.php?wg_abbrev=security, retrieved 22/09/2009

OASIS. (2009). *Web services atomic transaction (WS-AtomicTransaction).* Retrieved from http://docs.oasis-open.org/ws-tx/wsat/2006/06, retrieved at 22/10/2009

OECD. (2001a). *Cities for citizens: Improving metropolitan governance* (pp. 39–43). Paris: OECD Publications.

OECD. (2001b). *Citizens as partners: Information, communication and public participation in policy making* (pp. 20–22). Paris: OECD Publications.

Pistore, M., Traverso, P., Paolucci, M., & Wagner, M. (2009). From software services to a future internet of services. In Tselentis, G. (Eds.), *Towards the future Internet.* IOS Press.

Prahalad, C. K., & Ramaswamy, V. (2000). Co-opting customer competence. *Harvard Business Review, 78*(1), 79–87.

Prahalad, C. K., & Ramaswamy, V. (2003). The new frontier of experience innovation. In Rosenberg, J., & Remy, D. (Eds.), *Securing Web services with WS-Security: Demystifying WS-Security, WS-Policy, SAML, XML signature, and XML encryption.* Pearson Higher Education.

Prahalad, C. K., & Ramaswamy, V. (2004). *The future of competition: Co-creating unique value with customers*. New York, NY: Harvard Business School Press.

Rust, R. T., & Kannan, P. K. (2003). E-service: A New paradigm for business in the electronic environment. *Communications of the ACM, 46*(6), 37–42. doi:10.1145/777313.777336

Rust, R. T., & Lemon, K. N. (2001). E-service and the consumer. *International Journal of Electronic Commerce, 5*(3), 85–101.

Sawhney, M., Balasubramanian, S., & Krishnan, V. V. (2003). Creating growth with services. *Sloan Management Review, 45*(2), 34–44.

Sawhney, M., & Parikh, D. (2001). Where value lives in a networked world. *Harvard Business Review, 79*(1), 79–90.

Shirky, C. (2003). Social software: A new generation of tools. *Esther Dyson's Monthly Report, 10*.

The Helsinki Manifesto. (2006). Retrieved from http://elivinglab.org/files/Helsinki_Manifesto_201106.pdf

Tyagi, S. (2006). *RESTful Web services*. Retrieved October 22, 2009, from http://java.sun.com/developer/technicalArticles/WebServices/restful/

Walters, D., & Lancaster, G. (1999). Value and information: Concepts and issues for management. *Management Decision, 37*(8), 643–656. doi:10.1108/00251749910291613

ADDITIONAL READING

Avramidis, G., Manolopoulos, C., Sofotasios, D., Spirakis, P., & Stamatiou, Y. (2008). *PNYKA e-voting system*.

Bouras, C., Giannaka, E., Karounos, T., Priftis, A., Poulopoulos, V., & Tsiatsos, T. (2008). *A unified framework for political parties to support e-democracy practices: the case of a Greek party*.

Breindl, Y., & Francq, P. (2008). *Can Web 2.0 applications save e-democracy? A study of how new internet applications may enhance citizen participation in the political process online*.

Fraunholz, B., & Unnithan, C. (2009). *Anti-apathy approaches in representative democracies: e-governance and web 2.0 – facilitating citizen involvement?* Klein, H. (January 1999). Tocqueville in cyberspace: Using the internet for citizens associations. *The Information Society, 15,* 213–220.

Manolopoulos, C., Efstathiadou, R., & Spirakis, P. (2009). *The impact of the Web and political balance to e-democracy.*

Meneklis, V., & Douligeris, C. (2010). *Studying the interaction of the epistemology in e-government, organization studies and information systems.*

Norris, P. (2001). *Digital divide: Civic engagement, information poverty, and the Internet worldwide.* Cambridge, UK: University Press.

Ntaliani, M., Karetsos, S., & Costopoulou, C. (2006). *Accessing e-government services via TV.*

Paganelli, F. (2010). *Telep@b project: A model for eParticipation and a case study in participatory budgeting.*

Panagis, Y., Sakkopoulos, E., Tsakalidis, A., Tzimas, G., Sirmakessis, S., & Lytras, M. D. (2008). *Techniques for mining the design of e-government services to enhance end-user experience.*

Triantafillou, V., & Kalogeras, D. (2010). *E-democracy: The political culture of tomorrow's citizens.*

Xenakis, A., & Loukis, E. (2009). *Using structured e-forum to support the legislation formation process.*

KEY TERMS AND DEFINITIONS

Best Practice: One technique, method, process, activity, incentive or reward which is considered to be the most efficient and effecting in delivering a particular outcome among the other already existing solution is called best practice. Undoubtedly, the desired outcome can be achieved with fewer problems after a series of proper processes, checks, and testing. Even if the processes are continuously improved, a best practice is considered as a business buzzword used to describe the "methodology" and the standards for the development in cases of multiple organizations related to management, policy, and especially software systems.

Citizen-centric: After the "Helsinki Manifesto" (2006) put the "human-centric way" at the very centre of the measures needed "for turning the Lisbon Strategy

(2000) into a living reality", citizen-centric is meant to denote any approach related with or focused to the co-creative collaboration with the forthcoming users of products and / or services under development. This is especially useful in the field of (private and Government) e-Services, where the people can be considered as "twice" beneficiaries, namely of public services as such – impacting per se on their lives and businesses – and of ICT based or supported services, where the question becomes to which extent this novel user-centric approach can improve customization (if not "tailoring") to individual needs and requirements.

Contextualization: It is considered as the first amd most important part of the Living Lab configuration process. It builds on the exploration of both the technological and social challenges implied by a technology or a service under investigation. From a methodology point of view two alternative methods can be applied for its execution: (i) a technological scan, giving an overview of current and future technologies but also to map the specific functionalities and characteristics related to them; (ii) a (state-of-the-art) study in order to determine the socio-economic implications of the research focus (framework as well as topic).

eDemocracy: Direct democracy tries to find the solution to the democracy deficit from the quantity of direct citizen participation in decision-making. E-democracy comes for the combination of the words "electronic" and "democracy". In particular it includes the use of electronic communications technologies such as the Internet in enhancing democratic processes within a democratic republic, representative democracy or any other democratic model. It is a political development still in its infancy, as well as the subject of much debate and activity within government, civic-oriented groups and societies around the world.

Policy: Typically, the term policy is used to describe a deliberate plan of action to monitor and moderate decisions and achieve rational outcome(s). Sectors such as government, private sector organizations and groups, and individuals are using the term policy. Besides, the term policy is appropriate when it refers to the process of taking crucial decisions, including the recognition of several different alternatives such as programs or spending priorities, and finally the selection of the basic ones according to the impact they have. Policies are considered as management, political, financial, and administrative mechanisms that meet the explicit goals.

Policy Life Cycle: It includes three stages namely *formulation* (agenda setting), *implementation*, and *evaluation*.

This work was previously published in Cases on Adoption, Diffusion and Evaluation of Global E-Governance Systems: Impact at the Grass Roots, edited by H. Rahman, pp. 282-302, copyright 2011 by Information Science Reference (an imprint of IGI Global).

Section 2
Public Management Issues

Chapter 7
Agile Knowledge-Based E-Government Supported by SAKE System

Andrea Kő
Corvinus University of Budapest, Hungary

Barna Kovács
Corvinus University of Budapest, Hungary

András Gábor
Corvinus University of Budapest, Hungary

EXECUTIVE SUMMARY

The evolution of e-Government services moves quickly. There is a limited time for adaptation to the new environment in terms of legislation, society, and economy. Maintaining reliable services and a secure IT environment is even more difficult with perpetual changes like mergers and acquisitions, supply chain activity, staff turnover, and regulatory variation. The nature of the changes has become discontinuous; however, the existing approaches and IT solutions are inadequate for highly dynamic and volatile processes. The management of these challenges requires harmonized change management and knowledge management strategy. In this chapter, the selected change management strategy, the corresponding knowledge management strategy, and their IT support are analyzed from the public administration point of view. SAKE project (FP6 IST-2005-027128 funded by the European Commission) approach and IT solution are detailed to demonstrate the strategic view and to solve the knowledge management and change management related problems and challenges in public administration. The current situation of economic downturn

DOI: 10.4018/978-1-4666-0981-5.ch007

and political change forces public administration to follow the reconfiguration of existing resources strategy, which is appropriate on the short run; moreover, the combined application of personalization and codification strategy can result in long-term success.

BACKGROUND

Public administration (PA) has to cope with permanent changes in the political, economic and legal environment. Additionally, previous years' economic crisis has hit Eastern-European countries, like Latvia, Hungary, and Poland particularly hard, since the vulnerability of their economic environments. These fluctuations affect public administration processes and systems as well and require fast, agile responses in decision making. Public servants suffer from increasing information overload, which jeopardizes the organizations' capability to adapt to economic or market changes, endangers competitive edge or can also cause overloading of employees. The increasing complexity of information, the rising amount and the various alternatives of information systems available for a certain problem area make information management more difficult (Bray, 2008; Himma, 2007). New decisions, regulations have to operate fast; "time-to-market" is reduced, so public administration needs support to produce agile responses to changes. Changes in one part of the information assets can cause difficulties in other part of the e-government system; therefore change management should be done in a systematic way (Abrahamson, 2000; Kotter, 1995). The unpredictable and volatile environment requires adaptive, fast and knowledge-based decisions (Riege, 2006). Knowledge has been and is still government's most important resource (Heeks, 2006), so its management is a crucial task. Several examples illustrate the high priority of knowledge management in public administration, like the UK Government's Knowledge Network, which is a government-wide electronic communication tool helping government department to share knowledge and collaborate online with colleagues across government; or the knowledge management initiatives in the Federal Government in US (Barquin, 2010).

In order to comply with the permanent renewal need of knowledge, special knowledge management techniques and systems are needed (Jashapara, 2004; Kő & Klimkó, 2009). These systems have to cope with the fast changing, context-sensitive character of knowledge; meanwhile they have to support the externalization of knowledge (Holsapple, 2003).

Our research aimed to a) analyse change management and knowledge management related challenges of public administration; b) investigate the change management and knowledge management strategies' relationship from public administration view and c) provide a holistic framework and tool for an agile knowledge-based e-government that is reflecting the challenges collected in a) and expected to be sufficiently flexible to adapt to changing and diverse environments and needs for public administration.

The proposed holistic framework and tool is the result of SAKE project (IST-2005-027128 funded by the European Commission's 6th Framework Programme), which comprised: (a) a semantic-based change notification system, (b) semantic-based content management system, (c) a semantic-based groupware system (d) a semantic-based workflow system (e) a semantic-based attention management system. The paper will be structured as follows:

First, knowledge management and change management related problems and challenges in public administration are detailed. Next, relationships between change management and knowledge management strategies are discussed and analysed from the public administration perspective, followed by their appropriate IT support. SAKE project approach and IT environment is presented as an example of compliance with needs arising from change management and knowledge management strategies. Finally, an overview about the Hungarian trial is provided, validating the SAKE solution in real life situations.

SETTING THE STAGE

Change management, knowledge management and information technology are overlapping each other, they are interwoven in practice. The change management strategy applied by the organization influences the types of knowledge that it will draw upon, which will take effect on the knowledge management strategy, which, in turn, determines information technology used in the organization.

This section discusses the nature of changes and change management issues, main knowledge management strategies, and relationships between change and knowledge management strategies while highlighting their IT support.

Knowledge is a strategic resource of companies, also being a decisive factor of public administrations' success. All knowledge management initiatives, such as implementing new technical solutions, reorganization or promoting knowledge-sharing culture provide substantial challenges. Continuous challenges force companies to take the approach of change management into consideration. Different approaches and success factors of changes are hot topics in the literature (Jashapara, 2004; Fehér, 2004). The nature of change became discontinuous from the 1970s (Jashapara, 2004), when the consequences of the rising oil price shocked companies and forced organizations to manage such unpredictable surprises. Public bodies are subject of change as well, especially nowadays considering economic restrictions and their effects. Employees often resist change, because they have to work in a different environment, give up their work and modify their behaviour. Personal response to change can be various, from shocking to adaptation, according to the transition phases in the cycle of change (Hayes, 2002). Commitment of employees has crucial role in the success of change management. According to Strebel, three dimensions are important to reach their commitment (Strebel, 1996): "formal dimension (job description, tasks and processes, relationships, compensation), psychological dimension (equity of work and compensation) and social dimension (unwritten rules, values)."

Kotter stated that organizations successfully change in a slow-moving world in a very calculated, controlled way that is mostly a management process (Kotter, 1997). He analysed the failure factors of change processes (Kotter, 1995) and identified 8 steps of the change management process: feeling of urgency for change (which is a starting condition), forming a good team (supportive coalition), create a vision of change, communicate the vision, remove obstacles, change fast (create short term wins), consolidate results and keep on changing while embedding changes into culture. These steps require a knowledge management strategy that emphasizes the importance of tacit knowledge and long-term management.

Today, due to the fast-changing environment people are forced to take larger leap, like perform organization-wide reengineering projects. Lewin (1951) suggested three phases of change management for helping individuals, groups and organizations:

- *Unfreezing and loosening* current sets of behaviours, mental models and ways of looking problem.
- *Moving* by making changes in the way people do things, new structures, new strategies and different types of behaviours and attitudes.
- *Refreezing* by stabilizing and establishing new patterns and organizational routines.

Lewin's approach is cited frequently in the literature, as being general model of change management, which can be applied together with the decisive knowledge management strategies.

Several other change management theories and assumptions were published, like Lippitt's Phases of Change Theory (Lippitt, 1958), Prochaska and DiClemente's Change Theory (Prochaska & DiClemente, 1986), Social Cognitive Theory, and the Theory of Reasoned Action and Planned Behaviour.

Organizations facing the need of change management utilize a variety of resources supporting them in reaching their goal. Based on the Resource-Based View (RBV) of the firm, change management strategy has to focus on the acquisition and use of resources, like new competencies (Barney, 1991; Wernerfelt, 1984). According to this approach, organizations can select between the following alternatives (Bloodgood & Salisbury, 2001):

- Reconfigure existing resources;
- Acquire new resources with reconfiguration;
- Acquire new resources without reconfiguration, or they may;
- Preserve the status quo and engage in a business as usual strategy.

This Resource-Based View is applied in the analyses of relationships between change management strategy, knowledge management strategy and their IT support. The key question is what kind of information technology should be applied in the organization in order to support these strategies.

Knowledge Management Strategies

Based on the KM strategy literature and consultancy, common form of knowledge management strategies are codification and personalization strategies (Hansen et al., 1999). Codification strategy relies mainly on information technology and often uses databases to codify and store knowledge. This approach emphasizes the importance of explicit knowledge and externalization (Nonaka & Takeuchi, 1995). It is a risk-avoiding approach, because there is a little room for innovation and creativity, they use the tried and tested methods. Personalization strategy is more about people; the focus is on tacit knowledge and on its sharing. It is a creative, networking-based approach, which can result high profit through unique and innovative solutions. This strategy requires high level of rewards for knowledge sharing and dialogues. Form of strategy proposed is characterized as dialectic between the forces of innovation (personalization strategy oriented) and efficiency (codification strategy oriented) (Mintzberg, 1991).

Finding a proper ratio between personalization and codification is difficult for public administration since the obligatory tradition of codification, conforming to regulations and the nature of the work; but personalization is required by the rapid changes in their environment, like economic downturns and political changes.

Several other knowledge management strategies have been proposed in the literature emphasizing different aspects of knowledge management. Some KM strategies focus on the type of knowledge, others on the business processes/areas, and others on the end results. Wiig (1997) and the APQC (American Productivity and Quality Center) identified six emerging KM strategies, reflecting the different natures and strengths of the organizations involved (Wiig, 1997; Manasco, 1996). Day and Wendler (1998) of McKinsey & Company distinguished five knowledge strategies employed by large corporations. Knox Haggie and John Kingston provided guidance for KM strategy selection (Haggie & Kingston, 2003). Table 1 based on Bloodgood and Salisbury (2001) approach highlights relationships between change strategies, knowledge management strategies and their IT support.

Table 1. Relationships between change strategies, knowledge management strategies, and their IT support

Changestrategies	Knowledge type emphasized		Knowledge management strategy		Typical IT support
	Explicit	Tacit	Codification	Personalization	
reconfigure existing resources	Low	High	Low	High	Create networks
acquire new resources with reconfiguration	Moderate	Moderate	Moderate	Moderate	Create networks and codifying knowledge
acquire new resources without reconfiguration	High	Low	High	Low	Codifying knowledge

Reconfiguring existing resources strategy aims to achieve a better fit to the current external environment by changing the way existing resources are used by the organization. This approach mainly requires personalization, because knowledge assets of the organization have already been codified but the way of usage is different. Tacit knowledge and socialization have key role in this process. IT support is targeting network creation; forums, groupware are typical IT solutions used in this approach.

Acquiring new resources with reconfiguration strategy combines codification and personalization strategy; both explicit and tacit knowledge are emphasized. Socialization and externalization are appropriate approaches, making knowledge repositories and groupware suitable forms of IT support.

Acquiring new resources without reconfiguration strategy concentrates on explicit knowledge and emphasizes codification strategy. Competitive advantage is gained through fast knowledge transfer. This strategy focuses on IT usage, relying typically on knowledge repositories and ontologies.

Nowadays, the economic downturn forced public administration to apply reconfiguring existing resources strategy in most of the cases, increasing the importance of personalization strategy. IT support has to concentrate on network creation, emphasizing solutions assisting socialization.

SAKE IT solution provides an example of compliance with the needs arising from change management and knowledge management strategies. Before discussing its features an overview about the underlying knowledge management system development methodology is presented.

Knowledge Management System Development Methodologies

Different approaches to knowledge management can be distinguished on the basis of the investigated research questions, as the learning focused approach; the process focused approach; the technology focused approach; the environment focused (ecological) approach and the purpose focused approach (Klimkó, 2001). Researchers following the technology focused approach consider knowledge as a transferable object.

The first step of a technology based approach is often to set up a knowledge repository (Davenport, 1998), in which proper search capabilities has to be offered. A similar approach with different starting point is the one dealing with the so-called organisational memory, which is considered to be a real object that can be constructed with the tools of information technology. Abecker and his co-authors want to facilitate context-sensitive searching in the organisational memory by using different levels of ontologies (company, business area, information level) (Abecker et al., 1998).

In order to set up a knowledge repository (or sometimes referred as to build a knowledge-base or simply knowledge system) a proper methodology is required. One of the most wide-spread approaches among suitable methodologies is the CommonKADS method (Schreiber et al., 2000). The authors of CommonKADS wanted to provide a structured, verifiable and repeatable way for building a (software) system. Knowledge acquisition is done by engineering-like methods, with the help of knowledge engineering. The underlying assumption of CommonKADS is that knowledge engineering means description of the knowledge from different viewpoints, being a modelling activity where an aspect model is a proper abstraction of reality itself. CommonKADS assumes that knowledge has a stable internal structure that can be analysed by describing different roles and knowledge types. This assumption is analogous with the stability of data models in structured methodologies that help building up traditional data processing systems. The base of the methodology is a set of models consisting of six model types (Schreiber et al., 2000):

- **Organizational model:** describing the organizational environment.
- **Task model:** collecting tasks, which are considered relevant subsets of business processes. The task model globally analyses entire tasks: inputs, outputs, resources, conditions and the requirements of execution.
- **Agent model:** representing agents performing processes described in the Task model.
- **Communication model:** describing communication, information exchange, and interaction between agents.

- **Knowledge model:** consisting of an explicit, detailed description of the type and the structure of knowledge used in the course of execution.
- **Design model:** defining a technical system specification based on the requirements specification determined by the models detailed above.

Recently performed researches applying agile methods form the software engineering community (like eXtreme Programming) in the knowledge management (Hans, 2004) seem to be very promising for the management of changes. Indeed, the characteristic of agile methodologies is their attempt to shift the company's organisational and project memory from external to tacit knowledge, i.e., written documentation is replaced by communication among team members. In the SAKE project, this idea is extended by introducing semantic technologies that enable a formal and explicit representation of all factors that implement changes and their relations to knowledge and knowledge workers in order to resolve the problem of the consistent change propagation accounted in the previously mentioned system.

CASE DESCRIPTION

The SAKE methodology constitutes a hybrid composition of approaches and methodologies. Specifically, the proposed methodology takes in account a) the Know-Net method, that has been designed as a supporting tool to help the design, development, and deployment of a holistic Knowledge Management Infrastructure, b) the CommonKADS methodology (Schreiber et al., 2000), that supports structured knowledge engineering, and c) the DECOR Business Knowledge Method (Abecker et al., 2003) that constitutes a business process oriented knowledge management method consisting of a structured archive around the notion of the company's business processes which are equipped with active, context-sensitive knowledge delivery, to promote a better exploitation of knowledge sources. The *Know-Net method* elaborated by KNOW-NET (Esprit EP28928) project provides a holistic corporate knowledge management method and tool integrating content management and collaboration with advanced search and retrieval. The method is based on a knowledge asset centric framework combining the process-centred view of knowledge management (treating knowledge management as an interpersonal communication process) and the product-centred approach (which focuses on the artefacts for knowledge). The method claims that knowledge assets and knowledge objects are the common unifiers of a holistic organization-wide knowledge management environment that integrates process and content. This solution was further enhanced and tested in the LEVER project (IST-1999-20216) that helped four user companies set up knowledge repositories, facilitate knowledge exchange in communities of practice and implement procedures for capturing and diffusing best practices. CommonKADS methodology is detailed in the previous section. A structured archive has been provided by DECOR, enriching business processes with active, context-sensitive knowledge delivery to promote a better exploitation of knowledge sources. The core of the DECOR Business Knowledge Method is an extended Business Process Modelling method, including automatable knowledge retrieval activities, additional knowledge management tasks, sub-processes, and additional process variables. It provides methodological guidance for running a Business-Process Oriented Knowledge Management (BPOKM), which includes a) business process identification and analysis b) task analyses c) business process design d) ontology creation and refinement.

The objectives of the SAKE methodology are to:

- Facilitate the planning of necessary organisational changes (processes, actors, systems);
- Facilitate the (re-)structuring of PAs' knowledge resources (processes, actors, systems etc.);
- Support the adaptation of changes in policy, strategy and law from the public sector (e.g., continuous harmonization with EU regulations).

Figure 1 provides a diagrammatic overview of the SAKE methodology. The SAKE methodology consists of the following steps:

Figure 1. Overall SAKE methodology (adapted from Papadakis, 2006)

Step 1: Identify a process for testing SAKE	Step 2: Describe the selected process	Step 3: Detailed Knowledge sources analysis & ontology population	Step 4: Setting up of the SAKE solution in your organisation	Step 5: Develop your pilot plan	Step 6: Test & evaluate the SAKE solution
• Knowledge audit				• Decision making quality ontology	• Decision making quality assessment
• Selection of most promising focus area(s) and target solution		• Detailed knowledge sources analysis		• Assessment criteria	
• Processes	• Task analysis (process breakdown)	• Process and profile ontology	• Enhancement of bp models	• Trial planning	
• People	• Community & people analysis	• PA ontology	• CoP building		
• Knowledge	• Knowledge assets analysis	• Information & domain ontology	• Content annotation		
• KM business case					

- Knowledge "as is" analysis aiming to identify the current state of the Knowledge Infrastructure from the perspectives of currently existing and missing elements.
- Knowledge sources analysis involving the identification and specification of knowledge sources existing in the organization (PA).
- Ontology creation and population that involves the design and development of pilot-specific extensions and instances of the pre-developed ontologies that realize the conceptual framework of SAKE approach.
- Deployment of basic functionality and process modelling aiming the deployment of the basic functionality of Groupware and Content Management Systems in order to get a hands-on understanding of the basic SAKE functionality and provide user feedback on functionality issues.
- Testing, evaluating pilot solution.

Focus of the SAKE system itself is the integration of information, meaning homogeneous treatment of various kinds of information pieces. As a simplified example from the user's perspective, this means to be able to find and manage all relevant information in a set of systems by using a common user interface. Treating all information in a homogeneous manner requires information to be either homogeneous—which cannot be realized considering the variety of systems—or having homogeneous metadata. This latter method is viable and is extensively used in data warehouse systems for example (Inmon, 1996; Chaudhuri & Dayal, 1997; Jarke et al., 2003). According to Stojanovic et al. (2008), *information integration* requires first the integration of information sources by determining the methods of acquiring all potentially relevant information enabling smooth connection of information that can be relevant for a decision making process of an organization. Second requirement is the integrated processing of all information, ensuring a common view in order to get the most useful outcome for the decision making process. Finally, the integration of information flow with the current process and user context is necessary for defining the importance of information to the user. Information integration provides a framework for knowledge repositories needed to serve knowledge codification, acquisition and leveraging. SAKE system itself aims the realization of these requirements through offering an IT environment providing appropriate answers to the challenges of the public administration. The system consists of various components reflecting to these requirements, offering solutions to the above-mentioned problems of the public administration by being enhanced via means of information integration.

Overview of SAKE System Components

This section provides an overview about SAKE system main components, presenting them from the viewpoint of the functionalities. Figure 2 depicts system components and their interactions. Already existing, standalone open-source systems have been employed as components of the SAKE system. Their integration has been realized by specifically developed adaptors, attaching them to a homogeneous, ontology-based information bus, which is represented on the figure as the semantic layer. Adaptors are responsible capturing and transmitting all the information and user behaviour data created inside the individual components to the semantic layer. All these information are stored homogeneously in the ontologies of the semantic layer, moreover, they are interconnected by ontological relationships. Information stored in the ontologies is used by the attention management component, which extracts new information of this structured data set. In addition to the one-way information transmission to the semantic layer, functionalities of the components are also extended by ontology-based functions that are detailed later. These functions realize integration between the components themselves. On the top, a homogeneous, web-based common user interface applying portal technologies has been developed.

Figure 2. SAKE system components (adapted Stojanovic et al., 2008)

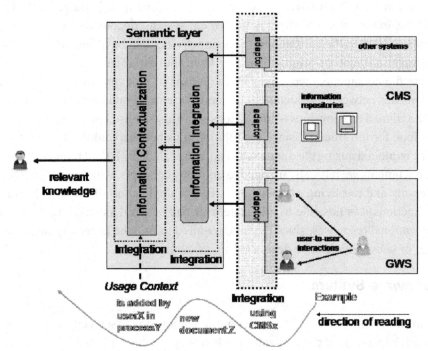

In the followings, details of the components are presented, also emphasizing the compliance for the requirements detailed before.

Content Management System

Most frequent sources of knowledge in an organization are various textual content, or in other words, documents. This form is used widely, is usually understood by every partners in a communication process, it is easy to update, index and provide searching facilities based on its content, and can be processed by humans and software as well. Content management systems can also manage other types of content like audio or video, querying facilities however are inadequate to cope with them effectively. Currently, full-text search is one of the most used means to retrieve information stored in textual form; however, it has several shortcomings, like homonyms, synonyms and other linguistic problems, also including the problem of different languages. By the introduction of ontologies as part of a semantic layer behind the components, it is possible to homogenize information stored in various types of content in the content management system, as well as to enrich the stored content with contextual information, including the current business process, activity, and task; as well as user information. The availability of this additional information enables several features that can support the work of public administrators. The typical overload situation of the administrators can be alleviated by filtering information according to the contextual information available in the semantic layer. This way, in the case of content management system, documents and knowledge that are relevant to the current processes or activities can be offered automatically. Necessary information originates either from the usage patterns of other users, or from the documents themselves by the means of indexing and by establishing relationships between the document or content elements and ontological concepts. These assigned relationships – annotations – can also be used in the cases when the users look for information, since the relationships between ontology concepts can also be exploited during the queries (Stojanovic et al., 2007). By having this annotation, documents are basically mapped to ontology concepts, which can also ease the processing and retrieving of documents. By the application of these technologies and functions it is possible to attenuate overload, as well as enabling more agile organizational responses, since the time required to find the necessary information pieces or knowledge can be decreased significantly.

Groupware System

The information that is hidden in communication processes can also provide a great added value to the organization, when they can be exploited to some extent.

Groupware system supports communication and collaboration activities by offering common facilities like discussion forums, shared calendars and notification services. This component also employs the functions of the semantic layer, meaning that all information created in the component's facilities is also stored in the ontologies, together with contextual information that was detailed in the case of content management system. As an additional feature, annotation is also present in this component via the means of ranking, indicating the usefulness of a conversation item for solving the targeted problem. Besides, usage patterns are also recorded in the ontologies, which contribute to the preciseness of information retrieval. Facilities of the groupware system contribute to the preservation of knowledge as communication in the organization usually contains the fastest reflections to the changes of the environment. This component contributes therefore to the adaptation to the changes as well as to the externalization of the knowledge, since knowledge is formed in a more-or-less tangible form during conversations.

Change Notification System

Main role of change notification system is to monitor the environment of the organization. Its current implementation focuses on textual information sources, although it can be extended according to the needs. Common application of CNS is the monitoring of changes in legal regulations that affect public administration organizations or commercial companies as well. This facility provides a deeper integration of the organization in its economic environment with a minimal amount of human attention, contributing this way to the competence of fast adaptation of the organization. The changes noticed in the monitored environment are delivered to the ontologies and are processed by the public administrators, since it is still not a realistic requirement to have the external sources automatically processed and incorporated into the common knowledge of the organization.

Workflow Management System

Business processes are key points in SAKE system operation as providing contextual information to other components, as well as guiding the users during problem solving processes. In a public administration environment processes are determined strictly by legal regulations. These processes can be described in a process model and a workflow can be built upon that. In the case of SAKE system, processes are modelled using an ontological description in order to be able to integrate them with other information in the system through the ontologies. This model is converted into an executable format and fed to a workflow engine, which offers a performance gain as compared to an ontological execution. During the process execution, all information provided by the users and all events happened in the context of the process are stored in instances of the process in the ontology. Ontology always provides this way an adequate picture of the current state of the process, constituting also the business context, which is used by every other component as described before. It has to be considered, however, that knowledge-intensive processes cannot be described fully in a formal way. In the case of the Hungarian pilot detailed below, a ministerial proposal has to be developed by a consulting body, which involves mainly experts' discussion. In this case, support of the workflow system is limited to the frames of the process, while the components of the system are used upon need, providing all additional semantic information as described above. According to the discussion above, having well-defined processes and workflows contribute to the transparency of the operation of public administration institutions. This approach also represents a way to preserve organizational knowledge crystallized in best practices by means of formalizing them into processes.

Attention Management System

The attention management system (AMS) component of the SAKE system provides information according to the semantic information stored in the ontologies of the semantic layer. AMS employs a reasoner (KAON2 has been selected in the project for performance reasons) and executes various predefined and ad-hoc queries, delivering information to the user that are thought to be relevant according the rules. AMS is used for providing the semantics-related functions described above, like the delivery of context-related documents and discussions in a given environment, as well as finding content-related information to a specific domain.

SAKE components support acquiring new resources with reconfiguration change strategy; they facilitate network creation (e.g., groupware component) and knowledge codification (e.g., content management component) as well. Next section details SAKE solution validation through the Hungarian pilot.

The Hungarian Pilot: Higher Education Portfolio Alignment with World of Labour Needs

SAKE solution was validated on three cases of PA organizations located in three different countries: Hungary, Poland, and Slovakia. Pilots were set up and organized according to SAKE methodology described above.

Higher education in Hungary had to face several challenges recently, like decreasing student population, stronger competition between higher education institutes, capacity overflow and compliance to the reforms of European Higher Education initiated by Bologna declaration. Hungarian Government decided a large-scale reform aiming to modify the Hungarian higher educational system, both the educational structure and the operating model. By connecting to the European Higher Education Area, Hungary needs to modernize operating processes, improve quality radically, and introduce strategic human resource management. The labour market demands three times more persons from vocational training, compared to the graduated number of students. Structure of the higher education shifted towards the humanities, arts, legal studies and business administration in Hungary and in most countries of Europe, compared to engineering and education in applied sciences. Structural problems require restructuring the educational portfolio and a sharp modification in teachers' education. Restructuring is also a strategic human resource management task with several risks. Hungarian case in SAKE project aimed higher education portfolio alignment with world of labour needs, which means the support of validation. Purpose of validation is to match the individual's competences with the needs of the labour market (Thomsen, 2008). The alignment process is a "strategic" problem at the field of education, which consists of knowledge intensive tasks. Different domains and cultural backgrounds of the players in the pilot process require unified and consistent interpretation, which is provided by underlying ontologies. Additional challenge is the reconciliation of the central planning and higher educational institutes' autonomy.

Main steps in Hungarian pilot process were the following:

- Description of the educational output by the Higher Education Manager (supported by SAKE semantic layer and CMS).
- Updating the database containing the actual figures of education (like number of students, who can start their studies in a certain year).
- Data collection about job opportunities, labour requirements (supported by SAKE CMS and CNS).
- Job profiling (supported by SAKE semantic layer and CMS).
- Comparison of existing job profiles and educational output (supported by SAKE semantic layer).
- Labour market forecast preparation for 3-5 years (supported by SAKE groupware and CMS).
- Job profiling – determination of world of labour needs (supported by SAKE groupware and SAKE semantic layer).
- Comparison of forecasted job profiles and educational output (supported by SAKE semantic layer).
- Planning further actions (supported by SAKE Groupware and CMS).

All steps were supported by workflow component. Higher education portfolio means the offer for the students in order to achieve their smooth integration to the labour market after their graduation. Higher education portfolio is normally prepared by public servants five or three years before the exact needs and situation of the labour market demands are known. Educational output (educational offer) is determined by higher educational portfolio, it contains the details of degree programs. Job profiling provides a job profile document for SAKE system. Job profiles are stored by CMS and their annotations are maintained in the semantic layer. Forecasting of labour market needs is a must, meanwhile codification of demands are also needed. Two primary roles are decisive in the pilot process, the Higher Education Manager and Educational Planner. Higher Education Manager is responsible for the educational output, while Educational Planner prepares the job profiles, detailing educational demand of labour market. SAKE system is an excellent candidate to support PA employees in the above mentioned pilot process, because of the following reasons:

- Higher Education Manager and Educational Planner are facing with information overload; educational output, job profiles, regulation, economic environment have to be processed during the planning process.
- More accurate planning is needed, due to the fast changing demographic and economic tendencies.
- Pilot process requires collaboration and cooperation among the partners involved in the process.
- Knowledge used in the pilot needed codification.
- "Matching" had no IT support earlier.
- Pilot process requires a conceptual framework.
- Pilot process needs documentation and strong control.

Higher educational portfolio determines the higher education offer, which consists of graduated students. From the labour market perspective the most important characters of the offers are the graduated students' competencies, namely their skills, abilities and knowledge, which make them a proper candidate to comply with a certain job. These competencies are defined by higher education degree programs. World of labour needs is the educational demand of labour market, which is described by job profiles collected from the publicly available resources, like recruitment databases and decisive Hungarian job portals. Educational output (degree programs), the offer and the job profiles the demand are compared in terms of competencies. Competencies are used as specific statements of areas of personal capability that enable to perform successfully in their jobs by completing tasks effectively (Mentzas et al., 2006).

Development of domain ontology for the Hungarian pilot was the most important task of system implementation and customization. This ontology contained descriptions of the above-mentioned competencies and educational outputs. In this phase of implementation, domain experts have been invited to cooperate on the development of ontology to ensure a common model. In addition, documents of accredited qualifications and courses have been processed in order to determine detailed competencies offered and get adequate data on higher educational output.

During the operation of the system, job profiles have been processed as annotated documents, during which relationships have been established between the job profiles and competencies. Ontological reasoning have been employed to realize the matching between educational outputs and annotated job profiles in order to provide input for the rest of decision making preparation process. Figure 3 showcases a screenshot from the SAKE system.

The following user scenario presents SAKE system's support for Higher Education Manager during the educational planning process.

Higher Education Manager is preparing the educational output, which he already did many times before. However, the corresponding law (Act on Higher Education, 2004) has been changed recently, so that CMS system warns him that he should be more careful in the resolution. Indeed, the context of the case is recognized and the module Attention Management searches for the semantically relevant recent changes in documents that are related to the given case, in order to inform the user. Moreover, the changed parts of relevant documents can be highlighted (Figure 4).

Figure 3. Screenshot from SAKE system

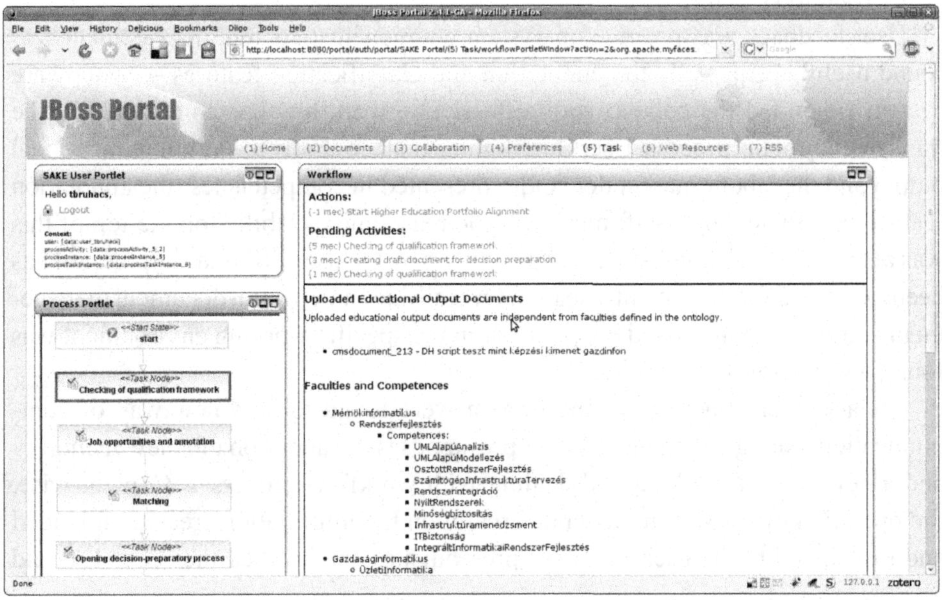

Figure 4. Higher education manager is coping with changes in law

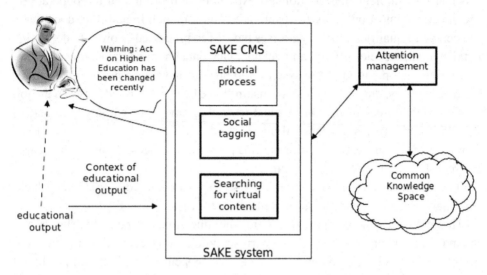

Users' Experiences and Feedback

The Hungarian trial team comprised of labour market experts, higher education experts and ministry staff responsible for higher education development. Overall, users were satisfied with the system capabilities. Several improvements were identified as a result of SAKE's intervention, as the possibility of involving more stakeholders in the process in timely manner; or making complex decision making easier (Samiotis, 2009).

User feedback was positive on system components: content management was found useful – especially the annotation and classification features –, groupware system supported the collaboration effectively; workflow has contributed to the transparency of the process. Users highlighted that the ability to have the educational output and the labour market demand represented in competencies (the annotation feature) is valuable by itself; moreover the reasoning capability on the top of this was also found very interesting and promising by the users. Similar impression has been expressed for the semantic search. Overall, having a central document management solution and improved cooperation in the specific working environment was found a very useful approach.

Collaboration functions of the system were found to be a new way of communication among colleagues, which presupposes the adoption of a new mentality and a new way of working and dealing with workflow processes. Content-wise, the operation of the system depends greatly on the information created, uploaded and exchanged by its users. If these prerequisites are fulfilled then SAKE could act and react to users' requests responsively and timely. Users have found pushing of information as a strong feature of SAKE, although it should be refined more in the future. As a conclusion, it is agreed that effectiveness of this feature depends largely on the users' contribution.

On the negative side, users have mentioned difficulties of navigation inside the system as well as the immature graphical user interface, which are caused by the fact that during the prototype development, more attention was paid to the functionalities than to the user experience.

The knowledge management-based approach of this pilot process was beneficial for PA's from several aspects:

- It helped to refine knowledge and change management strategy of the PA
- Pilot process became more transparent, faster, documented and controlled easier than before
- Knowledge used by the pilot process was codified and available as explicit knowledge for another processes
- Matching of educational output and labour market demands got IT support
- Common conceptual framework was provided.

Higher education portfolio planning got useful feedback from the system, e.g., by highlighting those competencies, which are required by the labour market, but not available in the higher education. Important experience of the pilot was that the introduction of an innovative solution, like SAKE requires special knowledge management related techniques, like the customization of organizational culture in order to make public servants more committed and motivated. Hungarian pilot highlighted that SAKE system can support lowering the unemployment rate through the more precisely planning of higher education portfolio.

SUMMARY AND CONCLUSION

SAKE main components provided several tangible, beneficial features for PA organization and its employees as well; amongst other it supported to refine their change management and knowledge management strategy. Satisfying the need for adaptive, fast and knowledge-based decisions was facilitated by semantically-enhanced components. Change management component has provided quick discovery of changes in the environment of the organization. Semantic-enhanced content management system has offered more effective information retrieval via mapping content elements to ontology concepts. Groupware system has facilitated decision preparatory discussions by annotation functions. Workflow system has orchestrated the decision preparation process by offering the framework of activities. Finally, attention management system has filtered semantic information captured in all other components during the operation of the system by applying pre-defined and ad-hoc rules. SAKE system provided several added values for public administrators' work, like the improved communication and collaboration quality. Threads, "comment on comment" support has made communication more structured. SAKE system provided a framework for knowledge externalization; educational demand and job profiles are structured, organized and annotated. Semantic layer offered common terminology and taxonomy, which are important where several stakeholders with different background are working in the same process. Another useful feature is the notification of potentially interesting changes. Main results of SAKE project were the following:

- SAKE methodology;
- SAKE ontologies;
- SAKE components (code and documentation);
    ◦ Semantic Layer;
    ◦ Attention Management System;
    ◦ Change Management System;
    ◦ Workflow Management System;
    ◦ Content Management System;
    ◦ Groupware System.

CURRENT CHALLENGES

Nevertheless, SAKE's propositions for work were not assimilated by the end users to the desired level. This finding has a huge value for this project and also for other similar initiatives. It proved again that technological interventions cannot be capitalized unless the organizational environment is prepared to do so. One way to tackle this problem is to offer methodological support in all phases of the technology intervention, from introduction, familiarization, adaptation, rethinking, up to operalization, then to re-invention and back to adaptation again. This issue was attempted to be addressed by the SAKE methodology, but further work should be done for the confrontation of organizational barriers and the prescription of countermeasures.

SAKE trials have proven that despite any difficulties it is worthwhile to invest in knowledge management. SAKE as an ICT tool realizes in its functionalities i.e., content management, groupware, workflow, all basic KM manifestations for the creation, sharing and application of knowledge. It also introduces a novel approach in KM through the notion and implementation of attention management, which is shifting KM's support from pull-based to push-based approach.

It has been concluded that ontology engineering is a difficult task and can be a bottleneck in knowledge acquisition, but the chosen methodology has a decisive role regarding the quality of the end product and facilitates development. Building ontology is a cooperative task of many experts requiring a collaborative environment during the development. By the inclusion of the environmental changes, SAKE system supports the creation of a common organizational knowledge repository, which helps avoiding knowledge inconsistencies and ambiguities in the organization. SAKE system had some disadvantages as well, like ignorance of recipients against continuous notifications. Lack of computer skills or missing trust can cause difficulties in the systems' operation. The system may appear too complicated, which can hinder its usage. Lessons learnt, experiences gained in SAKE project can be applied in several other fields, especially the way of managing information overload seems to be beneficial for other PA organizations.

SAKE knowledge management solution provided effective and efficient approach for the management of challenges and problems detailed in the first section. It provided appropriate support for all discussed change management strategic approaches. *Reconfiguration of existing resources* is supported through groupware component and the collaborative document editing feature of content management system which are the functions focusing on the utilization of the tacit knowledge of PA experts. *Acquiring new resources without reconfiguration* is supported by the ontologies, which have been used to preserve explicit knowledge; as well as by the content management system serving as a knowledge repository. *Acquiring new resources with reconfiguration* is supported via the combination of the previous approaches. The current situation of economic downturn and political change forces public administration to follow the reconfigure existing resources strategy, which is appropriate on the short run, however the authors are convinced that the combined application of personalization and codification strategy results in long-term success. Ratio between personalization and codification strategy is influenced by environmental effects and change management strategies.

According to the experiences gained during the system development, ontology development is one of the most complex and time consuming tasks that requires professional experience involving a lot of expert discussions and efforts. On its technological side, currently available ontology reasoners applied in the system require many resources in terms of computing time and operative storage capacities. Development of more efficient reasoning engines or enabling parallel processing of ontologies can encourage the development of information integration solutions, like the one depicted in this article.

Results of the SAKE project can be applied on other fields as well. It can be used by organizations to improve their change management or knowledge management practices; or other research projects can build on the foundation of SAKE project. In the case of the ongoing OntoHR project (LLP -1 - 2009-1-HU-LEONARDO-LMP), experiences and products of the Hungarian pilot case of SAKE have been extensively used. In UbiPOL project (FP7-ICT-2009-4, ICT-2009.7.3: ICT for Governance and Policy Modelling), the approach of SAKE workflow solution was investigated in workflow modelling.

SAKE approach to ontology-based matching can also be exploited in similar matching tasks, like matching between assembly plant and suppliers, which also forms a worthwhile research direction.

There is also a great potential in the presented ontology-based information integration approach. On one side, information push approach realized by Attention management system was found useful, which implies on one hand that further research should be conducted on how to extract information by using ontological reasoning. On the other hand, positive user experiences noted that there is a need for a homogenization among these complex systems and functions, and this approach is capable of realizing a general-purpose approach of system integration and homogenization.

ACKNOWLEDGMENT

Project SAKE (IST-2005-027128) is funded by the European Commission's 6th Framework Programme. This publication reflects only the author's views. The European Community, represented by the Commission of the European Communities is not liable for any use that may be made of the information contained herein. Further information regarding SAKE can be found at http://www.sake-project.org/. TÁMOP-4.2.1/B-09/1/KMR-2010-0005 is a research and innovation program of the Corvinus University of Budapest aiming ICT-based analyses of knowledge transfer, sharing and knowledge codification fields.

REFERENCES

Abecker, A., Bernardi, A., Hinkelmann, K., Kühn, O., & Sintek, M. (1998). Toward a technology for organisational memories. *IEEE Intelligent Systems*, *13*(3), 40–48. doi:10.1109/5254.683209

Abecker, A., Mentzas, G., Ntioudis, S., & Papavassiliou, G. (2003). Business process modelling and enactment for task-specific information support. *Wirtschaftsinformatik, 1,* 977–996.

Abrahamson, E. (2000). Change without pain. *Harvard Business Review,* 75–79.

Barney, J. B. (1991). Firm resources and sustained competitive advantage. *Journal of Management, 17*(1), 99–120. doi:10.1177/014920639101700108

Barquin, R. (2010). *Knowledge management in the federal government: A 2010 update.* Retrieved from http://www.b-eye-network.com/view/14527

Bloodgood, J. M., & Salisbury, W. D. (2001). Understanding the influence of organizational change strategies on information technology and knowledge management strategies. *Decision Support System Journal, 31,* 55–69. doi:10.1016/S0167-9236(00)00119-6

Bray, D. A. (2008). *Information pollution, knowledge overload, limited attention spans, and our responsibilities as IS professionals.* Paper presented at the Global Information Technology Management Association World Conference, Atlanta, GA.

Chaudhuri, S., & Dayal, U. (1997). An overview of data warehousing and OLAP technology. *SIGMOD Record, 26*(1), 65–74. doi:10.1145/248603.248616

Davenport, T. H., Long, D. W., & Beers, M. C. (1998). Successful knowledge management projects. *Sloan Management Review, 39,* 43–57.

Day, J. D., & Wendler, J. C. (1998). Best practice and beyond: Knowledge strategies. *The McKinsey Quarterly, 1,* 19–25.

Fehér, P. (2004). Combining knowledge and change management at consultancies. *Electronic Journal of Knowledge Management, 2*(1), 19–32.

Haggie, K., & Kingston, J. (2003). Choosing your knowledge management strategy. *Journal of Knowledge Management Practice,* 1-24.

Hans, D. D. (2004). Agile knowledge management in practice. In G. Melnik & H. Holz (Eds.), *Proceedings of the 6th International Workshop on Advances in Learning Software Organizations* (LNCS 3096, pp. 137-143).

Hansen, M. T., Nohria, N., & Tierney, T. (1999). What's your strategy for managing knowledge? *Harvard Business Review,* 106–116.

Hayes, J. (2002). *The theory and practice of change management.* Basingstoke, UK: Palgrave.

Heeks, R. (2006). *Implementing and managing e-government*. London, UK: Sage.

Himma, K. (2007). The concept of information overload: A preliminary step in understanding the nature of a harmful information-related condition. *Ethics and Information Technology, 9*(4), 259–272. doi:10.1007/s10676-007-9140-8

Holsapple, C. W. (2003). Knowledge and its attributes. In *Handbook on knowledge management 1: Knowledge matters*. Heidelberg, Germany: Springer-Verlag.

Inmon, W. (1996). The data warehouse and data mining. *Communications of the ACM, 39*(11), 49–50. doi:10.1145/240455.240470

Jarke, M., Lenzerini, M., Vassiliou, Y., & Vassiliadis, P. (2003). *Fundamentals of data warehouses*. Berlin, Germany: Springer-Verlag.

Jashapara, A. (2004). *Knowledge management: An integrated approach*. London, UK: Prentice Hall/Pearson Education Limited.

Klimkó, G. (2001). *Mapping organisational knowledge*. Unpublished doctoral dissertation, Corvinus University, Budapest, Hungary.

Kő, A., & Klimkó, G. (2009). Towards a framework of information technology tools for supporting knowledge management. In Noszkay, E. (Ed.), *The capital of intelligence - The intelligence of capital* (pp. 65–85). Budapest, Hungary: Foundation for Information Society.

Kotter, J. P. (1995). Leading change: Why transformation efforts fail. *Harvard Business Review*, 59–67.

Kotter, J. P. (1997). On leading change: A conversation with John P. Kotter. *Strategy and Leadership, 25*(1), 18–23. doi:10.1108/eb054576

Lippitt, R., Watson, J., & Westley, B. (1958). *The dynamics of planned change*. New York, NY: Harcourt Brace.

Manasco, B. (1996). Leading firms develop knowledge strategies. *Knowledge Inc., 1*(6), 26–35.

Mentzas, G., Draganidis, F., & Chamopoulou, P. (2006). *An ontology based tool for competency management and learning path*. Paper presented at the I-KNOW Conference, Graz, Austria.

Mintzberg, H. (1991). The effective organization: Forces and forms. *Sloan Management Review, 32*(2), 57–67.

Nonaka, I., & Takeuchi, H. (1995). *The knowledge-creating company: How Japanese companies create the dynamics of innovation.* New York, NY: Oxford University Press.

Papadakis, A. (2006). *D5 - As is analysis.* Geneva, Switzerland: SAKE Project.

Prochaska, J. O., & DiClemente, C. C. (1986). Toward a comprehensive model of change. In Miller, W. R., & Heather, N. (Eds.), *Treating addictive behaviors: Processes of change* (pp. 3–27). New York, NY: Plenum Press.

Riege, A., & Lindsay, N. (2006). Knowledge management in the public sector: Stakeholder partnerships in the public policy development. *Journal of Knowledge Management, 10*(3), 24–39. doi:10.1108/13673270610670830

Samiotis, K. (Ed.). (2009). *D28 evaluation report.* Geneva, Switzerland: SAKE Project.

Schreiber, G. (2000). *Knowledge engineering and management, the CommonKADS methodology.* Cambridge, MA: MIT Press.

Stojanovic, N., Apostolou, D., Dioudis, S., Gábor, A., Kovács, B., Kő, A., et al. (2008). *D24 – Integration plan.* Retrieved from http://www.sake-project.org/fileadmin/bro-chures/D21_2nd_iteration_prototype_of_semantic-based_groupware_system.pdf

Stojanovic, N., Kovács, B., Kő, A., Papadakis, A., Apostolou, D., Dioudis, D., et al. (2007). *D16B – 1st iteration prototype of semantic-based content management system.* Retrieved from http://www.sake-project.org/fileadmin/filemounts/sake/D16B_First_Iteration_Prototype_of_SCMS_final.pdf

Strebel, P. (1996). Why do employees resist change? *Harvard Business Review,* 86–92.

Thomsen, R. (2008). *Elements in the validation process.* Retrieved from http://www.nordvux.net/page/481/cases.htm

Wernerfelt, B. (1984). A resource-based view of the firm. *Strategic Management Journal, 5,* 171–180. doi:10.1002/smj.4250050207

Wiig, K. M. (1997). Knowledge management: Where did it come from and where will it go? *Expert Systems with Applications, 13*(1), 1–14. doi:10.1016/S0957-4174(97)00018-3

This work was previously published in the Journal of Cases on Information Technology, Volume 13, Issue 3, edited by Mehdi Khosrow-Pour, pp. 1-20, copyright 2011 by IGI Publishing (an imprint of IGI Global).

Chapter 8

Analysis–Sensitive Conversion of Administrative Data into Statistical Information Systems

Mariagrazia Fugini
Politecnico di Milano, Italy

Mirko Cesarini
Università degli Studi di Milano-Bicocca, Italy

Mario Mezzanzanica
Università degli Studi di Milano-Bicocca, Italy

EXECUTIVE SUMMARY

This chapter presents a case study concerning the development of a Statistical Information System (SIS) out of data coming from administrative archives of the PAs. Such archives are a rich source of up to date information, but an attempt to use them as sources for statistical analysis reveals errors and incompatibilities among each other that do not permit their usage as a statistical and decision support basis. These errors and incompatibilities are usually undetected during administrative use, since they do not affect their day-by-day use in the PAs; however they need to be fixed before performing any further aggregate analysis. The reader is engaged with the basic aspects involved in building a SIS out of administrative data, such as design of an integration model for different and heterogeneous data sources, improvement

DOI: 10.4018/978-1-4666-0981-5.ch008

of the overall data quality, removal of errors that might impact on the correctness of statistical analysis, design of a data warehouse for statistical analysis, and design of a multidimensional database to develop indicators for decision support. Finally, some examples are presented concerning the information that can be obtained by making use of a SIS constructed out of Registry and Income Office archives.

ORGANIZATION BACKGROUND

Public Administrations (PAs) are facing profound institutional and organizational changes requiring managers, stakeholders, and responsible statesmen to increase their ability in quick decision making processes. In this context, information related to individual and collective needs plays a large and relevant role, and therefore a deep knowledge of the observed phenomena and an increased degree of timeliness, quality, and efficiency is required.

The case study described in this article concerns the development of a *SIS* out of data coming from administrative archives managed by some PAs, namely the Registry Office of a large municipality and the Income Office of the country (for privacy reasons we refer to the municipality with the *M* tag and to the country with the *C* tag). The project described in this case study aims at integrating the information contents of the archives to provide to the decision makers a set of accurate and up-to-date information describing some characteristics of the population living in *M*.

Here we summarize some descriptive data about the PAs and the statistical research center involved:

Registry of *M*
- ○ Type of business: **PA services**
- ○ Products/services provided: **Registry activities**
- ○ **City dimensions:** about 1,300,000 resident inhabitants

Income office of country *C*
- ○ Type of business: **PA services**
- ○ **Products/services provided:** tax collection, tax related documentation collection

Statistical Research Center that developed the *SIS*
- ○ **Type of business:** non profit organization
- ○ **Products/services provided:** statistical analysis, statistical information system design, and management

A huge amount of changes occurred in the economical and social context in the last year in *C*, and, consequently, traditional and well known static scenarios in PAs have been replaced by more complex and dynamic ones. The PA, as well as the political decision makers, are currently faced with various management and organizational issues, and hence they need accurate and up-to-date information on some specific topics and sectors affected by the decision they are called to make.

SETTING THE STAGE

The development of a *SIS* can provide answers to the information needs, by providing support to analysis, monitoring, and control activities. Still, the only available data in the context of National-level statistics come from National Observatories, and are mainly constructed on the basis of *sample surveys*. The significance of these data decreases relevantly when small territorial environments are investigated (and this is the case of the *M* object of our study, with respect to the whole country *C*). On the contrary, PA *administrative sources* are very good representative data sets of the whole population and contain "fresh" data. Statistical analysis applied to them allows obtaining up-to-date information on the whole population. Moreover, the introduction of ICT has empowered the availability and fruition of administrative databases, making information accessible to organizations and institutions for further surveys (Sundgren, 1996). Some international experiences show that the integrated use of tax-related databases together with Registry databases enables to obtain rich information regarding both income trends and citizens (StatisticsDenmark, 2000). However, this possibility has not been fully exploited yet, because administrative data are often incorrect and unsuitable, in their format and contents, to be used for statistical and decision making. Hence, data need to be cleaned up from errors and pre-processed in several ways before being reversed into statistical databases.

Within an organization, a *SIS* is loaded and continuously fed using data sources derived from the administrative and management systems. Its role is the management of organizational and administrative data to extract knowledge, and to support domain exploration, verification, and control. An official definition of a *SIS* is given in UNECE (2000), where a *SIS* is described as "an informative system aimed at collecting storing, managing, and distributing statistical information."

On the basis of this definition, a *SIS* has two main purposes:

1. To support decision-making processes through the construction of *directional indicators* which are the final result of data collection, analysis, and processing activities

2.   To return information to the management systems useful for improving data quality along time

A *SIS* should meet requirements of availability, reliability, impartiality, pertinence, privacy, transparency, minimal overhead, and efficiency. Moreover, a *SIS* has to evolve along time in order to integrate data coming from new sources, with new data which may be the result of a new provision of a previously integrated archive or a completely new archive.

Before describing the issues related to *SIS* development, some related works is presented. In recent years, a marked tendency is reported towards re-using statistical data, notably administrative sources (Hoffmann, 1995), (Thomson & Holmy, 1998). This, in turn, has sharply increased the demand for easy access to a variety of pre-existing data sources (Sundgren, 1996). Some works address the issue of integrating existing data sources of national or regional statistical offices, or in general of data providers of comparable nature (Denk & Froeschl, 2000), (Hatzopoulos, Karali, & Viglas, 1998). These works focus on semantic integration and context translation of different sources into a uniform schema, which can then be used to perform composite analysis.

Other works leverage metadata classification to drive the data integration and elaboration (Papageorgiou, Pentaris, Theodorou, Vardaki, & Petrakos, 2001). Another category of works refer to quality of data (IQ1, 2005), and to specific quality assurance for census data (CensusBureau, 2005). These works rely on the existence of sources of data sets already formatted for statistical analysis; this is not the case of administrative data. The production of statistics is a further ancillary use of administrative data: this means that the measuring procedure is often out of the statistician's control and that administrative concepts are usually incompatible with statistical ones.

In Buzzigoli (2002), an experience is reported on how a *SIS* can be fed using PA's or large enterprises' archives; it focuses on the organizational issues necessary to build an efficient information system inside a PA structure. However a discussion concerning data quality, consistency, and archive integration is still an open issue in the research area concerning the elaboration required to turn administrative data into statistical archives.

The phases involved in the *SIS* design are presented in the next subsection.

Building a Statistical Information System

A *SIS* is usually built starting from heterogeneous data sources, in particular, data stored in *administrative archives*, which are the storage schema used by processes executed by *management and administration systems* of organizations. Administrative data are differently characterized, depending on the managed information contents, on the database design, and on the management and organizational choices taken to build the information repositories. Consequently, *SIS* development requires to integrate data coming from many sources and to ensure that the integration result meets some given *quality requirements*. The first operation in building a *SIS* is a detailed study of the source archives. Subsequently, each single archive is inspected for internal errors and inconsistencies, and if necessary, cleansed through a data cleansing step. Afterwards, the various archives are cross-checked for mutual inconsistencies, undergoing a second set of cleansing operations. Finally, data are integrated into a global archive, whose data structure has been designed in the meanwhile. Cleansing and integration operations, although described separately, are executed in combination within the overall process workflow. Data integration and cleansing issues are now analyzed; then, data quality and filtering issues are discussed.

Data Integration and Cleansing

In order to build a *SIS* out of heterogeneous data sources, the first step consists in analyzing the available source archives. Subsequently, a global integrated schema has to be developed. Data coming from different archives are structured according to different, most often incompatible, local schemas. Thus, the need arises for a global integrated schema. When constructing the integrated schema, two cases can occur:

1. If the provisioning is an *update of a previously integrated archive*, the data model to be adhered to is already set up. In such case, a large part of the analysis effort consists in re-organizing data, to make them compatible with the adopted model. The archives structures can evolve along time; this requires a tuning of the mappings between the global and the local level schemas.
2. If the provisioning comes from a *newly adopted archive*, a new global integrated schema must be designed, with proper definitions of the involved information entities and their relationships.

In both cases, *metadata* of the single archives need to be mapped into the common standard adopted for the global integration schema. The adoption of a common metadata *dictionary* is a key premise to perform comparisons among metadata related to different archives.

Further steps are the definition of a mapping schema between the global integrated schema and the local schemas. Finally, the plan of data migration towards the integrated archive (an instance of the global integration schema) is detailed.

During *data migration*, low quality data issues may arise, such as inconsistency, incorrectness, low timeliness, or misalignment. Moreover, data loaded into the global integration schema instance might reveal unsuitable for the analysis needs. Both issues should be addressed before proceeding with the analysis. Sometimes changes to the global integration schema are required. For these reasons, the whole process is usually managed iteratively, aimed at progressively tuning the global integration schema and the migration procedures.

The criteria used to match elements of heterogeneous schemas are based on heuristics that are not always easily captured in a precise mathematical way. Thus, schema matching is often subjective. Moreover, the schema descriptions may not completely capture the semantics of the described data, and there may be several plausible mappings between two schemas. This subjectivity makes it valuable to have the user input driving the match and the user contribution in validating the results. This guidance may come via an initial mapping employing a *dictionary* or *thesaurus*, such as a library of terms and of known mappings. Then an algorithm should be selected to transfer data values between corresponding elements, according to the schema correspondence previously generated.

Data Quality Improvement

One of the main problems in using administrative databases for statistical and decision making purposes is the presence of errors, duplications, inconsistencies, or unsuitability that do not affect the regular use of the archive for *administrative purposes* (Helfert & Herrmann, 2005), but highly impact the meaningfulness of the archive for *statistical purposes*. Such errors are hardly noticed in administrative activities, and, even when discovered, they are usually tolerated. However, these errors, together with low quality of data, can negatively affect further statistical analysis. In fact administrative databases are employed to access information describing a *single item* at a time (e.g., the address of a person), while statistical analysis deals with *collection of items* (e.g., number of people live within a given area). This different use may unveil simple errors, like duplicate records, or complex errors, for example, citizens who, according to the Registry Office, live in a town different (e.g., a suburb) from the actual residence town. This can happen when the Registry Office of a town manages the registries of small neighbour Municipality, and citizens living close to the boundaries are erroneously assigned to the wrong town.

Low data quality problems range from *simple syntactical inconsistencies* (e.g., different abbreviations for the same data item) or misspelled items, to missing associations among items, which prevent from a correct interpretation of data for statistical analysis. Typically, statistical analysis requires exploring *relationships* within archives, which were originally designed with no care for integration aims. Hence, *correspondences* and *dependencies* across and within the sources may be not well defined, or the schema or semantics might be missing, which leads to unpredictable trustworthiness of the results of the integration step. Two data *quality dimensions* should be investigated, according to the framework proposed in Wang & Strong (1996), namely: a data- intrinsic dimension and a process-specific dimension. Intrinsic data quality dimensions relate to properties that depend on the very nature of the data item; an example is whether the family status of a citizen is up-to-date. Process-specific quality dimensions describe properties that depend on the process where data are used. Data intrinsic qualities are related to: Syntactic and Semantic Accuracy, Completeness, Currency, Internal Consistency, Duplicate Records, and Missing Records; while process-specific qualities are related to Timeliness, Source Reliability, Confidentiality, and Partially Invalid Record Groups. More information about the two data quality sets can be found in appendix A.

Some of the outlined problems may be fixed by performing *data cleansing actions*. Data cleansing methods intended for issues related to *single sources*, that refer to errors and inconsistencies in the actual data (and that are not visible at the schema level), and methods that address *multi-source* issues, are distinguished between. Depending on the kind of conflicts to be resolved and on the available additional information, various methods of data cleansing can be applied, classified as *inference based*, where cleansing is performed by discovering patterns within the data and using such patterns to derive data cleansing rules, and *data based*, usually applied to clean a specific type of data according to a pre-specified set of rules, usually domain dependent.

Since data cleansing methods deliver results with a certain degree of reliability, results must be validated manually, by employing various data quality metrics such as accuracy, consistency, completeness, or timeliness (*integration quality* criteria). In the integration step, a deeper knowledge of the archives is gained. This process may be repeated several times, achieving better results and deeper knowledge on the archives at each iteration step. The activity of data filtering starts by choosing quality criteria. A filter may be summarized as a black box that takes a set of data records in input and provides two distinct output sets: the *filtered data* and the *rejected data records*. The first set is the result of selection and data manipulation operations, while the second set is composed of records discarded by some selection operations. A record may be rejected for many reasons: for example, the filtering criteria could not be applied, or some inconsistencies have been found, or no quality criteria were fulfilled. The lower the quality of the original data is, the stricter the quality criteria, and the larger the amount of the discarded records.

CASE DESCRIPTION

The concepts illustrated so far, are now presented within the context of a specific case study. As previously outlined, the case mainly focuses on the integration of the information content of two PA archives: the Registry Office of M and the Income Office of the including country C. The Income Office is managed at the national level, while the Registry Office is managed independently by each city. The Income Office provides fine-grained and up-to-date information about citizens, while the Registry Office provides information about the address where people live and the family relationships (concerning the latter, although some information can be guessed from the Income Office data as well, the Registry Office can provide richer and more up-to-date information). The involved PAs extracted data from their databases and provided such data to a Research Centre in charge of executing the statistical analysis and to build the *SIS*. The data sets provided by the involved PAs will be described in more detail.

Data provided by the Income Office have been delivered by means of a set of files organized according to a form type division, namely every file containing all the information related to a single form type managed by the Income Office. The form type division is related to the forms used by citizens to declare their income and to compute their taxation rates and amounts. Three different forms are available[1]: a generalized form (A), a simplified version (B) of form A, useful for employed or retired people who do not have other incomes, and a form (C) filled in by the employer in place of the employees. A citizen working for two or more employers is reported in as many C forms as the number of employers which he/she works for. Moreover, a worker may submit an A form which declares some additional types of income (e.g., real estate rental incomes). The worker has to declare in the A form all the incomes he/she earns, even those already declared by the employers in the C form. Consequently, the forms managed by the Income Office are likely to contain duplicate information: if a person works for two or more companies, the same person will fill form A, declaring both incomes, while each company will fill an instance of form C, each reporting only the income provided by the company.

Although the Income Office provided three different data files for the analysis (one for the each form type), the data structure was the same for all files. The data structure was conceived as a superset of all information contained within the forms. An example of data record is reported in Figure 1. Concerning data provided by the Registry Office, these have been provided as flat text files, with a record structure similar to the one reported in Figure 2.

Information derivable from the Income Office refers to three basic macro-information types: 1) total incomes, grouped by income sources 2) deductions and detractions 3) physical person taxation rates, necessary to determine the tax drag.

Figure 1. Record structure of the data set provided by the Income Office of C. The data structure is common to all the data files provided by the Income Office (simplified version).

Field Name	Description
FiscalYear	The fiscal year to which the income is related
DeclarationForm	Type of declaration form (it can be either A or B or C)
SSN	Social Security number, this field univocally identifies a person
FamilyName	The family name of the person declaring her/his income
FirstName	The first name of the person
DateOfBirth	The date of birth
PlaceOfBirth	The place of birth
Gender	The gender of the person
Marital Status	It can be single, married, divorced, legally separated, …
Citizenship	It describe the citizenship of the person
AddressOfResidency	The Address of residency
TotalAgrarianIncome	The total income resulting from farming
TotalRentalIncome	The total income resulting from renting
RaisingIncome	The total income resulting from animal raising
EmploymentIncome	The income resulting from employment (except self-employment)
SelfEmploymentIncome	The income resulting from self employment
CompanyEarnings	The income resulting from entrepreneurship
FinancialGain	The income resulting from financial investment
OtherIncomes	The income types not listed before
Deductions	Costs which contributes to lower the sum of incomes upon which taxes are calculated
SumOfTaxableIncome	The sum of incomes upon which taxes are calculated
Detractions	Cost which lower the taxes to pay
FamilyTaxDetractions	Bonus related to the family composition which lower the taxes to pay

The reference population set has been provided by the Registry Office of the *M*. Data on such population are fundamental, since it is almost impossible to obtain data linked to a geographic area, for example, with a territorial meaning, from the Income Office, since that archive is managed at the national level. The required information is provided by a cross reference between the Registry and the Income archives. Information managed within the two archives can be linked by means of the citizens' Social Security number.

From the contents of these two archives, the *SIS* can be built according to the approach outlined previously. The approach comprises various and independent phases: from data integration and quality analysis, to the definition of statistical indicators, via the analysis of information sources, the database design, the transformation and data management process, and finally the definition of a multidimensional model for

Figure 2. Record structure of the data set provided by the Registry Office (simplified version)

Field Name	Description
SSN	Social Security number
RegistryID	ID used by the Registry Office
FamilyID	ID used to identify family members
FamilyRole	father, mother, daughter, son, grandfather, …
Gender	Person gender
MaritalStatus	single, married, divorced, legally separated, …
Citizenship	Person citizenship
DateOfBirth	Date of birth
PlaceOfBirth	Place of birth
ImmigrationDate	Date of last immigration
PlaceOfImmigration	Place reached by the last immigration
EmigrationDate	Date of last emigration
PlaceOfEmigration	Place reached by the last emigration
Address	Actual residence address

data analysis as a decisional support. The process of data interpretation, cleansing, and normalization, applied both to single sources and to integrated data, has required a great effort and a deep domain analysis. The income archive holds information about people (e.g., address, marital status, date of birth, gender citizenship) that is also present in the Registry Office.

When processing information of the Income Archive also present in the Registry data, priority has been given to data of the Registry archive, since these are usually more up-to-date. In fact, citizens quickly notify changes, such as address changes, to the Registry Office, while the Income Office is notified once per year, in the tax declaration form. Once different records concerning the same individual have been identified, further information (e.g., profession, qualification, education, and so on) derived from other archives is used, which might be significant for analysis and that is not present in the Income Archive. However, the scarce freshness of some archives would violate information quality criteria; thus, such additional information has not been included in the analysis.

Concerning information coming from the Income Office, three basic *macro-information* types can be identified:

1. The total incomes grouped by income source
2. The deductions and detractions

Figure 3. An overview of the global data integration model

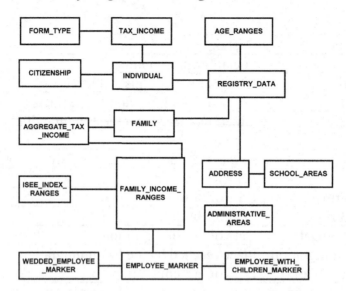

3.   The physical person taxation rate necessary to determine the tax drag

Around this information core, an integration model has been constructed able to drive the data migration activities (from the source data provisions to the integrated archive) and to highlight information relevant for statistical analysis. An overview of the model is reported in Figure 3. The core entity of the model is the INDIVIDUAL entity, which flows into the Registry data via the REGISTRY_DATA entity, and into the income data via the TAX-INCOME entity. REGISTRY_DATA also collects the individuals into the FAMILY group of instances. The ISEE_INDEX_RANGES entity is used to group families in categories, on the basis of a *welfare index* considering both the income deriving from work, and income deriving from patrimonial aspects. Finally, some entities have been introduced to identify some people categories: the EMPLOYEE_MARKER entity is used to identify the families whose income is fully originated from dependent work; the WEDDED_EMPLOYEE_MARKER identifies the wedded employees (which is a subcategory of the previous one); the EMPLOYEE_WITH_CHILDREN_MARKER entity identifies another subset, namely the families of employees with children.

Integration Model

A model for data restructuring was created, starting from the provided data sets. The developed global integration model is oriented to preserve information about the income form used by people to declare their tax-income. The rationale is that the form model used for the declaration provides information about the income type (i.e., dependent employment vs. self employment, although the distinction provided by the forms is not always very precise). This information is valuable for analysis. Using archives coming from different PAs usually brings about redundancy and incompatibilities. For example, the family relationships classifications used in the tax-income archives differ from the one used in the Registry archives. Registry information has been privileged since more up-to-date. Once the integrated archive has been designed, the delivered data sets undergo a pre-processing aimed at improving the *quality and reliability* of information, and aimed at framing the classifications to the adopted standards. Two types of pre-processing procedures are used: *semantic* and *syntactic cleansing*.

Examples of semantic cleansing are the *validation process* of the SSN (which, according to the law of the involved country, is not a progressive numeric identification but rather an alphanumeric string generated through a hash function onto the person's main data), and the *check of addresses* by means of area maps. Examples of syntactic cleansing are the consistency checks of income-tax returns (compatibility between imposable incomes, detractions, and tax indexes), revenue computation on the basis of the declared data, or separation of joint income-tax returns.

The cleansing procedures have been designed to be reused, in order to handle data provisions related to other years. To allow the provision of a new year's data, the integration tasks have been arranged at *two different levels*: integration at a single archive level, regarding provisioning over different years, and integration at a global level where different archives are involved.

1) *Integration at a single archive level*: Provisions over different years of the same archive can comprise heterogeneous information, since the data structure of the archive can undergo changes during the time. Hence the single archive instances must be reconciled to a unique data model taking into account information common to the different deliveries. The *selection* of the common information is *driven by the analysis* to be performed later, privileging relevant information or data present over different years, and hence comparable. A meaningful example in this case is the delivery of an archive from the Income Office: In the considered years, the tax laws have undergone many changes which caused the tax computation algorithm to change every year. For this reason, the adopted global model outlines the significant data common to the various deliveries, maintaining data related to specific tax information within the single annual stocks. The described integration phase can be considered as a *selective fusion* among data models reporting the same information type but expressed using different formats and according to different modalities. As a result of the analysis of the single archives, a data model is obtained for

every information source (in the case under exam, a model for the Income Office archives and a model for the Registry archive), reporting a subset of information relevant for the needed analysis purposes. The data models describing the sources are expressed as Entity-Relationship models, which allow an easily identification of subsets of information and permit to focus the analysis, thus drastically reducing analysis times. For example, it is possible to identify, within the whole set of income income-tax returns, those reporting an income "lower than a given threshold," and to restrict the analysis only to a selected subset, hence improving the overall analysis performance. This selection process can be adapted and reviewed depending on the statistical needs originating in the subsequent steps: Data considered as less relevant at a first analysis can be later included into the global data model.

2) *Integration in the system*: A second integration level includes the link among different information, coming from distinct sources. The goal of this step is to enrich the information content of the subjects to be analyzed (and consequently the range of possible queries) by collecting different information about the same subject, which is scattered among different sources. This integration is achieved by means of keys identifying connections among data. In this case, such connection occurs via the SSN which allows linking the tax income-tax return and the Registry information about an individual.

The process described in the previous steps can be summarized in terms of the flow reported in Figure 4.

Figure 4. Data loading and cleansing workflow

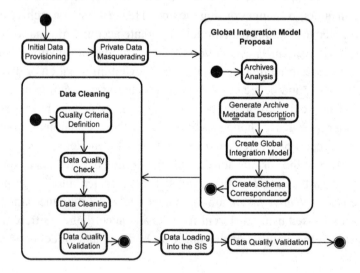

Quality Improvement

Data cleansing operations should be driven by *quality criteria*, which state the desired quality level to be reached. The quality criteria that have been defined for the *SIS* project are now illustrated.

- **Syntactic and Semantic Accuracy:** Syntactic errors are common when exploiting large administrative databases, even trivial ones, for example when using different abbreviations for the same location, which complicates the analysis based on geographic classification. Syntactic accuracy can be easily checked by comparing data values against those stored in reference dictionaries. Regarding semantic accuracy, the decisions has been taken case by case, both in an automatic and semi-automatic way, on the basis of the source archive that was considered as the one storing the correct value.
- **Completeness:** Some issues related to completeness can arise on some fields which content is not mandatory to declare. For example, some citizens may decide to expose medical costs, while others prefer not to do that for the sake of simplicity. This fact is acceptable from an administrative point of view; however it can bias statistical analysis.
- **Currency and Timeliness:** As far as currency is concerned, the *SIS* project required to move several huge databases to the same level of currency, which has not been a trivial job. Most of the time such operation is difficult from both a conceptual and an operative point of view. Statistical analysis contributes to overcome such problem since it involves other data sources, thus contributing to align the different archives values. For example, as mentioned before, address changes are more up-to-date in the Registry Office archives than in the Income Office, and hence the two archives do not share the same currency. Moreover, when currency issues arise, it means that different archives provide a snapshot of the same information at different time instances. In particular, when information is used within a business process, not all the archives are ensured to meet the time-related constraints expressed by the process, thus leading to timeliness problems. For example, the reclassification of incomes by city areas has been based on Registry address data which has been given preference with respect to the address field of the tax data, having the latter a low timeliness quality value. Different archives managing the same information are updated at different times, leading to currency problems. An example of low timeliness is the presence of many centenarian citizens in the Income Office archive, since deceases are communicated once per year (at tax declaration time). Problems related to timeliness are difficult

to be solved; in most cases, they can be solved only by leveraging knowledge of the domain, or information coming from different sources.

- **Internal Consistency:** These quality criteria have been checked in the *SIS* project based on semantic constraints derived from domain knowledge. A meaningful example is the discovering of a group of persons aged 140 years and over. For these people (obviously dead), the death certification had not been communicated to the Registry Office.
- **Duplicate records:** These have been identified across the different archives by using the SSN as a primary key. In this way, several duplicate records have been discovered in the Income Office database.
- **Missing records:** Missing records are present in the Income archives since some categories of citizens are allowed not to submit any tax declaration form (e.g., unemployed or below a given income threshold). This issue actually cannot be addressed directly and effectively; hence, the *SIS* project is being extended to include other data sources, such as the archives of the Provincial Employment Centres (responsible for distribution of unemployment subsidy), which are able to provide accurate information on most of the people who do not submit any tax declaration forms.

Process specific quality dimensions describe properties that depend on the process in which data are used; in the study case reference domain, for example, the timeliness of data between the income and the Registry data is a fundamental parameter to measure the efficiency and effectiveness of the overall taxation process. Concerning confidentiality, the personal name and the family name have been replaced with a progressive number that allows the identification of records only for maintenance and for updating the relationships with other archives. The partially invalid records issue arose when statistical analysis was conducted by communities of foreign people. These groups lose their significance when analyzed from an income point of view due to the fact that many of them do not submit a tax declaration form, because many have a (low) income falling in the "no-tax" area.

Multidimensional Data Model

Once the contents of the single information sources has been loaded into an integrated archive and quality has been improved, different analysis types can be executed. Due to the large number of treated information and of examined subjects, it is desirable to first perform a selection/aggregation of information to be used for further analysis. For example, it is possible to identify family groups (using Registry data), and to aggregate the income revenue for the whole family group. The level of aggregation/selection of the information needs to consider the trade off between the required computation and the desired granularity. However, by acquiring both knowledge and additional data about the specific topic of an analysis action, data can be re-processed to obtain more suitable aggregations/selections. For example, data can be analyzed/aggregated along these directions:

- On the basis of the *delivery year*, integrating the information source related to the same analysis year
- On the basis of the *analysis domain*, merging information coming from different annual stocks related to the same domain and introducing a *temporal* dimension for analysis
- By information *reprocessing* with *grouping*, computing, for example, the family groups
- By combining *subsequent aggregation steps*, until a global database is obtained, reporting synthetic information related to all the stocks and domains, on which flow analysis can be performed

The adoption of a multidimensional data model at information source integration time introduces and outlines the statistical information needs of the *SIS*. Both the data model designed for each single source and the global model put into evidence a set of possible subjects of analysis, and a set of dimensions along which the analysis can be performed, by aggregating or detailing the information, according to the different analysis needs. To ameliorate the subsequent analysis steps, the final phase

Figure 5. Facts: Family income tax

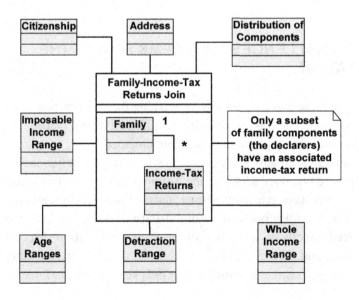

Figure 6. The SIS data warehouse

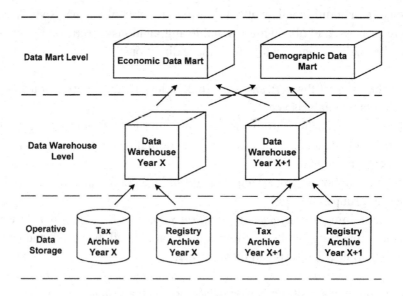

of data model design includes the definition of *facts of interest*, of their respective *dimensions*, and of *aggregation levels* along which it is possible to combine the data. An example of *fact* identified within the *SIS* project is illustrated in Figure 5.

A Data Warehouse was designed in order to host the results of the integration phases. Data within the Data Warehouse is organized along fact of interest for the statistical analysis to be performed. In Figure 6, an overview of the Data Warehouse is reported.

CURRENT CHALLENGES/PROBLEMS FACING THE ORGANIZATION

This article has presented a case study concerning the construction of a *SIS* out of administrative data. The link between an administrative and management system and a *SIS* is strong, although often poorly implemented.

The presented case study shows how this link can be better constructed and exploited. In the envisioned scenario, the Administrative and Management System should feed the *SIS* at given instants of time, and the Statistical System in turn, should be able to provide indicators to the Administrative System on how amelioration can be enforced directly on the data sources. Such amelioration first of all regards error prevention and filtering, in that, more strict analysis of data entry, or more precise definition of semantic constraints or data keys, can be enforced a priori, in order to facilitate the data conversion and merging. A second consideration regards the derivation of indicators about the granularity of data to be collected (e.g., those regarding territory, geographic areas, groups of subjects, and so on) in order to collect data that are really meaningful for statistical analysis. In fact, often—and this is a critical factor in manipulation of administrative data- administrative systems are designed using an self-justifying logic that privileges the definition of services that are functional to the organizational model rather than to the stakeholders (e.g., citizens, politicians) or to the statisticians. This reflects in expensive activities needed to normalize data, to ensure their quality, and to standardize them, as shown in the presented case.

In general, an enabling factor for a *SIS* construction is to encourage the PAs to cooperate and take into account the transversal, reciprocal acknowledgement, and agreement of data concepts, although used in different administrative processes, and also to require that such concepts are in relation with standard codifications.

Another key factor is related to the quality of documentation provided by the sources. This documentation is often scarce, or even not present, hence making the conceptual design phase of the *SIS* more complex.

A current undergoing development of the presented project regards the use of social security data, in particular data related to subjects receiving social security contributions. Tax income declaration is not mandatory for people receiving a subsidy; thus, tax registries do not store any data at all about these citizens, who are practically unknown. A recent survey in the *M* city area (performed by different public institutions) has reported the presence of large sets of missing records. By using social security data, one can correctly identify the wealth of a larger set of citizens; moreover, by continuing investigating data present in (and missing from) different archives, it will be possible to establish the poverty levels with a higher precision rate with respect to the currently available statistics.

A second development issue regards data quality. The criteria presented in the article are being refined, enlarged, and formalized using standard methodologies (e.g., IP-MAP and its extension with UML specifications, as presented for instance in Scannapieco, Pernici, & Pierce (2005).

REFERENCES

Buzzigoli, L. (2002). The new role of statistics in local public administration. In *Proceedings of the Conference on Quantitative Methods in Economics (Multiple Criteria Decision Making XI)* (pp. 28-34). Faculty of Economics and Management, Slovak Agricultural University, Nitra (SK).

Castano, S., Fugini, M., Martella, G., & Samarati, P. (1995). *Database security*. Addison Wesley.

Census Bureau. (2005). *Information quality guidelines, Office of Management and Budget, guidelines for ensuring and maximizing the quality, objectivity, utility, and integrity of information disseminated by federal agencies.* (Section 515). Retrieved from http://www.census.gov/quality/

Denk, M., & Froeschl, K. (2000). The IDARESA data mediation architecture for statistical aggregates. *Research in Official Statistics, 3*(1), 7–38.

Eppler, M. (2003). *Managing information quality.* Springer Verlag.

Hatzopoulos, M., Karali, I., & Viglas, E. (1998). Attacking diversity in NSIs' storage infrastructure: The *ADDSIA* approach. In *Proceedings of the International Seminar on New Techniques and Technologies in Statistics* (pp. 229-234). Sorrento.

Helfert, M., & Herrmann, C. (2005). Introducing data-quality management in data warehousing. In Wang, R. Y., Pierce, E., Madnick, S. E., & Fisher, C. W. (Eds.), *Information quality.* AMIS.

Hoffmann, E. (1995). We must use administrative data for official statistics—But how should we use them? *Statistical Journal of the United Nations/ECE, 12,* 41-48.

Information Quality I. (2005). *Principles and foundation, the MIT total data quality management program.* (2005, October 31-November 4). Retrieved from http://web.mit.edu/tdqm/www/index.shtml

Papageorgiou, H., Pentaris, F., Theodorou, E., Vardaki, M., & Petrakos, M. (2001). A statistical metadata model for simultaneous manipulation of both data and metadata. *Journal of Intelligent Information Systems, 17*(2-3), 169–192. doi:10.1023/A:1012805713392

Scannapieco, M., Pernici, B., & Pierce, E. (2005). IP-UML-A methodology for quality improvement based on information product maps and unified modeling language. In *Vol. Information Quality.* AMIS.

Statistics Denmark. (2000, June). *The use of administrative sources for statistics and international comparability (invited paper).* Presented at the Conference of European Statisticians, 48th Plenary Session, Paris.

Sundgren, B. (1996). Making statistical data more available. *International Statistical Review, 64*(1), 23–38. doi:10.2307/1403422

Thomson, I., & Holmy, A. (1998). Combining data from surveys and administrative record systems—The Norwegian experience. *International Statistical Review, 66*(2), 201–221.

UNECE. (2000). *Statistical metadata.* Presented at the Conference on European Statisticians Statistical Standards and Studies (no. 53), Geneva (CH).

Wand, Y., & Wang, R. Y. (1996). Anchoring data quality dimensions in ontological foundations. *Communications of the ACM, 39*(11). doi:10.1145/240455.240479

Wang, R. (1998). A product perspective on total data quality management. *Communications of the ACM, 41*(2). doi:10.1145/269012.269022

Wang, R. Y., & Strong, D. M. (1996). Beyond accuracy: What data quality means to data consumers. *Journal of Management Information Systems, 12*(4).

ENDNOTE

[1]   Some more tax declaration forms are managed by the income office, however they are not relevant for the case

APPENDIX A: DATA QUALITY ASPECTS

- **Data Intrinsic Quality:** Quality dimensions concerning data values are only referred to, while aspects concerning the quality of logical schemas are not dealt with (Eppler, 2003). In the following definitions, schema elements as the elements for which dimensions are defined are referred to. Examples of elements are: an entity in an Entity-Relationship schema or a class in an object oriented schema expressed in the Unified Modelling Language.

  - **Syntactic and Semantic Accuracy:** Accuracy refers to the proximity of a value v to a value v' considered as correct, with a distinction between syntactic and semantic accuracy. Let us consider the following examples: Person is a schema element with Name as the attribute of interest, and p is an instance of Person. If p.Name has a value v = JON, while the correct value is v' = JOHN, this is a case of a low syntactic accuracy as JON is not an admissible value according to a dictionary of English names; if p.Name has a value v = ROBERT, while v' = JOHN, this is a case of a low semantic accuracy, as v is a syntactical admissible value but the person whose name is stored as ROBERT has a name which is JOHN in the real world. Syntactical errors are mostly due to mistyping during data input and to different abbreviation conventions. Mistyping may be not noticed during data input, especially when it affects less important field in a data record (e.g., the name of a profession, city names, etc.). Abbreviation conventions are used to shortly write some worlds or sentences (e.g., St for street, NYC for New York City), most of the times more than one convention is used for the same subject (e.g., Union Sqr. or Union Sq. for Union Square), this way leading to a data representation that prevents automatic data classification. Semantic accuracy is more difficult to be quantified since the terms of comparison have to be derived from the real world, and hence verification of semantic accuracy may be very expensive. Semantic accuracy can be also checked through a process that aims at identifying similar instances in different databases, composed of two phases: 1) A searching phase, in which possibly matching instances are identified 2) A matching phase, in which a decision about a match, a non-match or a possible match is taken.

  - **Completeness:** This is an indicator of how many fields have been left blank or with nonsense value. In evaluating completeness, it is important to evaluate whether the attribute is mandatory, optional, or inapplicable: A null value for a mandatory attribute is associated with a lower completeness, whereas completeness is not affected by optional or inapplicable null values. For example, a null value for the e-mail attribute may have different meanings, that is (1) The specific person has no e-mail address, and therefore the attribute is inapplicable (this case does not impact on completeness) or (2) The specific person has an e-mail address which has not been stored (this case reduces completeness). Completeness issues arise when statistical analysis focuses on optional or inapplicable attributes. For example, an analysis aimed at evaluating the skills in computer science of a population may count the amount of people having an e-mail address. If the e-mail field has been considered optional information for administrative purposes, the employees that manually input the data may have omitted to ask this information to the persons having the business intelligence of this aspect. Low completeness can heavily affect the result of statistical analysis. In fact, lacking could only be guessed from other archives or leveraging knowledge of the specific domain.

- **Currency:** This refers to data values that may vary in time. As an example, the values of Address may vary in time, whereas the DateOfBirth can be considered invariant. Therefore currency can be defined as the age of a data-value, namely: Currency is the distance between the instant when a value is last updated and the instant when this value is used. It can be measured either by associating to each value an update time stamp or a transaction time in temporal databases. The records in a database may have different currencies, for example because the records of the database are updated at different periods of the year. While for administrative purpose it is sufficient that all the records related to a subject share the same currency, statistical analysis requires all the subjects involved within an analysis to share the same currency, especially where time concerns are important for the analysis.

- **Internal Consistency:** Consistency implies that two or more values are not in conflict. This means that all values that are compared in order to evaluate consistency satisfy some semantic constraints that must hold among values of attributes of a schema element, depending on the application domain modelled by the schema element. As an example, if we consider Person with attributes Name, DateOfBirth, Sex, and DateOfDeath, some possible semantic rules to be checked as satisfied are: the values of Name and Sex are coherent; if Name has a value v = JOHN and the value of Sex is FEMALE an internal consistency error exists; the value of DateOfBirth must precede the value of DateOfDeath. Statistical analysis may require data to enforce stricter consistency rules than the one required by administrative domains. Moreover, consistency rules may be poorly checked for optional fields of a schema. For this reason, some records in an administrative archive may fail the consistency checks required by statistical analysis. Sometimes consistency issues may be easily solved (e.g., an e-mail address where the @ character is missing because has been replaced with the "at" word); in some other cases, the consistency check failure will lead to discard the record.

- ○ **Duplicate Records:** In huge administrative and statistical databases some duplicate records, namely record that refers to the same subject, may be present in huge quantities. The use of a primary key within the archive being analyzed that does not provide strong duplication recognition (e.g., a progressive number) contributes to the proliferation of duplicate records. Duplicate records may be originated during data input, when some wrong data are inserted and the operation is not aborted but a new record is added with the correct information. The merging of databases may cause duplicate records as well. Merge operations are executed for many reasons: for example, during archive renovations and during integration with data provisioning of different years. The duplicate records have not necessarily the same contents; some may be either incomplete or not updated. PAs' databases are usually accessed looking for a subject per time (e.g., the tax payment balance of a single worker, the marriage status of a person, etc.). The operations that would highlight the presence of duplicate records like listing more subjects per time are rarely executed. Moreover, information related to a subject scattered among different archives is accessed climbing up relationship chains and most of the times duplicate records are outside these chains. Duplicate records affect statistical analysis involving counting operations over a population. They may be identified by comparing a field or combination of fields that have the properties of a primary key.

- ○ **Missing Records:** Some archives may lack the data describing some subset of a population. This is the most widespread low quality data dimension. There are many different causes strictly related to the application domain.

- ○ For example, people living closer to the town boundaries may have been registered as inhabitants of a neighbour town. Administrative procedure is not affected because citizens are somewhere registered although not in the right town. However, statistical analysis may be biased by this lack. The lack can be overcome by comparing or merging different data sources.

- • **Process Specific Quality:** Process specific parameters show how quality is related also to the usage of data and to its evaluation in an administrative database and in a *SIS*. As regards intrinsic data quality dimensions, a subset of the ones proposed in the literature are referred to, by considering the most important ones (Wand & Wang., 1996) and the requirements of statistical analysis. Wang (1998) highlights the need for data quality dimensions dependent on the context; for this purpose, it is observed that in administrative and statistical applications, the context is the cooperation among different PA processes and data quality dimensions are related to the evolution of data during time and within the process. Therefore, some of the dimensions proposed in Wang (1998) have been chosen and adapted (timeliness and source reliability), and in addition, new dimensions dependent on Public Administration processes which are distributed and cooperative, are proposed (importance and confidentiality). Process specific dimensions are tied to specific data exchanges within the process, rather than to the whole process. Hence, in all the following definitions, a data exchange as associated to a triple < source organization i, destination organization j, exchange id >, representing the cooperating organizations involved in the data exchange and the specific exchange, are considered.

○ **Timeliness:** It can be defined as the availability of data on time, which is within the time constraints specified by the destination organization. For example, a university lesson schedule provided to students after the semester has begun, has a very low timeliness. Administrative archives may be updated far behind the time when events in the real time occur. Some archives are updated periodically; periodicity may range from few times to once per year, thus changes will be reflected to the archive only after many months in the worst case.

○ **Source Reliability:** It is the credibility of a source organization with respect to specific provided data. It can be clarified through an example: the source reliability of the Italian Department of Finance as regards Address is lower than the one of City Councils; whereas concerning the Fiscal Code (FC, whose role is similar to the Social Security number in the US), its source reliability is the highest among all Italian administrations. For some types of administrative data, the higher the source reliability, the lower the effort required to process the data for statistical analysis.

○ **Confidentiality:** It indicates whether data must be protected from access by non authorized users. In an administrative as well as in a statistical process, sensitivity concerns protecting data from accidental and fraudulent misuse. Depending whether data processing is performed within a trusted or untrusted domain of subjects, the archives may be required to undergo an obscuration process (Castano, Fugini, Martella,

& Samarati, 1995) through which all the data identifying a single person are either discarded or replaced with identification keys. Fields not useful for further elaboration are dropped, while fields that should be used for further elaboration are replaced with values that do not prevent the subsequent elaborations but that prevent people identification.

o **Partially Invalid Record Groups:** This last dimension regards data that have a meaning when they are part of a group and the group is complete (namely all the data describing the elements of the group are present) or almost complete according to some domain dependent criteria. As an example, if a district collects data coming from various municipalities on its territory, some data regarding municipalities that spread over the district border lines might be missing. In that case, some criteria should be used to decide whether to consider or not the population of the municipalities whose data are partially missing.

APPENDIX B: MAIN RESULTS AND OUTCOMES

In this section, the main results achieved so far in the project are reported by presenting summary tables regarding the statistical data and the Data Warehouse that has been designed to host the *SIS* data. The data and charts presented in this section are the results of the elaborations executed by a statistic research centre, on data provided by the municipality *M*, and by the Income Office of the (including) country *C*. By December 31, 2000 the population residing in *M* enrolled in the municipal Registry, excluding large cohabitations (e.g., barracks or hospitals) was 1,378,083 citizens, 723,146 were women and 654,937 were men. Such population, whose data could not been integrated directly with data belonging to the Income Office, has been cleaned from some typologies of citizens, thus obtaining the net population, used as a basis for integration procedures. Table 1 reports, respectively, the various

Table 1. Total net population of M by 12/31/2000

	Total population of M by 12/31/2000 - initial	Nowhere to be found	Residents abroad	Over 110	Belonging to cohabitations	With no stable residence	Total population of M by 12/31/2000 – net
Women	723,146	19,279	14,403	49	10,062	6,750	678,434
Men	654,937	28,208	15,734	30	9,693	6,940	600,937
Total	**1,378,083**	**47,487**	**30,137**	**79**	**20,564**	**13,690**	**1,279,371**

cases that have been excluded and the cardinality of the final population set (equal to 1,279,371 residents, 678,434 women and 600,937 men).

The match between the net population and data coming from tax-return declarations has evidenced 847,871 residents (representing 66.3% of the total population) to whom a tax declaration form could be associated (see Figure 7). As pointed out, these declarers do not represent the whole number of income receivers resident in *M*, since the administrative archives involved in the project do not consider the incomes resulting from illegal work, from autonomous or temporary work, (whose amount does not imply a mandatory tax-return declaration), from other incomes, such as severance pay or retirement bonus, and from social-level pensions, invalidity pensions, or support bonus. That information can be obtained by considering the retirement agency archives. Figure 8 layers the typology of the tax-income declaration forms on the basis of the gender of workers and indicates the total and average income amount for each layer. Globally, the 847,871 tax-declaring citizens expose an imposable income equal to 19,9 billion €, corresponding to an average income of 23,423 €. It is evidenced a higher income for men than for women, by analyzing the average incomes for each tax declaration form type.

Individual Incomes

Figure 9 compares the incomes, re-classified on the basis of the income-ranges used for tax calculation on the year 2000, respectively for men and women. The number of women with imposable income lower than 10,329 € is almost double the number of men. For the subsequent two ranges, no special differences emerge, while for the last two ranges a strong male prevalence emerges.

By layering the average imposable income by gender and age ranges (Figure 8), a strong difference exists between the value of incomes produced or declared by

Figure 7. Distribution of citizens

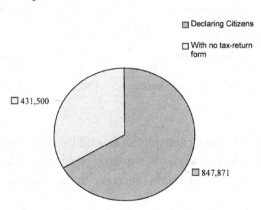

Figure 8. Average taxable income layered by age ranges and gender

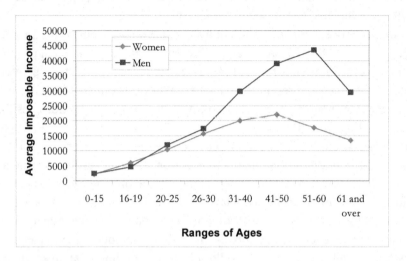

Table 2. Total tax-return submitters by different typology of the submitted forms and layered by gender

		Citizens with tax-return form				
		Number of submitters	Sum of submitted imposable income €	Sum of submitted imposable income %	Declared average Income	Standard deviation
Women	B Form	146,226	2,517,881,306	34.2	17,219	12,821
	C Form	134,099	1,505,901,944	20.5	11,230	72,975
	A Form	155,173	3,135,567,135	42.6	20,207	107,906
	Total	**435,498**	**7,159,350,385**	**97.4**	**16.439**	**76.534**
Men	B Form	129,772	3,638,384,192	28.3	28.037	26.893
	C Form	118,883	1,879,070,417	14.6	15.806	72.661
	A Form	163,718	7,183,275,072	56.0	43,876	704,123
	Total	**412,373**	**12,700,729,680**	**98.9**	**30,799**	**445,779**
Total	B Form	275,998	6,156,265,497	30.5	22,305	21,361
	C Form	252,982	3,384,972,361	16.8	13,380	72,864
	A Form	318,891	10,318,842,207	51.1	32,359	510,237
	Total	**847,871**	**19,860,080,065**	**98.4**	**23,423**	**315,768**

the male population with respect to those declared by the female population. The distribution of income has an analogous trend, increasing for both genders in the youngest range; after the 30's, a notable increase in the incomes of the male popu-

Figure 9. Number of income receivers grouped by income range

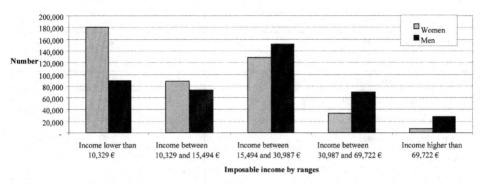

lation is present, whose curve reaches its top in the age range between 51 and 60 years. The curve for women increases at a lower pace until 45; afterward, the trend is inverted.

The usage of a Data Warehouse allowed layering the incomes and the declaring individuals on the territory, enriching the analysis with added value. In Table 4, individuals and incomes have been grouped by city areas. Area 1, corresponding to downtown, shows an anomalous situation characterized by a low number of resident citizens and of income receivers, but an average imposable income double with respect to the average total of the whole city. The other zones do not show relevant differences, and the average income is scarcely different from the average total.

By computing the average income for citizen groups, it emerges that the highest values are associated to residents coming from North America and Oceania, as reported in Figure 10.

The classification reported in Table 3 groups people according to the type of income sources and not by the imposable income. People have been classified according to their prevalent income source. Among the 78.9% of the residing citizens of *M* who present the considered tax-return forms, the main income type is the dependant work type. By layering the main income source by gender, dependant work type is prevalent for women.

Facts: Families

The number of families of residents in municipality *M*, their composition, their distribution on the municipal territory has been identified using the information provided by the Registry Office. A group of individuals that cohabitate is considered a family by the Registry archive. Moreover, using the individual income data, it has been computed for each family the sum of all the incomes produced by each

Table 3. Main income sources of the citizens of M (column: % of persons)

	Women	Men	Total
Prevalence of income from dependant work	79.20	76.91	78.09
- of which only incomes from dependant work	72.26	67.02	69.71
Incomes (positive) from self employed work	5.02	8.54	6.73
Incomes (positive) from entrepreneurship	2.41	7.27	4.77
Only negative incomes from enterprise of self employment	0.23	0.37	0.30
Other typologies of income	4.29	2.99	3.66
Only patrimonial income	7.91	2.46	5.26
Unclassified	0.94	1.45	1.19
Total	**100**	**100**	**100**

component. Such information is a relevant issue in the analysis of the wealth of a given territorial area. Also in this case, the lack of income elements (e.g., elements not present in the tax-return declaration models), might bring about an underestimation of the actual family income. Still, the analyses represent a helpful support for decision makers, who could take advantage of information on the whole universe, rather than on sample, ad hoc surveys only. For each family, various indicators have been extracted, such as the number of components, their incomes, and the net tax drag by family and by family typology, determined starting from the relationship with the householder declared in the Registry data.

Table 4. Tax declaring citizens distributed over the nine zones of the municipality

	Total population	Total declaring citizens	Declaring/ Total Population	Imposable Income	Average Imposable Income	Standard Deviation
1	98,110	61,215	62.4	3,188,887,780	52.093	1,108,689
2	131,873	87,026	66.0	1,782,449,591	20.482	40,776
3	138,877	91,702	66.0	2,238,679,456	24.413	74,837
4	147,466	98,187	66.6	2,062,707,120	21.008	37,540
5	115,654	76,679	66.3	1,509,008,797	19.680	53,509
6	147,664	98,993	67.0	2,045,297,819	20.661	191,536
7	167,839	111,103	66.2	2,658,576,851	23.929	185,539
8	173,077	116,115	67.1	2,423,221,411	20.869	48,443
9	158,546	106,777	67.3	1,949,606,631	18.259	68,081
Address not available	265	74	27.9	1,644,608	22.224	23,022

Figure 10. Average imposable income citizenship for residents of M

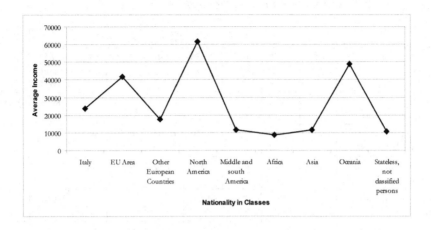

Globally, 634,289 families were identified, of which 278,631 (44% of the total number) are composed of one member. Figure 11 also shows that the percentage of families composed of two members is equal to 26%, while around 30% of families are composed of three or more components. The classification frame used in Figure 11 (as long as in all other figures and tables we are presenting) has been borrowed from the *C* National Institute of Statistics. The structure of the information provided by the Registry archive did not allow the system to reach a perfect alignment with the one used by the National Institute of Statistics.

The strong presence of mono-personal families is most probably related to taxation. Many familiar groups' components get a residence in a second real estate property different with respect to the usual living site, achieving in this way a light

Figure 11. Resident components of families in M (%)

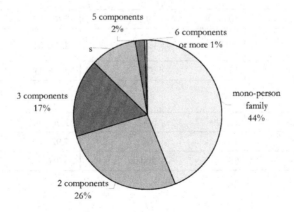

Table 5. Main income sources classified by age classes (column %) – The first column (0-15) refers to incomes related to heritages

	Age classes								Total
	0-15	16-19	20-25	26-30	31-40	41-50	51-60	61 and over	
Prevalence of income from dependant work	85.22	85.44	77.36	74.71	71.75	70.23	68.93	89.78	78.09
- of which only incomes from dependant work	84.55	83.58	71.57	66.79	63.18	61.22	59.21	81.72	69.71
Incomes (positive) from autonomous work	0.08	1.52	4.92	8.89	11.12	9.92	7.37	2.51	6.73
Incomes (positive) from enterprise	0.38	0.72	2.66	4.59	6.96	7.75	7.40	1.61	4.77
Only negative incomes from enterprise of autonomous work	-	0.09	0.30	0.45	0.52	0.48	0.33	0.04	0.30
Other typologies of income	1.88	7.06	9.18	6.76	4.23	3.61	4.08	1.48	3.66
Only patrimonial income	6.98	3.38	2.79	2.35	3.53	6.43	10.94	4.38	5.26
Unclassified	5.48	1.79	2.78	2.25	1.90	1.57	0.94	0.19	1.19
Total	**100**	**100**	**100**	**100**	**100**	**100**	**100**	**100**	**100**

Table 6. Average income for each family typology

	N. of families	Column %	Average income by typology	Standard Deviation
Mono-person families	216,752	39.4	23,653.85	585,627.23
Singles with children	60,323	11.0	32,803.34	82,799.05
- of which with other components	10,260	1.9	38,166.64	55,545.17
Pairs with no children	104,858	19.1	37,628.52	72,825.71
- of which with other components	2,972	0.5	44,362.01	75,448.03
Pairs with children	149,540	27.2	54,706.11	269,598.96
- of which with other components	5,544	1.0	50,108.78	100,920.23
Other types of families	18,829	3.4	32,667.46	110,335.57
Unclassifiable	4	0.0	77,926.50	20,667.47
Total	**550,306**	**100.0**	**36,066.53**	**396,446.05**

Table 7. Average familiar income

	Income < 10,329 €	Income between 10,329 and 15,494 €	Income between 15,494 and 30,987 €	Income between 30,987 and 69,722 €	Income >= 69,722 €	Total
	Absolute Values					
Mono-person families	64,474	46,139	73,140	25,714	7,285	216,752
Singles with children	31,338	12,377	12,901	3,08	629	0,323
- of which with other components	6,688	1,681	1,373	420	98	10,260
Pairs with no children	41,156	24,404	26,447	10,271	2,580	104,858
- of which with other components	1,573	623	563	178	35	2,972
Pairs with children	69,855	34,642	33,291	9,516	2,236	149,540
_ of which with other components	3,636	1,011	676	181	40	5,544
Other types of families	8,868	4,099	4,499	1,124	239	18,829
Unclassifiable	-	2	2	-	-	4
Total	**215,691**	**121,663**	**150,280**	**49,703**	**12,969**	**550,306**
	Row %					
Mono-person families	29.7	21.3	33.7	11.9	3.4	100.0
Singles with children	52.0	20.5	21.4	5.1	1.0	100.0
- of which with other components	65.2	16.4	13.4	4.1	1.0	100.0
Pairs with no children	39.2	23.3	25.2	9.8	2.5	100.0
- of which with other components	52.9	21.0	18.9	6.0	1.2	100.0
Pairs with children	46.7	23.2	22.3	6.4	1.5	100.0
_ of which with other components	65.6	18.2	12.2	3.3	0.7	100.0
Other types of families	47.1	21.8	23.9	6.0	1.3	100.0
Unclassifiable		50.0	50.0			100.0
Total	**39.2**	**22.1**	**27.3**	**9.0**	**2.4**	**100.0**

taxation on the second property. From the analysis point of view, this means that an actual family composed of two (or more) members can result as two (or more) mono-personal families, because one (or more) of the members has his/her residence at the second real estate property).

90.5% of families are composed of individuals having both the *C* citizenship, 8.4% have foreign citizenships, while only 1.1% of the families show cohabitation between national and foreign individuals.

Table 7 aims at classifying the families based on their components and on their income.

This work was previously published in the Journal of Cases on Information Technology, Volume 9, Issue 4, edited by Mehdi Khosrow-Pour, pp. 58-82, copyright 2007 by IGI Publishing (an imprint of IGI Global).

Chapter 9
The Significance of Government's Role in Technology Standardization:
Two Cases in the Wireless Communications Industry

DongBack Seo
University of Groningen, The Netherlands

EXECUTIVE SUMMARY

For first generation (1G) wireless communications technology standards, the Japanese government's early decision provided an opportunity for its national manufacturers to be first movers in the global market, while the late development of wireless communications in Korea made the Korean market dependent on foreign manufacturers by adopting the U.S. standard (AMPS). Moving toward the 2G wireless technology market, both countries decided to develop standards instead of adopting a technology from outside their regions. Japan developed its own standard, PDC, while Korea developed CDMA systems with Qualcomm, the U.S. technology provider. Although these governments' decisions on technologies looked only slightly different, the socio-economic consequences were greatly distinctive. The Korean success brought not only the rapid development of its domestic market but also opportunities for its manufacturers to become global leaders, while the PDC standard only provided the fast growth of the Japanese domestic market without

DOI: 10.4018/978-1-4666-0981-5.ch009

any opportunities for the Japanese manufacturers to grow further internationally in the 1990s. By the end of 1990s, two nations again had to decide a 3G technology standard with vast challenges and pressures.

ORGANIZATIONAL BACKGROUND

While it has always been true that governments play a critical role in the economy when they drive decisions about standards, today's rapidly changing and technology-dependent business environment has made the role of the government in standardization even more important. Some governments play their roles actively, whereas others leave it over to industries or a number of lobbyists.

A standard declared by a government is considered as a *de jure* standard, while a standard emerges from market competitions is *de facto*. De Vries (2006) points out that this classification is confusing and provides more detail and specific definitions and a typology of IT standards by suggesting various aspects related to subject matter, standards development, and standards use. For the cases of Korea and Japan in this paper, standards refer to governmental standards that are set by a governmental agency in the classification related to organizations, according to the category of De Vries (2006).

Governments, especially those in developing countries or with planned economies, often nurture certain industries to drive the national economy. In order to do so, some choose to use their regulatory power to mandate standards in technology-dependent industries. This eliminates the need for companies to expend resources in competing to establish a standard through market forces, allowing them to focus instead on creating economies of scale, and developing complementary products. If the standard successfully creates network externalities and is cost-effective, the standard can diffuse to other nations. Then companies enjoy the benefits of being developers or early adopters, and can use their domestic market to develop subsequent technologies and test marketing strategies to export to other countries. They have the advantage of being able to innovate and move the market to the next generation technology before later adopters can catch up. End-users in the countries that adopt the technology earlier enjoy benefits as well, with lower prices and greater variety of products or services.

However, a government has power to mandate a standard only for its juridical region. There is no international organization to force any country to adopt a particular standard. Thus, to diffuse a standard to other nations (or make an international standard), a governmental standard in one nation has to go through competition in the international market (Funk & Methe, 2001). This process is often very competitive because other nations tend to push their governmental standards to be international standards as well.

For this reason, governments, like companies, can bet on the wrong standard. In this paper, the importance of the government's role will be illustrated by looking at two cases: South Korea (Note: it will be referred to Korea in the rest of paper) and Japan, in their choice of a national technology standard for wireless communications (governmental standards). Some countries like the United States have settled on standards in their wireless communication industry through open competition (*de facto* standards through company or consortium standards); many others, however, including Korea and Japan, have had a history of tight regulation of their telecommunications industries and only privatized them in the last few decades. Because of similarities in the Korean and Japanese wireless communication markets, these two cases provide a stark comparison of governments' roles and the economic and social consequences of the governments' decisions in technology standardization.

Japan

Japan, as a defeated nation in World War II, was devastated, so the first priority of the Japanese government was reconstructing the nation. With scarce resources and capabilities, the Japanese government was heavily involved in developing certain industries such as motorcycles, sewing machine, steel, and shipbuilding through directing necessary resources (Porter, 1990). Companies in these industries were able to gain competitive advantages under the government's support, protection from foreign competitors, and policies like market liberation in a timely manner. Although there were other factors such as demand conditions and disciplined workers, the role of Japanese government was significant in reviving its industries.

The Japanese government also encouraged companies to develop related and supporting industries for the industries that it directly involved in. For example, the Temporary Measures Law for Machinery and Electronics between 1971 and 1978 contributed to develop these industries rapidly (Porter, 1990). Through these kinds of government policies, many Japanese electronics companies quickly developed their competitive capabilities to become a global firm such as Sony and NEC.

The Japanese government's role has changed as its industries have evolved. It is not involved as directly and actively as it used to be, but it still influences industries with regulations and public policies. Considering the history of the Japanese government's involvement in its industries, it is not surprising that the Japanese government has participated in the wireless telecommunications technology standardization.

Korea

During the Cold War period, Korea was not seen as an attractive country to invest in by foreign investors. After Park Chung Hee gained power with a military coup in 1961, the Korean government started to create economic development policies to achieve public support and cover their illegitimate power. The Korean market could not have free competition like the United States or western European countries, because there weren't any Korean players who could compete against foreign giant companies that had been in the market for a long time. The only way to develop the Korean economy was to execute a deliberate strategy by the Korean government to grow certain industries one by one in a protectionist manner.

The Korean government started by borrowing money from other countries and developing light industries for export, like the garment industry. With the capital accumulated from the development of this sector of the Korean economy, the Korean government was able to move into heavy industries like the auto industry. The companies that had close relationships with the Korean government were able to get into these industries and grow quickly under the government's wing.

Of course, all of this has changed dramatically through international pressure to open the Korean market, along with the political change from military dictatorship to democratic government, the Asian financial crisis in 1997, and other factors. The Korean market has become an open market and companies have become independent. The Korean government can't intervene into industries and markets directly, but they still can direct them by providing regulations as other governments do.

SETTING THE STAGE

Before the fifteenth century, people exchanged messages between distant regions through various methods such as beacon fires, messengers, and flags. The main purpose of most messages was related to military and sovereign matters of rulers. The development of the wireless telecommunications industry is an extension of the evolution of postal service, telegraphy and telephony. They were all designed to communicate more quickly over long distances as the socio-economic conditions of human activities changed.

Although individuals invented telephony technologies and founded private telephony companies, governments in many countries nationalized landline telephone networks in the late 1890s and early 1900s through World Wars I and II (Noam, 1992). Even before the liberalization and privatization of wireless telecommunications operators in the 1980s and 1990s, many governments ran their national telephone industry through their *Post, Telegraphy and Telephony* (PTT) bureaus. The timing and the development of liberalization and privatization varied across nations.

Japan

The Japanese government has played a significant role in its wireless communications industry. Japan was the first country that installed a cellular telephony system in 1979, but the market grew slowly at that time. After observing the development of wireless telecommunications technologies in Europe and the United States that moved to the second generation (2G) wireless telephony based on digital technology, the Japanese government decided to upgrade its infrastructure to 2G in 1989 (Bekkers, 2001). Instead of adopting one of the existing 2G technologies – Global System for Mobile (GSM), which would be used widely in Europe and around the world, or Time Division Multiple Access (TDMA) used in the United States—the Japanese government decided to create its own technology standard (Komiya, 1993). It felt confident in doing so, drawing on the strength of its technological capabilities and established track record in becoming the world leader in other industries, for example, consumer electronics. It also invited foreign companies such as Ericsson, Motorola and AT&T to develop the standard with its national companies like NEC. Its ambition was to make this wireless communications technology an international standard by exporting the technology to other countries, especially other Asian countries, so that Japanese companies could have benefits from this proprietary technology standard.

Japan thus developed Personal Digital Cellular (PDC) with its national manufacturers as a standard. NTT DoCoMo, which was used to be the Japanese national Post, Telegraph, Telephony (PTT), started to provide digital wireless communication services using the PDC standard in 1993. Initially, NTT DoCoMo was not enthusiastic about moving its network to 2G (Bekkers, 2001). This attitude stimulated the Japanese government to allow two more companies to be wireless service providers (Digital Tu-Ka Kyushu and Japan Telecom Digital Phone (Garrard, 1998). This government's decision has made the Japanese domestic wireless communications market more competitive with in total five wireless service providers. In addition to the three mentioned, there were IDO and DDI. This free competition could encourage wireless service providers to competitively upgrade their networks with next generation technologies.

One thing to remember is that the standardized PDC was not as radical compared to other technologies. It was technologically close to TDMA developed in the United States (Bekkers, 2001). This technological limit also affected the prosperity of PDC. This aspect will be discussed in the next section.

The first goal for the Japanese government was to provide more advanced services to its domestic market. The Japanese domestic market was enthusiastic about the new standard and fully embraced it. The number of wireless communication subscribers grew quickly, from less than 2 million at the end of 1993, to around 9 million at the end of 1995, and then to 42 million (about 33% of the total population) by mid-1999 (Bekkers, 2001).

On the other hand, the standardization of PDC was not internationally successful. Originally, PDC stood for Pacific Digital Cellular. As you can see from this original meaning, the Japanese government had obvious ambition to make PDC as an international standard, at least for Pacific-Asian region. However, this second goal was not achieved, which will be explained more in the next section—'CASE DESCRIPTION.'

Korea

Like the Japanese government, the Korean government has played a major role in the development of the Korean wireless industry from the beginning. The first wireless communications company in Korea was founded by the Korean government in March 1984 and named Korean Wireless Telecommunication. It started wireless telecommunications service in May 1984 through adopting the AMPS technology (Advanced Mobile Phone Service) from the United States. This adoption made the Korean wireless telecommunications market dependent on the foreign companies (e.g. Motorola) for systems.

The Korean government had four choices of technologies for its future 2G wireless industry: GSM, TDMA, PDC, and Code Division Multiple Access (CDMA). GSM, TDMA and PDC were easy to implement because they had been used in other markets, but it would have made the Korean wireless market dependent on foreign wireless companies again. The CDMA technology was developed by Qualcomm in 1989 but had not been introduced in any market at the time.

Although CDMA had not been proven in a commercial market yet, it would give a great advantage to the first company or market that tried it, by giving a chance to build CDMA networks, handsets, etc. The Korean government decided to go for CDMA to boost its electronics industry and have a better chance to keep its wireless industry independent, even though they had to pay royalties to Qualcomm for use of the CDMA technology. At that time, Pactel (former Verizon) and Southwestern Bell (former SBC), who were willing to be CDMA pioneers in United States, asked the Korean government whether it would be interested in waiting and buying a complete CDMA system from U.S. companies to deploy the CDMA technology, but the Korean government rejected this idea, even though it didn't know when it could develop its own CDMA systems (Lee, 2001). This incident indicated the willingness of the Korean government as a developer, not as a simple adopter, to develop, implement, and diffuse the CDMA systems.

In May 1991, the Electronics and Telecommunications Research Institute (ETRI)— founded by the Korean government in 1976 as a research institute—and Qualcomm agreed to jointly develop CDMA systems. This agreement implied that the Korean government and industry would invest enormously in financial means and other resources to develop and commercialize all the necessary CDMA systems. When the CDMA development did not go smoothly, Ericsson approached the Korean government and offered the deployment of GSM equipment for the Korean market without initial payment, but the Korean government did not approve this proposal (Lee, 2001). The Korean government had a very strong will to develop its own CDMA system to protect its wireless communications market. If the Korean government would fail, it would end up losing a lot of investment and time, and would have to build its wireless infrastructure again using one of the other technologies (GSM, TDMA, or PDC). Although the Korean government faced many challenges in developing and implementing CDMA-based systems, through diligent efforts from 1991 to 1995, it was finally able to launch commercial CDMA wireless service in 1996.

In the same year, the Korean government licensed three more companies as Personal Communication Service (PCS) providers based on the CDMA network, totaling five number of companies to compete in the Korean wireless communications market. In 1994, when the Korean government decided to privatize government-owned Korean Wireless Telecommunication, which was renamed SK Telecom in 1997, it also allowed another company, Shinsegi Telecommunication, to enter the wireless communications market, creating two private companies. These privatization and liberalization policies brought more competition to stimulate the Korean wireless communications market.

CASE DESCRIPTION

Up until this point, Korean and Japanese wireless communications industries have seemed to be in similar positions. They both took a chance on technology standards not being used outside their country, in order to develop their domestic companies' capabilities and give them the advantage of being a first mover in the global market. At the same time, they liberalized their market to grow with free competition.

However, while CDMA was subsequently adopted by other companies and markets, PDC remained isolated in Japan. There were two main factors that made CDMA more attractive to other markets than PDC. First, it was known that CDMA was technologically more advanced (Mock, 2005). CDMA could accommodate more subscribers in the same size network due to the effective frequency usage, the more efficient battery usage in handsets, and the better security (Mock, 2005). Furthermore, CDMA-based networks cost less to implement and maintain (Mock, 2005). Companies in other countries had been aware of the technological advantage of CDMA, even when they did not have confidence in its commercialization (Lee, 2001). Once they saw its commercial success in Korea, some of them were willing to implement it such as several U.S. companies (e.g. Verizon and Sprint).

Second, the biggest attraction of CDMA was about the natural migration path to third generation (3G) technology. When wireless telecommunications markets, at least in the developed countries, became mass markets for large customer populations, based on the 2G technologies from niche markets in the 1G period, as well as Internet emerged with great popularity, governments and companies realized that 3G technologies should provide wireless broadband to deliver large data in a speedy manner (Seo & Lee, 2007). Considering possible migration paths from existing 2G technology standards, CDMA was the most superior technology to provide the wireless broadband at the time. Seeing the advantage of ease migration path to 3G technology along with other factors including political reason, less developed countries that were still in the 2G stage have decided to open up their markets for CDMA along with their existing GSM networks. Thus, China and India started commercial CDMA service in 2002, expanding significantly the CDMA global market due to these countries' sizes and economic growths (Seo & Mak, in press).

Consequently, the choice of CDMA as a wireless communications technology standard has greatly impacted the Korean economy, even though the commercial debut of CDMA was much later than those of GSM and TDMA. Despite the small share of the CDMA standard in the global market, Korean government's decision has allowed major Korean electronic companies like Samsung and LG to become some of the world's leading wireless handset makers. These handset manufacturers have expanded their capabilities to produce GSM handsets as well, learning from their CDMA handset experience (Figure 1).

In contrast, no other countries have adopted PDC. Although the Japanese government, NTT DoCoMo, and NEC promoted PDC for the Asian market with the helps from Ericsson and Motorola in 1992, the Japanese wireless industry became technologically isolated from the global 2G wireless communication market (Bekkers, 2001). This standard was not so attractive to other nations. First, the PDC technology was not distinguishably innovative from GSM and TDMA. Second, the GSM standard, with noticeably roaming capability and the support of many European nations, already started to gain its global market share. Third, the PDC systems were more expensive and proprietary than others (Garrard, 1998). Considering these factors in the competitive international market, other countries tended to adopt the

Figure 1. Korean exports of wireless handsets and systems (1998-2002)

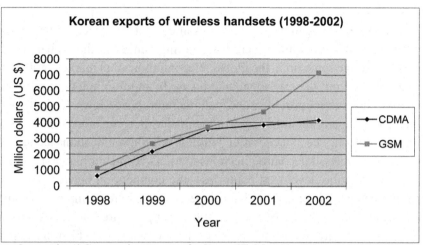

(Source, International Cooperation Agency for Korea IT, Monthly IT Export – 2003/10; Original source, Ministry of Information and Communication in Korea (MIC) 2003/09)

GSM technology that could bring the economy of scale for lower costs and would provide more options for systems, unless countries had a political and economical tie with a nation that hosted a certain standard. For example, many countries in Central and South America used to adopt U.S. technology standards because of the historically close relationship with the U.S. government (Funk & Methe, 2001).

The failure of PDC as an international standard also influenced the Japanese telecommunications system manufacturing industry. The Japanese electronics companies had gained significant market shares for the telecommunications-related systems as first movers under the supportive policies of the Japanese government during the 1G wireless telecommunications technology period (1980s). For example, in 1989, NEC and Fujitsu were ranked 5 and 9 respectively by the telecommunications-related sales in the global market (Bekkers, 2001). However, this success was doomed by the technologically isolated standard, PDC. While the Japanese companies such as Sony and Panasonic gained leading global brand names in the consumer electronics market, Nokia, Ericsson, Samsung, and LG pushed away these Japanese companies from the center of the world wireless communications market during the 2G period (1990s). As a result of the decision to develop its own technology standard, the Japanese electronics industry did not effectively expand its market globally, which has led to loss of economic opportunities for them and disadvantages for end-users. Because no other companies entered the Japanese market, lack of sustained competition meant higher prices and less variety of handsets and services.

CURRENT CHALLENGES

By the late 1990s, governments witnessed some standards successfully becoming international standards, while others were falling behind in the global standards competition. At the same time, the global telecommunication market evolved to be de-monopolized from the state-owned industry. In addition, the tight relationship between wireless service providers and manufacturers broke down. Considering this dynamic environment, the role of governments has become more significant than ever in standardizing the 3rd generation wireless telecommunications technologies.

As the 2G wireless telecommunications market became more mature and saturated—at least in the developed countries—the competition between companies became more intense. From the market perspective, this fierce competition naturally led to price erosion and loss of revenue. For example, wireless service providers set lower prices to attract customers from their competitors, which increased the costs for recruiting new customers and for maintaining existing customers. As a result, Average Revenue Per User or Unit (ARPU) deteriorated. Thus, both service providers and manufacturers were motivated to look for new sources of revenue. It showed the market need to develop a 3G wireless telecommunications technology. This situation has put more pressure on governments in terms of allocating necessary frequencies, opening their markets, and setting appropriate technology standards policies (Steinbock, 2003).

The questions were again what technology a government should pursue, and whom should it collaborate with for the upcoming 3G technology market. These were particularly important matters to the Korean and Japanese governments, because the CDMA and PDC markets were very small compared to the European standard, GSM, which dominated more than 70% of the global 2G market (see Figure 2).

While the European manufacturers were prospering with the success of the GSM standard, the Japanese manufacturers had to satisfy themselves with their domestic market, because Japan's 2G standard PDC was not adopted anywhere else. Even the second largest wireless service provider in Japan, KDDI abandoned its PDC infrastructure and adopted CDMA for its network in 1999. Nevertheless, the Japanese domestic market grew rapidly and became quickly saturated. Therefore, to move forward, the Japanese government and all the wireless communications related Japanese companies were keen on realizing 3G as soon as possible. The Japanese government did not want its electronics manufacturers to be again excluded from the future global 3G wireless communications market. Therefore, the Japanese government actively sponsored a study group and invited non-Japanese organizations as well as Japanese manufacturers to research and coordinate plans for 3G. The Japanese government hoped that the participation of non-Japanese organizations would help make whatever 3G technology it promoted internation-

Figure 2. The configuration of 2G standards in mid-1990s

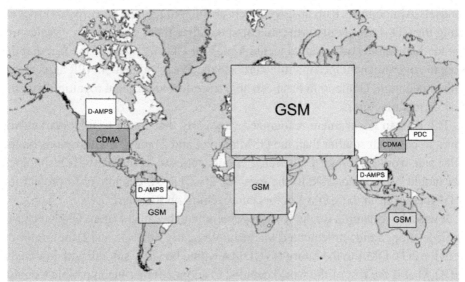

(Note: this picture is simplified and does not show all standards adopted by every country)

ally recognized. However, the Japanese government had to answer many difficult questions to move forward quickly such as:

- Whether the 3G technology should be migrated from its existing PDC market, otherwise, the switching cost would be very high for wireless service providers to implement whole new systems;
- Whether Japan should develop its own technology as it did for the 2G market, if so, then how Japan should advocate it in the global market;
- Whether Japan should adopt a technology from others, if so, then from whom, what technology, and when it should adopt the technology;
- Whether Japan should adopt a basic technology and develop it further, or wait and adopt the fully developed technology.

These questions put the Japanese government in dilemma, but it did not have time to sit and ponder the questions. The Japanese government should move very fast to provide first mover advantages to its national companies.

Through standardizing the CDMA technology, Korea has become the world's most advanced wireless market, and Korea's electronics industry grew to be highly sophisticated and successful. However, the large financial resource from this prosperity flowed to Qualcomm, because Qualcomm owned the essential Intellectual Property Rights (IPR) on the CDMA technology and the Korean manufacturers had to pay royalties to Qualcomm when they produced the CDMA systems including handsets. Although the Korean government and manufacturers participated in developing the CDMA systems further to commercialize them successfully, Qualcomm already had patents on essential technologies for CDMA. Despite the fact that the Korean government helped manufacturers to receive advantageous IPR agreements with Qualcomm, Qualcomm has been able to collect significant royalties from the Korean manufacturers.

The Korean government recognized very early that 1) the CDMA market was going to be much smaller than the GSM market and 2) many organizations on the GSM side would leverage their strategies and tactics to develop the 3G technology that would be incompatible to the existing 2G CDMA technology to protect the GSM market from the CDMA actors encroaching on their turf.

It was a big dilemma for the Korean government, because 1) the CDMA technology it developed and implemented was technologically superior; and 2) the migration from the 2G CDMA to the future 3G CDMA would be fairly smooth with low costs; but 3) what if the rest of the world decided to adopt another incompatible technology, while the Korean government would let its industry move toward the natural migration path to the 3G CDMA. If this happened, the Korean market would be technologically isolated and its companies would stay in the niche market. Therefore, the Korean government should also consider many questions. For example:

- Whether the Korean government should propose to develop its own 3G based on the natural migration path from its existing 2G CDMA technology, while minimizing the technology dependence on Qualcomm to avoid the large royalty fees, and then try to make an international standard;
- Whether Korea should abandon its 2G standard and adapt the 3G standard that GSM actors will develop;
- If the Korean government chooses an incompatible 3G standard from the 2G CDMA, how will it persuade the Korean wireless service providers to adopt new systems based on the new standard.
- Whether it chooses its own standard or adapts a standard from others, whom Korea should cooperate with in developing the 3G standard.

These were the questions that the Korean government had to answer for building standards strategies for the 3G wireless telecommunications technology. It should decide and act soon; otherwise, the window of opportunity would be closed in a very short time period.

REFERENCES

Bekkers, R. (2001). *Mobile telecommunications standards: GSM, UMTS, TETRA, and ERMES*. Boston, MA: Artech House.

De Vries, H. J. (2006). IT standards typology. In Jakobs, K. (Ed.), *Information Technology standards and standardization research* (pp. 1–26). Hershey, PA: Idea Group Publishing. doi:10.4018/978-1-59140-938-0.ch001

Funk, J. L., & Methe, D. T. (2001). Market- and committee-based mechanisms in the creation and diffusion of global industry standards: The case of mobile communication. *Research Policy, 30*, 589–610. doi:10.1016/S0048-7333(00)00095-0

Garrard, G. A. (1998). *Cellular communications: Worldwide market development*. Boston, MA: Artech House.

Komiya, M. (1993). Personal communications in Japan and its implications for Asia. *Pan-European Mobile Communications, Spring*, 52-55.

Lee, W. C. Y. (2001). *Lee's essentials of wireless communications*. New York, NY: McGraw-Hill.

Mock, D. (2005). *The Qualcomm equation: How a fledgling telecom company forged a new path to big profits and market dominance*. New York, NY: AMACOM.

Noam, E. M. (1992). *Telecommunications in Europe*. New York, NY: Oxford University Press.

Porter, M. E. (1990). *The competitive advantage of nations*. New York, NY: The Free Press.

Seo, D., & Lee, J. (2007). Gaining competitive advantage through value-shifts: A case of the South Korean wireless communications industry. *International Journal of Information Management, 27*(1), 49–56. doi:10.1016/j.ijinfomgt.2006.12.002

Seo, D., & Mak, K. T. (in press). Using the thread-fabric perspective to analyze industry dynamics: An exploratory investigation of the wireless telecommunications industry. *Communications of the ACM*.

Steinbock, D. (2003). Globalization of wireless value system: From geographic to strategic advantages. *Telecommunications Policy, 27*, 207–235. doi:10.1016/S0308-5961(02)00106-4

This work was previously published in the Journal of Cases on Information Technology, Volume 12, Issue 1, edited by Mehdi Khosrow-Pour, pp. 63-73, copyright 2010 by IGI Publishing (an imprint of IGI Global).

Chapter 10
Using Web Sites to Improve Fiscal Transparency:
The Case of Turkish Municipalities

Tolga Demirbaş
Uludag University, Turkey

EXECUTIVE SUMMARY

Fiscal transparency today is considered as an essential element of both good governance and e-governance. Therefore, in the new public management and budgeting reforms made by governments, it is clearly observed that fiscal transparency is one of the key elements. E-government technologies, and especially the internet, are supportive to the efforts on the part of governments offering unprecedented opportunities to public administrations enabling the dissemination of fiscal information and improving the e-governance system. In Turkey, where there is the tradition of Continental Europe, the reforms made through new laws in early 2000 contain various legal and institutional regulations to improve fiscal transparency and encourage the public administrators to use websites in an attempt to enhance fiscal transparency. This chapter, within the context of evaluating the endeavors in question, examines the websites of municipalities in Turkey in terms of fiscal transparency and eventually presents some suggestions for the improvement of the e-governance system.

DOI: 10.4018/978-1-4666-0981-5.ch010

INTRODUCTION

E-governance, the latest trend in the governance process, can be defined as using information and communication technologies (ICTs) to improve the delivery of information and services, encourage the public to participate in the decision-making process and make the government more accountable, transparent and efficient (Prabhu, 2005; Palvia & Sharma, 2007). While e-governance is a concept beyond a government website only in the Internet (Backus, 2001), it is also an interactive network that brings the public, non-governmental organizations (NGOs), businesses and other units in the community together with the government on the plane of ICT. Therefore, it encapsulates new policy formulation models, new forms of citizenship, new power and relationship patterns, new options for economic development and new ways in order to bring the public together with the political process (Chandra, 2003). Briefly, e-governance is the use of ICTs to strengthen good governance describing a significant transformation.

The realization of the benefits expected from the e-governance system and the ability of the government, an important agent in this system, to be able to improve its capacity to meet the needs of the public (Shiang, 2008), depends on the generation of sufficient and intelligible information by the agents in the system and especially by the government and on the easy access of this information by the agents. In other words, the efficiency of e-governance system is directly related to "transparency".

ICTs and especially the Internet offer policy makers and administrators unprecedented opportunities in order to strengthen transparency, a fundamental element of e-governance (Justice, Melitski, & Smith, 2006). However, some high costs have had to be paid globally for raising awareness for those opportunities. Towards the end of the last century, the financial crises that broke out because the fiscal information produced by governments was not standard, clear and comparative, had a negative impact on many countries and led to some serious economic and social costs. Therefore, fiscal transparency has started to occupy an indispensable place on the reform agendas of international financial organizations and states. Almost all governments have made some important technical reforms in order to improve paper-based transparency and have encouraged the dissemination of fiscal information produced via the Internet. Thus, public administrations have started to use the Internet more to take the opportunity of making their fiscal information more accessible, reaching more and more people simultaneously in an economical way (Wescott, Pizarro, & Schiavo-Campo, 2000).

In addition to this research, there have been a very few studies on how efficiently the public administrations use the Internet to increase fiscal transparency and it has been found that majority of the existing studies have been limited to developed countries. Therefore, Turkey, with its Continental European Tradition and still maintaining its accession talks with the European Union (EU), is an important subject of study to carry out in this sense. After the financial crises that followed early in the year 2000, some vital reforms were made in Turkey in order to improve the fiscal transparency of the state. Many legislations and regulations passed within the framework of the reforms in question have prescribed the preparation of comprehensive documents and reports inclusive of fiscal information of public administrations. Moreover, the new legal regulations encourage the publication of those relevant documents on internet sites and thus aim to contribute to the effectiveness of a local e-governance system. For this reason, this chapter, in the context of the latest developments, aims to measure to what extent the municipalities in Turkey use the Internet to disseminate fiscal information on their websites, focus on some of the variables explicating the results of these measurements, and thus present some important suggestions in an attempt to improve the local e-governance system at the grass roots.

In this framework, this chapter briefly explicates the concept and significance of fiscal transparency at first and emphasizes the part websites play in the improvement of fiscal transparency. Thereafter, what follow is the reforms made in Turkey in order to improve fiscal transparency and the regulations made in an attempt to disseminate fiscal information in the Internet. In the case part of the study, the websites of 207 municipalities in Turkey are evaluated using a fiscal transparency index. After the analysis of some of the variables capable of explicating the success of the municipalities, various problems hindering the use of websites in order to strengthen fiscal transparency of the municipalities are highlighted. In the final section, some suggested solutions for the improvement of the e-governance system are discussed.

THE CONCEPT OF FISCAL TRANSPARENCY AND ITS SIGNIFICANCE

Fiscal transparency is defined as generating reliable, comprehensive, timely, understandable and internationally comparable information regarding the accounts and operations of the government and making it as accessible as possible (Kopits & Craig, 1998). Fiscal transparency is regarded as a fundamental norm in public fiscal administration (Schick, 1999) since it allows the public to see and assess to what extent public institutions use fiscal resources (Premchand, 2002); it helps the administrators ensure fiscal discipline (Bushman & Smith, 2003) and enables the prevention of corruption through the curtailment of powers of public workers (Klitgaard, 1998). The financial crises that occurred at the end of the 1990s in Latin America and Asia generating significant macro global economic instabilities caused fiscal transparency to become internationally more important. The studies carried out revealed the extent of the importance of the lack of fiscal transparency such as the insufficiency of information regarding the accounts and operations of the governments, and the hidden obligations not visible in the accounts, in the deepening of the fiscal crises in question (Parry, 2007). Therefore, the International Monetary Fund (IMF) in an effort to ensure fiscal stability on a global scale, developed the Code of Good Practices on Fiscal Transparency (1998) in an attempt to make the fiscal information produced by governments more reliable and comparable. Today, whether and to what extent countries comply with those standards is announced in the national assessment reports of the IMF (IMF, 2007). After IMF developed these standards, a similar enterprise was started by the Organisation for Economic Co-operation and Development in 1999 (OECD, 2000) and the World Bank today provides governments with technical and financial assistance in an attempt to enhance fiscal transparency. The fact that fiscal transparency has gained international importance has increased the pressures on governments to make their fiscal systems more transparent and fiscal transparency has become one of the cornerstones of the public finance management reforms in almost every country.

Fiscal transparency is regarded as an indispensable reform element for the new public management (NPM) movement postulating the information problems between the principal and agent as a reference point (Kettl, 2005). Accordingly, public administrations are in possession of knowledge of how resources can be used effectively. However, the strict control and procedures on the administrators and financial resources fail to provide the necessary encouragement. Therefore, the NPM reforms, based on reliability, allow administrators some flexibility. This flexibility is also supported by the tools that will enable public administrators to be more accountable for the results (Kettl, 1997). One of the most prominent tools is the creation and announcement of comprehensible information about the operations of public administrations which is accessible by the public for evaluation (Bovaird, 2003). As has been seen so far, both the international financial institutions and the new conception of public administration regard fiscal transparency as an important tool. Therefore, the pressure on public administrations and administrators to improve fiscal transparency is gradually increasing.

The most effective tool which increases the pressure on public administrators and also offers them important opportunities to enhance the level of transparency is the advance in information technology and use of the Internet. In a world where internet use is spreading rapidly, any public administration without a website will be judged negatively by citizens. This demand forces change upon the structures of public administrations which have been traditionally self-enclosed refusing to share information with the public. Therefore, it is possible to argue that the most important function of e-government in general and the internet specifically is to make government more transparent.

THE ROLE AND IMPORTANCE OF THE WEBSITES
IN IMPROVING FISCAL TRANSPARENCY

Governments have been adopting reforms, especially since the 1990s, in an attempt to improve fiscal transparency, which has been proved to have key importance for both the global economy and global citizens. However, many of the tools used in these reforms enable complex and detailed information produced mostly for experts. To give an example, medium term budgets, performance reports of up to thousands of pages, a comprehensive classification of expenditure according to international standards, all enhance fiscal transparency for experts in this field but are very difficult to understand for the average citizen who has no detailed technical knowledge of budget and financial management issues. In this respect, the internet enables public administrators to submit fiscal information related to budget and accounting processes for public in a comprehensible form. Thus, it becomes possible for citizens who are most certainly not as knowledgeable as a budget expert to be informed about the process and, therefore, paves the way for the strengthening of public accountability (Justice et al., 2006).

Citizens may be reluctant to take part in the decision-making process of the government. Attending meetings, producing formal feedback and filling out questionnaires on public services may require time commitment and cost for citizens, which they may be unwilling to give (Hoo, 2002). Since the production of information via the internet has the quality of being a public good in terms of political economy, it has important potential to overcome those difficulties. The production of information by public administration via websites is a public good that has the qualities of relative nonexcludability and nonrivalness. Everyone has access to the information posted on the website and the access of one user mostly does not impede the access of another user (Weare, Musso, & Hale, 1999). Thus, it becomes possible for the citizens who are unwilling due to the intensity of the everyday life and can not afford to access the information to have quicker, more economical, easier access to this information 24/7 (Justice et al., 2006; Heeks, 2000). Above and beyond, since the internet allows a citizen to access the fiscal information of more than one public administration quickly, there is the opportunity to make a comparison between the administrations. Therefore, the public has the opportunity to compare and interpret the information such as budget figures and annual accounts of more than one public administration, and can eventually produce new information based on the information obtained (Justice et al., 2006).

Civil servants, on the other hand, who are faced with time pressure from the daily tasks of government, may regard contact with the public and proactive cooperation with them as an unnecessary and unwelcome burden (Hoo, 2002). It has even been stated that some civil servants may be so unwilling to share information with the public that they impede the intensive demand for government information (Heeks, 2000). This contributes to the disappointment of citizens who have spent time and money trying to access information. Websites help to remove this obstacle between the public administration and citizens. As PC ownership and internet usage increase, there is a greater demand for the spread of information from public administrations via websites, and administrations without a website or those that do not operate properly are negatively assessed (Hoo, 2002).

The key role that websites play in enhancing fiscal transparency has also attracted the attention of international financial institutions. Therefore, both the IMF and the OECD crucially lay emphasis on the fact that public administrations publish information and documents on fiscal transparency on the internet free of charge (OECD, 2000; IMF, 2007).

THE EFFORTS TO IMPROVE FISCAL TRANSPARENCY IN TURKEY AND THE INTERNET

The Republic of Turkey, founded in 1923 upon the collapse of the Ottoman Empire, is a unitary state that functions as a bridge between Asia and Europe and whose 70-million population is mostly composed of young people. The fiscal transactions of the government and public administrations in Turkey were for a long time subjected to the general accounting law which were adopted from France in 1927. Since it was an important goal in the early years of the Republic not to pave the way for financial corruption, the tradition of Continental Europe was adopted, where all expenditure of the administration was centrally controlled. This tradition proved to be very successful during the period concerned (Bayar, 2003). However, after this period, in order to be able to operate freely, some institutions were formed that were not subjected to the strict limitations and parliamentary control of the general accounting law. Revolving capital enterprises, extra budgetary funds, foundations and associations are examples of such institutions in Turkey. The fact that there was no proper reporting system regarding institutions that were extrabudgetary damaged the public's right to obtain information and the accountability of government. Besides, similar to other developing countries, the treasury guarantees were not directly reflected in the budget, operational losses of state banks and state economic enterprises became areas of expenditure whose cost was not known and that had not been budgeted for. All these developments caused the total size of public expenditure in Turkey to be unknown and, therefore, there was unaccountability of a significant amount of expenditure (State Planning Organization, 2000).

This state of affairs, which significantly damages fiscal transparency, was not properly questioned until the last ten years. This had been due to the fact that budget and government's accounts required some expertise and was boring to the public, there were a few non-governmental organizations that were equipped to inform the public about these issues, there was little awareness of questioning how and where taxes paid by the public were spent and an unwillingness on the part of politicians and bureaucrats to reveal the true financial situation of the government. The problem of transparency in public finance management in Turkey came to the forefront after two critical financial crises that occurred in November 2000 and in February 2001. The on-time unpaid operational losses of the state banks, since they did not appear in the public accounts, played an important role in these crises and eventually resulted in a debt of about 40 billion dollars, and debt being taken over by the government (Emil & Yılmaz, 2004).

Having been awarded EU candidate status at the 1999 Helsinki summit, Turkey started, after the two crises mentioned, to deliver the commitments she had made to the EU and within this framework, strengthen her fiscal transparency. In addition, the IMF and the World Bank provided financial aid to Turkey on condition that Turkey improved her fiscal transparency. Therefore, a new public financial law that was in line with the requirements of the new century was drafted. Thanks to the influence of some external institutions and then later approved by the Turkish Parliament. The most important feature of the Public Financial Management and Control Law (PFMCL), all provisions of which came into effect in early 2006, made public administrations and their administrators more accountable for their operations and guaranteed "fiscal transparency" as its fundamental insurance. The new law differed from the previous one in that it acknowledged fiscal transparency both as a main goal of public financial management and as a basic principle of budgeting (Article 1 & 13). In addition, the law includes many significant institutional arrangements. Accordingly,

- Preparing three-year budgets (Article 17 & 18),
- Making strategic plans (Article 9),
- Preparing annual performance programs (Article 9),
- Preparing annual activity reports (Article 41),
- Publishing the six-monthly budget execution results mid year (Article 30),
- Informing taxpayers of their rights and obligations (Article 36/d),
- Being clear about the tasks, powers and responsibilities (Article 7/a),
- Preparing the financial statistics in line with the standards and publishing them regularly (Article 52 & 53),
- Imposing fines on administrative officials who fail to submit them to the Ministry of Finance (Article 53),
- Public access to the reports (Article 7/b),

are among the important recent changes introduced by this law in terms of producing fiscal information and sharing it with the public.

Another development supportive of enhanced transparency in fiscal administration in Turkey is the right to information law that came into force in 2004. This law legally secured the right of every citizen to acquire information and ensured "the information acquisition units" to be established, and thanks to a specific regulation (The Regulation on the Procedures, 2004) made within this framework. This regulation also encouraged the institutions and organization to prepare informative and instructive brochures and publications about their organizational structures, tasks and services, and required annual activity reports together with the budgetary reports to be made available for public scrutiny (Article 6).

As is seen, some important legal changes have been made in Turkey in recent years in an attempt to enhance fiscal transparency and strengthen citizens' rights to obtain information. These changes can be regarded as significant steps toward changing the self-enclosed structure of the government previously unwilling to share information. One common important feature of the laws concerned is the increase in the responsibilities of public administrations and their administrators in terms of producing information and making it available to the public. The PFMCA remarks that public institutions are responsible for making the necessary arrangements to ensure fiscal transparency and taking the necessary measures, and all these points are under the scrutiny of the Ministry of Finance (Article 7). The right to information law confirms these remarks as follows:

The institutions and organizations are obliged to take the necessary administrative and technical measures in an attempt to make all kinds of documents apart from those indicated in the Law available for the use of those demanding it and finalizing the applications for obtaining information in a quick and correct manner (The Right to Information Law, 2004, Article 5).

The internet, the most effective tool of information sharing today, is in a position to become the most efficient instrument for public administrators in Turkey to use in order to improve fiscal transparency. The regulation related to the right to information law (The Regulation on the Procedures, 2004) based on this particular fact imposed the condition that public institutions with no web page should set up their own websites and institutional e-mail addresses by 24th of June, 2004 (Temporary Article 4). According to the regulation, it is compulsory for the relevant e-mail addresses and application forms for obtaining information to be posted on their websites (Article 6 & 10). For the right of obtaining information to be used effectively and to decrease the workload stemming from those applications, the regulation also encourages budgetary documents and statistics as well as information about tasks and services to be made available to the public on their websites (Article 6 & 7). Although it is optional to publish all this information on the internet, a regulation of PFMCA (The Regulation on Activity Reports, 2006) has made it compulsory for the annual activity reports of the public administrations to be posted on their websites. This compulsion is regarded as an important revolution in order for the local community to assess the activities and operations of public administrations.

THE EFFORTS OF THE MUNICIPALITIES IN TURKEY TO SPREAD FISCAL INFORMATION OVER THE INTERNET: AN EMPIRICAL STUDY

Methodology

Public administrations in Turkey, within the tradition of Continental Europe, are held responsible, in terms of the producing and spreading of fiscal information, for taking the necessary measures in accordance with the provisions in law, and are encouraged to disseminate the fiscal information through their websites. The aim of this study is reveal to what extent the public administrations in question make use of their websites for this purpose and offers some solution suggestions for the quality of e-governance system. The municipalities in Turkey, despite the centralized structure of the government, are among the most expedient local governments that are relatively very close to the public and powerful units. Especially in recent years, some arrangements have been made in order to increase the financial resources of municipalities and the service provision capacities of these administrations have been strengthened within the framework of "fiscal decentralization". The other reason why municipalities have been dealt with in this study is that the municipalities have gradually begun to perceive that "the internet" is an important window opening into the local community. While the internet was introduced in Turkey for the first time in 1993, there were only 30 municipalities with a website in March 1999 (Yıldız, 1999). This number rose to 92 in June 2000 (Bensghir, 2000) and to 1298 in September 2008 (Naralan, 2008). This trend is very positive for local e-governance in Turkey.

In this study, in order to be able to understand how effectively the municipalities use websites as a tool to enhance fiscal transparency, a total of 219 municipalities with a population of 50 000 and over have been examined[1]. The main reason for this is that the laws in Turkey made it an obligation for these municipalities to prepare a strategic plan (Municipality Law, Article 41). The strategic plan, an essential document for the efficient management of resources, is an administrative tool that determines the mid-term objectives and targets of the administrations linking them to the resources. The fact that the municipalities concerned have the competence to be able to use this tool also provides them with an important source of motivation to strengthen fiscal transparency.

In this study, in order to measure the degree of the municipalities' use of their websites for the purposes of fiscal transparency, a fiscal transparency index (FTI) has been used. Since there is no index with a general validity in the field of local governments which can be used for this purpose, Pérez, Hernández, & Bolívar (2005), Pérez, Bolívar, & Hernández (2008) and Justice et al. (2006) have been used extensively to establish the index used in this study. Accordingly, FTI is composed of three categories:

The first category is based on the fact that the basic documents (and reports) legally obligatory to be prepared by the municipalities and containing fiscal information be available for public scrutiny. It is noteworthy to remember that this is an issue significantly emphasized by both the PFMCA and the IMF. Within this framework, a measure has been set as to whether four basic documents are available to view and/or download from their websites. These documents are the strategic plan, the annual performance program, the original budget (or a comprehensive summary) and the annual activity report.

Even though the fact that the documents in the first category are available on the website can be regarded as an indication of fiscal transparency, it may not essentially reflect the reality. There may not be crucial information available in these documents, or a municipality may choose to publish some fiscal information on its website without publishing these documents. Therefore, the second category of the index is related to the content and characteristics of the information available both in the documents concerned and, apart from those documents, on the website of the municipality. In this context, the four important characteristics found in the definition of fiscal transparency have been established as four separate criteria. These are, possessing complete information about the current and past activities of the municipality (comprehensiveness); the characteristics of fiscal information being comparable across the past years and administrations (comparability); the characteristics of fiscal information being understandable and clear to the public (comprehensibility) and finally, the characteristics of fiscal information being published in periods of less than a year (timeliness) when they are out (IMF, 2007).

The third category of the index is related to the design and user-friendliness of the website. The ease of accessing fiscal information, presentation of the data in different formats to the user, availability of choice of accessing fiscal information in a foreign language (English) and availability of various ways for users to contact the municipality about fiscal information have been established as the criteria of this group.

The criteria and sub-criteria together with their categories are shown in Table 1. In this study, all the categories were weighted based on a total of 24 points. Therefore, the total of 12 criteria available in the three categories gives us the fiscal transparency index (FTI):

$$FTI = DOCUMENT - INFO = \frac{1}{4} \sum_{i=1}^{4} Vi + CONTENT$$

$$- CHARACT = \frac{1}{4} \sum_{i=5}^{8} Vi + NAV - DES = \frac{1}{4} \sum_{i=9}^{12} Vi$$

In this equation, the Vi's are the values obtained by each criterion as a result of examining municipality websites. The Vi value takes values of 2 and 0 based on the documents available on the municipality's website (document-info), content and characteristics of the information (content-charact) and the design of the website and its user-friendliness (nav-des). While the totality of high index scores illustrate that municipalities use their websites in order to enhance fiscal transparency, the low scores describe the exact opposite situation.

FTI ranks the municipalities in terms of online fiscal transparency, but it does not reveal the factors effective in this sequencing. Specially, political economy and diffusion literature show the variables that can be effective in a municipality spreading information through its website as in the following (Weare et al., 1999): population size, the number of internet users, per capita income, municipality size, the level of fiscal capacity, the rate of political participation and the number of social elites. Unfortunately, in this study, due to lack of data, it is not possible to analyze all the variables in question for all the municipalities. Therefore, in this study, the effect of the variables of population size, political participation, per capita income, education and municipal expenditures on the level of fiscal transparency of the 66 municipalities in the FTI is analyzed. In this study, multivariate linear regression analysis is to be used. The specification of the model is as follows:

$$FTI = \alpha_0 + \beta_1 (PolPar) + \beta_2 (PerCI)$$
$$+ \beta_3 (MunExp) + \beta_4 (Edu)$$
$$+ \beta_5 (MunPop) + \varepsilon_i$$

The fiscal transparency index (FTI) in the model is the dependent variable. The five independent variables respectively are, the rate of political (or electoral) participation (PolPar), per capita income in the municipality (PerCI), municipality

Table 1. Fiscal transparency index for Turkish municipalities

	Measures	Score
A.	**The Basic Documents being available for Public Scrutiny and accessible (DOCUMENT-INFO)**	**8**
	1. The updated strategic plan is available on the website.	2
	2. There is the current (2009) performance program or the original budget / its comprehensive summary on the website.	2
	3. The current activity report (2008) is available on the website.	2
	4. Any one or more of the past documents (those indicated in A1, A2 and A3) are available.	2
B.	**The Content and Characteristics of the Information Available on the Web Site and in The Basic Documents (CONTENT-CHARACT)**	**8**
	5. Comprehensive information	2
	a. Resource allocations in line with aims and objectives are available	0,33
	b. Budget expenditures together with types	0,33
	c. Budget revenues together with types	0,33
	d. Projections for two years following the budget (multi-year budget)	0,33
	e. Budgetary results	0,33
	f. Balance sheet	0,33
	6. Understandable information	2
	a. There is a citizens' guide to explain the main features of the budget	0,66
	b. Tasks, powers and responsibilities are explicated	0,66
	c. Percentages and graphics are provided together with interpretations	0,66
	7. Comparable information	2
	a. The user has a chance to compare the fiscal data with each other	1
	b. Data of at least three years old are comparatively available on the website or in the fiscal document	1
	8. Timely information	2
	a. Three-monthly (quarterly) data are periodically published	1
	b. Six-monthly data are periodically published	1
C.	**Navigation and Design of the Web Site (NAV-DES)**	**8**
	9. Ease of Accessing the Data	2
	a. There is a special part on the website allowing access to most of the fiscal information and very easy to notice	1
	b. Searching within the website is possible	0,50
	c. A site map is available	0,50
	10. Ease of Data Management	2
	a. Format: html	0,50
	b. Format: pdf or doc	0,50
	c. Format: xls	1

continued on following page

Table 1. Continued

Measures	Score
11. Ease of Use within International Context	2
a. Fiscal information in English on the website is available	2
12. Interaction with the User	2
a. E-mail addresses and legal on-line application documents of the information acquisition unit is available	0,66
b. Apart from the information acquisition unit and webmaster, e-mail addresses / telephone numbers for requesting fiscal information and enquiry is available	0,66
c. It is possible for taxpayers to have access to their personal obligations (such as debt inquiry, paying tax)	0,66

expenditure (MunExp), the percentage of those in the municipality population over 23 years of age with a university degree (Edu) and the municipality population (MunPop). ε_i refers to a random error term'.

Findings and Discussion

In order to determine to what extent the municipalities in Turkey use their websites to enhance fiscal transparency, initially the websites of 219 municipalities were examined in July 2009[2]. Of these, 12 were excluded from this examination since they did not have a website or their existing websites did not operate properly. The websites of the remaining 207 municipalities were subjected to content analysis in terms of the criteria specified in the FTI and the results were recorded. To achieve greater clarity, the index scores were converted into percentages.

The FTI results indicate that the index scores of the 207 municipality websites in Turkey are on average 23.84%. Perez et al. (2008), who examined the websites of 65 municipalities in Spain, found this percentage as 14.36%[3] and the authors described this percentage as quite low. Therefore, it is possible to indicate that the average of the index is high for a developing country like Turkey. According to the index, the 5 municipalities meeting the criteria the most are; Çanakkale municipality (83.83%), Istanbul metropolitan municipality (78.25%), Konak municipality (72%), Mersin metropolitan municipality (69.92%) and Kocaeli metropolitan municipality (69.33%). It is an interesting result that the Çanakkale municipality with its population of 66 000 people outstripped 16 metropolitan municipalities. The municipalities that failed to meet the criteria are Merzifon, Gemlik, Ergani, Siverek, Esenyurt and Atakum municipalities.

According to the first category of the index indicating whether the basic documents containing fiscal information are available on the website, the performance of the municipalities is 26.45%. The number of municipalities that never published any of the documents in question on their websites is only 12. The remaining 195 municipalities published at least one of the basic documents on their websites. It is believed that the legal changes made in Turkey have had an important contribution to the performance achieved.

The second category of the index regarding the content and characteristics of the fiscal information showed a value of 20.18%. Based on this value, it is possible to say that the municipalities, when compared to their publishing of the fiscal documents on their websites, are less successful in achieving information quality. One of the interesting points in this category is the fact that the majority of the municipalities (69%) published their tasks, powers and responsibilities on their websites as required by fiscal transparency. Many municipalities publish the relevant laws in this issue on their websites. Apart from these, for most of the basic fiscal documents mentioned above, there are some relevant parts. Another interesting point in this category is the accessibility and availability of the budget practice results in 44% of the municipalities. It is observed that the basic fiscal documents have a role to play in this issue. Contrary to these successful ones, there are also some issues that should be available in those fiscal documents, but the municipalities fail to provide. For instance, while the percentage of the municipalities whose strategic plan can be accessed on their website was 29%, the percentage of the municipalities that provided resource allocation related to the necessary objectives in the plan (and in the performance program) was lower (14%). This shows that some of the municipalities were short of the capacity in preparing a strategic plan. Çetinkaya (2008), who drew attention to this particular issue, indicated that the administrations lacked both staff and knowledge in this area (p.248). In this category of the index, only the Istanbul metropolitan municipality published a guide document explicating the municipality's budget process on its website.

In the third and last category of the index, the success rate of the municipalities was 24.89%. In this part, the criterion where the municipalities were most successful was interaction with the users (62.1%). Due to the influence of the right to information law, in 70.5% of the municipalities, it is possible to reach the e-mail addresses and application forms related to information acquisition. In addition, the percentage of access to the staff in the municipalities via e-mail and telephone from whom fiscal information could be requested was 61.4% and the percentage of the taxpayers who could access their personal financial information was 55.8%. Another interesting point in the third category is the fact that the fiscal information on the websites of the municipalities was placed under headings that were not easy to find or difficult to notice. For instance, some municipalities such as Nazilli municipality, Kuşadası municipality and Alanya municipality presented the information related to their budgets to their local communities under the link of council decisions.

Table 2. Spearman correlation matrix of independent variables (n=66)

	1 PolPar	2 PerCI	3 MunExp	4 Edu	5 MunPop
1 PolPar	1				
2 PerCI	0.35	1			
3 MunExp	-0.11	0.47	1		
4 Edu	0.04	0.66	0.52	1	
5 MunPop	-0.26	0.28	0.79	0.40	1

Interestingly, in Fatsa municipality, the performance program of the municipality was published in the "online services" section on its website. Nevertheless, in 52% of the municipalities, it is possible to make a "site search" and 27% of them have a site map. The most important factor that reduces the performance level of the municipalities in the third category is the criterion of presenting fiscal information in English. Out of the municipalities examined, only Kocaeli municipality could meet this criterion. Finally, most of the information and documents (42%) published by the municipalities were in pdf or doc format. The percentage of xls format, which facilitates analysis, is only 1.9%.

Clearly, FTI shows the degrees of the municipalities' fiscal transparency on the web. Nevertheless, it requires a separate analysis to work out why some municipalities have obtained high scores and others low scores. Therefore, in order to test some of the variables by which one can explicate the FTI in this study, the model author specified in the methodology section has been used. There has been an important data problem regarding local governments in Turkey. In this model, the rates of political participation and municipal expenditures are based on the 2004 data of the Turkish Statistical Institute. The population information on the basis of municipalities for the year 2004 have been estimated by the author (through the interpolation technique). Due to insufficiency of data, for the figure of the income per capita, the data of the year 2001 and for the percentage of those with a university

Table 3. Regression model results

FTÎ = - 1.21 + 0.001 PerCI + 0.533 Edu + 0.09 PolPar + 0.03 MunExp				
T (- 0.13)	(1.840)	(1.529)	(0.097)	(1.903)
Sig.	(0.071)*	(0.132)	(0.923)	(0.062)*
			$R^2 = 0.324$ $\check{R}^2 = 0.279$ $F = 7.299$ $P = 0.000$	

degree, the data of the year 2000 were used. Those data are appropriate for only 66 municipalities out of 207.

The Spearman correlations of the independent variables are found in Table 2.

The highest correlations were found between municipal population and municipal expenditure (0.79), education and per capita income (0.66). The approach was to use all available data. So, at first author chose to omit only the municipal population variable that has the highest correlation with municipal expenditure from the model. Thus, in the estimation process this research used all four variables (political participation, per capita income, municipal expenditure and education). Several regression models were estimated. Finally, the regression model (see Table 3) results were found to be appropriate.

The estimation above shows that per capita income and municipal expenditure are statistically significant at 10% level (See the significances marketed with *). Although these two variables are statistically significant, political participation and education are not. The coefficients of two significant variable signs were all found as expected (positively). The coefficient of determination was found to be 0.324. This value shows that the 32% change of the FTI was explained with the four independent variables that were used above. The significance of F statistic was found to be 0.000. This value shows that the variables fit well to the model. When author look at the estimation results, it was seen that the impact of the variables of per capita income and municipal expenditure on the transparency index is quite low (0.1% and 0.3% respectively).

According to these findings, the significance of the variable of per capita income seems to be compatible with the literature of e-government in general. For instance, Weare et al. (1999) found that as the welfare of the local community in 454 cities in California increased, website adoption increased as well. The articles of Musso, Weare, & Hale (2000), Huang (2006), Hoo (2002) and La Porte, Demchak, De Jong (2002) demonstrate that the variable of income had an impact on the quality of a website and its design. Although the variable in question in Turkey seems to have a little impact on the spread of fiscal information by municipalities on their websites, it is rather difficult to test how this impact operates. This is because the relevant literature claims that those individuals with high income will make more demands regarding e-government (La Porte et al., 2002), thus the public administrations will make more effort to meet this demand (Weare et al., 1999). Insufficiency of data on the basis of municipalities regarding internet users in Turkey makes it difficult to test this claim.

The variable of municipal expenditure is an important indicator of municipality size. The fact that one municipality can spend more in comparison to another one is an indication of its (purchasing) power. As this power increases, the likelihood of making more e-government investment may also increase (La Porte et al.,

2002). The fact that this study found a positive impact, though little, (0.3%) of the municipal expenditure on fiscal transparency on the web is supportive of this argument. However, it is not yet known how much e-government investment is made by municipalities in Turkey.

Theoretically, university graduates are expected to be more interested in the fiscal information of local governments. Nonetheless, in addition to those in the literature who found positive relationships between the level of education and e-government adoption like Huang (2006), there are also studies that found no positive relationship (Pérez et al., 2008). According to a survey in Turkey, university graduates are at the top amongst internet users (Turkish Statistical Institute, 2009). Therefore, the finding that the level of education had no positive impact on transparency is incompatible with the existing theory.

Municipalities that are units of local governments are the essence of democracy; the rate of participation to municipality elections, on the other hand, is an important indication of the level of democracy and transparency. This study, contrary to the expectations, found that political participation had no impact on the dissemination of municipalities' fiscal information on their websites. This particular state of affairs can be regarded as the result of a governmental tradition that has continued until the present day from the time of the Ottoman Empire. On the other hand, this centralized governmental tradition also plays an important role in municipalities in Turkey spreading the fiscal information on the web as we have seen in this chapter.

CURRENT CHALLENGES

In Turkey, just like in other countries, various obstacles negatively affect the municipalities' efforts in the dissemination of fiscal information on their websites. It is vitally important to reveal these obstacles in terms of the improvement of local e-governance.

The Problem of Leadership and Coordination

Since Turkey has the tradition of Continental Europe, "legislative framework" comes to have a primary significance in public administration reforms. Thus, the legislations passed in recent years have encouraged the municipalities and other public administrations to set up a website and disseminate their fiscal information and have become partially successful in this. However, it is vitally important for these legislative frameworks to be accomplished within the context of detailed plans and a strong institutional structure. Unfortunately, it is clearly observed that there has not been sufficient progress for planning, organizing, implementing and monitoring the efforts enabling e-transformation of the local governments in Turkey. Although a document of "information society strategy (2006-2010)" that displays a medium and long term strategy and targets aimed at enabling a transformation into an information society has been prepared with a participatory approach, this strategy has not yet been implemented at the local level. In this strategy document, it is stated that the Ministry of Interior, General Directorate for Local Authorities is responsible for the coordination between local governments, for sharing the technology in similar technology applications together with ensuring efficiency in investments and for monitoring and assessing the applications (State Planning Organization, 2006a). Also, in the action plan prepared based on the relevant strategy document, it is proposed that the measurement of performance in the provision of local services is carried out by the collective efforts of the State Planning Organization, local governments and the relevant NGOs under the supervision of the same General Directorate (State Planning Organization, 2006b). All the same, as was stated in the evaluation report in relation to the action plan dated March 2009, it is clearly seen that no action has yet been taken with regards to the activities in question (State Planning Organization, 2009).

Funding Problems

Funding issues are the main problems negatively affecting the entrepreneurship efforts of the public administrations. As has been mentioned before, municipalities in Turkey are local administrative units that are closest to the public and the most powerful in comparison to other local administration units. Some legislative regulations have recently been made in an attempt to increase the revenues of municipalities and efforts have also been exerted to enhance their service provision capacities. Nevertheless, the proportion of the expenditure made by the municipalities with regards to Gross Domestic Product (GDP) is approximately 3.2% (Ministry of Finance, 2009) and the municipalities in Turkey fall behind those in the EU. Moreover, almost half of the revenues of the municipalities are constituted by the funds transferred from the central government (Ministry of Finance, 2006), thus negatively affecting their fiscal autonomy. This condition, certainly, constitutes a huge obstacle especially for small-sized municipalities to start their e-governance initiatives and to be able to employ qualified personnel. In fact, the results of a survey conducted by Turkish Statistical Institute in 2005 revealed that the most important problems encountered by municipalities while providing services on the web are respectively lack of qualified personnel and the high cost of hardware and software programs (Turkish Statistical Institute, 2006).

Digital Divide

Digital divide is an important problem in terms of e-governance in Turkey as is the case in many other developing countries. According to the results of ICT Usage Survey on Households and Individuals done in April 2009, only 30% of households in Turkey had access to the Internet (Turkish Statistical Institute, 2009). This percentage is on average 60% in European Union countries (Eurostat, 2009). Moreover, the Internet usage percentages of individuals in the age group 16 to 74 are respectively 48.6% in males and 28.0% in females. Similar differences exist in rural and urban areas as well (Turkish Statistical Institute, 2009). These limitations result in not all the citizens being able to make full use of the websites of the municipalities and being unable to deliver their democratic requests and demands on the web. This condition, without a doubt, may negatively impact the municipalities' motivation to disseminate information on the web.

The Level of Public Interest in Fiscal Information

The interest of the local communities in fiscal information is one of the most important elements determining the dissemination of fiscal information via the website of a municipality. The citizens in Turkey, as is the case in many other countries, find issues related to government budgeting and financial management complex and boring in general, and do not show enough interest in them. In fact, according to a survey, the percentage of citizens in Turkey using the internet for the purpose of obtaining information from public institutions is 23.5% and is an indication of the lack of interest in question (Turkish Statistical Institute, 2007). In the research part of this study, the fact that the university graduates who constitute the group of people using the internet the most in Turkey did not make any significant contribution to the online fiscal transparency level of municipalities can be interpreted as the result of this lack of interest in fiscal information. The fact that there is an insufficient number of NGOs that will encourage the public in the pursuit of transparency informing them about financial issues and the tradition of centralized state are among the most important reasons behind the lack of interest in fiscal information. As a natural result of all these reasons, it is clearly observed that accountability of the municipalities to the public is not strong enough.

SOLUTIONS AND RECOMMENDATIONS

The pursuit of the municipalities in Turkey to reach the public and pay attention to what they have to say via the internet generally proceeds by means of their own efforts away from a clear vision. Therefore, a strong vision and strategy have to be urgently developed by central government and put into effect in a decided manner. The General Directorate for Local Authorities has to play a more active part in this issue. There are many steps that can be taken under the leadership of this Directorate. Developing some standards for municipalities for setting up websites and online transparency and measuring and publishing the performance of the municipalities in disseminating fiscal information via the web can be among the first of these steps to be taken. Such an approach may encourage municipalities to compete with one another, enabling them to enhance their performances.

It is necessary to strengthen the technological capacities and human resources of Turkish municipalities in order to support them to disseminate their fiscal information on the web at an institutional level. The most viable long term strategy on this issue is to enhance the individual revenues of the municipalities, thus strengthening their autonomy. However, since small-sized municipalities suffer more from such problems, it can be a short and medium term solution that they be supported by a fund to be set up by central government.

Public participation in the processes of administration and budget in local administrations is a crucial tool in meeting the demands of local needs and strengthening transparency. Therefore, encouraging "participatory budgeting" and efforts of "e-democracy" to be accomplished by the participation of the municipality, public and NGOs at the local level can be a viable approach in terms of improving the local e-governance system. Indeed, the fact that the municipality of Çanakkale occupying the first place on the transparency index developed in the research part of this study is the municipality which commenced the application of the very first participatory budget (Benyamor, 2007) supports this hypothesis. The city councils that have developed as a model of governance throughout the process of Local Agenda 21 in Turkey appear as ideal structures in terms of municipalities preparing a participatory budget and drawing the attention of the public and NGOs to fiscal issues (Economic Policy Research Foundation of Turkey, 2007). The functioning of this process also supported by the medium of the Internet can make crucial contributions to the improvement of transparency and e-governance.

Municipalities, just as is the case with other public institutions, do not have the motivation to adapt to the technological developments either, unlike private sector institutions. Problems such as digital divide and lack of technical capacity decrease this motivation even further. However, municipalities should remember that they are not in a position to choose their own citizens and that accessing information is a basic right of all citizens (Beckette-Camaratta, 2002). Therefore, it is vitally important that the administrators in municipalities be more sensitive to the dissemination of information via websites, making use of the existing resources and possibilities more efficiently. The familiarity of the administrators in municipalities with the technology and their occupations may play a part in this sensitivity.

CONCLUSION

This study, for the first time, comprehensively examined the websites of municipalities in Turkey in terms of transparency and rated 207 municipalities based on their performance. Accordingly, it was found that the level of municipalities improving their fiscal transparency through their websites was quite high (23.84% on average) for a developing country like Turkey. Given the fact that only 30 municipalities in Turkey in 1999 had billboard-type websites that were not updated regularly (Yıldız, 1999), it is possible to say that the municipalities have gone a long way in the last ten years. Without a doubt, in reaching this particular level today, the new laws that have both motivated the municipal administrators and imposed some obligations via some of their clauses have made a huge contribution. Therefore, it is possible to say that "the approach of law" in general is successful in Turkey, which has the tradition of Continental Europe. All the same, there is still a long way to go for the municipalities in terms of fiscal transparency. Under the leadership of a strong political and administrative command, the steps to be taken in this issue by the participation of the public, NGOs, the private sector and other agents are sure to enhance the quality of e-governance at the grass roots.

REFERENCES

Backus, M. (2001). *E-governance in developing countries.* (Research Brief No 1). Retrieved October 21, 2009, from International Institute of Communication & Development: http://www.ftpiicd.org/files/research/briefs/brief1.pdf

Bayar, D. (2003). Kamu Mali Yönetimi ve Kontrol Kanunu Ne Getir(m)iyor? [What does public financial management and control law yield (or not)?]. *Maliye Dergisi, 144,* 47–62.

Beckette-Camaratta, J. (2002, October). *Assessing e-budgeting in US local governments: A case study.* Paper presented at the Korean Association For Public Administration Conference, Seoul, S. Korea.

Bensghir, T. K. (2000). Web'deki Belediyelerimiz: Bursa Büyükşehir Belediyesi [Our municipalities on the Web: Bursa metropolitan municipality]. *Çağdaş Yerel Yönetimler, 9*(4), 106-118.

Benyamor, G. (2007, April 10). Türkiye'nin İlk Katılımcı Bütçesi Çanakkale Belediyesinden [First participatory budget in Turkey from Çanakkale municipality]. *Hürriyet Gazetesi*. Retrieved October 22, 2009, from http://hurarsiv.hurriyet.com.tr/goster/haber.aspx?id=6300902&yazarid=20

Bovaird, T. (2003). The changing context of public policy. In Bovarid, T., & Löffler, E. (Eds.), *Public management and governance* (pp. 13–23). London, UK: Routledge.

Bushman, R. M., & Smith, A. J. (2003). Transparency, financial accounting information, and corporate governance. *Federal Reserve Bank of New York Economic Policy Review, 9*(1), 65–87.

Çetinkaya, Ö. (2008). Kamu İdarelerinde Hazırlanan Stratejik Planlarda Mevzuata Aykırı Oluşan Durumlar [Legal problems related to strategic plans of public administrations]. *Yaklaşım, 16*(192), 244–248.

Chandra, R. (2003). *Information technology in 21st century: Ethics and governance of the internet*. Delhi, India: Kalpaz Publications.

Economic Policy Research Foundation of Turkey. (2007). *İyi Yönetişim İçin Örnek Bir Model: Katılımcı Bütçeleme* [A representative model for good: Participatory budgeting]. Yönetişim Etütleri Programı, Ankara. Retrieved October 21, 2009, from http://www.tepav.org.tr

Emil, M. F., & Yılmaz, H. H. (2004). *Mali Saydamlık İzleme Raporu* [Fiscal transparency monitoring report]. Ankara, Turkey: TESEV.

Eurostat. (2009). *Households who have Internet access at home*. Retrieved October 21, 2009, from http://epp.eurostat.ec.europa.eu

Heeks, R. (2000). Government data: Understanding the barriers to citizen access and use. *iGovernment Working Paper Series (Paper No 10)*. Manchester, UK: Institute for Development Policy and Management.

Hoo, A. T. K. (2002). reinventing local governments and the e-government initiative. *Public Administration Review, 62*(4), 434–444. doi:10.1111/0033-3352.00197

Huang, Z. (2006). E-government practices at local levels: An analysis of U.S. counties' websites. *Issues in Information Systems, 7*(2), 165–170.

International Monetary Fund. (2007). *Manual on fiscal transparency*. Washington, DC: Fiscal Affairs Department.

Justice, J. B., Melitski, J., & Smith, D. L. (2006). E-government as an instrument of fiscal accountability and responsiveness: Do the best practitioners employ the best practices? *American Review of Public Administration*, *36*(3), 301–322. doi:10.1177/0275074005283797

Kettl, D. F. (1997). The global revolution in public management: Driving themes, missing links. *Journal of Public Policy Analysis and Management*, *16*(3), 446–462. doi:10.1002/(SICI)1520-6688(199722)16:3<446::AID-PAM5>3.0.CO;2-H

Kettl, D. F. (2005). *The global public management revolution*. Washington, DC: Brookings Institution.

Kickert, W. (2007). Public management reforms in countries with a Napoleonic state model: France, Italy and Spain. In Pollitt, C., van Thiel, S., & Homburg, V. (Eds.), *New public management in Europe: Adaptation and alternatives* (pp. 26–51). Great Britain: Palgrave MacMillan.

Klitgaard, R. (1998). International cooperation against corruption. *Finance & Development*, *35*(1), 3–6.

Kopits, G., & Craig, J. (1998). *Transparency in government operations*. Occasional Paper. Washington, DC: IMF.

La Porte, T. M., Demchak, C. C., & De Jong, M. (2002). Democracy and bureaucracy in the age of the Web: Empirical findings and theoretical speculations. *Administration & Society*, *34*, 411–446. doi:10.1177/0095399702034004004

Ministry of Finance. (2006). *Belediyeler Seçilmiş Mali Büyüklükler*. [Municipal fiscal accounts]. Ankara. Retrieved October 21, 2009, from http://www.muhasebat.gov.tr

Ministry of Finance. (2009). *Kamu Hesapları Bülteni* [Public accounts report]. Ankara. Retrieved October 21, 2009, from http://www.muhasebat.gov.tr

Municipality Law. (2005). *Laws of Turkish Republic, No 5447 of 2005*. Retrieved October 21, 2009, from http://www.tbmm.gov.tr

Musso, J., Weare, C., & Hale, M. (2000). Designing Web technologies for local governance reform: Good management or good democracy? *Political Communication*, *17*, 1–19. doi:10.1080/105846000198486

Naralan, A. (2008). Belediyelerin Resmi İnternet Sitesi Sahipliği ile Siyasi Partiler ve Nüfus Arasındaki İlişki [Relations among website ownership of municipalities, population and political parties]. *Cumhuriyet Üniversitesi İktisadi ve İdari Bilimler Fakültesi Dergisi, 9*(2), 63–77.

OECD. (2000). *OECD best practices for budget transparency.* Public Management Service Public Management Committee.

Palvia, S. C. J., & Sharma, S. S. S. (2007). *E-government and e-governance: Definitions/domain framework and status around the world.* Paper presented at the Fifth International Conference on E-Governance, Hyderabad, India. Retrieved October 21, 2009, from http://www.iceg.net/2007/books/1/1_369.pdf

Parry, T. (2007). *The role of fiscal transparency in sustaining growth and stability in Latin America.* Working Paper (Paper No WP/07/220), IMF, Washington D.C.

Pérez, C. C., Bolívar, M. P. R., & Hernández, A. M. L. (2008). E-government process and incentives for online public financial information. *Online Information Review, 32*(3), 379–400. doi:10.1108/14684520810889682

Pérez, C. C., Hernández, A. M. L., & Bolívar, M. P. R. (2005). Citizens' access to on-line governmental financial information: Practices in the European Union countries. *Government Information Quarterly, 22*, 258–276. doi:10.1016/j.giq.2005.02.002

Prabhu, C. S. R. (2005). *E-governance: Concepts and case studies.* Delhi, India: Prentice Hall of India Private Limited.

Premchand, A. (2002). *Fiscal transparency and accountability: Idea and reality in United Nations. Globalization and new challenges of public finance: Financial management, transparency and accountability.* New York, NY: Department of Economic and Social Affairs.

Public Financial Management and Control Law. (2003). *Laws of Turkish Republic, No 5018 of 2003.* Retrieved October 21, 2009, from http://www.tbmm.gov.tr

Regulation on Activity Reports of Public Administrations. (2006). *Regulations of Turkish Republic, No 26111 of 2006.* Retrieved October 21, 2009, from http://www.bumko.gov.tr

Regulation on the Procedures and the Methods Related to Implementation of the Right to Information Law. (2004). *Regulations of Turkish republic, No 25445 of 2004.* Retrieved October 21, 2009, from http://www.mevzuat.gov.tr

Right to Information Law. (2003). *Laws of Turkish Republic, No 4982 of 2003.* Retrieved October 21, 2009, from http://www.tbmm.gov.tr

Schick, A. (1999). *A contemporary approach to public expenditure management.* World Bank Institute: Governance, Regulation, and Finance Division.

Shiang, J. (2008). *Change and adaptation of stakeholder relationships in e-governance.* Paper presented at Fourth International Conference on e-Government, Melbourne, Australia. Retrieved October 21, 2009, from http://web.thu.edu.tw/jshiang/www/iceg2008.pdf

State Planning Organization. (2000). *Kamu Mali Yönetiminin Yeniden Yapılandırılması ve Mali Saydamlık Özel İhtisas Komisyonu Raporu* [The special experts commission report on reinventing public financial management and fiscal transparency]. Ankara.

State Planning Organization. (2006a). *Bilgi Toplumu Stratejisi (2006-2010)* (Pub. No. 2699). [Information society strategy], Ankara.

(2006b). *State Planning Organization* (pp. 2006–2010). Ankara: Bilgi Toplumu Stratejisi Eylem Planı.

State Planning Organization. (2009). *Bilgi Toplumu Stratejisi Eylem Planı (2006-2010) Değerlendirme Raporu 3* [Evaluation report 3 of the information society strategy action plan (2006-2010)], Ankara.

Turkish Statistical Institute. (2006, January). 2005 Yılı Belediye Web Hizmetleri Araştırması, [Municipality Web services survey 2005]. *Haber Bülteni.* Retrieved October 21, 2009, from http://www.tuik.gov.tr

Turkish Statistical Institute. (2007, August). *2007 Yılı Hanehalkı Bilişim Teknolojileri Kullanım Araştırması Revize Sonuçları* [Revised results of the information and communication technology usage survey on households and individuals 2007]. Retrieved October 22, 2009, from http://www.tuik.gov.tr

Turkish Statistical Institute. (2009, August). 2009 Yılı Hanehalkı Bilişim Teknolojileri Kullanım Araştırması Sonuçları, [The results of 2009 information and communication technology usage survey on households and individuals]. *Haber Bülteni.* Retrieved October 21, 2009, from http://www.tuik.gov.tr

Weare, C., Musso, J. A., & Hale, M. L. (1999). Electronic democracy and the diffusion of municipal web pages in California. *Administration & Society, 31*(1), 3–27. doi:10.1177/009539999400935475

Wescott, C., Pizarro, M., & Schiavo-Campo, S. (2000). The role of information and communication technology in improving public administration. In S. Schiavo-Campo & P. Sundaram (Eds.), *To serve and to preserve: Improving public administration in a competitive world* (pp. 673-701). Retrieved October 21, 2009, from http://www.adb.org/documents/manuals/serve_and_preserve

Yıldız, M. (1999). Yerel Yönetimde Yeni Bir Katılım Kanalı Internet: ABD'de ve Türkiye'de Elektronik Bilgi Ağları [A new way to participation in local government (Internet): Electronic information networks in USA and Turkey]. *Çağdaş Yerel Yönetimler, 8*(4), 144-156.

ADDITIONAL READING

Armstrong, E. (2005). *Integrity, transparency and accountability in public administration: Recent trends, regional and international developments and emerging issues.* United Nations: Economic & Social Affairs.

Bolívar, M. P. R., Pérez, C. C., & Hernández, A. M. L. (2007). E-government and public financial reporting - The case of Spanish regional governments. *American Review of Public Administration, 37*(2), 142–177. doi:10.1177/0275074006293193

Brito, J. (2008). Improving government transparency online. *Public Management, 37*(1), 22–26.

Bushman, R. M., Piotroski, J. D., & Smith, A. J. (2004). What determines corporate transparency? *Journal of Accounting Research, 42*(2), 207–252. doi:10.1111/j.1475-679X.2004.00136.x

Cheng, R. H. (1992). An empirical-analysis of theories on factors influencing state government accounting disclosure. *Journal of Accounting and Public Policy, 11*(1), 1–42. doi:10.1016/0278-4254(92)90013-N

Cuillier, D., & Piotrowski, S. J. (2009). Internet information-seeking and its relation to support for access to government records. *Government Information Quarterly, 26*(3), 441–449. doi:10.1016/j.giq.2009.03.001

Gutierrez-Nieto, B., Fuertes-Callen, Y., & Serrano-Cinca, C. (2008). Internet reporting in microfinance institutions. *Online Information Review, 32*(3), 425–436. doi:10.1108/14684520810889709

Kelton, A. S., & Yang, Y. W. (2008). The impact of corporate governance on Internet financial reporting. *Journal of Accounting and Public Policy, 27*(1), 62–87. doi:10.1016/j.jaccpubpol.2007.11.001

Norris, D. F., & Moon, M. J. (2005). Advancing e-government at the grassroots: Tortoise or hare? *Public Administration Review, 65*(1), 64–75. doi:10.1111/j.1540-6210.2005.00431.x

OECD. (2007). *OECD e-government studies: Turkey.* Paris, France: OECD.

Ogurlu, Y. (2007). E-government applications and its effects on public service in Turkey. In D. Remenyi (Ed.), *Proceedings 7th European Conference on E-Government,* (pp. 395-404). England.

Pallot, J. (2001). Transparency in local government: Antipodean initiatives. *European Accounting Review, 10*(3), 645–660.

Pina, V., Torres, L., & Royo, S. (2007). Are ICTs improving transparency and accountability in the EU regional and local governments? An empirical study. *Public Administration, 85*(2), 449–472. doi:10.1111/j.1467-9299.2007.00654.x

Pina, V., Torres, L., & Royo, S. (2008, October). *E-government evolution in EU local governments: A comparative perspective.* Paper presented at the Fourth International Conference on E-Government, Melbourne, Australia.

Piotrowski, S. J., & Van Ryzin, G. G. (2007). Citizen attitudes toward transparency in local government. *American Review of Public Administration, 37*(3), 306–323. doi:10.1177/0275074006296777

Relly, J. E., & Sabharwal, M. (2009). Perceptions of transparency of government policymaking: A cross-national study. *Government Information Quarterly, 26*(1), 148–157. doi:10.1016/j.giq.2008.04.002

Roy, J. (2008). Service, security, transparency, and trust: Government online or governance renewal in Canada? In Norris, D. (Ed.), *E-government research: Policy and management* (pp. 314–335). Hershey, PA: IGI Publishing.

Serrano-Cinca, C., Rueda-Tomas, M., & Portillo-Tarragona, P. (2009). Factors influencing e-disclosure in local public administrations. *Environment and Planning. C, Government & Policy, 27*(2), 355–378. doi:10.1068/c07116r

Serrano-Cinca, C., Rueda-Tomás, M., & Portillo-Tarragona, P. (2009). Determinants of e-government extension. *Online Information Review, 33*(3), 476–498. doi:10.1108/14684520910969916

Shakespeare, T. (2008, October 15). Information, Information, Information: Improving Access to Information for Local Areas. *Localis,* Research Notes 2. Retrieved July 18, 2009, from http://www.localis.org.uk/article/122/Information-Information-Information.htm

Stanforth, C. (2006). *Analysing e-government implementation in developing countries using actor-network theory.* iGovernment Working Paper Series (Paper No 17), Manchester: Institute for Development Policy and Management.

Vishwanath, T., & Kaufmann, D. (2001). Toward transparency: New approaches and their application to financial markets. *The World Bank Research Observer, 16*(1), 41–57. doi:10.1093/wbro/16.1.41

Welch, E. W., Hinnant, C. C., & Moon, M. J. (2005). Linking citizen satisfaction with e-government and trust in government. *Journal of Public Administration: Research and Theory, 15*(3), 371–391. doi:10.1093/jopart/mui021

West, D. M. (2004). E-government and the transformation of service delivery and citizen attitudes. *Public Administration Review, 64*(1), 15–27. doi:10.1111/j.1540-6210.2004.00343.x

KEY TERMS AND DEFINITIONS

Annual Activity Report: This is a report comprehensively demonstrating especially the past one-year activities of the public agencies comparatively, together with the targets and the agency is obliged to publish it on its website.

Continental European Tradition: This is a hierarchical and centralist tradition of public administration in which administrative law strongly governs the acts of public agencies (Kickert, 2007).

Fiscal Information: Information available in such documents and reports as the budget and annual activity report; also information related to the accounts and operations of the government and the other public administrative units.

Fiscal Transparency Index (FTI): This is an index with a maximum of 24 scores demonstrating the usage performance for the municipalities to improve their websites' fiscal transparency.

Fiscal Transparency: The accounts and operations of the government and the other public administrative units are to be made accessible to the general public, and they are clear and comprehensible.

New Public Management: This is a reform movement that grants authority and responsibility to administrators so that the public administrations can operate more efficiently and deal with the public on an interactive basis, which leads to greater transparency and accountability.

Performance Program: This is an annual document prepared by a public administration according to a strategic plan and basically demonstrating the performance targets, resource allocations and fiscal information.

Strategic Plan: This is a document demonstrating the vision, mission, quantitative and qualitative objectives of the public agencies; it is also a fundamental element of strategic management.

ENDNOTES

[1]   The number of municipalities with a population of 50 000 and over has been calculated based on the 2007 census. According to the latest regulations, the number of the municipalities in Turkey is 2903.

[2]   The website addresses of the municipalities were searched in the following addresses http://www.devletana.com, http://www.yerelnet.org.tr and the following search engine http://www.google.com.

[3]   Using the average index value, it was converted into percentage by us.

This work was previously published in Cases on Adoption, Diffusion and Evaluation of Global E-Governance Systems: Impact at the Grass Roots, edited by H. Rahman, pp. 171-191, copyright 2011 by Information Science Reference (an imprint of IGI Global).

Chapter 11
Vision Impairment and Electronic Government

Reima Suomi
Turku School of Economics, Finland

Irene Krebs
Brandenburgische Technische Universität, Germany

EXECUTIVE SUMMARY

The visually-impaired are in a distinctive disadvantage when using computer screens based on visual presentation of data. Their situation becomes increasingly critical, as most society services, including issues such as e-Commerce, e-Business, e-Health, and e-Government go on-line. Yet modern technologies can too offer solutions to their problems, both at hardware and software level, and often with reasonable cost. Effective ICT can open up new communication channels and functionalities for say totally blind people, which would not have been available for them otherwise. General sensitivity for this issue, and especially, sensitivity among designers of governmental e-services must be developed. E-Government is an especially demanding activity area as it comes to all sorts of imparities (not just vision impairment), as governmental services are often in a monopoly service delivery situation: citizen have to use them, and there is often no other alternative. The issue binds it to the wider discussion on digital divide, where vision impairment is one cause for digital divide, and often very devastating, especially if still combined with other sources of digital divide.

DOI: 10.4018/978-1-4666-0981-5.ch011

ORGANIZATION BACKGROUND

Vision impairment is vision loss (of a person) to such a degree as to qualify as a handicap through a significant limitation of visual capability (Arditi & Rosenthal, 1998). It is a form of disability. Countries around the globe are acting to promote e-governance, so that people with disability are increasingly able to get access to information on the Internet. However, it is always a difficult commitment for many countries to reach the whole community (AHRC, 2009), and majority of the websites in the education, cultural and business sectors are still inaccessible to people with vision impairment. (HKBU, 2006).

Currently, there is less than 6% percent of printed material that is accessible for those citizens who are vision impaired or have other print disabilities. Moreover, people with vision impairment report frustration that they must continually request that government documents are presented online in multiple formats apart from PDF such as RTF, MS Word, and HTML (ACCAN, 2009; BSI, 2006). The system should be able to consider the needs of people with disabilities, such as providing alternative keyboard navigation, animated displays, color and contrast setting, and other means of making the system usable to people with vision impairment (Govt. of US, 2007). In addition to these blind, deafblind and vision-impaired people have particular needs. Skill development programmes must not be designed solely for people who can see and read standard print, and who can use software without altering its on-screen appearance or using adaptive technology. (NZ Foundation, 2009; EATT Project, 2003). Foremost, there should be studies to identify factors accounting for why some states or countries are more responsive than other states or countries to the needs of people with disabilities in their use of e-government (Rubaii-Barrett & Wise, 2008).

In this context, digital divide could be termed as the inequality in assessing services of the information society (Brodie, Flournoy et al. 2000; Compaine 2001; Norris 2001; Siochrú, Girard et al. 2002; Akhter 2003), and one form of digital divide is caused by vision impairment, that can take several forms from total blindness to minor shortcomings say in colour recognition. The number of people with visual impairment worldwide in 2002 was in excess of 161 million, of whom about 37 million were blind (Resnikoff, Pascolini et al. 2004).

The case is discussing governmental support for vision impairment in two well-developed countries, Germany and Finland. It is well clear that the problems might be totally different in less-developed countries, in which vision impairment can too be even more a severe problem; especially the area of e-Government is looking at. By e-Government this research means the delivery of governmental services to citizen through electronic means, mainly the Internet. In this perspective, parts of the government activities are; providing the needed regulation and legislation for both public and private organizations to deliver good services for vision impaired through electronic means; and delivering robust and well-designed government services to citizen with vision impairment. If the government fails in providing these services, pressure to serve citizen with vision impairment materializes strongly in other service channels.

SETTING OF THE STAGE

Vision Impairment

Equality of citizen is a central value in modern societies. In reality, the equality is of course eroded by many factors. Most permeating factors causing inequality are of course permanent physical capabilities of individuals. Alongside conditions such as deafness, dumbness, inability to move normally because of missing limbs etc. or failures in the neural system, vision impairment, at its worst form totally blindness, is a key source of inequality. The term often used in this connection is vision impairment.

In worldwide statistics vision impairment officially touches upon 160 million people (Resnikoff et al., 2004), but in reality the figure is most likely much bigger. The amount of totally blind people is expected to be around 37 million (Resnikoff et al., 2004).

The most common causes of blindness around the world are (World Health Organisation, 2009):

- cataracts (47.8%),
- glaucoma (12.3%),
- uveitis (10.2%),
- age-related macular degeneration (AMD) (8.7%),
- trachoma (3.6%),
- corneal opacity (5.1%), and
- diabetic retinopathy (4.8%).

In this chapter, authors discuss the activities public authorities need to take when assisting vision impaired people, especially in the field of eGovernment. In Table-1 they have provided some basic vision impairment statistics from those two case countries, Finland and Germany. These countries were selected to be the sample countries in this research of piloting character, as the authors are from these countries and have access to documentation at the local language. Of course it must be noted that the two countries are very much alike, and drawing conclusions based on this discussion to less developed countries is not possible.

One form of visual impairment is that of colour blindness. Colour blindness can for example harm the interpretation of maps and other visual information sources. There is nowadays a tool called vizcheck (http://www.vischeck.com), which can be used to study the colour schemes of web portals. The study by showed that there were no major shortcomings as it comes to colour use in the studied governmental www-pages (Choudrie, Ghinea, & Weerakkody, 2004). Other automated tools to evaluate the user friendliness of www-sites as it comes to visual impairment are Dottie and Usability Enforcer (Becker, 2004).

E-Government

eGovernment is usually presented as using IT to (Grönlund, 2002):

- Provide easy access to government information and services for citizens and businesses
- Increase the quality of services, by such things as increased speed, completeness and process efficiency
- Give citizens opportunities to participate in the democratic process.

eGovernment is a generic term meaning all electronic contacts between citizens and their government. It is divided into two main areas: first, eDemocracy, catering for democratic processes in government, and secondly, eAdministration, containing many applications such as health care (eHealth), taxation, public procurement and police operations.

Silcock (2001) defines eGovernment as follows: "...*the use of technology to enhance the access to delivery of government services to benefit citizens, business partners and employees.*" Banerjee & Chau (Banerjee & Chau, 2004) provide the following illustration of the fast development of eGovernment: in 1996, less than

Table 1. Vision impairment in Germany and Finland, some statistics from 2007 (combined from (Ojamo, 2008) and (Bertram, 2005)

Aspect	Germany	Finland
Total population	82,3 Mio	5,3 Mio
Vision impaired people total*, percent of total population	1.000 000; 1,34	80 000; 1,5
Totally blind people*, percent of total population	160 000; 0,2	10 000; 0,19

50 official government homepages could be found on the World Wide Web. In 2001, it was estimated that globally there were well over 50 000 official government websites. Of the 190 UN Member States, 169 were providing some degree of information and services on-line.

In the US, the State eGovernment strategy delivers the following summary of proceedings in the field: *"Federal information technology spending in the United States will exceed $48 billion in 2002 and $52 billion in 2003... a good portion of current federal IT spending is devoted to Internet Initiatives, yielding over 35 million web pages online at over 22,000 web sites."*

Goverment and thus eGovernment activities take place at different levels: munipality, area, state/nation, federal and international. Yet the national level is often a natural level to study, as many important decisions, such as most of regulation and legislation. Different public-private partnerships are easily blurring the boundaries of eGoverment, as well as the tendency of public administration to work increasingly in a business way, approaching practices of eBusiness. The third sector adopting different responsibilies from the public authorities if further mixing the cards. A national government cannot always take the lead in eGovernment. As (Jarvenpaa, Tiller, & Simons, 2003) put it: *"The role of government varies, and at times it reverses from its typical stance in public choice as a supplier of regulation to being a customer of regulation."*

SUPPORT FOR VISION IMPAIRED PEOPLE

In this section we study what the Finnish and German authorities have made to support vision impaired people.

Finland

In Finland a person is entitled to help equipments based on vision impairment, when the vision of his/her better eye is after best available glass correction less than 0,3, or the total vision scope of both eyes is less than 60 grades, or the total invalidated defined in her/his case is at least 50% because of blindness.

As other health care services too, health care services are organized by individual municipalities. The government sets the regulation and laws for handicapped people. There is little disease-specific legislation, but rather general government guidance. This leads to a situation in which the real services individual get can vary a lot between different municipalities.

By law services without co-payment from vision impaired people are definition of the need for help equipment, tuning of the needed equipment, use education, follow-up and needed maintenance. Devices are given to the vision impaired either for use of for ownership, depending on the case and policy of the municipality.

Eyeglasses are of course the basic device for most vision impaired. Being as standard and wide-scale service, it is covered with a complicated and detailed legislation. We do not dwell into the details of providing eyeglasses for vision impaired people in Finland.

Help equipment is provided at two levels: Municipal health centers provide standard devices, such as white sticks, audio devices and audio enhancements to mobile phones. Luckily, such programs most often nowadays are a standard part of mobile phone operating and user interface systems. Municipal health centers are not allowed to refund any acquisitions vision impaired people have made themselves.

Central hospitals cater for expensive and non-standard devices for vision impaired people. These items might be special devices for reading normal paper-based text or extra lenses that are attached to normal televisions. Many of these devices however have to do with normal personal computers, to which non-standard extensions for vision impaired people can be given. These are items such as:

- Scanner
- Speech synthesizer
- Braille displays
- Special software for helping reading the screen contents

An expensive item decided upon by the central hospital is the need for a guide dog. In Finland, 10 special journals distributed in point writing are provided.

Germany

Hardly for any other group the paradigm shift in Germany in institutions and authorities for social care is so important than for people with disabilities. Not any action of the authoritarian state as well as a patronized and super coordinated care by institutions shall determine the everyday life, but self-determination, participation and equality must be focused more and more. This can be a step toward greater transparency and openness in dealing with disabled people, especially with visually impaired and blind people. Dignity, equality and participating are key concepts of human living together in Germany.

About ten percent of the German population has a handicap which complicates the access to computer and Internet. These include blind, impaired, deaf / hard of hearing, physically and motor-driven disabled persons, mentally and psychically disabled persons as well as intellectually disabled and people with learning difficulties. But also elder people and people with a temporary handicap often find barriers on the Internet which complicate the use for them. Just for these target groups the Internet illustrates an ideal platform to take part in the modern information society. And, however, not only differs the availability of technical preconditions for each of these persons as a user (e. g. browser versions or input devices), but there are also individual needs that should be taken into consideration with the programming of a web page.

A big part of the barriers towards the access to the Internet can be overcome thanks to modern technology and program-technical capabilities. However, the implementation often fails according to the fact, that this is widely unknown. The German Act on Equality for People with Disabilities here refers in § 4 as following: „Free of barriers are (…) systems of the data processing, acoustic and visual sources of information and communication facilities as well as other living spaces if they are accessible and usable to handicapped people in the general usual way, without special difficulty and basically without foreign help and support" (ibid.) At present, many cities and municipalities work at the launching of „Guiding Principles and Participation Action Plans" as well as resulting legal recommendations in this sense.

The use of e-health and information and communication technologies (ITK) in the public health sector has been recognized and particularly great hope regarding process optimization and saving is set on the voluntary application of the electronic health card.

The use of the electronic health card (obligatory applications "Transfer of insurance data" as well as "Electronic prescription transport") is highly appreciated in the study on health economy and e-health in Germany. The highest benefit is seen in the storage of emergency data and medicine documentation (Wegweiser GmbH Berlin, 2007).

The German National Ministry of Research has announced a major funding program for ambient assisted living (AAL). There are 16 million people in Germany now who are older than 65. In the year 2050 there will be 23 million. This means that with increasing age people's eye sight will continuously deteriorate. For this reason, €125m will be invested in 17 AAL projects over the next year. The goal is to develop IT-solutions that help elderly and chronically ill people to stay in their own flat or house as long as possible.

In Germany develop a lot of towns and villages, policy guidelines and local strategies, and out of it resultant list of recommendations in this spirit.

In Germany, some special journals distributed in point writing are provided, e.g. Electronic Journal of e-Government, eGovernment computing, Sonderpädagogik, eHealth International.

CURRENT CHALLENGES FACING THE ORGANIZATION

Governmental service provision is increasingly turning into electronic channels, under the phenomenon of eGovernment. This means that services have to be well designed and state-of-the art in the way that they are self-explaining without or with minimal human intervention. This creates challenges as such, but especially for services meant for impaired – say vision impaired – people. Governmental agencies are in a big pressure, as they should be good examples even for other actors in cyberspace – such as private companies.

SOLUTIONS AND RECOMMENDATIONS

Technical means to provide eGovernment and other services through the web to vision impaired are already on the market, and the selection of tools is increasing all the time. Yet market scan necessitates resources, and some tools might need financial resources in an amount becoming critical even for big organizations. A mostly important issue is in government as well as in private sector sensitivity to the needs of impaired people. Services can be well designed for vision impaired people, but first the wake-up to this issue must take place, and then the organizations must strengthen their service orientation even towards the vision impaired citizen.

Overcoming the handicap and digital divide caused by vision impairment necessitates actions at many levels, so even in the case of eGovernment. Many technological solutions are already there, and they are so powerful that they can crucially help even totally blind people However, technology is yet not used to its full extend, and awareness and availability of different solutions can vary considerably between different population groups.

Designers of eGovernment services have to be especially sensitive to different impairment, including vision impairment, as their services affect everyone in the society, and are often obligatory for citizen to use. Making these services available through well-designed web-interfaces is at their own interest too, because ignoring the design on good web-services will manifest itself in pressure in other, often more expensive and inefficient, delivery channels.

REFERENCES

AAL Ambient Assisted Living Programme. (2009). Retrieved from http://www.aal-europe.eu/about-aal

ACCAN. (2009). *Submission to government 2.0 taskforce secretariat. Australian Communications Consumer Action Network*. Australia: ACCAN.

AHRC. (2009). *Web accessibility and Government 2.0 Australian Human Rights Commission submission to the Government 2.0 Taskforce – Towards Government 2.0, an issues paper.* Retrieved from www.humanrights.gov.au

Akhter, S. H. (2003). Digital divide and purchase intention: Why demographic psychology matters. *Journal of Economic Psychology, 24*(3), 321–327. doi:10.1016/S0167-4870(02)00171-X

Arditi, A., & Rosenthal, B. (1998). Developing an objective definition of visual impairment. *In Vision '96: Proceedings of the International Low Vision Conference* (pp. 331-334). Madrid, Spain: ONCE

Banerjee, P., & Chau, P. Y. K. (2004). An evaluative framework for analysing e-government convergence capability in developing countries. *Electronic Government, 1*(1), 29–48. doi:10.1504/EG.2004.004135

Becker, S. A. (2004). E-government visual accessibility for older adult users. *Social Science Computer Review, 22*(1), 11–23. doi:10.1177/0894439303259876

Bertram, B. (2005). *Blindheit und Sehbehinderung in Deutschland: Ursachen und Häufigkeiten. Der Augenarzt, 6.* Dezember.

Brodie, M., & Flournoy, R. E. (2000). Health information, the Internet, and the digital divide. *Health Affairs, 19*(6), 255–266. doi:10.1377/hlthaff.19.6.255

BSI. (2006). *Guide to good practice in commissioning accessible websites. British Standards Institution*. UK: BSI.

Choudrie, J., Ghinea, G., & Weerakkody, V. (2004). Evaluating global e-government sites: A view using web diagnostic tools. *Electronic Journal of E-Government, 2*(2), 105–114.

Compaine, B. M. (Ed.). (2001). *The digital divide: Facing a crisis or creating a myth?* Cambridge, MA: MIT Press.

EATT Project. (2003). *Equal access to technology training. UK Literature Review*. UK: Royal National Institute of the Blind.

Foundation, N. Z. (2009). *Digital strategy 2.0 submission - Royal New Zealand Foundation of the Blind.* Auckland, New Zealand.

Govt. of US. (2007). *FY 2007 report to Congress on implementation of The E-Government Act of 2002.* Office of Management and Budget, Government of the USA.

Grönlund, Å. (2002). Electronic government - Efficiency, service quality, and democracy. In Grönlund, Å. (Ed.), *Electronic government: Design, applications and management* (p. 62). Hershey, PA: Idea Group Publishing. doi:10.4018/978-1-930708-19-8.ch002

HKBU. (2006). *HKBU's views & comment on the digital 21 strategy 2007.* Hong Kong: The Hong Kong Blind Union.

Jarvenpaa, S., Tiller, E. H., & Simons, R. (2003). Regulation and the Internet: Public choice insights for business organizations. *California Management Review, 46*(1), 72–85.

Norris, P. (2001). *Digital divide: Civic engagement, information poverty, and the internet wordwide.* Cambridge, UK: Cambridge University Press.

Ojamo, M. (2008). *The Finnish register of visual impairment. Annual statistics 2007: National research and development centre for welfare and health in Finland and the Finnish federation of the visually impaired.*

Resnikoff, S., Pascolini, D., Etya'ale, D., Kocur, I., Pararajasegaram, R., & Pokharel, G. P. (2004). Global data on visual impairment in the year 2002. *Bulletin of the World Health Organization, 82*, 844–851.

Rubaii-Barrett, N., & Wise, L. R. (2008). Disability access and e-government: An empirical analysis of state practices. *Journal of Disability Policy Studies, 19*(1), 52–64. doi:10.1177/1044207307311533

Silcock, R. (2001). What is e-government. *Parliamentary Affairs, 54*, 88–91. doi:10.1093/pa/54.1.88

Siochrú, S. Ó., & Girard, B. (2002). *Global media governance. A beginner's guide.* Lanham, MD: Rowman & Littlefield Publishers.

Wegweiser GmbH Berlin. (2007). *Monitoring eHealth & Gesundheitswirtschaft 2007/2008.*

World Health Organisation. (2009). *Causes of blindness and visual impairment.* Retrieved April 14, 2009, from http://www.who.int/blindness/causes/en/

ADDITIONAL READING

Becker, S. (2005). E-government usability for older adults. *Communications of the ACM, 48*(2), 104. doi:10.1145/1042091.1042127

Buch, H., Vinding, T., la Cour, M., Appleyard, M., Jensen, G., & Vesti Nielsen, N. (2004). Prevalence and causes of visual impairment and blindness among 9980 Scandinavian adults The Copenhagen City Eye Study. *Ophthalmology, 111*(1), 53–61. doi:10.1016/j.ophtha.2003.05.010

Bundrick, M., Goette, T., Humphries, S., & Young, D. (2006). An examination of web site accessibility issues. *Communications of the IIMA, 6*(2), 9–18.

Choudrie, J., Ghinea, G., & Weerakkody, V. (2004). Evaluating global e-government sites: A view using web diagnostic tools. *Electronic Journal of E-Government, 2*(2), 105–114.

Congdon, N., Friedman, D., & Lietman, T. (2003). Important causes of visual impairment in the world today. *Journal of the American Medical Association, 290*(15), 2057. doi:10.1001/jama.290.15.2057

D'Allura, T. (2002). Enhancing the social interaction skills of preschoolers with visual impairments. [JVIB]. *Journal of Visual Impairment & Blindness, 96*(08).

Dandona, L., & Dandona, R. (2006). What is the global burden of visual impairment. *BMC Medicine, 4*(6), 1741–7015.

Jackson, W., Taylor, R., Palmatier, A., Elliott, T., & Elliott, J. (1998). Negotiating the reality of visual impairment: Hope, coping, and functional ability. *Journal of Clinical Psychology in Medical Settings, 5*(2), 173–185. doi:10.1023/A:1026259115029

Kocur, I., & Resnikoff, S. (2002). Visual impairment and blindness in Europe and their prevention. *The British Journal of Ophthalmology, 86*(7), 716. doi:10.1136/bjo.86.7.716

Rahmat, L., Yaakop, S., Mara, U., Tamil, E., & Idna, M. (2006). *The experiences of blind & visually impaired users with the Malaysian government ministries website.* Paper presented at the Conference on Social Science and ICT.

Reinhardt, J. (1996). The importance of friendship and family support in adaptation to chronic vision impairment. *Journals of Gerontology Series B, 51*, 268–278. doi:10.1093/geronb/51B.5.P268

Rubaii-Barrett, N., & Wise, L. (2008). Disability access and e-government: An empirical analysis of state practices. *Journal of Disability Policy Studies, 19*(1), 52. doi:10.1177/1044207307311533

Šimonová, S. (2005). *E-government and approaches of e-inclusion.* Paper presented at the 5th WSEAS International Conference on Applied Informatics and Communications table of contents.

Šimonová, S. (2006). E-inclusion and disabled-people-friendly web. *Scientific Papers of the University of Pardubice Series D,* 164–168.

Tielsch, J., Sommer, A., Katz, J., Quigley, H., & Ezrine, S. (1991). Socioeconomic status and visual impairment among urban Americans. *Archives of Ophthalmology, 109*(5), 637. doi:10.1001/archopht.1991.01080050051027

Wang, J., Mitchell, P., Smith, W., Cumming, R., & Attebo, K. (1999). Impact of visual impairment on use of community support services by elderly persons: The Blue Mountains eye study. *Investigative Ophthalmology & Visual Science, 40*(1), 12.

Weih, L., Hassell, J., & Keeffe, J. (2002). Assessment of the impact of vision impairment. *Investigative Ophthalmology & Visual Science, 43*(4), 927.

West, S., Rubin, G., Broman, A., Munoz, B., Bandeen-Roche, K., & Turano, K. (2002). How does visual impairment affect performance on tasks of everyday life? The SEE Project. *Archives of Ophthalmology, 120*(6), 774.

Wood, J., & Troutbeck, R. (1994). Effect of visual impairment on driving. *Human Factors: The Journal of the Human Factors and Ergonomics Society, 36*(3), 476–487.

KEY TERMS AND DEFINITIONS

Act on Equality for People with Disabilities: In German Behindertengleichstellungsgesetz (BGG), is a German Federal law from year 2006. The purpose of this law is to abolish and prevent any discrimination against persons with disabilities, to ensure their equal participation in social activities and to enable them to lead a normal life.

Ambient Assisted Living (known as AAL): Includes methods, concepts, (electronic) systems, devices as well as services that are providing unobtrusive support for daily life based on context and the situation of the assisted person.

Braille Display: A computer input/output device supporting the Braille system. The Braille system is a leading method used by blind people to read and write.

Colour Blindness: Limited capability to differentiate between different colours, as to what can be expected from a similar individual or cohort.

eGovernment: Refers to the usage of modern information and communication technologies to enhance the scope of communication and to make it more efficient between authorities and citizens, for mutual benefit.

Speech Synthesizer: A software component that turns written text in digital form into speech. Typical user options are for example male/female voice. Speech synthesizers should too be adapted to different languages.

Vision Impairment: Refers to a condition of an individual or group, where the individual's or group's seeing capability is less than what can be expected from a similar individual or cohort.

This work was previously published in Cases on Adoption, Diffusion and Evaluation of Global E-Governance Systems: Impact at the Grass Roots, edited by H. Rahman, pp. 273-281, copyright 2011 by Information Science Reference (an imprint of IGI Global).

Chapter 12

The Characteristics, Responsibilities, and Future of Chief Information Officers in the Public Sector

Rachel Lawry
Deakin University, Australia

Dianne Waddell
Deakin University, Australia

Mohini Singh
RMIT University, Australia

EXECUTIVE SUMMARY

This chapter presents a model that depicts the critical factors and assists in understanding the demands and effectiveness of Chief Information Officers (CIO) in public sector organisations. The chapter explores the literature on public sector CIO addressing personal and professional characteristics. It also reviews the literature pertaining to the responsibilities, career advancement, and future directions in government departments. The authors adopt a qualitative methodology, by which semi-structured interviews are conducted with CIO representatives from a State Government in Australia. From collation of the interview results, utilising a mind mapping strategy, the chapter identifies a model that adequately reflects the critical factors required for a public sector CIO. The chapter concludes that there are

DOI: 10.4018/978-1-4666-0981-5.ch012

certain unique characteristics and responsibilities that a public sector CIO must possess yet a private sector CIO does not require. The chapter also acknowledges the importance of outlining a future direction of the role, something that is neglected by the literature.

INTRODUCTION

With an increased dependence by governments on Information Technology for internal management, delivery of services to citizens and meeting the demands of the digital environment, the importance of the CIO role in this sector has become prominent. The CIO role within the public sector is still at a formative stage whereas in the private sector it is well developed. The aim of this chapter is to understand the demands on CIOs in government and what characteristics are indicative of their effectiveness. The intention of this study is to compare the data gathered in an extensive literature review with information gleaned from practitioners. It is then possible to develop a model which bridges the gap between public and private sector experiences. This chapter is founded on the premise that one cannot fully execute a role, particularly an executive role, without fully recognising the fundamentals of what the role is designed to do. With the main role of the public sector being service delivery, it is expected that there needs to be clarity on the characteristics and responsibilities of the CIO role along with a shared vision for the roles future development in order for those in the CIO position to contribute the greatest value to the public sectors bottom line.

In the following sections we discuss the background to this research, a review of extant literature, a discussion of the public sector context, research methodology, findings and implications for the important yet emerging role of the CIOs in the public sector.

BACKGROUND

The need for the CIO role arose out of the 1970s information technology (IT) revolution. This era saw increased investment in information technology systems (ITS). There was also an increasing awareness of competitors using information and its associated technology to gain a unique competitive advantage in an increasingly global marketplace (Porter & Millar 1985). Executives could no longer view IT as an add-on to the business, but rather a function that required equal strategic importance and consideration to that of finance, human resources, operations and marketing.

The CIO was first coined by Synott & Gruber in 1981 as the "senior executive responsible for establishing corporate information policy, standards, and management control over all information resources" (p. 66). Since the coining of the term in the early 1980s, private sector enterprises have been successfully implementing the role within their organisational structures. They have reaped the benefits of the new executive who manages the unique organisational asset of information for near twenty years. In contrast, the public sector had only established the CIO role in the early 2000s.

Australian government, at both Federal and State levels, is considered to be 'leading the pack' with regard to establishing credibility and authority for the CIO´s role (Bushell 2006). Interestingly, Australia's first Whole-of-Government (WoG) CIO was not appointed until June 2005 (Nairn MP 2005). Victoria was the first Australian State Government to appoint a CIO, but it did not do so until 2003 (Department of Premier and Cabinet 2006). The Victorian Government has also endured a turnover in the WoG CIO position for two out of the three years of its establishment (Department of Premier and Cabinet 2006). This is a significant turnover rate for a position that is still in its infancy stages of development. The situation within the Victorian Government is not confined to the state of Victoria or even Australia, but is evident of issues surrounding the implementation of the CIO role within the public sector worldwide.

The situation highlighted above signifies a twenty-year gap between the establishment of the CIO role within the private and public sectors. It is clear that the CIO role is significantly more developed and ingrained within the private sector. In the public sector it is still within the formative stages of development.

LITERATURE REVIEW

The literature surrounding this issue is substantial, however the models have only been established in the last twenty years and the amount of available literature reflects such a time frame. Also, the chapter explores the contextual issue (private and public sector), and its impact on the CIO. In this area, the literature is more limited.

Existing Models of CIO Effectiveness

The literature describes many models which attempt to measure the effectiveness and success of CIOs in organisations. Feeny, Edwards & Simpson (1992) presented one of the first well-conceptualised models in the literature, which aimed to observe the relationship between the CEO and CIO in order to determine the components of a successful two-way relationship. Later, Earl and Feeny (1995) conducted a review of research studies they had previously conducted. As an outcome of this review, the authors identified several common areas that outlined where the CIO added value to an organisation. Earl and Feeny's (1995) model is somewhat similar to that presented by Feeny *et al* in 1992, but does make up, unconvincingly however, for the discounting of proactively planning for the future. They have addressed the concept of proactive planning by incorporating a 'shared vision for IT'. While this is still a limited representation, they are at least acknowledging that without planning for IT in the organisation's future they would suffer greatly in terms of total value added by the CIO.

One of the only Australian focused research papers (Pervan, 1998) focussed on key information system management issues as they are perceived by CEOs and CIOs. The aim was to identify if there existed any commonalities in the importance levels of the issues. The results of the study indicated there was some agreement between CEOs and CIOs on certain IS/IT issues. Just as equally however, there were distinct differences, "particularly in relation to the quality and effectiveness of systems and processes and also how CIOs perceive the IT knowledge of the CEOs" (Pervan, 1998: 95). While this study differs from the previous two models presented by Feeny *et al.* (1992), and Earl and Feeny (1995) in the respect that it does not present concrete components that can be tested, it does present issues that are real and prevailing, and could be argued to provide a greater representation of future expectations.

Melarkode, From-Poulsen & Warnakulasuriya (2004) focused on how CIOs can deliver agility within the organisation through the utilisation of IT. Discussion in the paper included an analysis of the old role of the CIO and how this has transformed into a new role. Their comparison of the old and new CIO role is similar to Pervan's (1998) study in that it presents contentious issues related to the CIO role that have evolved over time. They argue that the CIO is uniquely positioned within organisations where "they increasingly have the opportunity to participate in corporate and business strategy planning and work across business units in identifying opportunities to improve value via IT" (Melarkode et al., 2004: 46). The model presented by Melarkode et al. (2004) also ties in closely with the value added framework presented by Earl and Feeny (1995), particularly through the emphasis on value creation. Similar to the model presented by Melarkode et al. (2004), Capella (2006) presented a model depicting the dual role of the CIO. Capella's (2006) model establishes the importance of quickly establishing a vision for the role due to the evolving nature of CIO responsibilities and IT.

As evident from both the literature discussed on the role characteristics, responsibilities, future, and from the models found in the available literature, there are certain commonalities. By isolating the recurring themes regarding components to assist success in the CIO role, this study will be able to amalgamate the models and literature to formulate a holistic model for use in studying the public sector CIOs. However, to fully address the problem of this research study, an insight into the development of the CIO in the private and public sector is crucial. This will serve to provide context to this chapter and aid understanding of the issues at hand.

Context: Public versus Private

There is a detailed history regarding how the private and public sectors are characterised, and there are many varied opinions concerning the similarities and differences between the two sectors. In order to understand this chapter, it is important to not only comprehend the components of the CIO, but to recognise and realise how and possibly why the role has evolved differently in the private and public sector.

The private sector is made up of small, medium and large-scale organisations where ownership is held either by an individual or a group of entrepreneurs, more commonly referred to as shareholders (Budhwar and Boyne 2004). As a result of the ownership of private sector organisations, the funding for the organisation within the private sector comes directly from one of two sources: fees paid directly by the customer purchasing a good or service, or from shares purchased by shareholders in listed companies which signifies claim to part ownership and a share of profits. As such there is no claim for public funds in order for the business to operate. The control within the private sector lies in the economy, or market forces (Boyne 2002). Accordingly, the ability to perform, operate and succeed are constrained or imposed by market forces, such as barriers to entering new markets, exchange rates, interest rate fluctuations and the like.

The Australian Bureau of Statistics (1998) defines the public sector as "enterprises which the Commonwealth Government, State/Territory and local Governments, separately or jointly have control over. It includes local Government authorities and all Government departments, agencies and authorities created by, or reporting to, the Commonwealth Parliament and State Parliaments" (p.1). When defining the public sector, the same three points of difference used above to define the private sector can be referred to in the same vain. Public sector agencies are owned, funded and controlled collectively by members of political communities at different levels of government (Budhwar & Boyne 2004). Funding within the public sector is generated by taxes, where citizens at the Local, State and Federal level pay taxes to the Government in return for essential services (Boyne 2002). Where market forces control the private sector, the public sector is subject to the imposition of political forces and the follow-through of political systems (Schneider & Vaught 1993), such as changes of political party leaderships.

Although the two sectors differ inherently in terms of ownership, funding and control, a considerable amount of similarities exist. In essence, both the private and public sectors function similarly with regards to management (Schneider & Vaught 1993). For example, whether or not one is operating in the private or public sector, management still consists of establishing an organisational purpose, developing objectives, planning, managing and motivating the human resources, and controlling the organisation's performance both internally and externally (Schneider & Vaught, 1993; Budhwar & Boyne, 2004).

While the actual process of management is similar between the two sectors, the conditions and constraints under which the management processes are conducted is where the differences between the private and public sector lie (Schneider & Vaught, 1993), for instance, time perspectives, performance measurement, media relations, authority, legal constraints, and personnel constraints. There are three *internal* characteristics of the public sector however, that serve as clear points of difference:

- **More Bureaucracy:** greater amount of formal procedures for decision making, and are less flexible and more risk-averse than their private sector counterparts (Bozeman & Kingsley, 1998; Farnham & Horton, 1996),
- **More Red Tape:** implies that the public sector operates with an unnecessary and counter-productive amount of rules, and relies more on rules and processes rather than results and outcomes (Boyne, 2002), and
- **Lower Managerial Autonomy:** the public sector allows managers less freedom to react as they see fit to circumstances when they arise, which is exemplified by public managers' discretion over human resource issues which generally involves complex and time consuming processes to follow in hiring, firing and promotion, that, as a preferred alternative, is generally avoided (Baldwin, 1987; Boyne, 2002). <-APA

In considering the above definitions of the private and public sector, it is clear that private sector organisations operate on the basis of filling a need or want for a product or service where they are compensated by fees or shares. On the other hand, the public sector provides products and services as an obligation to taxes paid to them by the citizens they serve. From these definitions it is appropriate to assume that the management of IS in either private or public organisations is both multidimensional and complex (Loukis and Tsouma 2002). Furthermore, the public sector plays a primary role in the life and economy of its citizens at local, state and federal levels. Despite the similarities between the two sectors, the three internal characteristics of the public sector – bureaucracy, red tape and autonomy – serve as possible impediments to the productivity and effectiveness of the CIOs role and responsibilities, namely, ICT project execution and investment.

The literature up until this point with regards to CIOs has been heavily focused on private sector studies. There have been very few studies conducted where the management of IT and IS issues has been raised in a public sector context. It is clear that more research is necessary in this area due to the critical role the public sector plays in the economic and social life of all countries, and also the growing realisation, reliance and importance of ICT on public sector productivity and effectiveness (Loukis & Tsouma 2002).

From the above discussion, it is clear that there is a striking difference between the development of literature from the private and public sector. The private sector has a twenty-year advantage over the public sector with regards to role evolution, and it appears that the advantage extends to development in academic literature too. The literature available regarding CIOs has made one faux pas clear: the CIO is not a position that is exclusive to the private sector. The CIO is not an executive position that discriminates between organisations with regards to importance; regardless of being small or large in size, domestic or international in scope, or private or public sector based, the CIO is a critical executive.

There are no models to date that have been specifically developed for the public sector, nor is there cohesion surrounding the personal and professional characteristics, list of responsibilities and method for proactively planning the future for public sector CIOs. Yet it is evident through the discussion on the components of the CIO and the difference between public and private sector literature, that this is an increasingly crucial role. Moreover, the position within the public sector is so new that it is impossible to claim if the role is a success or failure. As a consequence of this, those that are establishing the position in Government bodies today will no doubt have a lasting impact on how the role will be seen by the public sector in the future. The early success will reinforce the CIO role for the future years to come, whereas high-profile fails will weaken the CIO outlook (Fabris 1998). By combining the key points from the discussion on the CIO function, and the CIOs context within the public sector, an adapted model can be devised. This model takes the key findings from the personal and professional characteristics, responsibilities and future of the CIO, and places them within the public sector context. This model will be confirmed or amended through the responses from the interviews with CIOs from the Victorian Government. Figure 1 represents the amalgamation of the literature thus far.

METHODOLOGY

In order to compare current practice with existing literature a qualitative research approach was adopted. The major reason why this method was selected revolves around the inadequacy of quantitative methods when pursing an exploratory research approach. Qualitative research methods have also made a resurgence in studies of

Figure 1. Model for measuring CIO in public sector from the literature

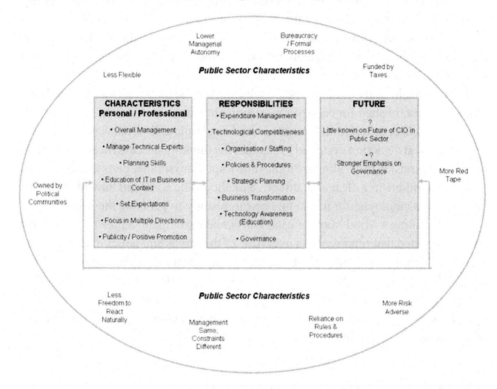

Information Technology (IT), Information Systems (IS) and Information Communication Technology (ICT) in academic literature. There has been a general shift in IT, IS and ICT issues from the technical side to the managerial side, and the methods by which these areas are studied has accommodated this shift in focus are also changing from statistical methods of analysis to qualitative methods (Myers 1997).

Ten semi-structured interviews took place with individuals from the Victorian Government, Australia, who hold the CIO title or perform the CIO function. An interview agenda was created and was emailed to the participants prior to the interview taking place to alert them to the topics for discussion. The interview agenda was devised to provoke discussion on six areas:

- Participant's educational background and work history;
- Current perception of their position;
- Perception of the role within Government;
- Predictions for the future direction of the role within Government;
- Personal future career goals or direction; and
- Critical success factors deemed important to their role.

Each area covered in the agenda was aimed at collating the data deemed necessary to translate into information for the purpose of answering the research questions. Ten interviews are regarded as saturation point, whereby adequate new information was collected from a range of areas within the Victorian Government so as to represent a diverse range of valid opinions.

In order to aid analysis of the codes isolated from the interview transcripts, Mind Maps were established for each of the participants' interview results. A Mind Map helps to organise, generate and present ideas in a simple and visual way; in essence, it is a graphical depiction designed to abstract the thinking process for an individual. Mind Maps assisted in dividing the topics and issues into smaller parts to help convey concepts to others in a clear and attractive method. The ConceptDraw MINDMAP program was employed for use in this research study to generate the Mind Maps.

After creating a Mind Map for each individual participant, a holistic Mind Map was constructed that represents an overview of the topics and issues discussed. The individual Mind Maps and the holistic Mind Map are used to aid discussion of the results as they highlight those topics and issues of greatest concern to the participants at this point in time. The Mind Maps were then integrated into the pre-existing model gleaned from the literature to present a new model which incorporates all facets identified by the interviewees.

RESEARCH FINDINGS AND DISCUSSION

The individual mind maps offered a clear and concise depiction of the topics and issues discussed by the individual participants. Each mind map varied in the topics and issues discussed, and also varied in depth and breadth of discussion. Some of the mind maps were limited in responses, whereas other cases appeared more varied in the responses. This is not a direct reflection on the individual respondent, their position, their experience or their knowledge on the subjects. It is merely the result of discussing a unique topic with ten very unique and individual people who have CIO responsibilities. It is natural in qualitative research to attract a wide variety of responses and patterns in responses.

While on their own the individual mind maps tell an interesting story, it is when they are amalgamated from ten individual mind maps into one holistic mind map, that they are most valuable and provide the most information. Figure 2 is a diagrammatic representation of the amalgamated model of the ten interviews into one mind map. It shows the twenty-two topics discussed by the ten participants of this study. Each topic was discussed in many different contexts and some commanded more discussion or attention than others.

Figure 2. Holistic participant mind map

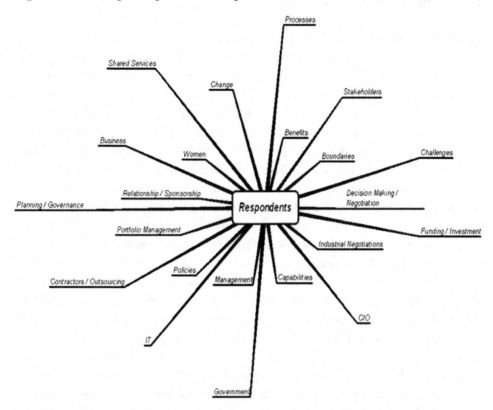

As can be observed from the Mind Map (Figure 2), there were twenty-two major topics identified by CIO practitioners. Some topics demanded more attention than others, and this research can conclude that the most frequently discussed topics are the ones that represent the truest picture of the CIO in the public sector at this point in time. By synthesising the topics discussed, authors identified the seven major topics of this research study to be: the unique role of the CIO; impact of IT; Funding / Investment Management; Governance; Shared Services; Stakeholders; and Outsourcing /Contracting. These seven major topics reflect the issues of most concern to those currently fulfilling the position of the CIO within the Victorian Government, and can be used to generalise on the situation of the CIO in the public sector. Each of the seven topics is discussed below with regards to their importance and their link with the established literature of the public sector CIO.

The Unique Role of the CIO

The CIO role within the public sector is still within the early stages of formation and is being defined within the changing perception of the role from technical guru to strategist. While it is theoretically understood that there is a distinction between the CIO and the IT Manager, where the CIO sits on the strategic side of IT and the IT Manager deals with the operations of IT, there still exists the belief that the position of some Departmental CIOs is just the renaming of the IT Managers. There are also some cases where the IT Manager is actually doing the CIO role, yet lacks the official title. It is evident that there is no clear idea of what the CIO does, and there is little available literature that acknowledges the public sector as having difficulty with implementing the role and establishing the role's difference to that of the several other IT positions that exist within Government.

The literature clearly identifies the CIO as a strategic business partner that should be situated within the CEO circle of executives. The CIOs within the various Departments of the VPS sit at different levels within the Departmental structures, and, therefore, the intended function of the role as a strategic business partner is diluted. An additional consequence of the structure of the CIO within the VPS Departments is that those in the CIO position believe that outside their office, there are very few external groups who know what the CIO is and what the office of the CIO deals with. If the role was situated at its intended level, perhaps such a situation would not occur and clarity over the role could begin to form. The literature also acknowledges that the CIO must have a strong relationship with the other senior executive positions such as the CFO and the CEO. Due to the lack of clarity surrounding the role and the CIOs structure within the Departments across Government, it is no wonder that many CIOs lack a strong relationship with the executive roles within Government, and, therefore, lack the impact they could have in promoting the value added by their role. What the literature fails to acknowledge is that the structure of Government is unlike that of a private enterprise. Therefore, the equal of a CEO or CFO is the Premier or Department of Treasury and Finance respectively, and access to such positions is filtered by Secretaries and their Deputies. The Victorian Government has sought a way to rectify part of this issue by creating the Office of the CIO (OCIO) at a WoG level; however, there is no clear reporting line from the Departmental CIOs to the OCIO and, therefore, the value that could be added by this central body is missing.

The literature acknowledges several personal and professional characteristics required by the individual filling the CIO position, however there are a few characteristics that the literature fails to recognise as important, and this is most likely due to the literature being private sector dominated. There are six key characteristics of the CIO role that are missing from the literature and from the synthesised literature model presented earlier, yet are evident in this study. They are: knowledge of the workings of Government; trustworthiness, a focus on the clients' needs, empathetic side, strategic thinker, and patience.

There is considerable discussion in the literature on what responsibilities constitute the domain of the CIO, however there are a few responsibilities that are not recognised in the literature. This is most likely due to the focus on the private sector throughout the majority of the literature. There are six key areas of the CIOs responsibility that the literature fails to adequately acknowledge yet they are evident through the findings of this study: centralising IT under the CIO function, providing advice, reducing duplication and exploiting common capabilities, service delivery, managing risk, and managing outsourcing agreements.

The Impact of IT

Apart from the Polanksy, Inuganti and Wiggins (2004) study, there were very few studies that recognised IT at the top of the CIO's priority list. As previously discussed, the CIO is an executive management position; however at the core of their management is information, communication and technology. While the literature acknowledges that the CIO must have a hand in IT strategy development and the management of IT projects, the literature does not acknowledge sufficiently the challenge of identifying the value of IT in the public sector. Many of the CIOs struggle within an environment that must be transparent and accountable to the public and are constantly battling to prove that the reputation of IT projects as a consumption rather than a production of money is actually a false reputation.

The CIOs from the public sector should only support business projects rather than IT projects, as this is one way of getting around the mindset of those outside the CIO office that IT projects are doomed to fail. In fact, there should be no IT projects developed without them being linked to a business solution. Creating IT procedures for IT's sake is a waste of money and time, and the reason why duplication of processes generally occurs. Through linking IT with a business outcome, the role of IT then becomes the enabler of a business initiative, and the benefits realised are business focused rather than IT focused. This point lacks emphasis in the literature, and needs to be recognised as a core characteristic of the role: being able to work with a business view and a WoG perspective.

As previously mentioned, some of the literature does acknowledge the role of IT in the CIOs job; however, it is generally focused on the technology side of IT and fails to acknowledge that information also plays a large part. The CIO must not only deal with technology, but also information, and be responsible for the diffusion of information throughout Government. The CIO is responsible for making sure the right information is available at the right time and is provided under the appropriate security measures. This is a missing component of the role in the literature available at present. While technology is the tool by which information is diffused, it is the CIOs job to ensure that the processes by which the information is collated, the channels by which information is transported, and the security procedures that ensure the information is safe, are established in accordance with Departmental and Government rules.

Funding/Investment Management

The literature acknowledges that a large part of the CIOs role is ensuring cost effectiveness and increasing value for money (Earl & Feeny 1995). As a result, investment management is key area of the CIO function, which is being realised in reality, not just in theory. Given the previous discussion on the IT component of the CIO role and the battle over changing perceptions on IT, it is understandable why investment management has grown in significance for the CIO and has become the true essence of the role. As with any executive managerial position, dealing with finances is crucial, and this is no exception with the CIO, as without full understanding of the money around the function there is little chance that any outcomes would be produced.

As the literature is predominately private sector focused, there is a large gap with regards to the CIO attaining funding in the public sector. One of the fundamental differences between the private and public sectors is the bureaucracy, processes and red tape that government departments face when obtaining funding. Many of the troubles faced by the CIOs in the public sector are that the time frames and procedures that need to be met strain getting the projects off the ground. This links very closely with the issues discussed in the previous two sections on the CIO and IT, as without the strong relationship with other executive members, without proving the value is added, and without changing the external mindsets of IT as a waste of money, attaining funding is near impossible. Similarly to the discussion on IT and with regards to developing business projects rather than IT projects, CIOs in the public sector must ensure that the business unit attains the funding for the business project, and that the CIO is only commissioned to source the way in which ICT can assist the overall outcome of the business initiative.

Governance

Governance is a critical part of the CIO role in the Government sector that is little acknowledged within the available literature. Some of the literature acknowledged that governance would become a core part of the role in the future (Bushell, 2006), but much of the literature – mostly likely due to the focus of the literature on the private sector – failed to acknowledge its ingrained importance in the role (Boyne, 2002). This is particularly true of the CIO in the public sector, as the major stakeholders are the citizens at large who dictate the public sectors need for transparency and accountability.

The key aspect of governance that relates to the CIO in the public sector is its link with project planning. The stereotype of IT projects failing and wasting money was not founded on false details. The public sector has experienced the consequences of poor project planning such as projects being under prepared, projects not meeting requirements, projects not producing intended benefits, and in some extreme cases, project failure. It is, therefore, the case that the governance structures set up in Government are predominately focused on project planning. The planning stage of a project is the most crucial stage as it outlines the intended outcome, the investment structure, and the benefits to be received. As can be concluded, this critical stage is linked heavily with investment management previously discussed, and aids in promoting the positive aspects of ICT. As there are no pure IT projects, planning for the project must be conducted in partnership with the business unit from which the initiative originates, and must be communicated in business terms.

Shared Services Centre

The Shared Services Centre (SSC) is a Victorian Government initiative to create an internal service provider so common applications and infrastructures can be joined together to service the whole rather than the individual Departments. The SSC at present joins four Departments together so that common and basic ICT functions can be carried out essentially once for four. The available literature implies that the CIO should reduce duplication and promote consolidation of processes; however, the literature fails to recognise how important this function is in the public sector.

Due to the long establishment of Government and its 'silo structure', there exists the challenge of dealing with duplicated processes and archaic systems. Due to poor planning, there are little checks in place to ensure that a new investment with the aim of solving an identified problem, is not just a re-investment in a new system that performs the same function as the one already operational. The SSC aims to address this characteristic of the public sector by joining together four Departments with similar economies of scale so that common systems and processes can be handled by an internal service provider, and then the remaining strategic functions can be handled individually to suit the needs and goals of the Departments. It exploits the commonalities that exist between Departments so that for example, common licensing agreements can be bought just once, instead of four times for four Departments which all come from the same State Government.

Stakeholders

The importance of delivery to and working with key stakeholders is a key function of the public sector and is an area that is not adequately explored within the available literature on this topic. The key function of the public sector is service delivery and their key stakeholder is the community and citizens at large. In the case of the Victorian Government, it is the Victorian citizens who are heavily invested in the actions of the Victorian Government. For this reason the Government must be held accountable for their actions and must be transparent in their activities. The private sector is short of this requirement as their fundamental concern is return on investment and, therefore, what needs to be reported to key stakeholders is much more tangible. Consequently, stakeholder management is a key part of the public sector CIOs role and at the same time plays a key part in project planning, as stakeholder identification must be considered.

Apart from the stakeholder who reaps the end benefits of Government initiatives, there are other stakeholders within Government whom the CIO must report to and have interaction with. It is through stakeholder reporting lines that projects and initiatives being worked on by individual Departments can be shared and talked about, so that opportunities for collaboration can be explored. Key internal stakeholders of the CIO include other Departmental CIOs, IT Directors, Chief Technology Officer, Secretaries, and Deputy Secretaries. By interacting and sharing with these key internal stakeholders, clarity and consistency in the service provided by the CIO can be achieved. It is also an avenue for promoting the benefits of the CIO and for increasing the profile of the CIO to assume the position of strategic business partner; its rightful position.

Outsourcing/Contracting

The role of outsourcing and contracting is a topic overlooked by the available literature, and this could be due to the fact that the literature is centred on private sector studies that do not deal with external service providers to the same extent that the Government relies upon them. As the public sector cannot compete with the IT salaries that the private sector provides and, therefore, cannot recruit the skills and expertise needed to deal with the projects on the level the Government runs, they compensate by outsourcing non core activities or by employing contractors.

There are two key issues with this situation. Firstly the Government has not established the required skill base for the CIO to be a successful office, and secondly, the cost of outsourcing and contracting is most likely equal to costs associated with increasing the salary structure of Government to recognise the price of IT professionals. The benefits, however, of outsourcing non core activities is that it leaves the

Departmental CIOs time to deal with strategic issues, and outsourcing agreements are secured by contractual arrangements thus securing the job be done as utmost priority. The benefit observed by contractors is that they have more enthusiasm and passion for the tasks at hand, and are experts in their field, thus the public sector benefits from their contributions and experience. A challenge with recruiting into the public sector is that many of the IT professionals that do fit within the prescribed Victorian Public Service remuneration structure lack the experience and maturity of dealing with large business projects that have core ICT components. Also, external "wanna-be" IT professionals discard the public sector as a viable workplace, thinking they do not offer the same type and range of jobs that the private sector does. This is entirely unfounded as the public sector deals in a range of areas – indicated by the range of different Departments – and the scale of the projects ranges from the small to the very large.

Managing outsourcing agreements and contractors have become a key area of the CIOs responsibilities. It is an area that has been forced upon the CIO due to the structure of Government and the competitiveness of the private marketplace, and initiatives such as the SSC are internal Government initiatives to move away from a strong reliance on external service providers. While the benefits of using external service providers cannot be discounted, the extent to which they are employed within the public sector needs reviewing and possible restructuring so that the most effective value for money can be achieved.

The seven major topics that were isolated from the research are indicative of the concerns of CIOs in the public sector. Through discussing the CIO, IT, Funding/Investment Management, Governance, Shared Services, Stakeholders, and Outsourcing/Contracting, it became clear that there were aspects of each topic that failed to be acknowledged adequately in the available literature. The common cause for their abandonment in the literature is that the literature is predominately founded on private sector studies. The following figure outlines the key findings from the previous discussion and is an improved representation of the CIO in the public sector from that provided from the literature. Figure 3 recognises the major findings of the study and also rectifies the shortcomings of the current literature on the CIO in the public sector.

IMPLICATIONS FOR CIO MANAGERS

From the findings of this study, in particular the model developed to outline the critical factors required of a CIO in the public sector, there are certain implications that can be identified. There exists a clear need for clarity and consistency on the CIO role and the situation of the role within the public sector. There also exists a need

Figure 3. Model of the CIO in the public sector

for distinction between the CIO role and the many other IT management positions within Government. A consistent position description endorsed by the Office of the CIO (OCIO) would assist in achieving this consistency and clarity. Clear reporting, sharing and communicating lines should also be established between the OCIO and the Departmental CIOs to aid clarification of the role and to also provide support for those Departmental CIOs who are new to the role and are embedding it in the public sector for the first time.

This chapter also highlights the need for public sector CIOs to be aware when reading academic literature and industry publications, that they are generally private sector focused and they, therefore, do not acknowledge adequately that there are some components of the CIO role that require more focus in the public sector. Comparing private sector based literature to the role of the CIO in the public sector would only foster annoyance and frustration. The role can be just as effective and efficient as it is in the private sector, as long as those in the public sector recognise there are certain areas of the role that require more attention than it would in the private marketplace.

Furthermore, CIOs in the public sector need to be more creative and proactive in dealing with the policies and procedures of Government. It became clear through discussion with interviewees that the challenges of the role generally originate in the characteristics of the public sector. While these characteristics are intrinsic in the working environment of the CIO, the CIO can still be creative in how to work within policy and procedure constraints of Government. There is a sense of tradition in Government, and there are some policies and procedures that require removal, and their removal will only occur if the existence of such policies and procedures is challenged. The CIO, who is in a position of change and evolution, is the perfect role to champion such transformation and can provide substitute policies that are more flexible and accommodating to the types of projects and initiatives that the CIO deals with.

CONCLUSION

This chapter is qualitative and exploratory in nature. The topic took an under-researched area, the CIO in the public sector, and employed qualitative techniques to gather information from CIOs in the public sector arena to shed a brighter spotlight on the struggles surrounding the role. The overall value of this research is that the gap in the literature regarding the public sector CIO has been bridged. The plight of the public sector CIO has been addressed to adequately examine the personal and professional characteristics of the role, the responsibilities that befall the CIO, and the future direction of the role. Through analysis of these areas, through the combining of theory and reality, and through critical discussion on the results of this study, clarity and consistency on the role in the public sector has been acquired, and can continue to be acquired.

REFERENCES

Australian Bureau of Statistics. (1998). *Paid work: Public sector employment.* Canberra, Australia: Author.

Baldwin, N. (1987). Public versus private: Not that different, not that consequential. *Public Personnel Management, 16,* 181–193.

Boyne, G. (2002). Public and private management: What's the difference? *Journal of Management Studies, 39*(1), 2322–2380. doi:10.1111/1467-6486.00284

Bozeman, B., & Kingsley, G. (1998). Risk culture in public and private organisations. *Public Administration Review, 58,* 109–118. doi:10.2307/976358

Budhwar, P., & Boyne, G. (2004). Human resource management in the Indian public and private sectors: An empirical comparison. *International Journal of Human Resource Management, 15*(2), 346–370. doi:10.1080/0958519032000158554

Bushell, S. (2006). *Government CIO role still developing, but Australia ahead of pack.* Retrieved from http://www.cio.com/index.php?id=401118652&eid=-601

Capella, J. (2006). The CIO's first 100 days. *Optimize, 5*(3), 46–51.

Department of Premier and Cabinet. (2006). *About the office of the chief information officer.* Retrieved from http://www.dpc.vic.gov.au/

Earl, M., & Feeny, D. (1995). Is your CIO adding value? *The McKinsey Quarterly, 2*, 144–161.

Fabris, P. (1998). *Odd ducks no more.* Retrieved from http://www.cio.com/archive/111598/index.html

Farnham, D., & Horton, S. (1996). Managing public and private organisations. In Farnham, D., & Horton, S. (Eds.), *Managing the new public service.* London, UK: Macmillan.

Feeny, D., Edwards, B., & Simpson, K. (1992). Understanding the CEO/CIO relationship. *Management Information Systems Quarterly, 16*(4), 439–448. doi:10.2307/249730

Loukis, E., & Tsouma, N. (2002). Critical issues of information systems management in the Greek public sector. *The International Journal of Government and Democracy in the Information Age, 17*(1), 65–83.

Melarkode, A., From-Poulson, M., & Warnakulasuriya, S. (2004). Delivering agility through IT. *Business Strategy Review, 15*(3), 45–50. doi:10.1111/j.0955-6419.2004.00327.x

Myers, M. (1997). Qualitative research in information systems. *Management Information Systems Quarterly, 21*(2), 241–242. doi:10.2307/249422

Nairn, M. P. G. (2005). *New Australian Government Chief Information Officer.* Australia: Media Release, Senator the Hon Eric Abetz, Special Minister of State.

Pervan, G. (1998). How chief executive officers in large organisations view the management of their information systems. *Journal of Information Technology, 13*, 95–109. doi:10.1080/026839698344882

Polanksy, M., Inuganti, T., & Wiggins, S. (2004). The 21st century CIO. *Business Strategy Review, 15*(2), 29–33. doi:10.1111/j.0955-6419.2004.00310.x

Porter, M., & Millar, V. (1985). How information gives you competitive advantage. *Harvard Business Review, 63*(4), 149–174.

Schneider, D., & Vaught, B. (1993). A comparison of job satisfaction between public and private sector managers. *Public Administration Quarterly, 17*(1), 68–83.

Synnott, W., & Gruber, W. (1981). *Information resource management: Opportunities and strategies for the 1980s.* New York, NY: John Wiley & Sons.

ADDITIONAL READING

Anonymous,. (2000). Gartner predicts "zero-budget" CIO. *Information Management Journal, 36*(4), 8.

Highbarger, J. (1998). What's the proper role for the CIO? *Management Review, 77*(3), 53–54.

Holmes, A. (2005). *Where there's a person, there's a problem.* Retrieved March 16th 2009, from http://www.cio.com/archive/040105/index.html

Kost, J. (2005). *Government CIO position continues to mature.* Retrieved March 30th 2009, from http://www.gartner.com

Mayor, T. (2003). *From private to public.* Retrieved March 16th 2009, from http://www.cio.com/archive/050103/index.html

McDonald, M. P., & Blosch, M. (2003). *CIO credibility: Proven practices from the public sector.* Retrieved March 30th 2009, from http://www.gartner.com

McDonald, M. P., & Tucker, C. (2004). *Making time: The office of the CIO.* Retrieved March 30th 2009, from http://www.gartner.com

Passino, J. H. Jr, & Severance, D. G. (1988). The changing role of the Chief Information Officer. *Planning Review, 16*(5), 38–42.

Remenyi, D., Grant, K. A., & Pather, S. (2005). The chameleon: A metaphor for the Chief Information Officer. *Journal of General Management, 30*(3), 1–11.

Rockart, J. F., Ball, L., & Bullen, C. V. (1982). future role of the information systems executive. *Management Information Systems Quarterly, 6*(4), 1–14. doi:10.2307/248989

Stephens, C. S., Ledbetter, W. N., Mitra, A., & Ford, F. N. (1992). Executive or functional manager? The nature of the CIO's job. *Management Information Systems Quarterly, 16*(4), 449–467. doi:10.2307/249731

Varon, E. (2000). *Uncle Sam wants you.* Retrieved March 16, 2009, from http://www.cio.com/archive/080100/index.html

Chapter 13
E–Government Policy:
A Case Study of E–Filing System

Abdul Raufu Ambali
University Technology MARA, Malaysia

EXECUTIVE SUMMARY

The emergence of faster delivery service required a faster mechanism of transaction between government and its people. But such a transaction is not without issues that have to be addressed by the governments of the public sectors. The primary issues addresses by this chapter include the relationships between the perceived: security tightening, facilitating conditions, usefulness, eases of using e-filing system, and users' retention. The second issue addressed by the chapter is differences in gender of the users with respect to factors that influence their state of retention. The findings of the study show a strong relationship between the predicting factors and user's intention to continuing using the system. The findings also show that the retention of users is highly affected by the differences in the gender of the users. This research would like to recommend that a faster transaction mechanism between the government and the people enhances the e-governance system and in this context, this chapter focuses on some potential implications of e-filing system of Malaysia.

ORGANIZATION BACKGROUND

Lembaga Hasil Dalam Negeri (LHDN) or the Inland Revenue Board of Malaysia is one of the potential agencies under the Ministry of Finance (MOF) in the country. The agency was established on 1st March 1996 and has been charged with collection of revenues in the country. It was established in accordance with the Inland Revenue

DOI: 10.4018/978-1-4666-0981-5.ch013

Board of Malaysia Act 1995 and the Income Tax Act 1967 to enhance the quality and effectiveness of tax administration. The agency also act as an agent of the Government and provide services in administering, assessing, collecting and enforcing payment of income tax, petroleum income tax, real property gains tax, estate duty, stamp duties and any other taxes as may be agreed between the Government and the Board. The agency has also been charged to participate in or outside Malaysia in respect of matters relating to taxation and advice the government accordingly. It also extends its function by liaising with the appropriate Ministries and statutory bodies on taxation matters and acts as a collection agent for and or behalf of any body on matters relating to the recovery of loans due for repayment under any written law.

Corporate Culture of IRBM

The Inland Revenue Board of Malaysia has been known to be the foremost tax administration agency and the best government income tax representative body in the Malaysia. The overall corporate culture of IRB can be envisaged from creation of a just, transparent and respectable tax management system. The vision of the board includes sensitivity to the welfare of its employees, career advancement opportunities for each employee and recognition of individual excellence. It is part of the Board's corporate culture to be committed towards excellence achievements and/or efficient client service provider. It also committed to a high degree of fairness of the country's tax system. IRB also focuses on continued improvements through development of appropriate skills and efficient workforce that is equipped with the high level of professionalism. Board vows to constantly upgrading income tax administration to become easier while simultaneously simplifying tax laws. The agent believes in offering fair and transparent service to people in the country at all time and always strive to encourage voluntary compliance of the taxpayers (see: www.hasil.gov.my).

Taxation Policy in Malaysia

Under the Malaysian tax policies, income tax is a fact of life and compulsory for resident that is due for its payment. However, Malaysian taxation policy is quite brightening and exciting for many reasons. *First* there is no capital gains-tax in the country. *Second*, there is no gift, inheritance nor estate taxes in Malaysia as well. *Third*, even the only capital gains tax in Malaysia related to the Real Property Gains Tax has been withdrawn for disposals made on 1 April 2007 (see: Budget Commentary & Tax Information 2009, PWC Tax Booklet 2007-2009).

Income tax in Malaysia is 'territorial' in nature because only income accruing in or derived from Malaysia is taxed. In other word, other form of incomes such as foreign remitted income into the country whether by resident or non-resident is exempted from taxation policy system. Generally speaking, there are several categories of income tax as described and delineated by section 4 of the Malaysian Income Tax Act, 1967. These categories include: gains or profits from business; income from employment; dividends interest and discounts; rents, royalties or premiums; pensions, annuities or other periodical payments; and gains or profits not falling under any of the above.

Manual Income Tax-Filing of Returns

Before the implementation of e-filing system in Malaysia, tax filing returns used to be done manually under a Self Assessment System (SAS). The taxpayer him/herself is responsible to correctly compute manually the amount assessable on a form and file the return to the Inland Revenue Board of Malaysia (IRBM). He or she then makes payment of any tax due and payable within the stipulated deadline to the respective IRBM's branches in the country. There are two categories of manual income tax returns forms. The first is employment income delineated as Form BE while the second is business income and/or other income form known as Form B. The due dates are usually 30th of June for business income tax purpose and 30th of April for non-business income tax every year.

Chargeable Income Tax

The chargeable income tax is described as tax residency. Individuals are regarded as tax resident if he or she is in Malaysia within certain periods of time. For example, an individual is a tax resident if he or she has spent at least 182 days in the country per year; or spent a period less than 182 days but the time spent is linked to another period following or preceding where he was present in Malaysia for 182 or more consecutive days. In addition, if a person has spent 90 days or more during the year and was present in Malaysia for at least 90 days in any 3 of the 4 immediate preceding years. The tax residential status of an individual citizen or non-citizen is important because it determines the rate of tax; it also determines if the person is entitled to personal relief and rebate and the income on which the person suppose to be taxed (see: see: Budget Commentary & Tax Information 2009, PWC Tax Booklet 2007-2009).

Joint Assessments

Following the amendment to Section 45(2) of the Income Tax Act, 1967 in Malaysia, a wife is automatically assessed separately on her income. However, the husband or the wife is given the opportunity to put in writing before 1 April every year if they want their income to be jointly assessed. In a situation where the spouse is not resident, this opportunity is applicable. In other words, spouse may decide only if he or she is a citizen or resident. Under the combined assessment, a spouse will be given a relief of RM3, 000 and a further RM3, 500 if the spouse is disabled. This is applicable if the spouse elects for joint assessment under his or her name, or the spouse has no source of income.

The chapter highlights some potential implications of the findings necessary for policy makers to achieve a successful e-filing system in the country. As reflected in the findings, it is imperative for all agencies' staff charged with e-government policy implementations to equip themselves with more sophisticated ICT tools to guide the users. The fact is that the gaps in IT infrastructure can affect people's intention (i.e., retention) to continue to use or not use the system provided by the government. Above all, the findings show that users must perceive the technology somehow useful, easy and friendly as well as security guaranteed.

In addition, the chapter also sheds light on the importance of ensuring technology readiness among the public users of the system in order to eliminate the external difficulties in terms of Internet access, ICT literacy among the public as these can also affect the user's retention. Finally, the chapter suggest that (i) more IT infra-structures and other incentives should be provided to encourage the public to use the system; (ii) effective program such as capacity building for the agency's staff that can facilitate readiness of the people to use the system is highly needed, if e-filing is to become a successful policy program. Thus, agency's staff must play effective roles to respond to the public perceptual complaints about the e-filing system and government must pay attention to gender differences in retention to use the system.

SETTING THE STAGE

E-Government and E-Filing System

The launching of Multimedia Super Corridor (MSC) in August 1996 by the Malaysian government was part of a major strategy to accelerate the country's entry into the Information Age. Thus e-government was introduced as one of the seven flagships of the MSC (Muhd Rais and Nazariah, 2003). In 1997, the Malaysian Government launched the Electronic Government initiative, generally known as e-Government, to reinvent itself to lead the country into the Information Age. E-government is one of the seven flagship applications introduced in MSC with the objectives of accelerating the growth of MSC, enhance national competitiveness and reduce digital divide (Ambali, 2009).

E-governments is about a process of reforming the way government works, shares information, delivers services to internal and external clients and specifically harnesses information technologies to transform its relations with citizens businesses and other arms of government. These technologies can serve a variety of ends and better delivery of government services to citizens. They can also be used to empowerment citizens through access to information or a more efficient government-citizen management (Bhatnagar, 2004).

Moreover, e-Government seeks to enhance the convenience, accessibility and quality of government's interactions with the public and businesses at large, (Shaidin). This would enable the government to be more responsive to the needs of its citizens. Hence, the principal aim of implementing e-government policy in various public sectors is to facilitate the effectiveness of government delivering services through electronic system and to create a strong relationship between government and its people at large. As such, several programs were launched by government to support the implementation of e-government, which includes e-filing system for taxpayers. In fact, e-filing is a reflection of government commitment to quality service delivery to people in the country.

Under the e-government flagship, seven main projects were identified to be the core of the e-government applications. The e-Government projects are Electronic Procurement (eProlehan), Project Monitoring System (PMS), Electronic Services Delivery (eServices), Human Resource Management Information System (HRMIS), Generic Office Environment (GOE), E-Syariah and Electronic Labour Exchange (ELX). Besides these seven main projects under e-government flagships, several government agencies has taken initiatives to introduced online services for the public, with aims to increase the ease and efficiency of public service to the people. Among them were Public Services Portal (myGovernment), e-Tanah, e-Consent, e-Filing, e-Local Government (e-PBT), e-Kehakiman, Custom Information System (SMK), Pensions Online Workflow Environment (POWER), and Training Information System (e-SILA) (Shaidin, 2007; Ambali, 2009).

Growing Population of Workforce and E-Filing Alternative

The data below shows that Malaysia labours force is increasing since 1980 until 2003. Although it seems decreased in 2003, but still achieves the level of above 8 million persons. In other words, it shows an increasing trend since 1985 to 2002. On the other hand, the unemployment rate recorded a lower percentage within the same periods as compared to 1980's as indicated in figure 1.

One important point to ponder from the increasing trend of workforce is the capability of the IRB officers to handle all income tax file returns manually with the growing population of such labour force today. As the population of those em-

Figure 1. Labor force and unemployment rate

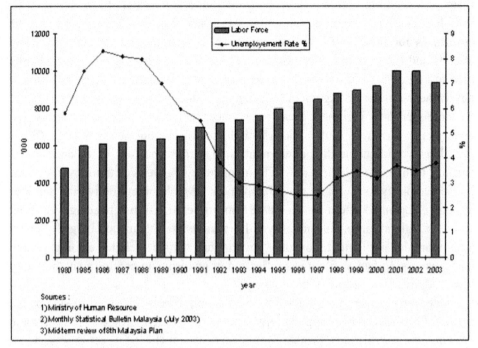

Graph source : Poon Wai Ching (2006); The development of Malaysia Economy, Prentice Hall

ployed among the growing labour force is increasing, the number of tax payers is also expected to steadily rise (see: labour force graph above). According to the department of statistic in Malaysia (2008), the predicted number of the population that is expected to be within the age group of 25-55 year in 2010 is expected to rise to 12 million. This implies that the cost that would be borne by IRB for manually processing every individual tax file return form will be at an average figure of RM10 ringgit. The immediate implication of this is that the IRBM has to handle approximately 10 million employed citizens' tax returns every year manually.

Technology and Components Concerns for E-Filing System

E-filing implementation was introduced by a government agency called LHDN (Lembaga Hasil Dalam Negeri). It allows taxpayers to submit their income tax details online and is considered as an alternative to the usual manual paper submission (i.e., BE or B forms). E-filing was first introduced in 2006 and has since undergone a progressive improvement with a more robust system promised to the users via Internet Explorer browsers technology. Today, the e-filing application is not only limited to Internet Explorer browsers like before; taxpayers can now also use other browsers like Firefox and Opera to reach LHDN wherever they are in the country. In terms of technology, a big picture of e-filing system in Malaysia is that it integrates tax preparation, tax filing and tax payment, which serves as a major advantage over traditional manual procedures. With the e-filing system, taxpayers and tax practitioners can file income tax returns electronically via the enabling technologies, rather than through mail or by physically visiting the tax offices. This is believed to make the art of tax filing returns easier by some users.

However, there has been some question of concerns on the authenticity of the transaction among the citizens and non-citizen taxpayers. In addition, the security loop holes have been discovered in the past but the Lembaga Hasil Dalam Negeri (LHDN) known as Internal Revenue Board (IRB) folks were very quick to address the issues and resolve them in a timely manner. Again, with the specter of the growing digital divide looming large, the significance of technology acceptance assumes paramount position in the roadmap towards e-government applications in public sector. Therefore, the implementation of e-government in any country would therefore require an environment that is very conducive to realize its potential for development. Ideally, an environment that is more 'e-ready', people are in general more comfortable with the new technologies and thus e-filing initiatives can be easily accepted and adopted.

Management and Organizational Concerns

From managerial and organizational perspectives, there were twofold concerns of implementing e-filing system by the charged agency LHDN. *First*, is for the agency to become more effective in the operational and processing tasks involving tax filing returns. For example, it has been realized that using manual system limits the ability to process tax files expeditiously and subsequently causing a lot of delay in income tax collections. In addition, given that the volume of taxpayers is increasingly risen up in the country, additional manpower and time are required to screen tax returns and enter the data manually into the system. Thus it is believed that implementation of e-filing system would significantly streamline the process, improve the accuracy of the tax returns and reduce transcribing error that characterized the manual base system. *Second* is to better serve the interest of the taxpayers by overcoming their difficulties in using paper base or manual system and to encourage voluntary compliance of the taxpayers in submitting their tax returns. Thus implementation of e-filing system serves as another additional channel for taxpayers to reach the agency. In other words, implementation of e-filing system is expected to provide greater convenience for taxpayers in the sense that it allows them to file their tax returns at anytime and from anywhere within the stipulated tax filing period.

CHALLENGES AND ISSUES IN THE LITERATURE

This section of the case examines the various challenges and issues pertaining to implementation of e-filing in Malaysia. The current challenges include how many and which segment of the population is using the system; perception of users towards it; perceived barriers, gender effect, age; security issue technology acceptance and readiness, perceived usefulness and ease as well as simplicity of the website of the service provider. This section covers both experience in Malaysia and elsewhere in the world with respect to theories and practices. This section begins with the challenges and/or issues can be found in practice and supported them with related theories in the literature.

Since 2006, both Malaysian and non-Malaysian citizens have been given the opportunity to choose either manual tax-filing or the internet-based called e-filing method of filing their tax-returns. However, the number of taxpayers using e-filing system is far below the expectation. According to an empirical report in newspaper, the user of e-filing in Malaysia only reached 448,742 users from 6.4 million taxpayers in the country (Izatun, 22/4/08, The Star). In an exploratory research conducted Ramayah et al (2006), the result has shown that many taxpayers did not use e-filing system to file their tax returns. One of the major issues identified in that study was related to *the 16-digit PIN number* that an e-filer must obtain directly from the income tax office. Furthermore challenges found include the queuing up at income office to get the PIN number; lack of step by step explanation on how to use the e-filing system as well as e-filers' skeptical of security and privacy of their personal data furnished in the online e-filing system. In terms of demographic effects the findings in Ramayah's study have shown that e-filers are *"predominantly female, aged 30-55 years old, married, Chinese with a bachelor or masters degree, earning more than RM 3000 per month and working in private sector" (p.4)*. However, access to computer and network facilities at home and at work was not a problem for both manual and online users in that study.

One obvious scenario is that though adoption of e-filing systems may seem to benefit taxpayers in many ways, however, the importance of understanding and influencing citizens' acceptance of this system is critical. The e-filing system may offer potential benefits to improve administrative commitments towards efficiency and quality of service delivery, but the benefits gained may be obstructed by tax users' unwillingness to accept and use the available electronic services for many reasons that worth to be researched.

Learning from the experience of overseas tax agencies, one may say that the move to embrace an e-filing system is not hassle free and is not well accepted by all parties in society. Thus, worldwide, tax users' resistance and under-utilization of the e-filing system remains a great concern and still plagues various tax agencies who are embracing electronic tax administration systems (see: ETAAC, 2002).

According to one survey on Success and Failure Rates of e-government policy in developing countries only 15% are successful, while 35% and 55% are total/ partial respectively (eGovernment for Development; Heeks, 2003). The result of a survey conducted by H.D. Vest Financial Services, Inc, - a US largest provider of financial products and services delivered through tax professionals in 2000 - has shown that majority of Americans are comfortable with e-filing.

In fact the acceptance of e-filing has given rise to an increased comfort with web preparation and it seems that Americans are catching on to the e-filing system and more swiftly than expected. To substantiate this point, the report has shown that over half of the country says that they are very comfortable by e-filing their tax returns. Fifty-four percent of American taxpayers (65 million) say that they are comfortable filing their tax returns electronically, which is more than twice the number that actually e-filed their tax returns in the previous year (30 million).

An almost identical proportion expressed the same level of comfort in receiving their refunds electronically. Not surprisingly, younger Americans in particular are more likely to e-file their tax returns and receive refunds electronically than citizens aged 65 or older who are significantly less comfortable with e-filing system. The nation's elderly are also uncomfortable with receiving a refund electronically in spite of the fact that many have already been receiving direct deposit of their Social Security payments electronically. The study also found that men are much more willing than women to use the Internet for tax preparation and e-filing.

In Asia, Taiwan is an example of country practicing e-government services where the citizen has been using the e-filing system for their personal income tax. However, there is a clear difference in willingness between men and women e-filers in terms of its usefulness, cost saving, and the ease of use (Jen et al, 2006). Many other studies have also reported similar cases of this kind and pointed to several factors such as technology readiness of the people, perception of the public in terms of technology usefulness, ease of use, and security of their information provided online (James, 1987; Davis, 1989; Parasuraman, 2000; Parasuraman and Colby, 2001; and Yurcik and Sharma, 2004).

People's Acceptance of Technology and Readiness Theory

People's acceptance of e-filing is highly related to their level of technology readiness on the one hand, ease and usefulness of e-filing system as well as security and facilitating support on the other. Technology readiness is defined as people's propensity to embrace and use new technologies for accomplishing certain tasks. The people's propensity towards e-filing system has to do with their level of optimism, innovativeness, discomfort, and security tightening in the system. Parasuraman and Colby (2001) highlighted that technology readiness is an overall state of mind and not a measure of competency and has pointed to some important issues surrounding human aspects of technology readiness. First, technology readiness varies from one individual to another. Some people can be consumer of a technology, but some may seek technology actively, whilst others may need special help or coaxing depending on the level of their readiness. Second, technology readiness can be used to predict and explain people's responses towards new technologies. Empirical findings also indicate that technology readiness correlates with actual use and intention to use the technology-based products and services in varying degrees (Parasuraman and Colby, 2001). In addition, an individual with a higher level of technology readiness has higher usage intention and more experience in using the technology based products and services in varying degrees. Similarly, prior studies by Dabholkar (1994) and Mick and Fournier (1998) also demonstrated that people with more positive beliefs are more receptive and ready to use the various new technologies.

People's Perceived Usefulness of Technology, Security, and Acceptance Theory

The perceived usefulness is a prospective user's subjective probability that using a specific application system will increase his or her job performance within an organizational context (Davis et al. 1989). As far back as 1989, Davis et al had developed a theoretical assumption relating to technology acceptance model (TAM) to explain the computer usage behaviour and had adopted the generic Fishbein and Ajzen's Theory of Reasoned Action (TRA) model to the domain of user acceptance of computer technology. The goal of TAM was to provide an explanation for the determinants of computer acceptance. He contends that this would generally capable of explaining behaviour across a broad range of end-users of computer technologies. In other words, TAM is usually used for explaining the relationship between usages [both self-reported and anticipated future usage] and perceived usefulness as well as perceived ease of use.

According to TAM, usage and acceptance of technology is a direct function of behavioural intention, which in turn a function of attitude toward actual usage. This will reflect feelings of favourableness or unfavourableness toward using any particular technology. The perceived usefulness will reflect the belief that using the technology will enhance performance. From such theoretical assumption, one may likely to conclude that behavioural intention of using, continuing to use, and actual usage of a any technological device for carrying out any transaction is determined jointly by perceived usefulness and perceived ease of use. In the same line of argument, Mathieson (1991); Adams, Nelson and Todd (1992); Segar and Grover (1993); Igbaria et al. (1995, & 1997); Ndubisi et al (2001); Jackson (1997); Ramayah et al. (2004) and Livari et al, (1997) had all shown that the three factors especially perceived usefulness and security have a direct influence on technology usage intention.

In addition, the Unified Theory of Acceptance and Use of Technology (UTAUT) by Venkatesh et al. (2003) have also been used to explain users' intention to use Information System and subsequent usage behaviour. The theory holds that four key constructs related to performance expectancy, effort expectancy, social influence, and facilitating conditions are direct determinants of usage intention and behaviour of the people. In UTAUT model, gender, age, experience, and voluntaries of use, are posited to moderate the impact of the four key constructs on usage intention and behaviour (see: Venkatesh et. al., 2003). The theory was developed through a review and consolidation of the constructs of eight models that earlier researchers had employed to explain Information Systems usage behaviour, such as theory of reasoned action; technology acceptance model; motivational model; theory of planned behaviour; a combined theory of planned behaviour/technology acceptance model; model of PC utilization; innovation diffusion theory; and the social cognitive theory. Subsequent validation of UTAUT in a longitudinal study found it to account for 70% of the variance in usage intention studied by Venkatesh et al, (2003).

As far as security issue is concerned it is obvious that people rarely worry about security in the physical world. Most of them, even while filing the paper-based tax returns, never bother to find out who is in charge of the post office where they will post their returns nor worry about the percentage accuracy of postage delivery services. But, when it comes to e-filing, people go out to extraordinary length to worry about the security of their information required in the system. The reason for such inconsistent behavior is that security violations in Internet-based systems have received much notoriety in the popular sections of press and mind of the people.

It is this perception of security in the online transactions that causes majority of the tax payer population to be reluctant to use this alternative medium of filing tax returns. People may perceive current facilities in electronic tax filing website not adequately secure and/or helpful. This may also lead to a general belief that electronic transaction are inherently insecure and that any hacker/geek, if he/she wants, can break into the computer system and can steal and misuse their confidential personal data information. Perhaps, it is this general paranoia that has gripped the public taxpayers.

In other words, electronic tax filing has been, without any doubt, gaining a lot of popularity in these days, but a lot of users go to this system and try to get a 'feel' of how to file electronically but poor navigability and sense of uncertainty about the functionality and security concerns for their sensitive information result in the users 'giving up' the idea of electronically filing tax returns in despair. Thus, even though these websites may initially attract a large number of people, the retention may be low.

In line with such view, Pfitzmann's work (2001) has shown that to perceive security and credibility of a website a person makes assessment of both trustworthiness to arrive at conclusion that the website is credible or not and to whether he/she should use it or not. If the user is able to feel that the system is well secured and trustworthy he/she will be able to put trust into the website and use it. One can easily argue that public users will have no doubt in trusting Malaysian federal and state government websites for providing information. However, users can still be sceptical in the manner the agency is going to transmit or store their personal information provided to them.

People's Perception of Ease and Simplicity of the Site

Another crucial issue related to users' perception, acceptance and usage of the e-filing system is the concern for simplicity of the site and availability of support. If the system matches the users' mental model and users can find it intuitive with nothing strange or unlikely happening, they feel more confident about the e-filing tax site. If they feel ease of using it and safe, they don't mind providing information about themselves. A sense that nothing is hidden or obscure on the e-filing tax website is a very important factor for the users to be able to perceive it as secure and trustworthy and have intention to continuing using it.

Thus the ease of use and users' feeling of control of the e-filing tax system would give them confidence about the system. Finally, a user's perception about genuineness of the tax web, authenticity and trustworthiness of the process of filing tax returns can also be enhanced if user feels ease about what he/she is doing when they are filing their tax returns. Thus, the users' awareness and experience also help enhance the users' retention dramatically.

To sum up, first people may have a positive view (optimistic) of e-filing and belief in the benefits of it in terms of time, cost efficiency and enhancement of their compliance. Second, they may be discomfort about it when they perceived themselves to be lack of control over technology and non confidence in using the new technology properly. Third is insecurity, which can lead to distrust of technology-based transactions and skepticism about its ability to work effectively for their needs.

CURRENT ISSUE EXAMINED IN THIS CHAPTER: A RETENTION PROBLEM

This section of the case study investigates the current challenges and issues in Malaysian e-filing system. The section seeks to confirm the relevance of some of the potential issues and challenges highlighted in the theoretical literature to Malaysian e-filing system with respect to users' retention and gender effect issues. As such this section of the chapter examines the user's perceptual retention and gender difference on the new electronic income-tax-paying or filing system in Malaysia, as an alternative to the traditional paper-base. The section begins with methodology and approach to the investigation. It then discusses the details of the finding about the new current challenge. Finally, it discusses the implications of the findings for the policy-makers with some recommendations for improvements.

Methodology and Approach to the Investigation of Retention Issue

The Design and Source of Data

The study is designed in a cross-sectional survey to obtain information from respondents over a period of time about their perceived usefulness, perceived security, facilitating condition, ease of using e-filing technology system to file their income tax returns and retention. Hence, the unit of analysis for the study is every individual taxpayer that has used the e-filing system and hoping to re-use it again. The study limits its scope to two geographical locations in Kuala Lumpur and Shah Alam for data collection.

A survey of questionnaire was distributed to participants and supported by unstructured interview for an in-depth investigation about the perceived ease, usefulness, security, facilitating conditions and retention for e-filing system. A sample size of 450 taxpayers was purposively and randomly chosen to participate in the study over a period of two months (March-April, 2009) of data collection. But, out of the 450 questionnaires distributed, only 302 were returned. Again, out of the 302 returned questionnaires only 300 were appropriately completed with valid information. The remaining 2 questionnaires were not used in the analysis due to too many omissions or non-completeness of the questions and more than two answers were chosen or ticked for some questions in the 2 questionnaires. As such they were dropped in the subsequence analysis.

Measurement and Instrumentation

Methodologically, the chapter employs a survey of the users of the new electronic system. The questionnaire covers the perceptual retention of the users to continue using e-filing system on the basis of the perceived level of security in using the e-filing system. The measurement of security variable embraces a lot of dimensions which include whether: use of e-filing may cause personal income tax information to be stolen or not; users do not consider it safe to give out bank account number through e-filing; users feel uneasy psychologically if they use e-filing; users do not think it is safe to use e-filing because of the privacy concerns; and overall, users find e-filing to be secured in preparing and filing tax returns. The rationale behind covering the perceived security is logical as it can affect the perceptual intentions (retention) of the users to use or continuing to use the system.

In addition, the survey questions also focus on the facilitating conditions/supports that are in place to encourage the users to use the system. For this variable the measurement includes availability of: the necessary resources such as computer and internet to use e-filing; the Internet knowledge of the users to use e-filing; a step by step guideline on how to use e-filing by the agency's staff; the easy of getting support when the users have problems, in using the e-filing, from the staff. The survey also went further to capture the ease of use of the e-filing system. The dimensions of this variable includes whether e-filing is: easy to learn; easy to master; easy to operate; has instructions that are easy to follow; easy for users to input and modify data; easy to use in general; clear and/or understandable to the users.

Above all, the survey items also cover another potential variable referred to as perceived usefulness. This variable is measured in different dimensions in terms of whether the system: enables users to accomplish the tasks more quickly; enhances effectiveness in preparing their income tax filing; simplifies the process of filing income tax return; enables users to reduce error in their tax filing process; reduces communication and filing costs; and overall users find e-filing useful in preparing their income tax at large. Finally, the survey questions also look at the natural characteristic factor, such as gender, that can shape users' perceptions in using e-filing system as a moderating effect. All questionnaire items except demographic variables are measured on 5-point likert scale, 1= strongly disagree, 2 = disagree, 3 = undecided, 4 = agree, and 5 = strongly agree.

Goodness of Data

The goodness of data starts from consistency of the items with the concepts being measured in the survey. In other words, consistency indicates how well the items measuring a concept hang together as a set for any constructs and must be tested.

Internal consistency and reliability of the survey instrument used was tested via Cronbach's alpha. Cronbach's alpha is computed in terms of the average inter-correlations among the items measuring the concepts.

The results confirm the suitability and validity of the designed survey instruments in this study with a value ranging from 0.8-0.9 and thus indicate the goodness of the items in the survey and their appropriateness (De Vaus, 2006). The Cronbach's alpha value exceeded the 0.7 standard proposed by Nunnaly (1978). The reliability coefficient values is categorized ranging from 0.6 acceptable to excellent (> 0.7) according to George and Mallery (2001) and hence the scale instrument is found to be adequate and well reliable in this study as indicated in Table 1.

Statistical Approach and Assumptions

At the inception of the OLS (ordinary least square) approach to this work, various assumptions such as normality of the data distribution, homoscedasticity and collinearity are examined and satisfied (see Aiken and West, 1991, Aguinis, 2004). Normality test is a prerequisite for any inferential statistical technique. As argued by Coakes and Dzidic (2006), there are a number of ways to explore this assumption graphically by histogram, stem and leaf plot, box-plot, normal probability plot. There are also a number of statistical methods to test such assumption which includes Kolmogrove-Smirnov with Lillifors significance level and Shapiro-Wilk as well as Skewness and Kurtosis.

Essentially, skewness and kurtosis are the two statistics used to summarize the shape of the distribution of the variables in this study. According to Hair et al (2006), the degree to which a distribution is asymmetrical is indicated by the skewness values whilst kurtosis meanwhile suggests the degree of flatness or peakness in data distribution relative to the shape of a normal distribution. Thus, Hair et al (2006) suggested that a normal distribution should occupy a range within an acceptable ± 2. In this study, the results for all items are well below such value ± 2 and thus indicate normality of the data distribution. In addition, other indicators of

Table 1. Internal consistency, validity, and reliability of the survey instrument

Variable	Cronbach's Alpha	No of Items
Perceived usefulness	0.86	6
Perceived ease of use	0.91	7
Facilitating conditions	0.80	5
Users' retention	0.88	4
Perceived Risk/security	0.82	5

Table 2. Normality test

Variables	Skewness	Kurtosis	Kolmogrove Smirnov	Sig.
User's retention	-0.297	0.830	0.049	0.2000*
Perceived usefulness	0.321	0.013	0.065	0.2000*
Perceived ease of use	0.181	0.613	0.070	0.197*
Facilitating conditions	0.055	-0.106	0.027	0.2000*
Perceived security	-0.232	-0.086	0.052	0.2000*

*>0.05 alpha value

normality of data distribution for using inferential statistics as in this study are the Kolmogrove-Smirnov and Shapiro-Wilk with p-value > 0.05 (see Table 2)

Furthermore, the multi-collinearity assumption is examined through a partial correlation statistics between variables. The result in Table 3 shows an absence of collinearity among all independent variables. In fact a lower values of correlation (r) (Mallery, 2001) among independent variable, which range from 0.2 to 0.4, as well as tolerance values between 0.7 and 0.8 indicate absent of multi-collinearity problem.

Statistical procedures of realizing the objective of this study began with the use of mean and standard deviation to assess the level of users' perceived usefulness, security, facilitating conditions and ease of using e-filing system (independent variables). Then, the causal relation between the levels of users' perception and retention i.e., an intention to continue using e-filing to file their tax returns (dependent variable) was examined through OLS (Regression) analysis. As such, a causal relation equation was derived as follows:

Table 3. Correlations among independent variables to examine collinearity assumption

	Perceived Usefulness	Perceived ease of use	Facilitating conditions	Security	Tolerance
Perceived usefulness	1				0.70
Perceived ease of use	0.422(**)	1			0.81
Facilitating conditions	0.353(**)	0.438(**)	1		0.75
Security	0.319(**)	0.391(**)	0.222(**)	1	0.80
N=300					

**Correlation is significant at the 0.01 level (2-tailed).

(a) First Order Analysis

Estimated Users' Retention: $(UR) = \alpha + \beta_1$ perceived usefulness $+ \beta_2$ perceived ease of use $+ \beta_3$ facilitating condition $+ \beta_4$ security + error term.   (1)

Where $\beta 1 - 4$ are the estimated coefficient values of the users' retention and a constant α.

This is used with entry method to see the overall effects of predictors, while controlling for all demographic variables.

(b) Second Order Analysis

The likely question on which type of genders has retention for e-filing system should be addressed. That is, is male or female feeling that: e-filing is a useful alternative; is easy to use; facilitating conditions are well in place; is very secure or safe to use among the taxpayers? This allows us to know specific intension to continuing using e-filing tool in relations to each of the predicting factors. As such, a block method was used to allow us to see the effect of each specific predictor, while controlling for all demographic variables except gender variable in order to test its moderating effect between each predictor and users' retention. The fact is that people by nature do not perceive and/or feel things in the same way.

Hence, new equations were generated for estimating the users' retention as follows:

$UR = \alpha + \beta_1$ perceived usefulness $+ \beta_2$ gender $+ \beta_3$ usefulness*gender   (2)

$UR = \alpha + \beta_1$ perceived ease of use $+ \beta_2$ gender $+ \beta_3$ ease of use*gender   (3)

$UR = \alpha + \beta_1$ perceived facilita-Condition $+ \beta_2$ gender $+ \beta_3$ facilita-Cond*gender (4)

$UR = \alpha + \beta_1$ perceived security $+ \beta_2$ gender $+ \beta_3$ security*gender.   (5)

Where usefulness*gender; ease of use*gender; facilita-Cond*gender and security*gender are the product terms in each respective equation.

To estimate a moderating effect, the equation must proceed from first order of each predictor to the second order, which involves a product term between the predictor and the moderator as can be seen in the equations 2 to 5 (see: Aguinis, 2004). The moderator in this study is coded with binary or a dummy coding system (effect order: male = 0 and female = 1). Finally, as mere statistical change in the value of R-square may not clearly show the effect with respect to each type of gender and therefore graphical moderating effect of gender is drawn to further shed lights on the effect.

The Findings of the Study

Level of Usage of E-Filing System in Filing Tax Returns

With reference to Table 4, the findings show that 45% (135) of respondents have used e-filing technology to file their tax returns, while a large number of respondents (55%) never use the e-filling services provided. In other words, it is a reflection that many still prefer to use their traditional manual to the new modern technology system!

Perceived Usefulness, Ease of Use, Facilitating Condition, Security Level of E-Filing System and Perceptual Retention of Users

On perceptual users' retention the research questions were measured on a 5-point likert scale to have a good sense of usage intention of e-filing system by taxpayers. The result shows that the level of respondents' retention is not very high but within moderate point (mean M= 3.23, std. Deviation SD= 0.62). This indicates that the majority of the respondents have moderate intentions of continuing using e-filing system. However, respondents have lower level of perceived security and safety about their personal data with mean 2.6 and std. deviation of 0.62.

In contrast, an examination of the result for perceived level of usefulness, ease of use and facilitating conditions in using e-filing system by respondents reflects a very high level except for security variable that below moderate (M= 4.58 SD= 0.57; M=4.43, SD=0.56; M=4.41, 0.54 and M=2.60, 0.63 respectively) as indicated in Table 5. A mere reflection on these results indicates that elements of perceived usefulness, ease of use and facilitating conditions for effective use of e-filing system could serve as driving forces that capture the taxpayers' retention or intentions to continue to use e-filing system to file their tax returns, since 2006 till the present time.

First Order Effect of Predictors on Users' Retention of E-Filing System

An examination of the results in Table 6 reflects that all the independent variables ranging from perceived usefulness to security or risk association are good predictors

Table 4. Percentage level e-filing usage

Usage of e-filing system usage	Frequency	% of e-filing
Yes	135	45
No	165	55

Table 5. Descriptive statistics of predictors with users' perceptual retention

Variable Deviation	Minimum	Maximum	Mean	Std.
User's retention	1.20	4.00	3.23	0.62
Perceived usefulness	2.50	5.00	4.58	0.57
Perceived ease of use	2.17	5.00	4.43	0.56
Facilitating conditions	2.28	5.00	4.41	0.54
Perceived security	1.22	3.00	2.60	0.63
Valid N = 300				

of users' retention for e-filing system in this study. In fact, as the results indicate, perceived usefulness is the most significant predicting factor that determine users' retention followed by perceived ease of use (Beta = 0.53, t = 6.3; and Beta = 0.24, t = 2.90) respectively. Facilitating condition and perceived security issue associated with the system (Beta = 0.12, t = 2.14; and 0.13, t = 2.24) are also good predictor of users' retention but on a lower rank compared to perceived usefulness and ease of using the e-filing system. Overall, as indicated by the result of the R-square, 62% of users' retention for e-filing system is explained by the whole predictors in our regression equation (1) put forward in this study.

Assessing the Moderating Effect of Gender

An examination of Table 7 gives a clear reflection on moderating effect of gender of users with respect to their relative perceived impact of each predictor against their intention to continuing using e-filing system. The effect is clearly shown through a change in R-square values when gender was used to moderate the relationship between each predicting factor and users' retention as indicated in model 1 and model 2 of the Table 7 respectively.

Thus, with moderating effect of gender there is a significant change from 48.7 to 49.5 for perceived usefulness. The same applies to perceived ease, facilitating condition and perceived security level from 59.3 to 59.8, 21.5 to 22.1 and 68.3 to 68.6 R-sq respectively.

However, these significant changes, due to moderating effect of gender (model 2), in the values of R-square may not be well appreciated in the sights of the readers for twofold reasons. First, it is ordinary minute figures to non-statisticians and therefore difficult to see the impact clearly. Second, these minute changes in R-square values again do not reflect the magnitude of such effect in relation to the type of gender of the users. Therefore, I have taken a one step further to show the impact of gender

Table 6. Estimated users' retention by predictors (first order effect)

Variables	Standarized Beta	t	Sig.
Perceived usefulness	0.529	6.310	0.000
Perceived ease of use	0.235	2.896	0.004
Facilitating conditions	0.123	2.144	0.034
Perceived security/risk	0.128	2.240	0.012
$R^2=0.63$**			
Adj $R^2=0.62$			

**P<0.05

graphically to account for those two reasons that R-square values cannot be able to tackle and to provide answers to questions on gender differences among the users.

So by computation of the previous equations 2 to 5 with the substitutions of all parameters from Table 4 yielded the following moderating effect of gender of the users on the relationships between the predictors and the users' retention as the graphs illustrate.

Figure 2a shows the moderating effect of gender between the perceived usefulness of e-filing and users' intention to continuing using the system to file their tax-returns. As clearly indicated by the graph, gender play a significant effect in intention to use e-filing. In fact, the result of this graphical representation of such effect shows that the degree of perceived usefulness of e-filing is higher for female e-filers than the male counterparts, wherein the slope of the female is quite steeper than the male, indicating a higher level of females' retention of e-filing system in relation to its perceived usefulness.

In addition, as indicated by the gradient of the slope, both genders have positively perceived the usefulness of e-filing system as enabler to file their tax returns as compared to traditional manual procedure or way. However, looking at perceived usefulness of e-filing system for female e-filers, the intention to continuing using

Table 7. Estimated users' retention by predictors and moderating effect of gender (2nd order effect)

	without gender	with effect of gender			
Variables	Model 1 (R^2)	Model 2 (R^2)	α	β_1	β_2	β_3
Perceived usefulness	48.7	49.5	-2.05	0.70	3.06	-0.14
Perceived ease of use	59.3	59.8	-1.94	0.72	2.74	-0.11
Facilitating conditions	21.5	22.1	4.22	0.11	0.02	-0.03
Perceived security/risk	68.3	68.6	-1.06	1.03	1.90	-0.11

the system (UR) ranges from 3.7 approximately to 4.5 as compared to male's retention level between 0. 7 and 1.6 as the graph indicates.

Just like perceived usefulness of e-filing system, the finding in Figure 2b shows that female e-filers have high retention to continuing using the system as compared to male e-filers. In other words, as perceived ease of use of e-filing system increases so also the users' retention for both genders, but that of female is extremely higher, ranging from 3.2 to 4.0 as compared to male between 0.9 and 1.7 approximately. Interestingly, the estimated minimum retention (UR) for female is even higher than maximum retention for male users as can be clearly seen in the graph with about 2.3 values difference.

In terms of facilitating conditions and/or supports put in place to enhance the using of e-filing system by e-filers, the results in Figure 2c shows an opposite trend to the way the gender perceived the first two variables (usefulness and ease of using the system), where the female e-filers have the highest degree of retention for using e-filing due to a highly perceived usefulness and ease of using the system. However, in the case of facilitating condition component, although both genders have positively perceived that there are a lot of facilitating conditions and supports, but the male e-filers' retention is slightly higher than the female counterparts as indicated by the graph. As the results indicate the lowest or minimum retention for both genders, regardless of their differences, ranges from 4.64, 4.65 to 4.73, 4.76 respectively when compared with perceived usefulness and ease of use component variables.

By looking at the graphical indicator (Figure 2d) of the users' retention with respect to perceived security associated with using e-filing, both male and female are differ in retention as indicated by the gradient of the slopes. Just like all other predicting factors, both of the slopes for male and female e-filers are paralleled but unequally steepened. In other words, both genders of the users have the same impressions regarding the extent to which their personal data submitted online can be protected or saved from being exposed to unauthorized people who may likely take advantage of making use of their data wrongly within and outside the country.

However, for female users, the degree of their perceived security tightening in e-filing is higher as compared to their male counterpart users. Thus, the female' retention for e-filing system is much higher ranging from 2.7 to 4.1 as compared to the male e-filers with retention between 0.9 and 2.3 approximately. In other words, the higher the perceived security tightening and protection of their personal information, the higher their retention to continue using e-filing system in filing their tax returns. Overall, differences in gender perceptions about the usefulness; ease of use of e-filing; enough facilitating conditions/supports; and level of security have a significant effect on each type of users' gender. In other words, both genders do not have the same feeling for e-filing system in filing their tax returns.

Figure 2. (a) Moderating effect of gender by perceived usefulness of e-filing system; (b) Moderating effect of gender by perceived ease of use of e-filing; (c) Moderating effect of gender perceived by facilitating conditions; (d) Moderating effect of gender security tightening in e-filing

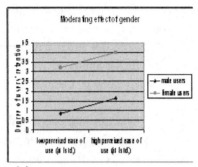

(a) Moderating effect of gender by perceived usefulness of e-filing system

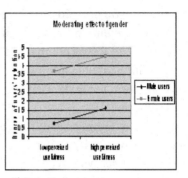

(b) Moderating effect of gender by perceived ease of use of e-filing

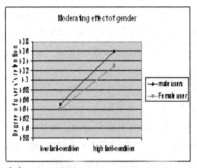

(c) Moderating effect of gender perceived by facilitating conditions

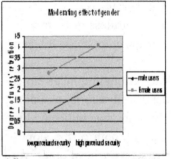

(d) Moderating effect of gender security tightening in e-filing

DISCUSSION OF FINDINGS AND RECOMMENDATIONS

There is no doubt that in this era of fast moving world, better services from respective governments or agencies to their citizens are highly needed. Therefore, creating a fast, reliable and safe service should be the main priorities of any governments in the world. Thus, adapting technology into the public service delivery system is one of the ways to create fast reliable and safe services. In Malaysia, e-government flagship was launched to cater for these technological needs of its citizens under which e-filing system is becoming a popular method for the citizens to file their tax returns. However, one thing is to provide a technology system for people to speed up the service processes, but it is another thing for people to accept and perceived it as something useful, easy, convenient, and enhance their situation as compared to the manual form.

In relation to the findings of this study, one can obviously say that the overall level of the e-filing usage among taxpayers is still low, despite many campaign activities by LHDN to increase the level of e-filing usage in the country. This finding is very similar to the statistical reports on the usage record for the previous years and also inline with similar disappointing numbers of the e-filing users reported by Izatun (2008) in one of the local news paper as discussed the section on literature review of this study. However, such disappointing lower number of usage of e-filing system by taxpayers to file their income tax returns is not confined to Malaysia, but also to some other developed countries including USA as discussed in the literature.

Regarding the other crucial issues of security level, holding the gender of the users constant, a lower mean level of using e-filing system shows some elements of negative perceptions of the users, which may likely affect their retention and/ or a continuing usage of e-filing system in the nearest futures. This equally shows that many taxpayers are still not satisfied with the e-filing service security. Hence, it implies that many of the participant taxpayers still have less trust in the system or agency in protecting their personal data. In the same line of argument a work conducted by Yurcik and Sharma (2004) has reinforced trustworthiness to be among the factors that influence the respondent perceptions on the online security. As far as security level is concerned in this study trustworthiness and security must achieve a reliable stage where federal government's web would not be questioned. It is true that taxpayers may have due respect for the federal or state government's website however; users can still be sceptical in the manner the information provided is going to be managed, transmitted or stored by the agency.

Since perceived ease of use is the degree to which a person expects the use of certain technology system be free of effort (Davis et al., 1989), there is a direct significant effect of perceived ease of such technological tool on users' retention as the finding of this study indicates and also ascertained by Hong et al., study in 2002. Thus, in general, if a technological tool is easy to use, it requires a less effort on the part of users thereby increasing the likelihood of its acceptance and usage (Teo, 2001). So as the result of this study shows that ease of use of e-filing is one of the key significant determinants of level of users' retention, the e-filing system should be made easy to use by the taxpayers in filing their tax returns.

With regards to facilitating conditions the finding of the study, apart from being a potential factor that challenge the users' retention, reflect how imperative is for all government agencies charged with e-government policy implementations to equip themselves with more sophisticated ICT skills in order to provide necessary guideline and support to the users. In other words any gaps in IT infrastructure can affect people's intention to use the system provided by the government. Such gap for example, may include the difficulty of Internet access, ICT literacy among the public, which can influence the public masses to use or neglect the system. Therefore, it is important to close the gaps by providing adequate IT infrastructure to encourage the public to use the system. Thus, it means there is a need for government to come out with better effective program for capacity building of the agency's staff and to ensure readiness of the people in society to use the system so that e-government implementation may realize its primary objectives in the country.

As far as perceived usefulness of e-filing is concerned, the findings in the chapter implied that it is a key influential and potential contributing factor of users' retention. Such a finding indicates that any technological devices provided in enhancing the service interface between the government and its citizens must be found useful, less complicated. Thus, e-filing system must be further seen to be more useful alternative, to the people, in terms of time and cost save as well as more convenience compared to manual; otherwise it wouldn't make any difference from the usual traditional manual system.

Finally, as the findings of the study show, there is a profound moderating effect of gender difference on the relationship between perceived usefulness, ease of use, facilitating conditions and security and users' intention to continue using the e-filing system. As the findings indicate, the female users have positively perceived a high usefulness of e-filing, ease of use and security level for e-filing and as such possessed a high retention level for the system. The male counterparts have the opposite of this perceptual feeling in all cases except for facilitating conditions variable. This result also confirms Ramayah's et al (2008) report where the e-filers are predominantly female with ratio 2 to 3 (see: Table 8).

In other words, it is a typical reflection of man's nature to be very rigid in mind and may not be easily convinced as compared to woman. Thus, there is a lot more to be done to convince and encourage more male taxpayers to use the new electronic system for tax returns. However, in some other parts of the world the finding is opposite. For example, the results of a survey conducted by H.D. Vest Financial Services show that most e-filing users in America are males.

Overall, there is a need for improvement in the implementation of the online e-filing to ensure that the system conform to the public e-filers' satisfaction as the result for users' retention only indicate moderate level. Perhaps, this might be due to the finding on security issues in e-filing system. It is argued that e-filing is associated with accountability of the government agencies in delivering quality services, while protecting detail data of the users.

Finally, e-filing must be seen and recognized as a means to promote electronic form of financial transaction as well as a value addition for enhancing the e-governance

Table 8. Profile of the respondents

Variables	Frequency	Percentage
Gender		
Male	120	40
Female	180	60
Age		
18-30	90	30
31-55	204	68
>55	6	2
Marital status		
Single	114	38
Married	186	62
Race		
Malay	60	20
Chinese	135	45
Indian	51	17
Others	54	18
Sectors		
Government	90	35
Private	195	65
Monthly Income		
RM2000-RM3000	54	18
RM3001-RM4000	84	28
>RM4000	162	54
Computer & Network Facilities at work		
Have no computer	39	13
Computer, no Internet	60	20
Computer & Internet	84	28
Dial up	66	22
Broadband	51	17

system of the country. Paying and e-filing income tax is a social responsibility of every citizen of a country; however, they must be impressed and encouraged to discharge such responsibility with the best and fast electronic devices.

REFERENCES

Adams, D. A., Nelson, R. R., & Todd, P. A. (1992). Perceived usefulness, ease of use and usage of information technology: A replication. *Management Information Systems Quarterly, 6*(2), 227–247. doi:10.2307/249577

Aguini, H. (2004). *Regression analysis for categorical moderators.* New York, NY: The Guilford Press.

Ajzen, I., & Fishbein, M. (1980). *Understanding attitudes and predicting social behaviour.* Prentice-Hall.

Ambali, A. R. (2009). Digital divide and its implication on Malaysian e-government: Policy initiatives. In Hakikur, R. (Ed.), *Social and political implications of data mining: Knowledge management in e-government.* Hershey, PA: Information Science Reference (an imprint of IGI Global). doi:10.4018/978-1-60566-230-5.ch016

Bhatnagar, S. (2004). *E-Government: From vision to implementation – A practical guide with case studies.* London, UK: Sage Publications Pvt. Ltd.

Coakes, J. S., & Lyndall, S. (2007). *SPSS version 16 for Windows: Analysis without anguish.* Australia: Jon Wiley and Sons, Ltd.

Davis, F. D. (1989). Perceived usefulness, perceived ease of use, and user acceptance of information technology. *Management Information Systems Quarterly, 13*(3), 319–340. doi:10.2307/249008

Davis, F. D., Bagozzi, R. D., & Warshaw, P. R. (1989). User acceptance of computer technology: A comparison of two theoretical models. *Management Science, 35*(8), 982–1003. doi:10.1287/mnsc.35.8.982

De Vaus, D. (2006). *Analyzing social science data.* London, UK: Sage Publications, Ltd.

eGovernment for Development (eGov4Dev). *Success and failure rates of egovernment in developing/transitional countries.* Retrieved February 20, 2009, from http://www.egov4dev.org/success/sfrates.shtml

ETAAC. (2002). *Electronic tax administration advisory committee (ETAAC) annual report to Congress.*

George, D., & Mallery, P. (2001). *SPSS for Windows step by step: A simple guide and reference* (3rd ed.). Boston, MA: Allyn and Bacon.

Hair, J. F., Black, W. C., Babin, B. J., Anderson, R. E., & Tatham, L. R. (2006). *Multivariate data analysis*. Upper Saddle River, NJ: Pearson Education International.

H.D. Vest Financial Services, Inc. (2000, March 22). Acceptance of e-filing gives rise to increased comfort with Web. *Irving, Texas-Business Wire*. Retrieved March 2, 2009, from http://www.icrsurvey.com/Study.aspx?f=hdvest.html

Heeks, R. (2003). *E-government for development: Causes of e-government success and failure, factor model*. IDPM, University of Manchester UK. Retrieved March 2, 2009, from http://www.egov4dev.org/causesfactor.html

Hong, W., Thong, J. Y. L., Wong, W. M., & Tam, K. Y. (2002). Determination of user acceptance of digital libraries: An empirical examination of individual difference and system characteristic. *Journal of Management Information Systems, 18*(3), 97–124.

Igbaria, M., Livari, J., & Marogahh, H. (1995). Why do individuals use computer technology: A finish case study. *Journal of International Management, 29*, 227–238.

Igbaria, M., Zinatelli, N., Cragg, D., & Cavaye, A. (1997). Personal computing acceptance factors in small firms: A structural equation model. *Management Information Systems Quarterly, 29*(3), 278–305.

Inland Revenue Board. Malaysia (IRBM). (2008). *The e-filing website*. Retrieved August 21, 2009, from http://e-hasil.org.my/index/e-hasil.asp

Izatun, S. (2008, April 22). Almost half a million taxpayers now using e-filing. *The Star.*

Jackson, C. M., Chow, S., & Leitch, R. A. (1997). Toward an understanding of the behavioural intention to use an information system. *Decision Sciences, 28*(2), 357–389. doi:10.1111/j.1540-5915.1997.tb01315.x

Jen, R., F., Cheng, K. F., Wen, P. C. (2006). Acceptance of electronic tax filing: A study of taxpayer intentions. *Information & Management, 43*(1), 109–126. doi:10.1016/j.im.2005.04.001

Karim, M. R., & Nazariah, A. K. (2003). *E-government in Malaysia*. Kuala Lumpur, Malaysia: Pelanduk Publications (M) Sdn. Bhd.

Livari, J., & Igbaria, M. (1997). Determinants of user participation: A Finnish survey. *Behaviour & Information Technology, 16*(2), 111–121. doi:10.1080/014492997119950

Mathieson, K. (1991). Predicting user intention: Comparing the technology acceptance model with the theory of planned behaviour. *Information Systems Research, 12*(3), 173–191. doi:10.1287/isre.2.3.173

Ndubisi, N. D., Jantan, M., & Richerdson, S. (2001). Is the technology acceptance model valid for entrepreneurs? Model testing and examining usage determinants. *Asian Academy of Management Journal, 6*(2), 31–54.

Nonnaly, J. C. (1978). *Psychometric theory*. New York, NY: McGraw Hill.

Parasuraman, A. (2000). Technology readiness index (TRI): A multiple-item scale to measure readiness to embrace new technologies. *Journal of Service Research, 2*(4), 307–320. doi:10.1177/109467050024001

Parasuraman, A., & Colby, C. L. (2001). *Techno-ready marketing: How and why your customers adopt technology*. New York, NY: The Free Press.

Pfitzmann, A., & Wolf, G. (2000). Properties of protection goals and their integration into a user interface. *International Journal of Computer and Telecommunication, 32*(6), 669–683.

Ramayah, T., Ramoo, V., & Amlus, I. (2008). Profiling online and manual tax filers: Results from an exploratory study in Penang Malaysia. *Labuan e-Journal of Muamalat and Society, 2*, 1-8.

Segars, A. H., & Grover, V. (1993). Re-examining perceived ease of use and usefulness: A confirmatory factor analysis. *Management Information Systems Quarterly, 17*(1), 517–725. doi:10.2307/249590

Sekaran, U. (2003). *Research methods for business: A skill building approach*. India: John Wiley & Son, Inc.

Shafie, S. (2007). *E-government initiatives in Malaysia and the role of the national archives of Malaysia in digital records management*. The 8th General Conference of Development of E-Government and Digital Records Management.

Teo, T. S. H. (2001). Demographic and motivation variable associated with internet usage activities. *Internet Research: Electronic Networking Application and Policy, 1*(2), 125–137. doi:10.1108/10662240110695089

Venkatesh, V., Morris, M. G., Davis, G. B., & Davis, F. D. (2003). User acceptance of information technology: Toward a unified view. *Management Information Systems Quarterly, 27*(3), 425–478.

Yurcik, W., Sharma, A., & Doss, D. (2002). *False impressions: Contrasting perceptions of security as a major impediment to achieving survivable systems*. IEEE/CERT/SEI Fourth Information Survivability Workshop (ISW-2002). Vancouver, Canada: IEEE Computer Society Press.

ADDITIONAL READING

James, G. J. (1987). *The ecological approach to visual perception.* New York, NY: Lawrence Erlbaum Associates.

Kahan, S. (1998). Is widespread e-filing inevitable? *The Practical Accountant, 31*(11), 22–29.

Kocakulah, M. C., & Grower, G. M. (2000). Modernizing the bureaucracy: Government information systems and technology. *The National Public Accountant, 45*(8), 24–25.

Lee, E. (2002). Merge, acquire and prosper. *Akauntan Nasional, 15*(6), 12–17.

Legris, P., Ingham, J., & Collerette, P. (2003). Why do people use information technology? A critical review of the technology acceptance model. *Information & Management, 40,* 191–204. doi:10.1016/S0378-7206(01)00143-4

Lindsay, P. H., & Norman, D. A. (1977). *Human information processing* (2nd ed.). New York, NY: Academic Press.

MIA. (2000, November). Income tax (Amendment Bill 2000). *Malaysian Institute of Accountants (MIA) Circular, 20.*

Mick, D. G., & Fournier, S. (1998). Paradoxes of technology: Consumer cognisance, emotions and coping strategies. *The Journal of Consumer Research, 25*(2), 123–143. doi:10.1086/209531

Newsberry, K. J., Reckers, P. M. J., & Wyndelts, R. W. (1993). An examination of tax practitioner decisions: The role of preparer sanction and framing effects associated with client condition. *Journal of Economic Psychology, 14*(2), 439–452. doi:10.1016/0167-4870(93)90010-I

NTRS. (2000). *The 2000 national technology readiness survey.* Retrieved from http://www.technoreadymarketing.com

Nunnally, J. C. (1978). *Psychometric theory.* New York, NY: McGraw Hill.

Parasuraman, A., & Rockbridge Associates Inc. (1999). *Technology readiness index: Instructions for use in a survey.*

Rogers, E. M. (1995). *Diffusion of innovations* (4th ed.). New York, NY: The Free Press.

SGATAR. (2001). *Creating a paperless environment in tax administration.* Paper presented at the 31st Study Group on Asian Tax Administration and Research (SGATAR) Conference, Kuala Lumpur, Malaysia.

Sheppard, B. H., Hartwick, J., & Warshaw, P. R. (1988). The theory of reasoned action: A meta-analysis of past research with recommendations for modifications and future research. *The Journal of Consumer Research, 15*(3), 325–343. doi:10.1086/209170

Zmud, R. W. (1979). Individual difference and MIS success: A review of the empirical literature. *Management Science, 25*(10), 966–979. doi:10.1287/mnsc.25.10.966

KEY TERMS AND DEFINITIONS

E-Filing: The process of submitting your tax returns to the government agency through the Internet, using computers and tax preparation software.

E-Government: The use of information technology to enhance, service provision, digital democracy, and economic development of a country. This definition covers a broad definition of e-government and applies to all customers of local, state and federal governments in a country, including all interactions and transactions between government and the public (G2P) or government and business (G2B); or government and other government agencies (G2G), and between government and its own employees (G2E). A definition of e-government is not complete until it embodied all of its stakeholders.

E-Service: A broad definition for all services done through the Internet. In our definition, e-services include all e-commerce transactions such as online orders. It also includes any processing or applications that are obtainable through the Web and/or online.

Retention: A condition or an intention of retaining and reusing something. Therefore, in this chapter it is refers to intention of users to continuing re-using e-filing system as means of filing their tax returns to government agency.

Security: Generally the state of being and/or feeling secure. It includes freedom from fear, anxiety, danger, doubt, and sense of safety or certainty. Specifically in e-filing, it is the combination of user's data integrity and data confidentiality.

Tax: A sum of money required of a person or business group or company by the Government of a country to pay as contributions to support its source of revenues. Hence, is a government levies upon individual incomes or property or sales, etc. which are taxable within the domain of government.

Technology: Referred to devices which are purposefully designed to enhance information, production and services and the organization of human activities.

Users: Persons who make use of something. Therefore, someone who uses or employs something is referred to as a user. For example, people who are using e-filing system to file their income tax returns via online in this chapter are referred to users.

This work was previously published in Cases on Adoption, Diffusion and Evaluation of Global E-Governance Systems: Impact at the Grass Roots, edited by H. Rahman, pp. 57-78, copyright 2011 by Information Science Reference (an imprint of IGI Global).

Section 3
Issues and Constraints

Chapter 14
E-ZPass and the Ohio Turnpike:
Adoption and Integration of Electronic Toll Collection

Eliot Rich
University of Albany, USA

EXECUTIVE SUMMARY

"Stop Stopping, Get Going." The commonwealth of Virginia's Web site slogan (2005) tells much of the E-ZPass story.[1] E-ZPass uses computer technology to automate vehicle toll collection and payments across most of the northeastern and eastern sections of the United States. E-ZPass participants have radio frequency identification (RFID) tags installed in their cars to signal their trip through a tollbooth. Each entry and exit is recorded in a database and charged against an account on file. Bills for tolls may be paid automatically through a credit card charge or from deposits in a cash account. Electronic toll collection reduces delays at tolls, eliminates fumbling for change, trims air pollution from idling vehicles, and accelerates travel. By most accounts, E-ZPass has been a resounding success. Within the northeastern and midwestern United States, over 9 million account holders subscribe to the program, recording over 2 billion transactions each year for road, bridge, and tunnel use in 2006. Customer satisfaction is high, and program enrollments continue to grow. E-ZPass represents a state-of-the-art practice in electronic toll collection as well as a significant success in the use of RFID technology for consumers (U.S. Federal Trade Commission, 2005).

DOI: 10.4018/978-1-4666-0981-5.ch014

ORGANIZATION BACKGROUND

The State of Ohio seems a likely spot for E-ZPass. The Ohio Turnpike, the major toll road through the state, collects tolls from over 50 million vehicles each year. Ohio lies between states that have already implemented E-ZPass successfully. The costs and overhead associated with its implementation are significant, however, and it is difficult to make a case purely from direct economic benefit to Ohio drivers.

After many years of rumination and reluctance, the Ohio Turnpike Commission announced its intention to implement the E-ZPass technology by 2009 (Ohio Turnpike Commission, 2007). This decision will render the roadway toll collection technology compatible with that of its neighbors. It will also strain its traditional fee-for-service financial model to pay for the estimated $40-50 million required for new toll plaza redesign and toll collection technology.

This case study considers the decision to implement E-ZPass on the Ohio Turnpike. The first section presents the history and current operations of the roadway. The OTC's position as a late technology adopter of electronic toll collection technology is examined. A discussion of the New York state E-ZPass implementation, an early and successful adopter, provides insight into the types of information technology needed to support electronic tolling and integration into the regional network. The case ends with a discussion of public sector technology adoption and issues facing the OTC as part of their decision.

The Ohio Turnpike, officially opened in 1955, runs for 241 miles across the northern part of the state. At its eastern border, the turnpike connects with the Pennsylvania Turnpike, a toll road. It travels through Cleveland, the state's second largest city, follows the coast of Lake Erie to Toledo, and continues across to the western border to the Indiana Toll Road, which is also near the border with Michigan. These connections in turn, link to major toll roads from Massachusetts, New York, and Illinois. All of these states are major manufacturing and commercial centers, and the turnpike serves both trucking and passenger vehicles traveling across the state.

In 2006 the roadway maintained 31 interchanges across its length, 20 from its initial launch, with 11 added since 1991. Alongside the roadway are 16 service centers that provide meals, sanitary facilities, and repair centers for motorists. At the end of 2005 the Ohio Turnpike Commission (OTC) employed about 1,300 full-time and part-time employees, of which about 900 were unionized staff responsible for toll collection and roadway maintenance. Concessionaires run many of the service center activities and pay rental fees to the roadway.

The OTC oversees turnpike operations. The seven members of the commission, appointed by the governor and legislature, serve 8 year terms. The executive director of the commission directly supervises 900 full-time and 430 part-time employees who collect tolls, maintain the roadways, and control the financial operations of the turnpike. Many of these employees are unionized, and while the current labor situation is stable, there have been recent periods of tension between management and labor. Some activities, such as safety patrols, food service, and towing, are outsourced.

There are other important government organizations with which the OTC collaborates. The Ohio Department of Transportation (ODOT) is responsible for the maintenance and development of other major highways and roadways in the state. ODOT is funded directly by the state budget and does not collect tolls on its roadways. Patrol and traffic enforcement on the turnpike is the responsibility of the Ohio State Highway Patrol. The OTC also works with the communities through which it travels to produce local benefits from the roadway.

SETTING THE STAGE

The use of innovative technology has long been seen as a critical enabler to competitiveness (Hammer & Champy, 1993), though the discussion of its ability to sustain leadership has been disputed (Carr, 2003). In the public sector, however, competitive pressures are less important than the provision of services to the public in a useful and cost-effective manner. The absence of a financial "bottom line" makes the analysis of the value of a public sector IT investment more challenging and subject to multiple and subjective interpretations. In addition, limited budgets and technical resources can constrain the range of options available to a public agency (Dawes et al., 2004). There are also concerns about privacy of personal information (Hinnant & O'Looney, 2003), particularly when it can be combined with legal or financial records. These factors all contribute to the challenges faced when governments decide when and how to adopt technology.

The E-ZPass system is a remarkably successful introduction of innovative technology in the public sector (U.S. Federal Trade Commission, 2005; Vollmer Associates, 2000). Drivers appreciate the convenience of automated toll collection, allowing them to move quickly through a toll plaza without fumbling for exact change or waiting on long lines. Highway officials improve operations by replacing paper toll tickets with electronic data collection. Audit and control managers maintain better records and see reduced opportunities for fraud and lost revenue. In addition, the collection of transaction data identifies the travel habits of millions of consumers. This RFID-based electronic toll collection technology, along with others with different names, has been widely adopted across most of the United States.

CASE DESCRIPTION

While the E-ZPass system has been in stable operation for over a decade, the Ohio Turnpike Commission has only recently decided to consider implementing it on its roadway. Understanding its reluctance to implement E-ZPass requires an examination of the management philosophy of the OTC and its operations history.

Management Philosophy of the Ohio Turnpike Commission

The OTC's mission statement encapsulates the management principles of the roadway: "To operate and maintain a user-fee supported highway with sound financial management that provides motorists and travelers with safe, modern, and helpful services." Over its 5 decades of operation, the Ohio Turnpike Commission has identified three themes that guide its decision-making and structure its operations. Each year, when the OTC reports on its activities, they are re-asserted and amplified in the context of that year's objectives and constraints.

Economic Self-Sufficiency

For its entire history, the turnpike has relied almost exclusively on user tolls to pay for operations and to pay off capital debt, supplemented with fuel tax rebates, toll permits, and concession payments. It receives no levies from the general funds of the State of Ohio or the Federal government. This self-sufficiency is quite appealing politically, as the direct costs of the roadway are paid for by its users, rather than taxpayers. To some extent, it also reduces potential conflicts with other organizations for revenues from the state budget.

This approach greatly influences the capital investment decisions made by the turnpike. All current renovations are paid for by the users of the roadway or through bonds backed by future tolls, which usually limits innovations to those that are financially balanced. Its recent experiments in the use of toll machines and pre-paid toll cards, discussed in more detail, reflect this low-cost approach to innovation and productivity improvement.

Safety and Reliability

Maintenance and improvement of the roadway and off-road facilities are a high priority for the commission. Much of its maintenance funding each year is spent on snow removal, surface repair, and safety engineering changes. In addition, outreach activities, such as Safety Days, featuring free auto inspections and car seat checks, demonstrate the concern for drivers. All 16 service plazas on the turnpike provide support for disabled vehicles as well as access to emergency services every day, throughout the year. Ongoing capital improvement programs have expanded the roadway's capacity and increased operating efficiency.

Leadership in the Toll Industry

The annual reports of the commission document its pride in its service to the state. It has received numerous awards for its safe operations and engineering achievements. In addition, the commission's bonds were among the highest rated in the government world, reflecting its financial strength and stability (Ohio Turnpike Commission, 2002).

By its own measure, the OTC believes that it is a premier roadway. In its 2006 internal review, its administration notes that its toll rates are near the lowest in the country, its maintenance costs compare well with comparisons inside and outside the state, and that it has worked diligently to keep costs under control. It also emphasizes the need to continue its revenue stream or face problems with its credit rating and its ability to complete its improvement plans (Ohio Turnpike Commission, 2005).

Turnpike Operations: Rising Demand, Rising Costs, Falling Revenues

The demand for turnpike services has steadily increased since 1998 (Figure 1). The number of vehicles using the road has increased by about 17% between 1998 and 2005. Most of the vehicles on the roadway are passenger cars, averaging about 80% of the total volume. In terms of revenue, however, commercial traffic has a much greater impact on the roadway. Trucks travel further on the road than do passenger cars, and represent about 57% of the roadway revenue, as truckers pay about triple the rate of passenger vehicles, due largely to a toll rate schedule that charges a premium for heavier vehicles.

A review of the roadway's financial position tells a story of emerging financial stress (Figure 2). Operating revenues, those resulting from tolls and direct roadway collections, have increased by 14.7%, but operating expenses have risen by 56.0% over the same period. The costs of toll operations and maintenance, the two largest activity-related expenses, jumped as the roadway opened new interchanges, widened the roadway, and increased staffing. The cost of running an interchange is about $1 million, and some of the new interchanges do not have sufficient traffic to pay salaries and benefits to their staff (Ohio Turnpike Commission, 2005).

When faced with an operating deficit, fee-for-service organizations often take a combination of three actions: increase fees, reduce expenses, and defer capital investment. Given the existing commitments to expand the number of interchanges,

Figure 1. Ohio Turnpike operating statistics 1998-2005

	2005	2004	2003	2002	2001	2000	1999	1998	% Change
Number of Vehicles (000s):									
Passenger Cars	40,149	40,364	39,196	38,614	37,036	36,289	35,903	35,064	14.5%
Commercial Vehicles	11,000	9,796	9,086	9,093	8,864	9,286	9,154	8,525	29.0%
Total	51,149	50,160	48,282	47,707	45,900	45,575	45,057	43,589	17.3%
Percentage of Vehicles:									
Passenger Cars	78.50%	80.50%	81.20%	80.90%	80.70%	79.60%	79.70%	80.40%	NA
Commercial Vehicles	21.50%	19.50%	18.80%	19.10%	19.30%	20.40%	20.30%	19.60%	NA
Number of Miles (000s):									
Passenger Cars	1,963,967	2,021,519	2,019,385	1,994,626	1,913,889	1,851,766	1,820,823	1,797,105	9.3%
Commercial Vehicles	1,025,542	889,986	814,385	814,978	803,853	850,533	836,591	772,424	32.8%
Total	2,990,509	2,911,505	2,833,770	2,809,604	2,717,742	2,702,299	2,657,414	2,569,529	16.4%
Percentage of Miles:									
Passenger Cars	65.70%	69.40%	71.30%	71.00%	70.40%	68.50%	68.50%	69.90%	NA
Commercial Vehicles	34.30%	30.60%	28.70%	29.00%	29.60%	31.50%	31.50%	30.10%	NA
Toll Revenue (000s):									
Passenger Cars	$76,892	78,985	78,837	77,904	74,710	72,356	71,017	64,480	19.2%
Commercial Vehicles	102,193	110,716	101,151	101,296	99,616	104,416	105,413	91,695	11.4%
Total	179,085	189,701	179,988	179,200	174,326	176,772	176,430	156,175	14.7%
% of Toll Revenue:									
Passenger Cars	42.90%	41.60%	43.80%	43.50%	42.90%	40.90%	40.30%	41.30%	NA
Commercial Vehicles	57.10%	58.40%	56.20%	56.50%	57.10%	59.10%	59.70%	58.70%	NA
Average Miles per Trip:									
Passenger Cars	48.9	50.1	51.5	51.7	51.7	51	50.7	51.3	-4.7%
Commercial Vehicles	93.3	90.9	89.6	89.6	90.7	91.6	91.4	90.6	3.0%
Average Toll Revenue per Trip:									
Passenger Cars	$1.92	1.96	2.01	2.02	2.02	1.99	1.98	1.84	4.3%
Commercial Vehicles	$9.29	11.3	11.13	11.14	11.24	11.24	11.52	10.76	-13.7%
Average Toll Revenue per Mile:									
Passenger Cars	$0.04	0.04	0.04	0.04	0.04	0.04	0.04	0.04	0.0%
Commercial Vehicles	$0.10	0.12	0.12	0.12	0.12	0.12	0.13	0.12	-16.7%

Source: Ohio Turnpike Commission (2006).

the OTC attempted to address its weakening financial position by economizing on operations and raising tolls. The most recent efficiency review of the roadway found that the turnpike's efforts to control maintenance costs have been successful, as they compare well to other similar roadways even with additional lane-miles in place, and that its tolls are some of the lowest in the country.

The roadway has not increased tolls, however, as the last set of increases had unexpected side effects on the roadway and the surrounding communities. From 1995 to 1999 the roadway increased tolls between 9% and 20% annually. Most of the increase fell onto commercial traffic, as it represented the larger share of the roadway's traffic base. The response of some of these drivers was to leave the toll road. From 2000 to 2003 commercial revenues were lower than in previous years, reflecting in part the price sensitivity of these key drivers.

The shift of trucking traffic to secondary roads was not well received by the towns neighboring the highway. When large trucks ride on roads not designed for their weight and size, maintenance costs rise. A spot check in 2003 found that 90% of the trucks exiting at one interchange for local roads were overweight. This also created great concerns for roadway safety and accessibility in these small towns.

In 2004 and 2005 the OTC refocused its efforts to bring trucks back to the highway. At the request of the governor of Ohio, the toll increases of the previous decade were temporarily reversed, and roadway speed limits were increased from 55 to 65 MPH. The result was a 9% increase in truck traffic, bringing volume back to the levels seen before the toll changes. This program, called "Trucks to

Figure 2. Ohio Turnpike statement of revenues, expenses, and changes in net assets (000s) for the years ended December 31, 1998-2005

	2005	2004	2003	2002	2001	2000	1999	1998	% Change
Operating Revenues									
Tolls	$179,085[1]	189,701	179,988	179,200	174,326	176,772	176,430	156,175	14.7%
Special Toll Permits	2,929	2,750	2,752	2,540	2,614	2,692	2,731	2,748	6.6%
Concessions	14,204	13,793	13,704	12,340	11,547	10,538	7,949	7,406	91.8%
Leases and Licenses	867	797	634	640	555	369	424	1,198	-27.6%
Other Revenues	486	386	399	268	407	223	254	282	72.3%
Total Operating Revenues	197,391	207,427	197,477	194,988	189,449	190,594	187,788	167,809	17.6%
ODOT Purchase of Capacity	15,600								NA
State Fuel Tax Allocation	2,772	2,698	2,780	2,669	2,328	2,360	2,381	2,274	21.9%
Investment Income	3,634	1,646	1,876	4,755	9,498	16,783	15,936	16,307	-77.7%
Total Revenue	219,397	211,771	202,133	202,412	201,275	209,737	206,105	186,390	17.7%
Operating Expenses:									
Administration and Insurance	8,193	7,982	7,166	6,432	6,099	8,555	7,640	7,044	16.3%
Maintenance of Roadway and Structures	34,185	30,957	29,127	27,677	24,441	27,559	27,140	21,746	57.2%
Services and Toll Operations	48,585	46,449	43,769	42,068	37,305	36,420	33,405	27,882	74.3%
Traffic Control, Safety, Patrol and Communications	13,565	12,902	13,136	12,474	11,966	10,900	11,430	10,566	28.4%
Major Repairs and Replacements	(79)	(277)	3,775	5,580	5,219	3,384	2,271	1,210	-106.5%
Depreciation	51,023	50,428	52,541	47,888	43,225	39,062	34,576	31,216	63.5%
Total Operating Expenses	155,472	148,441	149,514	142,119	128,255	125,880	116,462	99,664	56.0%
Loss On Disposals/ Write-offs of Capital Assets	720	1,605	1,859	1,957	4,092	4,006	4,502	4,502	-84.0%
Interest Expense	36,708	37,892	40,306	31,113	32,404	33,126	32,126	32,783	12.0%
Total Expenses	192,900	187,938	191,679	181,189	164,751	163,012	153,747	128,298	50.4%
Operating Income	41,919	58,986	47,963	52,869	61,194	64,714	71,326	68,145	-38.5%
Total Income	26,497	23,833	10,454	21,223	36,524	46,725	52,358	58,092	-54.4%

Note 1: 2005 Revenues include toll reduction program for commercial traffic and ODOT Purchase of Capacity program.
Source: Ohio Turnpike Commission (2006).

the Turnpike," included a payment of over $15 million to the OTC from the state to compensate for the revenue lost from the toll rollback. This payment partially reversed the downward trend in operating income, but there is no guarantee that these payments will continue.

Other programs were launched to attract drivers. Service area modernization programs were launched that targeted the needs of professional drivers, with showers, full-service restaurants, and Wi-Fi. In 2004, half of the service areas dated back to the opening of the turnpike, and reconstruction was needed. Other capital plans were deferred to help fund these plans.

E-ZPass: The Ohio Turnpike Commission Perspective

While there seems to be little doubt that E-ZPass technology has streamlined toll collection for drivers across the Northeast, the OTC has always been concerned about the costs and benefits of electronic toll collection. One recent publication anticipated that implementing E-ZPass in Ohio would cost $40-50 million, as much as it spends on roadway maintenance each year. A recent study cited in the OTC 2006 operating budget noted that less than 15% of vehicles on the turnpike are equipped to use E-ZPass, implying that it will not be possible to eliminate toll collectors, and largely limiting the efficiency benefits of the program to out-of-state drivers, rather than Ohio residents. On the other hand, the IAG reports that E-ZPass states process between 30% and 60% of their transactions and user adoption rates of up to 70%, indicating great demand for the technology once it is established.

Instead of investing in E-ZPass, the OTC has been developing less expensive options to simplify toll collection and provide discounted travel for Ohio residents and frequent travelers. The Ready Pass program, unveiled in 2002 and unique to the Ohio Turnpike, uses a prepaid toll account linked to a credit card. Enrollees receive a Ready Pass card to present to toll collectors at entry and exit points to the roadway. Tolls are charged against their account, and the associated credit card is debited as the prepaid balance decreases. The turnpike also provides a Commercial Charge Account Program for volume customers. This charge program provides a 15% discount on tolls in excess of $1,000 per month. Prepayment is not required, though participants must provide documents that ensure payment. From the driver's perspective the charge program is similar to the Ready Pass program. The BESTPASS program, administered through the New York State Motor Truck Association trade group, has negotiated a discount program for smaller commercial companies (www. bestpass.org) that is similar to the Commercial Charge Program. The OTC estimates that these discount programs have brought additional traffic to the turnpike, but at a cost of $5-6 million per year (Ohio Turnpike Commission, 2005).

In 2005 the turnpike purchased two automated toll payment machines as part of a trial program to accept bank-issued cards, currency, as well as their own Ready Toll cards. These machines were installed in existing lanes, and gates were added to discourage drivers from exiting the roadway without paying. The initial public reaction to these machines was positive, and the OTC hoped that this technology can reduce toll collection costs. As with the existing programs, drivers still need to stop at the toll booth for each transaction

All these programs reflect the low-technology toll automation approach employed by the OTC through 2006. In their estimation, these innovations provide value to Ohio drivers and limit capital costs to the roadway. As these programs are specific to the Ohio Turnpike, however, travelers from other states gain nothing unless they enroll in these particular programs.

E-ZPass: The View from Other States

Before E-ZPass, most toll roadways used a combination of human personnel, toll machines, and paper tickets to collect and account for payments. This fairly low-tech approach has the feature of a simple computer infrastructure, focused on cash accounting. For automobile drivers, transactions started and ended at the toll plaza. For volume users or commuters, a small back office operation was commonly employed to support pre-paid accounts or discount programs.

With the introduction of E-ZPass, however, toll collection moves from a single transaction and towards the servicing of repeating customers, with a new focus on customer service and support. A sophisticated software application must be in place to capture toll transactions, establish and maintain customer accounts, and bill and accept payments for charges and violations. As RFID tags represent the mechanism for billing, recordkeeping for tags must be secure. In addition, staff must be available for customer inquiries and dispute resolution. The transition is a move towards automated government service delivery, where toll charges accrue and payments are made with as little human interaction as possible.

E-ZPass had its beginnings in 1987 when seven state agencies in the northeastern United States began examining techniques to automate the processing of toll collections. In 1991, transportation officials in Pennsylvania, New York, and New Jersey formed the E-ZPass Interagency Group (IAG), a consortium that defined a vision of an inter-state electronic toll system. The goals of this group were to:

- Create and deploy a system that was compatible across all the participating states;
- Ensure an transaction accuracy rate of 99.5% or greater;
- Process millions of daily transactions with appropriate financial controls;
- Manage the distribution and maintenance of automobile identification devices;
- Identify and manage the organizational change that followed the introduction of technology into a unionized workplace; and
- Maintain high levels of consumer satisfaction.

One of the great achievements of the E-ZPass implementation was the coordination of efforts by multiple agencies to create a seamless technology (Gifford, Yermack, & Owens, 1995a, 1995b).[2] Drivers from one E-ZPass state who use their tags in other participating states receive a consolidated bill reflecting all their charges. Each participating agency shares transaction information with the other agencies to facilitate billing and revenue exchange. Violation data, reflecting improper use of E-ZPass facilities, is also shared.

Coordination and collaboration in design was absolutely essential to the success of their efforts. At the same time, each agency had its own set of requirements to meet, based on the needs of their customers and agency staff, as well as the various types of toll models that were in place. Rather than solve all these problems, the Interagency Group agreed to a common technical infrastructure, with each state being responsible for its own collections and account procedures. This model is still in use today: States develop (or contract out the development of) billing and collections software; a standard input file is used to capture and disseminate charges from any

Figure 3. E-ZPass geographic coverage (as of September 2005)

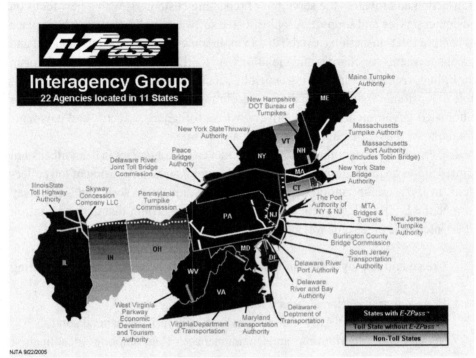

IAG participant to any other participant. Each state collects their own charges and is responsible for forwarding any out-of-state payments back to the originating IAG member. The original working group has expanded to include most of the north-eastern United States and is moving to include states in the Midwest (Figure 3).

Implementing E-ZPass

There are three interrelated requirements for a successful E-ZPass implementation. First, vehicles using E-ZPass must be identified as they accrue tolls during travel. Second, tolls must be billed and collected from customers. Third, an infrastructure supporting the seamless interchange of data among E-ZPass agencies to support out-of-state use must be in place.

Vehicle identification is accomplished through the installation of radio frequency identification tags (RFID) tags. RFID technology comes in various forms to suit the requirements of a particular implementation (U.S. Federal Trade Commission, 2005). Passive tags, which reflect radio emissions back to an antenna, are often used in consumer and warehousing applications; they are inexpensive, but have limited range. For toll collection, most applications use active tags, which contain their own battery power, often mounted to the vehicle windshield (Figure 4). While there are a number of different technologies available, the current E-ZPass system has settled on a standard tag type across the network.

Recording the use of an E-ZPass for tolls requires interaction between the RFID tag and hardware installed in traffic lanes (Spasovic et al., 1995). When a vehicle approaches a toll it receives a signal from a roadside communications device (Figure 5). In response, the tag transmits a unique identifier, which is then recorded and verified as a valid tag. If the toll station is equipped with a gate, a successful tag read is followed by lifting of the gate. In other situations a signal device shows the driver an acknowledgement of the toll or a message indicating a problem. If a driver travels through the lane with an invalid tag or without a tag at all, the trip is considered a violation of law and a camera photographs the vehicle and license for later enforcement. The collected data, with the tag id, date, time, and toll location, is stored for upload to a central computer later in the day.

The original implementations of E-ZPass added the necessary transceivers, gate controls, and cameras to exiting toll plazas. These plazas required drivers to slow or stop at each toll to ensure the safety of the toll staff, who needed to cross through

Figure 4. E-ZPass tag

Source: New York State Thruway Authority

Figure 5. E-ZPass toll collection

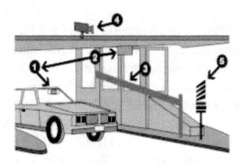

Source: New York State Thruway Authority.

lanes of traffic to get to the remaining cash lanes. Over the last decade, many agencies have redesigned toll plazas to eliminate gates and allow faster transit through dedicated electronic toll lanes. In the most modern implementations, vehicles can proceed through a toll zone without slowing at all, thus eliminating traffic delays and reducing the accumulation of vehicle emissions at plazas. The PrePass system, also using RFID technology, allows trucks to drive through a sensor net that records their tonnage without having to stop at a weigh station. Over 400,000 trucks use this technology across the nation, and a recent cross-marketing agreement now permits PrePass tags to substitute for E-ZPass tags, simplifying billing and boosting customer acceptance.

The second element of an E-ZPass implementation is the development of a customer service center (CSC) that accounts for tolls, bills customers, distributes tags, and maintains account information. Each agency supports the tags it issues; charges and tolls it receives for out-of-state tags are sent to the issuing agency and a complex set of financial guarantees and inter-agency agreements ensure that reciprocal payments, toll, and enforcement data are expeditiously shared.

The CSC is also responsible for telephone, Internet, and in-person support of its customers. Customers may inquire about the charges on their account, request new or replacement tags, close their accounts, modify their method of payment, set passwords, and in general, conduct any typical service activities. In addition, the CSC generates planning and control reports, tabulations of funds due and expected from other agencies in the E-ZPass network, as well as tag inventories. Today there are nine centers with several serving multiple agencies, with some smaller participants manage processing collectively. Some of the larger states have outsourced CSC to private vendors under closely monitored contracts.

The third element is the transfer of data among the various collaborating agencies. Reciprocity for toll collection is an absolute necessity for successful inter-state operations. The IAG provides a secure infrastructure for the transmission of data among its participants. There are a number of datasets exchanged among the agencies. Toll information, as collected at each source, is sent to the agency that issued the tag for collection. Each tag has its issuing agency embedded in its unique identifier, and each transaction includes this data. A second dataset includes the status of tags issued by an agency, so that other participants will know which tags are valid and which are not. Other datasets contain registration or driver contact information for violation enforcement.

The New York State Thruway Example

One of the first and most successful implementations of E-ZPass was performed by the New York State Thruway Authority, a toll road that spans the state. It serves as an illustration of the process that is needed to support electronic tolling and billing. The first step for a consumer is to apply for an E-ZPass tag. Each vehicle is issued a tag for its specific use. Applicants also choose how they wish to pay for tolls. They may request a cash- or check-based account or a credit account. In either case, the CSC charges the account an initial amount and toll charges are applied against these funds. When this initial amount nears depletion, cash customers see a signal when they exit the roadway advising them to send in funds. Credit customers authorize the CSC to charge their cards whenever needed to maintain a small balance in the account. Commercial customers have higher limits and are processed somewhat differently. There are different types of charges that occur on an NYSTA E-ZPass account. The first is a simple toll, where a customer uses a bridge, tunnel, or other facility that has a fixed price per usage. The second charge type is a paired charge, where both the entry and exit point for the vehicle are needed to calculate the toll; in upstate New York, for example, most charges for thruway travel are based upon both entry and exit points. A third type of charge is for miscellaneous fees, such as tag replacement and late payments. In addition, different types of vehicles (e.g., passenger vehicles, trucks, buses, tandem trucks) are assigned to their own class, and charged different rates per transaction. Violations of roadway rules, such as speeding through collection lanes, are grounds for cancellation of the E-ZPass account.

In New York, the E-ZPass CSC provides online access to the customer's account information. A summary account page describes the account, the replenishment type, and the most recent transactions (Figure 6). In addition, the customer may see an online quarterly summary of their detailed activity (Figure 7). This information is also mailed to the account holder each quarter. Customers have the right to dispute any charges applied to their accounts. The NYSTA E-ZPass telephone center is available during extended business hours. While most customers conduct business by mail, several walk-in centers exist across the state as well.

Figure 6. A sample customer record (abridged)

Account Balance		Address	
Account No:	23892309	**Type:**	MAILING
Name:	JONES, JAMES	**Street 1:**	1 WESTERN AVE
Balance:	$25.91	**Street 2:**	
Account Status:	GOOD	**City:**	ALBANY
Last Replenishment		**State:**	NY
Method:	AMEX	**Zip Code:**	12208 - 9999
Amount:	$20.00	**Country:**	US
Credit Card No:	xxxxxxxxxxxx4000	**Day Phone:**	(518)442-0000
Date:	28-Sep-2005 00:49:00	**Evening Phone:**	(518)442-0000

Latest Tolls (last 3 transactions)

Transaction Date	Tag	Entry Plaza	Entry Lane	Exit Plaza	Exit Lane	Status	Toll
25-Sep-2005 21:47:25	99999999997	CANAAN	02E	HUDSON-RENSSELAER	05N	ETOL	$0.63
25-Sep-2005 09:50:15	99999999997	HUDSON-RENSSELAER	02E	CANAAN	09E	ETOL	$0.63
21-Sep-2005 11:26:19	99999999999	W/ROUTE 128(I-95)	10	WEST STOCKBRIDGE	1	POST	$2.70

Detailed entry and exit information are uploaded regularly from toll booths across the state to the CSC and sent back out to the lanes. There each entry and exit transaction is matched and posted to the account of the tag holder. Where a lane match is not possible, the CSC attempts to make a match. Unmatched or improper transactions, such as the use of invalid tags through the E-ZPass lanes are also recorded, and a photo of the vehicle and license recorded in the database for later prosecution. In New York each E-ZPass exit lane has a list of all valid tags throughout the IAG network. This permits rapid validation of the customer's tag and identification of low balance or tag failures while the car is in the exit lane.

Figure 7. Sample transaction detail

Account No: 23892309   **Name:** JONES, JAMES

E-ZPass Transactions for Period   04/10/2005 – 06/10/2005

POSTING DATE	TRANSACTION DATE	TAG NUMBER	AGENCY	JONES PLAZA	JAMES TIME	EXIT PLAZA	TIME	AMOUNT	BALANCE
04/19/05	04/28/05	99999999997	MassPike	15	14:44:10	1	17:48:22	$ 3.60	$ 2.74
04/27/05	04/26/05	99999999997	MassPike	-	00:00:00	19	19:50:53	$ 1.00	$11.89
05/08/05	05/07/05	99999999999	NYSTA	25	22:30:58	24	22:38:00	$ 0.20	$17.34
05/08/05	05/07/05	99999999999	NYSTA	24	19:25:15	25	19:31:37	$ 0.20	$17.54
05/01/05	05/01/05	Prepaid Toll Deposit						$15.00	$17.74

Tolls against external tags that are not part of the NYSTA E-ZPass are identified through the tag's unique code. Each IAG participant has an established set of tag codes so that it is possible to create a file of transactions and charges for each agency. Each day the NY CSC forwards a file of transactions to each participating IAG member. E-ZPass receives a similar file from each of the other participating agency. Finally, the CSC sends a daily (or more frequent) file detailing the tags and toll data collected for other states' transactions to that state, and receives commitments for funds in return from out-of-state collections.

CURRENT CHALLENGES / PROBLEMS FACING THE ORGANIZATION

Incorporating the Ohio Turnpike into the E-ZPass consortium is expensive and complex. After many years of choosing and testing alternatives, the Ohio Turnpike Commission has tentatively decided to join with neighboring roadways in the E-ZPass system. It has established contacts with the IAG and hopes to attain full membership shortly. It has also begun soliciting bids and concept papers on how to implement the system across the state. This section discusses the timing of this decision as well as factors that need to be addressed over the next few years, if and when the project continues.

Public Sector Technology Adoption

As noted earlier, early adoption behavior in the private sector often stems from the desire to create competitive advantage and product differentiation. For the public sector, however, competitive advantage is not an issue in the speed of innovation. The absence of a competitive market for government activities reduces the drive to innovate or adopt change (Bretschneider, 1990). Empirical studies have found that innovation takes a back seat to cost-effectiveness and service enhancement (Bugler & Bretschneider, 1994). In addition, the high degree of accountability in the public sector creates formality and transparency in procurement that can slow the adoption and development of public sector technology deployment relative to the private sector (Caudle, Gorr, & Newcomer, 1991), though in some cases highly innovative procurement approaches are employed to bypass perceived red tape (Moon & Bretschneider, 2002). Public sector organizations also tend to spend less on IT than their private sector counterparts (Rocheleau & Wu, 2002), reducing the resources available to develop and deploy technologies early. More recent research indicates that the priorities of public sector and private sector CIOs may be aligning, driven by the emergent commoditization of IT technology, pressure to adopt private-sector operating techniques, the use of outsourcing, and changes in management application (Ward & Mitchell, 2004).

There are innovative uses of technology in the public sector to solve uniquely public sector problems, E-ZPass being a prime example. The strategic and tactical differences between the early adopters and the late adopters of this technology help clarify where others have gone ahead while Ohio has delayed. In the New York and New Jersey areas there is continual growth in commuter traffic, with persistent and extended delays at many toll plazas. These delays can routinely amount to 30-45 minutes or more during peak periods. Delayed vehicles create tremendous amounts of pollution, unnecessary consumption of fuel, and great frustration on the part of drivers who find their time wasted each morning. The secondary impact of these drivers on the communities surrounding the tolls is tremendous, as idling trucks and cards spew fumes and particulates each day, as well as increasing local traffic as vehicles leave the roadway in search of faster alternatives.

In these states, the early adoption of E-ZPass was one part of a larger strategy, one that would allow more cars and trucks to efficiently use the existing roadway. Increasing the number of toll booths at entrances and exits was thought to be very difficult as space did not permit easy modification of traffic patterns. Instead, the implementation of electronic tolling reduced the time needed to collect tolls and increased the number of vehicles that passed through a toll station per hour. Early reports from New York cited the benefits of increased traffic throughput, decreased peak-hour congestion, and a delay in plaza expansion (Vollmer Associates, 2000).

The strategic perspective of these early adopters went beyond direct financial effects. Public sector organizations often have to work with multiple stakeholders and competing goals where conflicts in priorities are difficult to resolve (Dawes et al., 2004). Early adopters of E-ZPass found support from the communities surrounding the roadway and the consumers whose commutes would be shortened, and businesses whose trucks would be able to move more freely through toll stations. This broad perspective on the needs of its customers was one force behind a strategy for customer service that looked at E-ZPass as a means for expanding constrained roadway resources, even at the cost of higher tolls to subsidize its implementation.

The Ohio Turnpike Commission had a different perspective and strategy, focused on a narrower goal to remain both self-sufficient and provide low cost services. The first indication of problems with this approach surfaced when the toll increases of the late 1990s needed to cover increased expenses resulted in a decrease, rather than an increase in operating income, as commercial traffic left the roadway in search of cheaper alternatives. Further toll increases were not likely to reverse the trend and new ways for recovering commercial traffic and reducing operating costs were needed. The introduction of the "Trucks to the Turnpike" program, the development of

Ready Pass, and the recent experiments with toll collection machines are all attempts to fund expansion and maintenance by increasing volumes and reducing operating costs. These programs, while all well-developed and thoughtfully implemented, have not provided the anticipated revenues needed to keep the roadway profitable.

In his classic work on diffusion, Rogers (1995) notes that organizations must experience some conflict between expectation and performance prior to adopting change. The growing financial gap on the roadway was one conflict. A second arose when commercial traffic moved to local roads, and towns and villages were suddenly affected by the decisions of the roadway's management. These localities exerted political pressure to be recognized as stakeholders in the turnpike's strategy, with important and relevant concerns about traffic management as vehicles exited the roadway and traveled through their towns. There appears to be an emerging re-definition of a larger set of goals for the turnpike, one that recognizes both its financial goals, the behavior of its customers, and its effects on its neighbors. This re-definition resembles the configuration of forces that resulted in the successful adoption of E-ZPass in other states. The continued recognition of this larger set of stakeholders and needs will be a challenge in the future.

Costs and Benefits of Adoption

E-ZPass is expensive to implement, requiring new technology, new roadway in-frastructure, new operations, and incremental personnel to staff the service center as well as continue roadside collections. As noted earlier, the OTC anticipates that E-ZPass will cost upwards of $30 million, and has maintained that the benefits of the technology are insufficient to justify this investment. From recent history, they believe that increasing tolls to pay for this innovation will cause drivers to shift to local roads. While all these concerns have merit, a broader examination of costs and benefits shows that there are other indirect effects that may make the invest-ment worthwhile.

Cresswell (2004) notes that calculation of return on investment on information technology is not as simple as a tabulation of direct costs and anticipated revenues. There are intangible costs that should be considered from the perspective of the wider stakeholder group. Early reports from New York cited the benefits of increased traffic throughput, decreased peak-hour congestion, and a delay in the need for plaza expansion in its analysis of E-ZPass (Vollmer Associates, 2000). New Jersey estimated that their passenger trucks saved 2.1 million hours of toll-collection delays at an estimated value of $25 million to its drivers in the first year of operation (New Jersey Turnpike Authority & Wilbur Smith Associates, 2001). Both E-ZPass users and non-users benefit from intangible benefits such as shorter collection lines, and these benefits have continued to accrue as traffic volumes and system usage has increased throughout the Northeast.

Calculating the indirect and intangible benefits of improved traffic flow may develop new support for E-ZPass in Ohio, particularly among commercial drivers. The PrePass program estimates that a 5 minute driver delay for calculating truck weight costs $5 for fuel, salaries, and operator productivity. Reducing delays at toll booths may translate to lower out-of-pocket costs for drivers, which in turn will keep them from leaving the turnpike and moving to local roads. Using this simple metric as a guide indicates that eliminating a 5 minute delay for each of the 11 million commercial drivers each year would generate intangible benefits of $55 million, more than the anticipated implementation cost. Detailed analysis of traffic delays at the toll plazas and discussions with commercial fleet and local drivers would be a mechanism for calculating the benefits of convenience to drivers.

The OTC, as a late adopter, will benefit from the experience of those that preceded it. RFID technology is more mature than it was 20 years ago, with the characteristics of tags and transmitters clearly defined and more robust. The OTC will also be able to learn a great deal about the steps needed for toll collection customer service and may even choose to contract with an existing agency rather than develop its own center from scratch. As a cooperative and collaborative organization, it is in the best interest of the other IAG members to assist Ohio in developing robust systems; failure reflects on the industry and raises costs for all. In this case, imitation rather than innovation will serve their interests.

Developing the E-ZPass Infrastructure

Adopting E-ZPass will be the largest IT investment in the OTC's history. The development of such a complex IT application is well beyond the experience of its current operations staff. It will likely need to engage outside consultants to analyze, design, and develop the system. The OTC and its stakeholders will need to participate in a design process to identify its specific business requirements. Current best practices in this area include the use of stakeholder analysis to capture the diverse set of needs for all the potential users of the system (Dawes et al., 2004), use of case analysis to identify the specific procedures that will support these needs, and object design and interaction models that depict the specific data and technical requirements (Ambler & Jeffries, 2002). While not all organizations use these techniques consistently (Dobing & Parsons, 2006), some familiarity with them will be quite important to achieve superior results. Careful analysis and comparison of existing E-ZPass operations is also warranted. All of the existing E-ZPass agencies have developed the database, communications, application software, and operating procedure specifications, providing good models from which to build the Ohio version of the system. Similarly, there are already established standards and unofficial experience on how to adapt the physical infrastructure of existing toll plazas and design new installations to ensure safe E-ZPass field operations.

Whenever customer data is computerized, appropriate safeguards for privacy and security are necessary. There has been evidence of customer backlash against the tracking of retail information in Europe, and new government policies have been proposed in several states to protect the privacy E-ZPass information. The convenience of the service appears to outweigh concerns in the minds of consumers (Eckfeldt, 2005). Nevertheless, the ability to trace individual vehicles across toll roads may open concerns about the ability to travel without monitoring. Officials in New York acknowledge that the ability to trace routes and identify speeding vehicles is present, but that the data is not released without court order. The OTC will need to create policies that explicitly address privacy concerns related to its data (Boulard, 2005).

Employee Relations

If E-ZPass is implemented, the OTC will need to address the concerns of its current employees. Since 2001, turnpike toll collectors and maintenance employees of the roadway have been represented by the International Brotherhood of Teamsters, Local 436. These employees are covered by a collective bargaining agreement effective January 1, 2005 through December 31, 2007. This agreement has included wage increases ranging between 3% and 3.5% during the covered period (Ohio Turnpike Commission, 2006). The relationship between the union and the OTC has been strained since the outset (International Brotherhood of Teamsters, 2001, 2005). The 2005 negotiation focused on wage increases, health care, and changes to work rules. A strike was narrowly avoided, with the roadway ready to implement contingency plans to keep the roadway open with simplified tolls and temporary employees. Further changes in collector work rules or schedules enabled by E-ZPass will certainly become an important part of the next round of contract negotiation, as they have been in other states.

REFERENCES

Ambler, S. W., & Jeffries, R. (2002). *Agile modeling: Effective practices for extreme programming and the unified process*. New York, NY: John Wiley & Sons, Inc.

Boulard, G. (2005). RFID: Promise or peril? *State Legislatures, 31*(10), 22–24.

Bretschneider, S. (1990). Management information systems in public and private organizations: An empirical test. *Public Administration Review, 50*(5), 536–543. doi:10.2307/976784

Bugler, D., & Bretschneider, S. (1994). Technology push or program pull: Interest in new information technologies within public organizations. In Bozeman, B. (Ed.), *Public management—The state of the art*. Jossey-Bass.

Carr, N. G. (2003, March). IT doesn't matter. *Harvard Business Review, 81*, 41–49.

Caudle, S. L., Gorr, W. L., & Newcomer, K. E. (1991). Key information management issues for the public sector. *Management Information Systems Quarterly, 15*(2), 171–188. doi:10.2307/249378

Commonwealth of Virginia Department of Transportation. (2005). *Smart tag/E-Z Pass*. Retrieved from https://smart-tag.com/index.cfm

Cresswell, A. (2004). *Return on investment in information technology: A guide for managers (Technical Report)*. Albany, NY: Center for Technology in Government, University at Albany.

Dawes, S., Pardo, T., Simon, S., Cresswell, A. M., LaVigne, M. F., & Andersen, D. F. (2004). *Making smart IT choices: Understanding value and risk in government IT investments* (2nd ed.). Albany, NY: Center for Technology in Government, University at Albany.

Dobing, B., & Parsons, J. (2006). How UML is used. *Communications of the ACM, 49*(5), 109–113. doi:10.1145/1125944.1125949

Eckfeldt, B. (2005). What does RFID do for the consumer? *Communications of the ACM, 48*(9), 77–79. doi:10.1145/1081992.1082024

Gifford, J. L., Yermack, L., & Owens, C. (1995a). *The development of the E-Zpass specification in New York, New Jersey, and Pennsylvania: A case study of institutional and organizational issues*. Paper presented at the Steps Forward: The Second World Congress on Intelligent Transport Systems, Yokohama, Japan.

Gifford, J. L., Yermack, L., & Owens, C. (1995b). E-ZPass: Case study of institutional and organizational issues in technology standards development. *Transportation Research Record, 1547*, 10–14.

Hammer, M., & Champy, J. (1993). *Reengineering the corporation: A manifesto for business revolution*. HarperBusiness.

Hinnant, C. C., & O'Looney, J. A. (2003). Examining pre-adoption interest in online innovations: An exploratory study of E-service personalization in the public sector. *IEEE Transactions on Engineering Management, 50*(4), 436–447. doi:10.1109/TEM.2003.820133

International Brotherhood of Teamsters. (2001). *Local 436 demands entry ramp to Ohio Turnpike.* Retrieved April 15, 2007, from http://www.teamster.org/01newsb/hn_011011_2.htm

International Brotherhood of Teamsters. (2005). *Ohio Turnpike strike possibility looms large.* Retrieved April 15, 2007, from http://www.teamster.org/05news/hn_050118_3.htm

Moon, M. J., & Bretschneider, S. (2002). Does the perception of red tape constrain IT innovativeness in organizations? Unexpected results from a simultaneous equation model and implications. *Journal of Public Administration: Research and Theory, 12*(2), 273. doi:10.1093/oxfordjournals.jpart.a003532

New Jersey Turnpike Authority, & Wilbur Smith Associates. (2001). *Operational and traffic benefits of E-ZPass to the New Jersey Turnpike: Executive summary.* Trenton, NJ.

Ohio Turnpike Commission. (2002). *Comprehensive annual financial report for the year ended December 31, 2001.* OH: Berea.

Ohio Turnpike Commission. (2005). *2006 Operating budget and internal efficiency review.* OH: Berea.

Ohio Turnpike Commission. (2006). *Comprehensive annual financial report for the year ended December 31, 2005.* OH: Berea.

Ohio Turnpike Commission. (2007). *Frequently asked questions.* Retrieved April 15, 2007, from http://www.ohioturnpike.org/faq_index.html

Rocheleau, B., & Wu, L. (2002). Public versus private information systems: Do they differ in important ways? A review and empirical test. *American Review of Public Administration, 32*(4), 379–397. doi:10.1177/027507402237866

Rogers, E. M. (1995). *Diffusion of innovations* (4th ed.). New York, NY: Free Press.

Spasovic, L. N., Zhang, W., Bladikas, A. K., Pignataro, L. J., Niver, E., & Ciszewski, S. (1995). Primer on electronic toll collection technologies. *Intelligent Transportation Systems, 1516*, 1-10. Washington, DC: Transportation Research Board, National Research Council.

U.S. Federal Trade Commission. (2005). *RFID radio frequency identification: Applications and implications for consumers* (Workshop Report). Washington, DC.

Vollmer Associates. (2000). *E-ZPass evaluation report*. Retrieved April 16, 2007, from http://ntl.bts.gov/lib/9000/9400/9406/6L01.pdf

Ward, M. A., & Mitchell, S. (2004). A comparison of the strategic priorities of public and private sector information resource management executives. *Government Information Quarterly, 21*(3), 284–304. doi:10.1016/j.giq.2004.04.003

ENDNOTES

1   "E-ZPass," a service mark of the E-ZPass Interagency Group, is used by permission.

2   The term "agency" is used to describe an individual toll-charging organization. Some states, such as New York, have several different organizations that supervise various bridges, roadways, and tunnels. Each of these is considered a separate agency within the E-ZPass architecture.

This work was previously published in the Journal of Cases on Information Technology, Volume 10, Issue 1, edited by Mehdi Khosrow-Pour, pp. 32-51, copyright 2008 by IGI Publishing (an imprint of IGI Global).

Chapter 15
Exploring IT Opportunities:
The Case of the Dutch Elderly Policy Chain

Ronald Batenburg
Utrecht University, The Netherlands

Johan Versendaal
Utrecht University, The Netherlands

Elly Breedveld
Erasmus University Rotterdam, The Netherlands

EXECUTIVE SUMMARY

There is a growing belief that IT can improve public management in general. The Dutch policy and services with regard to the elderly are no exception. Obviously, IT opportunities in the healthcare domain play a central role in this, since the main objective of policies is to sustain the independent functioning of the elderly in everyday social life. In this research four IT opportunities for elderly policy in The Netherlands are explored through discussion meetings with elderly, and consultation of experts in the field of elderly policy and services. The IT opportunities are designed to align the different levels of motivation and skills of elderly to use IT. Four IT pilot projects are defined, which take into account the costs and benefits of these opportunities to improve the elderly policy chain in The Netherlands.

DOI: 10.4018/978-1-4666-0981-5.ch015

ORGANIZATION BACKGROUND

It can be recognized as a recent trend that national and European governmental organizations, as well as supranational organizations such as "Brussels," put priority on the improvement a public customer service, that is, strongly anticipate their citizen's needs and wishes. Clearly, this is driven by citizens that are more articulate and more aware of what governments can do for them. Also, citizens have access to information that has never been easier to disclose. The result is a need for better anticipation through what can be labeled as "demand driven policy" or "participatory policy networks" (Bongers, 2000; Mayer, 1997). On various levels we see governmental policies that want to adapt to the needs of their inhabitants. Like in many countries, most of the Dutch initiatives to reform public organizations originate from bridging the "gap" between government and citizens.

Looking specifically at the elderly citizens in The Netherlands, we observe that the rapid growing number of aged people have a dynamic life pattern, high expectations for the future, changing needs, wishes, and specific information demands (Ewijk, Kuipers, Ter Rele, & Westerhout, 2000). This results in a larger participation in sports, undertaking long trips, studying, and so forth. Consequently, this articulate group of elderly particularly prompts governments to be more citizen-focused. Traditionally, the elderly are a vulnerable group that strongly relies on governmental support. This includes all major policy domains, such as healthcare, housing, work and retirement, transport, social and cultural participation, and so on. Governments increasingly fail to communicate sufficiently with the elderly to meet these increasing demands. For example, in The Netherlands, recently the bottlenecks experienced by elderly people in relation to the government have been the main topic in a discussion meeting with the Minister of Governmental Renewal (Nieuwsbank, 2004). Major complaints concerned forms that are difficult to read as well as the many different forms that need to be dealt with by the elderly. Not only the content of governmental information is criticized, also the medium of communication. Governments tend to experiment with different kinds of information channels, such as video, Internet, and mobile devices, but seem to neglect that many elderly do not use such technologies.

In short, the coordination and execution of government policy concerning the elderly is perceived insufficient. In addition, it can be stated that an efficient and effective incorporation of the needs and wishes of the elderly by public bodies is still missing. To an important extend, this problem concerns the information flow between the elderly, the government, and public bodies. On the one hand, governmental information should be generated and processed efficiently between organizations, in order to reach citizens in a consistent, understandable, and accessible manner. In return, citizens' demands should flow backwards as organized and regular feedback. How can this exchange of information between citizens and governmental organizations be optimized through the application of IT? In particular, can public services for the elderly be improved by IT-driven solutions? This question is the main trigger for this article. We first present a framework that might be of use to approach end-user problems in the elderly policy chain. Then we present our data collection to evaluate a number of IT opportunities that potentially can overcome these problems, compare, and evaluate them. The last section closes with reflections and some suggestions for further research.

Setting the Stage

From the background of this article, we recall the general movement of the Dutch government to renew itself and turn its public bodies into an efficient chain of citizen-focused organizations. Customer satisfaction has become an explicit part of the strategy of public organizations (Whitehouse, Spencer, & Payne, 2003), including a service orientation that is aimed at delivering products and services "on demand" instead of "from stock" (Arnold & Chapman, 2003). In terms of the well-known value discipline theory of Treacy and Wiersma, public bodies cannot excel in product differentiation or cost leadership, but typically can follow the "customer intimacy" strategy (Treacy & Wiersma, 1993). Although the (competitive) conditions for public organizations remain quite deviant from these of private companies, many characteristics of customer intimacy are promoted by politicians and policy makers, including detailed segmentation, providing public servants with specific information related to a prospect or client, being responsive, empowerment of people working closely with customers, employees trained to respond to individual needs, and so on.

If we project these characteristics on an elderly-focused governmental strategy, the following requirements for apply:

1. Information is available and services are suitable (tailor-made) for an individual elder person
2. Groups of elderly are being segmented to such level that they are being served best against lowest costs
3. Elderly expectations are being well managed
4. Information about elderly persons are consistent, up-to-date, and easily accessible for those authorized
5. Elderly satisfaction is regularly evaluated, in order to issue improvements
6. Elderly can easily contact the government and stake holding companies

Although this list appears rather idealized, it expresses the practical implications of developing an elderly-focused policy and related services. Actually, it projects the goals for new initiatives as the advanced application of IS/IT between the elderly and public bodies. With regard to our conceptual framework, this list will serve to set the critical success factors for potential IT opportunities that aim to improve the coordination and communication between government, public bodies and the elderly. With this, the main "boundaries" of the framework are defined.

Next, to construct the "content" of the framework, the IT opportunities itself need to emerge from another leading principle. In line with mass customization and individualization as major societal developments, it appears useful to depart from *diversity* as the main concept (Czaja & Sharit, 1998; Vinken, Ester, & Dirven, 1993). Consequently, to account for the diversity of elderly people, IT opportunities should be determined by segments of elderly. We choose to segment according to two dimensions. The first dimension represents the motivation of the elderly to exchange information with the public bodies. This we entitled as "willing" to interact with governmental and public bodies. The second dimension represents the skills of the elderly to exchange information with these organizations. This we labeled "able" to interact with the government and public bodies. This classification of individuals or groups by both the "willing" and the "being able" dimension, originates from a number of social-psychological approaches. From a learning and coaching perspective, it is known as the "skill/will matrix" launched by, among others, Covey and Landsberg (2003). Earlier, it was developed in relation to leadership styles by Hersey and Blanchard (1977).

Here, the skill/will classification is primarily used to capture the diversity of citizens—not to manage or "steer" people as it was intended by the originators of the approach. It is particularly intended to cope with the question how it can be used to leverage IT opportunities to attack the noted problems between the elderly and public bodies. Reasoning from the four possible combinations, Table 1 shows how classification of the elderly leads to IT-driven opportunities to increase their involvement.

Given the structure of Table 1, we choose to support every type of elderly citizen with a different type of IS/IT and approach (Stephanidis, 1999). Elderly that do not want, nor can interact with policy organizations (Group 1) need to be provided with

Table 1. Segmentation of the elderly, according to the motivation and skills of the elderly, including proposed information exchange strategy

		Able	
		No	**Yes**
"Willing"	**No**	1. Provide alternatives (multi-channeling)	3. Convince to exchange information
	Yes	2. Provide ICT training and support	4. Challenge and involve in innovative IT initiatives

simple, common communication alternatives. This group will probably never benefit from IT to improve their position in the information exchange with public bodies. Group 2 within Table 1 specifically needs to be supported in use of IT, at home, or elsewhere. Senior-specific computer and Internet-training are the relevant initiatives here. Quite opposite, Group 3 needs to be approached. Since these elderly are skilled to use (modern) communication tools, the prior concern is to let them image government and public bodies as reliable, responsive and supportive organizations. Group 4, obviously, can be considered as the ideal category and might be an example for all the elderly to participate and interact to make a difference for the elderly policy.

The above segmentation is not to be considered as a static classification for a number of reasons. First of all, the same elderly person can be classified into different groups, when different types of IT skills are concerned. Also, the distinction between Yes and No as projected in the table will not always be clear cut. Still, the segmentation provides a framework for policy planning. From a policy intervention perspective, pilot projects and IS/IT initiatives should be directed to "shift" elderly towards the fourth quadrant. After all, the objective is to empower the elderly such that they are willing and able to exchange information with public bodies. This will enlarge the possible services to the elderly, as well as provide the elderly with new means to, for example, receive and use information. Of course this is an ambitious and probably long-term mission. Still, in searching for IT opportunities we will take the improvement of both the motivation and skills of elderly as the main starting point.

Case Description

The elder citizens that were invited to join the focus group meetings were interviewed in three different age groups: the so-called "current elderly" (age 70 years and older), the "next elderly people" (between age 50 and 70) and the "future elderly" (between age 30 and 50). Through this division, a relevant variety of motivation and skills was achieved within our target group of panel members (Czaja & Sharit, 1998). It also allows us to take generation and time effects into account. As is known from standard social research, age groups differ significantly in behavior and attitude because of changes during the life course, and, simultaneously, because of temporal conditions (e.g., the period of time in which they experienced their life events such as growing up, being educated, getting jobs, raising families, retiring, and so forth; Becker & Hermskens, 1993). With 8 or 9 persons per panel, a total of 28 people were involved in the three group discussion meetings.

The discussions were organized in an open and informal environment (i.e., "coffee meetings"), to ensure a low threshold for debating. For the group of the current elderly, the research project team organized a meeting at an elderly home.

The group of next and future elderly were invited at the office building of research organization. All meetings were organized in 3-hour sessions, facilitated by both older and younger members of the research team. During the meeting, a computer and beamer was used to demonstrate some Web sites, but most of the time the discussion was lead and structured orally, and by using colored post-its to generate ideas as in brown bag sessions.

Next to the elderly, group discussion sessions were held with experts, that is, professionals of public organizations in the field of ICT and elderly policy. These experts were invited to give their opinion on the main bottlenecks the Dutch elderly experience and perceive in interaction and communication with public organizations. In practice, over 35 representatives of central and local authorities, elderly associations, and institutions were randomly divided into three separate groups. These experts merely represent the field of active "stakeholders" in The Netherlands at the crossroad of the ICT, elderly, and policy domain. Representatives were present from several ministries, governmental authorities, housing and health corporations. In addition, specific organizations took part, as "SeniorWeb," an Internet provider hosting portals for the elderly, "Bij de Tijd," an association to improve the abilities of the elderly in modern society, and KITTZ, an association for palliative care.

In contrast to the elderly panels, these sessions were structured by using an Electronic Meeting Room and, during parts of the meetings, applying computer-supported decision-making. This technology appears to be very useful to support and intensify explorative group processes, especially if policy matters and professionals are involved (Bongers, 2000; Nunamaker, Dennis, Valacich, Vogel, & George, 1991). The meetings were planned likewise the elderly panel groups. The 3-hour sessions were facilitated by members of the research team, and demanded specific efforts because of the use of the groupware system. With regard to both outcomes and process, the expert sessions were evaluated as very successful. Using the groupware system in combination with traditional (computer-supported) brainstorming techniques appeared to be very satisfactory (Batenburg & Bongers, 2001; Fjermestad & Hiltz, 1999).

Consultation Round 1: Elderly and Experts Consultation on Public Services and IT

From the first round of group meetings it became clear that the elderly of 50-70 years and older did not consider IT as a possibility to improve the bottlenecks and problems they encounter in communication with policy institutions and public organizations. This group of elderly primarily articulated critics on the attitude of policy employees and civil servants, by quotes such as:

"They do not tell me where to go as they don't understand my question"

"I have the feeling that they are not telling me everything"

"It sometimes seems that they do not want to understand me"

"They use difficult words and small fonts"

"Sometimes, those youngsters behind the desk do not know how it works either!"

"I call these "organizations without a father or a mother", as they are act irresponsible and uninterested"

This group of elderly have less or no experience with IT, although some try very hard not to stay behind. Still they feel stressed by all kinds of commercials on radio and television that refer to Web sites and URLs (like: "go to (…) dot NL!" or "visit www(…)!" and so forth), while they have little or no idea how this would actually work. It appears to them that contacting institutions and companies by phone is discouraged, as it takes longer and longer to be connected to the appropriate person. They fear significant increase of their telephone costs.

In contrast, the panel group of future elderly (between 30 and 50 years) did recognize the possibility to use IT to improve communication and interaction. When asked, this group mentioned the costs and user friendliness of computers and Internet connection as practical bottlenecks. Many hesitate to purchase a broadband or cable connection as they want to control their Internet costs, that is, pay per use not through a flat fee.

In general, most elderly groups were highly interested in improving their IT skills. They realize, however, that they need to invest in equipment and training. It was suggested that the government should stimulate companies to donate their replaced computers after 2 or 3 years. Also, low level courses should be provided for the elderly at low costs. In addition, they had a large number of practical ideas as to how public bodies can improve their services, especially their front office.

During this first round of meetings, the groups of experts came up with many ideas to attack the bottlenecks and problems as experienced by the Dutch elderly. From their profession, they have a more prominent perspective on the possibilities of IT in this. The experts appeared to be not only concerned about the front office, but explicitly address the problems with regard to the back offices in their organizations. They particularly addressed the chain dependency of public organization as a complex barrier for digitizing and improving public services. Initiatives to set up Internet portals to share civil information by different public bodies through one single platform and database were considered too complex and therefore too risky because of its unforeseen organizational and managerial consequences. Still, all experts realize that the exchange of information within the policy chain needs to be improved in order to provide transparency and better service towards citizens. This is actually (i.e., primarily) a major organizational issue that requires an integrative redesign of governmental chains of services and processes. IT can support this, although some experts believe that IT can be more leading in reshaping the Dutch public services. Currently, a number of public bodies are founded to coordinate the IT policies and investments of Dutch governmental organizations. This includes, among other things, standards for data storage and exchange, e-forms, front office and mid office architectures, and Web site design.

Consultation Round 2: Elderly and Experts Consultation on Four Pilots of IT Opportunities

With the goals for defining appropriate IT opportunities at scope, we formulated four different opportunities to present at all the panel groups. On the one hand, the opportunities were based on current and proven technology, such as public and private Internet connections and networks. On the other, they were developed in such a way that it suited with the elderly segmentation on a one-to-one basis. In Table 2, we represent the segmentation matrix as presented earlier in Table 1, including the labels for four IT opportunities as a basic idea for improving the bottlenecks in a pilot project.

We elucidate the four IT opportunities as follows:

1. **Top box plus:** the elderly get a box attached to their television, which provides access to the Internet, and contains a videophone connection. Having the box combined with television is done to lower the threshold for Internet access. Public bodies can supply all kinds of services for the elderly and serve as a direct helpdesk.

2. **Elderly telepanel:** the elderly can get a Personal Computer, Internet access, and a basic training for free, in exchange for participating in polls and usabil-

Table 2. Positioning of the four IT opportunities in the elderly segmentation matrix

		Able	
		No	**Yes**
Willing	**No**	1. Top box plus	3. Elderly quality mark
	Yes	2. Elderly telepanel	4. Personal Web folio

ity tests of, for example, governmental Web sites and public writings for the elderly.

3. **Elderly quality mark:** for the rather skilled elderly, Web sites will be judged following heuristic evaluation techniques known from the human factors domain (Nielsen, 1993; Zajicek, 2004; Zaphiris, Kurniawan, & Ghiawadwala, 2006). For the elderly in the U.S., usability expert Nielsen has developed a set of guidelines to which Web sites for the elderly could adhere (Nielsen Norman Group, 2003). A likewise set of guidelines can be used for Europe. The motivation to use quality marked Web sites may be higher, than nonquality marked sites. This opportunity is comparable with the ISO 9000 certification series.

4. **Personal Webfolio:** the elderly will get secure access to a Web site with all their relevant personal data, they can (let) update their personal data. Also, authorized public bodies will be able to read relevant information and perform updates. With this, the elderly can ensure themselves that personal information is up-to-date from their part. Also, public bodies can now provide all updates of personal information via this channel.

As stated, the feasibility of the opportunities are directly linked to the specific elderly group. For instance, its low threshold makes the top box plus suitable for the first quadrant. We assume that the low threshold can imply that their attitude towards information exchange with public bodies will move to the other quadrants. With the elderly telepanel, skills of the elderly may increase while at the same time public bodies can create, for example, more usable Web sites. An elderly quality mark may be used to increase the quality of, for example, Web sites or other public services. Elderly not motivated to exchange information are often disappointed by the quality of the information exchange. As such, we assume that this IT-related opportunity supports the direction of moving the elderly to the fourth quadrant. Finally, the personal Webfolio inherits the possibility of making information of the elderly most up-to-date, by making both public bodies and the elderly responsible for maintaining the personal information through one channel.

The second round of consultation of the three elderly panels and the three groups of experts resulted into a general appreciation and support for all four IT opportunities. In general, our ideas behind the top box plus, elderly telepanel, and personal Webfolio solution were validated. Organizing an elderly quality mark for Web sites was judged as useful but not essential.

As could be expected, the elderly and expert panels placed different emphasis on the IT opportunities. With regard to the personal Webfolio idea, the elderly strongly expressed their concerns about usability, and also privacy and security. Although the improvement of transparency and communication with public bodies were highly appreciated, they plea for having a strong say in delivering which personal data should be available in such an additional layer of the system. As ICT is a black box for most of the elderly, their fear of losing control over their personal data is significant; to quote one of the panel members: *"one does not really know what they do behind your back"*. In line with the first consultation round, the experts stressed the difficulties of connecting several back office systems for the personal Webfolio idea, reorganizing responsibilities of data entry, storage and representation.

The elderly welcomed the top box plus idea for its applicability. They felt, however, that it should enable more personal services as was initially proposed, such as house alarm and personal contact through cameras and human voice. In this way, the top box plus could also provide additional social support. Usability of such a device remains their major concern, however. The experts also supported the idea, but put their question marks at the financial implication of implementing this in a project; not the technology, but staffing the helpdesk would create difficulties.

Setting up an elderly telepanel, the third IT opportunity, was appreciated by the elderly, especially because it could enable their IT skills. In addition, they mentioned opportunities to stimulate their fellow elderly to get acquainted with IT, once PC and Internet were installed in their very own home. Completing Web questionnaires and using the Internet, together with a more experienced person, could be another way to combine learning with social contact. The elderly are in favor of the idea that they obtain a computer and Internet connection for free, if they are prepared to contribute to panel activities like survey on a regular basis (*"it is obvious to expect something in return"* as one of the panel member stated it). Some of the experts suggested that the idea of an elderly telepanel should be combined with activities of existing research organizations, or should preferably be tested on a small (municipality) scale. This saves time and development costs.

In sum, the focus group consultation results in the proposition that IT provides opportunities to empower the position of different types of elderly towards elderly organization and public bodies—but only if it is tailored, tested, and embodied in specific pilot projects.

A Policy Portfolio Analysis of Four IT Opportunities

Although it has been concluded that both governmental bodies and the elderly are in favor of the proposed IT opportunities, these obviously differ in their potential benefits and costs. Inspired by Ward and Peppard (2002), we applied the portfolio approach to additionally analyze the IT opportunities from a policy implementation perspective. Doing so, we explored their potential for actually being part of a IS/IT strategy consulting the current Dutch elderly policy chain. In line with the previous, we defined two portfolios for the four IT opportunities: (i) a supply-oriented portfolio, and (ii) a demand-oriented portfolio.

The supply-oriented portfolio describes the value of the four IT opportunities for government and public bodies, in relation to the ease of implementation. The demand-oriented portfolio shows the value of the IT opportunities for the elderly themselves. Subsequently the two portfolios are discussed. In the consultation round, the experts underlined not only the benefits but also the (investment) costs. These two dimensions reflect the portfolio also described in (Crockett, 2003). Figure 1 shows the supply-oriented portfolio, with keywords for each of the four quadrants.

The personal Webfolio is positioned as the most strategic opportunity, with the highest impact and highest risks for implementation. Although government and public bodies can to a large extent benefit from the high quality of personal elderly information, not only the elderly need to be convinced of the usage of the Webfolio, but also the public bodies. Both the elderly telepanel and the top box plus are considered "low hanging fruit," while they expect to bring less benefits compare to the personal Webfolio. With Figure 1 we confirm that the elderly quality mark is primarily "easy" to implement against relative low value for stakeholders. In sum, the supply-oriented portfolio clearly shows differences in ease of implementation and hence illustrates the trade-off between benefits and costs.

With respect to the demand-oriented portfolio, the elderly highly emphasized the usability of the IT opportunities. Also in the literature, usability of IS/IT for the elderly is considered important (Browne, 2000; Czaja, 1988; Nielsen Norman Group 2003; Schneiderman, 1992; Zaphiris et al., 2006). Next to the value of the

Figure 1. Supply-oriented portfolio of IT opportunities

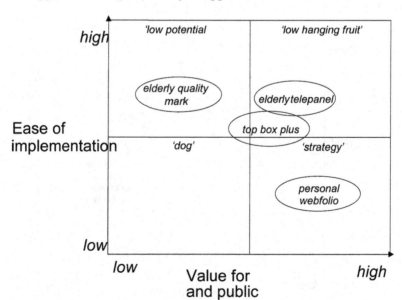

IT opportunities, the usability of the opportunities is defined as a dimension. Figure 2 shows the result of our demand-oriented portfolio analysis.

The positioning of the IT opportunities is different from the supply-oriented portfolio, but there are some similarities too. The elderly quality mark appears to be less useful, while the personal Webfolio can considerably contribute to the empowerment of the elderly. The Webfolio remains difficult in its implementation and use, however, even if investments are made in making the Webfolio user friendly. For the current group of the elderly, Figure 2 confirms that the top box plus is the most attractive option, followed by the elderly telepanel.

CURRENT CHALLENGES

In this article, the case of communication in the Dutch elderly policy chain is addressed by taking a combined IS/IT and policy perspective. Our approach does *not* depart from the idea that IS/IT holds the main solution for all the complex problems in the cooperation and communication between government, public bodies, and the elder citizens. Instead, our aim was rather to explore the opportunities and limits of the fast developments in IS/IT, and apply these to the case of the domain of the Dutch elderly policy. More specifically, the objective of this research was to define specific (pilot) projects that demonstrate the potential of IT to contribute to a more customer-oriented elderly policy and operation. At the same time, these IT

Figure 2. Demand-oriented portfolio of IT opportunities

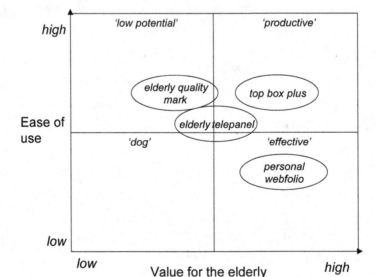

opportunities should contribute to solving existing bottlenecks in the cooperation and communication between government, public bodies, and the elderly.

Steered by our conceptual framework that combines (i) a citizen/elderly-focused government and (ii) segmentation of the elderly, four IT opportunities are developed: (1) the top box plus, providing a low threshold Internet access with additional features, (2) the elderly telepanel, offering a free PC, in exchange for usability testing of, for example, Web sites for elderly, (3) the elderly quality mark, consisting of a kind of ISO certification of Web sites for the elderly, and (4) the personal Webfolio, providing central access to personal information for both public bodies and an elderly person. It is expected that these four IT opportunities support the increase of motivation and skills of the elderly to exchange information with public bodies and the government.

We used group interview data collected from three elderly panels, and three panels of policy actors and stakeholders, applying the methods of focus group and expert consultation. In each panel round, the IT opportunities were discussed and evaluated by the elderly and expert panels. Validation of the four determined IT opportunities by consulting the elderly, the elderly experts, and stakeholders showed that, (except for the elderly quality mark) the IT opportunities were considered good candidates for pilot project initiation at the Dutch policy institutions.

Put into an international context, the opportunities described in this article match with several other European initiatives. Such is the case for the Service Orientated Programmable Smart Environments for Older Europeans (SOPRANO) project. Likewise the approach presented in this article, the aim of this project is to develop IT-based assisted living services to support the independence and quality of life of the elderly people—by explicitly recognizing the user acceptance of the applications (EU, 2007). Also, the British Health Sector panel of the Technology Foresight had been active since the late 1990s to promote the development of technology specific to the elderly as target groups (Newell, 1996). It will be an interesting subject for further research to compare the IT policy initiatives for the elderly in a cross-national comparison.

Next, there a number of other areas for future research. First, the actual piloting of the IT opportunities that can be monitored. One of the Dutch ministries is planning to pilot the personal Webfolio on a small scale, driven by the rapid increasing need for the electronic patient record. Especially with the personal Webfolio, it is interesting to measure the degree of adoption (by the elderly, and the public bodies) of using the Webfolio. The described conceptual framework may be further refined based on piloting in the field. Refinement may, for example, imply a more detailed segmentation, in line with the current e-business and Customer Relationship Management initiatives in healthcare (Crockett & Reed, 2003; Kertzman, Janssen, & Ruster, 2003). Finally, with the growing number of elderly in The Netherlands and many other European countries, it continues to be useful to look for (other) IT opportunities that can support increasingly elderly-focused governments. For certain, the usability and accessibility of these initiatives will remain a critical success factor (e.g., Browne, 2000; Stephanidis, 1999).

REFERENCES

Arnold, J. R. T., & Chapman, S. N. (2003). *Introduction to materials management.* New York, NY: Prentice Hall.

Batenburg, R. S., & Bongers, F. J. (2001). The role of GSS in participatory policy analysis. A field experiment. *Information & Management, 39*, 15–30. doi:10.1016/S0378-7206(01)00076-3

Becker, H. A., & Hermkens, P. L. J. (Eds.). (1993). *Solidarity of generations. Demographic, economic and social change, and its consequences.* Amsterdam, The Netherlands: Thesis Publishers.

Bongers, F. (2000). *Participatory policy analysis and group support systems.* Tilburg, The Netherlands: Tilburg University.

Browne, H. (2000). *Accessibility and usability of information technology by the elderly.* Retrieved July 25, 2008, from http://www.otal.umd.edu/UUGuide/hbrowne/

Crockett, B. K. (2003). CRM strategy: Capabilities for creating the customer experience. In Freeland, J. F. (Ed.), *The ultimate CRM handbook* (pp. 54–63). New York, NY: McGraw-Hill.

Crockett, B. K., & Reed, K. L. (2003). The foundation of insight: Three approaches to customer-centric understanding. In Freeland, J. F. (Ed.), *The ultimate CRM handbook* (pp. 78–84). New York, NY: McGraw-Hill.

Czaja, S. J. (1988). Microcomputers and the elderly. In Helander, M. (Ed.), *Handbook of human-computer interaction* (pp. 581–598). Amsterdam, The Netherlands: Elsevier Science Publishers.

Czaja, S. J., & Sharit, J. (1998). Age differences in attitudes toward computers. *The Journals of Gerontology. Series B, Psychological Sciences and Social Sciences, 53*, 329–340. doi:10.1093/geronb/53B.5.P329

EU. (2007). The SOPRANO project. *Information Society Technologies.* Retrieved July 25, 2008, from http://www.soprano-ip.org/

Ewijk, C., Kuipers, B., Ter Rele, M., & Westerhout, E. (2000). *Ageing in The Netherlands*. Den Haag, The Netherlands: SDU Uitgevers.

Fjermestad, J., & Hiltz, S. R. (1999). An assessment of group support systems experimental research: methodology and results. *Journal of Management Information Systems, 15*(3), 7–149.

Hersey, P., & Blanchard, K. H. (1977). *Managing of organizational behavior: Utilizing human resources*. Englewoods Cliffs, NJ: Prentice Hall.

Kertzman, E., Janssen, R., & Ruster, M. (2003). E-business in healthcare. Does it contribute to strengthen consumer interest? *Health Policy (Amsterdam), 64*, 63–73. doi:10.1016/S0168-8510(02)00139-2

Landsberg, M. (2003). *The Tao of coaching: Boost your effectiveness at work by inspiring and developing those around you*. Croydon, UK: Harper Collins.

Mayer, I. (1997). *Debating technologies. A methodological contribution to the design and evaluation of participatory policy analysis*. Tilburg, The Netherlands: Tilburg University Press.

Newell, A. F. (1996). Technology and the disabled. *Technology, Innovation and Society, 12*(1), 21–23.

Nielsen, J. (1993). *Usability engineering*. Boston, MA: Academic Press.

Nielsen Norman Group. (2003). *Web usability for senior citizens. 46 design guidelines based on usability studies with people age 65 and older.* Retrieved July 25, 2008, from http://www.nngroup.com/reports/seniors

Nieuwsbank. (2004). *Minister de Graaf wants the elderly involved to reduce administrative burden [Minister De Graaf wil ouderen betrekken bij vermindering administratieve lasten].* Retrieved July 25, 2008, from http://www.nieuwsbank.nl/inp/2004/03/01/R245.htm

Nunamaker, J., Dennis, A., Valacich, J., Vogel, D., & George, J. (1991). Electronic meeting systems to support group work. *Communications of the ACM, 7*, 40–61. doi:10.1145/105783.105793

Schneiderman, B. (1992). *Designing the user interface: Strategies for effective human-computer interaction*. Reading, MA: Addison-Wesley.

Stephanidis, C. (1999). Toward an information society for all: HCI challenges and R&D recommendations. *International Journal of Human-Computer Interaction, 11*, 1–28. doi:10.1207/s15327590ijhc1101_1

Treacy, M., & Wiersma, F. (1993). Customer intimacy and other value disciplines. *Harvard Business Review, 71*, 84–93.

Vinken, H., Ester, P., & Dirven, H.-J. (1993). Individualization of the life-course and cultural divergence between age groups. In Ester, P., Halman, L., & de Moor, R. (Eds.), *The individualizing society. Value change in Europe and North America* (pp. 183–196). Tilburg, The Netherlands: Tilburg University Press.

Ward, J., & Peppard, J. (2002). *Strategic planning for information systems*. Chichester, UK: John Wiley & Sons.

Whitehouse, C., Spencer, R. E., & Payne, M. (2003). Customer strategy: Whom do you what to reach? In Freeland, J. F. (Ed.), *The ultimate CRM handbook* (pp. 18–29). New York, NY: McGraw-Hill.

Womack, J., Jones, J., & Roos, D. (1990). *The machine that changed the world.* New York, NY: Rowson Associates. Zajicek, M. (2004). Successful and available: Interface design exemplars for older users. *Interacting with Computers, 16*, 411–430.

Zaphiris, P., Kurniawan, A. S., & Ghiawadwala, M. (2006). A systematic approach to the development of research-based Web design guidelines for older people. *Universal Access in the Information Society, 6*, 59–75. doi:10.1007/s10209-006-0054-8

APPENDIX

Utrecht University and IVA Tilburg have been assigned this research project by a joint effort of the Dutch Ministry of the Interior, the Ministry of Health, Welfare and Sports, the Ministry of Agriculture, Nature Management and Fisheries, the Ministry for Housing, Regional Development and the Environment, the Ministry of Education, Cultural Affairs and Science, the Ministry of Transport and Public Works, and the Ministry for Social Affairs and Employment.

This work was previously published in the Journal of Cases on Information Technology, Volume 10, Issue 4, edited by Mehdi Khosrow-Pour, pp. 65-76, copyright 2008 by IGI Publishing (an imprint of IGI Global).

Chapter 16
Emerging Forms of Covert Surveillance Using GPS–Enabled Devices

Roba Abbas
University of Wollongong, Australia

Katina Michael
University of Wollongong, Australia

M. G. Michael
University of Wollongong, Australia

Anas Aloudat
University of Wollongong, Australia

EXECUTIVE SUMMARY

This case presents the possibility that commercial mobile tracking and monitoring solutions will become widely adopted for the practice of non-traditional covert surveillance within a community setting, resulting in community members engaging in the covert observation of family, friends, or acquaintances. This case investigates five stakeholder relationships using scenarios to demonstrate the potential socio-ethical implications that tracking and monitoring will have on society. The five stakeholder types explored in this case include: (i) husband-wife (partner-partner), (ii) parent-child, (iii) employer-employee, (iv) friend-friend, and (v) stranger-stranger. Mobile technologies like mobile camera phones, global positioning system data loggers, spatial street databases, radio-frequency identification, and other perva-sive computing can be used to gather real-time, detailed evidence for or against a given position in a given context. Limited laws and ethical guidelines exist for

DOI: 10.4018/978-1-4666-0981-5.ch016

members of the community to follow when it comes to what is permitted when using unobtrusive technologies to capture multimedia and other data (e.g., longitude and latitude waypoints) that can be electronically chronicled. In this case, the evident risks associated with such practices are presented and explored.

BACKGROUND

The availability, prevalence, and proliferation of mobile tracking and monitoring solutions enable community members to independently gather location data for their own needs. In the market today are commercially available devices and technologies such as global positioning system (GPS) data loggers, spatial street databases, mobile camera phones, and radio frequency identification (RFID) tags, which facilitate the collection and capture of data related to the location of an individual. The information gathered from these devices can potentially be viewed in real-time, and may relate to habits, behaviors and/or trends. Furthermore, the devices support the compilation, display and manipulation of the location data, resulting in improved processing capabilities, and the application of the data and devices in novel situations, such as the use of covert surveillance from within a community setting. That is, technologies that were once considered to be used purely for the purposes of policing have now deviated from the policing realm, and are now increasingly available to community members at large. Effectively, this grants individuals complete power in conducting independent, covert surveillance activities within their social network. However, these practices lack the professionalism, checks and constraints afforded in the more conventional forms of (community) policing, thereby introducing exaggerated socio-ethical consequences. This case introduces and demonstrates the potential for covert surveillance in the community through a set of socio-ethical scenarios, which enable the ensuing implications of covert surveillance within the community to be investigated.

SETTING THE STAGE

This case explores the potential for covert surveillance within the community by way of demonstrative scenarios, which are supplemented by supporting literature, in order to draw out the emergent socio-ethical dilemmas. Scenarios have confirmed their value in previous studies regarding location-based and mobile tracking technologies to allow for an evaluation of the future social impacts of emerging technologies (Perusco & Michael, 2007) and to establish the need for privacy controls for location technologies (Myles et al., 2003), rendering them a fitting explanatory tool for the purposes of this case.

The scenarios developed below are based primarily on a societal relationships taxonomy, which defines the main social interactions or relationships amongst community members. The societal relationships taxonomy is modeled on categories utilized in a published study titled "The Next Digital Divide: Online Social Network Privacy", which focused on the use of online social networks (ONS) by young Canadians, and by organizations for commercial purposes (Levin et al., 2008). Importantly, the study evaluates the user's perception of risk and privacy protection in using OSN, requesting that respondents indicate their concern about who is granted access to their online information. The response categories provided are: (i) friends, (ii) parents, (iii) other family member, (iv) employer, and (v) people you don't know (Levin et al., 2008).

These categories have been adapted to form the societal relationships taxonomy for this case, as they offer a representation of the major social relationships that exist, and therefore offer guidance and a comprehensive approach to developing the socio-ethical scenarios relevant to covert and mobile tracking. However, while the aforementioned study is centered on perceptions of risk and additional concerns in an online setting, this research deals with each of the stakeholder categories in a physical setting and thus the categories have been modified to focus on the distinct physical interactions or relationships that may exist in a community social network. The five stakeholder types explored in this case include: (i) husband-wife (partner-partner), (ii) parent-child, (iii) employer-employee, (iv) friend-friend, and (v) stranger-stranger. Each of these stakeholder types is represented by a demonstrative scenario, which is constructed and explained using existing studies and literature.

FIVE SCENARIOS: THE POTENTIAL MIS(USE) OF GPS-ENABLED SMART PHONES BY COMMUNITY MEMBERS

This section discusses the stakeholder scenarios which are hypothetical cases whereby GPS-enabled smart phones might be used (or misused) by community members on one another for the purposes of covert surveillance.

Partner-Partner Context: The Suspected Cheating Husband

Ted Johnson had arrived home late from work three days in a row, and had not been himself for some time. After repeated attempts to find out what was wrong, Ted's wife Jenny was fed up with his claims that he was overloaded at work. After all, this was the first time in 17 years that Ted had worked overtime. Having heard about a new GPS logging device that could be purchased from Target at an affordable cost, Jenny placed the device in Ted's car, behind the tissue box next to the back window where he was unlikely to notice the thickset unit. What if Ted had been lying to her? Jenny could not wait to confront him with details of his whereabouts if he was to show up late for dinner again. She was convinced he had something to hide; now she would have the proof.

Parent-Child Context: Child Safety and Peace of Mind

The past week had been a trying one for the residents of a regional town in New South Wales, Australia. Word had spread of a near-kidnapping close to the public school. A white van was said to have been lingering around the grounds and had attempted to abduct several children before staff were formally on duty. Mr. and Mrs. Kumar were concerned about their eleven year old son's safety, as he had to walk home alone from school. The Kumars had recently emigrated and both had to work to make ends meet. Rachna felt guilty being a working mother and wanted to protect her son from all harm at all times. After speaking to some of her colleagues at work, Rachna believed that if she was able to monitor her son unaware until he had reached home, that she would have some peace of mind that he was okay and not have to rely solely on his promise that he would go directly home after school. In just a few Internet searches, Rachna had found her GPS child locator device and discussed the possibility with her husband. The Kumars agreed to subscribe to a monthly plan, sew the device into an inner lining of their son's schoolbag, and access the secure website while at work. Simple! The investment in the GPS, they thought, would be worth the safety of their only child.

Employer-Employee Context: Workplace Monitoring and Surveillance

Called into his manager's office, Tom slowly closed the door behind him. It was unlike Ms. Sanders to call one-on-one meetings with her staff, particularly members of the Delivery Team. This made Tom a little nervous. He had not been in a conflict with anyone and was generally happy with his occupation. "Tom it has come to my attention that you have been in breach of your contract. I regret to inform you that we will have to let you go." Ms. Sanders handed Tom a wad of documentation that looked something like mobile phone records with street addresses. The cover letter read, "Dear Mr. Clancy: After a 6 month investigation into the corporate use of your vehicle, we regret to inform you that your contract with ACME has been terminated. We provide evidence for your misconduct in the attached documentation. You will be escorted out of the premises by security without an opportunity to return to your desk."

Friend-Friend Context: Prankster | Gotcha!

This year, university friends Anna and Chris had been competing heatedly with one another to find out who could play the best practical joke. Having received a 'cool' GPS monitoring device for a class assignment about new innovations in IT, Anna thought it would be great to track Chris and show him that she knew where he had been, just like Big Brother! Step one was to hide the device without Chris knowing. This was easier than Anna had anticipated given how close they were and the fact that they would often work out at the university gymnasium together. Recovering the device two days later, Anna could not wait to show Chris a wall-sized spatial map with breadcrumbs and little annotated notes she had made making fun of particular points of interest (POI). Looking at the first three hours worth of data, she just had to laugh. Chris was so predictable! Looking on, Anna noticed Chris had not traveled to Sydney on Wednesday, as he had mentioned. Why did he tell her that he would be away all day?

Stranger-Stranger Context: Covert Tracking

Having recovered from his car accident, Benji had spent the last few weeks afraid to leave his home and even get behind the wheel. While his accident was minor and the damage to his car not even worth an insurance claim, Benji was a little disconcerted about the small external GPS device his mechanic claimed to have found under the body of his car. He lived in a friendly neighborhood and knew almost everyone there, so who could have an interest in tracking his every move? He pondered on the possibilities and while he had nothing to hide he did not know what to make of it all and whether or not he should even contact the police. Over the years he had had a few conflicts, both personal and professional, but it was unlikely that they would have warranted this conclusion, he thought.

THE SOCIAL IMPLICATIONS OF COVERT SURVEILLANCE

Having presented the five scenarios above, this section interprets the scenarios and presents a discussion of the socio-ethical consequences of covert surveillance by members of the community. Each scenario is in fact a stand-alone case in which readers can enjoy considering hypothetical possibilities, outcomes and solutions. The authors discuss the social implications of each case were it to occur in real life and use existing literature to support their claims.

Trust Implications in the Partner-Partner Relationship

The rapid development of mobile monitoring and tracking technologies is enabling a shift in adoption into new market segments. Traditionally covert surveillance technologies have been used by security/ law enforcement personnel but increasingly they are now being used by general members of the public. While noting the positive use cases of such technologies for law enforcement in particular, a number of concerns must still be addressed. Advanced technologies today are available commercially over the counter, normally require little knowledge to assemble or even to operate. Covert surveillance devices can be used for the purposes of spousal tracking (Dobson, 2009). Spousal tracking can be considered a form of "geoslavery". Dobson and Fisher (2003) define geoslavery as the ability to monitor and control the physical location of an entity, effectively empowering the 'master' who controls the other entity or entities (the 'slave').

When discussing the husband-wife scenario, a multitude of products, such as commercially available GPS tools and digital cameras/mobile phones (providing still and video footage) can be used to track the whereabouts of a partner, essentially diminishing the amount of control the victim or 'slave' possesses. To some degree this places the slave at the mercy of the controller and in a precariously powerless position. Furthermore, an individual can gather evidence for or against a particular position, as implied in the partner-partner scenario. Jenny seeks 'proof' for her husband's unusual absence, and her suspicions can be confirmed or refuted based on the findings coming through multiple information streams generated via technologies.

An immediate danger that can be observed in the partner-partner scenario or broadly in the tracking of family members is the threat of technology misuse (i.e., abuse in this context), and the potential to encourage suspicion and importantly distrust (Barreras & Mathur, 2007). In an article that describes the uses and privacy concerns pertaining to wireless location-based services, M.G. Michael is quoted as saying "[t]he very act of monitoring destroys trust, [and] implies that one cannot be trusted" (Ferenczi, 2009, p. 101). This trust implication is an underlying theme in the partner-partner scenario, as Jenny is convinced that her husband is deliberately concealing his whereabouts, jumping to the conclusion that he may be lying, and thereby questioning his trustworthiness.

Apart from the potential for misuse and the trust-related implications, privacy is an imminent concern when covert spousal tracking takes place. Individuals tend to lobby for increased privacy when institutional surveillance and monitoring activities take place, but are generally less wary of such activities being employed by families, notably within parent-child and spousal/partner-partner relationships (Mayer, 2003). Technologies such as internet-based tracking, GPS, miniature cameras and genetic tests are intended to be used to increase levels of safety for individuals within a family unit; however, Mayer (2003) believes that this can be damaging in terms of privacy and safety, and may also affect trust between family members.

In the case of the partner-partner scenario, the result of selective and continuous monitoring of partners must raise concern over potentially damaging outcomes. In selective situations, there is the danger of incriminating a partner based on an incomplete story/picture or incorrect details. Continuous monitoring activities which involve 24/7 observation and two-way communication (Dobson, 2009) run the risk of being interpreted as excessive surveillance eventuating to excessive levels of distrust. This is a harmful outcome. Moreover, data that has been collected using GPS-enabled devices is not always accurate and can be manipulated to provide information that is in conflict with reality (Iqbal & Lim, 2008). This is a particularly relevant consideration in the partner-partner and remaining stakeholder scenarios. This scenario encourages a number of questions: What are the relationship-related consequences in using covert surveillance techniques in a spousal situation? How will technological inaccuracies be factored into the decisions made based on the collected data? Can a partner take the law into their own hands? What actions are triggered by the assumptions made by the partner? How serious are the repercussions, for instance, physical violence, separation or even divorce?

Consent and Control Implications for the Parent-Child Relationship

The convenience associated with GPS monitoring and tracking technologies simplifies the ease with which such technologies can be used by family members, particularly in the parent-child scenario. That is, GPS technologies that come in the form of handheld, wearable and embeddable devices may be used to track the whereabouts of children such as the Wherifone wireless device (Michael et al., 2006) and the Verizon Wireless Chaperone (Ferenczi, 2009). These applications can be deployed in many different ways both overtly and covertly depending on the use of the subscriber who is usually the 'controller' and not the 'slave' as distinguished in the partner-partner scenario above. Generally, parent-child solutions are promoted as being technologies that increase safety levels. For example, Barreras and Mathur (2007) review family tracking software that is intended to provide knowledge of the location of family members, in order to maintain and provide protection. The solution is primarily attractive to parents who wish to monitor their child's movements, relying on continuous updates and the presentation of information on a secure website, as was the case in the above scenario. There is the perception that these solutions will ensure children are accountable for their behavior. Some parent-centric community groups view the technology as aiding and enhancing traditional parenting tasks and reinforcing ideals in children of what is right versus what is wrong.

The benefits of GPS technologies in the parent-child scenario are therefore specifically evident in two situations. The first situational context is that GPS technologies and monitoring applications can be used to protect young children who travel unescorted. The second situational context is that GPS technologies can monitor young adults (e.g., driving behavior) using commercial and portable systems that are fairly inexpensive to implement and are rather discrete in physical character (Mayer, 2003). This makes GPS and monitoring technologies ideal for covert uses. Commercially attainable GPS devices come in a number of forms, varying in size, capacity and complexity. These devices can be carried and worn in overt scenarios, and be placed amongst personal items within bags. Alternatively these devices can be obscured from view, within a vehicle or sewn into the inner lining of a very thick coat or bag, making the device virtually undetectable. If we deviate slightly from the scenario presented in the parent-child case and consider a situation where a parent just placed a device in full view in a pocket of the child's bag, the integrity of the solution is questioned, given that children can remove or ask a friend to carry the device. Still, even if the GPS device is sewn into the inner lining of the bag being completely unobtrusive, the risk of wrong GPS readings is ever-present—someone else could carry the bag of the child, the bag can be left behind after a child wanders off (e.g., a bus stop) and more. Such a scenario also assumes that a child has a bag with him/her all the time, which is not the case during recess or lunch in primary or infants school.

While such technologies have been used by law enforcement agencies for some time, it should be mentioned that the commercial alternatives do not require a high level of technical sophistication to implement. However, what are the resulting affects on trust, privacy and family relationships in general? A study on parental monitoring and trust maintains that a parent's trust in their child develops based on three types of knowledge: concerns/feelings which are linked to the beliefs or values a child possesses; information concerning past violations; and knowledge of a child's daily activities in varying situations which is linked to responsibility and judgment (Kerr et al., 1999). Importantly, the latter is weighted as an important form of knowledge, and information can be elicited in a number of ways. The information can be provided freely by the child, the parent can prompt the child for knowledge, or alternatively parental control techniques can be adopted where specific rules are imposed on the child. With the introduction of commercially attainable GPS technologies, the presented parent-child scenario proposes that a fourth method can be utilized to obtain knowledge of a child; that is, the use of commercial technologies implemented covertly. However, a major concern that emerges from this form of knowledge elicitation is: what contribution/impediment will this make to (a) parental trust, and (b) the trust a child has in their parent?

Applying these claims to covert tracking in the parent-child scenario, one can immediately pinpoint concerns regarding the covert tracking of children, particularly in view of trust. For instance, why did Rachna feel the need to use a device covertly, rather than rely on her son's account? Could she have been more transparent regarding her safety concerns? What would ensue if the child was to discover he was being tracked? Furthermore, what impact would excessive tracking have on the development of the child? Is child tracking eroding the idea of private space, and thus prohibiting children from developing fundamental skills? Michael and Michael (2009, p. 86) build on this notion of private space, in an article that discusses the privacy implications of "überveillance". Fundamentally überveillance is "an exaggerated, and omnipresent 24/7 electronic surveillance". The authors highlight the importance of being granted a private 'location' or space in which to flourish, develop and discover one's identity free from continual monitoring. With regards to the parent-child scenario, it is apparent that tracking technology may prohibit children from learning or developing 'street smartness' and other vital skills. Therefore, in an attempt to protect their child from 'society', parents can simultaneously be impeding their child's development, and the manner in which they view the role of trust (amongst other things) in relationships.

When considering the parental position, it is important to note that the perception of their child and the associated level of trust they have would also be affected/altered in the process of practicing independent policing-style surveillance activities. While from the parental perspective, the attainment of knowledge contributes to a trusting relationship, Kerr et al. (1999) found that the source of such knowledge is an essential factor. That is, the spontaneous disclosure of daily activities is favorable to other sources of knowledge gathering, and correlates to higher levels of trust on the part of parents. In gathering knowledge, family members often utilize monitoring and tracking technologies in the interest of the safety of their loved ones and with the best intentions, but this is generally conducted without consideration of the damaging nature of such activities, relinquishing trust and privacy in the process (Mayer, 2003). Similar articles review the use of child trackers to allow parents to identify the location of their child on a map or request the location of their child at any given time, also flagging the related privacy and trust issues (Schreiner, 2007).

In the context of covert surveillance within a community setting, a number of questions are pertinent. What consequences arise when a parent has knowledge of the daily activities of their child (for both parties)? How will GPS and other related techniques perform as valid knowledge gathering sources? Will the technologies contribute to or impede trust in parent-child relationships? Have the child's rights been considered? What will be the long term effects of parental monitoring and the covert policing of children? Does the use of parental monitoring solutions encourage a false sense of security for parents, particularly given the risk of a criminal 'breaking' into or compromising the system?

Implications for Employee Autonomy in the Workplace Relationship

Emerging technologies facilitate not only the collection of employee data but the storage and processing of such information, raising apprehension over information being used for purposes other than the intended use (Levin et al., 2006). A primary example is the use of unobtrusive GPS devices for covert surveillance applications. In this situation, an employer may utilize employee location details to incriminate individuals or to 'police' the activities of their subordinate in an unauthorized fashion. This was the case in Tom's situation in the employer-employee scenario. The implications of employee monitoring in general are discussed in numerous studies, a selection of which are presented here, providing insights into the associated risks.

Chen and Ross (2007) discuss the concept of electronic workplace monitoring, including the tracking of Internet usage and email communications. Specifically, their study focused on variations in individuals' personalities and demographic factors which affect the manner in which individuals respond to being monitored at work. The research discusses the use of electronic performance monitoring technologies, including GPS for vehicle location tracking, presenting both the positive and negative consequences that may result from such activities, while introducing a framework for evaluating individual differences in order to predict reactions to being monitored. In reviewing the literature, Chen and Ross (2007) identify gains such as reduced crime, enhanced customer relationships and productivity improvements. Similarly, the risks are articulated and include negative behavioral impacts, attitudinal effects and ethical concerns.

Other scholars elaborate on such perspectives, and offer additional examination of the risks associated with unwarranted levels of employee monitoring. Kaupins and Minch (2005) focus on the use of emerging technologies to monitor the location of individuals in a workplace setting, focusing on GPS solutions (outdoor, broader scale) through to sensor networks (indoors). The authors also point to the legal and ethical implications of having Internet/email communications and general work behaviors monitored by employees, citing security, productivity/performance enhancements, reputation and enhanced protection of third parties as being the encouraging facets of employee monitoring. Kaupins and Minch's (2005) inverse argument examines privacy, accuracy and inconsistency as being significant concerns of monitoring practices, with privacy also being cited by Townsend and Bennett (2003) as a chief concern, inevitably resulting in an undesirable work atmosphere between employer and employee. Weckert (2000) also reports on trust-related issues emerging from excessive monitoring of employees, contributing to deterioration in professional work relationships. Herbert (2010) offers a fresh perspective and important contribution with his balanced work on "Workplace Consequences of Electronic Exhibitionism and Voyeurism" where he discusses the legal implications of electronic voyeurism including employer surveillance of employee workplace computer use and employee off-duty blogs and social networking pages.

While the above discussion has focused on the implications of monitoring from an employee perspective, some studies examine employer attitudes regarding the workplace privacy and monitoring/surveillance debate. For instance, the study conducted by Levin et al. (2006) revealed that while employers admitted to using monitoring and surveillance techniques for benefits such as safety and security, fleet management, and employee training and development, they did not actively exploit the secondary uses of the monitoring technologies. With respect to the use of GPS technologies, the interviewed employers considered GPS technologies as a supply chain and fleet management solution first and foremost. Devices such as commercial mobility solutions (including GPS devices and in-car units), digital cameras and mobile phones, and electronic tags collect adequate information about an employee which can be used to promote efficient work practices and accountability, whilst providing employers with real-time access to information. However, this does not eliminate the fact that GPS technologies can be used for secondary purposes, and moreover in a covert manner. This is particularly true in cases where employers provide employees with a mobile phone for work purposes but use the technology surreptitiously because the functionality exists. In the United States persons who have had their employment contract terminated due to location data have had either an executive managerial level position or operational position.

The implications of employee monitoring have been briefly identified above. It is imperative then to consider the covert surveillance angle with respect to the workplace surveillance and monitoring context. Deceptive or concealed monitoring and tracking may result in trust being diminished in professional relationships, even in situations where high levels of trust are pre-existing. This is due to the fact that location information is often assured as accurate, despite the potential for inaccuracies to exist regarding the whereabouts of an employee. For instance, in deconstructing the employer-employee scenario, Ms. Sanders does not question the source and validity of her information. She was also not forthcoming with respect to how she came to be in possession of details to prove Tom was in 'breach' of his contract. Rather, she opted to act on the situational information immediately, concluding that her employee was 'guilty' of requesting remuneration for work he could not have completed, according to the logged location data.

Concerns inevitably escalate when covert means of tracking are present, based on the premise that secret or deceptive monitoring will affect openness between employer-employee relationships. This notion is alluded to by Herbert (2006) in a paper which examines the legal issues associated with human tracking technologies such as GPS, RFID, cellular technology and biometric systems. The author claims that tracking technologies enhance the power and control given to employers, and therefore secrecy is required to avoid employee backlash with respect to the installation of monitoring systems. Herbert further asserts that such systems allow employers to monitor not only work-related activities, but also personal data and habits, which can be compromised and result in subordinates seeking legal protection, and in essence rebelling against their employers. Therefore, it appears that there is the need for a more transparent approach. For example, Kaupins and Minch (2005) suggest the introduction of policy manuals and employee handbooks when implementing employee monitoring in the workplace. Other regulatory and policy issues need to be explored, and a practical and actionable solution be proposed, one which protects the interest of both stakeholders in the employer-employee scenario. The primary question posed is: How do employers reconcile the opposing ideas of protecting personal privacy with encouraging productive and efficient behaviors/attitudes in the workplace?

Privacy Implications in the Friend-Friend Context

Prior to engaging in a discussion of risks, it is necessary to reaffirm that GPS technologies are considered to add validity in particular contexts and an additional dimension and layer of precision that has previously not been available. If used in an overt manner, GPS monitoring devices can offer convenience in planning social events, and may in reality provide built-in safety and privacy features from a technical standpoint. As such, several GPS-based solutions and location technology vendors promote the safety angle in friend-friend scenarios, maintaining that privacy and safety are in fact enhanced, in that friends have power over who can access their location and assist in emergency or undesirable situations respectively (Schreiner, 2007).

However, the friend-friend scenario depicted in this case provides an alternative viewpoint with less desirable connotations. This scenario questions the amount of control individuals possess over their location data, specifically, who holds access to their personal location information and what they do with it. A valuable comparison is to evaluate similar concerns within the online social networking space, where individuals are able to select their 'friends' and define the level of access granted to them on an individual basis. This form of control is diminished in the friend-friend scenario. Anna was able to independently track Chris' location, while

Chris was seemingly unaware and did not have the power to restrict such activities, as two-way agreement was not reached.

Given the covert nature of such activities, concerns regarding control are significantly enhanced, as covert policing in the friend-friend scenario prohibits individuals from retaining the right to limit access to their details. The detrimental outcome of this situation is a loss of privacy.

In a related study on privacy and location-based services, Myles et al. (2003) explore the challenges associated with protecting personal information and privacy in using location-based technologies, through the development of a system which provides individuals with control over how they disseminate location information. The authors claim that individuals must possess such control and be notified of requests to access information in order to maintain privacy. In the presented scenario, control would be compromised, with the emergent risks extending beyond privacy to lack of trust, suspicion, obsessive behaviors and fundamental consequences to the very nature of the social fibers that bring individuals together to form a relationship.

This encourages an enquiry into the nature of friendships where covert surveillance practices are employed in the community setting, posing the following central questions: To what extent is the boundary between the physical world, in which traditional friendships are forged, affected by the electronic world of GPS data logs and potentially incorrect location information? Given that friendships are built on trust, is this not an erosion of this fundamental core value?

Personal Security Implications for the Stranger-Stranger Context

The idea of being tracked by a third party in a public space is not new; however, with technologies capable of determining location with pin-point precision, the potential for third party tracking is increased, and to some degree facilitated. In a study which distinguishes between location tracking and position aware services, Barkhuus and Dey (2003) explain that location tracking services result in added privacy concerns, when compared to their 'position aware' counterparts. That is, location tracking services require a third party to track the position of an individual, as opposed to position-aware services in which the device can determine its own location (Barkhuus & Dey, 2003). This finding was mentioned with reference to family and friends determining the physical position of an individual. Inevitably the concerns increase when the idea of a stranger is introduced into the scenario.

A recent study focusing on personal information in online social networks reported that individuals are generally unconcerned with friends accessing their profile. Yet these same individuals also expressed having anxiety over other people viewing and retrieving their personal information; the most disconcerting was that group of people that accessed the personal information of a respondent they were not acquainted with (Levin et al., 2008). When such a relationship is applied to the physical setting, and with the addition of mobile monitoring and tracking solutions, this interaction is represented by the stranger-stranger scenario. This has personal security implications.

The family, friend and employee-centric scenarios have expressed the ease with which commercial solutions, such as GPS data logging devices, can be installed and utilized. These factors are highly attractive in the stranger-stranger situation, providing a vehicle for individuals to ascertain details about persons they do not know or are unfamiliar with, in a similar manner to what Benji experienced in the scenario after his accident. Such situations are typically characterized by malicious intent and involve improper conduct, usually of a deceptive nature. For instance, parents may seek location information to maintain the safety of their dependents. Similarly, friends may request geographic details for convenience purposes or to organize gatherings within their social network. However, in the stranger-stranger scenario, such motivations are invalid, as the concept of 'stranger' itself suggests unfamiliarity, the unknown and the accessing of information without consent. This scenario demonstrates that the stranger-stranger interaction requires covert activity, deception and intrusion in its most fundamental form, due to the fact that individuals are unlikely to part with personal details, particularly location, to those they do not know. The aspect of 'intrusion' is further highlighted by the scenario where the outcome is that Benji possesses a feeling of fear and victimization. Additionally, the installation of the device itself suggests that the 'victim' remains unaware of the activities occurring which is another pivotal concern.

It is once again useful to look to social networking tools for insights into how emerging technologies are adopted by community members, as valid parallels can be drawn in the stranger-stranger scenario. This is applicable given the scenarios discussed throughout this case are based on social interactions which are present and have become more clearly defined on social networking sites.

In a study which focuses on the features, history and literature regarding social networking sites, Boyd and Ellison (2008) identify the term "networking" to refer to the initiation of interactions between strangers; however, they go on to state that this is not the primary aim of such technologies. That is, social networking technologies are intended to support existing social networks, while encouraging and facilitating the ability for strangers to form connections based on some common interest. Importantly, the authors examine visibility and the public display of information as central themes within social networking technologies. In theory, these technologies provide users with the ability to grant and/or restrict access to their profile.

When such concerns are applied to GPS and location monitoring software, the nature of the terms are altered. That is, visibility and the display of information are now controlled by the individual who installs and possesses the device and related software, rather than the individual about whom the data is collected. Furthermore, the primary intention of monitoring and tracking solutions are to determine location, as opposed to forming networks and relationships, although solutions exist that provide both functions.

Consequently, the risks in the stranger-stranger situation are amplified, as they imply sinister connotations such as stalking, sabotage, fraud, crime, and surveillance. These evident risks cannot readily be justified or masked in any way. Strangers are therefore empowered to perform covert policing techniques within the community setting, with the capability and tools to control or influence the behavior of others. Such risks urge that safeguards be introduced to protect individuals from assuming the role of the victim in such a scenario. Further research is required to determine the intricacies of this stakeholder type, and to propose an enforceable strategy or legal framework that minimizes the risks, and inhibits strangers from utilizing mobile tracking and monitoring solutions for ill purposes. However, this remains a challenging area due to the difficulty in identifying offenders, and implementing pragmatic strategies that can be imposed on them.

CHALLENGES AND CONCLUSION

In drawing out the major themes from the scenarios and the related literature, it is valuable to consider the methodological process underlying the concept of covert surveillance, vis-à-vis a type of covert policing but within a community setting. Thus it is no longer law enforcement agencies that are empowered with technology, but all consumers who can afford the systems and technologies that can be used to observe and to watch "without ceasing". Figure 1 provides a summary of this conceptual process. The diagrammatic representation allows the following findings to be extracted. First, the conceptualization of the process while applied to covert surveillance/policing in this instance, is also applicable to other areas. Second, in discussing the implications associated with emerging technologies, researchers and other individuals must consider the fundamental technical context, the social/environmental context in which the technologies are situated, in addition to the socio-ethical scenarios that will inevitably emerge. These scenarios can be sourced from real life events early on in the proliferation of the new technology, some of which find themselves being documented in the courtroom. Third, all the implications recognized must take into account the positive applications of devices, in conjunction with the less desirable effects, to ensure a balanced evaluation of the emerging technology in a given context. Fourth, future studies must consider the nature of the linkages between each of the identified elements and address the policy, regulatory and legal concerns.

Assessing the technical, social/environment and socio-ethical aspects allows us to draw a number of preliminary conclusions and themes from this study. First, GPS technologies contain vulnerabilities and are not error free. All systems can fail, and all systems are vulnerable. Thus in all the case scenarios, the 'victim' may be in-

Figure 1. Conceptualizing the notion of covert policing within a community setting

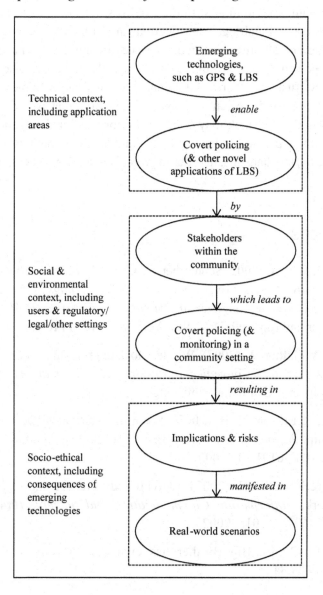

criminated or judged based on incorrect information and evidence. Incorrect data can yield inaccurate or false behavioral patterns. That is, a digital location chronicle of an individual may not necessarily match the physical reality, and thus assumptions cannot be made without accurate contextual information and discussions as supportive evidence. Technological concerns aside, in applying solutions that were originally intended for law enforcement and covert policing purposes to the community setting, risks relating to relationships and interactions between stakeholders surface. That is, the notion of covert activities almost always implies some form of deception and hidden agenda, which contributes negatively to social relationships within a community environment. In the case of strangers, the issue is magnified and the psychological and legal ramifications are of primary importance. Oppositely, when individuals are acquainted, the issues are intricately linked to changing the nature of personal relationships, concurrent with previously discussed factors such as privacy, trust and control. All scenarios point strongly to the need for some form of protection, and the introduction of safeguards that would minimize the adverse consequences, which may come in the form of legal (regulation), ethical (safeguards and/or privacy policies), or technological (default features such as warning systems) mechanisms, in order to protect the interests of community members.

REFERENCES

Barkuus, L., & Dey, A. (2003, September 1-5). Location-based services for mobile telephony: A study of users' privacy concerns. In *Proceedings of the 9th IFIP TC13 International Conference on Human-Computer Interaction (INTERACT 2003),* Zurich, Switzerland (pp. 709-712). New York, NY: ACM Press.

Barreras, A., & Mathur, A. (2007). Wireless location tracking. In Larson, K. R., & Voronovich, Z. A. (Eds.), *Convenient or invasive- The information age* (1st ed., pp. 176–186). Boulder, CO: Ethica Publishing.

Boyd, D. M., & Ellison, N. B. (2008). Social network sites: Definition, history, and scholarship. *Journal of Computer-Mediated Communication, 13*(1), 210–230. doi:10.1111/j.1083-6101.2007.00393.x

Chen, J. V., & Ross, W. H. (2007). Individual differences and electronic monitoring at work. *Information Communication and Society, 10*(4), 488–505. doi:10.1080/13691180701560002

Dobson, J. E. (2009). Big Brother has evolved. *Nature, 458*(7241), 968. doi:10.1038/458968a

Dobson, J. E., & Fisher, P. F. (2003). Geoslavery. *IEEE Technology and Society Magazine,* 47-52.

Ferenczi, P. M. (2009, February). You are here. *Laptop Magazine,* 98-102.

Herbert, W. A. (2006). No direction home: Will the law keep pace with human tracking technology to protect individual privacy and stop geoslavery? *I/S. Journal of Law and Policy, 2*(2), 409–473.

Herbert, W. A. (2010, June 7-9). Workplace consequences of electronic exhibitionism and voyeurism. In K. Michael (Ed.), In *Proceedings of the IEEE Symposium on Technology and Society (ISTAS2010),* Wollongong, NSW, Australia (pp. 300-308). IEEE Society on Social Implications of Technology.

Iqbal, M. U., & Lim, S. (2003). Legal and ethical implications of GPS vulnerabilities. *Journal of International Commercial Law and Technology, 3*(3), 178–187.

Kaupins, G., & Minch, R. (2005, January 3-6). Legal and ethical implications of employee location monitoring. In *Proceedings of the 38th Hawaii International Conference on System Sciences (HICSS'05),* Big Island, HI (pp. 1-10).

Kerr, M., Stattin, H., & Trost, K. (1999). To know you is to trust you: Parents' trust is rooted in child disclosure of information. *Journal of Adolescence, 22*(6), 737–752. doi:10.1006/jado.1999.0266

Levin, A., Foster, M., Nicholson, M. J., & Hernandez, T. (2006). *Under the radar? The employer perspective on workplace privacy.* Toronto, Canada: Ryerson University. Retrieved March 2009 from http://www.ryerson.ca/tedrogersschool/news/archive/UnderTheRadar.pdf

Levin, A., Foster, M., West, B., Nicholson, M. J., Hernandez, T., & Cukier, W. (2008). *The next digital divide: Online social network privacy.* Toronto, ON, Canada: Ryerson University, Ted Rogers School of Management, Privacy and Cyber Crime Institute. Retrieved March 2009 from http://www.ryerson.ca/tedrogersschool/privacy/Ryerson_Privacy_Institute_OSN_Report.pdf

Mayer, R. N. (2003). Technology, families, and privacy: Can we know too much about our loved ones? *Journal of Consumer Policy, 26*(4), 419–439. doi:10.1023/A:1026387109484

Michael, K., Mcnamee, A., & Michael, M. G. (2006, July 25-27). The emerging ethics of human-centric GPS tracking and monitoring. In *Proceedings of the International Conference on Mobile Business (ICMB2006),* Copenhagen, Denmark (pp. 34-42). Washington, DC: IEEE Computer Society.

Michael, M. G., & Michael, K. (2009). Uberveillance: Microchipping people and the assault on privacy. *Quadrant, 53*(3), 85–89.

Myles, G., Friday, A., & Davies, N. (2003). Preserving privacy in environments with location-based applications. *Pervasive Computing, 2*(1), 56–64. doi:10.1109/MPRV.2003.1186726

Perusco, L., & Michael, K. (2007). Control, trust, privacy, and security: Evaluating location-based services. *IEEE Technology and Society Magazine, 26*(1), 4–16. doi:10.1109/MTAS.2007.335564

Schreiner, K. (2007). Where we at? Mobile phones bring GPS to the masses. *IEEE Computer Graphics and Applications, 27*(3), 6–11. doi:10.1109/MCG.2007.73

Townsend, A. M., & Bennett, J. T. (2003). Privacy, technology, and conflict: Emerging issues and action in workplace privacy. *Journal of Labor Research, 24*(2), 195–205. doi:10.1007/BF02701789

Weckert, J. (2000, September 6-8). Trust and monitoring in the workplace. In *Proceedings of the IEEE International Symposium on Technology and Society, University as a Bridge from Technology to Society,* Rome, Italy (pp. 245-250). IEEE Society on Social Implications of Technology.

This work was previously published in the Journal of Cases on Information Technology, Volume 13, Issue 2, edited by Mehdi Khosrow-Pour, pp. 19-33, copyright 2011 by IGI Publishing (an imprint of IGI Global).

Chapter 17
Towards a Customer Centric E-Government Application:
The Case of E-Filing in Malaysia

Santhanamery Thominathan
Universiti Teknologi MARA, Malaysia

Ramayah Thurasamy
Universiti Sains Malaysia, Malaysia

EXECUTIVE SUMMARY

Information Communication Technology (ICT) has played an important role in today's global economy. Many countries have gained successful growth due to the implementation of ICT. In Malaysia, increased utilization of ICT has contributed significantly to the total factor productivity. One of the main contributing factors is the e-commerce and Internet based services. Therefore, this case study aims to examine the contribution of the newly introduced E-government application, namely E-filing system. E-filing system is a newly developed online tax submission services offered by the government to the tax payers in the country where they are able to easily, quickly and safely file their tax returns. The primary discussion in this case study concerns Malaysia's ICT revolution, followed by the introduction of E-Filing system, the challenges and barriers faced by the government, and the chapter concludes with future trends in the implementation of this system.

DOI: 10.4018/978-1-4666-0981-5.ch017

INTRODUCTION

Role of ICT

The advances in information and communication technologies (ICT) have raised new opportunities for the implementation of novel applications and the provision of high quality services over global networks. The aim is to utilize this "information society era" for improving the quality of life of all citizens, disseminating knowledge, strengthening social cohesion, generating earnings and finally ensuring that organizations and public bodies remain competitive in the global electronic marketplace (Hesson & Al-Ameed, 2007).

Developed economies are identified with countries that properly use technology for the creation of wealth and less developed economies are identified with countries lacking technological know-how necessary to create wealth (Khalil, 2000). As such, a proper management of technology also includes low-tech to high-tech to super-high technologies. Khalil (1993) asserted that a proper management of low or medium level technologies can still create a certain competitive advantage and be effectively used for wealth creation. This is especially evident in newly industrialized countries (NICs) such as Taiwan, Korea, Singapore and Malaysia.

In Malaysia, ICT has assimilated into people's lives in many ways such as communication, logistics or in their working environment. Malaysia has invested enormously in ICT over the years. For example in the Ninth Malaysian Plan (2006-2010), a total of US$6 billion was allocated for enhancing ICT diffusion throughout the country. This shows the importance given by the country for ICT accelerate the economic competitiveness of Malaysia (Kuppusamy et al.2009).

Impact of ICT on Economic Growth

Solow (1957) through his famous seminal research on the contribution of technology on productivity growth in the US had sparked great interest among scholars on the relationship between technology and economic progress.

Since then, various firms, industries and countries have undertaken studies to find out more on the relationship between technology and economic growth.

Based on the study of Jalava and Pohjola (2002), both the production and use of ICT have been the factors behind the improved economic performance of the United States in the 1990s. A further research done by Jalava and Pohjola (2007) proves that the ICT's contribution to the economic growth of Finland was three times larger than the contribution of electricity industry.

In relation to the study done on Korea's economic development from 1996-2001, it is proven that Korea's economic development in the 20th century are mainly due to the growth of industries related to ICT and also the government's treatment of ICT as a strategic focus for future development (Lee, 2003)

Kuppusamy and Shanmugam (2007) examined the impact of ICT on Malaysia over the periods of 1983-2004 and reveals that ICT investment has statistically improved Malaysia's economic growth. Antonopoulos and Sakellaris (2009) investigated the impact of ICT on Greece and found that the ICT has increased the total factor productivity and also benefited the finance, real estate and business services industries and the wholesale and retail industries in Greece.

This case study sets out to describe the approach adopted by the Malaysian government in enhancing the usage of ICT in the country. In particular, this case study will focus on the success of the newly introduced E-government services in Malaysia that is the E-filing System.

Literature Review on Technology Adoption

Previous studies have proven the various reasons affecting the technology adoption. Survey done by Lai et al. (2004) on the tax practitioners and the electronic filing system in Malaysia founds that there is a strong relationship between technology readiness and intention to use E-Filing system. Technology readiness is the main motivation in using the particular system. However, the survey also reveals that perceived insecurity could be an obstacle in promoting the E-filing system.

This survey is supported by another survey done by Lai et al. (2005) which claims that tax practitioners are willing to accept a technology which is easily to be used and can enhance their job performance; however the fear of Internet security has stopped many of them on filing tax online. This is also supported by study done by Sena and Paul (2009) which finds that the main reason for the decrease in the usage of Internet banking (IB) in Turkey are due to perceived risk on security features of IB.

Ramayah et al. (2008) posit that apart from less knowledge on how to use the E-Filing system, the main reason less people engaged in the system is because they are sceptical over the security and privacy of data transmitted through the web.

Furthermore, based on a study done by Azleen et al. (2009) on taxpayers' attitude, they found that education background of taxpayers plays an important role in encouraging the attitude of taxpayers to use E-filing. Meanwhile the gender of the taxpayers does not contribute any significant differences in the usage.

Conversely, study done on the selected working women in Malaysia to identify the learning barriers in ICT adoption among them finds that ICT skills of Malaysian women are lower than expected compared to their male counterpart although they do not face any serious learning barriers. One of the possible reasons given was may be due to the attitude of the women. (Junaidah, 2008)

In addition, based on the study done by David (2008) on the adoption of e-recruitment services among job seekers in Malaysia, concluded that job seekers widely accepted the e-recruitment services despite its perceived risk due to its ease of use, usefulness, application posting speed and advantages over other job application methods.

Another study conducted by Md Nor and Pearson (2007), posit that trust is another factor that can significantly affect the attitude of users in the acceptance of Internet Banking in Malaysia. According to a survey done by Abdullatif and Philip (2009) finds that one of the criteria on winning the customers trust in adopting a particular technology is the web features particularly the utilitarian (usefulness) and hedonic (attractiveness) features. This finding is similar with the findings by Irani et al. (2008) which indicate that factors such as utilitarian outcomes, perceived resources, social influence, self-efficacy and behavioural intentions are the most important factors in determining the decision on technology adoption.

The above research findings are also supported by another group of researchers Astrid et al. (2008) whose findings reveals that hedonic features (perceived enjoyment) is more powerful determinant of intention to use a technology compared to perceived usefulness. However, according to Raman et al. (2008), their study finds that despite the attractiveness of Internet Banking (IB), the core factor for adoption of IB in Malaysia is the quality of the services provided mainly on the ease of use and reliability (less time to download).

As such we can conclude that, consumers are ever willing to adopt a technology that is useful, ease to use, has hedonic and utilitarian features, higher security or lower perceived risk, trust and quality.

BACKGROUND: INFORMATION COMMUNICATION TECHNOLOGIES (ICT) AND EMERGING TECHNOLOGIES

ICT Revolution in Malaysia

For the past thirty years, Malaysia has undertaken various initiatives to enhance the ICT diffusion and its' economy. The initiatives can be divided into two categories, macro level and micro level initiatives.

Macro Level ICT Initiatives: The Multimedia Super Corridor (MSC)

With the advent of the IT revolution and its positive impact on economic growth and competitiveness, many countries including Malaysia are developing their very own regional development strategies through the dynamic of a high-technology cluster. Guided by the *Vision 2020*, Malaysia has embarked on an ambitious plan by launching MSC in 1996 as the macro level initiative. *Vision 2020* is the blueprint strategy that stated that Malaysia must be a fully developed and knowledge-rich society by the year 2020, among other visions. MSC is one of the main initiatives to achieve this vision.

Basically, MSC is a technology park with a dedicated corridor (15 km wide and 50 km long) which stretches from the one of the world's tallest Petronas Twin Towers at the Kuala Lumpur City Centre (KLCC) in the north to the new Kuala Lumpur International Airport (KLIA) in the south.

The development of MSC is a necessity as the new engine of economic growth to ensure Malaysia is moving in the right direction in embracing the IT revolution. This huge technology park is considered as the nucleus for the concentric development of the ICT and multimedia driven industries in Malaysia. In brief, MSC is the vehicle for transforming Malaysia - social and economic development levels – in to a knowledge-based economy. There are seven key flagship applications being

Figure 1. Vision 2020 (Source NEAC)

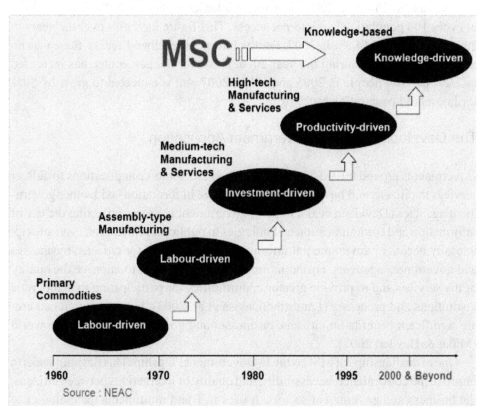

engineered to jumpstart in the development of MSC and also to create an ICT and multimedia utopia for producers and users of these technologies. These flagship applications are expected to expedite the diffusion of E-government and E-commerce activities in Malaysia. These applications are E-Government Flagship, Multi-Purpose card flagship, Tele-health Flagship, Smart School Flagship, R&D Cluster Flagship, E-Business flagship and Technopreneur Development Flagship.

Micro Level Initiatives: ICT Infrastructure

In order to support the ICT growth in Malaysia, the government also has concentrated on building the right and proper infrastructures to ensure speedy and efficient network of facilities and services for better transmission of ICT. During the 1980s, most of the ICT infrastructures investment went into provision of basic telephony services to rural and urban people. In the new millennium, Malaysia focused on increasing accessibility to Internet and its related services (Kuppusamy et al. 2009). As a result, there is a significant growth of the three ICT related services for the year 2000, 2005 and 2007. Based on the figure below, it can be seen that PC computers penetration rate per 100 populations was 9.4% in 2000, increased to 22.5% in 2005 and increase to 26.4% in 2007. In terms of internet access, in 2000 a total of 7.1% of every 100 population had internet access. This figure increases over the years in 2005 to 13.9% and 14.3% in 2007. For the Internet Broadband access, there was no access to broadband during the year 2000. However the percentage has increased to 2.2% per 100 people in 2005 and 5% in 2007 and is expected to grow by 50% for household penetration by 2010.

The Development of E–Government Application

Governments around the world have developed e-commerce applications to deliver services to citizens and business, and to exchange in formations with other government agencies (Davidson et al. 2005). E-government is a term reflecting the use of information and communication technologies in public administration in an attempt to easily access to governmental information and services for citizens, businesses and government agencies. Furthermore, it is always a target to improve the quality of the services and to provide greater opportunities for participating in democratic institutions and processes (Lambrinoudakisa et al. 2003). E-Government can create significant benefits for citizens, businesses and governments around the world (Mihar & Hayder, 2007).

One of the flagships of MSC is the E-Government Flagship. This flagship seeks to improve the convenience, accessibility, and quality of interactions between citizens, the business and government sectors. It uses ICT and multimedia technologies to

Figure 2. PC penetration rates (adapted from the National ICT Association of Malaysia (PIKOM))

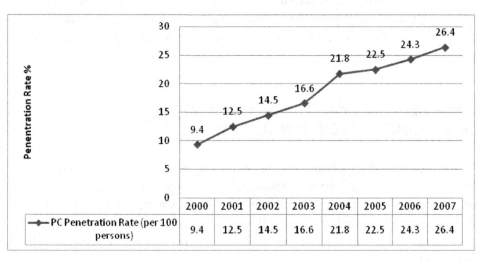

transform the way the government operates and improves the processes of policy development, coordination and enforcement. It includes Generic Office Environment (GOE), Electronic Procurement (eP), Project Monitoring System (SPP II), Human Resource Management System (HRMIS), Electronic delivery Services (E-services++), Electronic Labor Exchange (ELX) and E-Syariah.

Another prominent E-government application introduced in 2005 in Malaysia is the Electronic Tax- Filing (E-Filing) of income taxes. The electronic filing of income tax returns is an invaluable application that assists tax filers with the pro-

Figure 3. Internet and broadband penetration rates (adapted from PIKOM 2008)

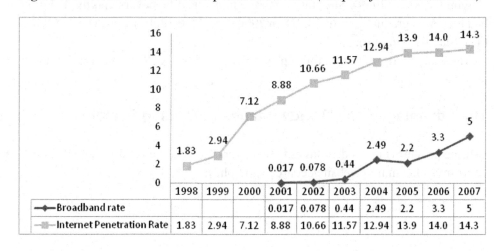

cess of collecting their personal tax information and provides them the ability to electronically transmit their return. According to Fu et al. (2006) electronic filing of income taxes has the potential of improving the overall process of tax filing for the individual filer while at the same time reducing the cost to both taxpayers and tax collection agencies.

CASE DESCRIPTION: THE DEVELOPMENT OF E-FILING SYSTEM IN MALAYSIA

In Malaysia currently there are two major tax filing methods: manually and E-Filing (Internet filing). Since 2005 the Malaysian government has moved aggressively to promote the Internet filing (E-Filing) with the aim for paperless transaction, efficient process and faster refunds. Traditionally the tax payers in Malaysia have to file their tax returns manually by receiving the B (companies) or BE (individuals) forms from the Inland Revenue Board (IRB) department. Then they need to fill up the forms, do a self- calculation on their tax, attach together all the payment receipts and send it over in person or by mail to the IRB branches and later the IRB will send to them the confirmation on the tax payment amount.

However a new paradigm has taken place when the Inland Revenue Board introduces the E-Filing system. The E-Filing system developed in 2005 was one of the remarkable businesses to consumer (B2C) E-government services established by the Malaysian government. Via E-Filing and Public Key Infrastructure features, the individual tax payers in Malaysia are able to easily, quickly and safely file their tax returns.

According to Inland Revenue Board public relations officer Najlah Ishak, the electronic filing (E-Filing) of the income tax returns have increased by 30% to 1.25 million this year (2009). She stated that the number of taxpayers making E-Filing had increased gradually from 78,718 in 2006 to 538,558 (2007) and 881,387 (2008) (The Star, 01/05/2009).

Basically there are four main steps involve in filing tax electronically. The steps are shown in Figure 4.

The Advantages and Disadvantages of E-Filing System

E-filing provides many advantages to taxpayers. Among the advantages are (http://www.mykad.com.my/Website/secureefiling.php):

Figure 4. How e-filing works (Adapted from: MSC Trustgate.com Sdn. Bhd)

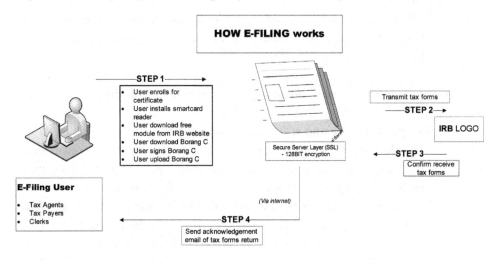

- **Immediate acknowledgement**
  - ◦ The tax filers will get immediate acknowledgement from IRB after submission online
- **Round the clock availability and convenience**
  - ◦ E-Filing is available round the clock daily. The submission work is not constrained by IRB' working hours. As long as the tax filers submit the tax forms before midnight on the due date, no late penalty will be payable.
- **Immediate processing time**
  - ◦ With E-filing submissions, the tax filers can enjoy the benefits of immediacy. There is no need to physically move tax forms or wait in queues for 20 minutes or more for manual processing.
- **Cost savings**
  - ◦ There are net savings in using E-Filing system - no physical movement of tax forms, no waiting time, no transport cost and no risk of losing tax forms. Instead, tax filers enjoy convenience, 24-hour accessibility, and fast, secured and accurate tax computation.
- **User friendly**
  - ◦ The look and feel of the E-Filing-system has been designed with a user-friendly interface to allow the tax filers to easily enter or amend any information before it is submitted to IRB.

- **Security**
  - ○ The tax filers can be assured on the security features that can prevent the hacker from altering your data as the main key features in assessing to the system will be your password and tax file number

However, E-Filing has its disadvantages as well. Some of the disadvantages are:

- **Minimum hardware and software requirement**
  - ○ In order for the E-Filing system to be executed at the filer's convenience the main important device is personal computer (PC). It is then must be followed by Internet access and Network configuration. The minimum requirement for the PC must also be installed with Windows XP or higher software and must have an Adobe reader application for the forms to be successfully downloaded. Failure to have all this features will enable the tax filers to access to the E-Filing website and perform the transactions.
- **Non-modification**
  - ○ Once the forms are sent to IRB, there will be no room for modification. If the tax filers have missed any information that are supposed to be included or excluded then they have to proceed with it manually by referring to the respective IRB branches.
- **Non-user friendly**
  - ○ There have been a lot of complaints from the tax payers that the time allowed to do the transaction is limited. Most of the time the key-in are stopped due to time elapsed and once the system is re-entered, all the data would have to be key in once again. This has created a problem for last minute filers. (http://thestar.com.my/news/story.asp?file=/2009/3/2/focus/3380923&sec=focus)

CURRENT CHALLENGES OF E-GOVERNMENT

Low Level of Personal Computer (PC), Internet, and Broadband Penetration

It can be seen that the cellular phone growth is much more pronounced than PC or internet or broadband. This may be due to the ease of application, versatility, and convenience of anytime and everywhere usage and ongoing price reduction resulting from stiff competition among service providers. Various reasons such as poor access, lack of adequate local content, low level of awareness and motivation and lack of affordability have been cited for the low uptake of PC, Internet and Broadband (The National ICT Association of Malaysia (PIKOM), 2008)

Mandatory Usage

Based on survey done by Skillman (1998) in United States, the tax accountants asserted that the only way to make their tax clients to use the E-Filing is by making it a mandated usage. However, this is not the case for Malaysia where mandating electronic filing too early will attract mush resistance and criticism due to the inequality of Malaysian citizens in terms of the digital divide; income level and age factor (Lai et al. 2005). The survey also finds that the traditional channels will still need to be retained for the need of social ties, human contact and for personalization.

According to Paul and Kim (2003) quoting the articles of Wang et al., if a person is unable to use the technologies that E-government relies upon, for lack of education or limited ability, that person cannot be denied access to government information and services. "If less-advantaged segments of the population are less able to access government on the Web, their other channels to government must not be closed off or contracted."

Availability of IT Workforce

It is widely believed that with respect to IT manpower resources, the tax authority is generally suffering from a shortage IT workforce. According to IRB's Annual Report 2006, the percentage of workforce distributed for IT tasks were only 2.6%. This figure has not increased much from 2001 where the percentage of IT workforce distributed in 2001 was 2.1% (IRB Annual Report, 2001). This low distribution of workforce could dampen the effectiveness of the IT related services offered by the tax authority.

Digital Divide

Low ownership of PCs and disparities in internet access are among the most important challenges Malaysia faces today in implementing E-government services. Efforts to narrow the digital divide will be further intensified. For example, more Medan Info Desa and Pusat Internet Desa will continue to be built and upgraded. The government has set target to provide at least one telecentre for each mukim by 2010. (Mid Term Review, 9MP)

BARRIERS TO E-GOVERNMENT ADOPTION

ICT Infrastructure

In order for a technology to be adopted successfully, any E-government initiatives must ensure that it has sufficient resources, adequate infrastructure, management support, capable Information Technology (IT) staff and effective IT training and support. Although with the introduction of E-government services the cost will be reduced but adequate IT infrastructure still a key barrier to e-government adoption. The infrastructure is composed of hardware and software that will provide secure electronic services to citizens, businesses, and employees. For example, Local Area Network (LAN), reliable server, and internet connections are important to build a strong foundation for E-government infrastructures (Zakareya & Zahir, 2005).

Security Concerns

Another most significant barrier in implementing E-government applications is the security of the particular system. According to Lai et al. (2005), concerns over security of online tax transactions constitute a tremendous barrier to technology adoption. Sena and Paul (2009) agreed that the main reason for the decrease in the usage of Internet banking (IB) in Turkey is due to perceived risk on security features of IB. These findings is also supported by Mc Clure (2000) who finds that E-government will only succeed when all its participants including the government agencies, private business and individual citizens feel comfortable using electronic means to carry out private sensitive transactions. Stories about the hacker attack, page defacement makes the general public reluctant to do "real" business over the Internet.

Change Factor

As with E-government, public sector administrations are required to change and re-engineer their business process to adapt new strategies and culture of E-government. Government staff should be prepared for new ways of dealing with new technologies that emerge with E-government. For example, they are used in dealing with physical papers and forms, paper receipts, and traditional physical signatures, while E-government allows citizens access to the organization back-office remotely to complete the transaction processing, which emerged with new technology solutions such as electronic forms, digital signatures, electronic receipts and certificates. This reluctant to change from traditional way of doing work to a new paradigm is a major barrier to adoption (Zakareya & Zahir, 2005).

Low Confidence in the Electronic Administration

According to Lai et al. (2005) one of the reasons for low usage of E-Filing system is due to low confidence in the electronic administrative capabilities of the tax authority in managing the E-Filing system successfully. The respondents perceived that the tax officers lack in the required skills, experience and competency as well as the ability in handling disaster recovery and technological crisis. Lai et al. also quoted Bird and Oldman's (2000) study which found that favourable attitude and trust in the tax authorities in managing electronic tax administration system has lead to high level of usage of E-Filing system in Singapore.

FUTURE TRENDS

Building a successful E-government adoption especially the E-Filing system may involve multiple approaches. There are general approaches and technical details. The general approaches will be first, bridging the digital divide. Government must always ensure that efforts are taken to bridge the difference in ICT supply and usage between the rural and the urban people. The Malaysian government in bridging the digital divide has constructed 108 Medan Info Desa in rural areas, 387 telecentres established, 42 Pusat Internet Desa was upgraded and targeted to provide at least one telecentre for each mukim by 2010 (PIKOM, 2008). Second approach is the IRB must create a long term marketing campaign strategy to convert reluctant taxpayers by tout that E-Filing is more convenient and less time consuming than sending paperwork via the mail, reduces preparation time, provide faster refunds, improves accuracy of returns and gives an acknowledgement-of-return receipt (Matthew, 2006). Third approach is by arranging programs such as Volunteer Income Tax Assistance and Tax Counselling for the Elderly in an effort to bring the elderly people to use the E-Filing system (Matthew, 2006). Fourth approach is on the security concerns; the normal procedure used to log in is the password and tax file number. This normal security codes are quite weak and passwords are often easy to guess, steal or crack.

In recent years, technical details approach is biometrics-based identification and authentication systems have become more widespread and have been considered for application in many application domains. Biometric techniques, such as fingerprint verification, iris or face recognition, retina analysis and hand-written signature verification, are increasingly becoming basic elements of authentication and identification systems (Zorkadis & Donos, 2004).

CONCLUSION

It is our tentative conclusion that the ICT industry in Malaysia is poised to grow positively in years to come. The role of the government in spearheading the deployment of ICT in major development corridors, continuing efforts to computerization of public services, globalization and market liberalization of financial and telecommunication verticals are among many other factors poised to contribute substantially to the economy (PIKOM 2008). The rate of increase in the number of tax filers using the E-Filing system shows the effectiveness and success of the system each year. However, for a better security, the third factor authentication process should be provided. The third authentication factor is the use of biometric such as iris or thumbprint recognition. As such, if passwords have been compromised, fraudsters need to get through another two levels of authentication to access a customer account. This would be difficult, if not, totally impossible.

REFERENCES

Abdullatif, I. A., & Philip, J. K. (2009). Rethinking models of technology adoption for internet banking: The role of website features. *Journal of Financial Services Marketing, 14*(1), 56–69. doi:10.1057/fsm.2009.4

Antonopoulos, C., & Sakellaris, P. (2009). The contribution of information and communication technology investments to Greek economic growth: An analytical growth accounting framework. *Information Economics and Policy, 21*, 171–191. doi:10.1016/j.infoecopol.2008.12.001

Astrid, D., Mitra, A., & David, M. (2008). The role of perceived enjoyment and social norm in the adoption of technology with network externalities. *European Journal of Information Systems, 17*, 4–11. doi:10.1057/palgrave.ejis.3000726

Azleen, I., Mohd Zulkeflee, A. R., & Mohd Rushdan, Y. (2009). Taxpayers' attitude in using e-filing system: Is there any significant difference among demographic factors? *Journal of Internet Banking and Commerce, 14*(1), 2–13.

David, Y. K. T. (2008). A study of e-recruitment technology adoption in Malaysia. *Industrial Management & Data Systems, 109*(2), 281–300.

Davidson, R. M., Wagner, C., & Ma, L. C. K. (2005). From government to e-government: A transitional model. *Information Technology & People, 18*(3), 280–299. doi:10.1108/09593840510615888

Economic Planning Unit (EPU). (2008). *The midterm review of the ninth Malaysian plan*: *2006-2010.*

Fu, J. R., Farn, C. K., & Chao, W. P. (2006). Acceptance of electronic tax filing: A study of taxpayers' intention. *Information & Management, 43*, 109–126. doi:10.1016/j.im.2005.04.001

Hesson, M., & Al-Ameed, H. (2007). Online security evaluation process for new e-services. *Journal of Business Process Management, 13*(2), 223–245. doi:10.1108/14637150710740473

Irani, Z., Dwivedi, Y. K., & Williams, M. D. (2008). Understanding consumer adoption of broadband: An extension of the technology acceptance model. *The Journal of the Operational Research Society*, 1–13.

IRB. (2001). *Annual report 2001*. Malaysia: Inland Revenue Board.

IRB. (2006). *Annual report 2006*. Malaysia: Inland Revenue Board.

Jalava, J., & Pohjola, M. (2002). Economic growth in the new economy: Evidence from advanced economies. *Information Economics and Policy, 14*, 189–210. doi:10.1016/S0167-6245(01)00066-X

Jalava, J., & Pohjola, M. (2007). The role of electricity and ICT in economic growth: Case Finland. *Explorations in Economic History, 45*, 270–287. doi:10.1016/j.eeh.2007.11.001

Junaidah, H. (2008). Learning barriers in adopting ICT among selected working women in Malaysia. *Gender in Management: An International Journal, 23*(5), 317–336. doi:10.1108/17542410810887356

Khalil, T. M. (1993). Management of technology and the creation of wealth. *Industrial Engineering (American Institute of Industrial Engineers), 25*(9), 16–17.

Khalil, T. M. (2000). *Management of technology: The key to competitiveness and wealth creation*. Singapore: McGraw Hill.

Kuppusamy, M., Raman, M., & Lee, G. (2009). Whose ICT investment matters to economic growth: Private or public? The Malaysian perspective. *The Electronic Journal on Information Systems in Developing Countries, 37*(7), 1–19.

Kuppusamy, M., & Shanmugam, B. (2007). Information communication technology and economic growth in Malaysia. *Review of Islamic Economics, 11*(2), 87–100.

Lai, M. L., Siti, N. S. O., & Ahamed, K. M. (2004). Towards an electronic filing system: A Malaysian survey. *eJournal of Tax Research, 5*(2), 1-11.

Lai, M. L., Siti, N. S. O., & Ahamed, K. M. (2005). Tax practitioners and the electronic filing system: An empirical analysis. *Academy of Accounting and Financial Studies Journal, 9*(1), 93–109.

Lambrinoudakisa, C., Gritzalisa, S., Dridib, F., & Pernul, G. (2003). Security requirements for e-government services: A methodological approach for developing a common PKI-based security policy. *Computer Communications, 26,* 1873–1883. doi:10.1016/S0140-3664(03)00082-3

Lee, S. M. (2003). Korea: From the land of morning calm to ICT hotbed. *Journal of the Academy Management Executive (USA), 17*(2).

Matthew, W. (2006). *E-file goals too ambitious.* FWC.com. Retrieved on 2/11/2009, from http://fcw.com/articles/2006/02/27/efile-goal-too-ambitious.aspx

Mc Clure, D. L. (2000). *Federal initiatives are evolving rapidly but they face significant challenges.* Testimony, United States General Accounting Office, GAO/T-AIMD/GGD-00-179.

Md Nor, K., & Pearson, J. M. (2007). The influence of trust on internet banking acceptance. *Journal of Internet Banking and Commerce, 12*(2), 2–10.

Mihyar, H., & Hayder, A. (2007). Online security evaluation process for new e-services. *Journal of Business Process Management, 13*(2), 223–246. doi:10.1108/14637150710740473

Paul, T. J., & Kim, M. T. (2003). E-government around the world: Lessons, challenges and future directions. *Government Information Quarterly, 20,* 389–394. doi:10.1016/j.giq.2003.08.001

Raman, M., Stephenaus, R., Alam, N., & Kuppusamy, M. (2008). Information technology in Malaysia: E-service quality and uptake of internet banking. *Journal of Internet Banking and Commerce, 13*(2), 2–17.

Ramayah, T., Ramoo, V., & Ibrahim, A. (2008). Profiling online and manual tax filers: Results from an exploratory study in Penang, Malaysia. *Labuan e-Journal of Muamalat and Society, 2,* 1-18.

Sena, O., & Paul, P. (2009). Exploring the adoption of a service innovation: A study of Internet banking adopters and non-adopters. *Journal of Financial Services Marketing, 13*(4), 284–299. doi:10.1057/fsm.2008.25

Skillman, B. (1998). Fired up at the IRS. *Accounting Technology, 14,* 12–20.

Solow, R. M. (1957). Technical change and the aggregate production function. *The Review of Economics and Statistics, 39*(3), 312–320. doi:10.2307/1926047

The STAR. (2009, May 1). Amount of Malaysian's choosing e-filing up by 30%. *The STAR.*

The, S. T. A. R. (2009). *It's time inland revenue board got real on e-filing.* Retrieved on June 19th, 2009, from http://thestar.com.my/news/story.asp?file=/2009/3/2/focus/3380923&sec=focus

The National ICT Association of Malaysia (PIKOM). (2008). *ICT strategies, societal and market touch.* Retrieved on June 24th, 2009. from http://www.witsa.org/news/2009-1/html_email_newsletter_jan09_b.html

Trustgate Sdn, M. S. C. Bhd. (2009). *Secure e-filing.* Retrieved on June 24th, 2009. from http://www.mykad.com.my/Website/secureefiling.php

Zakareya, E., & Zahir, I. (2005). E-government adoption: Architecture and barriers. *Business Process Management Journal, 11*(5), 589–611. doi:10.1108/14637150510619902

Zorkadis, V., & Donos, P. (2004). On biometrics-based authentication and identification from a privacy-protection perspective deriving privacy-enhancing requirements. *Information Management & Computer Security, 12*(1), 125–137. doi:10.1108/09685220410518883

KEY TERMS AND DEFINITIONS

Authentication: Is the process through which an Internet merchant can be established via a trusted third party that guarantees that the merchant is indeed whom he is.

E-Filing System: E-Filing system in Malaysia which is recently launched in 2006 is the way to submit the tax documents to the Inland Revenue Board through internet or online without the need to submit any paper documents. This system has provided an easy, faster and safer way of submitting the tax documents by the tax filers.

E-Government: E-government refers to electronic government which means governments in a particular country use ICT or internet base to provide their services. This is done in order to improve the quality of their services, interactions and transactions with customers and businesses mainly.

Economic Growth: Growth is the increase in the country's profit in terms of goods and services produced, monetary profits earned and increased in total productivity. Normally, economic growth is calculated based on the increase in Gross Domestic Product of the particular country.

Information Communication Technologies: ICT covers the use of advanced technologies in private and public sectors in order to give a better service to the customers. It includes the technologies such as broadcasting information and wireless mobile telecommunications.

Security: In the context of E-Filing System threats can be made either through network and data filing attacks or through unauthorized access to the tax file by means of false or defective authentication.

Technology Adoption: Technology Adoption refers to the rate of usage a particular technology by the consumers when it is introduced in the country either by the government or the private sectors. There are various reasons has been outline that can affect the usage or adoption of the particular system such as readiness, security concerns and level of education.

This work was previously published in Cases on ICT Utilization, Practice and Solutions: Tools for Managing Day-to-Day Issues, edited by M. Al-Mutairi and L. Mohammed, pp. 15-27, copyright 2011 by Information Science Reference (an imprint of IGI Global).

Chapter 18
ICT and Web 2.0 Technologies as a Determinant of Business Performance

Tanja Arh
Jožef Stefan Institute, Slovenia

Vlado Dimovski
University of Ljubljana, Slovenia

Borka Jerman Blažič
Jožef Stefan Institute, Slovenia

EXECUTIVE SUMMARY

This chapter aims at presenting the results of an empirical study, linking the fields of technology-enhanced learning (TEL), Web 2.0 technologies and organizational learning, and their impact on the financial and non-financial business performance. The chapter focuses on the presentation of the conceptualization of a structural model that was developed to test the impact of technology-enhanced learning and Web 2.0 technologies on the organizational learning and business performance of companies with more than 50 employees. The authors provide detailed definitions of technology-enhanced learning, Web 2.0 technologies, and technical terms related to it, its scope and the process of organisational learning, as well as a method for business performance assessment. Special attention is given to the findings related to the observed correlations between the aforementioned constructs. The results of the study indicate a strong impact of ICT and technology-enhanced learning on organizational learning and the non-financial business performance.

DOI: 10.4018/978-1-4666-0981-5.ch018

INTRODUCTION AND BACKGROUND

Success in a highly dynamic environment requires a more efficient response to customers from the side of the companies, more flexible approaches in facing their business circle and more focus on their core competencies (Smith, 2008). What are companies expected to do in order to introduce the necessary changes in the whole business circle? The answer definitely lies in people. The employees' knowledge and competencies significantly contribute to the company's ability to react to the requirements of the fast changes markets, customer needs and successful business processes. With this in view, companies are obliged to manage and maintain the knowledge of their employees. Maintaining the knowledge means to evaluate the employees' tacit and explicit knowledge, and provide knowledge within the company with the suitable tools (Reychav & Weisberg, 2009).

To perform this approach effectively, employees and all members of the company are expected to continuously refresh and enhance their skills and knowledge (Collins & Smith, 2006). As the human capital replacing the physical capital as the source of competitive advantage, organizational learning emerges as a key element for success (Varney, 2008). Only by making learning a truly strategic investment we can ensure an organization in which every person within the company is fully enabled to perform effectively and meet the ever changing demands.

When companies devise their strategies for the employee knowledge acquisition, they can find the most suitable solutions among the methods based on information and communication technologies (ICT), Web 2.0 technologies and technology-enhanced learning (TEL). Technology-enhanced learning as a way of acquiring knowledge and competences has been adopted by many companies as a promising time and cost saving solution providing learn-on-demand opportunities to individual employees, TEL enables workers to access various on-line databases, tools and e-services that help them find solutions for work-related problems (Zhang, 2002; 2003). The term Web 2.0 was coined by O'Reilly (2005) as a common denominator for recent trends heading towards the 'Read-Write Web', allowing everyone to publish resources on the web using simple and open, personal and collaborative publishing tools, known as the social software: blogs, wikis, social bookmarking systems, podcasts, etc. The main features of these tools are dynamism, openness and free availability. According to MacManus and Porter (2005), the power of social software lies in the content personalization and remixing with the other data to create much more useful information and knowledge. The continuously growing dissemination of social and open software in technology-enhanced learning is expected to reshape the technology-enhanced learning landscapes that are currently based on closed, proprietary, institutionalized systems. Thanks to the web evolution, the use of social and open software for learning is becoming an increasingly feasible alternative to these closed, proprietary, institutionalized systems.

However, earlier authors (Roach, 1987) argued that ICT still had not paid off in terms of the required productivity growth. The phenomenon was called the 'productivity paradox' and it asserted that the ICT investments did not result in productivity gains (Navarette & Pick, 2002). Carr (2003) believes that 'ICT may not help a company gain a strategic advantage, but it could easily put a company at a cost disadvantage.' Indeed, the latest empirical studies (Dewan & Kraemer 1998; Navarette & Pick 2002; Dimovski & Škerlavaj 2003) tend to reject the productivity paradox thesis – the phenomenon of organisational learning can be seen as a way out of the dilemma called the productivity paradox. In the last few decades the field of organisational learning has attracted a lot of interest from academics as well as practitioners. A key question in this context is the connection between ICT and organisational learning, and the impact they both have on the business performance (Škerlavaj & Dimovski, 2006).

In the past decade, quite a lot of research studies dealt with the influence of ICT (investments, usage, etc.) on (mainly financial) business performance. We can divide them into four streams of research based on the observed units: business, industry, national and international levels. The results were mixed. Some recent studies in our context (Dimovski & Škerlavaj, 2003) that analysed the influence of hardware, software, telecommunications and knowledge investments on value added per industry in Slovenia for the period 1996-2000, demonstrated a statistically significant, positive influence of hardware and telecommunication investments on value added (Škerlavaj & Dimovski, 2006). Dimovski (1994) confirmed the positive impact on both – the financial and non-financial performance aspects, using a one-industry research design and a stratified sample of 200 credit unions in Ohio, based on the asset size criterion (Škerlavaj & Dimovski, 2006). This study investigated the determinants, processes and outcomes of organisational learning, as well as the relationship between organisational learning and performance. Sloan et al. (2002), Lam (1998) and Figueireido (2003) also arrived at similar conclusions. Simonin (1997) found strong effects of learning on the financial and non-financial performance in the context of strategic alliances.

This chapter has four parts. The first section provides definitions of technology-enhanced learning and Web 2.0 technologies, technical terms related to it, its scope and the process of organisational learning, as well as a method for the business performance assessment in order to develop a set of constructs and an empirical basis for the relationships among them. In the second part, the model's operationalisation through the development of a measurement sub-model is presented. In the third section, the model is tested using a structural linear modelling technique. We conclude with a discussion on the implications of the results and offer some guidelines for future research.

CONCEPTUALISATION OF STRUCTURAL SUB-MODEL

A complete research model normally consists of two sub-models: measurement and structural (Jöreskog, Sörbrom, 1993). The measurement sub-model shows how each latent variable is operationalised through observations of corresponding indicators, and also provides data on validity and reliability of the variables observed. The structural sub-model describes relationships between the latent variables, indicating the amount of unexplained variance. Development of a quality model requires first to establish a structural framework, which is usually implemented in two steps: presentation of fundamental constructs and review of potential correlations between them. Results of the final analysis greatly depend on good conceptualisation of a research model (Jöreskog, Sörbrom, 1993).

Technology-Enhanced Leaning and Web 2.0 Technologies

Technology-enhanced learning is a term introduced along with the introduction of information and communication technology for educational purposes. Up to date companies have widely used this term as a synonym for e-learning (Arh, Pipan & Jerman-Blažič, 2006). Definitions of technology-enhanced learning are various, diverse and lack unity, consequently, it is of outmost importance to provide precise definitions of technology-enhanced learning and related notions. Hereby we refer to the process of studying and teaching as technology-enhanced learning when it includes information and communication technology, regardless of the mode or the scope of its use (Henry, 2001).

Kirschner and Paas (2001) defined technology-enhanced learning as a learning process in which the Internet plays the key role in the presentation, support, management and assessment of learning. Rosenberg (2001) defines technology-enhanced learning as a learning process in which information technology partially or fully undertakes the role of a mediator between different stakeholders involved in the learning process. We refer to the process of studying and teaching as technology-enhanced learning when it includes information and communication technology, regardless of the mode or the scope of its use (Henry, 2001; Dinevski & Plenković, 2002). Technology-enhanced learning extends the company out to ever-widening circles of impact. The companies are participating in a radical redefinition of industries, markets and the global economy itself. Today, organizations are investing great efforts into the making of proper adjustments to the changing business environment in order to enhance their competitiveness. In an attempt to keep up with the development of information technology and the Internet, many businesses are replacing traditional vocational training with e-learning to better manage their workforce. However, it is questionable whether training programs actually change employee behaviour after the implementation. In the case of the US companies, only 10-15% of training is applied to work (Sevilla & Wells, 1988).

When we talk about technology-enhanced learning we cannot overlook the impact of the Web 2.0 technologies on the process of technology-enhanced learning. The Web 2.0 technologies are changing the way messages spread across the web. A number of online tools and platforms are now defining how people share their perspectives, opinions, thoughts and experiences. The Web 2.0 tools, such as instant messaging systems, blogs, RSS, video casting, social bookmarking, social networking, podcasts and picture sharing sites are becoming more and more popular. One major advantage of the Web 2.0 tools is that the majority of them are free. There is a large number of the Web 2.0 tools, some of the more popular ones are: instant messaging systems, blogs, video-wiki and xo-wiki, Doodle, podcasting, RSS, etc.

Instant Messaging Systems (IMS)

The need for communication tools in the learning process is often underestimated by educators, especially those who feel comfortable with the traditional, instructive way of teaching. However, even with their 'traditional' approach learners need to communicate with each other when working together. At the beginning of the 90s, digital communication tools were rather limited: apart from the direct face-to-face meetings, the main way to communicate was through the plain old telephone. Sharing course materials was only enabled by a copy or a fax machine. However, these devices were rarely available in ordinary households. The only barriers to communication that exist today are the lack of skills needed to operate the new technologies. This barrier goes mostly unnoticed with the younger generations that have grown up as digital 'natives', rarely pulling themselves away from their computers (even out on the street they keep the mobile phones in their pockets), but it is definitely still a serious obstacle for many educators. However, the new technologies are inevitably permeating our everyday lives, and it is probably not necessary to explain the purpose of instant messaging to anyone in 2009. The number of users of the world top 10 instant messaging systems is counted in hundreds of millions according to the Wikipedia (2008) statistics, e.g. QQ 783 million total, 317.9 million active, 40.3 million peak online (mostly in China), MSN 294 million active, Yahoo 248 million active, Skype 309 million total, 12 million speak online, etc. The decisive factor for choosing an instant messaging system by an ordinary user is a friend recommendation (most people start using the same system the majority of their friends are already using). The IMS are used for any kind of information exchange including communication between employees or students regarding their study or learning environment. This is the reason this practice is included in the technology that contributes to the personalized learning environment.

Blogs

A blog is a type of a web site in which entries are made as in a journal or a diary and are displayed in reverse chronological order. Basically, an individual maintains his or her own weblog and it functions as a sort of a personal online diary. Regular entries such as comments, descriptions of events, or other types of materials combined with text, images, and links to other weblogs and web sites are the typical weblog ingredients. Blogs have attracted a lot of attention within the educational circles, where they are experienced as the tools that support several pedagogical aims and scenarios, ranging from an individual knowledge management and competence development to group-based learning activities. Therefore, blogs have become an important educational tool in recent years, providing an opportunity for both facilitators and employees to publish their ideas, essays, or simply providing a space to reflect upon their particular learning processes and reading materials. In the context of teaching and learning, blogs can do much more than just deliver instructions or course news items to employees. They can be an interesting collaboration tool for employees who can join relevant community and find people to collaborate with, give feedback to the management and others. In a learning environment blogs are most frequently used for content publishing and sharing. The blog technology can be improved by plug-ins such as the FeedBack tool used to track and integrate the content of other authors within one blog. FeedBack is a standard plug-in piece of code developed within the framework of the iCamp project (www.icamp-project. eu). In a simple way it is used to enable blog users to subscribe to each others' blogs. The blogging technology, in combination with innovations such as the FeedBack specification, has definitely a high potential to be considered a powerful tool for learning with others.

Video-Wiki and Xo-Wiki

Publishing or presenting someone's thoughts online usually means writing some text and illustrating it with pictures. Still, the most natural form of communication for humans is face to face, and for most people the majority of information is presented orally, directly facing the presenter, whose non-verbally communicated information is often even more important than the words they utter. Video could serve as a replacement for the face-to-face presentation, since it can convey the visible behaviour and important non-verbal information. In the past, recording a video and making sure it reached the target audience was quite a big challenge. Depending on the number of intended users, TV broadcasts or video tapes could be used. Employees taking part in an e-learning course work in groups, and are suggested to form groups by getting to know each other and discover some common topics. The mentor/tutor usually uses VideoWiki to record for ex. short self-introduction videos in which employees present their background, or explain their expectations regarding some specific topic for the group assignment. VideoWiki is based on the Red5 open-source Flash server written in Java and Flash. It allows video recording, searching and playback through the main system web page or via the standard URL links. VideoWiki also provides RSS feeds for each name, space or author, and videos can be embedded on any web page using special code snippets. Collaborative creation and maintenance of knowledge artefacts is one of the emerging phenomena of the online Internet communities, such as Wikipedia.org, MediaWiki.org, LyricWiki.org, Microformats.org and Wikitravel.org. A collection of web pages (a so-called wiki) can also be very useful for the teaching and learning purposes; for instance if learners need to collaborate to work on certain topics, or if facilitators wish to develop and share their learning content with others. Consequently, a contemporary approach to technology-enhanced learning requires tools which can enable learners to work on artefacts collaboratively, either by allowing them to publish small posts which can be reused and combined with others (see the blog-based solution presented in the previous section) or by providing real wiki functionality. XoWiki is one such wiki implementation, realized as a component of OpenACS (Open Architecture Community System), a framework for building scalable, community-oriented web applications. XoWiki includes a rich text editor for easy creation and editing of wiki pages, and provides features for structuring, commenting, tagging and visualisation of the wiki-based content.

Doodle

When employees work on a group project they need to divide tasks among the members of the group and monitor the progress of work. This requires the employees to engage in collaboration, discussion and decision making processes. In the context of bringing different cultures, educational systems, levels of teaching, languages and technology skills into a common virtual learning space, planning a series of meetings several weeks in advance may simply not work. Taking this into account, employees must adopt simple solutions to meet their needs. There are plenty of solutions which can help make a project run smoothly. One of them is Doodle. Doodle can be described simply as a web-based tool for finding suitable appointment dates.

Doodle allows employees to plan their meetings with partners, suppliers and other employees. In addition to time management, it can be used as a voting tool for any other issue that arises as a part of the distance learning process; for example, the literature that needs to be selected and analysed in order to complete a particular task.

Searching the Net: ObjectSpot

ObjectSpot is a meta-search engine designed to facilitate different types of research. It can be used to find publications and other learning resources on the web. ObjectSpot realizes federated searches over an ever-increasing number of digital libraries and learning object repositories. It provides access to more than 10 million learning objects spread across famous libraries such as the Directory of Open Access Journals (DOAJ), OAIster, EBSCO, ACM, CiteBase and IEEE. Some of these repositories are open access, whilst others require registration or subscription.

Organisational Learning

In recent years, the concept of organizational learning has enjoyed a renaissance among both academics and practitioners seeking to improve organizations. Early proponents (e.g. Argyris & Schön, 1978) found their ideas largely confined to the periphery of management thought during the 1980s, but the 1990s witnessed a rebirth of interest. The current renaissance is evident in the creation of a journal about organizational learning (*The Learning Organization*) as well as in the devotion of special issues of several journals to the topic (e.g., *Organization Science*, 1991; *Organizational Dynamics*, 1993; *Accounting, Management and Information Technologies*, 1995; *Journal of Organizational Change Management*, 1996). The appearance of several major review articles is testimony to organizational learning's growing stature in the research community (see Crossan, Lane & White, 1999; Dodgson, 1993; Fiol & Lyles, 1985; Huber, 1991; Jones, 2000; Levitt & March, 1998; Miner & Mezias, 1996). Moreover, a large number of articles in professional periodicals describing the design and management of learning organizations attest to the popularity of organizational learning and knowledge management among practitioners. New theories of knowledge creation have become prominent (Nonaka, 1994; Raelin, 1997), and formal knowledge management programs have been undertaken in many companies (Davenport, De Long & Beers, 1998). As we head into the twenty-first century, therefore, organizational learning promises to be a dominant perspective with influence on both organizational research and management practice (Argyris & Schön, 1996).

Defining Organizational Learning

Organisational learning is defined in numerous ways and approached from different perspectives. The pioneers (Argyris, & Schön, 1996; Senge, 1990) defined organisational learning as an individual's acquisition of information and knowledge, and development of analytical and communicational skills. Understanding organisational learning as a process, which can take up different levels of development, makes the learning organisational structure an ideal form of organisation, which can only be achieved once the process of organisational learning is fully optimised and the organisation is viewed as a system (Senge, 1990). Jones (2000) emphasizes the importance of organizational learning for the organizational performance, defining it as "a process through which managers try to increase organizational members' capabilities in order to better understand and manage the organization and its environment and accept the decisions that would increase organizational performance on a continuous basis." The aforementioned statements regarding the lack of unity of organisational learning definitions are also supported by the findings of Shrivastava, 1983 and Dimovski, 1994. The former states that extensive research carried out in the field of organisational learning has mostly been fragmented, while the latter adds the fragmentation lead to the multitude of definitions (for ex. Nonaka & Takeuchi, 1996 and Wall, 1998), differing according to the criteria of inclusion, scope and focus (Škerlavaj, 2003). Dimovski (1994) and Dimovski & Colnar (1999) provided an overview of previous research and identified four varying perspectives on organizational learning. Dimovski's model managed to merge informational, interpretational, strategic and behavioural approaches to organizational learning, and defined it as a process of information acquisition, information interpretation and the resulting behavioural and cognitive changes which should, in turn, have an impact on the company performance.

Development of our research model is based on DiBella and Nevis' model (DiBella & Nevis, 1998) of integrated approach, according to which the organisational learning factors are divided into study guidelines and study promoters, and on the Dimovski approach (Dimovski, 1994), which combines the aforementioned four aspects of organisational learning.

In this sense the organisational learning can be defined as a dynamic process of the acquisition, transfer and use of knowledge (Crossan, Lane & White, 1999; Dibella & Nevis, 1998), which starts at the core of the organisation – related to individual and team performance – and enable companies to strengthen the efficiency of the financial and non-profit (non-financial?) business achievements (Tippins & Sohi, 2003).

Business Performance

Business performance assessments have advanced over the past years, and developed from traditional, exclusively financial criteria, to modern criteria, which include also the non-financial indicators. Due to numerous disadvantages of the classical accounts and the growing need for quality information on company performance, the theory of economics started developing improved models for performance assessment, taking into account all shareholders: employees, customers, supplier employees and the wider community, also advocated by the Freeman's shareholders theory (Freeman, 1994; 1984). There are several approaches to the non-financial indicator selection, the most established of which is the Balanced Scorecard – BSC (Kaplan & Norton, 1992). The existing models, based on the accounting categories, combine with the non-financial data and the assessment of the so called 'soft' business areas, which mostly improve the assessment of companies' perspective possibilities. For a good performance of a modern company we need to introduce the non-financial indicators along with the financial ones.

Relationship among Constructs

Findings based on a rather wide overview and systematisation of literature has shown that we can expect positive impact of ICT and technology-enhanced learning on organisational learning and business performance. Robey et al. (2000) do warn that technology-enhanced learning and relative ICT may take either the role of a promoter or the role of an inhibitor of organisational learning, so the following hypothesis can be posed:

H_1. Technology-enhanced learning has positive impact on organisational learning.
H_2. Technology-enhanced learning has positive impact on financial performance.
H_3. Technology-enhanced learning has positive impact on non-financial performance.

Correlation between organisational learning and business success is often a controversial issue when we begin to deal with the company management (Inkpen & Crossan, 1995). Some authors believe better performance is related to organisational learning, though their definitions of business results differ greatly. In relation to this we can mention the capacity of organisational learning to have a positive impact on the financial results (Lei et al., 1999; Slater & Narver, 1995), on the results related to shareholders (Goh & Richards, 1997; Ulrich et al., 1993) and on the business results, such as innovativeness and greater productivity (Leonard-Barton, 1992). Mintzberg (1990) says the company performance is an important piece of feedback information on effectiveness and efficiency of the learning process. The study of Perez et al. (2004) has shown organisational learning has a significant impact on the company performance. On this basis, the following hypotheses can be put forward:

H₄: Organisational learning leads to improved financial results.
H₅: Organisational learning leads to improved non-financial results.

CONCEPTUALISATION OF MEASUREMENT SUB-MODEL

Having understood the hypothesized correlations between the latent variables, the following question is logically raised: 'How should these four constructs be operationalised and measured?' There are certainly various approaches available, since the number and the type of indicators to be used for the assessment of a certain construct, the number and the type of items to be included under an indicator and the methods for their integration are decided on the basis of validity and variability of specific measuring instruments. Table 1 presents constructs, indicators used for construct assessment, number of items summed up to give the value of an indicator and the theory or empirical research on the basis of which the measurement items were developed.

In short, the hypothesized model shall be composed of four constructs and 13 indicators, and will be of recursive nature, meaning that there shall be no cases of two variables appearing simultaneously, i.e. as a cause and a consequence to one another.

Table 1. Specification of constructs

Latent Variables	Indicators and Number of Items from Questionnaire
Technology-Enhanced Learning	Information and communication infrastructure (ICI) – 9 items Education technology (ET) – 10 items Learning contents (LC) – 3 items
Organisational Learning	Knowledge acquisition (KAc) – 9 items Knowledge transmission (KTt) – 10 items Use of knowledge (UoK) – 10 items
Financial Performance	Return on assets (FP1) – 1 item Return on capital (FP2) – 1 item Value added per employee (FP3) – 1 item
Non-Financial Performance	Employee fluctuation (NFP1) – 1 item Share of loyal customers (NFP2) – 1 item Number of customer complaints (NFP3) – 1 item Supplier relations (NFP4) – 1 item

Development of Research Instrument

The questionnaire used has been under constant development and validation for more than 10 years. Dimovski (1994) used it on a sample of Ohio credit unions in order to measure the organizational learning process as a source of competitive advantage. Škerlavaj (2003) upgraded it to include the measures of non-financial performance, while he replaced the industry-specific measures of financial performance with two measures valid for all companies. For this study the operationalisation of all four constructs involved was improved and applied on a sample of Slovenian companies with more than 50 employees in 2007. The reason to include smaller companies is to improve the generalizability of the research findings. The measurement instrument used in this study has 22 items for the technology-enhanced learning construct, 29 items for the organizational learning construct, 3 items for the financial and 4 items for the non-financial performance. The pre-testing procedures were conducted in the form of interviews and studies with managers and focus groups of research and academic colleagues.

RESEARCH HYPOTHESES AND MODEL

Once the theoretical frame of the model is devised, illustration of conceptualisation by the means of a flow chart is to be tackled (Arh, Dimovski & Jerman-Blažič, 2008). Flow chart is a graphical representation of interrelations between various elements of a model. Measurement variables belonging to exogenous latent variables are marked with an x, while their measurement deviations are marked with a δ. Endogenous latent variable indicators are marked with a y, and measurement deviations with an ε. Structural equation deviations are ζ, exogenous latent variables are ξ, endogenous constructs are η, and one-way influence of exogenous latent variables on exogenous are γ. To describe relations between latent variables and their indicators (measurement variables) we use λ. Figure 1 below is showing a conceptualised research model, presenting all basic constructs and hypothesized correlations between them. We aim at proving: (1) that the latent variable of technology-enhanced learning (TEL) has positive impact on organisational learning (OL), (2) financial (FP) and (3) non-financial performance (NFP); (4) that the latent variable of organisational learning (OL) as a process of knowledge creation leads to improved financial results (FP), as well as to (5) improved non-financial results (NFP); (6) that it is impossible to expect significant statistical correlations between financial performance (FP) and non-financial (NFP) performance.

Figure 1. Conceptualised research model

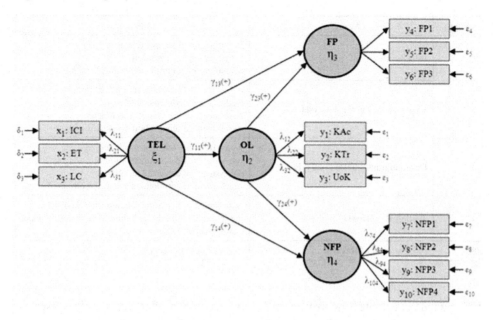

RESEARCH PROCEDURE

The methodology applied to test our research model was structural equation modelling (SEM). This involves a combination of confirmatory factor analysis (CFA) and econometric modelling, which aims to analyse hypothesised relationships among the latent constructs, measured with observed indicators (measurement variables). Table 2 provides the procedure for data analysis.

First, the item analysis was performed to describe the sample characteristics, to investigate the item means, and to assess item-to-total correlations. Second, exploratory factor analysis was performed to explore whether the items load highly on their intended latent construct, and have low cross-loadings. After the exploratory factor analysis, reliability of the underlying factors was discussed in terms of Cronbach's alphas. Third, confirmatory analysis (CFA) was performed to ensure that the constructs are valid and reliable; this refers to the measurement part of the model. Consequently, CFAs (without any structural relationships) were performed with LISREL 8.80 to check whether the items meet the criteria for convergent and discriminant validity, as well as construct reliability. Properties of the four research constructs in the proposed model (Figure 1) and the five hypotheses were tested using LISREL 8.80 and PRELIS 2.30 packages for structural equation analysis and procedures. As estimation method for model evaluation and procedures, the maximum likelihood (ML) method was utilized. Structural equation modelling (SEM)

Table 2. Research procedure

Stage	Analysis	Purpose
1.	**Item Analysis**	Investigation of sample characteristics Investigation of item means Investigation of item-to-total correlations
2.	**Exploratory Factor Analysis**	Exploration of loadings; removal of items with low loadings and high cross-loadings; Assessment of number of latent factors Assessment of reliability (Cronbach's alpha)
3.	**Confirmatory Factor Analysis**	Assessment of convergent validity Assessment of discriminant validity Assessment of construct reliability Assessment of correlations and multicollinearity
4.	**Testing Hypothesis**	Assessment of structural relationship (H1-H5) Parameter Estimates for Overall Measurement Model Convergent and Discriminant Validity
5.	**Presentation of Results**	Discussion of findings

is designed to evaluate how well a proposed conceptual model that contains observed indicators and hypothetical constructs explains or fits the collected data. It also provides the ability to measure or specify the structural relationships among the sets of unobserved (latent) variables, while describing the amount of unexplained variance. Clearly, the hypothetical model in this study was designed to measure structural relationships among the unobserved constructs that are set up on the basis of relevant theories, and prior empirical research and results. Therefore, the SEM procedure is an appropriate solution for testing the proposed structural model and hypotheses for this study.

Data Gathering and Sample

Based on the model's conceptualisation, a measurement instrument (questionnaire) was developed and sent in June 2007 to the CEOs or board members of all Slovenian companies with more than 50 employees, which accounted for 1215 companies. In the first three weeks 356 completed questionnaires were returned, five out of which were excluded from further analysis due to missing values. The response rate was 29.7%, which can be considered successful in the Slovenian context (using our primary data collection technique and no call backs). It is an indication that, beside academia, managers are also interested to know whether and in which circumstances investments in ICT and technology-enhanced learning pay off. We aimed at an audience of top and middle managers bearing in mind the idea of a strategic and to some degree even an interdisciplinary perspective of the companies in question, although there is some discrepancy between the desired and the actual structure of respondents. Based on the criterion of the average number of employees, in 2006 73.88% of the selected companies had between 50 and 249 employees, followed by 14.61% with 250 to 499 employees, while 11.51% of the companies had 500 to 999 employees. According to the company revenues in 2006, 33.15% of the Slovenian companies had the annual revenue of 2 to 7.3 million EUR. A somewhat smaller proportion (32.87%) of companies had the net income of 7.3 to 29.2 million EUR in this same period, 19.94% had the annual turnover of more than 29.2 million euro, and only 14.04% have not reached the annual revenue threshold of 2 million euro. The questionnaire was mostly completed by middle management respondents (directors of functional departments). The top and middle management were almost equally represented within the sample.

Table 3 demonstrates the industry structure of the companies in question. Our respondents reported in almost half of all cases that their main industry was manufacturing, followed by 13.8% of companies in the construction business and 11.5% in the wholesale & retail, repair of motor vehicles, personal & household goods. One out of fifteen industries have only one company representative, there was no company from the fishery sector and only two companies working the field of education. This is logical since we excluded the non-profit and small businesses from our analysis.

Table 3. Structure of respondents –by industry

	Industry (EU NACE Rev.1)	Frequency	Percent (%)
A	Agriculture, hunting and forestry	7	2
B	Fishing	0	0
C	Mining and quarrying	7	2
D	Manufacturing	158	44.4
E	Electricity, gas and water supply	15	4.2
F	Construction	49	13.8
G	Wholesale & retail, repair of motor vehicles, personal & household goods	41	11.5
H	Hotels and restaurants	12	3.4
I	Transport, storage and communication	14	3.9
J	Financial intermediation	7	2
K	Real estate, renting and business activities	16	4.5
M	Education	2	0.6
N	Health and social work	1	0.3
O	Other community, social and personal services	27	7.6

Parameter Value Estimates

The results of structural equation analysis by LISREL were utilized to test the hypotheses proposed in this study. As discussed in the previous section, the relationships between the constructs were examined based on t-values associated with path coefficients between the constructs. If an estimated t-value was greater than a certain critical value ($p < .05$, t-value $= 1.96$) (Mueller, 1996), the null hypothesis that the associated estimated parameter is equal to 0 was rejected. Subsequently, the hypothesized relationship was supported.

The maximum likelihood (ML) method was used to estimate the parameter values. In this phase, the hypotheses posed in the conceptualisation phase are tested. Even though several methods can be used for this purpose, ML is the one most often used and has the advantage of being statistically efficient and at the same time specification-error sensitive because it demands only complete data and does not allow for missing values. All methods will, however, lead to similar parameter estimates on the condition that the sample is large enough and that the model is correct (Jöreskog & Sörbrom, 1993). Figure 2 shows a path diagram of our model (with completely standardised parameter estimates).

The Tpu construct demonstrated a statistically significant, positive and strong impact on the Ou. Namely, the value of the completely standardised parameter almost equals the margin of 0.70. However, Tpu did not exhibit any statistically

*Figure 2. Research model (completely standardised parameter values, *significant at $p > 0.05$)*

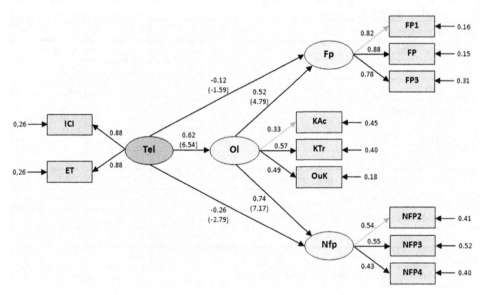

significant impact on the Fp, meaning that the hypothesis 2 must be rejected. The Ol construct demonstrated a statistically significant positive and strong impact on the Fp and an even stronger one on the Nfp. This means that the hypotheses 4 and 5 can be considered empirically supported by the data at hand.

Global Fit Assessment

Bollen (1989) explained that the model fit relates to the degree to which a hypothesised model is consistent with the available data – the degree to which the implicit matrix of covariances (based on the hypothesised model) and the sample covariance matrix (based on the data) fit. The aim of the global fit assessment is to determine to what degree is the model as a whole consistent with the data gathered. Over the years numerous global fit indices have been developed. To every researcher's regret, none of them is superior to the others. Different authors favour different measures. Diamantopoulos and Siguaw (2000) recommend using several measures and at the same time provide reference values for every one of them (Table 4).

The most traditional value is χ^2 statistics. Using this fit indicator we test the hypothesis that the implicit covariance matrix equals the sample covariance matrix. Our goal was not to reject this hypothesis, however, in our case this hypothesis must

Table 4. Fit indices

Fit Indices	Reference Value	Model Value	Global Fit
Chi-square ($\chi 2$) of estimate model	(χ^2/df < 2)	89.29 (df = 38) = 2.34	No
Goodness-of-fit index (GFI)	$\geq .90$	.96	Yes
Root mean square residual (RMR)	< .05	.023	Yes
Root mean square error of approximation (RMSEA)	$\leq .05$	.062	Yes
CAIC	CAIC saturated model CAIC independent model	281.79	Yes
Adjusted goodness-of-fit index (AGFI)	$\geq .90$	.92	Yes
Non-normed fit index (NNFI)	$\geq .95$	.97	Yes
Normed fit index (NFI)	$\geq .90$	.96	Yes
Parsimony goodness-of-fit index(PGFI)	$\geq .50$	.55	Yes
Comparative fit index (CFI)	$\geq .90$	.98	Yes
Critical (CN)	N = 248.77	356	Yes

be rejected (at a 5% level of significance). Nonetheless, quantifying the degree of misfit is often more useful than testing the hypothesis of exact fit, which χ^2 statistics are designed for. All other indices lead to the conclusion that the model is an appropriate representation of reality. The root means square error of approximation (RMSEA) is the most widespread measure of the global fit and in our case points to the acceptable fitness of the model. The consistent Akaike information criteria (CAIC) of the model needs to be compared against the CAIC of the saturated and independent model, where smaller values represent a better fit. Standardised root mean square residual (standardised RMR) is a fit index calculated on the basis of standardised residuals (differences between elements of the sample and implicit covariance matrixes). The goodness-of-fit (GFI) index and the adjusted goodness-of-fit (AGFI) index are absolute fit indices which directly assess how well the covariances based on the parameter estimates reproduce the sample covariances (Gebring &Anderson, 1993). All of the indices described above lead to the conclusion that the model can be regarded as an appropriate approximation of reality (at a global level).

SOLUTIONS AND RECOMMENDATIONS

The aim of this paper was to present the conceptualisation of a model for the assessment of the impact of technology-enhanced learning, and the respective information and communication technology on the business performance of Slovene companies with more than 50 employees. The theoretical and empirical grounds were studied in order to demonstrate the correlations between the aforementioned constructs with the basic aim to present a hypothesized research model as a concrete result.

The study focuses on the findings achieved through the estimation of the relations between information and communication technology and technology-enhanced learning, organizational learning and business performance, and their operationalisation. In accordance with stakeholder theory and balanced scorecard, both the financial and non-financial aspects of business performance are considered. Within this approach, a structural equation model was conceptualised based on the prior theoretical and empirical foundations.

In the study, five hypothesis were tested: (1) technology-enhanced learning has a positive impact on organizational learning, (2) technology-enhanced learning has a positive impact on the financial business results, (3) technology-enhanced learning has a positive impact on the non-financial business results, (4) organizational learning as a process of knowledge creation has a positive impact on the financial performance, and (5) organizational learning has a positive effect on the non-financial performance. A sample of data collected was used through the survey questionnaire, which was circulated among the CEOs and presidents of the management boards of Slovenian companies with more than 50 employees in June 2007. Out of a total of 1215 questionnaires sent, 356 correctly completed questionnaires were returned, which means that the response rate was 29.7%. The questionnaire was structured in four parts. The first construct (technology-enhanced learning) was based on 22 measurement variables, the second construct (organizational learning) on 29 measurement variables related to the acquisition of knowledge, knowledge transfer and the use of knowledge. The third and the fourth constructs were designed with the intention of measuring the financial and non-financial company results (three measurement variables for the financial and four measurement variables for the non-financial results). Equation modelling methodology was used for the analysis in the empirical part of the study. The methodology of structural equation modelling enabled us to concretely determine whether the hypothetical links between the constructs or latent variables are valid or not.

The results of the survey prove a statistically significant, strong and positive impact of ICT and technology-enhanced learning on organizational learning, and a decisive influence of organizational learning on the financial and non-financial business results. The companies which systematically incorporated various advanced educational tools and systems into their daily work, and ensured high quality information and communication technology equipment recognized the importance of organizational learning as the most effective process for the production, dissemination and application of knowledge. Furthermore, the positive effects of organizational learning on the financial and non-financial business results confirm that this concept really guarantees the achievement of higher performance both in financial and non-financial terms. Knowledge is definitely one of the most important criteria of the competitive advantage, which is confirmed by the results of the study.

The study contributes to the technology-enhanced learning and organizational learning base of knowledge in the following three dimensions: (1) theoretical, (2) methodological, and (3) practical. Technology-enhanced learning contributes to sustainable competitive advantage through its interaction with other resources. Recent literature suggests that organizational learning is a process that plays an important role in enhancing company's competitive advantage (Lei, Slocum & Pitts, 1999), which may benefit from the judicious application of technology-enhanced learning. It has also been argued that a prerequisite for the firms to be successful is the completion of Tel with Ol. Within the broader conceptual framework, this study focuses on the relationship between technology-enhanced learning, organizational learning and business performance. As such, the conceptual model offers several research opportunities and provides a solid base for further empirical testing of hypotheses related to technology-enhanced learning and organizational learning.

REFERENCES

Argyris, C., & Schön, D. A. (1978). *Organizational learning: A theory of action perspective*. Reading, MA: Addison-Wesley.

Argyris, C., & Schön, D. A. (1996). *Organizational learning II: Theory, method and practice*. Reading, MA: Addison-Wesley.

Arh, T., Dimovski, V., & Jerman-Blažič, B. (2008). Model of impact of technology-enhanced organizational learning on business performance. V. P. Cunningham & M. Cunningham (Eds.), *Collaboration and the knowledge economy: Issues, applications, case studies*, (pp. 1521–1528). IOS Press.

Arh, T., Pipan, M., & Jerman-Blažič, B. (2006). Virtual learning environment for the support of life-long learning initiative. *WSEAS Transactions on Advances in Engineering Education, 4*(4), 737–743.

Bollen, K.A. (1989). *Structural equations with latent variables*. New York, NY: Wiley.

Carr, N. G. (2003). IT doesn't matter. *Harvard Business Review, 81*(5), 41.

Collins, C. J., & Smith, K. G. (2006). Knowledge exchange and combination: The role of human resource practices in the performance of high-technology firms. *Academy of Management Journal, 49*(3), 544–560. doi:10.5465/AMJ.2006.21794671

Crossan, M., Lane, H. W., & White, R. E. (1999). An organizational learning framework: From intuition to institution. *Academy of Management Review, 24*(3), 522–537.

Davenport, T. H., De Long, D. W., & Beers, M. C. (1998). Successful knowledge management projects. *Sloan Management Review, 39*(2), 43–57.

Dewan, S., & Kraemer, K. L. (1998). International dimensions of the productivity paradox. *Communications of the ACM, 41*(8), 56–62. doi:10.1145/280324.280333

Diamantopoulos, A., & Siguaw, J. A. (2000). *Introducing LISREL*. London, UK: SAGE Publications.

DiBella, J. A., & Nevis, E. C. (1998). *How organizations learn – An integrated strategy for building learning capability*. San Francisco, CA: Jossey-Bass.

Dimovski, V. (1994). *Organisational learning and competitive advantage*. Unpublished doctoral dissertation, Cleveland State University.

Dimovski, V., & Colnar, T. (1999). Organizacijsko učenje. *Teorija in Praksa, 5*(36), 701–722.

Dinevski, D., & Plenković, M. (2002). Modern university and e-learning. *Media, Culture and Public Relations*, *2*, 137–146.

Dodgson, M. (1993). Organizational learning: A review of some literatures. *Organization Studies*, *14*(3), 375–394. doi:10.1177/017084069301400303

Figueiredo, P. N. (2003). Learning processes features: How do they influence inter-firm differences in technological capability - Accumulation paths and operational performance improvement? *International Journal of Technology Management*, *26*(7), 655–689. doi:10.1504/IJTM.2003.003451

Fiol, C. M., & Lyles, M. A. (1985). Organizational learning. *Academy of Management Review*, *10*(4), 803–813.

Freeman, E. R. (1984). *Strategic management – A stakeholder approach*. London, UK: Pitman.

Freeman, E. R. (1994). Politics of stakeholder theory: Some future directions. *Business Ethics Quarterly*, *4*, 409–422. doi:10.2307/3857340

Gerbing, D. W., & Anderson, J. C. (1988). An updated paradigm for scale development incorporating unidimensionality and measurement error. *JMR, Journal of Marketing Research*, *25*, 186–192. doi:10.2307/3172650

Goh, S., & Richards, G. (1997). Benchmarking the learning capability of organizations. *European Management Journal*, *15*(5), 575–583. doi:10.1016/S0263-2373(97)00036-4

Henry, P. (2001). E-learning technology, content and services. *Education + Training*, *43*(4), 251–259.

Huber, G. P. (1991). Organizational learning: The contributing processes and the literatures. *Organization Science*, *2*(1), 88–115. doi:10.1287/orsc.2.1.88

Inkpen, A., & Crossan, M. M. (1995). Believing is seeing: Organizational learning in joint ventures. *Journal of Management Studies*, *32*(5), 595–618. doi:10.1111/j.1467-6486.1995.tb00790.x

Jones, G. R. (2000). *Organizational theory* (3rd ed.). New York, NY: Prentice Hall.

Jöreskog, K. G., & Sörbrom, D. (1993). *LISREL 8: Structural equation modelling with the SIMPLIS command language*. London, UK: Lawrence Erlbaum Associates Publishers.

Kaplan, R. S., & Norton, D. P. (1992). Balanced scorecard – Measures that drive performance. *Harvard Business Review*, *1–2*, 71–79.

Kirchner, P. A., & Pass, F. (2001). Web enhanced higher education: A Tower of Babel. *Computers in Human Behavior, 17*(4), 347–353. doi:10.1016/S0747-5632(01)00009-7

Lam, S. S. K. (1998). Organizational performance and learning styles in Hong Kong. *The Journal of Social Psychology, 138*(3), 401–403. doi:10.1080/00224549809600392

Lei, D., Hitt, M. A., & Bettis, R. (1996). Dynamic core competencies through meta-learning and strategic context. *Journal of Management, 22*(4), 549–569. doi:10.1177/014920639602200402

Lei, D., Slocum, J. W., & Pitts, R. A. (1999). Designing organizations for competitive advantage: The power of unlearning and learning. *Organizational Dynamics, 27*(3), 24–38. doi:10.1016/S0090-2616(99)90019-0

Leonard-Barton, D. (1992). The factory as a learning laboratory. *Sloan Management Review, 34*(1), 23–38.

Levitt, B., & March, J. G. (1998). Organizational learning. *Annual Review of Sociology, 14*, 319–340. doi:10.1146/annurev.so.14.080188.001535

MacManus, R., & Porter, J. (2005): *Web 2.0 for design: Bootstrapping the social web*. Retrieved April 15th 2008, from http://www.digital-web.com/articles/web_2_for_designers

Miner, A. S., & Mezias, S. J. (1996). Ugly duckling no more: Pasts and futures of organizational learning research. *Organization Science, 7*(1), 88–99. doi:10.1287/orsc.7.1.88

Mintzberg, H. (1990). Strategy formation: Schools of thought. In Frederickson, J. W. (Ed.), *Perspectives of strategic management* (pp. 105–235). New York, NY: Harper Business.

Mueller, R. O. (1996). *Basic principles of structural equation modelling: An introduction to Lisrel and EQS*. New York, NY: Springer.

Navarette, C. J., & Pick, J. B. (2002). Information technology expenditure and industry performance: The case of the Mexican banking industry. *Journal of Global Information Technology Management, 5*(2), 7–28.

Nonaka, I. (1994). A dynamic theory of organizational knowledge creation. *Organization Science, 5*(1), 14–37. doi:10.1287/orsc.5.1.14

Nonaka, I., & Takeuchi, H. (1996). A theory of organizational knowledge creation. *International Journal of Technology Management, 11*(7/8), 833–846.

O'Reilly, T. (2005). *What is Web 2.0. Design patterns and business models for the next generation of software.* Retrieved November 10, 2009, from http://oreilly.com/web2/archive/what-is-web-20.html

Péréz López, S., Montes Peón, J. M., & Vázquez Ordás, C. (2004). Managing knowledge: The link between culture and organizational learning. *Journal of Knowledge Management, 8*(6), 93–104. doi:10.1108/13673270410567657

Raelin, J. A. (1997). A model of work-based learning. *Organization Science, 8*(6), 563–578. doi:10.1287/orsc.8.6.563

Reychav, I., & Weisberg, J. (2009). Good for workers, good for companies: How knowledge sharing benefits individual employees. *Knowledge and Process Management, 16*(4), 186–197. doi:10.1002/kpm.335

Roach, S. (1987). *America's technology dilemma: A profile of the information economy. Economics Newsletter Series.* New York, NY: Morgan Stanley.

Robey, D., Boudreau, M., & Rose, G. M. (2000). Information technology and organizational learning: A review and assessment of research. *Accounting, Management and Information Technologies, 10,* 125–155. doi:10.1016/S0959-8022(99)00017-X

Rosenberg, M. (2001). *E-learning, strategies for developing knowledge in the digital age.* New York, NY: McGraw-Hill.

Senge, P. M. (1990). *The fifth discipline: Art and practice of the learning organization.* New York, NY: Doubleday.

Sevilla, C., & Wells, T. D. (1988). Contracting to ensure training transfer. *Training & Development, 6*(1), 10–11.

Shrivastava, P. A. (1983). Typology of organizational learning systems. *Journal of Management Studies, 20,* 1–28. doi:10.1111/j.1467-6486.1983.tb00195.x

Simonin, B. L. (1997). The importance of collaborative know-how: An empirical test of the learning organization. *Academy of Management Journal, 40*(5), 1150–1173. doi:10.2307/256930

Škerlavaj, M. (2003). *Vpliv informacijsko-komunikacijskih tehnologij in organizacijskega učenja na uspešnost poslovanja: Teoretična in empirična analiza.* Unpublished Master's thesis. Ljubljana: Ekonomska fakulteta.

Škerlavaj, M., & Dimovski, V. (2006). Study of the mutual connections among information-communication technologies, organisational learning and business performance. *Journal for East European Management Studies, 11*(1), 9–29.

Slater, S. F., & Narver, J. C. (1995). Market orientation and the learning organization. *Journal of Marketing, 59*(3), 63–74. doi:10.2307/1252120

Sloan, T. R., Hyland, P. W. B., & Beckett, R. C. (2002). Learning as a competitive advantage: Innovative training in the Australian aerospace industry. *International Journal of Technology Management, 23*(4), 341–352. doi:10.1504/IJTM.2002.003014

Smith, R. (2008). Aligning competencies, capabilities and resources. *Research Technology Management: The Journal of the Industrial Research Institute*, September-October.

Tippins, M. J., & Sohi, R. S. (2003). IT competency and firm performance: Is organizational learning a missing link? *Strategic Management Journal, 24*(8), 745–761. doi:10.1002/smj.337

Ulrich, D., Jick, T., & von Glinow, M. A. (1993). High-impact learning: Building and diffusing learning capability. *Organizational Dynamics, 22*(2), 52–66. doi:10.1016/0090-2616(93)90053-4

Varney, S. (2008). Leadership learning: key to organizational transformation. *Strategic HR Review, 7*(1), 5–10. doi:10.1108/14754390810880471

Wall, B. (1998). Measuring the right stuff: Identifying and applying the right knowledge. *Knowledge Management Review, 1*(4), 20–24.

Zhang, D. (2002). *Media structuration – Towards an integrated approach to interactive multimedia-based E-Learning*. (Ph.D. dissertation, The University of Arizona. Zhang, D., & Nunamaker, J. F. (2003). Powering e-learning in the new millennium: An overview of e-learning and enabling technology. *Information Systems Frontiers, 5*(2), 207–218.

KEY TERMS AND DEFINITIONS

Balanced Scorecard – BSC: The balanced scorecard (BSC) is a strategic performance management tool – a semi-standard structured report supported by proven design methods and automation tools that can be used by managers to keep track of the execution of activities of staff within their control, and monitor the consequences arising from these actions. It is perhaps the best known of several such frameworks, and was widely adopted in the English speaking western countries and Scandinavia in the early 1990s. The BCS based on the use of three non-financial topic areas as prompts to aid the identification of the non-financial measures in addition to the one looking at the financial measures. The four perspectives are: financial, customer, internal business, and innovation and learning.

Confirmatory Factor Analysis: Confirmatory factor analysis (CFA) is a powerful statistical technique. CFA allows researchers to test the hypothesis of the existence of a relationship between the observed variables and their underlying latent construct(s). Researchers apply their theoretical knowledge, empirical research, or both, postulate the relationship pattern a priori and then tests the hypothesis statistically.

LISREL: LISREL is the pioneering software for structural equation modelling which includes statistical methods for complex data survey. LISREL was developed in 1970s by Karl Jöreskog and Dag Sörbom, both professors at the Uppsala University, Sweden.

Organizational Learning: Organizational learning is an area of knowledge within the organizational theory that studies models and theories about the ways an organization learns and adapts. Argyris and Schön (1978) were the first to propose models that facilitate organizational learning; others have followed in the tradition of their work. They distinguished between the single- and double-loop learning. In the single-loop learning, individuals, groups, or organizations modify their actions according to the difference between the expected and obtained outcomes. In the double-loop learning, entities (individuals, groups or organizations) question the values, assumptions and policies that led to the actions in the first place; if they are able to view and modify those, then the second-order or the double-loop learning has taken place. The double-loop learning is the process of learning about the single-loop learning.

Structural Equation Modelling: Structural equation modelling, or in short SEM, is a statistical technique for testing and estimating causal relationships using a combination of statistical data and qualitative causal assumptions. SEM allows both confirmatory and exploratory modelling, meaning it suits both theory testing and theory development. Factor analysis, path analysis and regression all represent special cases of SEM.

Technology Enhanced Learning: Technology-enhanced learning (TEL) refers to any learning activity supported by technology. TEL is often used as a synonym for e-learning, however, there are significant differences between the two; namely, TEL focuses on the technological support of any pedagogical approach that utilizes technology. However, it rarely includes the print technology or developments related to libraries, books and journals occurring in the centuries before computers.

Web 2.0: Web 2.0 is a category of new Internet tools and technologies created around the idea that those who consume the media, access the Internet, and use the web should not just passively absorb what is available; they should be rather active contributors, helping customize the media and technology for their own purposes, as well as those of their communities. Web 2.0 marks the beginning of a new era in technology – one that promises to help the nonprofits operate more efficiently, generate more funding, and affect more lives. These new tools include blogs, social networking applications, RSS, social networking tools, and wikis.

Chapter 19

Free Wireless Internet Park Services:
An Investigation of Technology Adoption in Qatar from a Citizens' Perspective

Shafi Al-Shafi
Brunel University, UK

EXECUTIVE SUMMARY

This chapter examines the adoption of free wireless Internet parks (iPark) by Qatari citizens as a means of accessing electronic services from public parks. The Qatar government has launched the iPark concept with a view of providing free internet access for all citizens while enjoying the outdoors. This concept is enabled by an ICT infrastructure and broadband facilities, which is considered as regional good practice. By offering free wireless Internet access, the Qatari government encourages its citizens to actively participate in the global information society with a view of bridging the digital divide. Using a survey based study this research set out to examine the Qatari citizens' perceptions of the iPark initiative. Results of the survey showed that there is a positive level of relation between the independent variables, usefulness, ease of use, Internet safety, and Internet speed/response time and one dependent variable, intention to use the iPark in Qatar. The chapter provides a discussion on the key findings, research implications, limitations, and future directions for the iPark initiative in Qatar.

DOI: 10.4018/978-1-4666-0981-5.ch019

ORGANIZATIONAL BACKGROUND

Since the advent of the internet some 40 years ago (Ho, 2002), the number of information and communication technology (ICT)-driven services has quadrupled, making today's society a technology and Internet-savvy one. While the 1990s saw the e-commerce revolution (UN, 2005) with private and multinational organisations, in the new millennium, we have witnessed public sector organizations embracing the same principles of e-business through the introduction of national e-government initiatives. Since the 1990s, ICT has played an important role in incrementally changing and shifting traditional and bureaucratic government models into the current e-government model, where services are delivered according to customers' needs.

While all developed countries have now implemented some form of e-government (Accenture, 2005; Al-Kibsi et al., 2001) with most having implemented transactional level services (see, for instance, Layne & Lee, 2001; Weerakkody et al., 2007) – the majority of developing countries are beginning to follow suit (Kurunananda & Weerakkody, 2006). Not surprisingly, wealthy Middle Eastern countries such as Dubai and Qatar have made plans to provide e-government services to citizens and businesses.

As in many countries, the national e-government focus in Qatar is to achieve the highest performance in executing governmental transactions electronically, through streamlined business processes and integrated information technology solutions (Qatar E-Government, 2007).

The socioeconomic structure in the state of Qatar is such that its population is made up largely of immigrant workers and professionals who are considered citizens of the country. Therefore, the largest proportion of recipients of e-government and early adopters are seen as those professional workers employed in numerous state, private, and multinational organizations. Consequently, the national e-government efforts are primarily focused towards these recipients (referred to as citizens).

The Internet, while being the primary mode of access to e-government services, has not been adapted globally at the same time or rate; some countries are considered as leaders (such as the United States and Singapore) and others simply follow (i.e., the Gulf region). More recently, wireless technologies have become a useful means of Internet connectivity and access to e-services. Wi-Fi for 'wireless fidelity' is a set of standards for wireless local area networks (WLAN) and provides wireless access to the Internet. Hotspots providing such access include Wifi-cafés, where one needs to bring one's own wireless-enabled devices such as a notebook or PDA. These services may be free to customers only or to all. A hotspot need not be limited to a confined location. In fact, as part of the government's ongoing efforts to provide free Internet access to all in Qatar, public parks are used as open spaces to offer free wireless Internet access to citizens. These parks are referred to as an iPark and the first such initiative was launched in March, 2007, in the city of Doha in Qatar. This iPark initiative is the first of its kind in the Arabian region.

In particular Wi-Fi has opened up new opportunities for e-commerce and e-government by allowing citizens, consumers and businesses to build connectivity, any time and at any place. Also, it helps to increase accessibility of services and to expand social, government, and business networks (Palen, 2002). Pyramid Research (2003) expected the number of Wi-Fi users worldwide to reach 707 million by 2008. However, wireless security remains the most important factor that challenges wireless Internet hot spots. As wireless Internet grows the security threat also increases rapidly and therefore the need to protect information becomes imperative (NIST, 1995). The security risk is mainly from hackers, who are individuals, that access into the system without any authorization and for personal gain.

Given this context, the rationale for this research is to gain a better understanding about the free wireless Internet park "iPark" initiative in Qatar. Using a pilot survey questionnaire, this study aims to investigate the intention of citizens to use iPark services in Qatar. This is achieved by examining their perceptions of 'ease of use' and 'usefulness' in relation to Internet access in the iPark. To pursue this line of inquiry, this research uses the technology acceptance model (TAM). TAM theorizes that an individual's behavioral intention to use a technology is determined by two factors: perceived usefulness and perceived ease of use (Gardner & Amoroso, 2004). TAM is one of the most influential research models in studies of determinants of IS/IT acceptance (Chau, 1996).

SETTING THE STAGE

With the popularity of e-government growing, various researchers have offered different definitions to explain the concept (Holden et al., 2003; Jain, 2002; Seifert & Peterson, 2002). However, these definitions differ according to the varying e-government focus and are usually centered on technology, business, process, citizen, government, or a functional perspective. For instance, Seifert and Peterson (2002) explain e-government with a functional focus, Burn and Robins (2003) define it with a citizen's focus, Zhiyuan (2002) views e-government with a technology focus, Wassenaar (2000) classifies it with a business focus, Wimmer and Traunmuller (2000) take a more government-centered view, and Bonham et al. (2001) define it with a process focus. The definition considered to be most suitable for the purpose of this paper is one that defines e-government as a radical change and strategic tool that supports and simplifies government for other stakeholders such as government agencies, citizens and businesses (Basu, 2004; Evans, 2003; Gupta & Jana, 2003).

Like e-business, e-government promises to deliver a number of benefits to citizens, businesses and governments. The most significant benefits of e-government, according to the literature, are delivering electronic and integrated public services through a single point of access to public services 24 hours a day, seven days a week (Reffat, 2003); bridging the digital divide so that every citizen in society will be offered the same type of information and services from government (InfoDev, 2002); rebuilding customer relationships by providing value-added and personalised services to citizens (Davison et al., 2005); fostering economic development and helping local businesses to expand globally; and creating a more participative form of government by encouraging online debating, voting and exchange of information (Bonham et al., 2001; Davison, et al., 2005; InfoDev, 2002; Reynolds & Regio, 2001;).

As with any other new technology or organizational concept, the introduction of e-government to a country will also result in a number of challenges for the citizens and the government alike (Margetts & Dunleavy, 2002; Seifert & Peterson, 2002; Zakareya & Irani, 2005). Overcoming these challenges would therefore be one of the biggest tests for the government and citizens of any country planning to implement the concept. Research on e-government has identified issues such as lack of awareness (Reffat, 2003), usability of e-government Websites (Porter, 2002; Sampson, 2002), lack of trust (Bhattacherjee, 2002; InfoDev, 2002; Navarra & Cornford, 2003; Silcock, 2001), security concerns (Harris & Schwartz, 2000; Javenpaa & Tractinsky, 1999), lack of skills and funding (Federal Computer Weekly, 2001), data protection laws (Bonham et al., 2003; Harris & Schwartz, 2000), lack of citizens' interest (Porter, 2002; Sampson, 2002); lack of government support (Karunananda & Weerakkody, 2006) and lack of strategy and frameworks (Reffat, 2003) as hindering the adoption of e-government in many countries.

In an e-government context, Moon (2002) proposed that IT and Web-based public services can help governments to restore public trust by coping with corruption, inefficiency, ineffectiveness and policy alienation. Conversely, lack of access to e-services (Chircu & Lee, 2005; Darrell, 2002; Fang, 2002; Silcock, 2001;) and digital divide (Carter & Bèlanger, 2005; Chen et al., 2006; Ifinedo & Davidrajuh, 2005; InfoDev, 2002; John & Jin-Wan, 2005; Silcock, 2001) are challenges that can impact on participation and thereby impede the further take-up of e-government services. To bridge the digital divide, Reffat (2003) suggests that governments could help by providing computer education especially to elderly and younger people. In this context, researchers have also found that younger people are accessing the Internet more compared to older citizens (Kurunananda & Weerakkody, 2006).

Some authors have also classified the challenges under the broader context of organizational and technical (Layne & Lee, 2001), and economical and social categories (Chesi et al., 2005; Oreste et al., 2005). The ultimate objective for governments should therefore be to ensure that e-government efforts successfully overcome these challenges and deliver to users (citizens) systems that are easy and convenient to use and, most of all, meet their expectations.

Technology Adoption: The Theoretical Background

Researchers in the field of information systems and information technology have for long been interested in investigating the theories and models that have the power in predicting and explaining behaviour. Many models have been proposed that have different sets of acceptance determinants (Venkatesh et al., 2003). For instance of these theories and models, the most widely accepted are: the theory of reasoned action (TRA), which is used to predict behavior; theory of planned behavior (TPB), which is used to predict intention and behavior in a wide variety of settings; innovation diffusion theory (IDT), that has been used to study a variety of innovations (Rogers, 1995); the unified theory of acceptance and use of technology (UTAUT), which was formulated with four core determinants of intention and usage, and four moderators of key relationships; and the technology acceptance model (TAM), (Venkatesh et al., 2003).

The technology accepted model is adapted from the theory of reasoned action (TRA) to the field of information systems. TAM was developed by Davis in 1989 (Davis, 1989) and uses TRA as a theoretical basis for specifying the linkages between two key beliefs: perceived usefullness and perceived ease of use and users' attitudes, intentions and actual usage behavior. According to Davis et al., (1989) the main goal of the model is to give an explanation of the determinants of computer acceptance, which resulted to an explanation of user behavior across a broad range of end-user computing technologies and user populations (Davis et al., 1989). Also, another key focus of TAM is to provide a base for determining or exposing the impact of external variables on internal beliefs, attitudes, and intentions. During previous years, TAM has received an extensive support through validation, applications, and replications for its power to predict use of information systems (Cheng et al., 2006).

Additionally, it is considered as a well-established, well-tested, powerful, robust, and parsimonious model for predicting user acceptance of technology (Venkatesh & Davis, 2000). Some examples of these technologies are electronic mail, text editors, and word processing systems and graphics software. Davis (1989) defined perceived usefulness as the degree to which a person believes that using a particular system would enhance his or her job performance. Also, he defined perceived ease of use as the degree to which a person believes that using a system would be free of efforts.

CASE DESCRIPTION

The state of Qatar is a peninsula with a strategic position at the centre of the west coast of the Arabian Gulf. The total land area is approximately 11,437 sq km. The population amounts to around 907,229; however, only a minority of the population is citizens by birth, while the rest are residents who live or work in Qatar and are not Qataris by birth (Al-Shafi & Weerakkody, 2007b).

E-government was launched in Qatar in July 2000. The vision of the Qatari e-government project was "*Qatar online services, anytime, anywhere, providing government transactions, information and knowledge*" (Al-Shafi & Weerakkody, 2007a). In the vision of the Qatar e-government project, the definitions of some key terms were as follows:

- *Anytime* means e-government services available 24/7.
- *Anywhere* means e-government transactions will be available through multiple Internet channels such as kiosks, wireless mobile, and digital TV.
- *E-government transactions* mean fully integrated transactions that are offered by the government agencies to be provided through Internet channels.

The Qatari e-government site offers many services, ranging from student registration and paying traffic violations to applying online for visas and permits (Al-Shafi & Weerakkody, 2007a). In global terms the UN global e-government readiness report (2008) ranked Qatar's e-government project as number 53 worldwide, where as in 2005 it was ranked as number 62 worldwide (Al-Shafi & Weerakkody, 2007a). In addition to this, the UN (2005) report considered the Qatari e-government project to be regional (West Asia) best practice. This implies that major improvements and developments have been made during recent times.

As part of Qatar government's ongoing efforts to increase accessibility to e-government services and bridge the digital divide, free wireless Internet access in public parks (iPark) initiative was launched in March 2007. This concept provides "Broadband for all" and aims to foster a knowledge based society. The primary goal of the initiative is to increase Internet usage by establishing "hot spots" in public parks (IctQatar, 2007). There are currently three designated wireless Internet hotspots throughout selected public parks in the city; these parks are targeting visitors who have Internet access available on their laptops, PDAs, and other Internet-ready devices (The Peninsula, 2007).

Figure 1. iPark adaption factors

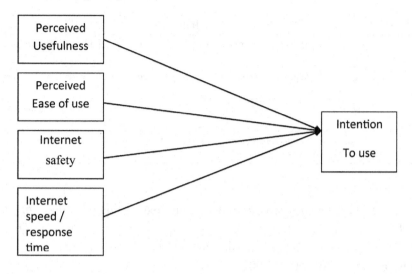

Research Model and Hypothesis

Based on the aforementioned and the theoretical context offered in section 2.1, a research model is proposed in figure 1 to examine the adoption of the iPark initiative by Qatari citizens. This model indicates that perceived usefulness; perceived ease of use, Internet safety, and Internet speed/response time has an impact on the intention to use the iPark initiative in Qatar. Based on these premises four hypotheses are proposed in table 1.

Data Collection

The only sources of published information on iPark in Qatar are official government reports and publications. Despite their significance, these publications do not provide an overall picture of the current iPark concept and its use by Qatari citizens in adequate depth. The purpose of this research is to investigate the current state of the Qatari iPark initiative and to examine its acceptance from a citizens' perspective. To explore the argument set out above and understand the context of the iPark initiative in Qatar, brief informal open-ended interviews (Yin, 1994) were conducted with three citizens (employees of commercial and government organizations) and one Academic (in higher education). The interviews lasted around 30 minutes and provided the context to formulate a detailed survey questionnaire that was to be used to investigate the citizens' perceptions of iPark in Qatar.

Table 1. Research hypothesis

NO.	Hypothesis
H1:	Higher levels of perceived usefulness will be positively related to higher levels of intention to use iPark services.
H2:	Higher levels of perceived ease of use will be positively related to higher levels of intention to use iPark services.
H3:	Higher levels of Internet safety will be positively related to higher levels of intention to use iPark services.
H4:	Higher levels of Internet speed/response time will be positively related to higher levels of intention to use iPark services.

After the questionnaire was designed, a limited testing was done using one researcher and four practitioners. This was important to improve the questions and to test respondents' comprehension and clarity before the actual survey was administered (Saunders et al., 2002).

The pilot testing led to the removal of one question and modification to another. Thereafter, the author e-mailed and delivered by hand the questionnaire to around 30 friends and colleagues in Qatar from different nationality, age, qualification, gender and professional backgrounds. Results of these questionnaires (23 out of the 30 responded) revealed that most respondents did not have any idea about the iPark initiative, or their location. Therefore, the results of the survey were unusable. Given this context, the author decided to visit the iParks physically and meet the visitors to these parks. The protocol followed was as follows: first, the author approached the iPark users, identified himself and provided a brief description of the research and the main purpose of the questionnaire; then, the process of completing the questionnaire began by the author distributing the questionnaire to users and briefly explaining the contents of the questionnaire; this was finally followed by collecting the questionnaires after a period of around 20 to 30 minutes.

This approach to data collection was followed as the distribution of the questionnaire by e-mail and hand outside of the iPark resulted in most respondents suggesting that they were unaware of the iPark concept and never used it. Therefore, approaching the citizens (users) physically in the iPark was considered as the most suitable method for data collection as the people who come to these parks can be considered as more aware of the service. The survey questionnaire was distributed to a total of 55 iPark users between the period of November and December 2007. Overall, a survey questionnaire approach was selected as it is inexpensive, less time consuming and has the ability to provide both quantitative scale and qualitative data from a large research sample (Cornford & Smithson, 1997). The questionnaire used had 26 closed-ended questions and used Likert scale type (5-point scale) questions, which were both quicker and easier to answer for the respondents (Saunders et al., 2002).

Data Analysis

The proposed model consists of four independent variables, usefulness; ease of use, Internet safety, and Internet speed/response time and one dependent variable, intention to use.

To check the responses of these questions, the first stage consisted of checking the responses and tagging them with a unique number. The author generated the descriptive statistics (percentage and tables) and used linear regression analysis by utilizing SPSS (Version 15.0). Descriptive data analysis provides the reader with an appreciation of the actual numbers and values, and hence the scale that researchers are dealing with (Dwivedi & Weerakkody, 2007).

CURRENT CHALLENGES

Of the 55 completed questionnaires that were returned, one questionnaire was discarded because it was not completed in full. This meant that the final sample of 54 questionnaires was used for all subsequent analysis. Of these 54 respondents, 13 (24 percent) had an Internet connection and accessibility in their homes only, 4 (7.4 percent) had at work only, and 23 (42.6 percent) had a connection at both places (work and home), while 2 (3.7 percent) did not have either connection. This meant that about (74 percent) of the free wireless Internet park users in Qatar had Internet connections in their home/work or both.

When examining the 'ease of use' of iPark services, 85 percent of the respondents mentioned that they found the service was easy for them, while 15 percent thought otherwise. Additionally, 78 percent of the respondents found that their interactions with the use of the free Internet park service were clear and understandable and only (5.5 percent) disagreed with this view.

In terms of age, the results revealed that the majority of respondents (37 percent) were found in the age group of 31-45, followed by the age group of 19-30 constituting around (31.5 percent) of the total respondents. In contrast, the younger groups (less than 18) and older age groups (46-60) consisted together of (16 percent) of the total respondents.

Within the respondents gender, (15 percent) of the 54 usable responses were females while 85 percent of the total respondents were males. As far as education is concerned, the majority of respondents (39 percent) hold postgraduate degrees (Masters or PhD), and (35 percent) hold undergraduate level qualifications and 26 percent hold secondary school certificates.

From a 'frequency of use' perspective, 78 percent of the users used iPark less than 5 times a week, while from the remaining 22 percent, 11 percent of the users used the iPark more than 20 time and the other 11 percent between 5-10 times a week.

Finally, the majority of respondents specified that they used iPark for: e-mails (76 percent); getting some information (54 percent); news (56 percent); e-government services (27 percent); chat (35 percent); and fun (43 percent).

As outlined in table-2, the average scores for respondents' perceived ease of use ranged from 4.07 to 4.37, (where 1 = minimum and 5 = maximum). Descriptive statistics show that these scores are quite high. For perceived usefulness, the score ranged from 3.85 and 4.54, which is quite high. With regards to perceived technology and Web security, the score ranged from 2.87 to 3.70, indicating that the scale is average. Also, for attitude towards iPark, the score ranged from 4.35 to 4.59, indicating that the scale is uniform. The last score ranged from 3.30 to 3.72 for intention to use.

Table 3 also shows that the correlation is significant to these three key factors, *perceived ease of use (0.258), perceived technology (response time) (0.405), and Web security (0.455)*. Whereas, perceived usefulness (0.178) was found to have insignificant impact.

Regression Analysis: Factors Influencing the Intention to Use iPark

A regression analysis was conducted with the use of iPark channels as dependant variable and perceived ease of use, perceived usefulness, perceived technology, and Web security as predictor variables. From a total of 54 cases that were analyzed a significant model emerged $\{F (4, 54) = 6.511, p < .001\}$ (Table-4). The second significant statistic that was obtained from the analysis is the R^2, which ranges from 0 to 1, with 1 being a perfect fit model. It was found that $R^2 = 0.347$ for this analysis. This factor explains 35 percent of the changes in the intention to use iPark. Other unidentified factors account for the remaining 65 percent. The R^2 of 35 (35 percent) is considered as a good value for a cross-sectional data involving many predictor variables. Also, Table 4 shows that of all the factors, the following have no significant impact on intention to use iPark: perceived ease of use ($\beta = 0.093$, $p= 0.489$); perceived usefulness ($\beta = 0.171$, $p= 0.243$); perceived technology($\beta = 0.262$, $p= 0.041$); and Web security($\beta = 0.362$, $p= 0.005$).

- **Predictors:** (Constant), Overall, I find the use of the iPark services easy, I would rate the speed of Internet/ Response time in the iPark is good, Overall, the iPark is a safe place to transmit sensitive information, I would find the iPark useful

Table 2. Descriptive statistics

	Mean	Std. Deviation
I use iPark frequently	3.43	1.238
I encounter problem frequently in using the iPark	2.70	1.218
I use iPark service frequently as source of information	3.51	1.187
Perceived Ease Of Use		
Using the iPark service is easy for me	4.07	.949
I find my interaction with the use of the iPark services clear and understandable	4.08	.917
It is easy for me to become skillful at the use of the iPark services	4.37	.853
Overall, I find the use of the iPark services easy	4.17	1.060
Perceived Usefulness		
Using the iPark would enable me to accomplish my tasks more quickly	3.89	1.144
Using the iPark would make it easier for me to carry out my tasks	3.85	1.139
I would find the iPark useful	4.54	.803
Overall, I would find using the iPark to be advantageous	4.50	.897
Perceived Technology and Web Security		
I would feel secure sending sensitive information across the iPark	2.91	1.336
I would rate the speed of Internet/ Response time in the iPark is good	3.70	.964
Overall, the iPark is a safe place to transmit sensitive information	2.87	1.275
Attitude		
Using the iPark is a good idea	4.59	.567
I would feel that Using the iPark is pleasant	4.43	.742
In my opinion, it would be desirable to use the iPark	4.35	.828
In my view, Using free wireless Internet from public parks is a wise idea	4.42	.936
Intention To Use		
I would Use the iPark channels for my government and personal needs.	3.72	1.140
Using the Web from iPark for handling my electronic government transactions is something I would do	3.30	1.207

Notes: SD = Standard Deviation.
Scores range from 1 to 5, where 1 = Strongly Disagree and 5 = Strongly Agree.

- **Dependent Variable:** I would Use the iPark channels for my government and personal needs.

Table 3. Correlations

		I would use the iPark channels for my government and personal needs.
1. I would find the iPark useful	Pearson Correlation	**.178**
	Sig. (1-tailed)	.099
2. Overall, I find the use of the iPark services easy	Pearson Correlation	**.258(*)**
	Sig. (1-tailed)	.030
3. I would rate the speed of Internet/ Response time in the iPark is good	Pearson Correlation	**.405(**)**
	Sig. (1-tailed)	.001
4. Overall, the iPark is a safe place to transmit sensitive information	Pearson Correlation	**.455(**)**
	Sig. (1-tailed)	.000

* Correlation is significant at the 0.05 level (1-tailed)
** Correlation is significant at the 0.01 level (1-tailed)

Table 4. Regression analysis results

			ANOVA			
Model		Sum of Squares	df	Mean Square	F	Sig.
Regression		23.889	4	5.972	6.511	.000(a)
			Regression	*Model*		
Model		R	R Square		Adjusted R Square	Std. Error of the Estimate
1		.589	.347		.294	.958
	Factors	*Affecting*	*Intention To Use*	*iPark*		
Intention To Use iPark Factor		Beta	Standardized Beta		T Statistics	Significance
(Constant)		.069			.083	.934
I would find the iPark useful		.244	.171		1.183	.243
Overall, I find the use of the iPark services easy		.103	.093		.697	.489
I would rate the speed of Internet/ Response time in the iPark is good		.312	.262		2.100	.041
Overall, the iPark is a safe place to transmit sensitive information		.330	.362		2.979	.005

CONCLUSION AND LESSONS LEARNED

E-government is widely accepted and seen as a growing trend worldwide. In the Middle East, most countries have implemented e-government services. However, the growth and adoption of e-government in a country will depend on basic prerequisites such as education, trust, marketing and awareness (Bhattacherjee, 2002; Navarra & Cornford, 2003; Reffat, 2003). The Qatari e-government project serves natural citizens, foreign residents and workers, and business and government agencies. As part of Qatar's wider national e-government program objectives to entice more users to access electronic government services, free wireless Internet access in public parks (iPark) initiative was launched in March 2007.

This article has presented the results of a survey that was conducted in Qatar during the last quarter of 2007 to examine the user adoption of the iPark initiative. The survey was targeted towards iPark users and the results from this research sample provide a representative account of the citizens' perceptions of the iPark project. While the availability and use of Wi-Fi networks continue to increase, for users, Wi-Fi facilitates greater mobility, information access, and flexibility in connectivity, improved efficiency, low cost, ease of use, and new applications, which could change the way they access electronic services, including e-government.

This research showed that there is a positive relationship between the independent variables, usefulness; ease of use, Internet safety, and Internet speed/response time and one dependent variable, intention to use iPark in Qatar. Therefore, it can be concluded that the iPark initiative in Qatar has been successful initially in promoting wider access to the Internet and thereby to electronic government services. Given this context, the author suggests that public parks (iParls) can be used to advertise and market the Qatari e-government national Website and raise e-government awareness among Qatari citizens. While the research findings are encouraging from a practical perspective for the Qatari government, from a theoretical perspective these results confirm that technology acceptance is influenced by key factors such as usefulness, ease of use and efficiency.

Although the survey sample used in this study was small (54), the results provide an early representative perspective of the Qatari iPark initiative from the citizens perspective. More research is planned in the second half of 2008.

REFERENCES

Accenture. (2005). *Leadership in customer service: New expectations, new experiences*. Retrieved from http://www.accenture.com/NR/rdonlyres/F45CE4C8-9330-4450-BB4A-AF4E265C88D4/0/leadershipcust.pdf

Adam, O., Werth, D., & Zangl, F. (2003). *Enabling Pan-European interoperability for the infocitizen*. Paper presented at the 3rd European Conference on E-Government, Trinity College, Dublin.

Al-Kibsi, G., De Boer, K., Mourshed, M., & Rea, N. (2001). Putting citizens online not in line. *The McKinsey Quarterly, 2*(1), 65–73.

Al-Sebie, M., & Irani, Z. (2005). Technical and organisational challenges facing transactional e-government systems: An empirical study. *Electronic Government, an International Journal 2*(3), 247-276.

Al-Shafi, S., & Weerakkody, V. (2007a). Implementing and managing e-government in the state of Qatar: A citizens' perspective. *Electronic Government, an International Journal, 4*(4), 436 - 450

Al-Shafi, S., & Weerakkody, V. (2007b, 24-26/06/2007). *Exploring e-government in the State of Qatar: Benefits, challenges and complexities*. Paper presented at the 2007 European and Mediterranean Conference on Information Systems (EMCIS), Valencia, Spain.

Alina, M. C., & Hae-Dong Lee, D. (2005). E-government: Key success factors for value discovery and realisation. *Electronic Government, an International Journal, 2*(1), 11-25.

Backus, M. (2001). *E-governance in developing countries*. Retrieved from http://www.ftpiicd.org/files/research/briefs/brief1.pdf

Bannister, F. (2005). E-government and administrative power: The one-stop-shop meets the turf war. *Electronic Government: An International Journal, 2*(2), 160–176. doi:10.1504/EG.2005.007092

Basu, S. (2004). E-government and developing countries: An overview. *International Review of Law Computers, 18*(1), 109–132. doi:10.1080/13600860410001674779

Bhattacherjee, A. (2002). Individual trust in online firms: Scale development and initial trust. *Journal of Management Information Systems, 19*(1), 211–241.

Bonham, G., Seifert, J., & Thorson, S. (2001). *The transformational potential of e-government: The role of political leadership*. Paper presented at the 4th Pan European International Relations Conference of the European Consortium for Political Research, University of Kent, Canterbury, U.K.

Burn, F., & Robins, G. (2003). Moving towards e-government: A case study of organisational change processes. *Logistics Information Management, 16*(1), 25–35. doi:10.1108/09576050310453714

Carter, L., & Bélanger, F. (2005). The utilization of e-government services: Citizen trust, innovation and acceptance factors. *Information Systems Journal, 15,* 5–26. doi:10.1111/j.1365-2575.2005.00183.x

Chandler, S., & Emanuels, S. (2002). *Transformation not automation.* Paper presented at the Proceedings Of 2nd European Conference on E-Government, St. Catherine's College Oxford

Chen, C., Tseng, S., & Huang, H. (2006). A comprehensive study of the digital divide phenomenon in Taiwanese government agencies. *International Journal of Internet and Enterprise Management, 4*(3), 244–256. doi:10.1504/IJIEM.2006.010917

Cheng, T., Lam, D., & Yeung, A. (2006). Adoption of internet banking: An empirical study in Hong Kong. *Decision Support Systems, 42,* 1558–1572. doi:10.1016/j.dss.2006.01.002

Chesi, F., Pallotti, M., & Oreste, S. (2005). *A working e-government experience: The Citel project CMG.* Paper presented at the Poland Annual Conference, Warsaw.

Chircu, A. M., & Lee, D. H.-D. (2005). E-government: Key success factors for value discovery and realisation. *E- Government, an International Journal, 2*(1), 11-25.

Cornford, T., & Smithson, S. (1997). *Project research in information systems: A student's guide.* London, UK: Macmillan Press.

Damodaran, L., Nicholls, J., Henney, A., Land, F., & Farbey, B. (2005). The contribution of sociotechnical systems thinking to the effective adoption of e-government and the enhancement of democracy. *Electronic Journal of E-Government, 3*(1), 1–12.

Darrell, W. (2002). *U.S. state and federal e-government full report.* Retrieved from http:// www.insidepolitics.org/egovt02us.pdf

Davis, F. D. (1989). Perceived usefulness, perceived ease of use, and user acceptance of information technology. *Management Information Systems Quarterly, 13,* 319–340. doi:10.2307/249008

Davis, F. D., Bagozzi, R. P., & Warshaw, P. R. (1989). User acceptance of computer technology: A comparison of two theoretical models. *Management Science, 35*(8), 982–1003. doi:10.1287/mnsc.35.8.982

Davison, R. M., Wagner, C., & Ma, L. C. (2005). From government to e-government: A transition model. *Information Technology & People, 18*(3), 280–299. doi:10.1108/09593840510615888

Deloitte Consulting and Deloitte & Touche. (2000). At the dawn of e-government: The citizen as customer. *Deloitte Research Report,* (pp. 88-101).

Dwivedi, Y., & Weerakkody, V. (2007). Examining the factors affecting the adoption of broadband in the Kingdom of Saudi Arabia. *Electronic Government, an International Journal, 4*(1), 43-58.

Evans, G. (2003). *Implementing e-government: An executive report for civil servants and their advisors.* Hampshire, UK: Gower Publishing Limite.

Eyob, E. (2004). E-government: Breaking the frontiers of inefficiencies in the public sector. *Electronic Government, an International Journal, 1*(1), 107-114.

Fang, Z. (2002). E-government in digital era: Concept, practice and development. *International Journal of the Computer. The Internet and Information, 20,* 193–213.

GAO (US Government Accountability Office). (2005*). Information security: Federal agencies need to improve controls over wireless networks.* Retrieved from www. gao.gov/cgi-bin/getrpt?GAO-05-383

Gardner, C., & Amoroso, D. (2004). *Development of an instrument to measure the acceptance of internet technology by consumers.* Paper presented at the 37th Hawaii International Conference on System Sciences, Hawaii, USA.

Goldkuhl, G., & Persson, A. (2006, June 12-14). *From e-ladder to e-diamond - reconceptualising models for public e-services.* Paper presented at the 14th European Conference on Information Systems (ECIS 2006), Göteborg, Sweden.

Gupta, M. P. a. J., D. (2003). E-government evaluation: A framework and case study. *Government Information Quarterly, 20,* 365–387. doi:10.1016/j.giq.2003.08.002

Harris, J. F., & Schwartz, J. (2000). *Anti drug website tracks visitors.*

Hazlett, T. W. (1990). The rationality of U.S. regulation of the broadcast spectrum. *The Journal of Law & Economics, 33,* 133–175. doi:10.1086/467202

Heath, W. (2000). *Europe's readiness for e-government.* Retrieved from http://www. dad.be/library/pdf/kable.pdf

Ho, A. (2002). Reinventing local governments and the 'e-government' initiative. *Public Administration Review, 62*(4), 434–444. doi:10.1111/0033-3352.00197

Holden, S. H., Norris, D. F., & Fletcher, P. D. (2003). E- government at the local level: Progress to date and future issues. *Public Performance and Management Review, 26*(4), 325–344. doi:10.1177/1530957603026004002

IctQatar. (2007). *Free wireless internet in Qatar's public parks.* Retrieved from http://www.ict.gov.qa/output/page422.asp

Ifinedo, P. A. D., R. (2005). Digital divide in Europe: Assessing and comparing the e-readiness of a developed and an emerging economy in the Nordic region. *Electronic Government: An International Journal, 2*(2), 111–133. doi:10.1504/EG.2005.007090

InfoDev. (2002). *The e-Government handbook for developing countries.* Retrieved from http://www.cdt.org/egov/handbook

Jain, P. (2002). The catch-up state: E-government in Japan. *Japanese Studies, 22*(3), 237–255. doi:10.1080/1037139022000036940

Jarvenpaa, S. L., & Tractinsky, N. (1999). Consumer trust in an internet store: A cross-cultural validation. *Journal of Computer-Mediated Communication, 5,* 1–36.

John, J., & Jin-Wan, S. (2005). E-government in South Korea: Planning and implementation. *Electronic Government, an International Journal, 2*(2), 188-204

Karvonen, D., & Parkkinen, J. (1999). *Signs of trust: A semiotic study of trust formation in the Web.* Retrieved from http://www.tml.tkk.fi/~kk/Papers/signs_of_trust_karvonen_parkkinen.pdf

Kurunananda, A., & Weerakkody, V. (2006, October, 2006). *E-government implementation in Sri Lanka: Lessons from the UK.* Paper presented at the 8th International Information Technology Conference, Colombo, Sri Lanka.

Layne, K., & Lee, J. (2001). Developing fully functional e-government: A four-stage model. *Government Information Quarterly, 18*(2), 122–136. doi:10.1016/S0740-624X(01)00066-1

Margetts, H., & Dunleavy, P. (2002). *Cultural barriers to e-government.* (Working Paper): University Collage of London and London School of Economics for National Audit Office.

Moon, M. J. (2002). The evolution of e-government among municipalities: rhetoric or reality. *Public Administration Review, 4,* 424–433. doi:10.1111/0033-3352.00196

Navarra, D. D., & Cornford, T. (2003). *A policy making view of e-government innovations in public governance.* Paper presented at the 9th Americas Conference on Information Systems, Tampa, Florida.

NIST. (1995). *An introduction to computer security: The NIST handbook*

Oreste, S., Chesi, F., & Pallotti, M. (2005, 7-9 June). *E-government: Challenges and opportunities.* Paper presented at the CMG Italy-XIX Annual Conference, Florence, Italy.

Porter Research. (2002). *The second annual report into key government web sites.* Retrieved from http://www.porter-research.com/govt2002.html

Qatar e-Government. (2007). *E- government portal.* Retrieved from http://www. qatar.e.gov.qa

Reffat, R. (2003). *Developing a successful e-government.* (Working Paper): University Of Sydney, Australia.

Reynolds, M. M., & Regio-Micro, M. (2001). The purpose of transforming government-e-government as a catalyst in the information age. *Microsoft E-Government Initiatives.* Retrieved from http://www.netcaucus.org/books/egov2001/pdf/EGovIntr. pdf

Rogers, E. M. (1995). *Diffusion of innovations.* New York.

Sampson, N. (2002). *Bank marketing international: Simplifying in(form)ation online.* Retrieved from http://www.mandoforms.com/news/coverage/bankmarketing.html

Saunders, M., Lewis, P., & Thornhill, A. (2002). *Research methods for business students* (3rd ed.). Harlow, MA: Prentice Hall.

Seifert, J., & Petersen, E. (2002). The promise of all things E? Expectations and challenges of emergent e-government. *Perspectives on Global Development and Technology, 1*(2), 193–213. doi:10.1163/156915002100419808

Silcock, R. (2001). What is e-government? *Hansard Society for Parliamentary Government. Parliamentary Affairs, 54,* 88–101. doi:10.1093/pa/54.1.88

Srinivasan, S. (2004). Role of trust in e-business success. *Information Management & Computer Security, 12*(1), 66–72. doi:10.1108/09685220410518838

The Peninsula Newspaper. (2007). *Minister launches iPark initiative.* Doha, Qatar.

UN. (2005). *World public sector report: Global e-government readiness, from e-government to e-inclusion.* New York.

UN. (2008). *World public sector report: UN e-government survey, from e-government to connected governance.* New York.

UN–DPEPA. (2002). *Benchmarking e-government: A global perspective, assessing the progress of the UN member states.* Retrieved from nettelafrica.org/docs/ NetTel percent20Safari@the percent20Equator percent20(Uganda percent202003)/ Benchmarkingegovt.pdf

Venkatesh, V., & Davis, F. D. (2000). A theoretical extension of the technology acceptance model: Four longitudinal field studies. *Management Science, 46*(2), 186–205. doi:10.1287/mnsc.46.2.186.11926

Venkatesh, V., Morris, M., Davis, G., & Davis, F. (2003). User acceptance of information technology: Toward a unified view. *Management Information Systems Quarterly, 27*(3), 425–478.

Wassenaar, A. (2000). E-governmental value chain models. *DEXA Conference,* (pp. 289-293).

Weerakkody, V., & Choudrie, J. (2005). Exploring e-government in the UK: Challenges, issues and complexities. *Journal of Information Science and Technology, 2*(2), 26–44.

Weerakkody, V., Janssen, M., & Hjort-Madsen, K. (2007). Realising integrated e-government services: A European perspective. *Journal of Cases in E- Commerce, 3*(2), 14-38.

West, D. (2004). E-government and the transformation of service delivery and citizen attitudes. *Public Administration Review, 64*(1), 15–27. doi:10.1111/j.1540-6210.2004.00343.x

Wimmer, M., & Traunmuller, R. (2000). *Trends in e- government: Managing distributed knowledge.* Paper presented at the 11th International Workshop on Database and Expert Systems Applications, New York.

Yin, R. K. (1994). *Case study research—Design and methods* (2nd ed.). London, UK: Sage Publications.

Zakareya, E., & Irani, Z. (2005). E-government adoption: Architecture and barriers. *Business Process Management Journal, 11*(5), 589–611. doi:10.1108/14637150510619902

Zakaria, N., Affendi, S., & Yusof, M. (2001). *The role of human and organizational culture in the context of technological change.* Paper presented at the IEMC '01.

Zhiyuan, F. (2002). E-government in digital era: Concepts, practice and development. *International Journal of the Computer, the Internet and Management, 10*(2), 1-22.

This work was previously published in the Journal of Cases on Information Technology, Volume 10, Issue 3, edited by Mehdi Khosrow-Pour, pp. 21-34, copyright 2008 by IGI Publishing (an imprint of IGI Global).

Compilation of References

(2006b). *State Planning Organization* (pp. 2006–2010). Ankara: Bilgi Toplumu Stratejisi Eylem Planı. [The action plan for information society strategy]

AAL Ambient Assisted Living Programme. (2009). Retrieved from http://www.aal-europe.eu/about-aal

Abdullatif, I. A., & Philip, J. K. (2009). Rethinking models of technology adoption for internet banking: The role of website features. *Journal of Financial Services Marketing, 14*(1), 56–69. doi:10.1057/fsm.2009.4

Abecker, A., Bernardi, A., Hinkelmann, K., Kühn, O., & Sintek, M. (1998). Toward a technology for organisational memories. *IEEE Intelligent Systems, 13*(3), 40–48. doi:10.1109/5254.683209

Abecker, A., Mentzas, G., Ntioudis, S., & Papavassiliou, G. (2003). Business process modelling and enactment for task-specific information support. *Wirtschaftsinformatik, 1*, 977–996.

Abrahamson, E. (2000). Change without pain. *Harvard Business Review*, 75–79.

ACCAN. (2009). *Submission to government 2.0 taskforce secretariat. Australian Communications Consumer Action Network.* Australia: ACCAN.

Accenture. (2005). *Leadership in customer service: New expectations, new experiences.* Retrieved from http://www.accenture.com/NR/rdonlyres/F45CE4C8-9330-4450-BB4A-AF4E265C88D4/0/leadershipcust.pdf

Ad Hoc Committee on E-Democracy of the Council of Europe (CAHDE). (2006). *Introduction to the Ad Hoc Committee on E-democracy (CAHDE).* Retrieved from http://www.coe.int/t/e/integrated_projects/democracy/02_activities/002_e-democracy/00%20Intro%20CAHDE_en.asp

Adam, O., Werth, D., & Zangl, F. (2003). *Enabling Pan-European interoperability for the infocitizen.* Paper presented at the 3rd European Conference on E-Government, Trinity College, Dublin.

Adams, D. A., Nelson, R. R., & Todd, P. A. (1992). Perceived usefulness, ease of use and usage of information technology: A replication. *Management Information Systems Quarterly, 6*(2), 227–247. doi:10.2307/249577

Agre, P. (2002). Real-time politics: The Internet and the political process. *The Information Society, 18*(5), 311–331. doi:10.1080/01972240290075174

Aguini, H. (2004). *Regression analysis for categorical moderators.* New York, NY: The Guilford Press.

AHRC. (2009). *Web accessibility and Government 2.0 Australian Human Rights Commission submission to the Government 2.0 Taskforce – Towards Government 2.0, an issues paper.* Retrieved from www.human-rights.gov.au

Ajzen, I., & Fishbein, M. (1980). *Understanding attitudes and predicting social behaviour.* Prentice-Hall.

Akhter, S. H. (2003). Digital divide and purchase intention: Why demographic psychology matters. *Journal of Economic Psychology, 24*(3), 321–327. doi:10.1016/S0167-4870(02)00171-X

Alina, M. C., & Hae-Dong Lee, D. (2005). E-government: Key success factors for value discovery and realisation. *Electronic Government, an International Journal, 2*(1), 11-25.

Al-Kibsi, G., De Boer, K., Mourshed, M., & Rea, N. (2001). Putting citizens online not in line. *The McKinsey Quarterly, 2*(1), 65–73.

Al-Sebie, M., & Irani, Z. (2005). Technical and organisational challenges facing transactional e-government systems: An empirical study. *Electronic Government, an International Journal 2*(3), 247-276.

Al-Shafi, S., & Weerakkody, V. (2007a). Implementing and managing e-government in the state of Qatar: A citizens' perspective. *Electronic Government, an International Journal, 4*(4), 436 - 450

Al-Shafi, S., & Weerakkody, V. (2007b, 24-26/06/2007). *Exploring e-government in the State of Qatar: Benefits, challenges and complexities.* Paper presented at the 2007 European and Mediterranean Conference on Information Systems (EMCIS), Valencia, Spain.

Ambali, A. R. (2009). Digital divide and its implication on Malaysian e-government: Policy initiatives. In Hakikur, R. (Ed.), *Social and political implications of data mining: Knowledge management in e-government.* Hershey, PA: Information Science Reference (an imprint of IGI Global). doi:10.4018/978-1-60566-230-5.ch016

Ambler, S. W., & Jeffries, R. (2002). *Agile modeling: Effective practices for extreme programming and the unified process.* New York, NY: John Wiley & Sons, Inc.

Amnesty International. (2004). *Country summary: Singapore.* Retrieved May 20, 2005, from http://www.amnestyusa.org/countries/singapore/document.do?id=ar&yr=2005

Anderson, C. (2006). *The long tail: Why the future of business is selling less of more.* New York, NY: Hyperion.

Antonopoulos, C., & Sakellaris, P. (2009). The contribution of information and communication technology investments to Greek economic growth: An analytical growth accounting framework. *Information Economics and Policy, 21*, 171–191. doi:10.1016/j.infoecopol.2008.12.001

Archmann, S., & Kudlacek, I. (2008). Interoperability and the exchange of good practice cases. *European Journal of ePractice, 2.*

Arditi, A., & Rosenthal, B. (1998). Developing an objective definition of visual impairment. *In Vision '96: Proceedings of the International Low Vision Conference* (pp. 331-334). Madrid, Spain: ONCE

Argyris, C., & Schön, D. A. (1978). *Organizational learning: A theory of action perspective.* Reading, MA: Addison-Wesley.

Argyris, C., & Schön, D. A. (1996). *Organizational learning II: Theory, method and practice*. Reading, MA: Addison-Wesley.

Arh, T., Dimovski, V., & Jerman-Blažič, B. (2008). Model of impact of technology-enhanced organizational learning on business performance. V. P. Cunningham & M. Cunningham (Eds.), *Collaboration and the knowledge economy: Issues, applications, case studies*, (pp. 1521–1528). IOS Press.

Arh, T., Pipan, M., & Jerman-Blažič, B. (2006). Virtual learning environment for the support of life-long learning initiative. *WSEAS Transactions on Advances in Engineering Education, 4*(4), 737–743.

Ari-Veikko, A. (2003). Building strong e-democracy: the role of technology in developing democracy for the information age. *Communications of the ACM, 46*(9).

Arnold, J. R. T., & Chapman, S. N. (2003). *Introduction to materials management*. New York, NY: Prentice Hall.

Associated Press. (2005). *Singapore delays launching casino tender*. Retrieved June 20, 2005, from http://www.forbes.com/associatedpress/feeds/ap/2005/06/16/ap2095993.html

Astrid, D., Mitra, A., & David, M. (2008). The role of perceived enjoyment and social norm in the adoption of technology with network externalities. *European Journal of Information Systems, 17*, 4–11. doi:10.1057/palgrave.ejis.3000726

Au, A. (2004, November 11). Casino decision: A bigger question looms. *The Strait Times*. Retrieved August 4, 2009, from http://www.wildsingapore.com/sos/media/041111-2.htm

Australian Bureau of Statistics. (1998). *Paid work: Public sector employment*. Canberra, Australia: Author.

Australian Security Industry Association Limited (ASIAL). (2010a). *Code of professional conduct*. Retrieved November 26, 2010, from http://www.asial.com.au/CodeofConduct

Australian Security Industry Association Limited (ASIAL). (2010b). *CCTV code of ethics*. Retrieved November 26, 2010, from http://www.asial.com.au/CCTVCodeofEthics

Azleen, I., Mohd Zulkeflee, A. R., & Mohd Rushdan, Y. (2009). Taxpayers' attitude in using e-filing system: Is there any significant difference among demographic factors? *Journal of Internet Banking and Commerce, 14*(1), 2–13.

Backus, M. (2001). *E-governance in developing countries*. Retrieved from http://www.ftpiicd.org/files/research/briefs/brief1.pdf

Badr, E. A. (2007, April 1). *ENPO Vice President for IT interview*.

Baldwin, N. (1987). Public versus private: Not that different, not that consequential. *Public Personnel Management, 16*, 181–193.

Banerjee, P., & Chau, P. Y. K. (2004). An evaluative framework for analysing e-government convergence capability in developing countries. *Electronic Government, 1*(1), 29–48. doi:10.1504/EG.2004.004135

Bannister, F. (2005). E-government and administrative power: The one-stop-shop meets the turf war. *Electronic Government: An International Journal, 2*(2), 160–176. doi:10.1504/EG.2005.007092

Barber, B. R. (1984). *Strong democracy: Participatory politics for a new age*. Berkeley, CA: University of California Press.

Compilation of References

Barber, B. R., Mattson, K., & Peterson, J. (1997). *The state of 'electronically enhanced democracy': A survey of the Internet*. New Brunswick, NJ: Walt Whitman Center.

Barkuus, L., & Dey, A. (2003, September 1-5). Location-based services for mobile telephony: A study of users' privacy concerns. In *Proceedings of the 9th IFIP TC13 International Conference on Human-Computer Interaction (INTERACT 2003)*, Zurich, Switzerland (pp. 709-712). New York, NY: ACM Press.

Barney, J. B. (1991). Firm resources and sustained competitive advantage. *Journal of Management, 17*(1), 99–120. doi:10.1177/014920639101700108

Barquin, R. (2010). *Knowledge management in the federal government: A 2010 update*. Retrieved from http://www.b-eye-network.com/view/14527

Barreras, A., & Mathur, A. (2007). Wireless location tracking. In Larson, K. R., & Voronovich, Z. A. (Eds.), *Convenient or invasive- The information age* (1st ed., pp. 176–186). Boulder, CO: Ethica Publishing.

Basu, S. (2004). E-government and developing countries: An overview. *International Review of Law Computers, 18*(1), 109–132. doi:10.1080/13600860410001674779

Batenburg, R. S., & Bongers, F. J. (2001). The role of GSS in participatory policy analysis. A field experiment. *Information & Management, 39*, 15–30. doi:10.1016/S0378-7206(01)00076-3

Bayar, D. (2003). Kamu Mali Yönetimi ve Kontrol Kanunu Ne Getir(m)iyor? [What does public financial management and control law yield (or not)?]. *Maliye Dergisi, 144*, 47–62.

Baym, N. K. (1995). The emergence of community in computer-mediated communication. In Jones, S. (Ed.), *Cybersociety* (pp. 138–163). Newbury Park, CA: Sage.

Becker, H. A., & Hermkens, P. L. J. (Eds.). (1993). *Solidarity of generations. Demographic, economic and social change, and its consequences*. Amsterdam, The Netherlands: Thesis Publishers.

Becker, S. A. (2004). E-government visual accessibility for older adult users. *Social Science Computer Review, 22*(1), 11–23. doi:10.1177/0894439303259876

Beckette-Camaratta, J. (2002, October). *Assessing e-budgeting in US local governments: A case study*. Paper presented at the Korean Association For Public Administration Conference, Seoul, S. Korea.

Bekkers, R. (2001). *Mobile telecommunications standards: GSM, UMTS, TETRA, and ERMES*. Boston, MA: Artech House.

Bensghir, T. K. (2000). Web'deki Belediyelerimiz: Bursa Büyükşehir Belediyesi [Our municipalities on the Web: Bursa metropolitan municipality]. *Çağdaş Yerel Yönetimler, 9*(4), 106-118.

Benyamor, G. (2007, April 10). Türkiye'nin İlk Katılımcı Bütçesi Çanakkale Belediyesinden [First participatory budget in Turkey from Çanakkale municipality]. *Hürriyet Gazetesi*. Retrieved October 22, 2009, from http://hurarsiv.hurriyet.com.tr/goster/haber.aspx?id=6300902&yazarid=20

Bertram, B. (2005). *Blindheit und Sehbehinderung in Deutschland: Ursachen und Häufigkeiten. Der Augenarzt, 6*. Dezember.

Bhatnagar, S. (2006). *Paving the road towards pro poor e-governance*, (pp. 26-27). UNDP, APDIP, UNCRD Workshop Report, Bangkok.

Bhatnagar, S. (2004). *E-Government: From vision to implementation – A practical guide with case studies*. London, UK: Sage Publications Pvt. Ltd.

Bhattacherjee, A. (2002). Individual trust in online firms: Scale development and initial trust. *Journal of Management Information Systems*, *19*(1), 211–241.

Bloodgood, J. M., & Salisbury, W. D. (2001). Understanding the influence of organizational change strategies on information technology and knowledge management strategies. *Decision Support System Journal*, *31*, 55–69. doi:10.1016/S0167-9236(00)00119-6

Bollen, K. A. (1989). *Structural equations with latent variables*. New York, NY: Wiley.

Bongers, F. (2000). *Participatory policy analysis and group support systems*. Tilburg, The Netherlands: Tilburg University.

Bonham, G., Seifert, J., & Thorson, S. (2001). *The transformational potential of e-government: The role of political leadership*. Paper presented at the 4th Pan European International Relations Conference of the European Consortium for Political Research, University of Kent, Canterbury, U.K.

Boulard, G. (2005). RFID: Promise or peril? *State Legislatures*, *31*(10), 22–24.

Bovaird, T. (2003). The changing context of public policy. In Bovarid, T., & Löffler, E. (Eds.), *Public management and governance* (pp. 13–23). London, UK: Routledge.

Bovet, D., & Martha, J. (2000). Value nets: Reinventing the rusty supply chain for competitive advantage. *Strategy and Leadership*, *28*(4), 21–26. doi:10.1108/10878570010378654

Boyd, D. M., & Ellison, N. B. (2008). Social network sites: Definition, history, and scholarship. *Journal of Computer-Mediated Communication*, *13*(1), 210–230. doi:10.1111/j.1083-6101.2007.00393.x

Boyne, G. (2002). Public and private management: What's the difference? *Journal of Management Studies*, *39*(1), 2322–2380. doi:10.1111/1467-6486.00284

Bozeman, B., & Kingsley, G. (1998). Risk culture in public and private organisations. *Public Administration Review*, *58*, 109–118. doi:10.2307/976358

Bray, D. A. (2008). *Information pollution, knowledge overload, limited attention spans, and our responsibilities as IS professionals*. Paper presented at the Global Information Technology Management Association World Conference, Atlanta, GA.

Bray, H. (2003, December 22). Open-source battle is heating up. *Boston Globe*. Retrieved August 4, 2008, from http://www.boston.com/business/technology/articles/

Bretschneider, S. (1990). Management information systems in public and private organizations: An empirical test. *Public Administration Review*, *50*(5), 536–543. doi:10.2307/976784

Brodie, M., & Flournoy, R. E. (2000). Health information, the Internet, and the digital divide. *Health Affairs*, *19*(6), 255–266. doi:10.1377/hlthaff.19.6.255

Bronitt, S. (1997). Electronic surveillance, human rights and criminal justice. *Australian Journal of Human Rights*, *3*(2). Retrieved January 1, 2011, from http://www.austlii.edu.au/au/journals/AUJ1HRights/1997/10.html

Browne, H. (2000). *Accessibility and usability of information technology by the elderly*. Retrieved July 25, 2008, from http://www.otal.umd.edu/UUGuide/hbrowne/

BSI. (2006). *Guide to good practice in commissioning accessible websites. British Standards Institution*. UK: BSI.

Budhiraja, R., & Sameer, S. (2009). *E-readiness assessment (India)*. Retrieved from unpan1.un.org/intradoc/groups/public/documents APCITY/ UNPAN014673.pdf

Budhwar, P., & Boyne, G. (2004). Human resource management in the Indian public and private sectors: An empirical comparison. *International Journal of Human Resource Management, 15*(2), 346–370. doi:10.1080/0958519032000158554

Bugler, D., & Bretschneider, S. (1994). Technology push or program pull: Interest in new information technologies within public organizations. In Bozeman, B. (Ed.), *Public management—The state of the art*. Jossey-Bass.

Burn, F., & Robins, G. (2003). Moving towards e-government: A case study of organisational change processes. *Logistics Information Management, 16*(1), 25–35. doi:10.1108/09576050310453714

Bushell, S. (2006). *Government CIO role still developing, but Australia ahead of pack*. Retrieved from http://www.cio.com/index.php?id=401118652&eid=-601

Bushman, R. M., & Smith, A. J. (2003). Transparency, financial accounting information, and corporate governance. *Federal Reserve Bank of New York Economic Policy Review, 9*(1), 65–87.

Button, M. (2002). *Private policing*. Cullompton, UK: Willan Publishing.

Button, M. (2007). Assessing the regulation of private security across Europe. *European Journal of Criminology, 4*(1), 109–128. doi:10.1177/1477370807071733

Button, M., & John, T. (2002). Plural policing in action: A review of the policing of environmental protests in England and Wales. *Policing and Society, 12*(2), 111–121. doi:10.1080/10439460290002659

Buzzigoli, L. (2002). The new role of statistics in local public administration. In *Proceedings of the Conference on Quantitative Methods in Economics (Multiple Criteria Decision Making XI)* (pp. 28-34). Faculty of Economics and Management, Slovak Agricultural University, Nitra (SK).

Cairo ICT. (2009). Retrieved March 20, 2009, from, www.cairoict.com

Caldwell, C. (2009). *Reflections on the revolution in Europe. Can Europe be the same with different people in it?* London, UK: Allen Lane, Penguin Books.

Campbell, D., & Campbell, S. (2007). *The liberating of Lady Chatterley and other true stories. A history of the NSW Council of Civil Liberties*. Glebe, NSW, Australia: NSW Council of Civil Liberties.

Canadian State Government. (2005). *Free and open source software—Cost comparison model*. Retrieved August 4, 2008, from http://www.tbs-sct.gc.ca/fap-paf/oss-ll/foss-llo/model-eng.asp

Capella, J. (2006). The CIO's first 100 days. *Optimize, 5*(3), 46–51.

Cardoso, J., & Sheth, A. P. (Eds.). (2006). *Semantic Web services, processes and applications*. Springer. doi:10.1007/978-0-387-34685-4

Carr, N. G. (2003). IT doesn't matter. *Harvard Business Review, 81*(5), 41.

Carter, L., & Bélanger, F. (2005). The utilization of e-government services: Citizen trust, innovation and acceptance factors. *Information Systems Journal, 15*, 5–26. doi:10.1111/j.1365-2575.2005.00183.x

Castano, S., Fugini, M., Martella, G., & Samarati, P. (1995). *Database security*. Addison Wesley.

Caudle, S. L., Gorr, W. L., & Newcomer, K. E. (1991). Key information management issues for the public sector. *Management Information Systems Quarterly, 15*(2), 171–188. doi:10.2307/249378

Census Bureau. (2005). *Information quality guidelines, Office of Management and Budget, guidelines for ensuring and maximizing the quality, objectivity, utility, and integrity of information disseminated by federal agencies.* (Section 515). Retrieved from http://www.census.gov/quality/

Çetinkaya, Ö. (2008). Kamu İdarelerinde Hazırlanan Stratejik Planlarda Mevzuata Aykırı Oluşan Durumlar [Legal problems related to strategic plans of public administrations]. *Yaklaşım, 16*(192), 244–248.

Chadwick, A. (2003). Bringing e-democracy back in: Why it matters for future research on e-governance. *Social Science Computer Review, 21*(4), 443–455. doi:10.1177/0894439303256372

Chandler, S., & Emanuels, S. (2002). *Transformation not automation.* Paper presented at the Proceedings Of 2nd European Conference on E-Government, St. Catherine's College Oxford

Chandra, R. (2003). *Information technology in 21st century: Ethics and governance of the internet.* Delhi, India: Kalpaz Publications.

Chaudhuri, S., & Dayal, U. (1997). An overview of data warehousing and OLAP technology. *SIGMOD Record, 26*(1), 65–74. doi:10.1145/248603.248616

Chen, C., Tseng, S., & Huang, H. (2006). A comprehensive study of the digital divide phenomenon in Taiwanese government agencies. *International Journal of Internet and Enterprise Management, 4*(3), 244–256. doi:10.1504/IJIEM.2006.010917

Cheney, S. (2007, May 22). Marina Bay Sands project on track for completion by 2009. *Channel News Asia.* Retrieved November 11, 2007, from http://www.channelnewsasia.com/stories/singaporelocalnews/view/277767/1/.html

Cheng, T., Lam, D., & Yeung, A. (2006). Adoption of internet banking: An empirical study in Hong Kong. *Decision Support Systems, 42*, 1558–1572. doi:10.1016/j.dss.2006.01.002

Chen, J. V., & Ross, W. H. (2007). Individual differences and electronic monitoring at work. *Information Communication and Society, 10*(4), 488–505. doi:10.1080/13691180701560002

Chesi, F., Pallotti, M., & Oreste, S. (2005). *A working e-government experience: The Citel project CMG.* Paper presented at the Poland Annual Conference, Warsaw.

Chia, S. (2004, November 26). Sizing up the casino critic. *The Strait Times.* Retrieved August 4, 2009, from http://www.wildsingapore.com/sos/media/041126-3.htm

Chircu, A. M., & Lee, D. H.-D. (2005). E-government: Key success factors for value discovery and realisation. *E- Government, an International Journal, 2*(1), 11-25.

Choudrie, J., Ghinea, G., & Weerakkody, V. (2004). Evaluating global e-government sites: A view using web diagnostic tools. *Electronic. Journal of E-Government, 2*(2), 105–114.

Chrissafis, T. (2005). *E-democracy: Challenges and actions in the EU*. TED Conference on e-Government Electronic democracy: The challenge ahead, Bolzano, Italy.

Cisco Systems. (1998). *Ontario Government pioneers next generation of e-government*. San Jose, CA: Cisco Systems, Inc.

Clift, S. (2004). *Online consultations and events - Top ten tips for government and civic hosts*. Retrieved November 20, 2004, from http://www.publicus.net

Coakes, J. S., & Lyndall, S. (2007). *SPSS version 16 for Windows: Analysis without anguish*. Australia: Jon Wiley and Sons, Ltd.

Coglianese, C. (2005). The internet and citizen participation in rulemaking. *I/S: A Journal of Law and Policy for the Information Society, 1*(1). Retrieved May 2, 2009, from http://www.is-journal.org/V01I01/I-S,%20V01-I01-P033,%20Coglianese.pdf

Cohen, J. (1989). Deliberative democracy and democratic legitimacy. In Hamlin, A., & Pettit, P. (Eds.), *The good polity* (pp. 17–34). Oxford, UK: Blackwell.

Coleman, S. (2004). Connecting parliament to the public via the Internet: Two case studies of online consultations. *Information Communication and Society, 7*(1), 1–22. doi:10.1080/1369118042000208870

Coleman, S., & Gøtze, J. (2001). *Bowling together: Online public engagement in policy deliberation*. London, UK: Hansard Society.

Collins, C. J., & Smith, K. G. (2006). Knowledge exchange and combination: The role of human resource practices in the performance of high-technology firms. *Academy of Management Journal, 49*(3), 544–560. doi:10.5465/AMJ.2006.21794671

Commonwealth of Virginia Department of Transportation. (2005). *Smart tag/E-Z Pass*. Retrieved from https://smart-tag.com/index.cfm

Compaine, B. M. (Ed.). (2001). *The digital divide: Facing a crisis or creating a myth?* Cambridge, MA: MIT Press.

Cornford, T., & Smithson, S. (1997). *Project research in information systems: A student's guide*. London, UK: Macmillan Press.

Cresswell, A. (2004). *Return on investment in information technology: A guide for managers (Technical Report)*. Albany, NY: Center for Technology in Government, University at Albany.

Crockett, B. K. (2003). CRM strategy: Capabilities for creating the customer experience. In Freeland, J. F. (Ed.), *The ultimate CRM handbook* (pp. 54–63). New York, NY: McGraw-Hill.

Crockett, B. K., & Reed, K. L. (2003). The foundation of insight: Three approaches to customer-centric understanding. In Freeland, J. F. (Ed.), *The ultimate CRM handbook* (pp. 78–84). New York, NY: McGraw-Hill.

Crossan, M., Lane, H. W., & White, R. E. (1999). An organizational learning framework: From intuition to institution. *Academy of Management Review, 24*(3), 522–537.

Cullen, R. (2007). E-government in Canada: Transformation for the digital age. *Information and Polity*, *12*(3), 187–191.

Curtis, K. (2007, November 20). *The social agenda: Law enforcement and privacy*. Paper presented at the International Policing: Towards 2020 Conference, Canberra, ACT, Australia.

Czaja, S. J. (1988). Microcomputers and the elderly. In Helander, M. (Ed.), *Handbook of human-computer interaction* (pp. 581–598). Amsterdam, The Netherlands: Elsevier Science Publishers.

Czaja, S. J., & Sharit, J. (1998). Age differences in attitudes toward computers. *The Journals of Gerontology. Series B, Psychological Sciences and Social Sciences*, *53*, 329–340. doi:10.1093/geronb/53B.5.P329

Dahlberg, L. (2001). Computer-mediated communication and the public sphere: A critical analysis. *Journal of Computer Mediated Communication*, *7*(1). Retrieved December 20, 2005, from http://jcmc.indiana.edu/vol7/issue1/dahlberg.html

Dahl, R. A. (1991). *Democracy and its critics*. New Haven, CT: Yale University Press.

Damodaran, L., Nicholls, J., Henney, A., Land, F., & Farbey, B. (2005). The contribution of sociotechnical systems thinking to the effective adoption of e-government and the enhancement of democracy. *Electronic. Journal of E-Government*, *3*(1), 1–12.

Darrell, W. (2002). *U.S. state and federal e-government full report*. Retrieved from http://www.insidepolitics.org/egovt02us.pdf

Davenport, T. H., De Long, D. W., & Beers, M. C. (1998). Successful knowledge management projects. *Sloan Management Review*, *39*(2), 43–57.

Davidson, R. M., Wagner, C., & Ma, L. C. K. (2005). From government to e-government: A transitional model. *Information Technology & People*, *18*(3), 280–299. doi:10.1108/09593840510615888

David, Y. K. T. (2008). A study of e-recruitment technology adoption in Malaysia. *Industrial Management & Data Systems*, *109*(2), 281–300.

Davis, F. D. (1989). Perceived usefulness, perceived ease of use, and user acceptance of information technology. *Management Information Systems Quarterly*, *13*(3), 319–340. doi:10.2307/249008

Davis, F. D., Bagozzi, R. D., & Warshaw, P. R. (1989). User acceptance of computer technology: A comparison of two theoretical models. *Management Science*, *35*(8), 982–1003. doi:10.1287/mnsc.35.8.982

Davison, R. M., Wagner, C., & Ma, L. C. (2005). From government to e-government: A transition model. *Information Technology & People*, *18*(3), 280–299. doi:10.1108/09593840510615888

Davitt, E. (2010). New laws needed to prosecute invasion of privacy cases. *Australian Security Magazine*. Retrieved from http://www.securitymanagement.com.au/articles/new-laws-needed-to-prosecute-invasion-of-privacy-cases-130.html

Dawes, S., Pardo, T., Simon, S., Cresswell, A. M., LaVigne, M. F., & Andersen, D. F. (2004). *Making smart IT choices: Understanding value and risk in government IT investments* (2nd ed.). Albany, NY: Center for Technology in Government, University at Albany.

Day, J. D., & Wendler, J. C. (1998). Best practice and beyond: Knowledge strategies. *The McKinsey Quarterly*, *1*, 19–25.

De Vaus, D. (2006). *Analyzing social science data*. London, UK: Sage Publications, Ltd.

De Vries, H. J. (2006). IT standards typology. In Jakobs, K. (Ed.), *Information Technology standards and standardization research* (pp. 1–26). Hershey, PA: Idea Group Publishing. doi:10.4018/978-1-59140-938-0.ch001

De Waard, J. (1999). The private security industry in international perspective. *European Journal on Criminal Policy and Research*, *7*, 143–174. doi:10.1023/A:1008701310152

Defence Sector Program. (2007). *Conference report on the regulation of the private security sector in Africa*. Pretoria, South Africa: Institute for Security Studies.

Deloitte Consulting and Deloitte & Touche. (2000). At the dawn of e-government: The citizen as customer. *Deloitte Research Report*, (pp. 88-101).

Denk, M., & Froeschl, K. (2000). The IDARESA data mediation architecture for statistical aggregates. *Research in Official Statistics*, *3*(1), 7–38.

Department of Premier and Cabinet. (2006). *About the office of the chief information officer*. Retrieved from http://www.dpc.vic.gov.au/

Dewan, S., & Kraemer, K. L. (1998). International dimensions of the productivity paradox. *Communications of the ACM*, *41*(8), 56–62. doi:10.1145/280324.280333

Diamantopoulos, A., & Siguaw, J. A. (2000). *Introducing LISREL*. London, UK: SAGE Publications.

DiBella, J. A., & Nevis, E. C. (1998). *How organizations learn – An integrated strategy for building learning capability*. San Francisco, CA: Jossey-Bass.

Dimovski, V. (1994). *Organisational learning and competitive advantage*. Unpublished doctoral dissertation, Cleveland State University.

Dimovski, V., & Colnar, T. (1999). Organizacijsko učenje. *Teorija in Praksa*, *5*(36), 701–722.

Dinevski, D., & Plenković, M. (2002). Modern university and e-learning. *Media. Culture and Public Relations*, *2*, 137–146.

Dobing, B., & Parsons, J. (2006). How UML is used. *Communications of the ACM*, *49*(5), 109–113. doi:10.1145/1125944.1125949

Dobson, J. E., & Fisher, P. F. (2003). Geoslavery. *IEEE Technology and Society Magazine*, 47-52.

Dobson, J. E. (2009). Big Brother has evolved. *Nature*, *458*(7241), 968. doi:10.1038/458968a

Dodgson, M. (1993). Organizational learning: A review of some literatures. *Organization Studies*, *14*(3), 375–394. doi:10.1177/017084069301400303

Dutta, S., Lopez-Claros, A., & Mia, I. (2008). *The global information technology report. INSEAD*. New York, NY: Oxford University Press.

Dwivedi, Y., & Weerakkody, V. (2007). Examining the factors affecting the adoption of broadband in the Kingdom of Saudi Arabia. *Electronic Government, an International Journal*, *4*(1), 43-58.

Earl, M., & Feeny, D. (1995). Is your CIO adding value? *The McKinsey Quarterly*, *2*, 144–161.

EATT Project. (2003). *Equal access to technology training. UK Literature Review*. UK: Royal National Institute of the Blind.

Eckfeldt, B. (2005). What does RFID do for the consumer? *Communications of the ACM,* *48*(9), 77–79. doi:10.1145/1081992.1082024

Economic Planning Unit (EPU). (2008). *The midterm review of the ninth Malaysian plan:* *2006-2010.*

Economic Policy Research Foundation of Turkey. (2007). *İyi Yönetişim İçin Örnek Bir Model: Katılımcı Bütçeleme* [A representative model for good: Participatory budgeting]. Yönetişim Etütleri Programı, Ankara. Retrieved October 21, 2009, from http://www.tepav.org.tr

Economist Intelligence Unit. (2008). *E-readiness rankings 2008: Maintaining momentum.* Retrieved August 10, 2009, from http://graphics.eiu.com/upload/ibm_ereadiness_2008.pdf

eGovernment for Development (eGov4Dev). *Success and failure rates of egovernment in developing/transitional countries.* Retrieved February 20, 2009, from http://www.egov-4dev.org/success/sfrates.shtml

Egypt Post. (2009). Retrieved March 25, 2009, http://egyptianpost.net/en/index.asp

El-Labban, D. N. (2007, April 1). *ENPO Director for International Relations interview.*

Elster, J. (1998). *Deliberative democracy.* Cambridge, UK: Cambridge University Press.

Emil, M. F., & Yılmaz, H. H. (2004). *Mali Saydamlık İzleme Raporu* [Fiscal transparency monitoring report]. Ankara, Turkey: TESEV.

Eppler, M. (2003). *Managing information quality.* Springer Verlag.

ETAAC. (2002). *Electronic tax administration advisory committee (ETAAC) annual report to Congress.*

EU. (2007). *Inclusive e-government: Survey of status and baseline activities.* European Commission, DG Information Society and Media, e-Government unit, December.

EU. (2007). The SOPRANO project. *Information Society Technologies.* Retrieved July 25, 2008, from http://www.soprano-ip.org/

Eurostat. (2009). *Households who have Internet access at home.* Retrieved October 21, 2009, from http://epp.eurostat.ec.europa.eu

Evans, G. (2003). *Implementing e-government: An executive report for civil servants and their advisors.* Hampshire, UK: Gower Publishing Limite.

Evans, K. (2011). *Crime prevention. A critical introduction.* Thousand Oaks, CA: Sage.

Ewijk, C., Kuipers, B., Ter Rele, M., & Westerhout, E. (2000). *Ageing in The Netherlands.* Den Haag, The Netherlands: SDU Uitgevers.

Eyob, E. (2004). E-government: Breaking the frontiers of inefficiencies in the public sector. *Electronic Government, an International Journal, 1*(1), 107-114.

Fabris, P. (1998). *Odd ducks no more.* Retrieved from http://www.cio.com/archive/111598/index.html

Fang, Z. (2002). E-government in digital era: Concept, practice and development. *International Journal of the Computer. The Internet and Information, 20,* 193–213.

Farnham, D., & Horton, S. (1996). Managing public and private organisations. In Farnham, D., & Horton, S. (Eds.), *Managing the new public service.* London, UK: Macmillan.

Farooq, O. (2010). *Company outsources work to Indian prison, plans to employ about 250 inmates.* Retrieved January 21, 2010, from http://www.news.com.au/business/breaking-news/company-outsources-work-to-indian-prison-plans-to-employ-about-250-inmates/story-e6frfkur-1225865832163

Feedback Unit. (2005). *Government consultation portal.* Retrieved January 10, 2005, from http://www.feedback.gov.sg

Feeny, D., Edwards, B., & Simpson, K. (1992). Understanding the CEO/CIO relationship. *Management Information Systems Quarterly, 16*(4), 439–448. doi:10.2307/249730

Fehér, P. (2004). Combining knowledge and change management at consultancies. *Electronic Journal of Knowledge Management, 2*(1), 19–32.

Ferenczi, P. M. (2009, February). You are here. *Laptop Magazine,* 98-102.

Figueiredo, P. N. (2003). Learning processes features: How do they influence inter-firm differences in technological capability - Accumulation paths and operational performance improvement? *International Journal of Technology Management, 26*(7), 655–689. doi:10.1504/IJTM.2003.003451

Fiol, C. M., & Lyles, M. A. (1985). Organizational learning. *Academy of Management Review, 10*(4), 803–813.

Fjermestad, J., & Hiltz, S. R. (1999). An assessment of group support systems experimental research: methodology and results. *Journal of Management Information Systems, 15*(3), 7–149.

Fleming, J., & Grabosky, P. (2009). Managing the demand for police services, or how to control an insatiable appetite. *Policing. Journal of Policy Practice, 3*(3), 281–291.

Foundation, N. Z. (2009). *Digital strategy 2.0 submission - Royal New Zealand Foundation of the Blind.* Auckland, New Zealand.

Fountain, J. (2001). *Building the virtual state: Information technology and institutional change.* Washington, DC: Brookings Institution Press.

Fox, R. (2001). Someone to watch over us: Back to the panopticon? *Criminal Justice, 1*(3), 251–276.

Freeman, E. R. (1984). *Strategic management – A stakeholder approach.* London, UK: Pitman.

Freeman, E. R. (1994). Politics of stakeholder theory: Some future directions. *Business Ethics Quarterly, 4,* 409–422. doi:10.2307/3857340

Fu, J. R., Farn, C. K., & Chao, W. P. (2006). Acceptance of electronic tax filing: A study of taxpayers' intention. *Information & Management, 43,* 109–126. doi:10.1016/j.im.2005.04.001

Funk, J. L., & Methe, D. T. (2001). Market- and committee-based mechanisms in the creation and diffusion of global industry standards: The case of mobile communication. *Research Policy, 30,* 589–610. doi:10.1016/S0048-7333(00)00095-0

GAO (US Government Accountability Office). (2005*). Information security: Federal agencies need to improve controls over wireless networks.* Retrieved from www.gao.gov/cgi-bin/getrpt?GAO-05-383

Gardner, C., & Amoroso, D. (2004). *Development of an instrument to measure the acceptance of internet technology by consumers.* Paper presented at the 37th Hawaii International Conference on System Sciences, Hawaii, USA.

Garrard, G. A. (1998). *Cellular communications: Worldwide market development.* Boston, MA: Artech House.

Gartner. (2006, February). *How to manage the consolidation of government IT infrastructure.* (Gartner Report # G00137407). Stamford, CT: Gartner.

George, D., & Mallery, P. (2001). *SPSS for Windows step by step: A simple guide and reference* (3rd ed.). Boston, MA: Allyn and Bacon.

Gerbing, D. W., & Anderson, J. C. (1988). An updated paradigm for scale development incorporating unidimensionality and measurement error. *JMR, Journal of Marketing Research, 25*, 186–192. doi:10.2307/3172650

Gifford, J. L., Yermack, L., & Owens, C. (1995a). *The development of the E-Zpass specification in New York, New Jersey, and Pennsylvania: A case study of institutional and organizational issues.* Paper presented at the Steps Forward: The Second World Congress on Intelligent Transport Systems, Yokohama, Japan.

Gifford, J. L., Yermack, L., & Owens, C. (1995b). E-ZPass: Case study of institutional and organizational issues in technology standards development. [Washington, DC: Transportation Research Board, National Research Council.]. *Transportation Research Record, 1547*, 10–14.

Gillingham, A. (n.d.). *Bulk mail takes notes and goes hi-tech.*

Gill, M., Owen, K., & Lawson, C. (2010). *Private security, the corporate sector and the police: Opportunities and barriers to partnership working.* Leicester, UK: Perpetuity Research and Consultancy International.

Gilmore, J. H., & Pine, B. J. (2000). *Markets of one: Creating customer-unique value through mass customization.* Boston, MA: Harvard Business School Press.

Goh, S., & Richards, G. (1997). Benchmarking the learning capability of organizations. *European Management Journal, 15*(5), 575–583. doi:10.1016/S0263-2373(97)00036-4

Goldkuhl, G., & Persson, A. (2006, June 12-14). *From e-ladder to e-diamond - reconceptualising models for public e-services.* Paper presented at the 14th European Conference on Information Systems (ECIS 2006), Göteborg, Sweden.

Gomez, J. (2000). *Self-censorship: Singapore's shame.* Singapore: Think Centre.

Govt. of US. (2007). *FY 2007 report to Congress on implementation of The E-Government Act of 2002.* Office of Management and Budget, Government of the USA.

Grabosky, P. (2004). Toward a theory of public/private interaction in policing. In McCord, J. (Ed.), *Beyond empiricism: Institutions and intentions in the study of crime* (*Vol. 13*, pp. 69–82).

Grönlund, Å. (2002). Electronic government - Efficiency, service quality, and democracy. In Grönlund, Å. (Ed.), *Electronic government: Design, applications and management* (p. 62). Hershey, PA: Idea Group Publishing. doi:10.4018/978-1-930708-19-8.ch002

Grönroos, C. (2000). Service management: A management focus for service competition. *International Journal of Service Industry Management, 1*(1), 6–14.

Grossman, L. (1996). *The electronic republic: Reshaping democracy in the information age.* New York, NY: Viking.

Compilation of References

Gupta, M. P. a. J., D. (2003). E-government evaluation: A framework and case study. *Government Information Quarterly*, *20*, 365–387. doi:10.1016/j.giq.2003.08.002

H.D. Vest Financial Services, Inc. (2000, March 22). Acceptance of e-filing gives rise to increased comfort with Web. *Irving, Texas-Business Wire*. Retrieved March 2, 2009, from http://www.icrsurvey.com/Study.aspx?f=hdvest.html

Habermas, J. (1984). *The theory of communicative action, volume one. Reason and the rationalization of society.* Boston, MA: Beacon Press.

Haggie, K., & Kingston, J. (2003). Choosing your knowledge management strategy. *Journal of Knowledge Management Practice*, 1-24.

Hair, J. F., Black, W. C., Babin, B. J., Anderson, R. E., & Tatham, L. R. (2006). *Multivariate data analysis.* Upper Saddle River, NJ: Pearson Education International.

Hammer, M., & Champy, J. (1993). *Reengineering the corporation: A manifesto for business revolution.* HarperBusiness.

Hans, D. D. (2004). Agile knowledge management in practice. In G. Melnik & H. Holz (Eds.), *Proceedings of the 6th International Workshop on Advances in Learning Software Organizations* (LNCS 3096, pp. 137-143).

Hansen, M. T., Nohria, N., & Tierney, T. (1999). What's your strategy for managing knowledge? *Harvard Business Review*, 106–116.

Harfield, C., & Kleiven, M. (2008). Intelligence, knowledge and the reconfiguration of policing. In Harfield, C., MacVean, A., Grieve, J., & Phillips, D. (Eds.), *The handbook of intelligent policing. Consilience, crime control and community safety* (pp. 239–254). Oxford, UK: Oxford University Press.

Harris, J. F., & Schwartz, J. (2000). *Anti drug website tracks visitors.*

Harris, R., & Kost, J. (2008, January). Dealing with roadblocks to centralized government IT. *Gartner Industrial Research*, G00151858. Retrieved August 4, 2008, from http://www.Cio.state.nm.us/content/cioCouncil/governmentITConsolidationDealingWithRoadblocks.pdf

Hatzopoulos, M., Karali, I., & Viglas, E. (1998). Attacking diversity in NSIs' storage infrastructure: The *ADDSIA* approach. In *Proceedings of the International Seminar on New Techniques and Technologies in Statistics* (pp. 229-234). Sorrento.

Hayes, B. (2009). *NeoConOpticon. The EU security-industrial complex.* Retrieved January 20, 2011, from http://www.statewatch.org/analyses/neoconopticon-report.pdf

Hayes, J. (2002). *The theory and practice of change management.* Basingstoke, UK: Palgrave.

Hayne, A., & Vinecombe, C. (2008, February). *IT security and privacy – The balancing act.* Paper presented at the Securitypoint 2008 Seminar.

Hazlett, T. W. (1990). The rationality of U.S. regulation of the broadcast spectrum. *The Journal of Law & Economics*, *33*, 133–175. doi:10.1086/467202

Heath, W. (2000). *Europe's readiness for e-government.* Retrieved from http://www.dad.be/library/pdf/kable.pdf

Heeks, R. (2000). Government data: Understanding the barriers to citizen access and use. *iGovernment Working Paper Series (Paper No 10).* Manchester, UK: Institute for Development Policy and Management.

Heeks, R. (2003). *E-government for development: Causes of e-government success and failure, factor model.* IDPM, University of Manchester UK. Retrieved March 2, 2009, from http://www.egov4dev.org/causesfactor.html

Heeks, R. (2006a). *Most E-government projects-for-development fail: How can risk be reduced?* Working Paper 14, IDPM, University of Manchester, UK.

Heeks, R., & Molla, A. (2009b). *Impact assessment of ICT-for-development projects: A compendium of approaches.* Working Paper 36, IDPM, University of Manchester, UK.

Heeks, R. (2006). *Implementing and managing e-government.* London, UK: Sage.

Helfert, M., & Herrmann, C. (2005). Introducing data-quality management in data warehousing. In Wang, R. Y., Pierce, E., Madnick, S. E., & Fisher, C. W. (Eds.), *Information quality.* AMIS.

Henry, P. (2001). E-learning technology, content and services. *Education + Training, 43*(4), 251–259.

Herbert, W. A. (2010, June 7-9). Workplace consequences of electronic exhibitionism and voyeurism. In K. Michael (Ed.), In *Proceedings of the IEEE Symposium on Technology and Society (ISTAS2010),* Wollongong, NSW, Australia (pp. 300-308). IEEE Society on Social Implications of Technology.

Herbert, W. A. (2006). No direction home: Will the law keep pace with human tracking technology to protect individual privacy and stop geoslavery? *I/S. Journal of Law and Policy, 2*(2), 409–473.

Hersey, P., & Blanchard, K. H. (1977). *Managing of organizational behavior: Utilizing human resources.* Englewoods Cliffs, NJ: Prentice Hall.

Hesson, M., & Al-Ameed, H. (2007). Online security evaluation process for new e-services. *Journal of Business Process Management, 13*(2), 223–245. doi:10.1108/14637150710740473

Himma, K. (2007). The concept of information overload: A preliminary step in understanding the nature of a harmful information-related condition. *Ethics and Information Technology, 9*(4), 259–272. doi:10.1007/s10676-007-9140-8

Hinnant, C. C., & O'Looney, J. A. (2003). Examining pre-adoption interest in online innovations: An exploratory study of E-service personalization in the public sector. *IEEE Transactions on Engineering Management, 50*(4), 436–447. doi:10.1109/TEM.2003.820133

HKBU. (2006). *HKBU's views & comment on the digital 21 strategy 2007.* Hong Kong: The Hong Kong Blind Union.

Hmelo-Silver, C. (2004). Problem based learning: what and how do students learn. *Educational Psychology Review, 16*(3), 235–266. doi:10.1023/B:EDPR.0000034022.16470.f3

Ho, A. (2002). Reinventing local governments and the 'e-government' initiative. *Public Administration Review, 62*(4), 434–444. doi:10.1111/0033-3352.00197

Hoffmann, E. (1995). We must use administrative data for official statistics—But how should we use them? *Statistical Journal of the United Nations/ECE, 12*, 41-48.

Holden, S. H., Norris, D. F., & Fletcher, P. D. (2003). E- government at the local level: Progress to date and future issues. *Public Performance and Management Review, 26*(4), 325–344. doi:10.1177/15309576030 26004002

Holsapple, C. W. (2003). Knowledge and its attributes. In *Handbook on knowledge management 1: Knowledge matters*. Heidelberg, Germany: Springer-Verlag.

Hong, W., Thong, J. Y. L., Wong, W. M., & Tam, K. Y. (2002). Determination of user acceptance of digital libraries: An empirical examination of individual difference and system characteristic. *Journal of Management Information Systems, 18*(3), 97–124.

Hoo, A. T. K. (2002). reinventing local governments and the e-government initiative. *Public Administration Review, 62*(4), 434–444. doi:10.1111/0033-3352.00197

Hoogenboom, B. (2006). Grey intelligence. *Crime, Law, and Social Change, 45*, 373–381. doi:10.1007/s10611-006-9051-3

Hoogenboom, B. (2010). *The governance of policing and security. Ironies, myths and paradoxes*. Houndmills, UK: Palgrave Macmillan. doi:10.1057/9780230281233

Huang, Z. (2006). E-government practices at local levels: An analysis of U.S. counties' websites. *Issues in Information Systems, 7*(2), 165–170.

Huber, G. P. (1991). Organizational learning: The contributing processes and the literatures. *Organization Science, 2*(1), 88–115. doi:10.1287/orsc.2.1.88

Hummer, D., & Nalla, M. (2003). Modelling future relations between the private and public sectors of law enforcement. *Criminal Justice Studies, 16*(2), 87–96. doi:10.1080/0888431 032000115628

Hummerston, M. (2007, October 2). *Emerging issues in privacy*. Paper presented at the SOCAP- Swinburne Consumer Affairs Course.

Iansiti, M., & Levien, R. (2004). *The keystone advantage: What the new dynamics of business ecosystems mean for strategy, innovation and sustainability*. Boston, MA: Harvard Business School Press.

IctQatar. (2007). *Free wireless internet in Qatar's public parks*. Retrieved from http://www.ict.gov.qa/output/page422.asp

Ifinedo, P. A. D., R. (2005). Digital divide in Europe: Assessing and comparing the e-readiness of a developed and an emerging economy in the Nordic region. *Electronic Government: An International Journal, 2*(2), 111–133. doi:10.1504/EG.2005.007090

Igbaria, M., Livari, J., & Marogahh, H. (1995). Why do individuals use computer technology: A finish case study. *Journal of International Management, 29*, 227–238.

Igbaria, M., Zinatelli, N., Cragg, D., & Cavaye, A. (1997). Personal computing acceptance factors in small firms: A structural equation model. *Management Information Systems Quarterly, 29*(3), 278–305.

InfoDev. (2002). *The e-Government handbook for developing countries*. Retrieved from http://www.cdt.org/egov/handbook

Information Quality I. (2005). *Principles and foundation, the MIT total data quality management program*. (2005, October 31-November 4). Retrieved from http://web.mit.edu/tdqm/www/index.shtml

Information Technology Division. (2006a). *Facts about information technology division.* Retrieved November 18, 2006 from http://www.mass.gov/portal/site/massgovportal/

Information Technology Division. (2006b). *Information domain – Enterprise technical reference model v.3.5.* Retrieved August 4, 2008, from http://www.mass.gov/portal/site/massgovportal/

Inkpen, A., & Crossan, M. M. (1995). Believing is seeing: Organizational learning in joint ventures. *Journal of Management Studies, 32*(5), 595–618. doi:10.1111/j.1467-6486.1995.tb00790.x

Inland Revenue Board. Malaysia (IRBM). (2008). *The e-filing website.* Retrieved August 21, 2009, from http://e-hasil.org.my/index/e-hasil.asp

Inmon, W. (1996). The data warehouse and data mining. *Communications of the ACM, 39*(11), 49–50. doi:10.1145/240455.240470

Interactive Policy Making Online Consultations website. (2007). *Report on interactive policy making.* Retrieved from http://ec.europa.eu/yourvoice/ipm/index_en.htm

International Brotherhood of Teamsters. (2001). *Local 436 demands entry ramp to Ohio Turnpike.* Retrieved April 15, 2007, from http://www.teamster.org/01newsb/hn_011011_2.htm

International Brotherhood of Teamsters. (2005). *Ohio Turnpike strike possibility looms large.* Retrieved April 15, 2007, from http://www.teamster.org/05news/hn_050118_3.htm

International Monetary Fund. (2007). *Manual on fiscal transparency.* Washington, DC: Fiscal Affairs Department.

Internet World Stats. (2009). *Asia Internet usage stats and population statistics.* Retrieved August 14, 2009, from http://www.internetworldstats.com/stats3.htm

Iqbal, M. U., & Lim, S. (2003). Legal and ethical implications of GPS vulnerabilities. *Journal of International Commercial Law and Technology, 3*(3), 178–187.

Irani, Z., Dwivedi, Y. K., & Williams, M. D. (2008). Understanding consumer adoption of broadband: An extension of the technology acceptance model. *The Journal of the Operational Research Society,* 1–13.

IRB. (2001). *Annual report 2001.* Malaysia: Inland Revenue Board.

IRB. (2006). *Annual report 2006.* Malaysia: Inland Revenue Board.

IST policy on the objective of ICT research for innovative Government website. (2004). Retrieved from http://cordis.europa.eu/ist/so/govt/home.html

IST-507767–QUALEG. (2004). *Deliverable 4.1 "marketing research."*

ITU. (2006a). *World telecommunication/ict development report 2006.*

ITU. (2007b). *World information society report, beyond WSIS.*

Izatun, S. (2008, April 22). Almost half a million taxpayers now using e-filing. *The Star.*

Jackson, C. M., Chow, S., & Leitch, R. A. (1997). Toward an understanding of the behavioural intention to use an information system. *Decision Sciences, 28*(2), 357–389. doi:10.1111/j.1540-5915.1997.tb01315.x

Jain, P. (2002). The catch-up state: E-government in Japan. *Japanese Studies*, *22*(3), 237–255. doi:10.1080/1037139022000036940

Jalava, J., & Pohjola, M. (2002). Economic growth in the new economy: Evidence from advanced economies. *Information Economics and Policy*, *14*, 189–210. doi:10.1016/S0167-6245(01)00066-X

Jalava, J., & Pohjola, M. (2007). The role of electricity and ICT in economic growth: Case Finland. *Explorations in Economic History*, *45*, 270–287. doi:10.1016/j.eeh.2007.11.001

Jarillo, J. C. (1988). On strategic networks. *Strategic Management Journal*, *9*(1), 31–41. doi:10.1002/smj.4250090104

Jarke, M., Lenzerini, M., Vassiliou, Y., & Vassiliadis, P. (2003). *Fundamentals of data warehouses*. Berlin, Germany: Springer-Verlag.

Jarvenpaa, S. L., & Tractinsky, N. (1999). Consumer trust in an internet store: A cross-cultural validation. *Journal of Computer-Mediated Communication*, *5*, 1–36.

Jarvenpaa, S., Tiller, E. H., & Simons, R. (2003). Regulation and the Internet: Public choice insights for business organizations. *California Management Review*, *46*(1), 72–85.

Jashapara, A. (2004). *Knowledge management: An integrated approach*. London, UK: Prentice Hall/Pearson Education Limited.

Jen, R., F., Cheng, K. F., Wen, P. C. (2006). Acceptance of electronic tax filing: A study of taxpayer intentions. *Information & Management*, *43*(1), 109–126. doi:10.1016/j.im.2005.04.001

Joh, E. (2006). The forgotten threat: Private policing and the state. *Indiana Journal of Global Legal Studies*, *13*(2), 357–398. doi:10.2979/GLS.2006.13.2.357

John, J., & Jin-Wan, S. (2005). E-government in South Korea: Planning and implementation. *Electronic Government, an International Journal*, *2*(2), 188-204

Johnston, L. (1999). Private policing in context. *European Journal on Criminal Policy and Research*, *7*, 175–196. doi:10.1023/A:1008753326991

Johnston, L., & Shearing, C. (2003). *Governing security*. London, UK: Routledge.

Jones, G. (2010, June 3). NSW government recording features for facial recognition. *Daily Telegraph*.

Jones, G. R. (2000). *Organizational theory* (3rd ed.). New York, NY: Prentice Hall.

Jones, Q., & Rafaeli, S. (2000). Time to split, virtually: Discourse architecture and community building as means to creating vibrant virtual publics. *Electronic Markets: The International Journal of Electronic Commerce and Business Media*, *10*(4), 214–223.

Jones, T., & Newburn, T. (2002). The transformation of policing? Understanding current trends in policing systems. *The British Journal of Criminology*, *42*, 129–146. doi:10.1093/bjc/42.1.129

Jöreskog, K. G., & Sörbrom, D. (1993). *LISREL 8: Structural equation modelling with the SIMPLIS command language*. London, UK: Lawrence Erlbaum Associates Publishers.

Junaidah, H. (2008). Learning barriers in adopting ICT among selected working women in Malaysia. *Gender in Management: An International Journal, 23*(5), 317–336. doi:10.1108/17542410810887356

Justice, J. B., Melitski, J., & Smith, D. L. (2006). E-government as an instrument of fiscal accountability and responsiveness: Do the best practitioners employ the best practices? *American Review of Public Administration, 36*(3), 301–322. doi:10.1177/0275074005283797

Kairys, D., & Shapiro, J. (1980). Remedies for private intelligence abuses: legal and ideological barriers. *Review of Law and Social Change. New York University, 10,* 233–248.

Kaplan, R. S., & Norton, D. P. (1992). Balanced scorecard – Measures that drive performance. *Harvard Business Review, 1–2,* 71–79.

Karim, M. R., & Nazariah, A. K. (2003). *E-government in Malaysia.* Kuala Lumpur, Malaysia: Pelanduk Publications (M) Sdn. Bhd.

Karvonen, D., & Parkkinen, J. (1999). *Signs of trust: A semiotic study of trust formation in the Web.* Retrieved from http://www.tml.tkk.fi/~kk/Papers/signs_of_trust_karvonen_parkkinen.pdf

Kaupins, G., & Minch, R. (2005, January 3-6). Legal and ethical implications of employee location monitoring. In *Proceedings of the 38th Hawaii International Conference on System Sciences (HICSS'05),* Big Island, HI (pp. 1-10).

Kearns, I., Bend, J., & Stern, B. (2002). *E-participation in local government.* London, UK: Institute for Public Policy Research.

Kempa, M., Stenning, R., & Wood, J. (2004). Policing communal spaces. A reconfiguration of the "mass property" hypothesis. *The British Journal of Criminology, 44*(4), 562–581. doi:10.1093/bjc/azh027

Kerr, M., Stattin, H., & Trost, K. (1999). To know you is to trust you: Parents' trust is rooted in child disclosure of information. *Journal of Adolescence, 22*(6), 737–752. doi:10.1006/jado.1999.0266

Kertzman, E., Janssen, R., & Ruster, M. (2003). E-business in healthcare. Does it contribute to strengthen consumer interest? *Health Policy (Amsterdam), 64,* 63–73. doi:10.1016/S0168-8510(02)00139-2

Kettl, D. F. (1997). The global revolution in public management: Driving themes, missing links. *Journal of Public Policy Analysis and Management, 16*(3), 446–462. doi:10.1002/(SICI)1520-6688(199722)16:3<446::AID-PAM5>3.0.CO;2-H

Kettl, D. F. (2005). *The global public management revolution.* Washington, DC: Brookings Institution.

Khalil, T. M. (1993). Management of technology and the creation of wealth. *Industrial Engineering (American Institute of Industrial Engineers), 25*(9), 16–17.

Khalil, T. M. (2000). *Management of technology: The key to competitiveness and wealth creation.* Singapore: McGraw Hill.

Kickert, W. (2007). Public management reforms in countries with a Napoleonic state model: France, Italy and Spain. In Pollitt, C., van Thiel, S., & Homburg, V. (Eds.), *New public management in Europe: Adaptation and alternatives* (pp. 26–51). Great Britain: Palgrave MacMillan.

Compilation of References

Kirchner, P. A., & Pass, F. (2001). Web enhanced higher education: A Tower of Babel. *Computers in Human Behavior*, *17*(4), 347–353. doi:10.1016/S0747-5632(01)00009-7

Klimkó, G. (2001). *Mapping organisational knowledge.* Unpublished doctoral dissertation, Corvinus University, Budapest, Hungary.

Klitgaard, R. (1998). International cooperation against corruption. *Finance & Development*, *35*(1), 3–6.

Kő, A., & Klimkó, G. (2009). Towards a framework of information technology tools for supporting knowledge management. In Noszkay, E. (Ed.), *The capital of intelligence - The intelligence of capital* (pp. 65–85). Budapest, Hungary: Foundation for Information Society.

Komiya, M. (1993). Personal communications in Japan and its implications for Asia. *Pan-European Mobile Communications, Spring*, 52-55.

Kopits, G., & Craig, J. (1998). *Transparency in government operations.* Occasional Paper. Washington, DC: IMF.

Korteland, E., & Bekkers, V. (2007). Diffusion of e-government innovations in the Dutch public sector: The case of digital community policing. *Information Polity*, *12*(3), 139–150.

Kotter, J. P. (1995). Leading change: Why transformation efforts fail. *Harvard Business Review*, 59–67.

Kotter, J. P. (1997). On leading change: A conversation with John P. Kotter. *Strategy and Leadership*, *25*(1), 18–23. doi:10.1108/eb054576

Kriss, E. (2005). *Informal comments on open document.* Retrieved August 4, 2008, from http://www.mass.gov/eoaf/open_formats_comments.html

Kuppusamy, M., Raman, M., & Lee, G. (2009). Whose ICT investment matters to economic growth: Private or public? The Malaysian perspective. *The Electronic Journal on Information Systems in Developing Countries*, *37*(7), 1–19.

Kuppusamy, M., & Shanmugam, B. (2007). Information communication technology and economic growth in Malaysia. *Review of Islamic Economics*, *11*(2), 87–100.

Kurunananda, A., & Weerakkody, V. (2006, October, 2006). *E-government implementation in Sri Lanka: Lessons from the UK.* Paper presented at the 8th International Information Technology Conference, Colombo, Sri Lanka.

La Porte, T. M., Demchak, C. C., & De Jong, M. (2002). Democracy and bureaucracy in the age of the Web: Empirical findings and theoretical speculations. *Administration & Society*, *34*, 411–446. doi:10.1177/0095399702034004004

Lai, M. L., Siti, N. S. O., & Ahamed, K. M. (2004). Towards an electronic filing system: A Malaysian survey. *eJournal of Tax Research*, *5*(2), 1-11.

Lai, M. L., Siti, N. S. O., & Ahamed, K. M. (2005). Tax practitioners and the electronic filing system: An empirical analysis. *Academy of Accounting and Financial Studies Journal*, *9*(1), 93–109.

Lambrinoudakisa, C., Gritzalisa, S., Dridib, F., & Pernul, G. (2003). Security requirements for e-government services: A methodological approach for developing a common PKI-based security policy. *Computer Communications*, *26*, 1873–1883. doi:10.1016/S0140-3664(03)00082-3

Lam, S. S. K. (1998). Organizational performance and learning styles in Hong Kong. *The Journal of Social Psychology*, *138*(3), 401–403. doi:10.1080/00224549809600392

Landsberg, M. (2003). *The Tao of coaching: Boost your effectiveness at work by inspiring and developing those around you*. Croydon, UK: Harper Collins.

Lauriat, S. M. (2007). *Advanced AJAX: Architecture and best practices*. Upper Saddle River, NJ: Prentice Hall PTR.

Layne, K., & Lee, J. (2001). Developing fully functional e-government: A four-stage model. *Government Information Quarterly*, *18*(2), 122–136. doi:10.1016/S0740-624X(01)00066-1

Lee, S. M. (2003). Korea: From the land of morning calm to ICT hotbed. *Journal of the Academy Management Executive (USA)*, *17*(2).

Lee, W. C. Y. (2001). *Lee's essentials of wireless communications*. New York, NY: McGraw-Hill.

Lei, D., Hitt, M. A., & Bettis, R. (1996). Dynamic core competencies through meta-learning and strategic context. *Journal of Management*, *22*(4), 549–569. doi:10.1177/014920639602200402

Lei, D., Slocum, J. W., & Pitts, R. A. (1999). Designing organizations for competitive advantage: The power of unlearning and learning. *Organizational Dynamics*, *27*(3), 24–38. doi:10.1016/S0090-2616(99)90019-0

Leman-Langlois, S., & Shearing, C. (2009). *Human rights implications of new developments in policing*. Retrieved January 20, 2011, from http://www.crime-reg.com

Leonard-Barton, D. (1992). The factory as a learning laboratory. *Sloan Management Review*, *34*(1), 23–38.

Levin, A., Foster, M., Nicholson, M. J., & Hernandez, T. (2006). *Under the radar? The employer perspective on workplace privacy*. Toronto, Canada: Ryerson University. Retrieved March 2009 from http://www.ryerson.ca/tedrogersschool/news/archive/UnderTheRadar.pdf

Levin, A., Foster, M., West, B., Nicholson, M. J., Hernandez, T., & Cukier, W. (2008). *The next digital divide: Online social network privacy*. Toronto, ON, Canada: Ryerson University, Ted Rogers School of Management, Privacy and Cyber Crime Institute. Retrieved March 2009 from http://www.ryerson.ca/tedrogersschool/privacy/Ryerson_Privacy_Institute_OSN_Report.pdf

Levitt, B., & March, J. G. (1998). Organizational learning. *Annual Review of Sociology*, *14*, 319–340. doi:10.1146/annurev.so.14.080188.001535

Lewis, S. (2008). Intelligent partnership. In Harfield, C., MacVean, A., Grieve, J., & Phillips, D. (Eds.), *The handbook of intelligent policing. Consilience, crime control and community safety* (pp. 151–160). Oxford, UK: Oxford University Press.

Linaa Jensen, J. (2003). Public spheres on the Internet: Anarchic or government sponsored – A comparison. *Scandinavian Political Studies, 26*(4), 349–374. doi:10.1111/j.1467-9477.2003.00093.x

Lippert, R., & O'Connor, D. (2006). Security intelligence networks and the transformation of contract security. *Policing and Society, 16*(1), 50–66. doi:10.1080/10439460500399445

Lippitt, R., Watson, J., & Westley, B. (1958). *The dynamics of planned change*. New York, NY: Harcourt Brace.

Lisbon Strategy. (2000). *Lisbon European Council 23 and 24 March 2000 presidency conclusions*. Retrieved from http://www.europarl.europa.eu/summits/lis1_en.htm

Livari, J., & Igbaria, M. (1997). Determinants of user participation: A Finnish survey. *Behaviour & Information Technology, 16*(2), 111–121. doi:10.1080/014492997119950

Loukis, E., & Tsouma, N. (2002). Critical issues of information systems management in the Greek public sector. *The International Journal of Government and Democracy in the Information Age, 17*(1), 65–83.

Macintosh, A., & Whyte, A. (2002). *An evaluation framework for e-consultations?* Paper presented at the International Association for Official Statistics conference, London, UK.

Macintosh, A., Robson, E., Smith, E., & Whyte, A. (2003). Electronic democracy and young people. *Social Science Computer Review, 21*(1), 43–54. doi:10.1177/0894439302238970

MacManus, R., & Porter, J. (2005): *Web 2.0 for design: Bootstrapping the social web*. Retrieved April 15th 2008, from http://www.digital-web.com/articles/web_2_for_designers

Maglio, P., & Spohrer, J. (2008). Fundamentals of service science. *Journal of the Academy of Marketing Science, 36*, 18–20. doi:10.1007/s11747-007-0058-9

Manasco, B. (1996). Leading firms develop knowledge strategies. *Knowledge Inc., 1*(6), 26–35.

Margetts, H., & Dunleavy, P. (2002). *Cultural barriers to e-government*. (Working Paper): University Collage of London and London School of Economics for National Audit Office.

Marx, G. (1987). The interweaving of public and private police undercover work. In Shearing, C., & Stenning, P. (Eds.), *Private policing* (pp. 172–193). Thousand Oaks, CA: Sage.

Mathieson, K. (1991). Predicting user intention: Comparing the technology acceptance model with the theory of planned behaviour. *Information Systems Research, 12*(3), 173–191. doi:10.1287/isre.2.3.173

Matthew, W. (2006). *E-file goals too ambitious*. FWC.com. Retrieved on 2/11/2009, from http://fcw.com/articles/2006/02/27/efile-goal-too-ambitious.aspx

Mayer, I. (1997). *Debating technologies. A methodological contribution to the design and evaluation of participatory policy analysis*. Tilburg, The Netherlands: Tilburg University Press.

Mayer, R. N. (2003). Technology, families, and privacy: Can we know too much about our loved ones? *Journal of Consumer Policy, 26*(4), 419–439. doi:10.1023/A:1026387109484

Mayo, S. (2004). *E-Government case study analysis: Unisys lays a services-oriented architecture foundation for the GSA. IDC Report, October (No. 32079)*. Framingham, MA: IDC.

Mc Clure, D. L. (2000). *Federal initiatives are evolving rapidly but they face significant challenges.* Testimony, United States General Accounting Office, GAO/T-AIMD/GGD-00-179.

McCahill, M. (2008). Plural policing and CCTV surveillance. *Sociology of Crime. Law and Deviance, 10*, 199–219. doi:10.1016/S1521-6136(07)00209-6

McGinley, I. (2007). Regulating "rent-a-cops" post 9/11: Why the Private Security Officer Employment Authorisation Act fails to address homeland security concerns. *Cardozo Public Law. Policy and Ethics Journal, 6*(129), 129–161.

Md Nor, K., & Pearson, J. M. (2007). The influence of trust on internet banking acceptance. *Journal of Internet Banking and Commerce, 12*(2), 2–10.

Melarkode, A., From-Poulson, M., & Warnakulasuriya, S. (2004). Delivering agility through IT. *Business Strategy Review, 15*(3), 45–50. doi:10.1111/j.0955-6419.2004.00327.x

Mentzas, G., Draganidis, F., & Chamopoulou, P. (2006). *An ontology based tool for competency management and learning path.* Paper presented at the I-KNOW Conference, Graz, Austria.

Michael, K., Mcnamee, A., & Michael, M. G. (2006, July 25-27). The emerging ethics of human-centric GPS tracking and monitoring. In *Proceedings of the International Conference on Mobile Business (ICMB2006),* Copenhagen, Denmark (pp. 34-42). Washington, DC: IEEE Computer Society.

Michael, M. G., & Michael, K. (2009). Uberveillance: Microchipping people and the assault on privacy. *Quadrant, 53*(3), 85–89.

Mihyar, H., & Hayder, A. (2007). Online security evaluation process for new e-services. *Journal of Business Process Management, 13*(2), 223–246. doi:10.1108/14637150710740473

Miner, A. S., & Mezias, S. J. (1996). Ugly duckling no more: Pasts and futures of organizational learning research. *Organization Science, 7*(1), 88–99. doi:10.1287/orsc.7.1.88

Ministry of Finance. (2006). *Belediyeler Seçilmiş Mali Büyüklükler.* [Municipal fiscal accounts]. Ankara. Retrieved October 21, 2009, from http://www.muhasebat.gov.tr

Ministry of Finance. (2009). *Kamu Hesapları Bülteni* [Public accounts report]. Ankara. Retrieved October 21, 2009, from http://www.muhasebat.gov.tr

Ministry of Information Technology. (2009). Retrieved from http://www.mit.gov.in/default.aspx?id=832

Ministry of Trade and Industry. (2004). *Social safeguards for integrated resort with casino gaming.* Singapore: Ministry of Trade and Industry. Retrieved June 20, 2005, from http://app.mcys.gov.sg/web/corp_press_story.asp?szMod=corp&szSubMod=press&qid=674

Ministry of Trade and Industry. (2005). *Proposal to develop integrated resorts.* Singapore: Ministry of Trade and Industry. Retrieved August 20, 2009, from http://app.mti.gov.sg/data/pages/606/doc/Ministerial%20Statement%20-%20PM%2018apr05.pdf

Mintzberg, H. (1990). Strategy formation: Schools of thought. In Frederickson, J. W. (Ed.), *Perspectives of strategic management* (pp. 105–235). New York, NY: Harper Business.

Mintzberg, H. (1991). The effective organization: Forces and forms. *Sloan Management Review, 32*(2), 57–67.

Mishra, D. C. (2007). *Sixty years of development of e-governance in India (1947-2007). Are there lessons for developing countries?* ICEGOV2007, December 10-13, Macao, ACM. 978-1-59593-822-0/07/12

Misra, H. K. (2009). Managing rural citizen interfaces in e-governance systems: A study in Indian context. *Proceedings of ACM ICE-GOV2009*, November 10-13, 2009, Bogota, Colombia, (pp. 155-162).

Misra, H. K., & Hiremath, B. N. (2009). *Livelihood perspective of rural information infrastructure and e-governance readiness in India: A case based study.* IRMA Working Paper Series 215, IRMA, Anand, India.

Misra, H. K. (2009). *Governance of rural information and communication technology: Opportunities and challenges.* New Delhi, India: Academic Foundation.

Misra, H. K., & Hiremath, B. N. (2006). Citizen-led participatory e-governance initiatives: An architectural perspective. IIM Lucknow. *Metamorphosis, 5*(2), 133–148.

Mock, D. (2005). *The Qualcomm equation: How a fledgling telecom company forged a new path to big profits and market dominance.* New York, NY: AMACOM.

Moon, M. J. (2002). The evolution of e-government among municipalities: rhetoric or reality. *Public Administration Review, 4,* 424–433. doi:10.1111/0033-3352.00196

Moon, M. J., & Bretschneider, S. (2002). Does the perception of red tape constrain IT innovativeness in organizations? Unexpected results from a simultaneous equation model and implications. *Journal of Public Administration: Research and Theory, 12*(2), 273. doi:10.1093/oxfordjournals.jpart.a003532

Moore, J. F. (1996). *The death of competition: Leadership and strategy in the age of business ecosystems.* Winchester, UK: J. Wiley & Sons.

Morison, J., & Newman, D. R. (2001). On-line citizenship: Consultation and participation in New Labour's Britain and beyond. *International Review of Law Computers & Technology, 15*(2), 171–194. doi:10.1080/13600860120070501

Mueller, R. O. (1996). *Basic principles of structural equation modelling: An introduction to Lisrel and EQS.* New York, NY: Springer.

Municipality Law. (2005). *Laws of Turkish Republic, No 5447 of 2005.* Retrieved October 21, 2009, from http://www.tbmm.gov.tr

Musso, J., Weare, C., & Hale, M. (2000). Designing Web technologies for local governance reform: Good management or good democracy? *Political Communication, 17,* 1–19. doi:10.1080/105846000198486

Myers, M. (1997). Qualitative research in information systems. *Management Information Systems Quarterly, 21*(2), 241–242. doi:10.2307/249422

Myles, G., Friday, A., & Davies, N. (2003). Preserving privacy in environments with location-based applications. *Pervasive Computing, 2*(1), 56–64. doi:10.1109/MPRV.2003.1186726

Naidu, S., Menon, M., Gunawardena, C., Lekamge, D., & Karunanayaka, S. (2007). How scenario based learning can engender reflective practice in distance education. In Spector, J. (Ed.), *Finding your voice online. Stories told by experienced online educators* (pp. 53–72). Mahwah, NJ: Lawrence Erlbaum & Associates.

Nairn, M. P. G. (2005). *New Australian Government Chief Information Officer.* Australia: Media Release, Senator the Hon Eric Abetz, Special Minister of State.

Naralan, A. (2008). Belediyelerin Resmi İnternet Sitesi Sahipliği ile Siyasi Partiler ve Nüfus Arasındaki İlişki [Relations among website ownership of municipalities, population and political parties]. *Cumhuriyet Üniversitesi İktisadi ve İdari Bilimler Fakültesi Dergisi, 9*(2), 63–77.

NASCIO. (2006, March). *IT consolidation and shared services: States seeking economies of scale, issue brief.* Retrieved August 4, 2008, from http://www.nascio.org/publications/documents/nascio-con_and_ss_issue_brief_0306.pdf

NASCIO. (2006, May). *Service oriented architecture: An enabler of the agile enterprise in state government, research brief.* Retrieved August 4, 2008, from http://www.enterprise-architecture.info/Images/Documents/NASCIO_SOA_Research_Brief_2006.pdf

Navarette, C. J., & Pick, J. B. (2002). Information technology expenditure and industry performance: The case of the Mexican banking industry. *Journal of Global Information Technology Management, 5*(2), 7–28.

Navaro, C., Gabriel, J., Dewhurst, F., Penalver, B., & Juan, A. (2007). Factors affecting the use of e-government in the telecommunications industry of Spain. *Technovation, 27*(10), 595–604. doi:10.1016/j.technovation.2007.03.003

Navarra, D. D., & Cornford, T. (2003). *A policy making view of e-government innovations in public governance.* Paper presented at the 9th Americas Conference on Information Systems, Tampa, Florida.

Ndubisi, N. D., Jantan, M., & Richerdson, S. (2001). Is the technology acceptance model valid for entrepreneurs? Model testing and examining usage determinants. *Asian Academy of Management Journal, 6*(2), 31–54.

NESSI. (2006). *Strategic research agenda, Vol. 1: Framing the future of the service.*

New Jersey Turnpike Authority, & Wilbur Smith Associates. (2001). *Operational and traffic benefits of E-ZPass to the New Jersey Turnpike: Executive summary.* Trenton, NJ.

Newburn, T. (2001). The commodification of policing: security networks in the late modern city. *Urban Studies (Edinburgh, Scotland), 38*(5-6), 829–848. doi:10.1080/00420980123025

Newell, A. F. (1996). Technology and the disabled. *Technology. Innovation and Society, 12*(1), 21–23.

Neyroud, P., & Beckley, A. (2001). *Policing, ethics and human rights.* Cullompton, UK: Willan Publishing.

Nielsen Norman Group. (2003). *Web usability for senior citizens. 46 design guidelines based on usability studies with people age 65 and older.* Retrieved July 25, 2008, from http://www.nngroup.com/reports/seniors

Nielsen, J. (1993). *Usability engineering.* Boston, MA: Academic Press.

Nieuwsbank. (2004). *Minister de Graaf wants the elderly involved to reduce administrative burden [Minister De Graaf wil ouderen betrekken bij vermindering administratieve lasten].* Retrieved July 25, 2008, from http://www.nieuwsbank.nl/inp/2004/03/01/R245.htm

Nina, D., & Russell, S. (1997). Policing "by any means necessary": Reflections on privatisation, human rights and police issues – Considerations for Australia and South Africa. *Australian Journal of Human Rights, 3*(2). Retrieved January 25, 2010, from http://www.austlii.edu.au/au/journals/AJHR/1997/9.html

NIST. (1995). *An introduction to computer security: The NIST handbook*

Noam, E. M. (1992). *Telecommunications in Europe*. New York, NY: Oxford University Press.

Nonaka, I. (1994). A dynamic theory of organizational knowledge creation. *Organization Science, 5*(1), 14–37. doi:10.1287/orsc.5.1.14

Nonaka, I., & Takeuchi, H. (1995). *The knowledge-creating company: How Japanese companies create the dynamics of innovation*. New York, NY: Oxford University Press.

Nonaka, I., & Takeuchi, H. (1996). A theory of organizational knowledge creation. *International Journal of Technology Management, 11*(7/8), 833–846.

Nonnaly, J. C. (1978). *Psychometric theory*. New York, NY: McGraw Hill.

Normann, R., & Ramirez, R. (1993). From value chain to value constellation: Designing interactive strategy. *Harvard Business Review, 71*(4), 65–77.

Norris, P. (2001). *Digital divide: Civic engagement, information poverty, and the internet wordwide*. Cambridge, UK: Cambridge University Press.

Noveck, B. S. (2005). The future of citizen participation in the electronic state. *I/S: A Journal of Law and Policy for the Information Society, 1*(1). Retrieved April 28, 2009, from http://www.is-journal.org/V01I01/I-S,%20 V01-I01-P001,%20Noveck.pdf

Nunamaker, J., Dennis, A., Valacich, J., Vogel, D., & George, J. (1991). Electronic meeting systems to support group work. *Communications of the ACM, 7*, 40–61. doi:10.1145/105783.105793

O'Malley, P. (2010). *Crime and risk*. Thousand Oaks, CA: Sage.

O'Reilly, T. (2005). *What is Web 2.0. Design patterns and business models for the next generation of software*. Retrieved November 10, 2009, from http://oreilly.com/web2/archive/what-is-web-20.html

OASIS. (2006). *Reference Model for Service Oriented Architecture 1.0*.Retrieved from http://www.oasis-open.org/committees/tc_home.php?wg_abbrev=soa-rm, accessed August 2006.

OASIS. (2009). *Business process execution language v 2.0*. Retrieved from http://docs.oasis-open.org/wsbpel/2.0/OS/wsbpel-v2.0-OS.html, retrieved 22/10/2009

OASIS. (2009). *Security assertion markup language (SAML)*. Retrieved from http://www.oasis-open.org/committees/tc_home.php?wg_abbrev=security, retrieved 22/09/2009

OASIS. (2009). *Web services atomic transaction (WS-AtomicTransaction)*. Retrieved from http://docs.oasis-open.org/ws-tx/wsat/2006/06, retrieved at 22/10/2009

OECD. (2000). *OECD best practices for budget transparency*. Public Management Service Public Management Committee.

OECD. (2001a). *Cities for citizens: Improving metropolitan governance* (pp. 39–43). Paris: OECD Publications.

OECD. (2001b). *Citizens as partners: Information, communication and public participation in policy making* (pp. 20–22). Paris: OECD Publications.

Office of the Privacy Commissioner. (2005). *Getting in on the act: The review of the private sector provisions of the Privacy Act 1988.* Melbourne, Australia: Author.

O'Hear, S. (2006, June 20). Web's second phase puts users in control. *The Guardian, Education*. Retrieved from http://education.guardian.co.uk/elearning/story/0,1801086,00.html

Ohio Turnpike Commission. (2002). *Comprehensive annual financial report for the year ended December 31, 2001*. OH: Berea.

Ohio Turnpike Commission. (2005). *2006 Operating budget and internal efficiency review*. OH: Berea.

Ohio Turnpike Commission. (2006). *Comprehensive annual financial report for the year ended December 31, 2005*. OH: Berea.

Ohio Turnpike Commission. (2007). *Frequently asked questions*. Retrieved April 15, 2007, from http://www.ohioturnpike.org/faq_index.html

Ojamo, M. (2008). *The Finnish register of visual impairment. Annual statistics 2007: National research and development centre for welfare and health in Finland and the Finnish federation of the visually impaired.*

Oreste, S., Chesi, F., & Pallotti, M. (2005, 7-9 June). *E-government: Challenges and opportunities.* Paper presented at the CMG Italy-XIX Annual Conference, Florence, Italy.

Organisation for Economic Co-operation and Development. (2001). *Engaging citizens in policy making: Information, consultation, and public participation*. Paris, France: OECD.

Palvia, S. C. J., & Sharma, S. S. S. (2007). *E-government and e-governance: Definitions/domain framework and status around the world*. Paper presented at the Fifth International Conference on E-Governance, Hyderabad, India. Retrieved October 21, 2009, from http://www.iceg.net/2007/books/1/1_369.pdf

Papadakis, A. (2006). *D5 - As is analysis*. Geneva, Switzerland: SAKE Project.

Papageorgiou, H., Pentaris, F., Theodorou, E., Vardaki, M., & Petrakos, M. (2001). A statistical metadata model for simultaneous manipulation of both data and metadata. *Journal of Intelligent Information Systems, 17*(2-3), 169–192. doi:10.1023/A:1012805713392

Parasuraman, A. (2000). Technology readiness index (TRI): A multiple-item scale to measure readiness to embrace new technologies. *Journal of Service Research, 2*(4), 307–320. doi:10.1177/109467050024001

Parasuraman, A., & Colby, C. L. (2001). *Techno-ready marketing: How and why your customers adopt technology*. New York, NY: The Free Press.

Parry, T. (2007). *The role of fiscal transparency in sustaining growth and stability in Latin America.* Working Paper (Paper No WP/07/220), IMF, Washington D.C.

Paul, T. J., & Kim, M. T. (2003). E-government around the world: Lessons, challenges and future directions. *Government Information Quarterly, 20*, 389–394. doi:10.1016/j.giq.2003.08.001

Péréz López, S., Montes Peón, J. M., & Vázquez Ordás, C. (2004). Managing knowledge: The link between culture and organizational learning. *Journal of Knowledge Management*, *8*(6), 93–104. doi:10.1108/13673270410567657

Pérez, C. C., Bolívar, M. P. R., & Hernández, A. M. L. (2008). E-government process and incentives for online public financial information. *Online Information Review*, *32*(3), 379–400. doi:10.1108/14684520810889682

Pérez, C. C., Hernández, A. M. L., & Bolívar, M. P. R. (2005). Citizens' access to on-line governmental financial information: Practices in the European Union countries. *Government Information Quarterly*, *22*, 258–276. doi:10.1016/j.giq.2005.02.002

Perry, W. (2001). The new security mantra. Prevention, deterrence, defense. In Hoge, J., & Rose, G. (Eds.), *How did this happen? Terrorism and the new war* (pp. 225–240). New York, NY: Public Affairs.

Perusco, L., & Michael, K. (2007). Control, trust, privacy, and security: Evaluating location-based services. *IEEE Technology and Society Magazine*, *26*(1), 4–16. doi:10.1109/MTAS.2007.335564

Pervan, G. (1998). How chief executive officers in large organisations view the management of their information systems. *Journal of Information Technology*, *13*, 95–109. doi:10.1080/026839698344882

Peterson, S. (2004). The open road. *Government technology*. Retrieved August 4, 2008, from http://www.govtech.net/magazine/story.php?id=87471

Pfitzmann, A., & Wolf, G. (2000). Properties of protection goals and their integration into a user interface. *International Journal of Computer and Telecommunication*, *32*(6), 669–683.

Pistore, M., Traverso, P., Paolucci, M., & Wagner, M. (2009). From software services to a future internet of services. In Tselentis, G. (Eds.), *Towards the future Internet*. IOS Press.

Planning Commission. (2001). *Government of India, report of the working group on convergence and e-governance for tenth five year plan (2002-2007),* (pp. 6-25). New Delhi, November.

Poland, P. (2001). *Online consultation in GOL-IN countries: Initiatives to foster e-democracy*. Amsterdam, The Netherlands: Ministry of the Interior and Kingdom Relations.

Polanksy, M., Inuganti, T., & Wiggins, S. (2004). The 21st century CIO. *Business Strategy Review*, *15*(2), 29–33. doi:10.1111/j.0955-6419.2004.00310.x

Porter Research. (2002). *The second annual report into key government web sites*. Retrieved from http://www.porter-research.com/govt2002.html

Porter, M. E. (1990). *The competitive advantage of nations*. New York, NY: The Free Press.

Porter, M., & Millar, V. (1985). How information gives you competitive advantage. *Harvard Business Review*, *63*(4), 149–174.

Prabhu, C. S. R. (2005). *E-governance: Concepts and case studies*. Delhi, India: Prentice Hall of India Private Limited.

Prahalad, C. K., & Ramaswamy, V. (2000). Co-opting customer competence. *Harvard Business Review*, *78*(1), 79–87.

Prahalad, C. K., & Ramaswamy, V. (2003). The new frontier of experience innovation. In Rosenberg, J., & Remy, D. (Eds.), *Securing Web services with WS-Security: Demystifying WS-Security, WS-Policy, SAML, XML signature, and XML encryption*. Pearson Higher Education.

Prahalad, C. K., & Ramaswamy, V. (2004). *The future of competition: Co-creating unique value with customers*. New York, NY: Harvard Business School Press.

Premchand, A. (2002). *Fiscal transparency and accountability: Idea and reality in United Nations. Globalization and new challenges of public finance: Financial management, transparency and accountability*. New York, NY: Department of Economic and Social Affairs.

Prenzler, T. (2001). *Private investigators in Australia: Work, law, ethics and regulation*. Retrieved from http://www.criminologyresearchcouncil.gov.au/reports/prenzler.pdf

Prenzler, T. (2009). Strike Force Piccadilly: A public-private partnership to stop ATM ram raids. *Policing: An International Journal of Police Strategies and Management, 32*(2), 209–225. doi:10.1108/13639510910958145

Prenzler, T., Sarre, R., & Earle, K. (2009). The trend to private security in Australia. *Australasian Policing. Journal of Professional Practice, 1*(1), 17–18.

Prochaska, J. O., & DiClemente, C. C. (1986). Toward a comprehensive model of change. In Miller, W. R., & Heather, N. (Eds.), *Treating addictive behaviors: Processes of change* (pp. 3–27). New York, NY: Plenum Press.

Public Financial Management and Control Law. (2003). *Laws of Turkish Republic, No 5018 of 2003*. Retrieved October 21, 2009, from http://www.tbmm.gov.tr

Qatar e-Government. (2007). *E- government portal*. Retrieved from http://www.qatar.e.gov.qa

Raelin, J. A. (1997). A model of work-based learning. *Organization Science, 8*(6), 563–578. doi:10.1287/orsc.8.6.563

Raman, M., Stephenaus, R., Alam, N., & Kuppusamy, M. (2008). Information technology in Malaysia: E-service quality and uptake of internet banking. *Journal of Internet Banking and Commerce, 13*(2), 2–17.

Ramayah, T., Ramoo, V., & Amlus, I. (2008). Profiling online and manual tax filers: Results from an exploratory study in Penang Malaysia. *Labuan e-Journal of Muamalat and Society, 2*, 1-8.

Rash, W. (1997). *Politics on the Net: Wiring the political process*. New York, NY: W.H. Freeman.

Rawls, J. (1971). *A theory of justice*. Cambridge, MA: Harvard University Press.

Reffat, R. (2003). *Developing a successful e-government*. (Working Paper): University Of Sydney, Australia.

Regulation on Activity Reports of Public Administrations. (2006). *Regulations of Turkish Republic, No 26111 of 2006*. Retrieved October 21, 2009, from http://www.bumko.gov.tr

Regulation on the Procedures and the Methods Related to Implementation of the Right to Information Law. (2004). *Regulations of Turkish republic, No 25445 of 2004*. Retrieved October 21, 2009, from http://www.mevzuat.gov.tr

Resnikoff, S., Pascolini, D., Etya'ale, D., Kocur, I., Pararajasegaram, R., & Pokharel, G. P. (2004). Global data on visual impairment in the year 2002. *Bulletin of the World Health Organization, 82,* 844–851.

Reychav, I., & Weisberg, J. (2009). Good for workers, good for companies: How knowledge sharing benefits individual employees. *Knowledge and Process Management, 16*(4), 186–197. doi:10.1002/kpm.335

Reynolds, M. M., & Regio-Micro, M. (2001). The purpose of transforming government-e-government as a catalyst in the information age. *Microsoft E-Government Initiatives.* Retrieved from http://www.netcaucus.org/books/egov2001/pdf/EGovIntr.pdf

Rheingold, H. (1993). *The virtual community: Homesteading on the electronic frontier.* Reading, MA: Addison Wesley.

Richards, L., O'Shea, J., & Connolly, M. (2004). Managing the concept of strategic change within a higher education institution: the role of strategic and scenario planning techniques. *Strategic Change, 13,* 345–359. doi:10.1002/jsc.690

Riege, A., & Lindsay, N. (2006). Knowledge management in the public sector: Stakeholder partnerships in the public policy development. *Journal of Knowledge Management, 10*(3), 24–39. doi:10.1108/13673270610670830

Riga Declaration. (2006). *Internet for all: EU ministers commit to an inclusive and barrier-free information society.* Press release of June, IP/06/769.

Right to Information Law. (2003). *Laws of Turkish Republic, No 4982 of 2003.* Retrieved October 21, 2009, from http://www.tbmm.gov.tr

Roach, S. (1987). *America's technology dilemma: A profile of the information economy. Economics Newsletter Series.* New York, NY: Morgan Stanley.

Robey, D., Boudreau, M., & Rose, G. M. (2000). Information technology and organizational learning: A review and assessment of research. *Accounting. Management and Information Technologies, 10,* 125–155. doi:10.1016/S0959-8022(99)00017-X

Rocheleau, B., & Wu, L. (2002). Public versus private information systems: Do they differ in important ways? A review and empirical test. *American Review of Public Administration, 32*(4), 379–397. doi:10.1177/027507402237866

Roger, W. (1999) *Postal service getting wired.* Retrieved May 31, 2009 from www.interactive-week.com

Rogers, E. M. (1995). *Diffusion of innovations* (4th ed.). New York, NY: Free Press.

Rosenberg, M. (2001). *E-learning, strategies for developing knowledge in the digital age.* New York, NY: McGraw-Hill.

Rubaii-Barrett, N., & Wise, L. R. (2008). Disability access and e-government: An empirical analysis of state practices. *Journal of Disability Policy Studies, 19*(1), 52–64. doi:10.1177/1044207307311533

Rust, R. T., & Kannan, P. K. (2003). E-service: A New paradigm for business in the electronic environment. *Communications of the ACM, 46*(6), 37–42. doi:10.1145/777313.777336

Rust, R. T., & Lemon, K. N. (2001). E-service and the consumer. *International Journal of Electronic Commerce, 5*(3), 85–101.

Sack, W. (2005). Discourse architecture and very large-scale conversation. In Latham, R., & Sassen, S. (Eds.), *Digital formations: IT and new architectures in the global realm* (pp. 242–282). Princeton, NJ: Princeton University Press.

Samiotis, K. (Ed.). (2009). *D28 evaluation report*. Geneva, Switzerland: SAKE Project.

Sampson, N. (2002). *Bank marketing international: Simplifying in(form)ation online*. Retrieved from http://www.mandoforms. com/news/coverage/bankmarketing.html

Sarre, R. (1994). The legal powers of private police and security providers. In Moyle, P. (Ed.), *Private prisons and police. Recent Australian trends* (pp. 259–280). Leichardt, NSW, Australia: Pluto Press.

Sarre, R. (2008). The legal powers of private security personnel: Some policy considerations and legislative options. *QUT Law and Justice Journal*, *8*(2), 301–313.

Saunders, M., Lewis, P., & Thornhill, A. (2002). *Research methods for business students* (3rd ed.). Harlow, MA: Prentice Hall.

Sawhney, M., Balasubramanian, S., & Krishnan, V. V. (2003). Creating growth with services. *Sloan Management Review*, *45*(2), 34–44.

Sawhney, M., & Parikh, D. (2001). Where value lives in a networked world. *Harvard Business Review*, *79*(1), 79–90.

Scannapieco, M., Pernici, B., & Pierce, E. (2005). IP-UML-A methodology for quality improvement based on information product maps and unified modeling language. In *Vol. Information Quality*. AMIS.

Schick, A. (1999). *A contemporary approach to public expenditure management*. World Bank Institute: Governance, Regulation, and Finance Division.

Schneider, D., & Vaught, B. (1993). A comparison of job satisfaction between public and private sector managers. *Public Administration Quarterly*, *17*(1), 68–83.

Schneiderman, B. (1992). *Designing the user interface: Strategies for effective human-computer interaction*. Reading, MA: Addison-Wesley.

Schneider, S. (2006). Privatising economic crime enforcement: Exploring the role of private sector investigative agencies in combating money laundering. *Policing and Society*, *16*(3), 285–316. doi:10.1080/10439460600812065

Schreiber, G. (2000). *Knowledge engineering and management, the CommonKADS methodology*. Cambridge, MA: MIT Press.

Schreiner, K. (2007). Where we at? Mobile phones bring GPS to the masses. *IEEE Computer Graphics and Applications*, *27*(3), 6–11. doi:10.1109/MCG.2007.73

Segars, A. H., & Grover, V. (1993). Re-examining perceived ease of use and usefulness: A confirmatory factor analysis. *Management Information Systems Quarterly*, *17*(1), 517–725. doi:10.2307/249590

Seifert, J., & Petersen, E. (2002). The promise of all things E? Expectations and challenges of emergent e-government. *Perspectives on Global Development and Technology*, *1*(2), 193–213. doi:10.1163/156915002100419808

Sekaran, U. (2003). *Research methods for business: A skill building approach*. India: John Wiley & Son, Inc.

Compilation of References

Sena, O., & Paul, P. (2009). Exploring the adoption of a service innovation: A study of Internet banking adopters and non-adopters. *Journal of Financial Services Marketing*, *13*(4), 284–299. doi:10.1057/fsm.2008.25

Senge, P. M. (1990). *The fifth discipline: Art and practice of the learning organization*. New York, NY: Doubleday.

Seo, D., & Lee, J. (2007). Gaining competitive advantage through value-shifts: A case of the South Korean wireless communications industry. *International Journal of Information Management*, *27*(1), 49–56. doi:10.1016/j.ijinfomgt.2006.12.002

Seo, D., & Mak, K. T. (in press). Using the thread-fabric perspective to analyze industry dynamics: An exploratory investigation of the wireless telecommunications industry. *Communications of the ACM*.

Sevilla, C., & Wells, T. D. (1988). Contracting to ensure training transfer. *Training & Development*, *6*(1), 10–11.

Shafie, S. (2007). *E-government initiatives in Malaysia and the role of the national archives of Malaysia in digital records management*. The 8th General Conference of Development of E-Government and Digital Records Management.

Sharma, S. (2007). Exploring best practices in public-private partnership (PPP) in e-government through select Asian case studies. *International Library Review*, *39*(3/4), 203–210.

Shearing, C. (1992). The relation between public and private policing. In Tonry, M., & Norval, N. (Eds.), *Modern policing* (pp. 399–434). Chicago, IL: University of Chicago Press. doi:10.1086/449198

Shiang, J. (2008). *Change and adaptation of stakeholder relationships in e-governance*. Paper presented at Fourth International Conference on e-Government, Melbourne, Australia. Retrieved October 21, 2009, from http://web.thu.edu.tw/jshiang/www/iceg2008.pdf

Shirky, C. (2003). Social software: A new generation of tools. *Esther Dyson's Monthly Report, 10*.

Shrivastava, P. A. (1983). Typology of organizational learning systems. *Journal of Management Studies*, *20*, 1–28. doi:10.1111/j.1467-6486.1983.tb00195.x

Shulman, S., Schlosberg, D., Zavestoski, S., & Courard-Hauri, D. Electronic rulemaking: New frontiers in public participation. *Social Science Computer Review*, *21*(2), 162–178. doi:10.1177/0894439303021002003

Silcock, R. (2001). What is e-government? *Hansard Society for Parliamentary Government. Parliamentary Affairs*, *54*, 88–101. doi:10.1093/pa/54.1.88

Simonin, B. L. (1997). The importance of collaborative know-how: An empirical test of the learning organization. *Academy of Management Journal*, *40*(5), 1150–1173. doi:10.2307/256930

Siochrú, S. Ó., & Girard, B. (2002). *Global media governance. A beginner's guide*. Lanham, MD: Rowman & Littlefield Publishers.

Si-young, H. (2007, June 11). Korea post utilizes cutting-edge IT. *The Korea Herald*.

Škerlavaj, M. (2003). *Vpliv informacijsko-komunikacijskih tehnologij in organizacijskega učenja na uspešnost poslovanja: Teoretična in empirična analiza*. Unpublished Master's thesis. Ljubljana: Ekonomska fakulteta.

Škerlavaj, M., & Dimovski, V. (2006). Study of the mutual connections among information-communication technologies, organisational learning and business performance. *Journal for East European Management Studies*, *11*(1), 9–29.

Skillman, B. (1998). Fired up at the IRS. *Accounting Technology*, *14*, 12–20.

Sklansky, D. (2006). Private police and democracy. *The American Criminal Law Review*, *43*(1), 89–105.

Slater, S. F., & Narver, J. C. (1995). Market orientation and the learning organization. *Journal of Marketing*, *59*(3), 63–74. doi:10.2307/1252120

Sloan, T. R., Hyland, P. W. B., & Beckett, R. C. (2002). Learning as a competitive advantage: Innovative training in the Australian aerospace industry. *International Journal of Technology Management*, *23*(4), 341–352. doi:10.1504/IJTM.2002.003014

Smith, R. (2008). Aligning competencies, capabilities and resources. *Research Technology Management: The Journal of the Industrial Research Institute*, September-October.

Solow, R. M. (1957). Technical change and the aggregate production function. *The Review of Economics and Statistics*, *39*(3), 312–320. doi:10.2307/1926047

Spasovic, L. N., Zhang, W., Bladikas, A. K., Pignataro, L. J., Niver, E., & Ciszewski, S. (1995). Primer on electronic toll collection technologies. *Intelligent Transportation Systems*, *1516*, 1-10. Washington, DC: Transportation Research Board, National Research Council.

Srinivasan, S. (2004). Role of trust in e-business success. *Information Management & Computer Security*, *12*(1), 66–72. doi:10.1108/09685220410518838

State Planning Organization. (2000). *Kamu Mali Yönetiminin Yeniden Yapılandırılması ve Mali Saydamlık Özel İhtisas Komisyonu Raporu* [The special experts commission report on reinventing public financial management and fiscal transparency]. Ankara.

State Planning Organization. (2009). *Bilgi Toplumu Stratejisi Eylem Planı (2006-2010) Değerlendirme Raporu 3* [Evaluation report 3 of the information society strategy action plan (2006-2010)], Ankara.

Statistics Denmark. (2000, June). *The use of administrative sources for statistics and international comparability (invited paper)*. Presented at the Conference of European Statisticians, 48th Plenary Session, Paris.

Steinbock, D. (2003). Globalization of wireless value system: From geographic to strategic advantages. *Telecommunications Policy*, *27*, 207–235. doi:10.1016/S0308-5961(02)00106-4

Stenning, P. (2009). Governance and accountability in a plural policing environment – The story so far. *Policing*, *3*(1), 22–33. doi:10.1093/police/pan080

Stephanidis, C. (1999). Toward an information society for all: HCI challenges and R&D recommendations. *International Journal of Human-Computer Interaction*, *11*, 1–28. doi:10.1207/s15327590ijhc1101_1

Stephens, S., McCusker, P., O'Donnell, D., Newman, D., & Fagan, G. (2006). On the road from consultation cynicism to energizing e-consultation. *The Electronic. Journal of E-Government*, *4*(2), 87–94.

Compilation of References

Stojanovic, N., Apostolou, D., Dioudis, S., Gábor, A., Kovács, B., Kő, A., et al. (2008). *D24 – Integration plan*. Retrieved from http://www.sake-project.org/fileadmin/brochures/D21_2nd_iteration_prototype_of_semantic-based_groupware_system.pdf

Stojanovic, N., Kovács, B., Kő, A., Papadakis, A., Apostolou, D., Dioudis, D., et al. (2007). *D16B – 1st iteration prototype of semantic-based content management system*. Retrieved from http://www.sake-project.org/fileadmin/filemounts/sake/D16B_First_Iteration_Prototype_of_SCMS_final.pdf

Strebel, P. (1996). Why do employees resist change? *Harvard Business Review*, 86–92.

Sundgren, B. (1996). Making statistical data more available. *International Statistical Review, 64*(1), 23–38. doi:10.2307/1403422

Sunstein, C. (2001). *Republic.com*. Princeton, NJ: Princeton University Press.

Swanton, B. (1993). *Police & private security: possible directions*. Trends & Issues in Crime and Criminal Justice.

Synnott, W., & Gruber, W. (1981). *Information resource management: Opportunities and strategies for the 1980s*. New York, NY: John Wiley & Sons.

Teo, J. (2004, November 26). Anti-casino groups keep up the fight. *The Strait Times*. Retrieved August 4, 2009, from http://www.wildsingapore.com/sos/media/041117-1.htm

Teo, T. S. H. (2001). Demographic and motivation variable associated with internet usage activities. *Internet Research: Electronic Networking Application and Policy, 1*(2), 125–137. doi:10.1108/10662240110695089

Thatcher, J., Waddell, C., Henry, S., Swierenga, S., Urban, M., & Burks, M. (2003). *Constructing accessible web sites*. San Francisco, CA: Apress.

The Helsinki Manifesto. (2006). Retrieved from http://elivinglab.org/files/Helsinki_Manifesto_201106.pdf

The National ICT Association of Malaysia (PIKOM). (2008). *ICT strategies, societal and market touch*. Retrieved on June 24th, 2009. from http://www.witsa.org/news/2009-1/html_email_newsletter_jan09_b.html

The Peninsula Newspaper. (2007). *Minister launches iPark initiative*. Doha, Qatar.

The STAR. (2009, May 1). Amount of Malaysian's choosing e-filing up by 30%. *The STAR*.

The Wallis Group. (2007). *Community attitudes to privacy*. Melbourne, VIC, Australia: Office of the Privacy Commissioner.

The, S. T. A. R. (2009). *It's time inland revenue board got real on e-filing*. Retrieved on June 19th, 2009, from http://thestar.com.my/news/story.asp?file=/2009/3/2/focus/3380923&sec=focus

Thomsen, R. (2008). *Elements in the validation process*. Retrieved from http://www.nordvux.net/page/481/cases.htm

Thomson, I., & Holmy, A. (1998). Combining data from surveys and administrative record systems—The Norwegian experience. *International Statistical Review, 66*(2), 201–221.

Tippins, M. J., & Sohi, R. S. (2003). IT competency and firm performance: Is organizational learning a missing link? *Strategic Management Journal, 24*(8), 745–761. doi:10.1002/smj.337

Townsend, A. M., & Bennett, J. T. (2003). Privacy, technology, and conflict: Emerging issues and action in workplace privacy. *Journal of Labor Research, 24*(2), 195–205. doi:10.1007/BF02701789

Treacy, M., & Wiersma, F. (1993). Customer intimacy and other value disciplines. *Harvard Business Review, 71*, 84–93.

Trustgate Sdn, M. S. C. Bhd. (2009). *Secure e-filing*. Retrieved on June 24th, 2009. from http://www.mykad.com.my/Website/secureefiling.php

Turkish Statistical Institute. (2006, January). 2005 Yılı Belediye Web Hizmetleri Araştırması, [Municipality Web services survey 2005]. *Haber Bülteni*. Retrieved October 21, 2009, from http://www.tuik.gov.tr

Turkish Statistical Institute. (2007, August). *2007 Yılı Hanehalkı Bilişim Teknolojileri Kullanım Araştırması Revize Sonuçları* [Revised results of the information and communication technology usage survey on households and individuals 2007]. Retrieved October 22, 2009, from http://www.tuik.gov.tr

Turkish Statistical Institute. (2009, August). 2009 Yılı Hanehalkı Bilişim Teknolojileri Kullanım Araştırması Sonuçları, [The results of 2009 information and communication technology usage survey on households and individuals]. *Haber Bülteni*. Retrieved October 21, 2009, from http://www.tuik.gov.tr

Tyagi, S. (2006). *RESTful Web services*. Retrieved October 22, 2009, from http://java.sun.com/developer/technicalArticles/WebServices/restful/

U.S. Federal Trade Commission. (2005). *RFID radio frequency identification: Applications and implications for consumers* (Workshop Report). Washington, DC.

Ulrich, D., Jick, T., & von Glinow, M. A. (1993). High-impact learning: Building and diffusing learning capability. *Organizational Dynamics, 22*(2), 52–66. doi:10.1016/0090-2616(93)90053-4

UN. (2005). *World public sector report: Global e-government readiness, from e-government to e-inclusion*. New York.

UN. (2008). *UN e-government survey, from e-government to connected e-governance*. New York, NY: UN.

UN. (2008). *World public sector report: UN e-government survey, from e-government to connected governance*. New York.

UN–DPEPA. (2002). *Benchmarking e-government: A global perspective, assessing the progress of the UN member states*. Retrieved from nettelafrica.org/docs/NetTel percent20Safari@the percent20Equator percent20(Uganda percent202003)/Benchmarkingegovt.pdf

UNECE. (2000). *Statistical metadata*. Presented at the Conference on European Statisticians Statistical Standards and Studies (no. 53), Geneva (CH).

United Nations. (1966). *International covenant on civil and political rights*. New York, NY: Author.

Universal Postal Union. (2003). *The role of postal services*. Bern: WSIS Summit.

Van Alstyne, M., & Brynjolfsson, E. (1996). *Electronic communities: Global village or cyberbalkans?* Paper presented at the17th International Conference on Information Systems, Cleveland, OH.

Varney, S. (2008). Leadership learning: key to organizational transformation. *Strategic HR Review*, *7*(1), 5–10. doi:10.1108/14754390810880471

Venkatesh, V., & Davis, F. D. (2000). A theoretical extension of the technology acceptance model: Four longitudinal field studies. *Management Science*, *46*(2), 186–205. doi:10.1287/mnsc.46.2.186.11926

Venkatesh, V., Morris, M. G., Davis, G. B., & Davis, F. D. (2003). User acceptance of information technology: Toward a unified view. *Management Information Systems Quarterly*, *27*(3), 425–478.

Vinken, H., Ester, P., & Dirven, H.-J. (1993). Individualization of the life-course and cultural divergence between age groups. In Ester, P., Halman, L., & de Moor, R. (Eds.), *The individualizing society. Value change in Europe and North America* (pp. 183–196). Tilburg, The Netherlands: Tilburg University Press.

Vollmer Associates. (2000). *E-ZPass evaluation report*. Retrieved April 16, 2007, from http://ntl.bts.gov/lib/9000/9400/9406/6L01.pdf

Von Hirsch, A. (2000). The ethics of public television surveillance. In Von Hirsch, A., Garland, D., & Wakefield, A. (Eds.), *Ethical and social perspectives on situational crime control* (pp. 59–76). Oxford, UK: Hart Publishing.

Von Hirsch, A., & Shearing, C. (2000). Exclusion from public space. In Von Hirsch, A., Garland, D., & Wakefield, A. (Eds.), *Ethical and social perspectives on situational crime control* (pp. 77–96). Oxford, UK: Hart Publishing.

W3C. (2009). *RDF annotations (RDFa)*. Retrieved October 22, 2009, from http://www.w3.org/TR/xhtml-rdfa-primer/

W3C. (2009). *RDF schema (RDFS)*. Retrieved October 22, 2009, from http://www.w3.org/TR/rdf-schema/

W3C. (2009). *Resource description framework (RDF)*. Retrieved October 22, 2009, from http://www.w3.org/RDF/

W3C. (2009). *Simple object access protocol (SOAP)*. Retrieved October 22, 2009, from http://www.w3.org/TR/soap/

Wakefield, A. (2000). Situational crime prevention in mass private property. In Von Hirsch, A., Garland, D., & Wakefield, A. (Eds.), *Ethical and social perspectives on situational crime control* (pp. 125–146). Oxford, UK: Hart Publishing.

Wall, B. (1998). Measuring the right stuff: Identifying and applying the right knowledge. *Knowledge Management Review*, *1*(4), 20–24.

Walters, C. (2007, September 22). There is nowhere to hide in Sydney. *Sydney Morning Herald*. Retrieved January 20, 2011, from http://www.smh.com.au/news/national/there-is-nowhere-to-hide-in-sydney/2007/09/21/1189881777231

Walters, D., & Lancaster, G. (1999). Value and information: Concepts and issues for management. *Management Decision*, *37*(8), 643–656. doi:10.1108/00251749910291613

Wand, Y., & Wang, R. Y. (1996). Anchoring data quality dimensions in ontological foundations. *Communications of the ACM*, *39*(11). doi:10.1145/240455.240479

Wang, R. (1998). A product perspective on total data quality management. *Communications of the ACM, 41*(2). doi:10.1145/269012.269022

Wang, R. Y., & Strong, D. M. (1996). Beyond accuracy: What data quality means to data consumers. *Journal of Management Information Systems, 12*(4).

Ward, J., & Peppard, J. (2002). *Strategic planning for information systems*. Chichester, UK: John Wiley & Sons.

Wardlaw, G., & Boughton, J. (2006). Intelligence led policing – The AFP approach. In Fleming, J., & Wood, J. (Eds.), *Fighting crime together. The challenges of policing and security networks* (pp. 133–149). Sydney, Australia: UNSW Press.

Ward, M. A., & Mitchell, S. (2004). A comparison of the strategic priorities of public and private sector information resource management executives. *Government Information Quarterly, 21*(3), 284–304. doi:10.1016/j.giq.2004.04.003

Wassenaar, A. (2000). E-governmental value chain models. *DEXA Conference,* (pp. 289-293).

Weare, C., Musso, J. A., & Hale, M. L. (1999). Electronic democracy and the diffusion of municipal web pages in California. *Administration & Society, 31*(1), 3–27. doi:10.1177/009539999400935475

Weckert, J. (2000, September 6-8). Trust and monitoring in the workplace. In *Proceedings of the IEEE International Symposium on Technology and Society, University as a Bridge from Technology to Society,* Rome, Italy (pp. 245-250). IEEE Society on Social Implications of Technology.

Weerakkody, V., Janssen, M., & Hjort-Madsen, K. (2007). Realising integrated e-government services: A European perspective. *Journal of Cases in E-Commerce, 3*(2), 14-38.

Weerakkody, V., & Choudrie, J. (2005). Exploring e-government in the UK: Challenges, issues and complexities. *Journal of Information Science and Technology, 2*(2), 26–44.

Wegweiser GmbH Berlin. (2007). *Monitoring eHealth & Gesundheitswirtschaft 2007/2008.*

Wellman, B. (1999). *Networks in the global village: Life in contemporary communities.* Boulder, CO: Westview Press.

Welsh, W. (2003, October 27). Open source riles software makers – Massachusetts ignites furor with new strategy. *Washington Technology, 18*(15). Retrieved August 4, 2008, from http://www.washingtontechnology.com/print/18_15/22000-1.html

Welsh, B., & Farrington, D. (2009). *Making public places safer. Surveillance and crime prevention.* Oxford, UK: Oxford University Press.

Wernerfelt, B. (1984). A resource-based view of the firm. *Strategic Management Journal, 5*, 171–180. doi:10.1002/smj.4250050207

Wescott, C., Pizarro, M., & Schiavo-Campo, S. (2000). The role of information and communication technology in improving public administration. In S. Schiavo-Campo & P. Sundaram (Eds.), *To serve and to preserve: Improving public administration in a competitive world* (pp. 673-701). Retrieved October 21, 2009, from http://www.adb.org/documents/manuals/serve_and_preserve

West, D. (2007). *Global e-government 2007.* Providence, RI: Center for Public Policy, Brown University. Retrieved August 20, 2009, from http://www.insidepolitics.org/egovt07int.pdf

West, D. (2004). E-government and the transformation of service delivery and citizen attitudes. *Public Administration Review, 64*(1), 15–27. doi:10.1111/j.1540-6210.2004.00343.x

Whitehouse, C., Spencer, R. E., & Payne, M. (2003). Customer strategy: Whom do you what to reach? In Freeland, J. F. (Ed.), *The ultimate CRM handbook* (pp. 18–29). New York, NY: McGraw-Hill.

Whyte, A., & Macintosh, A. (2001). Transparency and teledemocracy: Issues from an e-consultation. *Journal of Information Science, 27*(4), 187–198.

Wiig, K. M. (1997). Knowledge management: Where did it come from and where will it go? *Expert Systems with Applications, 13*(1), 1–14. doi:10.1016/S0957-4174(97)00018-3

Wilhelm, A. (2000). *Democracy in the digital age: Challenges to political life in cyberspace.* New York, NY: Routledge.

Williamson, G. (2010). The problem with privacy. *Australian Security Magazine,* 10-12.

Wimmer, M., & Traunmuller, R. (2000). *Trends in e- government: Managing distributed knowledge.* Paper presented at the 11th International Workshop on Database and Expert Systems Applications, New York.

Womack, J., Jones, J., & Roos, D. (1990). *The machine that changed the world.* New York, NY: Rowson Associates. Zajicek, M. (2004). Successful and available: Interface design exemplars for older users. *Interacting with Computers, 16,* 411–430.

Wood, J. (2006). Dark networks, bright networks and the place of police. In Fleming, J., & Wood, J. (Eds.), *Fighting crime together. The challenges of policing and security networks* (pp. 246–269). Sydney, Australia: UNSW Press.

World Health Organisation. (2009). *Causes of blindness and visual impairment.* Retrieved April 14, 2009, from http://www.who.int/blindness/causes/en/

World Summit on Information Society. (2009). Retrieved February 10, 2009, from www.wsis-egypt.gov.eg.

Wright, S. (2005). Design matters: The political efficacy of government-run discussion forums. In Oates, S., Owen, D., & Gibson, R. (Eds.), *The Internet and politics: Citizens, voters, and activists* (pp. 80–99). London, UK: Routledge.

Wright, S., & Street, J. (2007). Democracy, deliberation and design: The case of online discussion forums. *New Media & Society, 9*(5), 849–869. doi:10.1177/1461444807081230

Yıldız, M. (1999). Yerel Yönetimde Yeni Bir Katılım Kanalı Internet: ABD'de ve Türkiye'de Elektronik Bilgi Ağları [A new way to participation in local government (Internet): Electronic information networks in USA and Turkey]. *Çağdaş Yerel Yönetimler, 8*(4), 144-156.

Yin, R. K. (1994). *Case study research—Design and methods* (2nd ed.). London, UK: Sage Publications.

Yurcik, W., Sharma, A., & Doss, D. (2002). *False impressions: Contrasting perceptions of security as a major impediment to achieving survivable systems*. IEEE/CERT/SEI Fourth Information Survivability Workshop (ISW-2002). Vancouver, Canada: IEEE Computer Society Press.

Zakareya, E., & Irani, Z. (2005). E-government adoption: Architecture and barriers. *Business Process Management Journal, 11*(5), 589–611. doi:10.1108/14637150510619902

Zakaria, N., Affendi, S., & Yusof, M. (2001). *The role of human and organizational culture in the context of technological change.* Paper presented at the IEMC '01.

Zaphiris, P., Kurniawan, A. S., & Ghiawadwala, M. (2006). A systematic approach to the development of research-based Web design guidelines for older people. *Universal Access in the Information Society, 6*, 59–75. doi:10.1007/s10209-006-0054-8

Zedner, L. (2003). The concept of security: an agenda for comparative analysis. *Legal Studies, 23*(1), 153–176. doi:10.1111/j.1748-121X.2003.tb00209.x

Zedner, L. (2006a). Liquid security: Managing the market for crime control. *Criminology & Criminal Justice, 6*(3), 267–288. doi:10.1177/1748895806065530

Zedner, L. (2006b). Policing before and after the police. *The British Journal of Criminology, 46*, 78–96. doi:10.1093/bjc/azi043

Zekri, N. (2006, April 16). Transformation of the post organization. *Al-Ahram Newspaper.*

Zhang, D. (2002). *Media structuration – Towards an integrated approach to interactive multimedia-based E-Learning.* (Ph.D. dissertation, The University of Arizona. Zhang, D., & Nunamaker, J. F. (2003). Powering e-learning in the new millennium: An overview of e-learning and enabling technology. *Information Systems Frontiers, 5*(2), 207–218.

Zhiyuan, F. (2002). E-government in digital era: Concepts, practice and development. *International Journal of the Computer, the Internet and Management, 10*(2), 1-22.

Zorkadis, V., & Donos, P. (2004). On biometrics-based authentication and identification from a privacy-protection perspective deriving privacy-enhancing requirements. *Information Management & Computer Security, 12*(1), 125–137. doi:10.1108/09685220410518883

About the Editor

Christopher G. Reddick is an Associate Professor and Chair of the Department of Public Administration at the University of Texas at San Antonio, USA. Dr. Reddick's research and teaching interests are in information technology and public sector organizations. Some of his publications can be found in *Government Information Quarterly*, *Electronic Government*, and the *International Journal of Electronic Government Research*. Dr. Reddick has edited several books on e-government research. He is author of the book *Homeland Security Preparedness and Information Systems*, which deals with the impact of information technology on homeland security preparedness (IGI-Global). Dr. Reddick recently published the book *Public Administration and Information Technology* (Jones and Bartlett Learning), which examines the impact of information technology on public sector organization.

Index